To Inbal and Yael

The Jew in the Modern World

THE JEW IN THE MODERN WORLD

A Documentary History

Edited by

PAUL R. MENDES-FLOHR
Hebrew University of Jerusalem

JEHUDA REINHARZ
University of Michigan

New York Oxford
OXFORD UNIVERSITY PRESS
1980

Library of Congress Cataloging in Publication Data
Main entry under title:
The Jew in the modern world.
Includes bibliographical references and index.
1. Jews—History—17th century—Sources.
2. Jews—History—18th century—Sources.
3. Jews—History—1789-1945—Sources.
4. Judaism—History—Modern period, 1750- —Sources.
I. Mendes-Flohr, Paul R. II. Reinharz, Jehuda.
DS102.J43 909'.04'924 79-15050
ISBN 0-19-502631-4 ISBN 0-19-502632-2 pbk.

9 8 7 6 5

Printed in the United States of America

Preface

Peoples of the past, it has been ironically observed, did not live as self-consciously as we do—they did not even know whether they were living in the fifth or fourth century B.C.E. In contrast, we are distinctly conscious of our place in history, and undoubtedly this consciousness derives from a profound sense of being witness to a radically new era in human history. Heralded first in Western Europe, this new or modern period is marked by far-reaching transformations in almost every aspect of human culture. For the modern Jew this consciousness of history is perhaps even more pronounced than it is for others—if for no other reason than that the Jew's entry into the modern world was marked by a radical, sudden break with the past. Western Jews "did not enter modern European [and American] society in a long process of 'endogenous' gestation and growth, but they plunged into it as the ghetto walls were breached, with a bang, though not without prolonged whimpers."[1]

These whimpers express the modern Jew's bewilderment. Beyond the walls of the ghetto and the precincts of the Pale, the Jews found horizons that led them far from the world of their grandfathers. The modern, secular world has granted the Jews equality and has opened before them undreamt of opportunities for intellectual and personal development—opportunities that have immeasurably enriched the Jews. Moreover, the modern world has encouraged the development of new and rewarding forms of Jewish self-expression and collective organization. Yet this same new era has been for many Jews a veritable purgatory: in the Jews' passage through modernity their religion, culture and identity have suffered severely, and, tragically, they have borne the brunt of the most demonic enemies of modernity, the anti-Semites, who, eventually, leading an apocalyptic war to dismantle the modern

1. R. J. Zwi Werblowsky, *Beyond Tradition and Modernity: Changing Religions in a Changing World* (London: University of London, The Athlone Press, 1976), p. 42.

world—or at least what in their eyes were its most egregious features, democracy and Jewish emancipation—unleashed a Holocaust that devoured a third of the Jewish people. This trauma, in consonance with the contradictory rhythms of modern Jewish history, was quickly followed by the rebirth of the State of Israel and a renewal of Jewish pride and sense of community.

In light of the ambiguous quality of their recent history, the Jews of the modern age are profoundly perplexed. This perplexity has intrigued us, the editors, and many others, and has encouraged us to study, and, we hope, to understand, modern Jewish history. This book, the product of our study, is not, however, a "Guide to the Perplexed": it offers no release from the contradictions; but, rather, offers a guide through the dynamic forces that shape the modern Jewish experience.

The study of modern Jewish history is encumbered by many of the same processes that produced that history: rapid changes in Jewish life have pushed and pulled the Jews across numerous linguistic, cultural and political boundaries. The examination of modern Jewish history thus requires the knowledge of the many languages that have affected Jewish destiny in the recent past. Also required is an understanding of the dialectical tension between religious tradition and secularity. Likewise the comprehension of Jewish history rests on a knowledge of European, Near Eastern and American political, economic, cultural and social history, particularly of the Enlightenment, the formation of the modern nation-state, the development of democracy, liberalism, capitalism, socialism and the conservative and romantic reactions to these processes.

As teachers of modern Jewish history, our task is encumbered by the inaccessibility of many of the primary documents that illustrate the various processes at work in modern Jewish history. Hitherto no comprehensive attempt has been made to gather—either in the original languages or in translation—the relevant primary documents. For this reason we have selected over two hundred French, German, Hebrew, Portuguese, Russian and Yiddish documents—most of them especially translated for this volume—which we consider central and illuminating. The length of the documents varies: some briefly illustrate a point, others delve into the intricacies of a debate or process. Generally, a document speaks for itself, but when arcane references make it unintelligible, we have added explanatory numbered notes following the document. Notes original to the document are marked by symbols and appear at the bottom of the page. We have also woven the documents into a conceptual and narrative apparatus—explained in the introduction—which helps articulate their meanings. Although our selection and organization of the documents reveal a certain perspective, we do not propose a specific thesis. Rather, we seek to encourage a creative interplay between the documents and the reader. Thus, while not presuming to relieve the "perplexity" of readers, this volume is intended to aid them in understanding the experience of the Jew in the modern world.

We have adopted two technical guidelines in the selection of the documents in this reader. First, we have sought to minimize duplicating material found in volumes that are readily available.[2] Second, we have made an effort to include documents which, although frequently referred to in scholarly discussions of modern Jewish history, are not generally available in English translation.

Although scholars' lives are said to be solitary, they also participate in a special sharing, both with the subject of inquiry and with fellow scholars. The scholarly community bridges time and space and includes persons not personally known by the individual. Our indebtedness to the community of scholars is recorded in the text. In the preparation of this book we also enjoyed the personal encouragement and generosity of many colleagues and friends in the academic community: Lloyd P. Gartner, Arthur A. Goren, Michael Heymann, Jacob Katz, Otto Dov Kulka, Walter Z. Laqueur, Ezra Mendelsohn and George L. Mosse. We are most grateful for their assistance and sincere interest in our project.

We also wish to acknowledge the competent translations by Saul Fischer, Sylvia Fuks, Mark Gelber, Deborah Goldman, Jeffrey Green, Jacob Hessing, Rita Mendes-Flohr, Jeffrey Rubin, Laura Sachs, Arnold Schwartz, Saul Stampler, Stephen Weinstein and Rachel Weiss. We are grateful to Ann Joachim and Carole Wolkan for their help in preparing the first draft of the index, to Ann Hofstra Grogg for preparing the final version of the index and to Regina Alkalai for typing the manuscript. We particularly appreciate the intelligent, resourceful and devoted assistance of Stephen Weinstein.

Thanks are due also to the Horace H. Rackham School of Graduate Studies of the University of Michigan for financial assistance in the final stages of the preparation of the manuscript.

Finally, we would like to express our deepest gratitude to our former teachers at the Department of Near Eastern and Judaic Studies of Brandeis University: Professors Alexander Altmann, Nahum N. Glatzer and Ben Halpern. With scholarly eminence, sensitivity and wisdom they taught us that genuine scholarship is a moral and spiritual endeavor. We hope that this book will prove a worthy tribute to them.

Jerusalem
Ann Arbor, Michigan
April 1979

Paul R. Mendes-Flohr
Jehuda Reinharz

2. See Robert Chazan and Marc Lee Raphael, eds., *Modern Jewish History: A Source Reader* (New York: Schocken, 1974); Lucy Dawidowicz, ed., *The Golden Tradition: Jewish Life and Thought in Eastern Europe* (Boston: Beacon Press, 1967); Nahum N. Glatzer, ed., *The Judaic Tradition* (Boston: Beacon Press, 1967) pt. 3; Arthur Hertzberg, ed., *The Zionist Idea: A Historical Analysis and Reader* (New York: Atheneum, 1969); Eliezer L. Ehrmann, ed., *Readings in Modern Jewish History: From the American Revolution to the Present* (New York: Ktav Publishing House, 1977); Walter Ackerman, ed., *Out of Our People's Past: Sources for the Study of Jewish History* (New York: The United Synagogue Commission on Jewish Education, 1977).

Contents

III The Process of Political Emancipation in Western Europe, 1789–1871

IX The American Experience

X Zionism

XI The Holocaust

The Jew in the Modern World

Introduction

According to most empirical indices contemporary Jewish life in the West is markedly different from that which the Jews traditionally led. The overarching role of religion is no longer a feature of Jewish life. Integrated in western, secular culture, contemporary Jews do not, as their forbears did, conduct their lives according to norms and criteria exclusively derived from Judaism and the Jewish experience. Economically and vocationally the Jews' activity now has an immeasurably wider range and variety than formerly. Politically, the Jews have left the ghetto and they legally enjoy either civic parity in the country of their residence or political independence in the newly sovereign State of Israel. These transformations in Jewish life are structurally parallel to the process generally called modernization that has affected any number of traditional societies in recent times.[1]

Scholars differ, of course, regarding the exact definition of modernization, with varying components of the process being alternately emphasized. Dating the process is related to the question of definition, and it is thus no less controversial. Periodization in history is inevitably problematic, for history as a fluid, dynamic process is never uniform and unidimensional. A "period" is not intrinsic to history; it is imposed by the historian to bracket years that give witness to a process he or she deems salient. For example, Heinrich Graetz, one of the pioneers of Jewish historiography in the nineteenth century, characterized the "latest epoch"[2] in Jewish history as an intellectual-spiritual process which brought the Jews to a new level of historical

1. For a most illuminating discussion of modern Jewish history within the framework of a comparative analysis of the dialectical encounter of traditional cultures with modernization, see R. J. Zwi Werblowsky, *Beyond Tradition and Modernity: Changing Religions in a Changing World* (London: University of London, The Athlone Press, 1976), ch. 3, "Sacral Particularity: The Jewish Case, with a Digression on Japan."

2. H. Graetz, *Geschichte der Juden*, 2nd ed. rev. (Leipzig, 1900), vol. 2, p. 3.

self-awareness (*Selbstbewusstsein*).[3] This epochal leap beyond the preceding period of spiritual "exhaustion"[4] was quickened by an intense, but at its most genuine moments never self-abnegating, contact with liberal European culture. Graetz associated the beginnings of the modern epoch in Jewish history with Moses Mendelssohn—the son of a Torah scribe who without forfeiting his Jewish self-esteem enjoyed the friendship and intellectual fellowship of Gotthold Ephraim Lessing and other prominent figures of the German Enlightenment.[5] For the Russian Jewish historian Simon Dubnov, on the other hand, Mendelssohn and the Jewish Enlightenment (*haskalah*) in general were merely of transitional significance.[6] Dubnov held that "the principal processes of the most modern history of the Jews" were political and social, and not cultural.[7] The fact that Mendelssohn served as the prototype for "Nathan the Wise"—the literary figure which Lessing hoped would inspire political tolerance for the Jews and for all dissenters—was thus eminently more important, in Dubnov's view, than was Mendelssohn's cultural activity. Mendelssohn *qua* Nathan the Wise is a precursor, according to Dubnov, of the era of Jewish political emancipation (and the anti-Semitic reaction to it) ushered in by the French Revolution of 1789. The late Israeli historian Ben Zion Dinur had yet another conception of modern Jewish history.[8] The modern era, as he understood it, began in 1700 when Rabbi Judah Hasid led a band of some thousand pious Jews on a march to settle the Holy Land. Most of Rabbi Judah Hasid's followers did not complete the then difficult journey, but for Dinur their effort at "organized immigration" to the ancestral homeland signified the beginnings of the revolt against Jewry's millennial Exile—a revolt which steadily gained momentum, ineluctably culminating in the 1948 reestablishment of the Jewish commonwealth in the land of Israel.

There are other conceptions of Jewish modernity, of course, many of which we will make reference to in the course of the volume.[9] What is, however, manifest in all of these conceptions, despite their often extreme variation, is the conviction that the last two hundred years or so have witnessed a radical transformation of Jewish life. If we emphasize the aspect of transformation, it is to underscore that the process of modernization in Jewish Diaspora history is neither chronologically nor geographically uniform. Not all of Mendelssohn's contemporary German Jews were "modern," nor were most nineteenth-century East European Jews. The Jews of the

3. *Ibid.*, p. 1.

4. H. Graetz, "Die Construction der juedischen Geschichte," *Zeitschrift fuer die religioesen Interessen des Judentums*, 3 (1846).

5. H. Graetz, *Geschichte der Juden*, vol. 11, pp. 1–36.

6. S. Dubnov, *History of the Jews*, ed. and trans. Moshe Spiegel, 4th definitive, rev. ed. (New York: Thomas Yoseloff, 1971), vol. 4, pp. 325–47.

7. *Ibid.*, pp. 493–501.

8. Ben Zion Dinur, *Israel and the Diaspora* (Philadelphia: Jewish Publication Society, 1969), pp. 79–161.

9. For a fine survey of the leading trends in the historiography of modern Jewish history, see Michael A. Meyer, "Where Does the Modern Period of Jewish History Begin?" *Judaism*, 24, no. 3 (Summer 1975), pp. 329–38.

Orient have for the most part just begun to enjoy the ambiguous fortunes of modernization with their settlement in the twentieth-century State of Israel.[10] This uneven pattern of Jewish modernization explains the selection of the documents we have included in this volume. While the documents, arranged according to themes, illustrate the various dimensions—political, social, intellectual—of Jewish modernity which are generally considered significant, we have emphasized those aspects that point to a break with, or at least a weakening of, traditional values, institutions and socio-economic patterns of Jewish life. To understand the nature of this eclipse of tradition (both in its specific religious and broad cultural sense),[11] it is necessary to note that it is not fortuitous that Jewish modernity, regardless of which periodization is employed, roughly coincides with what are generally considered to be the temporal delimitations of the modern period in Europe. Indeed, the transformations in Jewish life are synchronized with and informed by the intellectual criteria and institutional patterns that regulated the changes in European culture and polity. This implies that both ideationally and institutionally, Jewish modernity derives its primary energy and legitimation from sources other than the sacred authority of Jewish tradition. With this in mind, the documents we have selected make little reference, for instance, to Hasidism, a movement of popular mysticism that emerged among eighteenth-century East European Jewry.[12] To be sure, the custodians of Jewish tradition—and

10. On the modernization of Oriental Jewry, see A. N. Chouraqui, *Between East and West: A History of the Jews of North Africa* (Philadelphia: Jewish Publication Society of America, 1968), pt. 3; S. Deshen and M. Shokeid, *The Predicament of Homecoming* (Ithaca, N.Y.: Cornell University Press, 1974); S. Eisenstadt, *Israeli Society* (New York: Basic Books, 1967); Harvey Goldberg, *Cave Dwellers and Citrusgrowers: A Jewish Community in Libya and Israel* (Cambridge: Cambridge University Press, 1972); A. Weingrod, *Reluctant Pioneers: Village Development in Israel* (Ithaca, N.Y.: Cornell University Press, 1966). Harvey Goldberg has recently published a manuscript of Mordecai Ha-Cohen (1856–1929), a *maskil* from Tripoli, Libya. Significantly, Ha-Cohen was inspired by the East European Haskalah; moreover, his community was unreceptive to his secular ideas. See *Higgid Mordecai* (in Hebrew), ed. Harvey Goldberg (Jerusalem: Ben Zvi Institute, 1978). See also Norman A. Stillman, *The Jews of Arab Lands: A History and Source Book* (Philadelphia: Jewish Publication Society, 1979).

11. For a discussion of the meaning of tradition in the Jewish context, see Nathan Rotenstreich, *Tradition and Reality: The Impact of History on Modern Jewish Thought* (New York: Random House, 1972), pp. 7–18; also Gershom Scholem, "Revelation and Tradition as Religious Categories in Judaism," *The Messianic Idea in Judaism, and Other Essays on Jewish Spirituality* (New York: Schocken, 1971), pp. 281–303. We may here briefly note that traditional Judaism may be comprehended under four C's: cult, creed, code and community. In the integral unity of these four C's, formally religious aspects merge with the social and the national.

12. Although historians generally agree that Hasidism had no direct impact on the shaping of Jewish modernity, it has been argued that Hasidism challenged, often quite effectively, traditional rabbinic institutions of authority and models of religious virtuosity. Hence, it is said that Hasidism indirectly—dialectically—prepared the way to the secularization of East European Jewish life, if by secularization is meant the weakening and eclipse of religious authority and traditions. See Jacob Katz, *Tradition and Crisis: Jewish Society at the End of the Middle Ages* (New York: The Free Press, 1961), ch. 22: Gershom Scholem, *Major Trends in Jewish Mysticism*, 3rd ed. (New York: Schocken, 1961), pp. 299ff. Both Katz and Scholem also attribute great significance to Sabbatianism—the messianic movement engendered by Shabbetai Zevi (1626–1676) and the concomitant antinomian mood that affected wide circles of Jewry—as a factor weakening traditional Jewish authority and religious practice. In that the alleged impact of Hasidism (and

the Hasidim were among the most forceful—did respond to modernity and were quick to note its "dangers," often with an impressive understanding of its radical nature. We have included some illustrations of their arguments.

The conception of modernization that guided our selection of documents should explain what might seem to be an inordinate emphasis on German and Central European Jewish experience. The transformations in traditional Jewish life occurred in a comprehensive way among the Jews of the Germanic lands first and in a particularly intense manner.[13] Hence the dynamic of Jewish modernization—with all its passion, ambiguity, promise and contradictions—is viewed in an especially clarion fashion in Germany and Central Europe. Moreover, the Jewry of these regions—the so-called *deutscher Kulturbereich*[14]—established many of the intellectual and institutional forms that were paradigmatic for Jewish modernity in general. We may mention, at random, Reform, Historical (or Conservative) and Neo-Orthodox Judaism; the academic study of Judaism (*Wissenschaft des Judentums*); political Zionism. Nonetheless, we have allotted separate sections for both American and East European Jewry, because of their special experience and response to modernity. Undoubtedly the most universal feature of the Jewish experience of modernity is anti-Semitism. As they sought integration in the cultural, economic and political life of modern society, the Jews met resistance. To be sure, this resistance was in part engendered by traditional Christian antipathy toward the alleged nation of deicides, but anti-Semitism in the modern period received a unique stamp. Again Germany provides the most intense and voluble expression of our subject. The selections on anti-Semitism are thus perforce largely German. Whether or not anti-Semitism inhered logically in the process of modernization is an immensely complex question. However pertinent and interesting the question is methodologically and philosophically, the historical fact is that in their encounter with modernity the Jews experienced anti-Semitism and, worse, the Holocaust.

Sabbatianism) on Jewish modernity is largely social-psychological, its significance is admittedly difficult to measure. On the other hand, Hasidism created institutions that manifestly served to reinforce traditional Judaism in the modern period. "However much Hasidism challenged some of the norms of rabbinic Judaism, it surely did not create the characteristics of Jewish modernity. On the contrary, it soon became the most vociferous opponent of Jewish modernity" (Meyer, op. cit., p. 336).

13. In this regard, see Gerson D. Cohen's pertinent observations in his "German Jewry as Mirror of Modernity," introduction to volume twenty of *Leo Baeck Institute Year Book* (1975), pp. ix–xxxi. Salo Baron traces the emergence of certain aspects of Jewish modernity to sixteenth-century Italy and eighteenth-century Holland. See S. Baron, *A Social and Religious History of the Jews* (New York: Columbia University Press, 1937), vol. 2, pp. 205–12; see also Isaac E. Barzilay, "The Italian and Berlin Haskalah," *Proceedings of the American Academy for Jewish Research*, 29 (1960–61), pp. 17–54.

14. The term *deutscher Kulturbereich* refers to the regions of Europe in which the German language predominated as the arbiter of middle-class culture. The term thus has primarily sociological and cultural connotations. One need only mention such urban centers as Budapest (at least until the latter part of the nineteenth century), Prague and Vienna—all of which are included in the *deutscher Kulturbereich*. It is important to note that in the process of modernization many middle-class Jews in Lemberg, Czernowitz and Posen sought to identify with German language and culture.

I

Harbingers of Political and Economic Change

The emergence in Europe of the centralized state—the so-called Absolute State—from the sixteenth to the eighteenth centuries marked the transition from the medieval, feudal era to what is called the modern period. This transformation of the European political structure is associated with the concentration of political, legal and economic authority in the hands of a single ruler independent of the nobility and the church. In this process two elements were crucial: the ruler's ready access to liquid assets and a bureaucracy controlled by him. In consonance with these requirements, the centralized state facilitated the development of mercantilism or early capitalism. The Jews, particularly in Central Europe, were in a unique position to benefit from this process. Bereft of political power, thus not a threat to the ruler, yet possessing the requisite skills to assist the "absolute monarch" to develop his treasury and economy, certain *individual* Jews acquired a new status as "court Jews." This unique institution flourished especially in the seventeenth century after the conclusion of the Thirty Years War (1648) when the 240 territories that constituted the Holy Roman Empire of the German Nation each sought to consolidate their newly gained autonomy in the spirit of absolutism and mercantilism. Most German princes had their court Jews. Because of their *utility* these Jews enjoyed privileges—privileges such as those delineated in the bill of patent by Emperor Leopold of the court Jew Samson Wertheimer (1658–1724).

The institution of the court Jews—there were several hundred of them—introduced a radically new and explicit criterion for determining the legal status of the Jew in Europe: utility rather than theology. The privileged status of the court Jew, however, was a matter of exception. Most of his brethren remained despised and *dis*privileged. But the mercantilism of the absolute state had an inner logic that led to a more "enlightened" policy. The commitment of the centralized state to economic independence eventually included a program of economic expansion, of increased industry and commerce and, as a corollary, of an increase of population. This program encouraged the augmentation of the number of "useful" subjects, including Jews. The policy of "enlightened absolutism" is illustrated by the declaration of the Estates General of the United Netherlands in 1657 and the charter concerning the Jews issued by King Frederick the Great of Prussia in 1750. Indicating an acute understanding of the new economic and political ethos, Rabbi Menasseh ben Israel based his appeal for the readmission of the Jews into England, "The Humble Addresses" (1655), on mercantilist arguments. John Toland (1670–1722), Irish Deist and political philosopher, echoed remarkably similar views when he argued that England would immeasurably benefit from attracting Jews to its shores. In his pamphlet, "Reasons for Naturalizing the Jews in Great Britain and Ireland" (1714), he maintained that the manifest faults of the Jew were not innate but circumstantial. Granted equal opportunity and dignity they would prove to be resourceful and loyal subjects.

The ideological rationale of this policy was refined by the German scholar Christian Wilhelm von Dohm. In his treatise, "Concerning the Amelioration of the Civil Status of the Jews" (1781), written at the behest of his friend Moses Mendelssohn, Dohm argues that the Jew is not inherently "evil," for the faults in the character of the Jew can be ascribed to the deleterious effects of repression and economic restrictions. He thus concludes that the removal of these negative conditions would render the Jews less "harmful" and, moreover, prepare them for a gradual increase of rights and improved conditions "if and when they may deserve them." The Edict of Tolerance (1782), issued by Joseph II, the emperor of Austria, emphasizes Dohm's proposition that civic betterment of the Jews requires that in exchange the Jews reform many of their cultural values and institutions. This *quid pro quo* exacted of the Jews indicates how far the Jewish policy of enlightened absolutism was from the democratic principles of civic parity as an intrinsic right to be granted the Jew as a human being. The remaining selections, which record the debate surrounding Dohm's treatise, underscore this point.

MENASSEH BEN ISRAEL[1]

1. How Profitable the Nation of the Jews Are

Three things, if it please your Highnesse, there are that make a strange *Nation* well-beloved amongst the Natives of a land where they dwell: (as the defect of those *three* things make them hatefull) viz. *Profit*, they may receive from them; *Fidelity* they hold towards their Princes; and the *Noblenes* and purity of their blood. Now when I shall have made good, that all *these three* things are found in the *Jewish* Nation, I shall certainly persuade your Highnesse, that with a favorable eye (Monarchy being changed into a Republicq), you shall be pleased to receive again the Nation of the Jews, who in time past lived in that Island: but, I know not by what false Informations, were cruelly handled and banished.

Profit is a most powerfull motive, and which all the World preferres before all other things: and therefore we shall handle that point first.

It is a thing confirmed, that merchandizing is, as it were, the proper profession of the Nation of the Jews. I attribute this in the first place, to the particular Providence and mercy of God towards his people: for having banished them from their own Country, yet not from his Protection, he hath given them, as it were, a naturall instinct, by which they might not only gain what is necessary for their need, but that they should also thrive in Riches and possessions; whereby they should not onely become gracious to their Princes and Lords, but that they should be invited by others to come and dwell in their Lands.

Moreover, it cannot be denyed, but that necessity stirrs up a man's ability and industry; and that it gives him great incitement, by all means to trie the favour of Providence.

Besides, seeing it is no wisedome for them to endeavour the gaining of Lands and other immovable goods, and so to imprison their possessions here, where their persons are subject to so many casualities, banishments and peregrinations; they are forced to use merchandizing untill that time, when they shall returne to their own Country, that then as God hath promised by the Prophet Zachary, *Their shall be found no more any marchant amongst them in the House of the Lord.*

From that very thing we have said, there riseth an infallible Profit, commodity and gain to all those Princes in whose Lands they dwell above all other strange Nations whatsoever, as experience by divers *Reasons* doth confirme.

I. The Jews, have no opportunity to live in their own Country, to till the Lands or other like employments, give themselves wholy unto marchandizing, and for contriving new Inventions, no Nation almost going beyond them. And so 'tis observed, that wheresoever they go to dwell, there presently the Traficq begins to florish. Which may be seen in divers places, especially in Lighorne, which having been but a very ignoble and inconsiderable City, is at this time, by the great concourse of people, one of the most famous places of Trafique of whole Italy. . . .

II. The Nation of the Jews is dispersed throughout the whole World, it being a chastisement that God hath layd upon them for their Idolatries, Deut. 28:69, Ezech. 20:23, Nehem. 1:8, Ps. 107:27. and by their other sinnes their families suffer the same shipwrack.

Now in this dispersion our Fore-fathers

Source: Menasseh ben Israel, "To His Highnesse the Lord Protector of the Commonwealth of England, Scotland and Ireland," *The Humble Addresses of Menasseh ben Israel* (1655), in *Menasseh ben Israel's Mission to Oliver Cromwell: Being a Reprint of the Pamphlets published by Menasseh ben Israel to promote the Re-admission of the Jews to England, 1649–1656*, ed. Lucien Wolf (London: Macmillan & Co., 1901), pp. 81–89. The original orthography has been retained.

flying from the Spanish Inquisition, some of them came in Holland, others got into Italy, and others betooke themselves into Asia; and so easily they credit one another; and by that means they draw the Negotiation where-ever they are, where with all of them marchandizing and having perfect knowledge of all the kinds of Moneys, Diamants, Cochinil, Indigo, Wines, Oyle, and other Commodities, that serve from place to place; especially holding correspondence with their friends and kinds-folk, whose language they understand; they do abundantly enrich the Lands and Countrys of Strangers, where they live, not onely with what is requisite and necessary for the life of man; but also what may serve for ornament to his civill condition. Of which *Traficq,* there ariseth ordinarily *Five* important benefits.

1. The augmentation of the Publiq Tolls and Customes, at their coming and going out of the place.

2. The transporting and bringing in of marchandises from remote Countries.

3. The affording of Materials in great plenty for all Mechaniqs; as Wooll, Leather, Wines, Jewels, as Diamants, Pearles, and such like Merchandize.

4. The venting and exportation of so many kinds of Manifactures.

5. The Commerce and reciprocall Negotiation at Sea, which is the ground for Peace between neighbour Nations, and of great profit to their own Fellow-citizens.

III. This reason is the more strengthened, when we see, that not onely the Jewish Nation dwelling in Holland and Italy, trafficqs with their own stocks but also with the riches of many others of their own Nation, friends, kinds-men and acquaintance, which notwithstanding live in Spaine, and send unto them their moneys and goods, which they hold in their hands, and content themselves with a very small portion of their estate, to the end they may be secure and free from danger that might happen unto them, in case they should fall under the yoke of the Inquisition; whence not onely their goods, but oftentimes also their lives are endangered.

IV. The love that men ordinarily beare to their own Country and the desire they have to end their lives, where they had their beginning, is the cause, that most strangers having gotten riches where they are in a forain land, are commonly taken in a desire to returne to their native soil, and there peaceably to enjoy their estate; so that as they were a help to the places where they lived, and negotiated while they remained there; so when they depart from thence, they carry all away, and spoile them of their wealth; transporting all into their own native Country: But with the Jews the case is farre different; for where the Jews are once kindly receaved, they make a firm resolution never to depart from thence, seeing they have no proper place of their own: and so they are alwayes with their goods in the Cities where they live, a perpetuall benefit to all payments. Which reasons do clearly proove, that it being the property of Citizens in populous and rich countries, to seeke their rest and ease with buying lands and faire possession of which they live; many of them hating commerce, aspire to Titles and Dignities: therefore of all strangers, in whose hands ordinarily Trafique is found, there are none so profitable and beneficiall to the place where they trade and live, as is the Nation of the Jews. And seeing amongst the people of Europ, the chiefest riches they possesse, from Spain, those neighbour Nations, where the Jews shall finde liberty to live according to their own Judaicall Laws, they shall most easily draw that benefit to themselves by means of the industry of our Nation, and their mutuall correspondence.

From hence (if it please your Highness) it results, that the Jewish Nation, though scattered through the whole World, are not therefore a despisable people, but as a Plant worthy to be planted in the whole world, and received into Populous Cities: who ought to plant them in those places, which are most secure from danger; being trees of most savory fruit and profit, to be alwayes most favoured with Laws and Privileges, or Prerogatives, secured and defended by Armes.

. . . The chiefest place where the Jews live, is the Turkish Empire, where some of them live in great estate, even in the Court of the Grand Turke at Constantinople, by reason there is no Viceroy, or Governour, or Bassa,[2] which hath not a Jew to manage his affaires, and to take care for his estate: Hence it cometh that in short time they grow up to be Lords of great revenues, and they most frequently bend the minds of Great ones to most weighty affaires in government.

The greatest Viceroy of whole Europe is the Bassa of Egypt; this Bassa always takes to him, by order of the Kingdome, a Jew with the title of Zarf-Bassa (*Thresurer*) viz. of all the Revenues of that government, who receaves purses full of money, seals them, and then sends them to the King. This man in a short time grows very rich, for that by his hands as being next to the Bassa, the 24 Governments of that Empire are sould and given, and all other businesses managed. At present he that possesseth this place, is called Sr. Abraham Alhula. The number of Jews living in this Kingdome of the Great Turke, is very great, and amounts to many Millions. In Constantinople alone there are 48 Synagogues, and in Salaminque 36, and more than fourescore thousand soules in these two Cities alone.

The first King gave them great privileges which they enjoy untill this day: for besides the liberty, they have every-where, of trading with open shops, of bearing any Office and possessing of any goods, both mooveable and immooveable, he yet graunted them power to judge all Civil causes according to their own Laws amongst themselves. Moreover they are exempted from going to Warres, and that souldiers should be quartered in their houses, and that Justice should take no place upon the death of any one that left no heir to his Estate. . . .

In Germany, there live also a great multitude of Jews, especially at Prague, Vienna and Franckfurt, very much favoured by the most mild and most gracious Emperours, but despised of the people, being a Nation not very finely garnished by reason of their vile cloathing: yet notwithstanding there is not wanting amongst them persons of great quality.

. . . But yet a greater number of Jews are found in the Kingdome of Poland, Prussia and Lethuania, under which Monarchy they have the Jurisdiction to judge amongst themselves all causes, both Criminal and Civil; and also great and famous Academies of their own. The chief Cities where the Nation liveth, are Lublin and Cracow, where there is a Jew, called Isaac Iecells, who built a Synagogue, which stood him in one hundred thousand Francs, and is worth many tons of gold. There is in this place such infinite number of Jews; that although the Cosaques in the late warres have killed of them above one hundred and fourescore thousand; yet it is sustained that they are yet at this day as innumerable as those were that came out of Egypt. In that Kingdome the whole Negotiation is in the hand of the Jews, the rest of the Christians are either all Noble-men, or Rustiques and kept as slaves.

In Italy they are generally protected by all the Princes: their principall residence is in the most famous City of Venice; so that in that same City alone they possesse about 1400 Houses; and are used there with much courtesy and clemency. Many also live in Padoa and Verona; others in Mantua, and also many in Rome it self. Finally they are scattered here and there in the chief places of Italy, and do live there with many speciall privileges. . . .

In all these places the Jews live (in a manner) all of them Merchants, and that without any prejudice at all to the Natives: For the Natives, and those especially that are most rich, they build themselves houses and Palaces, buy Lands and firme goods, aime at Titles and Dignities, and so seek their rest and contentment that way: But as for the Jews they aspire at nothing, but to preferre themselves in their way of Marchandize; and so employing their *Capitals*, they send forth the benefit of their labour amongst many and sundry of the Natives, which they, by the trafick of their Negotiation, do enrich. From whence it's easy to judge of the profit that

Princes and Common-wealths do reap, by giving liberty of Religion to the Jews, and gathering them by some speciall privileges into their Countries: as Trees that bring forth such excellent fruits.

So that if one Prince, ill advised, driveth them out of his Land, yet another invites them to his; and shews them favour. Wherein we may see the prophecy of Jacob fulfilled in the letter: *The staffe (to support him) shall not depart from Jacob, untill Messias shall come.* And this shall suffice concerning the Profit of the Jewish Nation.

NOTES

1. Menasseh (also Manasseh) ben Israel (c. 1604–1657), Dutch rabbi of Marrano parentage. He energetically sought to persuade the English to permit the return of the Jews to *their* country, from which they were expelled in 1290. He went to London in 1655 and presented a petition to Oliver Cromwell, Lord Protector of Great Britain. Although his mission was ostensibly unsuccessful, it did prepare the way for the resettlement of the Jews in England.

2. Earlier English for the Turkish word "Pasha."

JOHN TOLAND[1]
2. Reasons for Naturalizing the Jews in Great Britain and Ireland

Tis manifest almost at first sight, that the common reasons for a GENERAL NATURALIZATION, are as strong in behalf of the *Jews*, as of any other people whatsoever. They encrease the number of hands for labor and defence, of bellies and backs for consumtion of food and raiment, and of brains for invention and contrivance, no less than any other nation. We all know that numbers of people are the true riches and power of any country, and we have been often told, that this is the reason, why *Spain* (since the expulsion of the *Jews* and *Moors*) being continually drain'd of her inhabitants by the colonies in *America*, and all other Nations being in a manner kept out by the rigor of the *Inquisition*, is grown so prodigiously weak and poor: whereas, tho *Holland has comparatively but few native Inhabitants, and sends great numbers yearly to the East-Indies;* yet allowing an unlimited LIBERTY OF CONSCIENCE, and receiving all nations to the right of citizens, the country is ever well stockt with people, and consequently both rich and powerful to an eminent degree. . . .

My Purpose at present then, is to prove, that the *Jews* are so farr from being an Excresence or Spunge (as some wou'd have it) and a useless member in the Commonwealth, or being ill subjects, and a dangerous people on any account, that they are obedient, peaceable, useful, and advantageous as any; and even more so than many others: which last point, as seeming the least probable, I shall briefly demonstrate in two or three respects. And, in the first place, it is evident, that by receiving of the *Jews*, no body needs be afraid that any religious Party in the nation will thereby be weaken'd or enforc'd. The *Protestant Dissenters* have no reason to be jealous, that they shou'd join with the *National Church* to oppress them, since they have an equal Interest to preserve LIBERTY OF CONSCIENCE; and that the example of *Spain* and *Portugal*

Source: John Toland, *Reasons for Naturalizing the Jews in Great Britain and Ireland, On the same foot with all other Nations. Containing also, A Defence of the Jews against all Vulgar Prejudices in all Countries* (London, 1714), pp. 6, 10–15, 17, 20, 39–46. Original orthography and emphases are retained.

has taught 'em how dangerous a thing it is, that one sett of *Clergy-men* shou'd dispose and influence all things at their pleasure in any country. The *National Church* on the other hand, has no reason to be jealous that the *Jews* shou'd come in for snacks with them in sharing the Ecclesiastical Benefites; so that no candidate or expectant from the *University* needs shew his zeal on this occasion, to keep the *Jews* out of the nation (as has been done once on a time to keep the *Dissenters* out of the *Church*) lest he should be shoulder'd out of a Parish by some *Levite,* or be kept from a fat Bishoprick by a *Rabbi.* There's as little danger they shou'd ever join with any particular Body of *Dissenters* against the *National Church,* since they can expect no more favor from the one, than from the other; and that it is always their interest to preserve the legal Establishment, on which their own Security is grounded. For this reason likewise, they'll never join with any Party in civill Affairs, but that which patronizes LIBERTY OF CONSCIENCE and the NATURALIZATION, which will ever be the side of Liberty and the Constitution. But otherwise they are wholly devested of those engagements to WHIG and TORY, which are become hereditary in so many Families: and this holds as true of other Factions, which shou'd consequently recommend them to the favor of all Parties, would people but think for themselves; and not, like so many Brutes, be led or driven by a few self-interested Demagogues.

ANOTHER Consideration that makes the *Jews* preferable to several sorts of People, is, their having no Country of their own, to which they might retire, after having got Estates here; or in favor of which, they might trade under the umbrage of our NATURALIZATION, which I am certain will be done by many, unless prevented by proper Laws: for I have known several get themselves naturaliz'd before the late *Act,* yet without ever designing to live in *England,* or to become a part of the *English* Government; but to avoid in their Factorship paying Aliens duties, and for other reasons well known to the Merchants. But the *Jews* having no such Country, to which they are ty'd by inclination or interest as their own, will never likewise enter into any political engagements, which might be prejudicial to ours, as we have known (for Example) certain *French* Refugees to have done, notwithstanding their protection; nay, and to be ever pleas'd with any successes against us (which I say, without Prejudice to the more honest and more numerous part) as making for the greatness of their nation, wherein they still took a sort of pride, and to which, some of 'em are gone back again, after failing of their expectations here. The *Jews* therefore being better us'd with us, than any where else in the world, are sure to be ours for ever; which is more than we dare reasonably promise from any other nation, whatever may be expected from their posterity.

To ascend from these particular to more general Reasons, we may observe that Trade is by certain circumstances shar'd in such a manner, and parcell'd out among the inhabitants of the earth, that some, by way of eminence, may be call'd the Factors, some the Carriers, some the Miners, others the Manufactorers, and others yet the Store-keepers of the world. Thus the *Jews* may properly be said to be the Brokers of it, who, whithersoever they come, create business as well as manage it. Yet it is neither by any National Institution or Inclination (as many ignorantly believe) that they do now almost entirely betake themselves to business of Exchange, Insurances, and improving of money upon Security; but they are driven to this way of Livelihood by mere Necessity: for being excluded every where in *Europe,* from publick Employments in the State, as they are from following Handycraft-trades in most places, and in almost all, from purchasing immovable Inheritances, this does no less naturally, than necessarily, force 'em to Trade and Usury, since otherwise they cou'd not possibly live. Yet let 'em once be put upon an equal foot with others, not only for buying and selling, for security and protection to their Goods and Persons; but likewise for Arts and Handycraft-trades, for purchasing and inheriting of estates in Lands and Houses (with which they may as well be trusted as with Shares in the *publick Funds*) and then I doubt not, but they'll insensibly betake themselves to Building, Farming, and all sorts of Improvement like other people. . . . I envy not those whole streets of magnificent buildings, that the *Jews* have erected at *Amsterdam* and the *Hague:* but there are other *Jews* enow in the World to adorn *London* or *Bristol* with the like, the fifth part of the People in *Poland* (to name no other Country) being of this Nation. Nay, the very Original of their present numerous Settlement at *Prague* in *Bohemia,* is a Privilege granted them in the tenth Century, to build a Synagogue there, as a recompence for the valiant assistance they lent the inhabitants, in expelling the invading and depopulating Barbarians: And I fancy they could kill the enemies of our British Islands, when they become their own with equal alacrity. . . .

There are among the *Jews,* to be sure, sordid wretches, sharpers, extortioners, villains of all sorts and degrees: and where is that happy nation, where is that religious profession, of which the same may not be as truly affirm'd? They have likewise their men of probity and worth, persons of courage and conduct, of liberal and generous spirits. But one rule of life, which is willingly admitted, nay, and eagerly pleaded by all Societies in their own case (tho miserably neglected in that of others) is, *not to impute the faults of a few to the whole number;* which, considering the unavoidable mixture of good and bad in all communities, wou'd be no less want of charity, than want of justice. The *Jews* therefore are both in their origine and progress, not otherwise to be regarded, than under the common circumstances of human nature. The *Romans* were not less esteem'd for being descended from Shepherds and Fugitives (which original they had in common with the *Jews*) than are the *English* for being the progeny of barbarous pyrates. . . . The vulgar, I confess, are seldom pleas'd in any country with the coming in of Foreners among 'em: which proceeds first, from their ignorance, that at the beginning they were such themselves; secondly, from their grudging at more persons sharing the same trades or business with them, which they call *taking the bread out of their mouths;* and, thirdly, from their being deluded to this aversion by the artifice of those who design any change in the Government. But as wise Magistrates will prevent the last, and are sensible of the first: so they know the second cause of the people's hatred, to be the true cause of the land's felicity; and therefore, not minding those, who mind nothing but their selfish projects, they'll ever highly encourage a confluence of strangers. We deny not that there will thus be more taylors and shoomakers; but there will also be more suits and shoos made than before. If there be more weavers, watchmakers, and other artificers, we can for this reason export more cloth, watches, and more of all other commodities than formerly: and not only have 'em better made by the emulation of so many workmen, of such different Nations; but likewise have 'em quicker sold off, for being cheaper wrought than those of others, who come to the same market. This one Rule of MORE, and BETTER, and CHEAPER, will ever carry the market against all expedients and devices.

That the encrease of people encreases import and export, garrisons and armies, with the tillage that feeds, and the revenues that pay 'em, is, I hope, no longer a doubt or secret to any. But this only in order the more speedily and effectually to bring these things to pass, that I plead at present for the NATURALIZATION OF THE JEWS. This once accomplish'd, I have reason not only to believe that they'll fall to building, husbandry, navigation, and purchasing (as I hinted before) but that they'll come in greater numbers than other people from all countries hither. In several places they are still very hardly treated, tho their throats are not so familiarly cut as formerly. They are generally expos'd to the affronts and rapine of the Soldiery with impunity; whereas they wou'd be safe from all such rude Insults in the peaceable arms of *Britannia.* I have been in several Cities, where they are infamously lock'd up every night, in a quarter by themselves, under a peculiar guard, as at *Prague;* and in others, as at *Colen,* they are not permitted to dwell within the City, but whenever they come over from *Deuts,* on t'other side of the *Rhine,* they must pay so much for every hour they continue in the town, which they must also leave before Sun-set: whereas, if the Citizens of *Colen* understood their own interest, they shou'd rather give 'em immunities and privileges, with a *Synagogue* into the bargain, in order to inhabit among 'em. What a paltry fisher-town was *Leghorn,* before the admission of the *Jews?* What a loser is *Lisbon,* since they have been lost to it? I name these cities only for example-sake, having been a witness to such preposterous politics in many others. They are in most places forc'd to wear a distinct habit, and they do yellow hats at *Rome,* and red ones at *Venice;* they are often taxt for their passage, and lie under a great many other partial regulations. Tis true, that in *Turky* they enjoy immoveable property,. and exercise mechanic arts; they have likewise numerous Academies in *Poland,* where they study in the *Civil* and *Canon* Laws of their nation, being privileg'd to determine even certain criminal Causes among themselves: yet they are treated little better than Dogs in the first place, and are often exposed in the last to unspeakable Calamities.

Now the worse they are us'd on the foresaid and the like accounts in any country, the more they'll be dispos'd to transport themselves hither, where already they live promiscuously with the other Citizens, and without any distinction of habit, or imposition of tribute. They have neither many lucrative employments, nor immoveable possessions to quit in other places, excepting the latter in *Holland;* whereas here they may hope for both, and being once with us, will never leave us: since they cannot be allur'd by ampler privileges from any nation besides; or at least if they be, it must needs be solely our fault. Let no man mistake what I have said of employments: for in the *Church* as I have shewn above, they'll accept of none; and they are as much excluded from most preferments in the *State,* by reason of certain forms of oaths, and some other conditions, which consistently with their religion they cannot perform. But there are offices, where such qualifications are not requir'd; and which may indifferently be held by men of all religions, as many in the *Exchequer, Customs,* and *Excise:* nor can I see any reason, why the *Jews* may not be employ'd in several Affairs in the city, as to be Directors of the *Bank,* of the *East India Company,* or the like; and we know the nature of mankind to be such, as not seldom to be ambitious of even expensive employments, for the credit of the honor or the trust. In how many places, since their dispersion (tho not so frequently of late) have they enjoy'd considerable posts and offices? They have in some been *first Ministers,* high *Treasurers* in many, and *Envoys* in most. In a word they ought to be so naturaliz'd in *Great Britain* and *Ireland,* as, like the *Quakers,* to be incapacitated in nothing, but where they incapacitate themselves. A General Naturalization, and a Total Incapacity from Offices, are perfect inconsistencies: for as one, who understood this matter very well, says, *If few have been found ever since mankind existed, that wou'd for their own native country, without the expectation of any reward, expose their bodies to the weapons of their enemies; do you think there may be such a person found, that will undergo dangers for another Government, where not only he receives no reward, but that he is absolutely excluded from any?*[2] But the privilege of purchasing alone (especially since Titles are like to be generally secur'd by the gradual Introduction of *Registers*) will be the most powerful motive to bring the richest of the *Jews* hither: for it may be easily demonstrated, that the want of immoveable property is the true Reason, and not any pretended Curse or other ridiculous fancy, why none of the vast estates they so frequently acquire, seldom or ever descends to the third Generation; but are always floating and unfixt, which hinders their families from growing considerable, and consequently deprives them of the credit and authority, whereof all men of worth may be laudably ambitious.

NOTES

1. Influenced by Thomas Hobbes, Baruch Spinoza and John Locke, Toland (1670–1722) was one of the most radical followers of the Enlightenment in Great Britain. His pamphlet, published anonymously, was written during the public debate regarding the naturalization of foreign-born Protestants in Great Britain. Although it elicited little but derisive comment, Toland's essay was the earliest plea for the comprehensive toleration of the Jews, thus initiating the protracted literary struggle for Jewish civic equality.

2. Cicero, *Pro L. Cornelius, Balbo Ocatio,* ch. 10.

THE ESTATES GENERAL OF THE REPUBLIC OF THE UNITED PROVINCES

3. Declaration Protecting the Interest of Jews Residing in Holland (July 13, 1657)[1]

Upon the request of the elders of the Jewish nation, residing within the United Provinces, as well as those in the Province of Holland, also of those in the city of Amsterdam presented to Their Very Puissant [the Estates General] containing complaints about unjust and severe procedures applied to them for some time, by the King of Spain and his subjects with regard to their traffic and navigation as well as in other respects; the officials after deliberation do understand and declare that it should be understood and declared herewith that those of the aforementioned Jewish nation are truly subjects and residents of the United Netherlands, and that they also therefore must enjoy, possess and profit by the conditions, rights and advantages, provided by the Treaties of Peace and Navigation concluded with the aforementioned King of Spain, or other Treaties, Agreements, Alliances and Engagements with other Kings, Republics, Princes, Potentates, States, Towns, Cities, demanded and obtained in favor of the inhabitants of the State. Therefore, the rights and advantages of those of this nation will, in the aforementioned cases, as well as in other similar situations, be maintained, and wherever the contrary should be done or undertaken, it shall be prevented as it has been agreed.

NOTE

1. According to the Peace of Muenster (1648), Spain was obliged to permit the subjects of the Netherlands to reside and engage in commerce in Spain and Portugal. But the Spanish monarch adamantly held that this provision did not apply to the Jewish *residents* of the Netherlands. In response, the Estates General made the above declaration. Historians have usually regarded the declaration of July 13, 1657 as the first such statement on the part of any government. However, one ought to keep in mind that the Jews were always allowed to become burghers of Amsterdam and were regarded as residents of Holland from the very beginning of the seventeenth century. The declaration concerned the protection of the trade of residents of the province of Holland yet entailed no confirmation of citizenship, as such a concept did not yet exist. Moreover, similar declarations of protection had been made as early as 1603 (regarding the "Portuguese" merchants). See Daniel M. Swetschinski, "The Portuguese Jewish Merchants of Seventeenth-Century Amsterdam: A Social Profile" (Ph.D. diss., Brandeis University, 1979), pp. 590–91 and 107n.

Source: H. J. Koenen, *Geschiedenis der Joden in Nederland* (Utrecht, 1843), pp. 487–88. Raphael Mahler, ed. and trans., *Jewish Emancipation, A Selection of Documents by R. Mahler,* Pamphlet Series, Jews and the Post-War World, no. 1 (New York: The American Jewish Committee, 1941), pp. 10–11. Reprinted by permission of the American Jewish Committee.

EMPEROR LEOPOLD

4. The Appointment of Samson Wertheimer as Imperial Court Factor[1]

We, Leopold, elected Roman Emperor by the grace of God, in the name [of the House of Hapsburg], the name of our heirs and our descendants, with this letter proclaim publicly that we have graciously looked upon the industrious, indefatigable, efficacious, loyal and selfless services that have been rendered to the Holy Roman Empire and to our, the Imperial House of Austria—and especially on behalf of our Court Chamber and other princes and estates of the Roman Empire—by the Court Factor [*Ober Factor*][2] Samson Wertheimer,[3] chief rabbi of the Jews in our countries, throughout the last seventeen years. He has proven himself on various and important missions, here as well as in other places to which he was sent—especially in former Turkey, the Rhineland, France and Italy. When heavy fighting broke out over the issue of the succession to the Spanish Crown,[4] he came to the aid of the Roman Empire greatly expediting the military operations. He took care of expenses incurred by our Emperor, our beloved son, the King of Rome and Hungary, the Archduke Carl and the rest of the court. Further, in order to meet the innumerable and extraordinary expenses of the Imperial Court during the war, he not only spent in a wise and prudent manner the many millions provided him in cash by the War Treasury and the Court, but he also advanced [the Empire] several loans at [a low] interest. The loans were advanced partly by his personal credit, and partly with our principalities as collateral, such as our Archduchy of Silesia and others, but especially the salt-mines of Siebenbuergen. For the lease of these mines he immediately received a million ducats. To our great pleasure, he has managed to perform all these deeds by the allocation of subsidies, money, and work. Even today, he and his son are constantly busy serving us and the public; his only wish is the permission to continue his services. In the light of his well-known qualities, his high intelligence and his considerable skill this permission will gladly be granted. In grateful recognition of all this we have not only presented Samson Wertheimer and his son Wolff with our the Imperial chain of grace and our portrait; we have also honored him with a gift of one thousand ducats for the acquisition of some silver or golden dishes for his successful negotiations [in raising a dowry] on behalf of our beloved cousin and brother-in-law, the Count Palatini, Charles Philip. Furthermore, we have decreed that Samson Wertheimer be designated as our Imperial Court Factor, in which capacity he shall remain forever, and which title he shall hold before every man and authority our heirs and descendants included. But in order that our Court Factor Samson Wertheimer may enjoy our Imperial grace more fully, in order that he may accomplish his tasks with minimal hindrance and may peacefully travel, he and the members of his family, both in our Empire and in foreign lands, we have bestowed still another grace upon him: We have not only confirmed and ratified the protective privileges issued on June 1, 1683 and on May 28, 1695, including all clauses, articles, interpretations and terms contained therein, but have extended their validity for another twenty years beyond the time specified therein. This extension is granted

Source: David Kaufmann, *Samson Wertheimer, Der Oberhoffactor und Landesrabbiner, und seine Kinder* (Wien, 1888), pp. 29–33. Trans. here by J. Hessing.

within our rights as Roman Emperor and King and within our rights as a territorial prince: We wish our Court Factor Samson Wertheimer to be successful in all further service which he will render us and the electors of the Empire. We are cognizant that his indefatigable services during the last seventeen years have diminished his bodily strength, and we therefore allow him to dwell in our Roman lands and the lands of our crown—together with his son, daughter-in-law, grandchildren and whoever may dwell with him presently, and also all members of his family of either sex, wherever they may be, grandchildren, servants and others included—for another twenty years, starting on May 28, 1715. During this time he will be exempt from all tithes and taxes. He will have to pay neither protection-money [*Schutzgeld*] nor tolerance-money [*Toleranzgeld*].[5] Nor will he have to pay any duties, whether they be regular or irregular, or however they may be designated. In all the above-mentioned places he will enjoy our Imperial and Royal protection, or the protection extended to him in our capacity as a territorial prince, and everywhere we will guarantee his personal security and the freedom of his movement, be it in Vienna, the city of our Imperial residence, or in any other place. And wherever he may be, whether in the Empire or in our crown lands, whether with the members of his family or without them, their sojourn will be legal; they shall have the right to stay there with their people, their horses, their cattle, their wagons and the rest of their property. They shall be entitled to pay with their own money for room and board wherever they will find it convenient to do so. All this they shall be able to do in peace and security, in freedom and without fear, and no further and special decree from our Court shall be necessary to confirm their rights. Furthermore, they shall not be disturbed in the observance of their religious rites and the Mosaic laws as they appertain to their daily life as well as in matters of death; this right is in accordance with the custom laid down in the constitution of the Empire where similar rights are granted to the Jewish communities which he, Wertheimer, serves as our privileged rabbi. These rights, however, do not affect any other Jews outside these communities. . . . On acquisition of property, they shall have to pay the same duties as Christians do, and no more. In addition, we allow them to move about from place to place, on land or on water, with horse and carriage, without interference or disturbance, taking along their goods and cash assets in order to serve the Court or our military camps. They shall also be entitled to possess, without any restriction, any Hebrew books which he, Wertheimer, needs for the performance of his rabbinical duties. . . . In case any member of the Wertheimer family [men of age] dies before this privilege and letter of grace expires, all clauses and articles contained therein will remain in force for the widow, children and servants until the specified date. It is understood that you, Wertheimer, will be personally responsible for the conduct of the members of your family and the integrity of their commercial transactions. We hereby order all authorities under our jurisdiction, ecclesiastical and secular, of both the higher and lower echelons, and especially the magistrate and the Lord Mayor of Vienna, the city of our Imperial residence, to protect our Court Factor and Court Jew Samson Wertheimer as well as his sons-in-law, grandchildren and anybody else who may happen to be in his company, their wives and children included, until the date specified in this privilege, issued by our Imperial grace and within our capacity as a territorial prince: that they shall not be troubled, interfered with or harmed in any way, and that anybody who dares to do them any harm shall be punished by the withdrawal of our grace and a penal fine of thirty gold marks. We consider this to be a matter of great seriousness and put our Imperial seal to this document, issued in Vienna, our Imperial capital and city of residence, on August 29, 1703; the forty-sixth year of our Roman reign; the forty-ninth year of our Hungarian reign; the forty-seventh year of our Bohemian reign.

NOTES

1. Leopold I of Hungary (1640–1705), Holy Roman emperor (1658–1705), king of Bohemia (1656–1705), and king of Hungary (1655–1705). His hostility toward the Jews (whom he expelled from Vienna in 1670) was tempered by his sincere appreciation of court Jews in his service. Samson Wertheimer (1658–1724) was a court Jew, rabbi, scholar and patron of scholars. The preceding document not only delineates his privileges (to be seen in light of the disprivileged status of the Jewish masses), but also describes his varied activities on behalf of the crown—financial, commercial and even diplomatic.

2. A great variety of titles were used to designate court Jews, e.g., *Hofjude, Hoffactor, Hofprovedieteur, Hofagent, Kabinettfactor,* and *Kommerzienrat.*

3. The text consistently has Simsson Wertheimber.

4. The Peace of Utrecht (1713) was a settlement of decisive importance. In 1704, the British navy had captured Gibraltar; Utrecht guaranteed its possession. In addition, Britain gained firm foothold in America: Newfoundland, the Hudson's Bay Territory and Nova Scotia. While the Bourbon king of Spain, Philip V, was confirmed on the throne, the separation of the Spanish and French crowns was written into the peace, and Spanish possessions in the Mediterranean and the Netherlands were handed to the Austrian Hapsburgs and other members of the coalition. The Dutch too profited in military security. Even Eastern Europe entered into the settlement. Prussia obtained new territories, and the title of "king in Prussia" which the elector Frederick had taken in 1701, was officially confirmed.

5. In Austrian usage "protection money" was an annual tax exacted collectively on the Jewish community; "tolerance money" was a tax that individual Jews payed for the right of residence.

THE HOUSES OF PARLIAMENT
5. The Plantation Act (March 19, 1740)[1]

Whereas the increase of people is a means of advancing the wealth and strength of any nation or country: and whereas many foreigners and strangers from the lenity of our government, the purity of our religion, the benefit of our laws, the advantage of our trade, and the security of our property, might be induced to come and to settle in some of his Majesty's colonies in America, if they were made partakers of the advantages and privileges which the natural born subjects of this realm do enjoy; be it therefore enacted by the King's most excellent majesty, by and with the advice and consent of the lords spiritual and temporal, and commons, in this present parliament assembled, and by the authority of the same, That from and after the first day of June, in the year of our Lord one thousand seven hundred and forty, all persons born out of the ligeance of his Majesty, his heirs or successors, who have inhabited and resided, or shall inhabit or reside, for the space of seven years or more, in any of his Majesty's colonies in America, and shall not have been absent out of some of the said colonies for a longer space than two months at any one time during the said seven years, and shall take and subscribe the oaths, and make, repeat, and subscribe the declaration appointed by an act made in the first year of the reign of his late Majesty King George the First . . . before the chief judge, or other judge

Source: "An Act for Naturalizing Such Foreign Protestants, and Others Therein Mentioned, As Are Settled, or Shall Settle, in Any of His Majesty's Colonies in America," *Collection of Public Statutes* (London, 1740), vol. 13, pp. 167–71. The original orthography has been retained.

of the colony wherein such persons respectively have so inhabited and resided, or shall so inhabit and reside, shall be deemed, adjudged and taken to be his Majesty's natural born subjects of this kingdom, to all intents, constructions, and purposes, as if they, and every of them had been or were born within this kingdom. . . .

And whereas the following words are contained in the latter part of the oath of abjuration, Videlicet (upon the true faith of a christian),[2] and whereas the people professing the Jewish religion may thereby be prevented from receiving the benefit of this act; be it further enacted by the authority aforesaid, That whenever any person professing the Jewish religion shall present himself to take the said oath or abjuration in pursuance of this act, the said words (upon the true faith of a christian) shall be omitted out of the said oath in administering the same to such person and the taking and subscribing the said oath by such person professing the Jewish religion, without the words aforesaid, and the other oaths appointed by the said act in like manner as Jews were permitted to take the oath of abjuration, by an act made in the tenth year of the reign of his late Majesty King George the First, intituled, An act for explaining and amending an act of the last session of parliament, intituled, An act to oblige all persons, being papists, in that part of Great Britain called Scotland, and all persons in Great Britain refusing or neglecting to take the oaths appointed for the security of his Majesty's person and government, by several acts herein mentioned, to register their names and real estates; and for enlarging the time for taking the said oaths, and making such registers, and for allowing further time for the inrolment of deeds or wills made by papists, which have been omitted to be inrolled pursuant to an act of the third year of his Majesty's reign; and also for giving relief to the protestant lessees, shall be deemed a sufficient taking of the said oaths, in order to intitle such persons to the benefit of being naturalized by virtue of this act.

NOTES

1. The act was passed by both Houses of Parliament, without opposition, on March 19, 1740.

2. The removal of the required Christian oath in effect permitted the naturalization of Jewish residents of Great Britain's colonies in America, e.g., Jamaica, New York, Pennsylvania, Maryland and South Carolina.

FREDERICK II
6. The Charter Decreed for the Jews of Prussia (April 17, 1750)[1]

Revised General-Patent and Regulations of April 17, 1750 for Jewry of the Kingdom of Prussia, Electoral and Mark Brandenburg, the Duchies and Principalities of Magdeburg, Cleves, Farther-Pomerania, Krossen, Halberstadt, Minden, Camin, Moers, as well as the Counties and Territories of Mark, Ravensburg, Hohenstein, Tecklenburg, Lingen, Lauenburg, and Buetau—Explanation of the Causes for the further Regulation of Jewry:

Source: Jacob R. Marcus, ed. and trans., *The Jew in the Medieval World* (New York: Harper Torchbooks, 1965), pp. 84–97. Reprinted by permission of Dr. Jacob R. Marcus.

We, Frederick, by God's grace, King of Prussia, Margrave of Brandenburg, Chancellor and Electoral Prince of the Holy Roman Empire, sovereign and supreme Duke of Silesia, etc., etc., etc.,

Make known and order to be made known: We have noticed in our kingdom of Prussia . . . and particularly also in this capital [Berlin] various faults and abuses among the licensed and tolerated Jews, and have particularly observed that the rampant increase of these abuses has caused enormous damage and hardship, not only to the public, particularly to the Christian inhabitants and merchants, but also to Jewry itself. For this reason and because of the surreptitious entry of unlicensed Jews—foreigners [non-Prussian] and those who are all but without any country—many complaints and difficulties have arisen.

We, however, out of a feeling of most gracious paternal provision wish to establish and maintain, as far as possible, the livelihood and trades of each and every loyal subject under our protection, Christian as well as Jews, in a continually good and flourishing state.

For this reason we have found it necessary to make such provision that this, our most gracious purpose, may be attained, so that a proportion may be maintained between Christian and Jewish business opportunities and trades, and especially that neither [Jew or Christian] may be injured through a prohibited expansion of Jewish business activity. For this purpose we have again made an exact investigation of the condition, in our kingdom and in the other above mentioned imperial lands, of all Jewry, of their families, their means of subsistence, and their business activity. We have considered certain feasible proposals which have as their basis justice, fairness, and common safety, and have also deemed them useful for the attainment of our ultimate object and the attendant welfare of all inhabitants of the country who live by means of business activity. As a result of these proposals we wish to prepare and to put into effect a special regulation and constitution for all Jewry. Therefore we establish, regulate, and order, herewith and by virtue of this, that . . .

I. No other Jews are to be tolerated except those named in the lists that are attached to the end of these regulations.

II. List of the tolerated communal Jewish officials in Berlin: The following list of communal officials for the capital here in Berlin has been fixed:

1. One rabbi or a vice-rabbi.
2. Four assistant-judges.
3. A chief and assistant cantor with his basses and his sopranos. These latter must not be married.
4. Four criers, one of whom must report daily to the police office the arrival of foreign Jews. [These criers, or "knockers," used to call people to services at dawn by "knocking" on their doors.]
5. Two employees in the synagogal-school.
6. Six grave diggers who also do other work for the Jewish community.
7. One cemetery guard.
8. Three slaughterers.
9. Three butchers.
10. One secretary of the meat-market and his supervisor.
11. Three bakers and one restaurant-keeper.
12. A communal scribe.
13. Two doorkeepers and one assistant. [The doorkeepers at the city gates examined the papers of immigrant Jews.]
14. Two hospital attendants.
15. One physician.
16. One male and one female bath attendant.
17. A fattener of fowl and cattle.
18. Eight attendants for the sick.
19. Two Hebrew printers.
20. Two teachers for girls. Both must be married. . . .

V. Principles that are to be observed in the settlement of Jews. The following principles respecting the settlement of Jews shall be established and observed in the future. . . .

A distinction is to be made between Regular Protected-Jews and Special Protected-Jews who are merely tolerated during their life time.[2] . . .

Only those are to be considered Regular Protected-Jews who have the right to settle a child. . . .

The above mentioned Special Protected-Jews, however, are not authorized to settle a child [in business] nor are they to marry off a child by virtue of their privilege. . . .

In accordance with our most graciously issued cabinet-order of May 23, 1749, the fixed number of Jewish families at present is not to be exceeded except by our royal command. . . .

The Regular Protected-Jews, however, are allowed by virtue of their Letter of Protection to settle one child, a son or daughter, during their life time, but once they have made their decision they will not be authorized to change it in the future. This child may marry if it can first establish its identity legally. . . .

Foreign [non-Prussian] Jews are not allowed to settle in our lands at all. However, if one should really have a fortune of ten thousand Reichsthaler, and bring the same into the country and furnish authentic evidence of the fact, then we are to be asked about this and concerning the fee he is to pay. . . .

In order that in the future all fraud, cheating, and secret and forbidden increase of the number of families may be more carefully avoided, no Jew shall be allowed to marry, nor will he receive permission to settle, in any manner, nor will he be believed, until a careful investigation has been made by the War and Domains Offices together with the aid of the Treasury. . . .

Male and female servants and other domestics, however, are not allowed to marry. Should they attempt to do this they are not to be tolerated any longer. . . .

The children of [all] licensed Jews, whose fathers have died or have been impoverished, or are in such a condition that they, the children, have no right of "settlement," or do not possess the required fortune, are to be tolerated, even as are the widows of such people. However, when they come of age, they shall in no wise dare, under penalty of expulsion, to set up a business for themselves but they must either work for other licensed Jews, or go away and seek to be accepted somewhere else. They may, indeed, prepare themselves so that they take the place of Jewish communal officials who leave. Thus it will not be necessary to accept so many foreigners for this purpose. . . .

VII. No Protected-Jew can stay away from home for more than a Year without authorization; otherwise his place will be given to another. . . .

VIII. The Jews must pay their taxes quarterly and all the Jews are responsible as a body for the payment of the taxes. . . .

XI. The Jews must not pursue any manual trade. . . .We herewith establish, regulate, and order earnestly that in the future no Jew shall presume to engage in any manual trade, nor venture upon any except seal-engraving, [art] painting, the grinding of optical glasses, diamonds, and jewels, gold and silver embroidery, fine cloth needlework, the collecting of gold dust by a sieving process, and other similar trades in which vocational associations and privileged guilds are not found. Particularly are they enjoined not to brew beer nor to distill spirits. However, they are allowed to undertake the distilling of spirits for the nobility, government officials, and others, with the understanding that only licensed Jews and their sons are to be taken for this task. . . . However, those Jews who have received or may receive special concessions for the establishment of particular types of factories or for the sale of goods of Christian manufacturers are to be protected in the future as in the past.

XII. Jews are forbidden the smelting of gold and silver. . . .

XIV. The Jews in Berlin are not allowed to have dealings in raw wool or woolen yarns or to manufacture woolen goods. . . . [They were allowed, however, to sell the domestic finished product.]

XV. Jews are further allowed to sell one another beer and spirits... [but] with the exception of kosher wines they are not allowed to do any business in wines. ... [Jews must not, however, sell strong drink to non-Jews.]

XVI. Jews are not allowed to deal in raw cattle-and-horse hides, plain or dyed leathers, and foreign woolen wares except those which are specifically permitted in [paragraph XVIII].... [Cheap raw materials were to be reserved for Prussian manufacturers.]

XVII. Under special conditions they may sell choice groceries and spices to other Jews.... The Jews are forbidden to trade in raw tobacco, to manufacture tobacco, and to carry a line of [staple] groceries....

XVIII. Precisely the kind of goods with which the Protected-Jews are allowed to do business. In order that all Jews under our protection may be informed and instructed precisely in the business opportunities and trades allowed them, they are allowed to trade and to do business with the following, namely:

With gold-cloth, silver-cloth, fine fabrics and ribbons, native and foreign embroidered goods, domestic gold and silver laces manufactured in the Berlin Royal Gold and Silver Factory, neck bands of lace, Spanish lace, gold and silver thread and purl; likewise with jewels, broken gold and silver, ingots, all sorts of old pocket-watches, and similar things. Furthermore they are permitted to deal in money-exchange and pledges, money-brokerage, and the buying and selling of houses and estates for other people. They are also permitted to do business in all sorts of Brabant, Dutch, Silesian and Electoral-Saxonian fine cloth and silk textiles, in laces, muslin, and all-white domestic coarse linings, domestic linens, white linen thread, and tablecloths of linen and half-linen. They are also specially allowed to deal with domestic silk goods, also with foreign and native undyed, dressed leather, and with domestic velvet.[3] They are also allowed to deal in all sorts of all-wool and half-wool goods and cotton goods—by whatever name they may be called—manufactured here in this country, as well as with cotton and chintz goods made in our lands.

Furthermore they are permitted to deal in horses, in undressed calf and sheep hides, feathers, wigs, hair, also camel and horsehair, tallow, wax, and honey, Polish wares [pelts, potash, hemp, etc.], undressed and unfinished pelts, but not finished furriers' wares in those cities where furriers live, unless they can without hesitation give the name of the furriers from whom they bought the finished product for further sale. [Jews must not compete with the craft-guilds, such as the furriers.] They are also allowed to trade in tea, coffee, chocolate, and foreign and domestic manufactured snuff and smoking tobacco. They are also free to trade, exchange, and do business in all sorts of old clothes, old or used furniture, house and kitchen utensils; to sum up, with everything which is not generally and specifically forbidden in the above paragraphs, even though it is neither specified or mentioned in this special paragraph. But all this is permitted them only in their own homes and in those shops and booths that have been regularly assigned them.

However, with respect to foreign and domestic Jewish trade in our Kingdom of Prussia, the special constitution that has been made there will remain in force, inasmuch as the Polish and Russian business there is still dependent on both Christian and Jewish commerce....

XIX. The Jews must not trade in anything herein forbidden them, under threat of confiscation of their wares.... They may not peddle in cities except at the time of the fairs....

XX. No foreign [non-Prussian] Jews and Jewish boys shall do business in Berlin. Outside of exceptional cases herein specified, those who remain over twenty-four hours in Berlin must pay one specie-ducat to the Potsdam Orphan Home....

Now it has been noticed that many Jews and Jewish boys from other cities and provinces that are subject to us have tarried in

Berlin, year in and year out, and almost daily, constantly coming and going, and, as it were, relieving one another. Through private and public trading they have done tremendous damage, not only to the entire public, but particularly to the entire Christian and authorized Jewish trade, and have at the same time deceived and duped our treasuries through all sorts of fraud and malicious practices. Therefore, we establish, regulate, and order herewith by virtue of this, that except for the local fairs no Jew who does not belong to Berlin—whether he is otherwise licensed or non-licensed within our land—shall be allowed to come into the city with any wares except broken gold and silver. Also no foreign [non-Prussian] Jew, male or female, shall be allowed in except at the time of the fairs. . . .

XXI. All foreign [non-Prussian Jews] who do not arrive with the post-carriage or their own vehicles may enter into and leave Berlin by only two gates. . . .

XXII. What is to be done with Jewish beggars. It has already been decreed many times that Jewish beggars are nowhere to be allowed to cross our borders. We not only repeat this, but order that in the event such Jewish beggars nevertheless reach our capital surreptitiously, they shall be brought at once to the Poor-Jews House at the Prenzlau Gate. There they are to be given alms and on the following day evicted through the gate without being allowed to enter the city. . . .

XXIV. The Jews are allowed to lend out money on proper pledges. Inasmuch as the money-business is a particular source of Jewish support, Jews are therefore allowed to lend money on pledges now as in the past. They must not, however, accept pledges from any non-commissioned officer or soldier, or buy anything where they are not sufficiently assured that this is their lawful property and no part of their soldiers' equipment. And in every case they must demand a note from the company commander with respect to these things. Furthermore, the Jews must be very sure in all pawning and selling that the pledges were not stolen or secretly removed and then pledged, either by young folks from their parents, or by unfaithful servants from their employers. On each occasion, therefore, the pawnbrokers must make enquiries from the parents or the employers.

Furthermore, those Jews, their wives, or employees must not only surrender such pledges to the owner without compensation, but in case that they knew that the pledge was stolen or secretly removed, and shall be legally convicted of this, then, in accordance with the edict of January 15, 1747, the possessors of such pledges shall be regarded just like those who have wittingly purchased stolen goods. Such a pawnbroker shall lose all rights of protection, not only for himself, but also for his children if some of them have already been settled in business, for their Letters of Protection shall be annulled, and he and his family shall be removed from the country. Furthermore, no one else is to be settled in the vacancy created by that family, and, besides this, the transgressor is to be compelled to pay the full worth of the stolen or illegally received things to the lawful owner, who, if necessary, will take an oath as to their value.

If the offender cannot pay this because his Letter of Protection has been cancelled and his family already expelled, then the entire Jewry of the town is officially to be held responsible for the payment in cash—and without any protest—to the robbed owner of the value of the stolen or illegally received things. For this reason the Jews must watch one another and pay attention carefully when they find any of their people on the wrong road and immediately report such a person to the proper authorities. Jewry, therefore, and particularly the elders are required to anticipate any annoyance and damage by ridding the country of those receivers of stolen goods and the other rascally crew among them whenever they discover them. And when they submit their information they will be given all assistance. . . .

XXXIII. Concerning the observance of the general-patent for the Jews. In order that this general-patent for the Jews shall be contravened as little as possible, the War and Domains Offices of their respective Departments and local commissaries [the tax-councils] shall watch Jewry very carefully in the cities of the provinces and see to it that the said general-patent is everywhere exactly followed. They are particularly to see that the fixed number of families, communal officials, and Jewish-owned homes in every town is not increased, that no one is admitted without our royal concession, and least of all that no unlicensed Jew be tolerated. For this reason nothing is to be undertaken or conceded by the magistrates on their own authority; nor shall any Jew be permitted to live in the rural districts or in open towns where there is no excise office.

So done and given at Berlin, the seventeenth of April 1750.

NOTES

1. Frederick II (1712–1786), Frederick the Great, king of Prussia (1740–1786). Jacob R. Marcus observes in his *The Jew in the Medieval World* that the charter "is a curious combination of medieval and modern elements. It is modern in the sense that the Jew is thought to be no longer a ward of the king, but instead a subject of the state—albeit second class. The former Jewish autonomy is broken down and the Jew is brought closer to the state economically, politically, and culturally. The charter is medieval, however, in the sense that it is filled with a spirit of distrust of and contempt for the Jew, limiting him almost exclusively to commerce and industry" (p. 81).

2. This division of Jews according to their economic value to the state constitutes the unique feature of the charter. In 1763, Moses Mendelssohn became a Special Protected Jew; despite his fame he was never able to acquire the status of Regular Protected Jew (see documents 11 and 12 in this chapter).

3. Moses Mendelssohn was employed by a domestic silk firm.

THE HOUSES OF PARLIAMENT
7. "The Jew Bill"[1]

Whereas by an Act made in the Seventh year of the reign of King James the First, intituled, An Act that all such as are to be naturalized or restored in Blood, shall first receive the Sacrament of the Lord's Supper, and the Oath of Allegiance, and the Oath of Supremacy, every person who shall apply to be naturalized by Act of Parliament, being of the Age of Eighteen Years or upwards, is required to receive the Sacrament of the Lord's Supper, within One Month before such Naturalization is exhibited, whereby many Persons of considerable Substance professing the Jewish Religion, are prevented from being naturalized by Bill to be exhibited in Parliament for that Purpose: And whereas by an Act made in the Thirteenth Year of his present Majesty's Reign,[2] intituled, An Act for Naturalizing such Foreign Protestants, and others therein mentioned, as are settled, or shall settle in any of his Majesty's Colonies in America, Persons professing the Jewish Religion, who have inhabited and resided or shall inhabit and reside for the Space of

Source: "The Jewish Naturalization Act. An Act To Permit Persons Professing the Jewish Religion, To Be Naturalized by Parliament and for Other Purposes Therein Mentioned," *Collection of the Public General Statutes* (London, 1753), vol. 26, pp. 407–11.

Seven years or more, in any of his Majesty's Colonies in America, and shall not have been absent out of some of the said Colonies, for a longer space than two months at any One Time during the said Seven Years, are naturalized upon their complying with the terms therein mentioned, without their receiving the Sacrament of the Lord's Supper; Be it therefore enacted by the King's most excellent Majesty, by and with the Advice and consent of the Lords Spiritual and Temporal, and Commons, in this present Parliament assembled, and by the Authority of the same, That Persons professing the Jewish Religion may, upon Application for that Purpose, be naturalized by Parliament, without receiving the Sacrament of the Lord's Supper, the said Act of the Seventh Year of the Reign of King James the First, or any other Law, Statute, Matter or Thing to the contrary in any ways notwithstanding. . . .

Provided also, and it is hereby further enacted, That no Person shall be naturalized by virtue of any Act to be made or passed in pursuance of this Act, unless Proof shall be made by two credible Witnesses, that such Person professeth the Jewish Religion, and hath for Three Years past professed the same, the Proof in both cases before mentioned to be made in such Manner as is now practised in both Houses of Parliament respectively, when Proof is made that any Person hath received the Holy Sacrament, in order to [be naturalized].

And it is hereby further enacted by the Authority aforesaid,[3] That from and after the First Day of June, one thousand seven hundred and fifty-three, every Person professing the Jewish Religion shall be disabled, and is hereby made incapable to purchase, either in his or her own name, or in the Name of any other Person or Persons, to his or her Use, or in Trust for him or her, or to inherit or take by Descent, Devise, or Limitation, in Possession, Reversion, or Remainder, any advowson or Right of Patronage, or Presentation, or other Right or interest whatsoever of, in, or to any Benefice, Prebend,[4] or other Ecclesiastical Living or Promotion, School, Hospital, or Donative whatsoever, or any Grant of any Avoidance thereof; and all and singular Estates, Terms, and other Interests whatsoever of, in, or any Benefice, Prebend, or other Ecclesiastical Living or Promotion, School, Hospital, or Donative, which, from and after the said First Day of June, shall be made, suffered or done, to or for the Use or Behoof of any such Person or Persons, or upon any Trust or Confidence, mediately or immediately, to or for the benefit or Behoof of any such Person or Persons, shall be utterly void and of none Effect, to all Intents, Construction, and Purposes whatsoever.

NOTES

1. Enacted by Parliament in May 1753, this act, in face of the energetic opposition by Christian merchants of London, was repealed a year later.

2. The reference is to the Plantation Act. See document 5 in this chapter.

3. This paragraph is intended to allay fears that the granting to Jews of civil rights will obscure the social boundaries separating Jew and Christian.

4. Part of revenue of cathedral or collegiate church granted to canons as stipend.

CHRISTIAN WILHELM VON DOHM

8. Concerning the Amelioration of the Civil Status of the Jews[1]

What might be the reasons that induced the governments of almost all European states unanimously to deal so harshly with the Jewish nation? What has induced them (even the wisest) to make this one exception from the laws of an otherwise enlightened policy according to which all citizens should be incited by uniform justice, support of trade and the greatest possible freedom of action so as to contribute to the general welfare? Should a number of industrious and law-abiding citizens be less useful to the state because they stem from Asia and differ from others by beard, circumcision, and a special way—transmitted to them from their ancient forefathers—of worshiping the Supreme Being? This latter would certainly disqualify them from full rights of citizenship, and justify all restriction measures, if it contained principles which would keep the Jews from fulfilling their duties to the state, and from keeping faith in their actions within the community and with single members of the community; and if hatred against those who do not belong to their faith would make them feel an obligation to deal crookedly with others and to disregard their rights.

It would have to be clearly proved that the religion of the Jews contains such antisocial principles, that their divine laws are contrary to the laws of justice and charity, if one were to justify before the eyes of reason that the rights of citizenship should be withheld entirely only from the Jew, and that he should be permitted only partially to enjoy the rights of man. According to what has become known about the Jewish religion so far, it does not contain such harmful principles. The most important book of the Jews, the Law of Moses, is looked upon by Christians with reverence and it is ascribed by them to divine revelation. This belief in its divine origin alone must banish every thought that this law could prescribe any vicious thing, or that its followers must be bad citizens. But even those who did not start from this assumption have found after investigation that the Mosaic law contains the most correct principle of moral law, justice and order. . . .

It is natural that in the Jews of our time the sense of oppression under which they live mixes with the hostile feelings of their ancestors against other nations whose lands they were to conquer, feelings which were hallowed by their Law. It may be that some of them hold to the belief that it is permitted to hate as they hated the Canaanites those who, in their societies, scarcely give them permission to live. But these feelings are obviously derived from their old laws; and the natural reactions of the offended and oppressed seem to justify these. It is certain, however, that the present faith of the Jews contains no commandment to hate and offend adherents of other religions. Murder, theft, felony, even when commited by a non-Jew, still remains, according to their law, the same crime.* Con-

*One finds perhaps in the Talmud places where some rabbis endeavored to prove by sophistic conclusion that it is a minor misdemeanor to defraud a non-Jew. An example of such a kind is the statement that expounds the law to "love thy neighbor and not offend him" meaning only the Israelite. Some writers who are very prejudiced against the Jews have collected these items with many re-

Source: Christian Wilhelm von Dohm, *Ueber die buergerliche Verbesserung der Juden* (Berlin, 1781), a sequel appeared in 1783. In *Readings in Modern Jewish History,* ed. Ellis Rivkin and trans. Helen Lederer (Cincinnati, Ohio: Hebrew Union College-Jewish Institute of Religion, 1957), pp. 5–7, 9–22, 50–71. Reprinted by permission of Dr. Ellis Rivkin.

clusions of the kind I mentioned above are possible in all religions and, in fact, do occur in all religions. Each one boasts of being the only, or at least the safest and straightest, way to please God, to reach the goal of a blissful life in the hereafter. Each one boasts that its truth is founded on such clear, irrefutable proofs that only wilful shutting of the eyes could deny its shining light. So every religion instils in its adherents a kind of antipathy against adherents of other faiths, an antipathy which borders sometimes on hatred, sometimes more on contempt, and which manifests itself sometimes more, sometimes less, as political conditions influence the sentiments of the various religious groups towards each other and as the cultural level, the influence of philosophy and the sciences strengthen or weaken the impact of religious convictions. If therefore every religion severs the bond between man and man and makes men withhold affection and justice from those who are not of the same faith, if this is a natural consequence of the boasted superiority of every faith, then this phenomenon cannot be a valid reason for withholding the rights of citizenship from the adherents of any one faith....

So, even if actually in the faith of today's Jews there should be some principles which would restrict them too strongly to their special group and exclude them from the other groups of the great civil society; this would still not justify their persecution—which can only serve to confirm them in their opinions—so long as their laws are not contrary to the general principles of morality and do not permit antisocial vices. The only prerogative of the government in this case would be (1) to have an exact knowledge of those principles, or indeed only the conclusions drawn from religious principles, and the actual influence of these on their actions, and (2) endeavor to weaken the influence of these principles, by general enlightenment of the nation, by furthering and advancing its morals independently of religion, and, in general, further the refinement of their sentiments.

More than anything else a life of normal civil happiness in a well ordered state, enjoying the long withheld freedom, would tend to do away with clannish religious opinions. The Jew is even more man than Jew, and how would it be possible for him not to love a state where he could freely acquire property and freely enjoy it, where his taxes would be not heavier than those of the other citizens, where he could reach positions of honor and enjoy general esteem? Why should he hate people who are no longer distinguished from him by offensive prerogatives, who share with him equal rights and duties? The novelty of this happiness, and unfortunately, the probability that this will not in the near future happen in all states, would make it even more precious to the Jew, and gratitude alone would make him the most patriotic citizen. He would look at his country with the eyes of a long misjudged, and finally after long banishment, re-instated son. These human emotions would talk louder in his heart than the sophistic sayings of his rabbis.

Our knowledge of human nature tells us that conditions of this our actual life here have a stronger influence on men than those referring to life after death. History proves also that good government and the prosperity all subjects enjoy under such a government weaken the influence of religious principles and abolish the mutual antipathy which is only nourished by persecution....

Certainly, the Jew will not be prevented by

---

proaches against the Jewish nation, intending to justify thereby the hatred and persecution of Jews. If, however, as is undoubtedly true, these sayings of some single rabbis were never accepted by the nation; if the Mosaic law as well as the greatest Jewish rabbis make no difference at all between vices and crimes, committed against Jews or non-Jews; then it would be grossly unfair to make the whole nation responsible for the prejudices of some single rabbis and to judge their whole religious system by such sayings; just as it would be wrong to judge Christianity and the moral principles of today's Christians from the sayings of some Fathers of the Church (which often are quite unreasonable and misanthropic).

his religion from being a good citizen, if only the government will give him a citizen's rights. Either his religion contains nothing contrary to the duties of a citizen, or such tenets can easily be abolished by political and legal regulations.

One might oppose to all these reasons the general experience of our states of the political harmfulness of the Jews, intending to justify the harsh way our governments are dealing with them by the assertion that the character and spirit of this nation is so unfortunately formed that on this ground they cannot be accepted with quite equal rights in any civil society. Indeed, quite often in life one hears this assertion that the character of the Jews is so corrupt that only the most restricting and severest regimentation can render them harmless. To these unfortunates, it is said, has been transmitted from their ancestors, if not through their most ancient law, then through their oral tradition and the later sophistic conclusions of the rabbis, such a bitter hatred of all who do not belong to their tribe, that they are unable to get used to looking at them as members of a common civil society with equal rights. The fanatic hatred with which the ancestors of the Jews persecuted the founder of Christianity has been transmitted to their late posterity and they hate all followers of this faith. Outbreaks of this hatred have often shown themselves clearly unless held in check by force. Especially have the Jews been reproached by all nations with lack of fairness and honesty in the one field in which they were allowed to make a living—commerce. Every little dishonest practice in commerce is said to be invented by Jews, the coin of any state is suspect if Jews took part in the minting, or if it went frequently through Jewish hands. One hears also in all places where they were allowed to multiply in numbers, the accusation that they monopolize almost entirely the branches of trade permitted to them and that Christians are unable to compete with them in these. For this reason, it is further said, the governments of nearly all states have adopted the policy, in an unanimity from which alone it can be concluded that it is justified to issue restrictive laws against this nation and to deviate, in its case alone, from the principle of furthering a continuous rise in population. They could not concede to these people who are harmful to the welfare of the rest of the citizens the same rights, and had to adopt the stipulation of a certain amount of property for those permitted to settle down, as guarantee for compliance with the laws and abstinence from criminal activities.

If I am not entirely mistaken there is one error in this reasoning, namely, that one states as cause what in reality is the effect, quoting the evil wrought by the past erroneous policy as an excuse for it. Let us concede that the Jews may be more morally corrupt than other nations; that they are guilty of a proportionately greater number of crimes than the Christians; that their character in general inclines more toward usury and fraud in commerce, that their religious prejudice is more antisocial and clannish; but I must add that this supposed greater moral corruption of the Jews is a necessary and natural consequence of the oppressed condition in which they have been living for so many centuries. A calm and impartial consideration will prove the correctness of this assertion.

The hard and oppressive conditions under which the Jews live almost everywhere would explain, although not justify, an even worse corruption than they actually can be accused of. It is very natural that these conditions cause the spirit of the Jew to lose the habit of noble feelings, to be submerged in the base routine of earning a precarious livelihood. The varied kinds of oppression and contempt he experiences are bound to debase him in his activities, to choke every sense of honor in his heart. As there are almost no honest means of earning a living left to him it is natural that he falls into criminal practices and fraud, especially since commerce more than other trades seduces people to such practices. Has one a right to be surprised if a Jew feels himself bound by laws which scarcely permit him to breathe, yet he cannot break them without being punished? How can we demand willing obedience and affection for the state from him, who sees that he is tolerated only to the extent that he is a means of revenue? Can one be surprised at his hatred for a nation which gives him so many and so stinging proofs of its hatred for him? How can one expect virtue from him if one does not trust him? How can one reproach him with crimes he is forced to commit because no honest means of earning a livelihood are open to him; for he is oppressed by taxes and nothing is left him to care for the education and moral training of his children?

Everything the Jews are blamed for is caused by the political conditions under which they now live, and any other group of men, under such conditions, would be guilty of identical errors. . . .

If, therefore, those prejudices today prevent the Jew from being a good citizen, a social human being, if he feels antipathy and hatred against the Christian, if he feels himself in his dealings with him not so much bound by his moral code, then all this is our own doing. His religion does not commend him to commit these dishonesties, but the prejudices which we have instilled and which are still nourished by us in him are stronger than his religion. We ourselves are guilty of the crimes we accuse him of; and the moral turpitude in which that unfortunate nation is sunk—thanks to a mistaken policy—cannot be a reason that would justify a continuation of that policy. That policy is a remnant of the barbarism of past centuries, a consequence of a fanatical religious hatred. It is unworthy of our enlightened times and should have been abolished long ago. A look at the history and the origin of the present regulations concerning the Jews will make this clear. . . .

If this reasoning is correct, then we have found in the oppression and in the restricted occupation of the Jews the true source of their corruption. Then we have discovered also at the same time the means of healing this corruption and of making the Jews better men and useful citizens. With the elimination of the unjust and unpolitical treatment of the Jews will also disappear the consequences of it; and when we cease to limit them to one kind of occupation, then the detrimental influence of that occupation will no longer be so noticeable. With the modesty that a private citizen should always show when expressing his thoughts about public affairs, and with the certain conviction that general proposals should always be tailored, if they should be useful to the special local conditions in every state, I dare now, after these remarks, to submit my ideas as to the manner in which the Jews could become happier and better members of civil societies.

To make them such it is FIRST necessary to give them equal rights with all other subjects. Since they are able to fulfill the duties they should be allowed to claim the equal impartial love and care of the state. No humiliating discrimination should be tolerated, no way of earning a living should be closed to them, none other than the regular taxes demanded from them. They would have to pay all the usual taxes in the state, but they would not have to pay protection money for the mere right to exist, no special fee for the permission to earn a living. It is obvious that in accordance with the principle of equal rights, also special privileges favoring the Jews—which exist in some states—would have to be abolished. These sometimes owed their existence to a feeling of pity which would be without basis under more just conditions. When no occupation will be closed to Jews, then they should, in all fairness, not have a monopoly on any occupation in preference to other citizens. When the government will decide to fix the rate of interest by law, the Jew will not be able to ask for any more than the legal rate of interest. If it will be prohibited to private citizens to lend money on pawns, or do so only under certain conditions, the Jews will have to observe these rules.

Since it is primarily the limitation of the

Jews to commerce which has had a detrimental influence on their moral and political character, a perfect freedom in the choice of a livelihood would serve justice, as well as representing a humanitarian policy which would make of the Jews more useful and happier members of society.

It might even be useful, in order to achieve this great purpose, if the government would first try to dissuade the Jews from the occupation of commerce, and endeavor to weaken its influence by encouraging them to prefer such kinds of earning a living as are most apt to create a diametrically opposed spirit and character—I mean artisan occupations. . . .

The Jews should not be excluded from agriculture. Unless the purchase of landed property is restricted in a country to certain classes of the inhabitants, the Jews should not be excluded, and they should have equal rights to lease land. But I do not expect very great advantages from this occupation in respect to the improvement of the nation, because, as remarked above, it is too similar to commerce, it nourishes the spirit of speculation and profit-seeking. I do not wish to see the Jews encouraged to become owners of big estates or tenants (few of them have the necessary capital) but peasants working their own land. The funds which many states provide for colonists could in many cases be used to better advantage by settling the Jews of the country on vacant pieces of land, and by providing houses and money for agricultural implements. Perhaps it would help to reawaken the love for such work in the nation if the big Jewish tenants or owners of estates would be required to employ a number of Jewish farmhands.

From several sides the proposal has been made that the Jews should be allotted separate districts for settlement and be kept isolated there from the rest of the subjects. In my opinion it would not be advisable to make the religious difference more noticeable and probably more permanent by this step. The Jews, left entirely to themselves, would be strengthened in their prejudices against Christians, and vice versa. Frequent intercourse and sharing the burdens and advantages of the state equally is the most certain way to dull the edge of the hostile prejudices on both sides. The *Judengasse* (*Juiveries* in France) [ghetto] and restricted districts of Jewish residence in many cities are remnants of the old harsh principles. In many places (for instance, Frankfurt on the Main, where the *Judengasse* is locked up every night) the evil consequence is that the Jews are forced to build their houses many stories high and live under very crowded conditions resulting in uncleanliness, diseases, and bad policing, and greater danger of fire.

No kind of commerce should be closed to the Jews, but none should be left to them exclusively and they should not be encouraged by privileges. On the contrary, by encouraging skilled crafts and agriculture they should be drawn away from commerce, and in the intention of weakening the influence of this one occupation which for such a long time was their only one, it would even be permissible at least in the beginning, to restrict the number of Jews active in commerce, or subject them to special taxes and so establish a fund to encourage other occupations among the nation.

A useful new regulation, which has already been introduced in various states, would be to obligate the Jews to keep their books in the language of the land and not in Hebrew. This would facilitate communication with Christian merchants and in cases of litigation over these books the judges would have less difficulties. Fraud and crooked dealings in commerce should be represented to the Jews as the most heinous crime against the state which now embraces them with equal affection, and these crimes should be subjected to the harshest penalties—perhaps exclusion from the newly granted freedoms for a period of time or permanently.

Every art, every science should be open to the Jew as to every other free man. He, too, should educate his mind as far as he is able; he, too, must be able to rise to promotion, honor, and rewards by developing his talents. The scientific institutions of the State should be for his use, too, and he should be as free as other citizens to utilize his talents in any way.

Another question is whether in our states Jews should be admitted to public office immediately. It seems, in fact, that if they are granted all civil rights, they could not be excluded from applying for the honor to serve the government, and if they are found to be capable, from being employed by the state. I think, however, that in the next generation this capability will not yet appear frequently, and the state should make no special effort to develop it. In most countries there is no lack of skilled civil servants, and without any efforts on the part of the government there are enough applicants for public office. For some of these jobs early education and scholarship, which are hard to come by in the present educational setup for Jews, is required. Other jobs require that the applicant be far removed from any suspicion of misdemeanors due to greed, and this will probably not always be the case in the Jews of today and of the next generation. The too mercantile spirit of most Jews will probably be broken more easily by heavy physical labor than by the sedentary work of the public servant; and for the state as well as for himself it will be better in most cases if the Jew works in the shops and behind the plow than in the state chancelleries. The best middle way would probably be to allow the Jews, without especially encouraging them, to acquire the education necessary for public service, even to employ them in cases where they show special capability, if only to overcome the prejudice which will no doubt endure for a long time. But impartiality would demand that if a Jewish and a Christian applicant show equal capability, the latter deserves preference. This seems to be an obvious right of the majority in the nation—at least until the Jews by wiser treatment are changed into entirely equal citizens and all differences polished off.

It should be a special endeavor of a wise government to care for the moral education and enlightenment of the Jews, in order to make at least the coming generations more receptive to a milder treatment and the enjoyment of all advantages of our society. The state should not look further into their religious education than would perhaps be necessary to prevent the teaching of antisocial opinions against men of other persuasions. But the government should take care that, besides the holy teachings of his fathers, the Jew is taught to develop his reason by the clear light of knowledge, the science of nature and its great creator, and that his heart is warmed by the principles of order, honesty, love for all men and the great society in which he lives; that the Jew, too, is led at an early age to the sciences required more or less for his future profession. This would have to be done either in the Jewish schools, or if teachers and funds are for the time being lacking, the Jews should be permitted to send their children to the Christian schools (except for the hours reserved for religious instruction). As some Jews perhaps would be kept from making use of this permission by prejudice, they should even be required to send their children to certain classes in accordance with their future vocations. That department of the government which is in charge of public education (an office which should always belong to the state, not to a religious party) should extend its supervision over the education of the Jews, except only for their religious instruction. Regarding all other subjects Jewish schools should be organized just like the best Christian schools, or the Department should order the Jewish children to be admitted to these latter and take care to make sure that Jewish parents need not be afraid that their children might be lured away from the religion of their fathers. No doubt it would be useful for the education of the moral and civil character of the Jew if the government would arrange that in the synagogues, besides, the religious instruction which is not to be interfered with, instruction be given sometimes in the pure and holy truths of reason, and especially on the relationship of all citizens to the state and their duties to it. An institution which would, in fact, be highly desirable also for the Christians!

With the moral improvement of the Jews there should go hand in hand efforts of the Christians to get rid of their prejudices and uncharitable opinions. In early childhood they should be taught to regard the Jews as their brothers and fellow men who seek to find favor with God in a different way; a way they think erroneously to be the right one, yet which, if they follow in sincerity of heart, God looks at with favor. Other men should not quarrel with them about it, but try to lead them by love to still higher truths. The preachers should be required to repeat frequently these principles so much in accord with real Christianity, and they will do it easily if the spirit of love which rules in the fable of the Good Samaritan fills their hearts, if they, like the apostles of Christ, teach that any man of any nation who does right finds favor with God.

An important part of civil rights would be the right for Jews in all places of free worship, to build synagogues and employ teachers at their own expense. This freedom should be limited only in special cases, for instance for the reason that a synagogue would be too much of a financial burden on a very small Jewish community or that the support of too many teachers would cause too great a hardship; just like Christian communities have often to get along without their own teachers and churches. The care of the poor could either be left to the Jews alone, as until now, without help of the government, or the Jews should contribute proportionately to the general fund of these institutions and partake in their advantages. At any rate, government supervision of the Jewish poorhouses and hospitals would be useful, in order to assure the healthiest and best organization and the best utilization of the money appropriated for them. The Jewish community, just as any other organized religious society, should have the right to excommunicate for a period of time or permanently, and in case of resistance the judgment of the rabbis should be supported by the authorities. Regarding the execution of this ban, the state should interfere less when it does not go beyond a religious society and has no effect on the political society, for the excommunicated member of any church can be a very useful and respected citizen. This is a principle of general church jurisprudence which should no longer be doubtful in our times.

The written laws of Moses, which do not refer to Palestine and the old judicial and ritual organization, as the oral law are regarded by the Jews as permanently binding divine commandments. Besides, various commentaries to these laws and argumentations from them by famous Jewish scholars are held in the same respects as laws. Therefore, if they are to be granted full human rights, one has to permit them to live and be judged according to these laws. This will no more isolate them from the rest of the citizens of the state than a city or community living according to their own statutes; and the experience made with Jewish autonomy during the first centuries in the Roman Empire as also in some modern states has shown that no inconvenient or detrimental consequences are to be feared. Although this does not necessarily mean that the laws should be administered by Jewish judges, this would always be more agreeable to them and would avoid many difficulties arising from ignorance of the complicated Jewish jurisprudence in Christian judges which requires the knowledge of the Hebrew language and Rabbinics. It would therefore be better to leave litigation between Jew and Jew in civil cases to their own judges in the first instance, but also to permit the Jews to start court proceedings at the court of the regular Christian judges. These courts as well as the higher instances to which Jews might appeal from the decision of the Jewish judge, would of course have to decide according to Jewish laws; for if they would decide according to the common law great confusion would be unavoidable, and besides the litigants would have the unfair advantage that he could file his claim with the Judge whose decision he would expect to be favorable to him. I think, Jewish judges could also (like in Anspach and Baireuth, in Alsace and other countries) take care of the business of notaries and, under supervision of the authorities decide on inheritances, appoint guardians, etc. . . .

A constitution shaped according to these principles would, it seems to me, bring the Jews into society as useful members and at the same time would abolish the many ills that have been done to them and of which they were forced to make themselves guilty. Men of higher insight will decide if my assertions are correct, my proposals feasible. . . .

NOTE

1. Christian Wilhelm von Dohm (1751–1820). German scholar in constitutional law, statistics and modern history; active in the Enlightenment circles of Berlin, where he befriended Moses Mendelssohn. (See documents 11 and 12 in this chapter.) In 1779, he assumed a position in the Prussian government serving as the registrar of the secret archives and as councillor in the Department of Foreign Affairs. The title of Dohm's essay may also be translated as "On the Civil Improvement of the Jews." This translation underscores Dohm's argument that an amelioration of the Jews' civil status will bring about the "desired" improvement in their public morality. Dohm's plea for admitting the Jews to citizenship, which he wrote at the behest of Mendelssohn, coincided with the reform of Joseph II, the emperor of Austria, and thus helped give focus to the ensuing debate throughout Europe on the desirability of granting the Jews civil parity.

JOSEPH II
9. Edict of Tolerance[1]

We, Joseph the Second by the Grace of God, elected Roman Emperor, at all times the Enlarger of the Empire, King of Germany, Hungary and Bohemia, etc., Archduke in Austria, Duke of Burgundy and Lorraine, send Our Grace to all and graciously make known the following:

From the ascension to Our reign We have directed Our most preeminent attention to the end that all Our subjects without distinction of nationality and religion, once they have been admitted and tolerated in Our States, shall participate in common in public welfare, the increase of which is Our care, shall enjoy legal freedom and not find any obstacles in any honest ways of gaining their livelihood and of increasing general industriousness.

Since however the laws and the so-called Jewish Regulations [*Judenordnungen*] pertaining to the Jewish nation [*Nazion*] prevailing in Our hereditary countries in general and particularly in Vienna and Lower Austria are not always compatible with these Our most gracious intentions, We hereby will amend them by the virtue of this present edict in so far as the difference in times and conditions necessitates it.

Source: Alfred Pribram, *Urkunden und Akten zur Geschichte der Juden in Wien* (Vienna, 1918),vol. 1, pp. 494–500. Raphael Mahler, ed. and trans., *Jewish Emancipation, A Selection of Documents by R. Mahler,* Pamphlet Series, Jews and the Post-War World, no.1 (New York: The American Jewish Committee, 1941), pp. 18–20. Reprinted by permission of the American Jewish Committee.

The favors granted to the Jewish nation by this present amendment, whereby the latest Jewish Regulation of May 5, 1764, is fully repealed consist of the following:

As it is our goal to make the Jewish nation useful and serviceable to the State, mainly through better education and enlightenment of its youth as well as by directing them to the sciences, the arts and the crafts, We hereby grant and order: . . .

8. Graciously, that the tolerated Jews[2] may send their children to the Christian primary and secondary schools so that they have at least the opportunity to learn reading, writing and counting.

9. With regard to schools of higher degrees which were never forbidden to Jewish co-religionists, We hereby merely renew and confirm this permission.

10. In order to facilitate their future means of support and to prepare the necessary ways of gaining a livelihood We hereby most graciously permit them from now to learn all kinds of crafts or trades here as well as elsewhere from Christian masters, certainly also amongst themselves, and to this end to apprentice themselves to Christian masters to work as their journeymen, and the latter [the Christian craftsmen] may accept them without hesitation. This, however, should not be interpreted as if We wish to exercise any compulsion on Jews and Christians. We merely grant both sides full freedom to come to an understanding about this amongst themselves to their satisfaction.

11. We hereby further grant to the Jewish nation the general license to carry on all kinds of trade, without however the right of citizenship and mastership from which they remain excluded, to be carried on by them freely, only consequently as it is usual here and even then not before having obtained, same as Christians do, from the *Magistrat* in this city from the government of Lower Austria in the country. . . and We further

12. Grant to the Jewish co-religionists the completely free choice of all non-civic branches of commerce and authorize them to apply for the right of wholesale trade under the same conditions and with the same liberties as are obtained and carried on by Our Christian subjects. . . .

15. Considering the numerous openings in trades and manifold contacts with Christians resulting therefrom, the care for maintaining common confidence requires that the Hebrew and the so-called Jewish language and writing of Hebrew intermixed with German . . . shall be abolished.

16. In order to facilitate the tolerated Jews in their trades also with regard to the question of servants, it shall be permitted to them from now on to employ as many Jewish as well as Christian servants as their business requires. . . .

18. By the present Decree We hereby permit the existing restrictions with regard to definite Jewish houses to lapse and allow tolerated Jews to lease at their choice their own residences in the city as well as in the suburbs.

19. No less do We hereby completely abolish the head toll hitherto levied on foreign Jews and permit them to enter Our residence from time to time in order to carry on their business. . . .

23. Besides, We hereby completely remove the double court and chancellery fees hitherto in force only for Jews, and [We remove]

24. In general all hitherto customary distinctive marks and distinctions, such as the wearing of beards, the prohibition against leaving their homes before twelve o'clock on Sundays and holidays, the frequenting of places of public amusement and the like; on the contrary, it shall be permitted to wholesale merchants and their sons as well as to people of such rank to carry swords.

25. Since by these favors We almost place the Jewish nation on an equal level with adherents of other religious associations in respect to trade and employment of civil and domestic facilities, We hereby earnestly advise them to observe scrupulously all political, civil and judicial laws of the country to which they are bound as all other inhabitants, just as they remain subject with respect to all

political and legal matters to the provincial and municipal authorities within their jurisdiction and pertinent activities.

Done in our City of Residence Vienna, the second day of January, 1782, in the eighteenth year of Our reign in the Roman Empire and in the second year of reign in Our hereditary lands.

NOTES

1. Promulgated on January 2, 1782 by Joseph II (1741–1790), king of Germany (1764–1790) and Holy Roman emperor (1765–1790). This edict—appertaining initially to Lower Austria only—reflects Joseph II's policy of enlightened absolutism: religious tolerance, the encouragement of education, and unrestricted trade. This is the first of a series of edicts designed to end the social and economic isolation of the Jews and render them useful to the state. In 1781, Joseph II forbade the Jews the use of Yiddish and Hebrew in their public and commercial records. An edict of 1784 abolished rabbinical juridical autonomy; edicts in 1787 and 1788 made Jews liable for military service and obliged them to adopt German-sounding personal and family names, to be chosen from a government-prepared list. Although generally hailed by upper-class and educated Jews, the vast majority of Jews viewed these edicts as a sinister attempt to undermine their traditional way of life.

2. The edict confirmed the category of "tolerated Jew," and indeed maintained the restrictions regarding their number. The "tolerated Jews," however, were now granted new cultural and economic opportunities.

JOHANN DAVID MICHAELIS[1]
10. Arguments Against Dohm

Herr Dohm admits candidly that the Jewish brain is more harmful and more corrupted than that of other Europeans, an admission which several defenders of the Jews were hitherto unwilling to make. He seeks the reason for this, however, in the condition in which the Jew lives, reviled, oppressed, and forced to support himself almost exclusively from trade. Herr Dohm has probably no idea to what extent I agree with him in this matter; I wrote exactly the same thing thirty years ago in a piece in the *Goettingische gelehrte Anzeigen*. I would like to express my opinion as it was then and as it still is today. Mine goes one step further, however, than does that of Herr Dohm in that it takes account of the deceitfulness of the Jews.

We can see, principally from reports of investigations of thieves, that the Jews are more harmful than at least we Germans are. Almost half of those belonging to gangs of thieves, at least those of whose existence is known to us, are Jews, while the Jews are scarcely 1/25th of the total population of Germany. If this 1/25th part supplies the same number of riff-raff as the whole German people, or even more, then one must conclude that at least in respect to thievery, which I consider to be the lowest of vices, the Jews are twenty-five times as harmful or more than the other inhabitants of Germany.

I also agree with what Herr Dohm says about the praiseworthy aspects of the national character of the Jews and I would add

Source: Johann David Michaelis, "Herr Ritter Michaelis Beurtheilung," in Christian Wilhelm von Dohm, *Ueber die buergerliche Verbesserung der Juden* (Berlin & Stettin, 1783), vol. 2, pp. 33–51. Originally appeared in *Orientalische und Exegetische Bibliotek*, 19 (1782). Trans. here by L. Sachs.

only one comment: The Jews have a great deal of national pride, and not the least reason for this is their conception of themselves as God's Chosen People. It seems to me, however, that this pride has deleterious effects on their nation, preventing them from mingling with other peoples.

It is clear from several of Herr Dohm's remarks that he does not seek, as others do, to obtain special privileges for those who are Jews only in name or in origin and who do not believe in the Jewish religion, those who are known as Deists, or who are perhaps not even that. I agree with this completely. When I see a Jew eating pork, in order no doubt to offend his religion, then I find it impossible to rely on his word, since I cannot understand his heart.

After so much argument with Herr Dohm on basic issues it undoubtedly appears to my readers that I agree with him about granting citizenship to the Jews. But this is not the case and I must now express my reservations.

In mentioning the Law of Moses Herr Dohm considers that religion to be superior to mine. He sees nothing inimical in it, nothing that could incite the hatred of the Jews towards other people. No one could agree with him about this more than I; permit me nevertheless to raise a different question: Does the Law of Moses make citizenship, and the full integration of the Jew into other peoples, difficult or impossible? I think it does! The purpose of this Law is to maintain the Jews as a people almost completely separate from other peoples, and this purpose is an integral part of all the laws, down to those concerning kosher and non-kosher food, with the result that the Jews have lived as a separate group during 1700 years of dispersion. As long as the Jews continue to observe the Mosaic Laws, as long as they refuse, for example, to eat together with us and to form sincere friendship at the table, they will never become fully integrated in the way that Catholics, Lutherans, Germans, Wends, and French live together in one state. (I am not discussing isolated cases, but rather the Jews as a collective entity.) Such a people could be useful to the state in agricultural work or in various crafts, if the matter be handled wisely. But it will be impossible to consider the Jew as an equal of our citizens, and it is therefore impossible to grant him the same freedoms. For he will never be a full citizen with respect to love for and pride in his country (as Herr Dohm, for example, takes pride in his Prussian citizenship) and he will never be fully reliable in an hour of danger. . . .

One must mention something in addition to the Law of Moses, which Herr Dohm seems not to have considered, and which casts doubt on the full and steadfast loyalty of the Jews to the state and the possibility of their full integration, namely their messianic expectation of a return to Palestine. The Jews will always see the state as a temporary home, which they will leave in the hour of their greatest happiness to return to Palestine. For similar reasons their forefathers were suspect in the eyes of the Egyptians (Ex. 1:10). Passages in the sayings of the Prophets, even in those of Moses himself, seem to promise the Israelites a future return to Palestine, and the Jews at least hope for this return on the authority of those passages. And this is true not only for the simple masses, but also for the greatest commentators on the Bible who have been universally admired for many hundreds of years, men such as Rashi,[2] and others who are more objective such as Ibn Ezra[3] and David Kimchi,[4] whose names I cannot mention but to honor them. It is true that our Lutheran commentators often deny this, (not all, not the wise Phillip Jakob Spener[5] for example, whose arguments have almost the force of legal authority among jurists), and so do several others of different religions. But it is doubtful whether they will convince the Jews, particularly when philosophers of the greatest eminence (not necessarily Newton, who is too apocalyptic, but rather Locke) interpret these passages in exactly the same way. A people which nurses these hopes will lack, at the very least, a patriotic love for the fields [*Ackers*] of their fathers. There is even the danger that if the

Jewish people lives separately (for it will be necessary to provide special villages for Jewish agricultural settlers and to avoid placing them among the Christians) it may at some time be inflamed by a febrile vision, or led to destruction by some latter-day Pied Piper of Hamlyn.

And now I must state my principal objection. Herr Dohm's proposal to give the Jews rights of citizenship equal to our own, even to the poor Jew who does not bring money into the state, and to open to them all the professions such as agriculture, crafts, etc., would indeed be a blessing for them. But it would gravely weaken the state, even in the unlikely case that the Jews would bring wealth and money directly into the state, or attract them in the course of time. For the power of a state does not depend on gold alone, but rather, in large part, on the strength of its soldiers. And the Jews will not contribute soldiers to the state as long as they do not change their religious views. There are several reasons for this. First, the Jews will not fight on the Sabbath, for they are forbidden to do so if not attacked. . . . As long as they observe the laws about kosher and non-kosher food it will be almost impossible to integrate them into our ranks. No one would recommend forming special units for them, especially since the oath of the Jews is one of the most complicated matters in the world. Eisenmenger[6] is justified in complaining that it is highly doubtful whether the Jew respects an oath as we do. One must add to this a further physical argument, albeit a hypothetical one, which Herr Dohm seems not to have considered. It is held that the conduct of modern warfare requires a specific minimum height for the soldiers. Whether this claim is justified I am not qualified to judge. At any event this is accepted practice in the two most militarily powerful German states. If this claim be true, very few Jews of the necessary height will be found who will be eligible for the army.

NOTES

1. Johann David Michaelis (1717–1791), German Bible scholar and professor of Oriental languages at the University of Goettingen.

2. Rashi (acronym of *Rabbi Solomon Yitzhak* [1040–1105]) French rabbinical scholar and biblical exegete.

3. Abraham Ibn Ezra (1098–1164), Spanish Jewish scholar and poet.

4. David Kimchi (c. 1160–1235), Spanish Jewish grammarian, philologist and biblical exegete.

5. Phillip Jakob Spener (1635–1705), Protestant theologian. His *Pia desideria oder herzliches Verlangen nach gottgefaelliger Besserung der wahren evangel. Kirche* (1675) is a classic statement of Pietism, which he subsequently defended against the objections of orthodox theologians.

6. Johann Andreas Eisenmenger (1654–1704) author of *Entdecktes Judenthum* [Judaism unmasked], a work denouncing Judaism, including charges of using Christian blood for ritual purposes and of poisoning of wells. Eisenmenger supported his argument with citations from talmudic literature, which he had studied for nineteen years under the pretence of becoming a proselyte.

MOSES MENDELSSOHN
11. Response to Dohm[1]

While reasonable arguments are unanimous in adjudging also to the Jews a participation in the rights of man, it is not thereby understood that even in their present debased con-

Source: Moses Mendelssohn's Preface of 1782 to the German translation of Menasseh ben Israel's *Vindiciae Judaeorum,* in Mendelssohn's *Jerusalem* (a two volume collection of Mendelssohn's Jewish writings), trans. M. Samuels (London, 1838), vol. 1, pp. 90–99.

dition, they may not be useful to the state, or that their increase might possibly become injurious to it. On this too, Rabbi Manasseh's reasoning in this tract, well deserves attention, since in his days, he would seek for none but a very qualified admission of his brethren in England. Holland alone affords an example which may remove all doubts on that head. There, the increase of the Jews has never yet been complained of; although the means of getting a living are almost as scantily doled out to them, and their privileges are almost as stunted as in many a province of Germany. "Ay," it is said, "but Holland is a commercial country; and therefore cannot have too many trading inhabitants." Agreed. But I should like to know, whether it was commerce which drew people thither; or whether commerce was not rather drawn there by the people? How is it, that so many a city in Brabant and the Netherlands, with equal or perhaps superior commercial accommodations, comes so much behind the city of Amsterdam? What makes people crowd together on a barren soil, in marches not intended by Nature to be inhabited; and by industry and art metamorphose lone fens into a garden of God, and invent resources for a comfortable existence, which excites our admiration? What else but liberty, mild government, equitable laws and the hospitable manner in which men of all complexions, garbs, opinions, manners, customs and creeds, are admitted, protected and quietly allowed to follow their business? Nothing else but these advantages have produced, in Holland, the almost superabundant blessings and exuberance of prosperity, for which that country is so much envied.

Generally speaking, "Men superfluous to the state, men, of whom a country can make no use at all," seem to me terms which no statesman should make use of. Men are all more or less useful: they may be employed in this or that way; and more or less promote the happiness of their fellow creatures and their own. But no country can, without serious injury to itself, dispense with the humblest, the seemingly most useless of its inhabitants, and to a wise government, not even a pauper is one too many—not even a cripple altogether useless. Mr. Dohm, in the introduction to his work, has, indeed, tried to determine the quantity which population may not exceed, without overfilling the country and becoming injurious to it. But I think that, with any proviso whatever, no legislator should give this the least consideration; there is no arrangement to oppose the accumulation of souls, no measure to put a stop to increase, that does not tend far more to injure the improvement of the inhabitants, the destination of man and his happiness, than is done by the alleged superfluity. In this, let them depend upon the wise ordering of Nature. Let it quietly take its course, and on no account place impediments in its way, by unreasonable officiousness. Men will flock to places where they can get a living; they multiply and crowd together where their activity has free play. Population increases as long as genius can discover new means of earning. When the sources become exhausted, it instantly stops, of course; and if you make a vessel too full on one side, it will, of itself, discharge the superfluity on the other. Nay, I venture to assert, that such an instance never occurs; and that there never has been a thinning or emigration of the people, which was not the fault of the laws or the management of them. As often as, under any government whatsoever, men become a nuisance to men, it is owing to nothing but the laws of their administrators.

In some modern publications, there is an echo of the objection—"The Jews are an unproductive people; they neither till the ground, cultivate the arts, nor exercise mechanical trades; and, therefore, do not assist Nature in bringing forth, nor give her produce another form, but only carry and transport the raw or wrought commodities of various countries one to another. They are therefore, mere consumers, who cannot but be a tax upon the producer." Nay, an eminent, and, in other respects, a very acute author, the other day, loudly complained about the hardship of the producer having to maintain so many consumers, to fill so many useless stomachs. Mere common sense, thinks he, shows that the price of the products of nature, and of the arts, must be run up the greater the number of intermediate buyers and sellers, who themselves add nothing to the stock, yet will have them. Accordingly he gives the State this advice and friendly admonition, either not to tolerate Jews at all, or to allow them to exercise agricultural and mechanical trades.

The conclusion may be heartily well meant, but so much weaker are the premises, which appear so plain and irrefutable to the author. According to his ideas, who are precisely called *producers* and *consumers*? If he alone produces who co-operates in the composing of some tangible thing, or improves it by the labour of his hands, the largest and most valuable portion of the state consists of mere consumers. According to these principles, both the learned and military professions produce nothing, unless the books written by the former may be said to form an exception. From the trading and working classes, there are first to be deducted, merchants, porters, carriers by hand and by water, etc., and at the upshot, the class of producers, as they are called, will consist chiefly of ploughboys and journeymen mechanics. For landholders and master-manufacturers, now-a-days, rarely put their hands to the work themselves. Thus, with the exception of that carefully useful, but considerably minor portion of the population, the state would be composed of individuals who neither cultivate the productions of nature, nor improve them by the labour of their hands—that is, of mere consumers; and will it be therefore said also, of useless stomachs which are a burden to the producers?

Here the absurdity is palpable: and as the conclusion is just, the error must lodge somewhere in the antecedents. And so it does. Not only *making something* but *doing something* also, is called *producing*. Not he alone who labours with his hands, but, generally, whoever does, promotes, occasions, or facilitates anything that may tend to the benefit or comfort of his fellow-creatures, deserves to be called a producer; and, at times, he deserves it the more, the less you see him move his hands or feet. Many a merchant, while quietly engaged at his desk in forming commercial speculations, or pondering, while lolling on his sofa, on distant adventures, produces, in the main, more than the most active and noisy mechanic or tradesman. The soldier too produces; for it is he who procures the country peace and security. So does the scholar produce, it is true, rarely anything palpable to the senses, yet matters, at least, equally valuable, such as wholesome advice, information, pastime and pleasure. The expression, "that there is more produced by any Paris pastrycook, than by the whole Academy of Science," could have escaped a man like Rousseau, only in a fit of spleen. The well-being of a country at large, as well as of every individual in it, requires many things both sensual and intellectual, many goods both material and spiritual; and he who, more or less directly or indirectly, contributes towards them, cannot be called a mere consumer; he does not eat his bread for nothing; he produces something in return.

This, I should think, places the matter in a far clearer light to common sense. And as to immediate buyers or sellers, in particular, I will undertake to maintain, that they are not only far from prejudicial, either to the producer or consumer, provided abuses be prevented, but very beneficial and almost indispensable to both; nay, that through their agency, commodities become more useful, more in demand, and also cheaper; while the producer gains more, and is thereby enabled to live better and happier without any extraordinary exertion of his strength.

I imagine a workman who is obliged to go himself to the farmer for the raw material, and also to take the manufactured product to the wholesaler himself; who has to mind that he lays in, at a certain season of the year, an adequate stock of the former, and takes the latter, as often as he has occasion, to one who may just have a demand for it, and will become a purchaser. Compare to him, the workman to whom the intermediate dealer brings the raw material into his house, sells it for him for ready money or on credit, according to his present exigency and circumstances. At times he also takes the wrought articles off his hands, and disposes of them to the shopkeeper, at convenient opportunities. What a deal of time and trouble must not the former save, which he may devote to his in-door business, and which the latter is obliged to waste in chance travelling and tarrying about the country, in ever so many avocations, or convivialities, which either he dare not or cannot prevail upon himself to decline. How much more, then, will the former, with the same degree of exertion, work and produce; and thus be able to afford higher prices, and live comfortably notwithstanding? Will not real industry be promoted thereby, and does the intermediate dealer still deserve to be called a useless consumer? This argument in favour of the petty buyer and seller becomes still more forcible when applied to the wholesale dealer, to the merchant proper, who removes and transports the productions of nature and the arts from one country to another, from one hemisphere to another. He is a real benefactor to the state, to the human race at large, and therefore, every thing but a useless stomach living at the producer's charge.

I said, "provided abuses be prevented." These principally consist in the manoeuvres and tricks resorted to by the intermediate dealers in raw materials, to get the grower's fate into their power, and become the rulers of the prices of things, by depressing them in the hands of the first holder, and driving them up in their own. These are great evils, which crush the producer's industry and the consumer's enterprise, and which should be counteracted by laws and by police regulations. Not indeed summarily, by prohibiting, excluding, or stopping; and least of all, by granted or winked-at monopoly or forestalling. Such measures either aggravate the evils which it is intended to avert by them, or bringing on others still more ruinous. Rather let them seek to abate, as much as possible, all restrictions, abolish all chartered companies, abrogate all preferring and excluding exceptions, grant the humblest dealer and jobber in raw materials, equal rights and privileges, with the first house of commerce; in one word, let them every way promote competition, and excite rivalry, and, amongst the intermediate dealers, whereby the prices of commodities will be kept in equilibrium, arts and manufacturing encouraged on the one hand, and on the other, every one enabled to enjoy the industry of his fellow-creatures without excessive exertion. The consumer may live comfortably without luxury, and the artist yet maintain himself respectably. It is by competition only, by unlimited liberty, and equality of the laws of buying and selling, that those ends can be obtained; and, therefore, the commonest salesman or buyer-up, who takes the raw material from the grower to the workman, or the wrought from him to the grower, is of very considerable utility to the prosperity of the arts, industry, and commerce in general. He causes the raw material to maintain its price to the advantage of the grower, while, for the benefit of the workman, and the prosperity of trades, he seeks to spread the products of industry about in all directions, and to render the comforts of life more known, and more generally serviceable. On this consideration, the pettiest trafficking Jew is not a mere consumer, but a useful inhabitant (citizen, I must say), of the state—a real producer.

Let it not be said, that I am a partial advocate of my brethren; that I am magnifying everything which may go in their favour, or tend to their recommendation. Once more I quote Holland. And when the subjects treated of industry and commerce, what country in the world can be more aptly quoted? It is merely through competition and rivalry, through unlimited liberty and equality of the privileges of buyers and sellers, of whatsoever station, quality, or religious persuasion they be, that all commodities have their price there, but with a moderate difference as to buying and selling; while rivals and competitors bring both the parties to a mean, which tends to their mutual advantage. Hence, with a small sacrifice, you can buy or sell any article whatsoever, at all seasons of the year, and at all times of the day, nowhere better, and with greater ease, than at Amsterdam.

NOTE

1. Moses Mendelssohn (1729–1786), the central personality of the German Jewish Enlightenment. To strengthen the impact of Dohm's treatise, Mendelssohn induced Markus Herz (1747–1803) to translate Menasseh ben Israel's *Vindiciae Judaeorum*, the Dutch rabbi's 1656 refutation of objections advanced by British clergy against Jewish readmission to England. Mendelssohn's lengthy preface, intended as a supplement to Dohm's essay, also gave him the opportunity to correct some of Dohm's views. Mendelssohn, as we see from this excerpt, was particularly perturbed by Dohm's endorsement of the popular view of Jewish commercial and moral corruption—a corruption, Dohm contended, which would be eliminated with the Jews' admission to citizenship. Mendelssohn, of course, objected to this type of argument. Indicatively, he also rejected the term *buergerlichte Verbesserung* (the civil amelioration or betterment), preferring the term *buergerliche Aufnahme* (civil admission).

MOSES MENDELSSOHN
12. Remarks Concerning Michaelis' Response to Dohm

Ritter Michaelis does not seem to know any other vice besides fraud and roguery. I think, however, that where the wickedness of a people is to be evaluated one should not entirely overlook murderers, robbers, traitors, arsonists, adulterers, whores, killers of infants, etc.

But even if one where to judge [a people's] wickedness only by the quantity of thieves and receivers of stolen goods among them, this number should not be viewed in terms of that people's proportion of the entire population. The comparison should rather be made between traders and pedlars among the Jews on the one hand, and among other peoples on the other. I am sure that such a comparison would yield very different proportions. The same statistics, I do not hesitate to maintain, will also show that there are twenty-five times as many thieves and receivers of stolen goods among German pedlars as among Jewish. This is aside from the fact that the Jew is forced to take up such a calling, while the others could have become field marshals or ministers. They freely choose their profession, be it a trader, pedlar, seller of mouse traps, performer of shadow plays or vendor of curios.

It is true that quite a number of Jewish pedlars deal in stolen goods; but few of them are outright thieves, and those, mostly, are people without refuge or sanctuary anywhere on earth. As soon as they have made some fortune they acquire a patent of protection from their territorial prince and change their profession. This is public knowledge; when I was younger I personally met a number of men [Jews] who were esteemed in my native country after they had elsewhere made enough dubious money to purchase a

Source: Moses Mendelssohn, "Anmerkung zu des Ritters Michaelis Beurtheilung des ersten Theils von Dohm, ueber die buergerliche Verbesserung der Juden" (1783), *Moses Mendelssohns gesammelte Schriften*, ed. G. B. Mendelssohn (Leipzig, 1843), vol. 3, pp. 365–67. Trans. here by J. Hessing.

patent of protection. This injustice is directly created by that fine policy which denies the poor Jews protection and residence, but receives with open arms those very same Jews as soon as they have "thieved their way to wealth." Although he is inspired by Scripture, Herr Ritter Michaelis seems to have a bias against poverty. Among the Jews, however, I have found comparatively more virtue in the quarters of the poor than in the houses of the wealthy.

The hoped-for return to Palestine, which troubles Herr M. so much, has no influence on our conduct as citizens. This is confirmed by experience wherever Jews are tolerated. In part, human nature accounts for it—only the enthusiast would not love the soil on which he thrives. And he who holds contradictory religious opinions reserves them for church and prayer. In part, also, the precaution of our sages accounts for it—the Talmud forbids us *even to think* of a return [to Palestine] by force [i.e., to attempt to effect Redemption through human effort]. Without the miracles and signs mentioned in the Scripture, we must not take the smallest step in the direction of forcing a return and a restoration of our nation. The Song of Songs expresses this prohibition in a somewhat mystical and yet captivating verse (Song of Songs, 2:7 and 3:5):

> I charge you, O daughters of Jerusalem,
> By the gazelles, and by the hinds of the field,
> That you stir not up, nor awake my love,
> Till it please.

. . . I doubt the validity of Herr Michaelis' view that we are unfit for army service. Does he wish to say that religion should sanction wars of aggression? Let him name the one religion which is cursed enough to do so. Christianity, to be sure, does not. And are not Quakers and Mennonites tolerated and allowed many more privileges and rights than we are?

Herr Michaelis never speaks of Christians and Jews, but always of *Germans* and *Jews*. He does not content himself with establishing the religious differences between us; he prefers to see us as strangers who will have to agree to all conditions which the owners of the land are ready to concede to us. But this, in the first place, is a question to be decided: would it not be better for the owners of the land to accept those they now merely tolerate as citizens rather than bringing strangers at great cost, into their country[?] Secondly, we should also consider the following problem: for how long, for how many millennia, must this distinction between the owners of the land and the stranger continue? Would it not be better for mankind and culture to obliterate this distinction?

I think, moreover, that laws should not be influenced by personal convictions at all. Laws should take their inevitable course, proscribing whatever is not beneficial to the general good. When personal convictions conflict with the laws it is up to the individual to resolve this problem on his own. If then the fatherland is to be defended, everybody who is called upon to do so must comply. In such cases, men usually know how to modify their convictions and to adjust them to their civic duty. One merely has to avoid excessively emphasizing the conflict between the two. In a few centuries the problem will disappear or be forgotten. In this way, Christians have neglected the doctrines of their founders and have become conquerors, oppressors and slave-traders, and in this way, Jews too could be made fit for military service.

ABBÉ GRÉGOIRE

13. An Essay on the Physical, Moral and Political Reformation of the Jews[1]

But the Jews, I shall be told, are incapable of being reformed, because they are absolutely worthless. I reply, that we see few of them commit murder, or other enormous crimes, that call forth public vengeance; but their abominable meanness produces base actions. Mr. Michaelis[2] assures us, that in Germany, of twenty-five criminals imprisoned or condemned, twenty-four are always Jews. This is the assertion of Mr. Michaelis—but, in the first place, an assertion is no proof. The truth of this, however, might have been easily ascertained, by examining and producing the criminals. Secondly, supposing the circumstances to be as true as it is doubtful, this would prove nothing but against the German Jews; and lastly, it would still be necessary to establish as a certainty that this perversity proceeds immediately from their religion, or their natural disposition. That it is not inspired by the law, is evident; shall we believe, then, that it is innate? Some peevish philosophers, indeed, have pretended, that man is born wicked; but happily for the honor and comfort of humanity, this system has been banished to the class of absurd and mortifying hypotheses. So many laws made against the Jews, always suppose in them a natural and indelible worthlessness; but these laws, which are the fruit of hatred or prejudice, have no other foundation but the motive which gives rise to them. This perversity is not so inherent in their character as to affect every individual. We see talents and virtues shine forth in them wherever they begin to be treated as men, especially in the territories of the Pope, which have so long been their terrestrial paradise; in Holland, Prussia, and even among us. Hertz[3] and Block[4] render the Jewish nation illustrious at present in Germany; and the Hague is honored by a Pinto.[5] We must, therefore, believe these people susceptible of morality, until we are shown, that they have invincible obstacles in their physical organization, and in their religious and moral constitution.

Let us cherish morality, but let us not be so unreasonable as to require it of those whom we have compelled to become vicious. Let us reform their education, to reform their hearts; it has long been observed, that they are men as well as we, and they are so before they are Jews.

Mr. Michaelis objects also, that this nation being in constant opposition to general manners, will never become patriotic. We allow that it will be difficult to incorporate them into universal society; but between difficulty and impossibility, there is the same difference as between impossibility and possibility. I have myself remarked, and even proved, that hitherto the Jews have been invariable in their manners and customs; but the greater part of their customs are not contrary to civil functions; and with regard to those which may appear to be incompatible with the duties of the citizen, they are preserved only by the uniformity of that conduct, which all nations observe towards them. If we do not maintain, with Helvetius,[6] that the character and disposition of man depend altogether on his education, we at least allow, that in a great measure they are the result of circumstances. Can the Jews ever become patriots? This is a question proposed by those who reproach them with not loving

Source: Abbé Grégoire, *Essai sur la régénération physique, moral, et politique des Juifs* (Metz, 1789). Abbé Grégoire, *An Essay on the Physical, Moral and Political Reformation of the Jews,* translator not indicated (London, 1791), pp. 134–40.

a country that drove them from its bosom; and with not cherishing people who exercised their fury against them—that is to say, who were their executioners.

Flatterers, in every country, extol the attachment of the people to their sovereigns, and to their country; thus gratifying the vanity of the master at the expense of truth. Study the characters of men, in different countries, and you will find, that pleasure and interest are the grand springs by which they are actuated; provided the people sleep securely in their habitations, and enjoy there in peace, the fruits of their fields, which they cultivate at their ease, and provided they are not subjected to the scourge of the law, nor oppressed by the iron hand of despotism, they are satisfied; but under any other circumstances, they show something more than indifference with regard to their government, as well as to their sovereign: they even offer up secret vows for a revolution, because they imagine that a new order of things will procure them happiness; and they know nothing of patriotism but the name, except, perhaps, in places where they have a share, though at a distance, in the legislative or executive authority. We may, therefore, lay it down as a fact, that the character of the French, for two years past, has acquired more energy and displayed more patriotism than in the two last centuries.

The Jews, every where dispersed, yet no where established, have only had the spirit of a body which is entirely different from the spirit of a nation; for this reason, as had been observed, it is neither that of the English at London, nor that of the Dutch at the Hague, nor that of the French at Metz; they form always a state within a state,[7] because they are never treated as children of the country. In republics even, where the people taking an active part in the legislation, are subject only to themselves, the Jews are always passive, and counted as nothing; they possess no landed property; though commerce, which generally renders men citizens of the world, procures them portable riches, that afford them a small consolation of the opprobrium thrown upon them, and the load of oppressive laws under which they groan. You require that they should love their country—first give them one.

But, says Mr. Michaelis, they will always look towards Palestine, as the seat of their repose; and will never consider other countries but as places of passage, without ever attaching themselves to them. Whom must we believe, him or Boulanger?[8] The latter assures us, that the fanaticism of the Jews begins to cool; and that, in the process of time, it may be totally extinguished. They hope to return to Palestine, but they hope at the same time to conquer the whole world, which will secure to them the possession of other countries. Besides, this return is fixed at an uncertain epoch; the Talmud forbids them to think of it; and to take any step in consequence of their expectations, until prodigies announce the arrival of their deliverer.

At the moment when the weight of misfortune oppresses the Jew, and when he eats with trembling the bread of sorrow, he sights, perhaps the arrival of the Messiah. I say, perhaps, for all do not consider that event as a very favourable prospect; since, according to some Rabbis, a severe judgement must previously try those who are to be made partakers of the felicity that will thence arise to men. The exclamation of a certain doctor is well known, "let him come, provided I do not see him!" However this may be, his coming will appear less desirous to our Israelite, when the humanity of the world shall suffer him to breathe in peace under his paternal roof, become the abode of tranquility and happiness, which to him will possess all the charms of novelty. The comforts of the present life make people too often forget those promised in the next; the Jew has his sensations as well as we, and his hopes will never induce him to abandon present enjoyments, when he can obtain them. When he is once become a member of the state, attached to it by the ties of pleasure, security, liberty, and ease, the spirit of the body will become diminished in him; he will not be tempted to transport his riches elsewhere, when his landed property has fixed him in that country where he has acquired it and he will cherish his mother, that is to say his country, and interests of which will be confounded with his own.

NOTES

1. Abbé Henri Baptiste Grégoire (1750–1831), Jesuit priest, who despite his negative views of Judaism and "Jewish" commercial behavior, consistently advocated the granting of equal rights to Jews (and to other minorities). As a delegate to the French National Assembly he placed a motion for Jewish emancipation. (See "Motion en Faveur des Juifs par M. Grégoire, cure d'Embermenil, député de Nancy, précédée d'une notice historique sur les persécutions qu'ils viennent d'essuyer en divers lieux . . . ," Paris, 1789.) On the day on which his motion was considered by the Assembly, Grégoire exclaimed before the Assembly: "Fifty thousand Frenchmen arose this morning as slaves; it depends on you whether they shall go to bed as free men." Although Grégoire's arguments on behalf of Jewish civil parity are not original, they are significant because he advanced them as a professing Catholic and priest. Grégoire's essay was first submitted in a 1785 competition held by the Société Royale des Arts et Sciences at Metz on the question: "Are there possibilities of making the Jews more useful and happier in France?"

2. Johann David Michaelis, see document 10, note 1, in this chapter.

3. The reference is apparently to Markus Herz (1747–1803), German-Jewish physician, friend and disciple of Kant. See chapter 2, document 6.

4. The reference is apparently to Markus (Mordecai) Eliezer Bloch (1723–1797), German-Jewish physician, famed zoologist, friend of Mendelssohn.

5. Isaac de Pinto (1717–1787), philosopher and economist of Portuguese-Jewish descent; born in France, but lived most of his life in Holland. See chapter 7, document 2.

6. Claude Adrien Helvetius (1715–1771), French philosopher, one of the Encyclopedists.

7. This was a frequent charge of opponents of Jewish emancipation. See chapter 2, document 4.

8. The reference is apparently to Nicholas Antoine Boulanger (1722–1759), French philosopher and scholar. See his controversial *L'Antiquité dévoilée par ses usages, ou Examen critique des principales, opinions, cérémonies et institutions religieuses et politiques des differens peuples de la terre*, 3 vols. (Amsterdam, 1766).

II

Harbingers of Cultural and Ideological Change

On the cultural and ideological level a departure from the regnant medieval and theological attitude toward the Jew was evident in the Enlightenment, the seventeenth- and eighteenth-century intellectual movement which held that the ultimate arbiter of truth, both epistemological and moral, is reason as opposed to religion and tradition. Moreover, the Enlightenment celebrated reason as a universal attribute of man that transcends differences of religion and of national and social origin. Reason, accordingly, constitutes a universal bond between men. In adopting this premise the Enlightenment adumbrated the liberal and democratic values that would eventually embrace the Jew as a fellow man. The selections from Gotthold Ephraim Lessing (1729–1781) are representative of the Enlightenment as it relates to the Jew.

Parallel to the Enlightenment there was a shift in the attitudes of Jews toward their own religious tradition and the outside world. One may refer to this shift as a secularization of consciousness, or a disengagement of the consciousness of the individual from the authority of his religious tradition. Perhaps the first instance of this process was the circle of Daniel (Juan) de Prado (c.1615–c.1672) and Baruch Spinoza, or, as he is also known, Benedict de Spinoza (1632–1677), in the Jewish community of Amsterdam. These men questioned some of the basic tenets of Jewish faith, for example, the divine authorship of the Scripture, rabbinic authority and, most significantly, the relevance of ritual as divine service. In expressing these heretical views Prado and Spinoza revealed—and thus met violent opposition from the elders of their community—the spiritual turmoil of a community of former Marranos. Having lived for generations as Christians, the process of reconstructing their lives in accordance with the traditional patterns of Judaism was not simply an organizational one, but a complex cognitive process involving the acceptance of a new source of religious authority. Cognitively, Prado and Spinoza were marginal Jews and thus apparently receptive to the Deism and rationalism of the early Enlightenment. The texts of the ban of excommunication (*herem*) of Prado and of Spinoza, presented herein, reflect this situation. Prado recurrently sought to have the *herem* repealed and to be readmitted to the House of Israel. Spinoza, on the other hand, apparently accepted his banishment from Judaism without regret. He steadfastly refused, however, to adopt another positive religion. His rejection of Albert Burgh's appeal to embrace Catholicism illustrates both his Deistic rationalism and his insistence that a man of reason need not belong to a church. In that Spinoza left Judaism without adopting another faith he is said to be the first modern, secular Jew.

The selection "The Right To Be Different" from Moses Mendelssohn's *Jerusalem* (1783) illustrates an attempt to argue that participation in the secular culture of the Enlightenment need not involve a rejection of Judaism. In consonance with the proposition that the community forged by reason—the so-called *Gelehrterrepublik* (the republic of the learned, viz., those who developed their reason)—was ideally neutral to one's religious faith and background, Mendelssohn proudly pointed to his friendship with the leading personalities of the Enlightenment. "I have the good fortune to include among my friends," Mendelssohn wrote, "quite a number of fine men who are not of my faith. We have a genuine affection for each other, although we take it for granted that in matters of religion we have very different beliefs. I enjoy their company and feel enriched by it" (Letter to J. C. Lavater, December 12, 1769).[1] As is indicated by Immanuel Kant's letter to Markus Herz (document 6), these individuals just as enthusiastically esteemed their relationship with Mendelssohn. The reading from Naphtali Herz Wessely (1725–1805), who was like Mendelssohn an observant Jew, expresses ideas similar to Mendelssohn's in a programmatic fashion, emphasizing the need for a reform in Jewish education to encourage participation in the universal and secular learning of Europe. *Ha-Me'assef* [The gatherer], a journal published intermittently from 1784 to 1811, was founded by disciples of Mendelssohn and Wessely to propagate among Jewry the weltanschauung of the Enlightenment. Specifically, *Ha-Me'assef*, written in Hebrew, sought to re-orient the axis of Jewish concern from Talmud and Halakha (Jewish law) to the Bible and the Hebrew language—aspects of Judaism deemed more amenable to the values of the Enlightenment. Included herein are the prospectus of *Ha-Me'assef* and the lead article, "We Shall Not Be Deterred," of the fourth volume of the magazine. The custodians of traditional Judaism for the most part responded to the efforts of Mendelssohn and his followers with vehemence, for they feared that these new trends would undermine the integrity of the traditional Jewish way of life. The reading from Rabbi David (Tevele) ben Nathan of Lissa (d. 1792) is one of the milder responses on behalf of traditional Judaism.

With the rapid acculturation of German Jewry not only was the commitment to Talmud and Halakha eclipsed but so was the interest in the Hebrew Scripture and

1. See Jacob Katz, *Exclusiveness and Tolerance* (New York: Schocken, 1962), p. 173.

language. The Jewish votaries of Enlightenment quickly adapted to the situation and began to use German as a medium of expression. In that the exigent need was no longer to encourage Jewish adaptation to the spirit of the age, the message, of course, changed somewhat: the focus was now on how Judaism could be adapted and integrated into the secular life of the modern Jew. *Sulamith,* issued from 1806 to 1833 in Dessau, Germany, became a major organ of the Jewish Enlightenment. Not surprisingly *Sulamith* also became a forum advocating religious reformation, as the "Preface" from its first issue (1806) indicates. From the second issue (1808) the selection "Call for Religious Enlightenment," a proto-Reform proposal for a Judaism based exclusively on moral precepts, represents a weakening of tradition and the demand for a redefinition of Judaism compatible with the new cultural orientation of "enlightened" Jewry.

The passages from the writings of Saul Ascher (1767–1822) and Lazarus Bendavid (1762–1832), antedating those from *Sulamith*, represent early appeals to minimize the "ceremonial laws" of Judaism, which, they contended, obstructed the Jew's integration in the modern world. They differed sharply with Mendelssohn, who had previously argued (see document 14 in this chapter) that fidelity to Halakha was not incompatible with Enlightenment. Mendelssohn did, however, urge the dissolution of the legal autonomy enjoyed by the Jewish community since the Middle Ages, in order to underscore the Jew's commitment to the separation of church and state and to facilitate the Jew's integration in the unitary legal structure of the modern state.

This chapter concludes with David Friedlaender's (1750–1834) petition to the religious authorities of Berlin for a "dry baptism." Despairing of inner reform and of political emancipation, Friedlaender in the name of some of Berlin's leading Jewish families sought admission to the Church without the confessional obligation to affirm Christian dogma.

THE SEPHARDI COMMUNITY OF AMSTERDAM

1. The Writ of Excommunication Against Baruch Spinoza[1]

The Senhores of the Mahamad[2] make it known that they have long since been cognizant of the wrong opinions and behavior of Baruch d'Espinoza, and tried various means and promises to dissuade him from his evil ways. But as they effected no improvement, obtaining on the contrary more information every day of the horrible heresies which he practised and taught, and of the monstrous actions which he performed, and as they had many trustworthy witnesses who in the presence of the same Espinoza reported and testified against him and convicted him; and after all this had been investigated in the presence of the rabbis, they decided with the consent of these that the same Espinoza should be excommunicated and separated from the people of Israel, as they now excommunicate him with the following ban:

> After the judgment of the Angels, and with that of the Saints, we excommunicate, expel and curse and damn Baruch d'Espinoza with the consent of God, Blessed be He, and with the consent of this holy congregation [*Kahal Kados*] in front of the holy Scrolls with the 613 precepts which are written therein, with the anathema with which Joshua banned Jericho, with the curse with which Elisha cursed the youths, and with all the curses which are written in the Law. Cursed be he by day, and cursed be he by night; cursed be he when he lies down, and cursed be he when he rises up; cursed be he when he goes out, and cursed be he when he comes in. The Lord will not pardon him; the anger and wrath of the Lord will rage against this man, and bring him all the curses which are written in the Book of the Law, and the Lord will destroy his name from under the Heavens, and the Lord will separate him to his injury from all the tribes of Israel with all the curses of the firmament, which are written in the Book of the Law. But you who cleave to the Lord your God are blessed.

We order that nobody should communicate with him orally or in writing, or show him any favor, or stay with him under the same roof, or come within four ells of him, or read anything composed or written by him.

NOTES

1. After several warnings the writ of excommunication against Spinoza was proclaimed on July 27, 1656. The extant copy of the document does not include the signatories of the writ.

2. The term used by the Spanish-Portuguese Jewish (Sephardi) community to designate the governing council of the synagogue.

Source: J. Freudenthal, ed., *Die Lebengeschichte Spinozas in Quellenshcriften, Urkunden und nichtamtlichen Nachrichten* (Leipzig: Veit & Co., 1899), pp. 114–16. Trans. here by R. Mendes-Flohr.

THE SEPHARDI COMMUNITY OF AMSTERDAM

2. The Writ of Excommunication Against Daniel (Juan) de Prado[1]

Dr. Daniel de Prado, having been accused before the Senhores of the *Mahamad* of reverting to his evil and false beliefs against our Sacred Law and of having corrupted through these beliefs young students, obliged the said Senhores of the *Mahamad* to cross-examine several witnesses regarding the said Daniel de Prado. The accusation with which he had been charged was found to be true. The acceptance among us of a person so antagonistic to the doctrines and the customs of this holy congregation would cause us great damage. All the more so, considering that he was already condemned for the same transgression in 1656 by the Senhores of the *Mahamad* at the time (as can be seen in *The Book of Decisions*, p. 407), who ordered him to go up to the *tebah*[2] and ask pardon of the entire holy congregation and of the Holy Law (as was stated in the said decision). For all these reasons, the Senhores of this *Mahamad*, together with the rabbis, unanimously ordered that the said Daniel de Prado be placed under the ban of excommunication and separated from the Nation, and that, under penalty of the same action, no one may speak with him (this restriction does not pertain to members of his family). This decree was announced from the *tebah* on the fourteenth of last February.

The Senhores of the *Mahamad*, cognizant of the difficult situation of the members of Daniel de Prado's family and wanting to prevent a worsening of this situation, tried to find a way to send them overseas to regions where Judaism is practised. For this purpose they commissioned two *Parnassim*[3] who spoke with the said Prado, and endeavored to persuade him to agree to this, assuring him that the Community would aid him generously. But the said Prado, citing ill-founded arguments, refused to comply; on the contrary, he stressed that the excommunication should be lifted and that he should be allowed to do the required penance.

The Senhores of the *Mahamad* resolved to meet with the undersigned Senhores, the Elders of the Nation. This having been done, a meeting attended only by Senhores and the rabbis was devoted to reviewing the long account of all that had transpired concerning the said Daniel de Prado. All present unanimously decided that the excommunication would not be lifted, unless he were to go overseas, with or without his family, and then on the condition that, were he to come back to some place in the Low Countries, he would be placed again under the same *herem*. And so that what took place in this affair would become known to all, the Senhores of the *Mahamad* ordered, by the vote of seven out of seven, that a written declaration of this affair would be made in the current book and signed by all.

Joseph de los Rios
J. Selomo Abrabanel
Ishac Belmonte
Jacob Barzilay
Abraam Pereyra
Abraham Pharar
Abraham Nunes Henriques

Saul Levy Mortera
Ischac Abuab

Benjamin Mussaphia
Semuel Salom
Dr. Efraim Bueno
Immanuel Israel Dias
Izak Bueno
David Osorio
Abraham Telles

Source: C. Gebhardt, ed., *Chronicon Spinozanum* (Hague Comitis, curis Societatis Spinozanae, 1923), vol. 3, pp. 274–76. Trans. here by J. Rubin and R. Mendes-Flohr.

NOTES

1. Prado was first excommunicated in 1656, but he was readmitted to the community after he had publicly recanted his heretical views. The elders of the community, however, found him to be insincere, and excommunicated him a second time on May 22, 1657. The text here presented is that of the second writ of excommunication.

2. The Holy Ark in the synagogue in which the Scrolls of the Torah are kept.

3. Elders of the community.

BARUCH SPINOZA
3. Letter to Albert Burgh[1]

That, which I could scarcely believe when told me by others, I learn at last from your own letter; not only have you been made a member of the Roman Catholic Church, but you are become a very keen champion of the same, and have already learned wantonly to insult and rail against your opponents.

At first I resolved to leave your letter unanswered, thinking that time and experience will assuredly be of more avail than reasoning to restore you to yourself and your friends; not to mention other arguments, which won your approval formerly, when we were discussing the case of Steno,[2] in whose steps you are now following. But some of my friends, who like myself had formed great hopes from your superior talents, strenuously urge me not to fail in the offices of a friend, but to consider what you lately were, rather than what you are, with other arguments of the like nature. I have thus been induced to write to you this short reply, which I earnestly beg you will think worthy of calm perusal.

I will not imitate those adversaries of Romanism, who would set forth the vices of priests and popes with a view to kindling your aversion. Such considerations are often put forward from evil and unworthy motives, and tend rather to irritate than to instruct. I will even admit, that more men of learning and of blameless life are found in the Roman Catholic Church than in any other Christian body; for, as it contains more members, so will every type of character be more largely represented in it. You cannot possibly deny, unless you have lost your memory as well as your reason, that in every Church there are thoroughly honourable men, who worship God with justice and charity. We have known many such among the Lutherans, the Reformed Church, the Mennonites, and the Enthusiasts. Not to go further, you knew your own relations, who in the time of the Duke of Alva suffered every kind of torture bravely and willingly for the sake of their religion. In fact, you must admit, that personal holiness is not peculiar to the Roman Catholic Church, but common to all Churches.

As it is by this, that we know "that we dwell in God and He in us" (1 John. 4:13), it follows, that what distinguishes the Roman Catholic Church from others must be something entirely superfluous, and therefore founded solely on superstition. For, as John says, justice and charity are the one sure sign of the true Catholic faith, and the true fruits of the Holy Spirit. Wherever they are found, there is truth in Christ; wherever they are absent, Christ is absent also. For only by the Spirit of Christ can we be led to the love of

Source: The Chief Works of Benedict de Spinoza, trans. with an introduction by R. H. M. Elwes (New York: Dover Publications, 1951), vol. 2, pp. 414–18. Devices used for emphasis in original.

justice and charity. Had you been willing to reflect on these points, you would not have ruined yourself, nor have brought deep affliction on your relations, who are now sorrowfully bewailing your evil case.

But I return to your letter, which you begin, by lamenting that I allow myself to be ensnared by the prince of evil spirits. Pray take heart, and recollect yourself. When you had the use of your faculties, you were wont, if I mistake not, to worship an Infinite God, by Whose efficacy all things absolutely come to pass and are preserved; now you dream of a prince, God's enemy, who against God's will ensnares and deceives very many men (rarely good ones, to be sure), whom God thereupon hands over to this master of wickedness to be tortured eternally. The Divine justice therefore allows the devil to deceive men and remain unpunished; but it by no means allows to remain unpunished the men, who have been by that self-same devil miserably deceived and ensnared.

These absurdities might so far be tolerated, if you worshipped a God infinite and eternal; not one of whom Chastillon [in performing the rite of the Host], in the town in which the Dutch call Tienen, gave with impunity to horses to be eaten. And, poor wretch, you bewail me? My philosophy, which you never beheld, you style a chimera? Oh youth deprived of understanding, who has bewitched you into believing that the Supreme and Eternal is eaten by you, and held in your intestines?

Yet you seem to wish to employ reason, and ask me, "*How I know that my philosophy is the best among all that have ever been taught in the world, or are being taught, or ever will be taught?*" a question which I might with much greater risk ask you; for I do not presume that I have found the best philosophy, I know that I understand the true philosophy. If you ask me in what way I know it, I answer: In the same way as you know that the three angles of a triangle are equal to two right angles: that this is sufficient, will be denied by no one whose brain is sound, and who does not go dreaming of evil spirits inspiring us with false ideas like the true. For the truth is the index of itself and of what is false.

But you, who presume that you have at last found the best religion, or rather the best men, on whom you have pinned your credulity, you "*who know that they are the best among all who have taught, do now teach, or shall in future teach other religions. Have you examined all religions, ancient as well as modern, taught here and in India and everywhere throughout the world?* And, *if you have duly examined them, how do you know that you have chosen the best*" since you can GIVE NO REASON FOR THE FAITH THAT IS IN YOU? But you will say, that you acquiesce in the inward testimony of the Spirit of God, while the rest of mankind are ensnared and deceived by the prince of evil spirits. But all those outside the pale of the Roman Catholic Church can with equal right proclaim of their own creed what you proclaim of yours.

As to what you add of the common consent of myriads of men and the uninterrupted ecclesiastical succession, this is the very catchword of the Pharisees. They with no less confidence than the devotees of Rome bring forward their myriad witnesses, who as pertinaciously as the Roman witnesses repeat what they have heard, as though it were their personal expression. Further, they carry back their line to Adam. They boast with equal arrogance, that their Church has continued to the day unmoved and unimpaired in spite of the hatred of Christians and heathens. They more than any other sect are supported by antiquity. They exclaim with one voice, that they have received their traditions from God Himself, and that they alone preserve the Word of God both written and unwritten. That all heresies have issued from them, and that they have remained constant through thousands of years under no constraint of temporal dominion, but by the sole efficacy of their superstition, no one can deny. The miracles they tell of would tire a thousand tongues. But their chief boast is that they count a far greater number of martyrs than any other nation, a number which is daily increased by those who suffer with singular constancy for the faith they profess; nor is their boasting false. I myself knew among others of a certain Judah called the faithful,[3] who in the midst of the flames, when he was already thought to be dead, lifted his voice to sing the hymn beginning, "To Thee, O God, I offer up my soul," and so singing perished.

The organization of the Roman Church, which you so greatly praise, I confess to be politic, and to many lucrative. I should believe that there was no other more convenient for deceiving the people and keeping men's minds in check, if it were not for the organization of the Muhammadan Church, which far surpasses it. For from the time when this superstition arose, there has been no schism in its Church.

If, therefore, you had rightly judged, you would have seen that only your third point tells in favour of the Christians, namely, that unlearned and common men should have been able to convert nearly the whole world to a belief in Christ. But this reason militates not only for the Roman Catholic Church, but for all those who profess the name of Christ.

But assume that all the reasons you bring forward tell in favour of the Roman Catholic Church. Do you think that you can thereby prove mathematically the authority of that Church? As the case is far otherwise, why do you wish me to believe that any demonstrations [disproving the authority of the Church] are inspired by the prince of evil spirits, while your own are inspired by God, especially as I see, and as your letter clearly shows, that you have been led to become a devotee of this Church not by your love of God, but by your fear of hell, the single cause of superstition? Is this your humility, that you trust nothing to yourself, but everything to others, who are condemned by many of their fellow men? Do you set it down to pride and arrogance, that I employ reason and acquiesce in this true Word of God, which is in the mind and can never be depraved or corrupted? Cast away this deadly superstition, acknowledge the reason which God has given you, and follow that, unless you would be numbered with the brutes. Cease, I say, to call ridiculous errors mysteries, and do not basely confound those things which are unknown to us, or have not yet been discovered, with what is proved to be absurd, like the horrible secrets of this Church of yours, which, in proportion as they are repugnant to right reason, you believe to transcend the understanding.

But the fundamental principle of the "Tractatus Theologico-Politicus,"[4] that Scripture should only be expounded through Scripture, which you so wantonly without any reason proclaim to be false, is not merely assumed, but categorically proved to be true or sound; especially in chapter 7, where also the opinion of adversaries are confuted; see also what is proved at the end of chapter 15. If you will reflect on these things, and also examine the history of the Church (of which I see you are completely ignorant), in order to see how false, in many respects, is Papal tradition, and by what course of events and with what cunning the Pope of Rome six hundred years after Christ obtained supremacy over the Church, I do not doubt that you will eventually return to your senses. That this result may come to pass I, for your sake, heartily wish. Farewell. . . .

NOTES

1. Albert Burgh (c. 1650–c. 1700). a son of Konrad Burgh, a member of Amsterdam's aristocracy and a close friend of Spinoza, had written Spinoza a letter, dated September 3, 1675, explaining his recent conversion from Calvinism to Catholicism. He included therein a demand that Spinoza justify his refusal to affirm the truth of Catholicism. Spinoza's reply is dated "end of 1675."

2. Nicolaus Steno (1631–1686), a Danish scientist who renounced Lutheranism for Catholicism in Florence in 1669.

3. "Don Lope de Verz y Alarcon de San

Clemente, a Spanish nobleman who was converted to Judaism through the study of Hebrew, and was burnt at Valladolid on July 25,1644" (F. Pollack, *Spinoza, His Life and Philosophy*, 2nd ed. [London: Druckworth & Co., 1899], p. 75, n. 1).

4. "Tractatus Theologico-Politicus," published by Spinoza in 1670. It appeared unsigned and presented his critique of revealed religion, his justification for intellectual and religious freedom and his political theories. The work created a sensation everywhere, and Spinoza was accused of being an atheist.

GOTTHOLD EPHRAIM LESSING

4. The Jews[1]

Scene 21. (Baron, Traveller)

. . . .

BARON: But how should I, my dear friend, acknowledge my gratitude to you? Now, for yet a second time you saved me from danger—a danger as great as the first. I am indebted to you for my very life. I never would have discovered this near tragedy without you. My steward, a man whom I totally trusted with my property, was a godless accomplice [of the highway robbers]. I would have never suspected it. Had you departed today without . . .

TRAVELLER: It is true—but then the help I provided yesterday would have remained incomplete. I deem myself extremely fortunate that heaven brought me to this unexpected discovery [of the steward's complicity]. At this moment I am so overjoyed that I am trembling, just as before when I feared I made a mistake.

BARON: As much as I esteem your generosity of spirit I admire your love of man. *(Aside)* I may say that what [my housemaid] Lisette reported is true![2]

Scene 22. (Lisette, Baron, Baron's Daughter, Traveller, Christophe)

LISETTE: And why shouldn't it be true?

BARON: Come my daughter, come! Join your plea to mine. Entreat my saviour to take your hand, and together with your hand to accept my good fortune. What could be more precious to him as a token of my gratitude, than you, whom I love so very dearly. (*To the Traveller*) Aren't you surprised that I can make such a proposal to you? Your servant revealed your identity to us. Grant me the boundless joy of expressing my gratitude. My good fortune, as yours, is my [high] social standing. Here [under the protection of my family], you will be safe from your enemies. You will be with friends who will cherish you. Alone, you will surely be vanquished.

BARON'S DAUGHTER: Are you in doubt on my account? I assure you that I will gladly obey my father in this matter.

TRAVELLER: Your generosity astounds me. By the magnitude of the remuneration you offer me, I first realize how trifling my deed was. But how should I tell you? My servant did not speak the truth. And I . . .

BARON: Would to heaven that you aren't what he made you out to be! Would to heaven that your position be less than mine. Then, at least, my offer should seem all the more precious and you would be more disposed to accept it.

TRAVELLER: *(Aside)* Should I not disclose my true identity?—Dear Sir, your magnanimity touches me profoundly. As-

Source: Gotthold Ephraim Lessing, "Die Juden," *Saemmtliche Schriften*, ed. Karl Lachmann (Leipzig, 1853), vol. 1, pp. 381–84. Trans. here by M. Gelber.

cribe it to fate alone, not to me, that your offer is in vain. I am . . .

BARON: Perhaps already married?

TRAVELLER: No—

BARON: What then?

TRAVELLER: I am a Jew.

BARON: A Jew? Cruel misfortune!

CHRISTOPHE: A Jew?

BARON'S DAUGHTER: But, what difference does it make?[3]

LISETTE: Shush, Fraeulein, shush. I'll tell you later what difference it makes.[4]

BARON: So, there are times when heaven itself prevents us from being grateful?

TRAVELLER: You are already more than grateful, just by your desire to be so.

BARON: Then I will do at least as much as fate allows me. Take my entire wealth, I prefer to be poor but grateful, than rich and ungrateful.

TRAVELLER: This offer, too, is in vain, since the God of my fathers has granted me more than I need. I ask for no recompense, except perhaps that in the future you judge my people somewhat more leniently and with fewer generalizations. I didn't conceal my identity from you because I am ashamed of my religion. No! I saw that although you indicated hostility toward my nation, you were favorably disposed towards me. And, a man's friendship, whoever he be, shall always be invaluable to me.

BARON: I am ashamed of my conduct.

CHRISTOPHE: Only now after my initial astonishment, am I regaining my wits. How? You are a Jew and had the heart to take an upright Christian into your service? You should have served me. Then it would have been right according to the Bible. Good Heavens! You've insulted through me all of Christianity.—Hmm, I didn't know why the man wouldn't eat pork during our travels, for which he made a hundred silly excuses.—Don't think that I'll accompany you any further. And, moreover, I'll bring a suit against you.

TRAVELLER: I can't expect more from you than I can from the other Christian rabble. And, I'll not remind you of the pitiful circumstances from which I removed you in Hamburg. I don't wish to force you to remain with me any longer. Still, because I have been rather satisfied with your services and also for a time suspected you unfairly [of theft], take for recompense that which aroused my suspicions in the first place. *(He gives Christophe a snuff-box)* You may also have your wages. Go then where you will!

CHRISTOPHE: No! The deuce! Certainly there are also Jews who aren't Jews.[5] You're an upright man. By God, I'm staying with you! A Christian would have given me a kick in the ribs, not a [valuable] snuff-box.

BARON: All of your deeds enchant me. Come, let's make certain that those guilty are brought into custody. Oh, how commendable the Jews would be, if they were all like you!

TRAVELLER: And how worthy of love the Christians, if they all possessed your qualities!

(The Baron, his Daughter and the Traveller exit)

Last Scene. (Lisette, Christophe)

LISETTE: Now then, did my friend lie to me before?

CHRISTOPHE: Yes, and for two reasons. First, because I didn't know the truth, and second, because you can't speak much truth for a bribe that you have to give back in the end.

LISETTE: For that matter, how can he be considered a Jew if he conceals his identity?

CHRISTOPHE: For a maid, that's too curiously put! Come let's go. *(He takes her under the arm and they exit)*

NOTES

1. Gotthold Ephraim Lessing (1729–1781), dramatist, critic and philosopher. Aside from Immanuel Kant, Lessing is probably the best-known representative of the Enlightenment in German-

speaking Europe. This play was written in 1749, but first published in 1754; this translation is based on the revised edition of 1770. In addition to its dramaturgical innovations, the significance of the play lies in its unambiguous portrayal of a Jew as a virtuous individual. The preceding excerpts are taken from the play's denouement. The anonymous traveller, who on the previous day rescued the Baron and his entourage from the hands of highway robbers, initially assumed to be "damned Jews," now identifies the scoundrels as none other than the steward and the administrator of the Baron's own estate. Finally, the chivalrous traveller discloses his own identity.

2. At the Baron's behest, Lisette had solicited from the anonymous traveller's servant, Christophe, his master's identity. Although equally ignorant of his master's identity, Christophe was enticed by a promise of a bribe (the snuff box) and told Lisette that his master was a nobleman who had fled his native Holland after having killed an opponent in a duel.

3. The 1754 text reads: "What does that mean? You can certainly still marry me."

4. The 1754 text reads: "Be quiet, Fraeulein. I will explain later what that means."

5. "Es gibt doch wohl auch Juden, die keine Juden sind." The 1754 text reads. "No the deuce! The Jews are generous people."

GOTTHOLD EPHRAIM LESSING
5. A Parable of Toleration[1]

NATHAN: In days of yore a man lived in the East,
Who owned a ring of marvellous worth,
Given to him by a hand beloved.
The stone was opal, and shed a hundred lovely rays,
But chiefly it possessed the secret power
To make the owner loved of God and man
If he but wore it in this faith and confidence;
What wonder then that this man in the East
Ne'er from his finger took the ring.
And so arranged it should forever with his house remain,
Namely, thus: He bequeathed it to
The most beloved of his sons,
Firmly prescribing that he in turn
Should leave it to the dearest of his sons;
And always thus the dearest, without respect to birth,
Became the head and chieftain of the house
By virtue of the ring alone.
You understand me, Sultan?
SALADIN: I understand. Proceed.
NATHAN: The ring, descending from son to son,
Came to the father of three sons at last,
All three of whom obeyed him equally,
And all of whom he therefore loved alike.
From time to time indeed, now one seemed worthiest of the ring,
And now another, now the third,

Source: Gotthold Ephraim Lessing, *Nathan the Wise,* trans. William Jacks (Glasgow, 1894), scene 7.

Just as it happened one or other with him were alone,
And his o'erflowing heart was not divided with the other two;
And so to each one of the three he gave
The promise—in pious weakness alone—
He should possess this wondrous ring.
This then went on as long as it could;
But then at last it came to dying,
Which brings the father into sore perplexity.
It pains him much to practise such deceit
Upon two sons who rested so upon his word.
What can be done? In secret
He seeks out a skilful artist,
And from him orders two other rings,
Just to the pattern of his own.
And urges him to spare neither pains nor gold,
To make a perfect match.
The artist so succeeded in his task,
That, when he brought the jewels home,
The father even failed to tell which was the pattern ring.
Now, glad and joyous, he calls his sons—
But separately of course—gives each
A special blessing with his ring, and died,
You hear me, Sultan?
SALADIN: *(Somewhat moved, turns from him)*
I hear, I hear;
But pray get ended with your tale.
You soon will be?
NATHAN: I'm at the end,
For what follows is self-understood.
Scarce was the father dead,
When each one with his ring appears
Claiming each the leadership of the house.
Inspections, quarrelling, and complaints ensue;
But all in vain, the veritable ring
Was not distinguishable—
(After a pause, during which he expects the Sultan's answer)
Almost as indistinguishable as to us,
Is now—the true religion.
SALADIN: What? Is that meant as answer to my question?
NATHAN: This meant but to excuse myself, because
I lack the boldness to discriminate between the rings,
Which the father by express intent had made
So that they might not be distinguished.
SALADIN: The rings! Don't play with me.
I thought the faiths which I have named
Were easily distinguishable,
Even to their raiment, even to meat and drink.
NATHAN: But not yet as regards their proofs;
For do not all rest upon history, written or traditional?

And history can also be accepted
Only on faith and trust. Is it not so?
Now, whose faith and confidence do we least misdoubt?
That of our relatives? Of those whose flesh and blood we are,
Of those who from our childhood
Have lavished on us proofs of love,
Who ne'er deceived us, unless 'twere wholesome for us so?
How can I place less faith in my forefathers
Than in yours? or the reverse?
Can I desire of you to load your ancestors with lies,
So that you contradict not mine? Or the reverse?
And to the Christian the same applies.
SALADIN: By the living God, the man is right, I must be dumb.
NATHAN: Let us return unto our rings.
As said, the sons accused each other,
And each one swore before the judge
He had received his ring directly
From his father's hand—which was quite true—
And that, indeed, after having long his promise held,
To enjoy eventually the ring's prerogative,
Which was no less the truth.
Each one insisted that it was impossible
His father could play false with him.
And ere he could suspect so dear and true a father,
He was compelled, howe'er inclined to think
The best of them, to accuse his brothers
Of this treacherous act, to unmask the traitors,
And avenge himself.
SALADIN: Well, and the judge? I'm curious to hear what you will give
The judge to say, Go on.
NATHAN: The judge said this; Produce your father here
At once, or I'll dismiss you from this court.
Think you I'm here but to solve riddles?
Or would you wait till the true ring itself will speak?
But stop; I've just been told that the right ring
Contains the wondrous gift to make its wearer beloved,
Agreeable alike to God and man.
That must decide, for the false rings will not have the power.
Now which one do the other two love most?
Come, speak out; you're silent?
Do the rings work only backwards and not outwardly?
Does each one love himself the best?
Then you're all three deceived deceivers;
None of your rings are genuine.
The genuine ring is no doubt lost.
To hide the loss and to supply its place
The father ordered other three.
SALADIN: Splendid, splendid!
NATHAN: The judge went further on to say;

If you will have my judgment, not my advice,
Then go. But my advice is this;
You take the matter as it stands.
If each one had his ring straight from his father,
So let each believe his ring the true one.
T'is possible your father would no longer tolerate
The tyranny of this one ring in his family,
And surely loved you all—and all alike,
And that he would not two oppress
By favouring the third.
Now then, let each one emulate in affection
Untouched by prejudice. Let each one strive
To gain the prize of proving by results
The virtue of his ring, and aid its powers
With gentleness and heartiest friendliness,
With benevolence and true devotedness to God;
And if the virtue of the ring will then
Have proved itself among your children's children,
I summon them to appear again
Before this judgment seat,
After a thousand thousand years.
Here then will sit a judge more wise than I,
Who will pronounce. Go you.
So said the modest judge.
SALADIN: God, oh God!
NATHAN: Saladin, if now you feel yourself to be
That promised sage—
SALADIN: *(Rushes to him and seizes his hand, which to the end he does not let go)*
I dust? I nothing? Oh God!
NATHAN: What ails thee, Sultan?
SALADIN: Nathan, dear Nathan, your judge's thousand
Thousand years have not yet fled,
His judgment seat's not become mine.
Go, go; but be my friend.

NOTE

1. This play, first published in 1779, is based on the parable of the three rings, a story from Giovanni Boccaccio's *Decameron* (composed between 1348 and 1353). The play presents Judaism, Christianity and Islam as three sons of a benevolent father who gave each an identical ring, although each claims that his alone is authentic. Nathan, a Jew, is made the spokesman for the ideals of the Enlightenment, tolerance, brotherhood and love of humanity. Lessing regarded his close friendship with Mendelssohn as a testimony to these ideals. It is thus believed that Nathan was modeled after Mendelssohn.

IMMANUEL KANT
6. Letter to Markus Herz[1]

. . . Dearest Friend,

Today Herr Mendelssohn, your and my honorable friend—as I take pride in calling him—departed from here. Having a man of such gentle disposition, and good spirits and intelligence for a constant and intimate companion in Koenigsberg would be the kind of spiritual nourishment which is completely lacking here, and which, as I grow older, I increasingly miss. I did not [I must admit] know how to enjoy the company of such a rare person, or how to avail myself sufficiently of [his presence in Koenigsberg] in part because I was afraid to interfere with the business that had brought him here. The day before yesterday, he honored me by attending two of my lectures—*à la fortune du pot,* as one might say, since the table was not prepared for such a distinguished guest. The lecture, this time, must have seemed rather tumultuous to him; vacations had interrupted the previous one and most of the time, therefore, was spent on summarizing its content. The summary, naturally, lacked all the clarity and order of the lecture itself. I beg you to help me retain the friendship of this venerable man. . . .

NOTE

1. Immanuel Kant (1724–1804), German philosopher who articulated in a systematic manner the precepts of the Enlightenment. Despite his negative views of Judaism, he had many Jewish disciples and friends.

Markus Herz (1747–1803), German-Jewish physician, disciple of Kant, friend of Moses Mendelssohn and advocate of the Enlightenment among his fellow Jews. In August 1777, Mendelssohn (see chapter 1, documents 11 and 12 and chapter 2, documents 7, 14, 18 and 19) had made a business trip to Koenigsberg, the East Prussian city where Kant taught. Mendelssohn met Kant, with whom he quickly developed a friendship. This letter is dated August 20, 1777.

Source: Immanuel Kants Werke, ed. E. Cassirer (Berlin: Bruno Cassirer, 1918), vol. 9, pp. 158–59. Trans. here by J. Hessing.

MOSES MENDELSSOHN
7. The Right To Be Different[1]

Brethren! if it be genuine piety you are aiming at, let us not feign consonance, when manifoldness is, evidently, the design and end of Providence. None of us feels and thinks exactly alike with his fellow-man; then wherefore impose upon one another by deceiving words? We are, alas! prone enough to do so, in our ordinary transactions, in our general conversation, comparatively of no material importance; but wherefore also in

Source: Moses Mendelssohn, *Jerusalem,* trans. M. Samuels (London, 1838), vol. 1, pp. 170–72.

things involving our spiritual and temporal welfare, and constituting the whole purpose of our creation? God has not stamped on every man a peculiar countenance for nothing: why, then, should we, in the most solemn concerns of life, render ourselves unknown to one another, by disguise? Is not this resisting Providence so far as lies with us? Is it not frustrating the designs of creation, if it were possible, and purposely acting against our vocation and destiny, both in this life and that to come? Regents of the earth! if an insignificant fellow-inhabitant of it may be allowed to lift up his voice unto ye, O listen not to the counsellors, who, in smooth words, would misguide you to so pernicious an undertaking. They are either blind themselves, and cannot see the enemy of mankind lurking in ambush; or they want to blind you. If you hearken to them, our brightest jewel, freedom of conscience is lost. For your happiness' sake, and for ours, *religious union is not toleration*; it is diametrically opposite to it. For your happiness' sake, and for ours, lend not your powerful authority to the converting into a law any *immutable truth*, without which civil happiness may very well subsist; to the forming into a public ordinance any theological thesis, of no importance to the state. Be strict as to the life and conduct of men; make that amenable to a tribunal of wise laws; and leave thinking and speaking to us, just as it was given us, as an unalienable heirloom; as we were invested with it, as an unalterable right, by our universal father. If, perhaps, the connexion of privilege with opinion be too proscriptive, and the time have not yet arrived to do away with it altogether, at least, endeavour to mitigate, as lies with you, its deleterious influence, and to put wise bounds to prejudices now grown too superannuated; at least, pave, for happier posterity, the way to that height of civilization, to that universal forebearance amongst men, after which reason is still panting in vain. Reward and punish no doctrine; hold out no allurement or bribe for the adoption of theological opinions. Let every one who does not disturb public happiness, who is obedient to the civil government, who acts righteously towards you, and towards his fellow-countrymen, be allowed to speak as he thinks fit, to pray to God after his own fashion, or after that of his forefathers, and to seek eternal salvation where he thinks he may find it. Suffer no one to be a searcher of hearts, and a judge of opinions in your states; suffer no one to assume a right which the Omniscient has reserved to himself. "*As long as we are rendering unto Caesar the things which are Caesar's; render ye, yourselves, unto God the things which are God's. Love truth! Love peace!*"

NOTE

1. This call for religious tolerance and pluralism served as the peroration of Mendelssohn's *Jerusalem* (1783), his systematic demonstration of the compatability of traditional Judaism with the precepts of the Enlightenment.

NAPHTALI HERZ (HARTWIG) WESSELY
8. Words of Peace and Truth[1]

Said the wisest of men: "Educate a youth in the path he is to take [literally: "according to his way"], and even when he is old he will not depart from it" (Prov. 22:6). This state-

Source: Naphtali Herz Wessely, *Divrei Shalom ve'Emet* (Berlin, 1782), chaps. 1, 3, 4 and 5. Trans. here by S. Weinstein and S. Fischer.

ment has two parts. The first—"educate a youth," that is, one should be educated in his youth, when his heart is unsullied by the vanities of the world and by the perversities of strange ideas. For when his heart is like clean and smooth paper it shall be easiest to write words of truth upon it, and they shall be well inscribed. The second part—"according to his way," that is, according to his qualities and potential. For the disposition of men and their spiritual faculties are not the same; what is easy for one to receive and retain will be difficult for another, while other matters will be easy for the latter and difficult for the former. . . . And if he shall be educated in his youth, and the education will be according to his way, then "when he is old he will not depart from it."

Now, in order to educate the youths of Israel in the proper manner, two types of studies should be established. The first type is the study of "human knowledge" [*Torat ha'Adam*], that is, those matters which earn for their possessors the title "man" [*Adam*], since he who lacks this knowledge hardly deserves this title, as shall be explained. The second type is the study of the Torah of God, that is, God's laws and teachings, matters that are above human reason and that were made known to Moses through prophetic revelation. Had the Torah not come to us in this divine fashion, it would have remained hidden from even the most sagacious of men, for its contents cannot be deduced from the fixed laws of nature. Moreover, only the seed of Israel is obligated by the laws of the Torah. . . .

In general, "human knowledge" is comprised of etiquette, the ways of morality and good character, civility and clear, graceful expression; these matters and their like are implanted in man's reason. He who possesses "human knowledge" will gain much from the poetic expression of the divine Torah and from the ways of God that are written therein. . . . Similarly, history, geography, astronomy and the like—which are inscribed in the mind of man as innate "primary ideas" whose foundation is reason—produce truths in every matter of wisdom. Included in this category of knowledge are the natural sciences, which provide genuine knowledge about all things: animals, plants, minerals, the elements, meteorology (clouds and their effects), botany, anatomy, medicine, chemistry, etc. It is in man's power to study all of these phenomena by means of his senses and reason; he does not need anything divine to comprehend them. . . .

Now, "human knowledge" is anterior to the exalted divine laws. Hence it is proper that in his youth man should crown himself with the fear of God, with the rules of etiquette and with knowledge to which the appellation "human" is appropriate. With this knowledge he will prepare his heart to learn the laws and teachings of God. . . . From Adam to Moses twenty-six generations elapsed and during this time men acted according to "human knowledge" alone, that is according to the seven Noachide laws[2] and their details as they have been affirmed by the majority of sages, as well as the etiquette, to the arts and to the sciences, all of which are included in "worldly affairs." This "human knowledge" benefits the commonweal, as it teaches how to avail oneself of all things under the sun. It is responsible for man's success in all his worldly endeavors and provides a means for every man to be an aid to his fellow through his affairs and actions. Therefore he who lacks "human knowledge," even though he has learned the laws and teachings of God and lives according to them, gives no pleasure to others and this for two reasons. First, his fellowship is burdensome to other people. He will constantly err in the manners of men, his speech in worldly affairs will not be in conformity with reason, and his actions worse than useless, for they will be of no benefit and no service to other people. Second, even though the laws and teachings of God are far superior to "human knowledge" they are closely correlated to it; where "human knowledge" ends, the divine teaching begins, instructing us on what is beyond man's power of reason. Therefore he who is ignorant of the laws of God, but is versed in "human knowledge," even though the sages of Israel will not benefit from his light in the study of Torah, he will benefit the remainder of humanity. But he who is ignorant of "human knowledge," though he knows the laws of God, gladdens neither the wise of his own people nor the remainder of humanity. . . .

There is one people in the world alone who are not sufficiently concerned with "human knowledge" and who have neglected the public instruction of their youth in the laws of etiquette, the sciences and the arts. We, the children of Israel, who are dispersed throughout all of Europe and who live in most of its states, have turned our backs on these studies. Those among us who dwell in Germany and Poland have been especially negligent in this regard. Many among them are men of intelligence and great understanding, and many are also men of faith and piety, but from childhood their exclusive preoccupation has been God's laws and teachings. They have not heard of or studied "human knowledge." They are ignorant even of the grammar of the holy tongue, and they do not discern the beauty of its diction, the rules of its syntax and the purity of its style—which are wells from which spring wisdom and moral instruction. It goes without saying that they lack proper knowledge of the language of the peoples among whom they live. Many of them do not even know how to read or write the native language. Knowledge of the structure of the earth and the events of history are hidden from them, as are matters of civility, the sciences and the arts. They do not know or understand, for from the start nothing of all this was told to them, neither by their fathers nor by their teachers, who themselves were ignorant of these subjects. Even the fundamental principles of their faith were not taught systematically, so that all the youth might become conversant with them in an orderly fashion. Similarly, our youth were not taught ethics and psychology. Only some of the more outstanding students of God's Torah as they grew older perceived deficiency in matters of "human knowledge," and accordingly endeavoured to correct the fault committed by their teachers by gleaning knowledge either from books or from conversation, "here a little, there a little," but, alas, unsystematically and ineffectively. Their knowledge is like a lightweight coat on a cold day. Indeed, a clear knowledge in these subjects is not found except among individuals whose hearts and spirits moved them to listen to wisdom and pay heed to reason. They learned languages and read books with understanding and thus became like a fountain which replenishes and augments itself. They acquired this knowledge unassisted by their fathers and their superiors. They were driven solely by their love of truth. Such superior men, however, are few. . . .

Let it be understood, however, that we ourselves are not responsible for this state of affairs. We should not pour out our anger upon ourselves or direct our complaints against ourselves. Rather, it is the nations who have hosted us for more than a thousand years who are to blame for our misfortune, for they have terribly wronged us by the command of their kings and ministers. Inspired by many evil motives they have risen against us to destroy us and to humble us to the dust, for which purpose they subjected us to irrational decrees. They thereby acted contrary to "human knowledge," for they thrust our bodies to the dust and depressed the spirit within us.

The hearts of our community subsequently have grown dark. Seeing that we are treated with a heavy hand and that in the eyes of our oppressors we are beneath the rank of man, we have lost the inclination to pursue the study of "human knowledge." When our brethren saw that they had no share in all the good that God had provided for all his creatures from one end of the world to the other, they despised all worldly things. In their bitterness they disregarded and entirely neglected the laws and sciences concerning the administration of world affairs: knowledge of the movement of celestial bodies, of the cultivation of the earth, of the crossing of the seas, of the construction of cities and fortifications, of the governance of kings. For they said: "What have we to do with all this? The inhabitants of the land are our enemies, to our counsel they will not listen, to our valor they pay no heed; moreover, we do not possess fields and vineyards. Let us abandon these studies and occupy ourselves with trade and commerce to enable ourselves to live and feed our children, for only this have they left us. And even of this they have left us only in small measure and in a reduced way. Our Father in Heaven shall be our support and we will engage chiefly in those things which bring eternal life—the laws and teachings of God which we were commanded to obey and upon which God made a covenant with our fathers." The few superior individuals among them ceased to teach the people "human knowledge" for they knew that even the sweetest wisdom is bitter to the embittered soul. Were they to teach them the duty of loving all men, the crown of etiquette, the people would not heed them, since they live among peoples who daily conspire to do evil against them, who slander them in a mendacious and cruel fashion and who in return for their love give forth hate. Were they to teach linguistics so that they may marshal their words according to the rules of speech, to be pleasing to both kings and common men, the people would refuse to listen to them. For their enemies despise the logic of their words and cover them with shame. Were they to teach the people the arts and sciences they would abhor these, because they receive no advantage from them. They cannot work in field or vineyard, or in the construction of towers, fortresses and cities. These nations have not permitted them to work in any practical crafts. Once all these studies and disciplines were forgotten by our community with the passage of time, we have been unable to acquire them again even in those kingdoms ruled by generous kings, who lifted the iron yoke from upon our necks, for we had become alienated from these matters. We did not have books in the Hebrew language and we were not conversant in the language of the Gentiles, for in the times of great troubles . . . we had become estranged from the Gentiles and their languages. Thus we did not learn to read their books, and, it goes without saying, we did not learn to speak their language accurately. When, out of our great distress, we went from nation to nation and from kingdom to kingdom, we learned a bit of the language of one people and a bit of the language of another so that our speech became a jumble.

It is thus a source of thorough amazement how in spite of all the evil that has befallen us we have remained a people and how, notwithstanding the flow of mighty waters, we have nevertheless retained our humanity. It is the power of the divine Torah that is responsible for this. Despite our lack of all the above mentioned knowledge, the Torah stood by us and assured us of a human heart, protecting us thereby from the trait of cruelty and from truly evil actions, far be these sins from us! From the days of yore until now we were never in a rebellious association or in a wicked band who devises evil against men. In every generation we were faithful to the kings ruling over us and to the inhabitants of the land, and we besought God for the well-being of the monarchy of the land. If we found ourselves in the humblest of stations we consoled ourselves with the thought of our innocence and we said: "These are prejudices in the hearts of the people and their rulers, who are acting in the tradition of their fathers," and we hoped that God would change their hearts toward us for good, and have us find mercy in their eyes.

So matters developed generation after generation, and such remains the state of affairs today. To be sure, generous kings reigned in several kingdoms, and in this generation also there are kings of Europe who are wise, philanthropic and kind, treating us with kindness and mercy, may God remember them for good. Nevertheless, many of the iron laws that their cruel predecessors have decreed against us, laws which were intended to remove us from the society of men and which prevented us from performing those acts by means of which man aids his fellow man, . . . have not been abrogated. Rather, they have taken root in the hearts of the peoples and their leaders, and have become venerable to them with the passage of time. Therefore it is difficult for mercy to counteract them and for reason to become strong enough to argue with them and to overcome this perversion. Even if for one moment the heart sees that these are rash laws, habit will quietly extinguish the light of reason. No one has compassion for the many righteous and unfortunate souls who seek only peace and whose sole fault is that they were born Jewish and maintain the faith they had nursed from their mother's breast. We believe in one God who is the same God for all men; the same for our brothers, the men of Europe, and for our brothers, the men of Africa and Asia. Our Torah teaches the love of mankind and the way of life and peace which is the foundation and cornerstone of the religion of Europe and the religion of the Arabs. Nevertheless we were treated unkindly, and thus we despaired, imagining that for the rest of the Exile we would be oppressed.

However, it was not as man envisioned, for to everything there is a season, and a time for every purpose under the heaven. From the time the Creator, blessed be He, established heaven and earth, He ordered in His superior wisdom the appointed times of the universe, times of good and times of evil, for He proclaims the generations from the beginning and sees to the end of all existence. From generation to generation, knowledge that was hidden was revealed by wise men in the arts, sciences and crafts, such as the discovery of America, the inventions of printing, gunpowder, spectacles and so forth. In similar fashion, the Creator ordered every generation and its leaders from the beginning, raising kings to their thrones to be instruments of His craft and to work His decrees and designs. For behold, the prophet Isaiah lived about three hundred years before the destruction of Babylon, yet prophesied Israel's conqueror and named him, as he said: "Thus says the Lord to his annointed to Cyrus" (Is. 45:1); so, too, the man of God Jeroboam said two hundred years before the event: "Behold a child shall be born in the House of David, Josiah by name" (1 Kings 13:2). King Solomon enumerated times of good and evil that encompass all the inhabitants of the earth. Among these, he observed, there is "a time to love and a time to hate" (Eccles. 3:9). And so now, perhaps the time has come to remove hatred from the hearts of men, an unfounded hatred based on a quarrel which is not theirs and whose source lies in differences of faith and worship. O Generation! You have seen that God is good. He has raised up a great man, a saviour to mankind, the exalted emperor, His Majesty Joseph II. Aside from the tidings of his wisdom, his counsel and his military might, imperial statements that have recently issued from him have brought us tidings of even more heroic deeds. These statements—words of peace and truth to all his subjects—have been tried in the crucible of reason and are founded on the love of mankind. Moreover, in his many good works he has not forgotten a poor people, long abused, the Jews. He gave us many good and consoling commands, as a father does to his son, a teacher to his pupils and a [benign] ruler to his people. He has unshackled the disabling bonds by permitting the Jews to engage in all forms of cultivation of the land, to work in all crafts and to trade in all merchandise. In his interest he has also observed that few among us speak the German language accurately . . . and as a result cannot read books, neither history books nor books on etiquette, science and the arts. Neither can we speak in a clear fashion with the inhabitants of the land and their ministers. Taking this into consideration he has commanded us upon a righteous path. He has instructed the Jews to establish schools in which to teach their children to read and write the German language. He has also instructed them to write edifying books according to the Torah, to teach the children understanding and the rules of behavior in society. Arithmetic, geometry, astronomy, history and geography, however, are to be studied from the extant books used by the children of the kingdom, for these sciences do not impinge upon faith, and the ideas of all men concerning these subjects are identical. Knowledge of these subjects can only strengthen the House of Israel and mend the breaches made by the preceding rulers. . . . And thus, the children of Israel will also be men who accomplish worthy things, assisting the king's country in their actions, labor and wisdom.

NOTES

1. Naphtali Herz Wessely (1725–1805), poet, linguist, biblical exegete, pioneer of the revival of Biblical Hebrew and advocate of the Enlightenment among his fellow Jews. In this controversial work Wessely sought to marshal Jewry's support of the Edict of Tolerance issued by Emperor Joseph II of Austria in 1782 (reprinted here, see chapter 1, document 9).

2. Injunctions traditionally given to Noah and therefore binding upon Jew and Gentile alike. According to the Talmud there were seven such laws derived from the early chapters of Genesis.

DAVID (TEVELE) BEN NATHAN OF LISSA[1]
9. A Sermon Contra Wessely

We speak of an act by a sycophant, an evil man, a man poor in understanding, the most mediocre of mediocre of men. This man, Herz Wessely of Berlin, has addressed an epistle to those of the House of Israel who dwell in the land of His Majesty the Emperor.[2] This epistle, called "words of Peace and Truth," makes one's heart heavy. It consists of eight chapters of bootlicking. And, deeming himself unique in his generation, he offers his rash advice to wise, understanding, perfect and flawless men. The gist of his [insolent] remarks is that since His Majesty the Emperor commanded the Israelites to establish schools to teach their youths the German language and to educate them to do mighty deeds in all areas of knowledge, that he, this worthless man, will extend counsel to fulfill His Majesty the Emperor's wishes. I am thoroughly amazed and my heart skips many beats when I contemplate the audacity of this evil man. Aside from the fundamentals of the Hebrew language and a simple rudimentary knowledge of Scripture and the commentaries, this man is bereft of the sublime wisdom of Torah. He manifestly lacks an understanding of the profundities of the Talmud, the early commentaries and the Oral Torah—the testament of God, His laws and statutes. These sources of wisdom are obviously beyond the grasp of this fool. How dare he say, "I shall extend counsel to men of wisdom, understanding and knowledge"? How can one who does not possess any of the foundations of knowledge presume to teach the correct manner of study, proper conduct and the way of God to this people of God? Can one who is weak claim he is strong? Can a blind man say, "Hearken to me and I will teach you to read"? Or can a poor and ill man, whose house is empty of bread, say,"Come eat my bread"?

Beware! This man, Wessely, is an impious man. Beware, do not draw near to him! God, the Lord of Hosts, knows that for the sake of the glory of your Holy Torah I have come this

Source: Hebrew manuscript published by Louis Lewin, "Aus dem juedischem Kulturkampfe," *Jahrbuch der juedisch-Literarischen Gesellschaft*, 12 (1918), pp. 182–94. Trans. here by S. Fischer and P. Mendes-Flohr.

day to hew down he who tramples upon the heads of your Holy People, and to make known to You the evil machinations of this man. In my perusal of his small book I have noted that the spirit of sin animates it. This book seeks to lead the masses astray and to mislead children just out of the womb so that they will not know the paths of Torah and piety. Wessely's counsel is that of a renegade. So that the people should heed him, this imposter associates his sacrilegious ideas with the great and majestic thoughts of His Majesty the Emperor.

What the Emperor actually commanded and what never occurred to Wessely I shall now explain: in His infinite mercy the Lord, the God of Israel, has rendered our people pleasing to His Majesty the Emperor, who now urges each of us to cross the threshold of science and knowledge, [promising] us a place among the royal servants and ministers. The Emperor has commanded all his subjects the following: Every child shall be taught to speak and write the German language so that he will know the language of the land. Everyone shall [also] remain true to the rites and principles of his faith; no part of his faith shall be made alien to him. No Jew will be prevented from fulfilling the fundamentals of our faith, the Written and Oral Torah. (One Torah was spoken by God, although we heard two—may the Lord be blessed that He gave us both of them!) . . . His Majesty the Emperor wishes to teach our children an hour or two a day to speak and read the German language. [But he also wishes] to educate all who spring from the loins of Jacob in the manner of their traditions, for what is primary remains primary and what is secondary remains secondary. How great are his [the Emperor's] works and how precious is his kindness, for indeed all parents wish to provide their children with an education in every type of wisdom, science and craft. . . . But this imposter, Wessely, perverts and distorts the counsel of His Majesty, the Emperor, claiming that he commanded that Jewish children shall no longer attend schools [which teach a traditional Jewish curriculum]. . . . This is a prevarication. Far be it for any intelligent man to think this of the righteous and sincere lover of mankind and leader of nations, his most pious Majesty the Emperor. In the abundance of his righteousness he actually wishes to strengthen the fortress of religion, each man according to his faith.

Our children shall study the sciences as an adornment; however, the foundations of their education will be in accordance with the command of our ancient sages of the Talmud. Our children shall be taught Torah, ethics, Mishnah and Talmud. Wessely, a foolish and wicked man, of coarse spirit, is the one who lacks civility. A carcass is better than he! Whom does he seek to defame and abuse? He has interpreted the thoughts of His Mighty and wise Majesty, the Emperor in the light of his own schemes. Moreover, he has distorted the teachings of our holy sages. . . . Can his behavior be construed as proper etiquette or any other virtue? . . .

Wessely is a cunning man. He gives the impression that he is well versed [in the teachings of Judaism] and thus he is treated with the honor that befits a scholar. He has falsified the words of the Holy Torah. In chapter one [of his book] he glibly writes: " . . . he who lacks 'human knowledge,' even though he has learned God's laws and teachings and acts according to them, he does not please God, because he is certain to sin in the ways of man." May God punish this ever so glib tongue—a tongue that renders its master as disgusting as a creeping reptile. . . . Who of the pious students of God's laws—assuming that he is an intelligent, honest and understanding student of the Torah—is not a tribute to humanity, even if he has not learned etiquette and languages. Can such a man be lacking in "human knowledge"? The moral instruction of Scripture and the words of the holy sages of the Talmud teach [one] how to behave and converse [with his fellow men]. Indeed, does not the student of Torah study the words of Maimonides in the *Book of Knowledge*[3] and the codes of other masters which teach the path of righteous conduct, the path which is a holy path? Does not the student of Torah also study *Duties of the Heart*[4] and other books of ethical teaching? The roots of these works extend from the Prophets and the talmudic sages. [The ethical relevance of traditional Jewish studies is especially manifest if one considers] the divine statutes such as the prohibitions against theft, financial manipulations and the like. Even if one knows but a fraction of these laws he is awed by the depth of their ethical wisdom. How great are thy works O Lord, Your statutes are of great depth. . . .

Could it be that Wessely is directing his calumny against those who are immersed in spiritual meditation, and who have set themselves apart from the vanities of the world? If he has raised his hand against these individuals who have consecrated their lives to the service of God, let his hand wither! He has chosen to blaspheme God and those whom He has hallowed merely because they err in the customs of men [and do not] adorn themselves and paint their eyes. And the fool has said that God does not derive any pleasure from these men. You, Wessely, are a despicable man. Shame on you! May you be mocked by man! Woe to him who does not reprove you! Wessely has shorn his beard and therefore all who have beards and sidecurls are deemed by him to lack "human knowledge" and to deviate from the ways of humanity. This prattler thoroughly disgusts me. . . . It is a source of great consolation to learn from a reliable report that in Vilna, the great city of God,[5] they have burned Wessely's book in the streets. Before doing so they hung his book from an iron chain in the courtyard of the synagogue. Even though the Emperor's name and praises are mentioned numerous times therein, justice, in my opinion, was realized in Vilna.

NOTES

1. David ben Nathan (d. 1792), Rabbi of Lissa (Polish Leszno), center of rabbinic learning in Western Poland, from 1774 to 1792. In 1774, he gave his approbation to Wessely's *Yein Levanon*, a commentary on the Mishnaic tractate *Avoth*. Later when he perceived Wessely's program of Enlightenment to be a threat to the integrity of traditional Judaism, he became his bitter opponent.

2. Joseph II, emperor of Austria.

3. *Sefer ha-Madda*, the first part of Maimonides' (1135–1204) Mishnah Torah, which is devoted, among other matters, to ethics.

4. *Hovot ha-Levavot* by Bahya ben Joseph ibn Pakuda, an eleventh-century Spanish moral philosopher. This work discusses the Jew's duties to cultivate his inner spiritual and ethical life.

5. Because of its preeminence in rabbinical study, Vilna was reverently called by East European Jewry the Jerusalem of Lithuania.

HA-ME'ASSEF
10. The Stream of Besor[1]

This prospectus brings good tidings and greetings to every enlightened member of the congregation of Yeshurun [Israel] who seeks the truth and loves natural science. May the Lord be gracious unto him, now and forever more, Amen.

Source: "Nahal Besor" [Prospectus of *Ha-Me'assef*, April 13, 1783], *Ha-Me'assef*, 1 (1784), pp. 1–4, 11–14. Trans. here by L. Sachs.

The truly wise man, who yearns to know the nature and purpose of every thing from all its aspects, will divide his examination into five principal questions: What? Who? For whom? Why? How?

And now, gentle reader! When you see that a new journal is being published abroad, one that has never existed before, you will undoubtedly be eager to know its nature and curious to ask more about it: What is this new thing? Is it about the Law [*Halakhah*], or is it a collection of tales? Does it deal with matters of worldly knowledge [*hokhmah*],[2] with civility and etiquette and such matters? In order to explain our objectives in such a way that you will have no further doubts, we will answer our five principal questions one by one.

In answer to the question: What?:

The article you have before you is an introduction and a preface to a journal which will make its first appearance in a few days, God willing, and will thereafter appear monthly. This journal will be called *Ha-Me'assef* because it will gather a variety of different articles from all branches of natural science and ethics, articles which will be instructive to the soul that yearns for wisdom. It will have five sections:

In this section we will have poems in the Holy Tongue by select poets whose work has never before appeared in print and who, with God's help, will continue to write. These poems will be about worldly knowledge, ethics, beauty, friendship, and the blessings of love. Poems of passion and lust, however, are an abomination and will not be accepted. Also alien and unacceptable to us are the poems of a few new poets who chose the way of the Gentiles and write hymns to idols and appeal to pagan gods. This will be explained further in the letter of the eloquent Rabbi Hirsch Weisel,[3] may his light shine!

Essays and disquisitions. This section will separate into four streams.

At the source will be the words of men who are learned in languages in general and in the wisdom and character of the Hebrew language in particular. This section will illuminate subjects in Hebrew grammar, clarify problems of phraseology and rhetoric, chart a path in Hebrew poetry, and teach the reader to recognize the meaning of the individual root words.

The tributaries of this section will divide into interpretations of difficult passages in the Scripture. The opinions of ancient commentators will be examined, and where these are insufficient different interpretations will be offered. The understanding and honest reader must judge and decide whether the simple, true solution has been found. And in order to teach students to pay attention to the purpose of an article, and to demonstrate the way in which articles are analyzed and composed . . . we have chosen the method of question and answer as will be seen below in the answers to the questions: For whom?, and Why?

The springs of this section will pour forth short, clear, pleasant, and elegant studies, either from ancient wise men or from wise men of our generation, on those subjects of natural science and ethics that seem appropriate for presentation to enlightened Jews. There will also be translations from the languages of the Gentiles.

The streams of this section will flow into the sea of the Talmud in order to remove obstacles which have deterred many teachers of our people who are unacquainted with the Talmud and its problems and have never applied themselves to the study of the sources of wisdom, but rather stumble in the Talmud like the blind groping in the dark. Since they are ignorant of the source of Halakhah, these teachers have no profound understanding of the ideas of our sages of blessed memory. Moreover, in their teaching to their students they have yet to discuss this source.

And through the tributaries of this section will flow the rest of the things necessary to moral education. Nor will we avoid discussing physical education, for many of our artisans are sedentary and unaware of the importance of physical education. They do not know that the preservation of the body and its powers is an excellent way of preserving the soul and its powers.

Biographies of the great men of Israel. This will include biographies of rabbis, geniuses of the land, those who are great and famous for their worldly knowledge, honored scholars and wealthy men of the people who support the House of Israel and who present themselves before kings to speak for the good of their people. We shall describe the place and time of their births, the events of their lives, and the good that they have done for their fellowmen. And an enlightened man will understand of what great benefit this will be to enlightened youths, quite apart from the pleasure the soul takes in hearing about the events which occurred to famous men in different times and various circumstances.

News. Accounts of the events occurring among us in these days, the days of the first fruits of natural science and love in all the kingdoms of Europe. And the reader who is unable to read the language of the Gentiles will yet know the state of God's people in his times and the things which occur among them. The reader will hear in what way God will move the heart of kings for the good of the people. All these matters will be included in the journal.

Announcement of new books, which will be published for our edification and benefit, both in the Holy Tongue and in the languages of other peoples. Occasionally there will be critical reviews of these books, discussing their virtues and faults and whether or not they are beneficial. Each matter will be treated in its proper place, God willing, as regards its relevance for our actions.

And now, dear reader, you will certainly be curious to know who is putting out this journal and bringing these matters to print. Is it a famous man, or not? Is it one man or many? Is he young or old?

Be assured that this journal is not the work of one man or even of two, but rather of a community of enlightened men who have spent their lives in diligent study of the Torah and the sources of worldly knowledge. These include masters of the Talmud who know how to discuss the profundities of Halakhah in a clear and truthful manner, and wise men learned in foreign languages. Each one of them has spent long periods investigating and studying the characteristics of our Holy Tongue as it is used in the Holy Scriptures and in the writings of ancient authors. Each of these has written a book about the interpretations of Scripture, about its grammar, the language, rhetoric and poetry, and about the clarity of its stories and the gracefulness of its syntax and diction. These scholars have joined forces to master the Torah and worldly knowledge, as those of blessed memory said in the verses: "Listen and give ear Israel; today you have become a nation."[4] They formed groups and studied the Torah, for it can be mastered only in a group. And each man will bring the findings of his study to the daily meetings of the group, in order that the group may pursue its work in an orderly fashion.

Answer to the question: How?

And now enlightened reader! In order to answer the question How?, we will disclose to you the rules and conditions which were established in our councils.

The Society of the Friends of the Hebrew Language was founded on Sunday the seventh of the Hebrew month of Teveth, in the presence of all its members, and this was the gist of their decision:

Four men, whose signatures appear below, were chosen as chairmen and charged with a sacred duty; two will examine the articles to be printed, removing any impurity or blasphemy which may not be admitted to the House of God. The other two will oversee income and expenditures and the other needs of the group.

If a member of our congregation (may the Lord grace it with strength!) wishes to join us and become one of our group, he should announce his intention in writing to our confidential secretary, the enlightened Zanvil Friedlaender[5] and address the application to the Society of Friends of the Hebrew Language. At its next meeting he will be summoned to discuss the amount that will be fixed as his contribution to the Society's treasury.

Ha-Me'assef will appear monthly after the publication of this prospectus, "The Stream of Besor." For although matters of Torah and worldly knowledge are like a flowing spring—its waters may be drawn every day for they are unlimited and inexhaustible—nevertheless we cannot publish more than this, for the expenses are very heavy. This is particularly true in our area where there are no Hebrew type-setters and the printers raise their prices at whim. Also the font of type we have is not attractive and properly arranged, and we have been obliged to bring new type from Berlin in order to put out a work of finished craftsmanship. At the end of every three months a frontispiece on colored paper will appear with the names of all members of the Society and any noteworthy events which have occurred among them. Whenever it becomes possible to enlarge the scope of our publication we will do so. . . .

And now, dear reader! be you artisan or metalworker among the Sons of Israel! We depend on you! We know that you have works of worldly knowledge and ethics which shine forth like the brightness of the firmament to those who walk in darkness. Each one of you should search in his desk and send us what he finds there, and thus crown our efforts with success. Please strengthen and encourage our hearts with your friendship and learning. We shall listen to what you say and take you to our bosom that you may never leave us. We will applaud you with thanks, and God, He who is honored by men of wisdom, will grant you immortality.

These are the words of your servants who stand at the watch for the Society of Friends of the Hebrew Language, Tuesday the thirteenth of Nisan, 5544, in Koenigsberg, Friesen.

Mendel Breslav,[6] Zanvil Friedlaender, Isaac Euchel,[7] and Simon Friedlaender.

NOTES

1. *Ha-Me'assef* [The collector or The gatherer], a Hebrew magazine published intermittently from 1784 to 1811 by the Society of Friends of the Hebrew Language (*Doreshei Leshon Ever*) founded in Koenigsberg, East Prussia, in 1783. In 1787, the Society was renamed Friends of Goodness and Virtue and the Friends of the Hebrew Language (*Shoharei ha-Tov ve-ha-Tushiyyah ve-Doreshei Leshon Ever*). An occasional German supplement was also included. This little magazine, containing on the average twenty pages, served as the forum of German-Jewish followers of the Enlightenment. Specifically, *Ha-Me'assef* sought to revive biblical Hebrew, esteemed for its purity, as a means of elevating the aesthetic sensibility of the Jews and as a vehicle for introducing its readers to the value of the Enlightenment and to secular knowledge. Published in the midst of the debate concerning the Edict of Tolerance, *Ha-Me'assef* urged its readers to respond favorably to the edict, particularly the provision for the reform of the traditional Jewish educational system. Significantly, the portrait of Wessely graced the frontispiece of one of the first volumes of the magazine. *Ha-Me'assef* quickly became the symbol of the movement of Jewish Enlightenment (in Hebrew, Haskalah), whose votaries became known as "the generation of *Me'assfim*."

Nahal Besor, the name of a river in the Negev Desert in Israel, mentioned in 1 Sam. 30; it is here used as a pun on the Hebrew word *besora*, "good tidings."

2. Cf. "Wisdom [*hokhmah*] includes every occupation, study, activity, deportment that bring one closer to human perfection." "Preface," *Ha-Me'assef*, 4 (1787–88), p. 5 (reprinted here, see document 11 of this chapter). See Wessely's concept of human knowledge (*Torat ha'Adam*), document 8 of this chapter.

3. I.e., Naphtali Herz Wessely.

4. Deut. 27:5.

5. Zanvil (Samuel) Friedlaender and his brother Simon—brothers of David Friedlaender and sons of the wealthy Protected Jew Joachim Moses Friedlaender of Koenigsberg—gave *Ha-Me'assef* financial and administrative support.

6. Mendel Breslav (1786–1829), tutor in the Friedlaender family, Hebrew publicist, dramatist and co-editor of *Ha-Me'assef*.

7. Isaac Euchel (1756–1804), tutor in the Fried-

laender family, Hebrew writer and biblical exegete. Co-editor of *Ha-Me'assef* until 1790; published therein the first biography of Moses Mendelssohn, *Toledot Rabbenu he-Hakham Moshe ben Menahem* [The biography of our teacher, the sage Moses son of Menahem].

HA-ME'ASSEF
11. We Shall Not Be Deterred[1]

Sons of Israel who march to the forefront of worldly knowledge [*hokhmah*] without a guide to show you a path, incline your ear and listen to members of a Society who desire your well-being and take pleasure in your peace of mind. Examine the statements of your friends, draw your conclusions, and "Be Men!"[2]

We have seen many novices start out on the path in search of worldly knowledge fall into the pit of doubt, not knowing where to turn. For they listened to the talk of some pretenders to wisdom [*hokhmah*], different factions which conspire together and make speeches. The first faction says: "Why should you bother about vacuous knowledge of men, and the nonsense of the toil of the flesh. Do you not know the sayings of the wisest man: 'He who increases in knowledge [*da'at*] increases in suffering.' "[3] And the listener, in ignorance of the real intention of this wise king, and the real truth of his words, retreats backwards and stands before wisdom like a man stunned and terrified of jackals. This faction drives many away from "cleaving to the inheritance of wisdom"[4] and we shall call them the tormentors of the enlightened man.

The second faction is a group of men who have retained only a portion of what they learned as youths. They think that one can see at a glance all the branches of worldly wisdom and its secrets, for a few limited words from the books of worldly knowledge were sufficient for them. They say: "Now we know the path of wisdom [*hokhmah*] and its ways; it is sufficient. We will no longer seek to question and investigate through study, for such is an artifice. And in less time than a single day or a single night we can find anything that a scholar might find in long days and nights of study." When they are in doubt about matters of belief, the force of this worldly knowledge leads them to invent things which are untrue about God and His creation. And in the absence of any instruction or introduction to the natural sciences and worldly knowledge (for only the enlightened man who applies himself daily to the study of these subjects will know and understand them) they will mistake their random musings and fantasies for reality. Their sloth numbs their souls so that they no longer follow the path of disciplined inquiry and do not seek to correct distortions in their understanding. Every enlightened man who persists in learning and scholarship is contemptible in their eyes, for he is diligent about a matter they regard as trivial, and they consider him ignorant and simple-minded. These are the people we will call "the disparagers of the enlightened man."

The third group is composed of those for whom wisdom is alien, and who have no knowledge or understanding of it. When they see a wise man who is preeminent among his people and honored by large numbers, the fire of jealousy is ignited in their breast. They become quarrelsome and contentious towards him because his nature is alien to them, and they will hate him and

Source: "Preface," *Ha-Me'assef*, 4 (1787–88), pp. 1–8. Trans. here by S. Weinstein.

insult him, saying: "He is strange, and he must be forbidden to take part in the Holy, for he has looked to treacherous men, and cast away belief."[5] And they will talk about him and make false accusations against him, until they humiliate him and drive him from the community of the righteous. These are the despisers of the enlightened man.

The factions we have discussed have led many of our youths astray, youths of clean heart and innocent of the concept of wisdom [*hokhmah*], which will become alien and an anathema to them. In the course of time the number of enlightened men dwindled and that of the ignorant and the wanton and the vacuous increased. We became like a widower in the eyes of our neighbors who said of us: "They have lost their wisdom and none of them knows to what extent."

These are the reasons which aroused us to speak in this introduction about man and his creations, about wisdom and its concerns, and about the value of worldly knowledge to man, in order that beginning students may find a straight path to the temple and sanctuary of wisdom, and turn their backs on its slanderers.

From the substance of this introduction the enlightened reader will see what principles a man must obey if he desires life and wishes to sit securely in the tent of wisdom without slander or abuse. We, the collectors of the articles and notes which appear in this journal, published by us with God's help for the past three years, have adhered to these principles. And although *Ha-Me'assef* has not reached perfection, or attained freedom from blemish—for we are young in years and most of the members of our group are busy at their labors to earn their daily bread, some engaged in teaching youth, others in trade—yet the enlightened reader is aware of the extent of *Ha-Me'assef*'s activity to date. It has elucidated difficult passages in the Bible and in the works of our sages of blessed memory, and has published clear and eloquent articles in the Hebrew language. These will give young men thorough knowledge of the language. Questions about the customs of Israel were solved in consonance with the words of ancient sages. Biographies of the great men of our people were presented as an example for the enlightened man. And since the journal is published in its entirety every month, young men look forward to its appearance. In addition we have shown the community of Israel that we have not labored so hard to issue the journal for the profit that is to be found in publishing (as unfortunately is apparently the case with most authors), for it will be sold at a fair price. From now on thirty pages a year will cost 2 Reichsthalers, and we will include articles on natural science. Concerning natural science, history, etc., the kind reader is referred to the article entitled "The Program of the Society of the Friends of Goodness and Virtue," which will be published on the first day of Tamuz of the Hebrew year 5548. Thus every sincere man will know that we have performed this labor for the public good; we have taken this burden on our shoulders in order to spread Torah and wisdom [*hokhmah*]. The intention of our hearts is clear—we wish to light the path for the sons of our nation, who yearn to hear about ethics and knowledge [*da'at*]. Therefore we will not pay attention to the gossip which has been circulated by many in the camp of the Jews to slander and abuse us. We shall not fight with them, and shall not sully our lips with their names. . . . And we shall never fight anyone except on a matter of truth. . . .

NOTES

1. Title given by the editors of this book. *Ha-Me'assef* met with bitter opposition from traditional elements within the Jewish community. While following Wessely's advice to avoid open conflict with their opponents, the editors of *Ha-Me'assef* nonetheless resolutely maintained their commit-

ment to bring Enlightenment to the Jewish public.

2. *"Hay l'anashim!"* The authors of this article evidently have in mind the German word *Menschen*, which in the parlance of the Enlightenment meant not simply a human being, but human existence defined by that quality—viz., reason—which assures our inherent humanity and our bond with all men irrespective of religion and national origin.

3. Eccles. 1:18.

4. An allusion to 1 Sam. 26:19: "cleaving to the inheritance of the Lord." N.B., the emendation.

5. An allusion to Ps. 40:5: "Happy is the man who makes the Lord his trust and does not look to brutal and treacherous men."

JOSEPH WOLF
12. Preface to Volume One of *Sulamith*[1]

Religion is the essential intellectual and moral need of a cultured man. It is the purpose of *Sulamith* to expose this religion to the highest light. *Sulamith* desires to arouse the nation to a respect of religion, that is, of those truths which alone are worthy of the name of religion. It wants to revitalize the urgent need for religious sentiment and concepts, but at the same time it wants to point up the truth that the concepts and commands contained in the Jewish religion are in no wise harmful, either to the individual or to society. Further it desires to bring the Jewish nation back to its native level of education. It will demonstrate thereby that this education is entirely pure and that our religious concepts and teachings, as long as they have not been disfigured through superstitious additions, would never be an obstacle to any political constitution, but would rather be part of it, and that in those countries where total integration is not taking place, at least brotherly integration is possible. Finally, *Sulamith* wants to sort out truth from falsehood, reality from illusion, the useful from the corrupt. *It wants to enlighten the Jewish nation about itself*. It wants to strike the dry and hard rock and bring forth from it a spring of goodness which will then, by its own power, flow forth in its pristine clearness and purify the sap of the tree. In no wise do we desire, by vain artifices to graft foreign fruit upon this tree which could not grow by itself. Only in this manner do we believe that we can utilize for the best purposes the happy atmosphere which enlightenment and education have brought the souls of men and spread blessing and well-being on the whole Jewish nation.

Therefore, we issue an invitation to all those who want to take part in the spread of useful truths, in the advancement of general human welfare, in a pleasant and tasteful conversation amongst the readers; and we hope that they will participate with fitting contributions to this magazine in a manner adequate to its plan. Every truth, every inquiry which stems from pure intention, regardless from which pen it comes, will be welcome to *Sulamith*.

Source: Joseph Wolf, "Inhalt, Zweck und Titel dieser Zeitschrift," *Sulamith*, 1 (Leipzig, 1806), p. 9. W. Gunther Plaut, *The Rise of Reform Judaism: A Sourcebook of Its European Origins* (New York: World Union for Progressive Judaism, 1963), p. 13. Reprinted by permission of the World Union for Progressive Judaism.

NOTE

1. Full title: *Sulamith, Eine Zeitschrift zur Befoerderung der Kultur und Humanitaet unter der juedischen Nation* [A periodical for the promotion of culture and humanism among the Jewish nation]. In 1810, the words *Jewish nation* were replaced by the word *Israelites*. This first German-language periodical for Jews appeared intermittently from 1806 to 1833. It explicitly viewed itself as a continuation of *Ha-Me'assef*. While supporting Enlightenment among Jews, it also placed special emphasis on synagogal reform. The co-founders and first co-editors were David Frankel (1779–1865), director of a modern Jewish primary school in Dessau, and Joseph Wolf (1762–1826), scholar and translator of various books of Hebrew Scripture into German. He was a collaborator in nine volumes of *Sulamith* and ten of *Ha-Me'assef*.

SULAMITH
13. Call for Religious Enlightenment

Now we wish to define the concept of *religious* enlightenment. . . .

The task of *religious* enlightenment is to illuminate and elucidate the concept of man regarding religious truths, the existence of the Creator, providence, immortality, etc., and to clarify man's religious creed and free it from the additions and abuses of harmful fanaticism and foolish prejudices. Enlightenment teaches us that the essence of religion is not mere ceremony, not a mere matter of remembrance. Enlightenment banishes the low, slavish fear of the world's Ruler from our hearts. It shows us the true purpose of our existence; it also shows the proper relationship to the Invisible One, and to those who share with us a common origin, the same priorities and common destiny.[1] Enlightenment offers us the correct vantage point from which we must view our obligations, which originate from these relationships. It teaches us that serving one's fellow also means serving God, that loving him also means loving God. . . . Enlightenment teaches us that we must think liberally and act humanely, not offend anyone who thinks differently or worships differently than we; but, rather follow the example of the Creator, who embraces and preserves the entire host of Creation with the eternal bonds of love. Finally, it instructs us concerning the brevity of our existence; however, at the same time, enlightenment indicates that our future life stands in the closest connection to the present one, indeed, that it is a consequence of this one; it also indicates that the degree of perfection which we have attained here in this life will determine the degree of perfection which we will be capable of in future life. Accordingly, good care should be taken for our present and eternal well-being, which are one and the same.

NOTE

1. This is the only reference in the article, an indirect one at that, to Jews or Judaism.

Source: Anonymous, *Sulamith*, 2 (Leipzig, 1808), pp. 221–22. Trans. here by M. Gelber.

MOSES MENDELSSOHN

14. On the Curtailment of Jewish Juridical Autonomy[1]

I can scarcely conceive how a writer of Herr Dohm's great judgment could say: "As all other religious societies have a right of expelling members, either for a limited time or for ever; the Jewish should have it too; and, in case of resistance of the Rabbi's sentence, be supported by the civil authorities." All societies have a right of expelling members; religious ones only have not: for it runs diametrically contrary to their principle and object, which is joint edification and participating in the outpouring of the heart, by which we evince our thankfulness to God for the many bounties he bestows on us, and our filial trust in his sovereign goodness and mercy. Then, with what conscience can we deny entrance to dissenters, separatists, misbelievers, or sectarians, and deprive them of the benefit of that edification? For rioters and disturbers there is the law and the police; disorders of that kind may, nay must, be restrained by the secular arm. But a quiet and inoffensive attendance at the meeting may not be forbidden even to an offender, unless we purposely want to bar him from every road to reformation. The doors of the house of rational devotion require neither bars nor bolts. There is nothing locked up within, and, therefore, no occasion to be particular in admitting from without. Whoever chooses to be a tranquil spectator, or even to join in the worship, is right welcome to every pious man, at the hour of his own devotions.

Herr Dohm, on this occasion, has perhaps taken things as they are, and not as they should be. Mankind seems to have agreed to regard the external form of divine worship, that is the church, as a moral being, who has her own rights and claims or duties; and to grant to her more or less authority to assert those rights, and enforce them by external power. It is not thought contrary to common sense, to style, in every country, one of those beings. The *Dominant* treats her sisters just as the whim takes her; at times using, to oppress them, the power delegated to herself, and, at others, generous enough to *tolerate* them, and concede to them as much of her own prerogative, of her own pretensions and consequence, as she thinks proper. Now as anathematizing and excommunicating is always the first right with which a dominant church enfolds tolerated ones, Herr Dohm claims, for the Jewish religion, the same privileges which are granted to all other religious societies. As long as these still possess the right of expelling, he deems it an inconsistency, to put the Jewish under greater restrictions in that respect. But if, as it does evidently appear to me, religious claims to wordly things, religious power, and religious compulsory law, are words without a meaning—and if generally expelling must be called irreligious—then let us still be consistent, rather than heap abuses.

I do not find that the wisest of our forefathers ever did pretend to any such right as excluding individuals from religious exercises.

When King Solomon had finished the building of the Temple, he included in his sublime dedication prayer even strangers, a denomination in his days, of course, synonymous with idolators. He spread forth his hands towards heaven, saying: "Moreover concerning a stranger that is not of thy people Israel, but cometh out of a far country for thy name's sake (for they shall hear of thy great name, and of thy strong hand, and of thy stretched-out arm); when he shall come

Source: Moses Mendelssohn's Preface of 1782 to the German translation of Menasseh ben Israel's *Vindiciae Judaeorum*, in Mendelssohn's, *Jerusalem*, trans. M. Samuels (London, 1838), vol. 1, pp. 108–16.

and pray toward this house; hear thou in heaven thy dwelling-place, and do according to all that the stranger calleth to thee for: that all people of the earth may know thy name, as thy people of Israel; and that they may know that this house which I have built, is called by thy name."[2] In the same manner our Rabbis directed the voluntary gifts and votive offerings of idolators to be accepted in the Temple, and not turn away the sacrifice of even an offender belonging to the nation itself, as long as he had not positively abjured his religion; in order, said they, that he may have an opportunity and inducement to amend.[3] So *they* thought at a period, when they had a little more power and authority to be exclusive in religious matters: and yet shall we presume to shut out dissenters from our barely *tolerated* religious meetings?

I shall forbear speaking of the danger there is in entrusting *any one* with the power of excommunicating—with the abuse inseparable from the right of anathema, as indeed with every other form of church discipline, or ecclesiastical power. Alas! it will require ages yet, before the human race shall have recovered from the blows which those monsters inflicted on it. I can imagine no possibility of bridling false religious zeal; as long as it sees that road open before it; for a spur will never be wanting. Herr Dohm fancies he is offering us an ample guarantee from all the abuses, by taking for granted, that the right of anathema, entrusted to the colony, "will never reach beyond religious society, and have no effect at all on the civil; and this, because an expelled member of any church whatsoever may be a very valuable and estimable citizen notwithstanding: a principle in universal ecclesiastical law . . . which should be no longer questioned in our days."

But if universal ecclesiastical law, as it is called, at last acknowledges the important principle, in which I concur with all my heart, "that the expelled member of any and every church, may be a very useful and respected citizen notwithstanding," the evil is far from being remedied by that weak reservation. For, in the first place, this very estimable and useful citizen, who, perhaps, is also internally a very religious man, may not like to be debarred from all meetings for worship, from all religious solemnities; and may not like to be entirely without external religion. Now, if he have the misfortune to be thought a dissenter by the congregation he belongs to, and his conscience forbids him to join any other religious party established or tolerated in the state; must not this very useful and estimable citizen be exceedingly unhappy when his own congregation is allowed to exclude him, and he finds the doors of their religious assemblies shut against him? And it is possible, that he finds them so everywhere; for every religious community would perhaps turn him away by the same right. But how can the state allow any one of its useful and estimable citizens to be made unhappy by the laws? Secondly, what church excommunication, what anathema is entirely without secular consequences, without any influence whatever on, at least, the civil respectability, on the fair reputation of the excommunicated, on the confidence of his fellow citizens, without which no one can exercise his calling and be useful to the state? As the boundary-laws of this nice distinction between the civil and the ecclesiastical are barely perceptible to the keenest eye, it becomes truly impossible to draw them so firmly and precisely, in any state, as to make them obvious to every citizen, and cause them to have the desired effect in common civil life. They will remain dubious and undefined, and very frequently expose innocence itself to the sting of persecution, and blind religious zeal.

To introduce church-discipline, and yet not impair civil happiness, seems to me a problem, which yet remains for politics to solve. It is the answer of the Most High Judge to Satan: "He is in thine hand but save his life,"[4] or, as the commentators add; *Demolish the cask, but let not the wine run out. . . .*

I have that confidence in the more enlightened amongst the Rabbis, and elders of my nation, that they will be glad to relinquish so pernicious a prerogative, that they will cheerfully do away with all church and synagogue discipline, and let their flock enjoy, at their hands, even that kindness and forbearance, which they themselves have been so long panting for. Ah, my brethren, you have hitherto felt too hard the yoke of intolerance, and perhaps thought it a sort of satisfaction, if the power of bending those under you to such another yoke were allowed you. Revenge will be seeking an object; and if it cannot wreak itself on strangers, it even tortures its own flesh and blood. Perhaps, too, you let yourselves be seduced by the general example. All the nations of the earth, hitherto, appear to have been infatuated by the error, that religion can be maintained by iron force—doctrines of blessedness inculcated by unblest persecution—and true notions of God, who, as we all acknowledge, is love itself, communicated by the workings of hatred and ill-will only. You, perhaps, let yourselves be seduced to adopt the same system; and the power of persecuting was to you the most important prerogative which your own persecutors could bestow upon you. Thank the God of your forefathers, thank the God who is all love and mercy, that that error appears to be gradually vanishing. The nations are now tolerating and bearing with one another, while to you also they are showing kindness and forbearance, which, with the help of Him who disposes the hearts of men, may grow to true brotherly love. O, my brethren, follow the example of love, the same as you have hitherto followed that of hatred. Imitate the virtues of the nations whose vices you hitherto thought you must imitate. If you would be protected, tolerated and indulged, protect, tolerate and indulge one another. *Love, and ye will be beloved.*

NOTES

1. In his essay on Jewish civil rights, Christian Wilhelm von Dohm favored the retention of Jewish juridical autonomy, particularly the right of excommunication. Mendelssohn objected, for he strongly felt that Jewish Enlightenment and the liberalization of society in general required the relinquishment of traditional ecclesiastical juridical prerogatives such as that of excommunication. He elaborated this position in his preface to the German translation of Menasseh ben Israel's *Vindiciae Judaeorum*. Mendelssohn initiated the translation of the Dutch rabbi's 1656 refutation of objections advanced by British clergy against Jewish readmission to England, and he used the occasion of writing a preface to the volume, which he felt would strengthen the impact of Dohm's treatise, as an opportunity to both supplement and correct sections of Dohm's argument. Some of Mendelssohn's readers, for example, the author of "Search for Light and Right" (see document 16 of this chapter), interpreted his argument for the annulment of Jewish juridical autonomy to be an implicit admission that Judaism was an anachronistic religion.

2. 1 Kings 8:41–43.

3. Talmud, tractate *Chullin*, 5a.

4. Job 2:6.

DAVID FRIEDLAENDER[1]

15. On Self-Development and the Abolishment of Jewish Autonomy

I do not have to tell you about the conception of God which the rabbis define as religion. Three thousand years after the granting of the Torah, [these rabbis] are still busy pon-

Source: David Friedlaender to Meir Eger, March 19, 1792, in J. Meisl [Letters of David Friedlaender], *Historishe Schriften* (Vilna: Yiddisher Visinshaftlicher Institut, 1937), vol. 2, p. 402. Trans. here by J. Hessing.

dering the question whether on consumption of less than a morsel, one must recite the grace after meals or not. He who does [recite the grace] belongs to the Jewish religion, and he who does not make such a blessing, does not belong. It can easily be imagined what such masters of the Torah consider to be truth. The most noble gift of God, reason, is treated as a base handmaid; they are even impertinent enough to say that after the removal of the Torah from the Temple, a cloud of darkness and of fog descended upon the world. If this is what is taught by the "judges and the leaders" of the nation, what do you expect the masses to believe? Imagine all of Jewry assembled in one room and you and I standing at the threshold, asking everyone, Who exists? What is God? What is Judaism? What is virtue?! What is truth? Faith?! Only a few will be able to give a clear answer to any of these questions. We have here [in Berlin] a so-called *Torani*, one who studies [Torah] every day, day in, day out. He would give his life for the Jewish religion and would never taste [a morsel of food] without a blessing before and a blessing after eating. He is wealthy, possessing abundant assets and money, and, yet, a few years ago, this very man allowed his own brother to go begging. In short, we do not know anymore what religion is, and what is virtue. When we stand in front of the throne to be weighed on the scales of the Creator, it will be found that we have lived by the principles of cannibals. We speak the language of the [primitive] Hottentot, not that of the Torah of the living God which was given to us in glory and in honor!

The consequence of all this is obvious. We are living among the Gentiles, all of whom daily probe into their religions in order to eliminate the chaff, to purify their morals and to improve their faith. We, on the other hand, who have started out on the highest level, constantly deteriorate. The ignorance of our people accumulates in a most frightful manner, and in twenty years you will hardly find a man who is able to read the Torah. The Talmud is kept in dire contempt, and daily something is lost from the treasures of our Torah. The natural consequence of all this must be—my hairs bristle at the thought of it!—that our sons will first abandon Judaism and then convert to Christianity. Were our rabbis not completely blind, were they not confined within the four walls of the Halakhah—where they know as much about the things of the world as I know about the doings of the Nabob in Sanghar—they would think of repairing the breach. But nobody seems to notice. They think that by writing, "ours is a lost generation, may the Lord forgive us," they have done their duty. But, alas, what can they do, utterly ignorant as they are, superstitious and bent on closing their eyes to the facts? I have been watching all this for the last twenty years, and I have found only one possible solution: to throw off the heavy yoke under which the king and the judges of this country, who are not of our people, have harnessed us; to throw off, furthermore, that other yoke which we have taken upon us with the rule of our own rabbis and communal leaders. Only if we are free, neither afraid of the ruling party nor intimidated in our enlightenment, by the threat of excommunication and the refusal of burial rites, will it be possible to raise Israel's prestige, our Torah and the teachings of Moses from the dust.

NOTE

1. David Friedlaender (1750–1834), a wealthy and respected entrepreneur. He was also widely held to have inherited from his close friend Moses Mendelssohn the leadership of the movement of Enlightenment among German Jewry. His interest in this area was expressed in his activities on behalf of the religious reform of Judaism and his unflagging efforts in German Jewry's protracted struggle for emancipation. These interests are reflected in this document, a letter Friedlaender wrote to his business associate Meir Eger, an Orthodox Jew. Aside from a few select Hebrew expressions, the letter is written in German transliterated into Hebrew script.

16. Search for Light and Right[1]: An Epistle to Moses Mendelssohn

Estimable Sir,

There was a time, when I could not help blaming Lavater's[2] obtrusion, in calling upon you in so singularly solemn a manner to embrace his faith; or, in the event of declining the proposal, demonstrate the unsoundness of the Christian religion. That step having been made in consequence of what fell from you in the course of a friendly conversation, which, probably, was not meant to go forth to the public, is what I shall never cease to think unjustifiable.

Now, however, I scarcely can resist the temptation of wishing that Lavater would make another attack on you, with all the force of his emphatic adjuration, so as actually to make a convert of you, or provoke you to refute a religion, which it seems, you are neither willing, nor (from conviction) able to embrace.

At all events, certain candid expressions, in your excellent "Preface" to Rabbi Manasseh Ben Israel's *Vindication of the Jews*, give every searcher for truth a right to expect of you some further explanation; lest you should appear unintelligible on a comparison with former statements. . . .

In your former reply to Lavater, you all along insist on your adherence to the *Faith of your Forefathers*. But you never tell us what you properly mean by the *Faith of your Forefathers*. The substance of the Christian religion, too, is the Faith of your Forefathers, transferred to us, weeded of rabbinical institutions, and improved by additions, new, indeed; but nevertheless derived from the Faith of your Forefathers, and, interpreted as the consummation of Old-Testamentary prophecies.

In a wider sense of the term, the *Faith of your Forefathers* is that which the Christians profess; namely, the adoration of an only God; the keeping of the divine Ten Commandments delivered by Moses; and a belief in the gathering of all the nations of the earth, in one flock, under the universal sceptre of a Messiah announced by the prophets.

In a narrower sense, the expression, *Faith of your Forefathers*, comprises only the proper Jewish ecclesiastical system, together with all scriptural appointments, rabbinical interpretations thereof, and statutory laws thereon, the whole constituting the proper distinctive doctrine, which separates the Jews from the faith of all other nations, and also from Christians.

From that latter particular faith, my dear Mr. Mendelssohn, you have, in your remarkable preface, wrenched the corner-stone, by stripping, in dry words, the synagogue of its original power; by denying it the right of expelling from the congregation of the holy, the backslider from the Faith of your Forefathers, curtailing anathema and malediction on the heretic, and cutting him off from the people of Israel. It may consist with reason, that ecclesiastical law, in general, and the authority of spiritual courts to enforce or restrict opinion, is an inconceivable thing. . . .

In common sense, religion without conviction is not possible at all; and every forced religious act is no longer such. The keeping of the divine commandments from fear of the

Source: Anonymous, "Das Forschen nach Licht und Recht in einem Schreiben an Herrn Moses Mendelssohn auf Veranlassung seiner merkwuerdigen Vorrede zu Menasseh Ben Israel, 1792" [Search for light and right, an epistle to Moses Mendelssohn, occasioned by his remarkable "Preface" to Rabbi Menasseh ben Israel's *Vindiciae Judaeorum*], Moses Mendelssohn, *Jerusalem*, trans. M. Samuels (London, 1838), vol. 1, pp. 119–20, 122–41.

ecclesiastical penalties annexed to them is servile compliance, which, according to refined notions, cannot be acceptable to God. Still, it will not be denied, that Moses puts prohibitions and positive punishments on the neglect of religious observances. His statutes ordain that the Sabbath-breaker, the reviler of the divine name, and other infringers of his law shall be stoned, and their souls exterminated from amongst his people.

That rule, it is true, could be carried into practice, only so long as the Jews had an empire of their own; so long as their Pontiffs were princes, or such sovereign heads of the people, as created princes, and governed them. But cease it must, as did the sacrifices, upon the Jews having lost territory and power, and, depending on foreign laws, found their jurisdiction circumscribed by very narrow limits. Still, that circumscription is merely the consequence of external and altered political relations, whereby the value of laws and privileges, consigned to quiescence, cannot be diminished. The ecclesiastical law is still there, although it be not allowed to be put into execution. Your lawgiver, Moses, is still the drover, with the cudgel, who leads his people with a rod of iron, and would be sharp after any one who had the least opinion of his own, and dared to express it by word or deed....

Agreed and most unqualifiedly granted, that the foundation of such an ecclesiastical law is the most inconceivable thing in the world; that it does not answer the purpose of bringing the strayed back into the bosom of the church; but, on the contrary, removes them from it; that its object cannot be to reclaim but to undo them; that the rigour of ecclesiastical law, excommunication, and anathema, cannot be exercised without the most serious injury to civil happiness; that true worship ought to be a spontaneous homage, founded on one's own conviction, and practised out of love to the Father of all beings, and with perfect filial confidence in the mercy and goodness with which he lets his sun shine even for the erring, and his dew fertilise also the fields of the dissenter from religious dogmas; that servile awe, extorted by penalties, cannot be an acceptable offering on the altar of the God of Love. Granting and admitting all this, it certainly is very true, that the church has no need either of sword or scourge to bind the sceptic beneath a yoke—repugnant to the standard of his intellect—to reconcile the dissenter to articles of faith, or to ruin the rebellious. But then, what becomes of the rabbinical statutes, passed into laws which Judaism is strictly bound to obey? What becomes of even the Mosaic law, and of its authority derived immediately from God himself? Armed ecclesiastical law still remains the firmest groundwork of the Jewish polity, and the master-spring of the whole machinery. Then good Mr. Mendelssohn, how can you profess attachment to the religion of your forefathers, while you are shaking its fabric, by impugning the ecclesiastical code established by Moses in consequence of divine revelation? The public, whose attention you have excited, is entitled to both an explanation of—and instruction in—so important a point....

Allow me, good Sir, to submit to your opinion a few remarks, which appear to me of importance in the present age, when a great revolution in favour of your nation is dawning forth. You yourself speak, in your preface, of the unjust persecutions which have hung over the whole of your race ever since the destruction of their Capital, and the dispersion of the Jews amongst all the nations of the world. The Christian's silly hatred and absurd contempt of them [the Jews], has, during many ages, denied them all pretensions to the universal rights of man.... [But in our own times] the wise and reasonable amongst the Christians are willing to love as brethren the good amongst your nation. This your own experience must tell you, Mr. Mendelssohn. Do not Christian men, superior to nursery, schoolboy, or popularly vulgar impressions, come forward at this time, and openly plead with frankness and energy, the cause of humanity on behalf of your nation; men, who make it their business to couch the Christian rabble, both high and low, for the cataract of old and inveterate infection, in order to enable them to recognise Jews as God's goodly and rational creatures? Are there not now sovereigns who listen to such appeals of humanity, and give fair hopes that they will not let all pious wishes remain unfulfilled, in their dominions.

To what may it be owing, that brotherly love does not more generally unite two nations, both of the same nature and substance, both worshiping the same God, and both coinciding in the fundamental points of their religion?

The civil disabilities, the exclusion from common privileges, and from a participation in the reciprocal offices of men and brethren—those hardships, Mr. Mendelssohn, about which your nation can feel only in a certain measure, justly aggrieved, are not the fault of Christians. In the religion of your forefathers itself, there is a tremendous breach which keeps your nation far removed from an unqualified sharing in both the public and private advantages of social life, which, in a state, are enjoyed by all citizens alike.

I shall say nothing about your excessively strict keeping of the Sabbath, which is not the Sabbath of the nations amongst whom you dwell. That inconvenience, perhaps, may not be the one that least admits of mitigation, yet it will always be found impossible entirely to remove the difficulties which would attend the measure of employing Jews in those capacities, whereby the state and the public service must necessarily be sufferers, as long as the duties thereof remain incompatible with the uncompromising Sabbath Laws. It may, however, be asked, whether the solemnisation of the Rabbinical Sabbath, with all its nervous niceties and shivering scruples, should not be referred exclusively to the former territory and polity of the Jews; and amidst different relations, and under foreign dominion, be subordinate to the circumstances in which Providence itself has placed them since the abolition of their empire? The laws of sacrifices, I should think, were no less sacred and inviolable than those of the Sabbath; and yet they were discontinued on the breaking up of the Jewish State, because the practice could not be carried on under foreign governments. Then, why may not those of the Sabbath be equally subject to some modification, at least, when times, circumstances, and local situations, do not admit their full observance?

But of still greater importance is the obstacle which the Jewish law places in the way of a more general intermixture with Christians. The very scorn and contumely which furnish the Jew no unjust grounds of complaint against the Christian, form an article of faith of the Jewish religion; according to which all other nations are deemed unclean creatures, by a social intercourse with whom the people of God would be defiled. All victuals and certain drink prepared by the hands of a Christian, are, by law, an abomination to a Jew.

Those laws, no doubt in former times, were the offspring of pure precaution, to keep a people so prone to idolatry from associating with their pagan neighbours, and from being ensnared by them into the worship of idols. But that precaution has become quite supererogatory at present....

If it be possible to suppress, without any detriment to pure Judaism, ecclesiastical law, founded as it is on express Mosaic Statutes, why then should mere rabbinical reservations, subsequently devised, and opening so injurious a breach between Jew and Christian, not be set aside as well, for the good of the nation? But if the ecclesiastical laws, assumed to have been given by revelation, form a part of the Jewish religion, we must admit those Rabbinisms also to do so; and, in that case, you, good Mr. Mendelssohn, have renounced the religion of your forefathers. One step more, and you will become one of us.

As long as you forbear taking the other step now that you have taken the first, the public is most justly entitled to expect of you, either a reason for so glaring a discrepancy from the religion of your forefathers, or the statement of any cause you may have to show why you should not publicly embrace Christianity, or the production of an argument against Christianity.... This whole truth-loving public expect of every inquirer, "Light and Right," and long to hear an approved thinker speak, in the evening of his life, without reserve, of the most important human concerns. By a more particular explanation, you either will use your endeavours to relieve your nation from many an antiquated and paralysing constraint, and to regenerate them into freer, and less abashed beings, who will unite themselves by mutual ties more closely to their fellow-men of another persuasion—men who already evince a strong and cordial disposition to regard them too as men and brethren, in a greater degree than heretofore—or you will draw your brethren nearer to us, or, by removing our errors, ourselves to them.

At the present remarkable juncture, there is nothing whatsoever to deter you from unfolding to us your sincere and real conviction. Now that you have so heroically battered down the once impregnable steel gate of ecclesiastical authority, what should keep you from celebrating your ovation in the very essence of truth, which has been so long inaccessible to us? You have put your hand to the plough, as the saying is; and a man, firm in his conviction, as you are, and, on account of his extraordinary talents, called by Providence itself to the service and promulgation of truth, cannot possibly withdraw it again, and deprive the world of the final result of the long exercise of his mental energies, after having already given it, in his preface to Rabbi Manasseh Ben Israel's works, so beautiful a specimen, as one of the most elegant and valuable presents from the vast museum of his learning and information.

Your sincere admirer,

S.

Vienna, June 12, 1782

NOTES

1. The authorship of this anonymous epistle was until recently in doubt. The latest research, however, indicates that the epistle was written by August Friedrich Cranz (1732–1801), a German author of satirical essays. This epistle and the postscript by D. E. Moerschel (see document 17 in this chapter) prompted Moses Mendelssohn to break his resolve to eschew public debate on religious issues and to write his famous treatise, "Jerusalem, or On Religious Power and Judaism" (1783).

2. In 1769, John Caspar Lavater (1741–1801), a Swiss clergyman, publicly challenged Mendelssohn to defend the superiority of Judaism. In his published reply to Lavater, Mendelssohn politely declined to accept the challenge, indicating that polemics on religious questions were contrary to the spirit of tolerance and, moreover, imprudent for a Jew. "I am a member of an oppressed people," he reminded Lavater, "which must appeal to the benevolence of the government for protection and shelter.... Should [the Jews] therefore attack their protectors on an issue to which men of virtue are particularly sensitive? Or would it not be more fitting if they abstained from religious disputes with the dominant creed?" (Mendelssohn, *Jerusalem and Other Jewish Writings*, trans. and ed. A. Jospe [New York: Schocken, 1969], pp. 119–20.)

DAVID ERNST MOERSCHEL[1]
17. Postscript to "Search for Light and Right"

. . . I think I have discovered in your preface [to Menasseh ben Israel's *Vindication of the Jews*] certain characteristic remarks by which I feel myself perfectly warranted to regard you as removed from the religion in which you were born and educated, as you are from the one which has been transmitted to me by my own forefathers: and, having done so, I shall not charge you with untruthfulness for replying that you are equally as little inclined to Judaism as you are to Christianity, being as you are, an opponent of revealed religion in general. In order to show what grounds I have for my assertion, I shall refer you to the first paragraph of your preface, where you say: "The doors of the house of rational devotion require neither bars nor bolts. There is nothing locked up within, and, therefore, no occasion to be particular in admitting from without. Whoever chooses to be a tranquil spectator, or even to join in the worship, is right welcome to every pious man, at the hour of his own devotions." Let me add, that, on account of your personal merits, such an explanation as I beg of you, may become the occasion of meditations which speculative men cannot make too often. I say meditations, because, in religion, the infallible word of God can alone be admitted as a rule.

What is there, worthy man, to deter you from at once openly acknowledging to the world that you are a Jew or a Christian, or neither one nor the other? My request, indeed, is not important enough to betray you into confession; still I flatter myself, you will render to the call of truth, that homage, to which myself, simply an honest man, may not pretend.

Forgive my boldness, and be assured that it is with the sincere consent of my heart, that I call myself your reverer, although I have never yet intruded upon you, to declare by word of mouth, the esteem with which I am Cordially yours,

D. E. Moerschel
Berlin, September 3, 1782

NOTE

1. David Ernst Moerschel, a military chaplain from Berlin, took the occasion of the publication of "Search for Light and Right" to voice his opinion that Mendelssohn's endorsement of a universal, rational religion implied a rejection of divine revelation and *a fortiori* Judaism, a revealed, particularistic religion. Accordingly, Moerschel felt he detected an inconsistency in Mendelssohn's devotion to rational religion and his abiding loyalty to Judaism.

Source: David Ernst Moerschel, "Postscript to 'Search for Light and Right,'" Moses Mendelssohn, *Jerusalem*, trans. M. Samuels (London, 1838), vol. 1, pp. 144–45.

MOSES MENDELSSOHN

18. Judaism Is the Cornerstone of Christianity[1]

[The objections of the author of a "Search for Light and Right"] go to the heart; and I must admit, that, except for some intemperate expressions, the ideas he gives of Judaism are the same which even many of my brethren in the faith entertain. Now, could I be convinced of their being correct, I certainly would, with shame, retract my positions, and bend reason to the yoke of faith. O no! wherefore should I dissemble? If the word of God were so evidently contradictory to my understanding, the utmost I could do would be to impose silence on the latter; but my unrefuted arguments would, nevertheless, return to some secret recess of my heart, there change to harnessing doubts, and those would resolve into filial prayer, into fervent supplication for light. I would exclaim with the Psalmist: "O! send me thy light, and thy truth. Let them lead me unto thy holy mount, and to thy residence" (Ps. 43:3).

At all events, it would be hard and vexing, if, like the above anonymous writer, and him who wrote the postscript with the signature of Moerschel, the world should impute to me the scandalous design of subverting the religion which I confess, and of renouncing it, if not expressly, but, as it were, in an underhand manner. This practice of wresting meanings should be forever discarded from the conversation of the learned. *Not every one who concurs in an opinion, does, at the same time, concur in all the inferences drawn from it, though ever so correctly.* These kind of imputations are odious, and only cause exasperation and pugnacity, by which truth seldom gains anything.

Nay, the "Searcher," goes to the length of apostrophizing me in the following manner: "Or are we to presume," etc.

That imputation is expressed seriously and pathetically enough. But, my good sir, am I to take the step, without first considering whether it will really draw me out of the dilemma, in which, you think, I must find myself? If it be true that the corner-stones of my house are failing, and the building threatens to fall down, am I then right in shifting my effects from the lower story to the upper? Shall I be any safer there? Now Christianity, you know, is built on Judaism, and when this falls down, that must necessarily become one heap of ruins with it. You say, my conclusions undermine the foundation of Judaism, and you proffer me, for safety, your upper story. Must I suppose that you are mocking me? When there is the appearance of a contradiction between one truth and another, between Scripture and reason, a Christian, in earnest about "right and light," will not challenge a Jew to a controversy, but conjointly, with him, seek to discover the groundlessness of discrepancy. Both their causes are concerned in it. Whatever else they have to settle between themselves may be deferred to another time. For the present they must use their joint endeavours to avert the danger, and either discover the false conclusion, or show that it was nothing but a paradox which frightened them.

Thus I might now elude the snare, without engaging in any farther discussion with the "Searcher." But what would the subterfuge avail me?

NOTE

1. This excerpt from *Jerusalem* is Mendelssohn's explicit reply to the author of "Search for Light and Right," document 16 in this chapter.

Source: Moses Mendelssohn, "Jerusalem, or On Religious Power and Judaism" (1783), *Jerusalem*, trans. M. Samuels (London, 1838), vol.1, pp. 83–85.

MOSES MENDELSSOHN

19. Judaism as Revealed Legislation[1]

I must, however, do justice to [Herr Moerschel's] penetrating eye. He is, partly, not wrong in his observations. It is true. I *acknowledge no immutable truths, but such as not only may be made conceivable to the human understanding, but as also admit of being demonstrated and warranted by human faculties*. There only he is misled by an erroneous notion of Judaism, when he supposes that I cannot maintain this without deviating from the religion of my forefathers. On the contrary, this is just what I hold an essential point of the Jewish religion; and I think that this doctrine forms a characteristic difference between it and the Christian. To express it in one word, I believe that Judaism knows nothing of a revealed religion, in the sense in which it is taken by Christians. The Israelites have a divine legislation: laws, commandments, statutes, rules of life, instruction in the will of God, and lessons how to conduct themselves in order to attain both temporal and spiritual happiness: those laws, commandments, etc., were revealed to them through Moses, in a miraculous and supernatural manner; but no dogmas, no saving truths, no general self-evident propositions. Those the Lord always reveals to us, the same as to the rest of mankind, by *nature and by events*; but never in spoken or written words [of revelation]. . . .

Now I am able to concentrate my ideas of Judaism of former times, and bring them under one focus. Judaism consisted, or, according to the founder's design was to consist of:

1. Religious dogmas and propositions of *immutable truths* of God, of his government and providence, without which man can neither be enlightened nor happy. These were not forced on the belief of the people, by threats of eternal or temporal punishment, but suitably to the nature and evidence of immutable truths, recommended for rational consideration. They needed not be suggested by direct revelation, or promulgated by *words* or *writing*, which are understood only *in this or that place, at this or that time*. The Supreme Being revealed them all to all rational beings, by *events* and by *ideas*, and inscribed them in their soul, in a character legible and intelligible *at all times*, and *in all places*. Hence sings the frequently quoted bard:

> The heavens tell the glory of God; and the firmament showeth his handy work.
> One day streams this unto another, and night therein instructeth night.
> No lesson or words of which the voice is not heard; their chord rings through the entire globe; their discourse penetrates to the extremes of the inhabited world, where he set a tabernacle to the sun, etc. (Ps. 70:1).

Their effect is as universal as the salutary influence of the sun, which, while revolving round its orbit, diffuses light and heat over the whole globe, as the same bard still more distinctly declares in another place:

> From where the sun rises to where it sets,
> the name of the Lord is praised.

Or, as the prophet Malachi says, in the name of the Lord: "From where the sun rises to where it sets, my name is great among the Gentiles; and in all places, incense, sacrifice, and pure meat-offerings are offered unto my name, for my name is great among the heathen."

2. Historical truths, or accounts of the occurrences of the primitive world, especially memoirs of the lives of the first ancestors of the nation; of their knowledge of the true

Source: Moses Mendelssohn, "Jerusalem, or On Religious Power and Judaism" (1783), *Jerusalem*, trans. M. Samuels (London, 1838), vol. 1., pp. 89, 151–54.

God, even of their failings, and the paternal correction immediately following thereon; of the covenant which God entered into with them, and his frequent promise to make their descendants a nation dedicated to himself. These historical truths, contain the groundwork of the national union; and, as historical truths, they cannot, according to their nature, be received otherwise than *on trust*; authority alone gives them the necessary evidence. And they were, moreover, confirmed to the nation by miracles, and supported by an authority which sufficed to place *faith* beyond all doubt and hesitation.

3. Laws, judgments, commandments, rules of life, which were to be peculiar to that nation; and by observing which, it was to arrive at national—as well as every single member thereof, at individual—happiness. The lawgiver was God himself; God, not in his revelations as Creator and Preserver of the universe, but God, as Lord Protector and ally of their forefathers; as the liberator, founder, and leader, as the king and ruler of that people. And he gave the laws a sanction, than which nothing could be more solemn; he gave them publicly, and in a marvellous manner never before heard of, whereby they were imposed on the nation, and on their descendants for ever, as an unalterable duty and obligation.

These laws were *revealed*, that is, they were made known by the Lord, by *words* and *in writing*. Still, only the most essential part thereof was entrusted to letters; and without the unwritten laws, without explanations, limitations, and more particularly definitions, even these written laws are mostly unintelligible, or must become so in the course of time; since neither any words or written characters whatever retain their meaning unaltered, for the natural age of man.

As *directions to general practice*, and rules of conduct, both the written and unwritten laws have public and private happiness for their immediate object. But they must also be mostly considered as a mode of writing; and as *ceremonial laws*, there is no sense and meaning in them. They lead inquiring reason to divine truths; partly to eternal, partly to historical truths, on which the religion of *that* nation was founded. The ceremonial law was the bond for uniting practice with speculation, conduct with doctrine. The ceremonial law was to offer inducements to personal intercourse and social connexion between the school and the professor, the inquirer and the instructor, and to excite and encourage competition and emulation; and that purpose it actually did answer in the first times, before the polity degenerated, and human folly again intermeddled to change, by ignorance and misguidance, good to evil, and the beneficial to the hurtful.

NOTE

1. This passage from Mendelssohn's *Jerusalem* is in direct response to David Ernst Moerschel's "Postscript to 'Search for Light and Right,'" document 17 in this chapter. This response occasioned Mendelssohn's famous and controversial definition of Judaism as a divine legislation of ceremonial laws,. as opposed to a revelation of truths which either supersedes or superfluously duplicates the judgments of reason. Mendelssohn thus held that Judaism in no way interferes with the free use of one's reason, and contrary to Moerschel's assertion, one can be both an observant Jew and a consistent votary of Enlightenment.

SAUL ASCHER[1]

20. Leviathan

Finally, we will discuss Judaism in our era. Fortuitous circumstances compelled Mendelssohn to write his *Jerusalem* and declare his views on Judaism. This great spirit took a path that was absolutely different from his predecessors [e.g., Maimonides and Spinoza]. He placed—who can believe it?—reason in the shadow of faith. He neither explicated faith by means of the principles of reason, nor did he differentiate between faith and reason, rather he placed reason in the captivity of faith. He esteems only a faith which masters reason.

The path that he took is understandable. Mendelssohn had to be cautious. He had an adversary that set a trap for him. Consequently, he could not pursue a subtly reasoned argument, lest he forget to circumvent this trap. His opponent appealed to [creedal and scriptural] authority, obliging Mendelssohn to counter with similar arguments. Thus, already in the first round the debate came to an end over marginal issues. . . . [Mendelssohn] permitted extraneous issues to lead him to adopt extreme positions.

. . . And in order to save Judaism from the politicians, Mendelssohn dared to present it in such a manner that neither the politician, nor the philosopher, much less the common man, know what to make of it. Even if we assume that Judaism is indeed based on [divine] legislation, the question remains to be asked: To what end was the Law [of Moses] given? If as this sage, Mendelssohn, himself keenly argues the Jews were given the Law in order to preserve the nation in the knowledge [of the eternal, cognitive truths] possessed by their forefathers on the one hand, and, as one may assume, to maintain the memory of certain historical truths on the other, then fine. It would indeed be laudatory if reason, apprehending through the Law eternal truths and faith, offering the historical truths, would free the nation from the Law.

In order to prove the assumption that Judaism has no ecclesiastical laws [*Kirchenrecht*] Mendelssohn seeks to demonstrate that Judaism is essentially based on knowledge and on obedience. Does not he himself admit, however, the possibility of faith founded on historical truths? And could not this fact lead him to conclude that the laws [of Judaism] are also largely based on historical truths? The error lies in that Mendelssohn considered these laws strictly as statutory duties [*constituirte Pflichten*], and failed to differentiate correctly between the essence of law [*Gesetz*] and the essence of rule [*Anordnung*]. To be sure [given this error], he was right in his presentation of Judaism as revealed legislation and in his designation of what is merely a means to an end to be essential.

In general, as a psychologist, Mendelssohn should have clarified the nature of obedience and not confined the entire purpose of revelation in Judaism to the Mosaic constitution. Had he done so he would have had to reach—as he most certainly would have—a different conclusion. One may assume, however, that he would have tried to evade this conclusion, as may be anticipated from the limited goal he set for himself.

If the politician does not know what to do with [Mendelssohn's thesis], even less so does the philosopher. Mendelssohn contends that Judaism contains religious doctrines of eternal truths. According to his system, and in consonance with the purpose he assigns to the Law, it must be assumed that

Source: Saul Ascher, *Leviathan, oder ueber Religion in Ruecksicht des Judenthums* (Berlin, 1792), pp. 149–50, 157–60, 226–28, 232, 235–38. Trans. here by S. Fischer and P. Mendes-Flohr.

the eternal truths are made known to man through the Law. Are these eternal truths then only determined by what is arbitrary and revealed? Can reason ever deduce anything necessary from something contingent? Is not the meaning of this [proposition] to forsake the truths of reason to fortuity?

As may be assumed from Mendelssohn's argument, the Law, however, is also a symbol for eternal truths—again I do not understand how it is possible to identify eternal truths with the Law. Contingent as well as historical and moral truths can be expressed in various ways. However, to present eternal truths, which are imprinted in all men, in a symbolic manner has yet to appeal to any nation. The common man is totally confused. If the Law has a purpose, it is completely self-evident that when the purpose becomes obsolete the Law is rendered superfluous. If the purpose of the Law in Judaism, as might be assumed from Mendelssohn, is to establish a Mosaic constitution, Judaism must cease the moment that this constitution no longer exists. If the intention of the Law, however, is to bring men to faith and to knowledge of historical and religious or eternal truths, then the Law is only a method to guide men upon a certain path. If they are already walking upon this path, then it undoubtedly follows that they can forego this method, and nevertheless their descendants will remain on the same path.

How then did Herr Mendelssohn reach a conclusion which does not at all follow from his own system, and which, as it seems, he drew under duress: Whoever is born to the House of Jacob cannot in good conscience rid himself of the Law.

. . . Where do we find today a systematic doctrine of the essence of Judaism [from which] it may be learned how far one may go [to free himself from the Law]? Indeed, such a doctrine is precisely that which was missing until now. Transgression of the Law is deemed as an absolute abandonment of Judaism, and because those who have dared to transgress [the law] publicly were despised by their co-religionists, the significant aspects of Judaism have ceased to concern them. This process, which grows greater with each day, threatens us with a total disintegration of our faith, a faith whose *form* so bestows felicity and so uplifts the heart and which can render men so happy. This disintegration cannot be prevented unless we do away with the present constitution of Judaism and permit men unlimited use of their faculties, so that they may—without acting in opposition to the constitution of our religion—choose a position [*ein Beruf*] for himself in society.

In overthrowing the old constitution we must establish a new one which will maintain us in the faith of our fathers, teach us the true essence of Judaism, present in a vital way its objectives and guide us in the path upon which we can, at the same time, be good men and good citizens.

. . . I therefore ask whether I may be regarded a heretic or an enemy of our faith because I argue that morally our nation cannot hope for a genuine amelioration [of this situation] unless we begin a positive reformation in the area of the Law. How may this reformation be brought about? What should be the limits of this reformation? The theologian, i.e., the rabbi, must answer these questions.

I believe I have already adumbrated several replies to these questions in this essay in which I surveyed the entire scope of Judaism. I would like to summarize here the thoughts which I expressed because I believe that some of my suggestions may lead us upon the correct course. First, I contend that the only possible object of Judaism was to make men as happy as possible, and with this in mind to establish a society. Second, in Judaism the only component of revelation is faith. Third, as a result [Judaism] is not based on obedience to the Law, rather this obedience required by the All Mighty under certain circumstances is only a means to attain the higher aims of Judaism. Fourth, Judaism posits the true autonomy of the will. Fifth, the intention of the Allmighty was not to reveal laws to the Jews so as to undermine their autonomy. Sixth, the Law only establishes [the framework] of religion, but it does not constitute its essence. Seventh, the laws came into effect only as statutes for the sake of maintaining a society and as rules intended to preserve certain deeds and [the memory of certain] events.

If it were my intention to support these theses with authority, I would illustrate them with numerous references to the writing of the prophets and other authors. But the matter must speak for itself.... We do not understand the deep intention of the Allmighty which He made manifest to us in the word that was recorded by our fathers, which at the same time He inscribed in our souls and hearts. We fail to understand, however, that if our faith is strong we do not need symbols and if we make a genuine effort to achieve earthly happiness we can liberate ourselves from the Law. We do not understand that we are united among ourselves in faith alone, but in law [i.e., natural law] with all men.

Why did we not understand the intention of the Allmighty? Why? Because we considered the legal constitution of our faith to be its essence: because by keeping the Law we neglected the entire form of our faith . . . ; because those who received the constitution of our faith from the Eternal were not capable of achieving true faith and of establishing its true purpose.

Those who dared penetrate into the Holy of Holies of our faith are left to stand on its outer boundary only. They call to us: "Your religion is no longer good for our time, deny it and become men." Come to us, they intimate, and an abundance of bliss will be yours.

But no! Children of Israel, remain on the path of your fathers. Our religion is for every individual and is valid at all times. Show that your religion is capable of turning you into men, and soon you will be capable of developing yourselves into citizens, that is, if only the constitution of your religion were reformed. If we persist [in effecting such a reformation] we will become, in all corners of the earth and among all men, a people worthy of divinity....

[Reformation will not undermine the essence of the religion.] What, in fact, does this essence consist of? What distinguishes it? And how far must the new constitution go?... Judaism, like every revealed religion, is given to man in its entirety, as an undefined compendium of principles, doctrines and laws. It is incumbent upon us to develop certain disciplines to create some other therein. The designated task must first delineate systematically the sources, the principles of Judaism and the history of their development; from this will emerge Theoretical Dogmatics, or the science of the sources of our faith. Second, it is necessary to learn the skills to teach the truth of our religion.... From this will emerge Practical Dogmatics, or the science of the constitutive faith of our religion.... Through this type of constitution ... our faith will stand pure and ennobled and no adversary will dare to deny its sanctity. Moreover, the adherents of this constitution will not dare to violate it.

Our form of faith must be open before the world and coming generations like the Book of Nature.... Let the witness of faith step forward:

1. I believe in one God.

2. I believe in a unique God that revealed Himself to our forefathers, Abraham, Isaac and Jacob and promised our salvation.

3. I believe in a God who chose Moses and others who were pleasing to Him and gave them the gift of prophecy.

4. I believe in a God who at Mount Sinai gave to our forefathers laws.

5. We hereby believe that the observance of these laws was sacred to our fathers, and by their observance they were maintained on the same path upon which we march today solely through faith in God and His prophets.

6. We believe that this God is a God of love.

7. We believe that He rewards good and punishes evil.

8. We believe that He guides the world through providence and omnipotence.

9. We believe that He will turn our misfortune to good.

10. We hope for redemption through the agency of His Messiah, in this world or after our death, with those whom He will deem worthy of resurrection.

11. We are obliged to continue and maintain the covenant that the Eternal One made with our fathers through the rite of circumcision.

12. We are obliged to celebrate the Sabbath as a day that is sanctified to God.

13. We are obliged to renew through the holidays the memory of His acts of grace.

14. We are obliged to seek through repentance God's grace and purification.

This is the pristine constitution [*Organon*] of Judaism. It must be explicated clearly with the aid of Scripture and Tradition. Faith, trust and obedience—these constitute the bond that binds us and holds us together. True, as long as we are under the yoke of the present [rabbinic] constitution, our actions contrary to it are indeed improper. Therefore, I have shown the ways which we may, in a lawful manner, discard this constitution and introduce a new one, so that we will not be attacked as children who have forgotten their duties and violate the faith of their fathers. Thus we will not be placed in a position of being rebels against God, and of being mutineers who rely solely on their own arbitrary judgment, and further, we shall not be despised for forgetting all that has happened to our people, nor shall we be deemed—because of a lack of faith—the cause of the covenant's disintegration.

NOTE

1. Saul Ascher (1767–1822), a Berlin bookdealer who wrote widely on Jewish political and literary subjects. In so far as he regarded Judaism to be constituted by essential principles of faith (*Glaubenslehre*) and denied the eternal value of the *mitzvoth*, Ascher is considered a forerunner of Reform Judaism. The point of departure of Ascher's view on Judaism was his rejection of Moses Mendelssohn's definition of Judaism as essentially a religion of ceremonial laws.

LAZARUS BENDAVID[1]
21. Notes Regarding the Characteristics of the Jews

. . . I wish, then, to describe the four classes to which Jews today belong in order to derive therefrom the principal claim of this discussion, namely: " to the extent that the Jews do not take advantage of [the opportunity] to abrogate the ceremonial laws, which are meaningless and inappropriate for our time; to the extent that they do not establish a purer religion, more worthy of God—the pure teaching of Moses—they will perforce remain, even if baptized, apathetic citizens who are harmful to the state."

The four classes are the following: The first class, which is still the largest, is that which retains its loyalty to and its belief in the entire immense conglomeration of Jewish traditions. This class considers it to be a sin if it is doubted that the distance between the heel and the ankle of the foot of Og, King of Bashan, is less than thirty cubits or that

Source: Lazarus Bendavid, *Etwas zur Charackteristick der Juden* (Leipzig, 1793), pp. 45–53. Trans. here by S. Fischer and S. Weinstein.

Moses received on Mount Sinai from God Himself the melody of several of the hymns sung on the Day of Atonement. This class will remain forever irredeemable and its extinction is the only hope for the coming generations. For this class of Jews baptism and the acknowledgment of the Christian faith are of value only in that the zeal for bread is no more injurious to their existence than it is to the Christian who wants to be accepted into a particular guild. Aside from this, they pray with the rosary with the heart of a superstitious Jew, harboring resentment toward the Jews and contempt for the Christians. One rich fellow belonging to this gang who was baptized—for what reason I know not—recently wrote to another baptized Jew and invited him, although he was poor, to marry his daughter since he did not want her to marry a Christian.

Among those who remain steadfast in the faith of their forefathers, they are not infrequently to be found—in spite of their superstitions—exceedingly worthy men who, with respect to their sincerity and to the ardent zeal of their efforts for the good of their co-religionists truly embellish this class. I knew a director of a hospital in Berlin who was willing to share his last shirt with anyone who needed it. I knew another, a very poor man, who made it his business to collect donations for people even poorer than himself and who would have thought it the greatest sin to have taken even a penny of the money placed in his hands for his own use, even at the time of his greatest need.

The second class of Jews is that dissolute mob who have abandoned the ceremonial laws[2] because they were too much of a burden and because they prevented them from following unhindered their unbridled passions. Unfortunately, their number is still very great and will increase from day to day if a change does not soon take place. These, who in most cases were born to rich parents of the first class, were raised without a proper education and were led astray by love and wine. They consider themselves to be enlightened, but they merely arouse contempt. Their fathers are at least at peace with themselves, while they must suppress the voice of conscience at every moment. They simulate enlightenment, but are incorrigible, uninformed vagabonds. These are the ones who, for the most part, are responsible for the bad opinion the Christians have of the Jews. These are the ones who through their immoral way of life cause the best of the first and third classes to abhor enlightenment in any form. The majority go over to Christianity the moment they meet a Christian maiden who is more cunning and more beautiful than she is clever and eloquent. After baptism, were it possible, they would be prepared to undergo a second circumcision were the acceptance of the Jewish religion to confer as many advantages as those attained through the acceptance of the Christian religion.

The third class seems to me to be always worthy of respect, even though my outlook in religion is far removed from theirs, for they are good men. Their intellect has not been cultivated by proper education, but their hearts are without blemish. [Consequently] their intellect is not sufficiently strong to elevate them to that level of enlightenment that makes a man moral even without such a religion that constantly reminds him of his [moral] duties. They are, however, cognizant of this weakness. Through fear of immorality, they remain [embedded] in an unrefined Judaism. With respect to themselves, they are suspicious of every innovation, but do not in principle disallow innovation for others. They are deemed to be stubborn and unbending Jews, but if the Jews of the first class could read what is in their hearts they would accuse them of heresy. For the most part they have a system entirely their own in matters of religion. They persecute no one and act charitably toward everyone. They are faithful husbands, loving parents, true friends and good citizens. The countries of Prussia and Austria benefit greatly from their devoted and indefatigable industry. In the majority of cases—though not without exception—the state can rely on the sons of these noble men to be loyal, useful men.

The fourth class is composed either of the sons of the third class or of men who, owing to unfortunate circumstances, have been equipped by heaven with adequate mental powers and who have met with men of the better sort. This class, which combined all the virtues of the previous class with true enlightenment, is as removed from Judaism as it is from apathy [*Indifferentismus*]. They are disciples of the genuine natural religion. Sensing the necessity of the duty of believing with all the ardor that this religion instils in men of reason, they are nonetheless aware of the precarious pillars upon which civic security would rest and the superficial foundations upon which human happiness would lie were man prevented from believing in God, immortality or the advance toward further perfection after death. Their words are holy to them. A member of this class would be ashamed of himself were he to make a profession of faith—even if only *pro forma*—of that of which in his heart he was not convinced. He would think that such a profession of faith, such a mockery of man's most important possession, implies a different kind of belief, one which every upright man would abhor. He would in effect be saying: "Citizens and compatriots! I hereby betray my conscience for the sake of ephemeral happiness; I avow with my lips that which is not in my heart! Trust me not! Do not charge me with public office, for I have committed perjury and I could easily do so again were I to be prompted by equally powerful inducements!"

The men of this class cannot be very happy as long as they are considered by the Christians to be Jews because they are not Christians and they are considered by the Jews to be apostates because they are men. They cannot be very happy as long as their solicitude for the integrity of their own mode of life and for the upbringing of their children is beset by obstacle after obstacle. On the one hand they have no access to any branch of livelihood other than that open to the ordinary Jew, namely, to make money through money. Their demands for civic respectability, which, in spite of all philosophizing, are motivated by a strong and sincere uprighteousness, are either rejected, as in the case of the ordinary Jew, or are granted solely out of charity. Moreover, the state forces them to be wicked men who must act contrary to their convictions before it permits them (according to present regulations) to engage in even the lowest of occupations of the civil service. On the other hand, those who support the meaningless ceremonial laws still bind them with iron chains. The vagabonds who have also abandoned the ceremonial laws consider themselves to be like the members of this class, while the better Jews of the third class consider them to be apathetic and even wicked men who are willing to separate themselves from Judaism because of its obligations.

NOTES

1. Lazarus Bendavid (1762–1832), German-Jewish mathematician, philosopher and educator. Despite his love of philosophy (in 1801, the Royal Academy of Sciences in Berlin awarded him a prize for a study on Immanuel Kant's epistemology), he devoted himself largely to Jewish problems. He regarded a religious reform of Judaism as the only feasible means of stemming the growing tide of conversions.

2. In this work Bendavid advocates the abolition of the ritual or "ceremonial laws" of Judaism. Here he demonstrates a sensivity to Kant's criticism of Judaism as a "heteronomous" system of morally and spiritually vacuous ritual obligations. (Cf. Immanuel Kant, *Religion Within the Limits of Reason Alone* [1793], trans. T. M. Greene and H. H. Hudson [New York: Harper Torchbooks, 1960], pp. 115–90.) Kant misunderstood Bendavid's call for the reform of Judaism as intimating the desirability of conversion. He accordingly urged Bendavid to abandon the "pseudo-religion" of his forefathers and openly embrace Christianity. (See Kant, *Der Streit der Fakultaeten* [1798].)

DAVID FRIEDLAENDER

22. Open Letter to His Reverence, Probst Teller[1]

. . . In light of the wisdom of He who gave the Torah we may assume, even if this cannot be proved in detail in every instance, that each custom and each commandment had its own meaning, which went hand in hand with the welfare of the nation and its moral stature. From those [customs and commandments] whose purpose has been stated or is clearly discernible to the eye, it is reasonable to infer concerning all the others [that they too have purposes], which are likely to appear to us as aimless, trivial or even entirely ridiculous. Even those whose membership in that society obligated them to fulfil the commandments did not always have a clear knowledge of their purpose. It is sufficient for the lawgiver that for the present the fulfilment of the commandments contributed something to the happiness either of the group or of the individual. He who inquires [into these matters], however, was given cause for reflection or was provided with the opportunity to be enlightened by the sages and the leaders of the people. This is not an hypothesis that has been fabricated in order to save these laws. The very spirit of the entire system clearly demonstrates this. The written laws were few, and even these were for the most part unintelligible without oral commentary. It was axiomatic that it was forbidden to write down anything concerning the Law. [Indeed] it was explicitly stated: "The words transmitted orally thou art not at liberty to recite from writing."[2] The unwritten laws were thus learned only through oral transmission; for understandable and judicious reasons these laws remained vague. The teacher of the people in every generation was thereby given a free hand to alter and to adapt the commandments to the conditions of the time. No one could take a book of laws and contradict the teacher, for in this respect there were no written laws. "Even though these prohibit and these permit"—it is explicitly stated concerning the ceremonial laws [*Ceremonialgesetze*]—"these and these are the words of the living God."[3] This statement and many others in the Talmud demonstrate beyond any doubt that it was the intention of the first lawgiver that the sages of each generation would remain free to expand or limit the laws linked to time and place, to give them a more precise interpretation or to cancel them completely, all according to the needs of the time and to the moral behavior and the general progress of the nation. Not only is the cancellation of the laws linked to time and place grounded in the nature of the Law and evident throughout all of the Holy Scriptures, but even teachers of the people from such later periods, from whom the respect, spirit and authority of the first lawgiver had long since been withdrawn, acknowledged this as being fundamental. How else could they have cancelled and altered on their own authority many laws the fulfilment of which in foreign lands and in different climates either was of no use or subjected them to great difficulties? . . . The [Jewish] people, dispersed throughout the world and completely abandoned, with no permanent abode, no political sovereign and no spiritual leader, finally lost all touch with the values of reason and all inclination for the higher truths, which had constituted the foundation of their original religion. Instead, they fulfilled the ceremonial laws with a scrupulous exactness. The beautiful edifice of their reli-

Source: David Friedlaender, *Sendschreiben an seine Hochwuerdigen, Herrn Oberconsistorialrat und Probst Teller zu Berlin, von einigen Hausvaetern juedischer Religion* (Berlin, 1799), pp. 25–27, 30–34, 48–49. Trans. here by S. Weinstein.

gion was destroyed. Those who escaped the collapse embraced the ruins not of the Temple but of its scaffolding, that is, the external customs, the only thing which they saved. Had their spirit not been so profoundly distorted and their psychic powers so paralyzed, they would have learned in other lands and under other conditions to cancel the ceremonial laws as something that had become completely superfluous. Because of their state of mind at the time, however, their adherence to these laws grew increasingly stronger. The greater the persecutions were, the more anxiously their teachers, who lacked spiritual inspiration, urged the fulfilment of meaningless actions.

To all this the idea of a messiah was added, which completely clouded their minds and made all independent thought impossible. This idea arose quite early as a result of the mistaken interpretation of [certain] passages containing the inspired words of their prophets. In all these prophetic utterances the messiah, or the redeemer [of the people] from prevailing hardship and distress, appears as the customary figure of consolation. When the people repent of their sins—so proclaimed the prophets in all their oracles—they will be freed of the yoke of oppression and will return to the land of their fathers. This idea became ever more deeply rooted [in the minds of the people]. As the likelihood that redemption would take place by natural means decreased, the hope for a return to Jerusalem occurring by miraculous means grew stronger. If the people of God are to dwell once again in the land of their fathers, their return must be bound to the restoration of the ancient political order, to service in the Temple and to sacrifices. This delusion was much beloved by the people and was entirely in keeping with the spirit of the slogans of their seers and demagogues who in their vision of the future could not imagine—because of the situation at the time—the liberation of their nation by any other means. Accordingly, the strict fulfilment of the ceremonial laws was necessary for two reasons: first, in order to be worthy of the miraculous redemption through meritorious conduct and second, in order to be able, upon arriving in Jerusalem, to live according to the ancient political order and to fulfil the will of God.

This anticipation of [the coming of] the messiah and the return to the promised land fortified the inclination to direct all efforts and all thoughts to ancient history, service in the Temple, sacrifice and ceremonial laws. All faculties of the soul were devoted to these studies, all ingenuity was focused on hairsplitting musings. Their scholars multiplied and perverted [the obligations], increasing the yoke of the ceremonial laws, which in any case had been heavy. The separation from other peoples and from other subjects of human knowledge was thereby accentuated. The more meticulous [the fulfilment of] the ceremonial laws became, the more deserving became the people's demand for speedy redemption, for miraculous deliverance from misfortune. They overworked their brains and those of their contemporaries with responses to hairsplitting questions concerning the laws that will come into effect upon their return to Jerusalem or with the solution of the most trifling problems, which inclined to childishness and quixotry.

Given this frame of mind it is easy to perceive not only how the intellect and most likely the manners of the people were increasingly corrupted but also how even their external appearance took on a one-sidedness bordering on caricature. Accompanying this was an ever more rapidly increasing ignorance of their primordial language, Hebrew. That which was known [of Hebrew] through exegesis, together with the scarcely comprehensible translations [of Scripture] contributed to the dissemination of even more erroneous concepts. Moreover, the power of imagination [of the people], which in any case had been unrestrained, was provided with a new opportunity to generate fantastic notions and extravagant expectations. Under the circumstances in which the people found themselves, it was hardly to be expected that the teachers would cancel those ceremonial laws which had become inapplicable and replace them with other laws better suited to the spirit of the times. It was even less likely that these leaders, who were no longer capable of spiritual elevation and who had a scant knowledge of Hebrew, could extract the religious concepts and moral teachings expounded in the Holy Scriptures, order them systematically and present them to the best of their ability—even, if need be, in the adulterated language of the people—for the enlightenment and moral edification of the people.

Finally, what strengthened the yearning for Jerusalem and the hope for [the coming of] the messiah, and turned this into the most fervent wish of the people, was the fact that this yearning and this wish were transposed into the liturgy, becoming thereby an integral part of the worship of God and the prayer service. . . . The Jews' greatest gain [with the passing of time] lies no doubt in the fact that the yearning for the messiah and for Jerusalem has become removed ever further from their hearts in so far as reason has increasingly rejected these expectations as chimerical. It is always possible that certain isolated individuals, confined to their cloisters or in other respects alienated from worldly affairs, still preserve such wishes within their souls. [However,] with regard to the majority of Jews, at least those in Germany, Holland and France, this notion receives no support and the last traces of it will ultimately be eradicated. . . .

If the authority of the lawgiver and one's own discernment, wisdom and duty, if the innermost conviction of the rightness of the action all point toward a single aim, namely, toward the cancellation of the ceremonial laws, then one may ask [us]: Wherefore do you procrastinate? Wherefore do you hesitate to declare that these laws are no longer binding on you, that you are ready to abandon the religion of your fathers (in so far as it is understood as the fulfilment of these laws and customs) and to convert to Christianity?

Here, our worthy, virtuous friend, our conscience bids us pause. Here we face the abyss which we know neither how to circumvent nor how to leap over. In short, here is the point at which we seek your counsel, your assistance and your instruction.

With the same audacious candor with which we have presented the results of our investigations in the Law of Moses and the foundations of the Mosaic religion, with the same love of truth, we must confess that which is surely sufficiently clear from our presentation. To abandon the religion of our fathers, that is to say, the ceremonial laws, and to accept the Christian religion are to us two entirely different matters.

. . . [Beyond the ceremonial laws Judaism contains at its core principles] which we deem to be the foundation of every religion. The principles upon which the religion of Moses is built have for us the highest certainty. We do not doubt that the creed of the Church corresponds to the principles of our faith in spirit, if not in wording, and we would [be ready to] embrace it. [Moreover,] we would [be ready to] make a public confession of that which the Christian teacher [Jesus] has taught, for we do not [merely] believe in his teachings as an aggregate of truths but rather are convinced of their correctness. From this direction, therefore, there is no obstacle facing us and we need not fear that we would be repulsed [by the Church]. These [universal] principles are not all that we will bring with us from Judaism, however. In addition to them we shall bring other principles of the utmost significance, the truth of which is equally clear to us and which we are obligated to accept with equal conviction.[4] Will these principles conform to the teachings of the religious society that we are choosing? Will the teachers of the Christian Church be prepared if not to accept these principles then at least to display tolerance toward them, allowing us to publicly acknowledge these other principles which for us are convincing and beyond doubt? We do not venture to answer this question in the affirmative. At the very least we must not make a decision regarding this without the consent of a teacher of religion as respected, learned and noble as you, worthy Sir.

. . . That which we wish to do, with full conviction of the rightness of our action, our descendants—and perhaps even our contemporaries—will be forced to decide to do. Therefore why should we conceal the true condition of the great part of our brethren, above all those who reside in the large cities? The study of Hebrew and the Talmud declines among us day by day. The authority of the rabble is diminishing, and with the neglect of the ceremonial ritual laws it must continue to diminish. In every country the government, with great justice, has taken from these rabbis all power to make binding judgments and enforce the Halakha. For the application of the civil laws of Judaism in our time is no longer to be tolerated and the retention of the power of excommunication and similar punishments in the hands of the scholars and theologians would seriously retard the progress of the members of the [Jewish] community. At a time when all religious factions are complaining that the bonds of religion are becoming weaker, it is to be expected that the Jews, who have no genuine religious instruction and no worship of God aimed at increasing piety, would relate to these matters with ever-increasing thoughtlessness. The contact and the social ties with the Christians, which are becoming more numerous, together with the willingness of the Christians to accept Jews in their temples as fellow believers should have sufficed to have aroused the oppressed, abandoned and on occasion even despised Jew to cross over to the Christian religion without further scruples. By this means, through the recital of a few words, he could secure for himself all the advantages of life, all the civil liberties which even the most upright Jew could not attain through a lifetime of faultless behavior. This consideration is extremely depressing for every thinking man and perhaps even the ruling authorities are not indifferent to it.

[On the one hand] the thinking man dare not assume that his descendants will possess the unselfishness and the strength of character to persevere in the face of the powerful enticement of such great, and so easily attainable benefits. [On the other hand] the ruler cannot view as desirable the increase of such families who were either tempted out of rashness or forced by need to break all family ties and who without shame and solely out of self-interest took a step against which at one time there had been a general bias.

In this labyrinth, into which we have fallen because of the time and circumstances, we might almost say because of our very virtues we have recourse to you, worthy and venerable Sir. Instruct us how we can find our way out [of this impasse]. Tell us, noble lover of virtue, should we decide to choose the great Protestant Christian community as a place of refuge, what kind of public declaration would you, and the men who sit with you on the venerable council, demand of us? . . .

The number of people who, full of trust, are sending this epistle to you is quite small. However, unless we are mistaken there must be a sizable number of heads of families who find themselves in a similar position and who perhaps lack only an initial example to arrive at a similar decision. This is also demonstrated by the numerous attempts of individuals of our religion to outline proposals concerning how religious reform is to be instituted. Although we doubt the feasibility of these attempts, they nevertheless make manifestly clear the need felt by our heads of families to do away with the fetters of the ceremonial laws as well as their desire to be incorporated, one way or another, into the wider society of the state.

A positive pronouncement by a man of your stature and authority in the Christian Church can thus have the most auspicious consequences for a multitude of upright, truth-loving men. By your pronouncement, noble Sir, you can establish and promote the prosperity and well-being of creatures yet unborn who will be able to enjoy a life of happiness and for whom your name will remain an eternal blessing.

The very fact that we are not taking this step merely out of consideration for ourselves helps us meet the objections that can be raised against us. . . . We can be asked, for instance: Why are you not satisfied with disseminating morality and virtue among your brethren and leaving the future in the hands of Providence? The step that you are taking is astonishing. Would it not be more advisable to walk upon the slow path and to wait for time to unite all those who serve God in spirit and in truth? Further, we might be asked: Do you have such little trust in your wise and noble government and in the truly praiseworthy councillors of the consistory [Lutheran clerical board]? Will they not provide you with protection and assure you of tolerance once you declare your views in public? Why expose yourselves to the accusation that will inevitably be raised against you, namely, that you find fault with your fellow men?

We shall answer these questions frankly. Our circle of influence is small. However clear and pure the fundamental truths that we have made our own might be, however great and earnest our efforts to establish and spread these truths among our families might be, we nevertheless cannot help but fear that the purity and wholeness of these truths would not be preserved were they to be transmitted to future generations solely by oral means. In addition, we have never denied that our aim is to attain the rights of the citizen by means of our declaration and that it is our ardent wish that in this way we may see our descendants develop their intellectual and physical powers. Therefore, even if we concede that the assumption that the state will preserve and protect us is well grounded, we nevertheless will always exist merely as an intermediary body between Christians and Jews. We will be regarded and treated as an isolated sect without disciples which can offer [to its adherents] no more than a wretched existence. It would be far too much to hope that under these circumstances we could be accepted as citizens, attain [civil] liberties and enter society at large through matrimonial ties.

Finally, the history of all periods teaches that those principles which we have called eternal truths are indeed the religion of individual men, but cannot serve as the religion of the people, and certainly not for a prolonged period of time. In order to perpetuate them and preserve their salutary influence these delicate flowers of the power of thought require a vessel, the vessel of ways and means. These flowers wither easily, and the noblest creation of reason can in its decay be fatal for the spirit. Or, to use less figurative language, when sophistry and self-interest take possession of a person, our system, like every other, is subject to corruption and falsification. It therefore degenerates either into superstition and fanaticism or into heresy and atheism.

Without in the least seeking to forestall your opinion [of our proposal], venerable Sir, we [nevertheless] expect that within the wide circle of the true spirit of Protestantism we and our system can also find shelter and protection. In this way we will be able to attain the goal we have set for ourselves.

If the Protestant religion does indeed prescribe certain ceremonies, we can certainly resign ourselves to their performance as mere forms necessary for [our] acceptance as members of this society. Let it be understood that we are presupposing as a matter of principle that these ceremonies are required merely as actions, as customs that attest to the fact that the newly admitted member accepts the eternal truths out of conviction and that he submits to all the duties that result from this as a man and as a citizen. We do not regard this demand as a sign that he who performs the ceremonies is tacitly acknowledging that he accepts out of faith the dogmas of the Church. Should the demands of the Church be confined to formal ceremonies, we could accept these demands with a quiet conscience and fulfill them with total peace of mind.

The words of the prophet Zephania will thereby surely be consummated: "For then I will convert the peoples to a purer language that they may all call upon the name of the Lord, to serve Him with one consent."[5]

NOTES

1. David Friedlaender published this open letter to Probst Teller anonymously in the name of an unspecified number of heads of Jewish households in Berlin. The circumstances of the letter are not clear. Historians suggest that the letter indicates *inter alia* the despair of some German Jews in the struggle for civil equality, or that it perhaps bespeaks an attempt of well-to-do Jews to separate themselves from the Jewish masses and so improve their image and socio-economic position. Whatever the motive behind the letter, it clearly reflects the frustrations and dilemma of a generation of acculturated Jews prior to full emancipation. Friedlaender's proposal to accept Christianity, if he and they on whose behalf he spoke were freed from the confession of certain dogmas (e.g., the divinity of Jesus) and acceptance of sacraments, assumes a Deistic conception of reason as a self-sufficient means both to know God's will and to serve Him. Accordingly, he not only rejected the ritual precepts of Judaism, but also the dogmas Christianity deemed incompatible with reason. The eternal, principally moral, truths that are accessible to reason and that can serve as a basis for unifying enlightened Jews and Christians are, according to Friedlaender, identical with the original teachings of Moses. This argument indicates an ambivalence toward Judaism. On the one hand he is critical of the ritualism of Rabbinic Judaism; on the other, he is enthusiastic in his presentation of biblical faith or "pristine Judaism." As much as a proposal for conversion, the letter is then to be understood as an apologia for Judaism.

Wilhelm Abraham Teller (1734–1804), Protestant philosopher and scholar identified with the Enlightenment, was appointed dean (*Probst*) in the German Protestant Church, with a seat in the supreme consistory of Berlin, in 1767. In 1792, he issued his work *Die Religion der Vollkommenen*, an exposition of his theological position, in which he advocated at length the idea of the "perfectability of Christianity"—that is, of the ultimate transformation of Christianity into a scheme of simple morality with a complete rejection of all specifically Christian ideas and methods. Friedlaender thus apparently felt that Teller would respond favorably to his proposal for a "dry baptism." With the eyes of Berlin upon him, Teller, however, proclaimed that conversion to the Church required a confession of the superiority of Christianity to Judaism, and the acceptance of baptism and the sacraments as the indispensable symbols of the religion founded by Christ. The Jew entering the Church would have to become a Christian!

2. Babylonian Talmud, *Gittin* 60b.

3. The citation is a composite of a midrash in Eccles. 12:11, on *Fathers of Rabbi Nathan*, version A, ch. 18, and passages from the Jerusalem Talmud, *Berakhot*, Mishnah 7:1, p. 3a.

4. Friedlaender is referring here to principles of Judaism which cannot be verified by reason. In the succeeding paragraphs he calls these principles, which must be affirmed by belief alone, historical truths, following the distinction made by Mendelssohn in *Jerusalem* between eternal (or rational) and historical truths. This discussion is part of Friedlaender's attempt to justify his proposal for a qualified conversion to Christianity.

5. Zeph. 3:9.

III

The Process of Political Emancipation in Western Europe, 1789–1871

The process of legal emancipation [1] of the Jews was ambiguous. The granting of citizenship—or full equality of each individual before the law—did not necessarily signify a basic and widespread change in attitudes toward the Jew. The modern, democratic state of France, established in 1789 on the principles of equality before the law, initiated the ambiguous process of the emancipation of Jewry. After an initial hesitation to extend to the Jews "the Rights of Man and of the Citizen," the National Assembly of France decided that its founding principles would be seriously vitiated should the Jews be excluded from citizenship. Despite personal and moral reservations regarding the Jews, the constitution of the Republic made it *de rigueur* for the Assembly to grant the Jews citizenship (see documents 1–5). Indicative of the disparity between principle and personal attitudes toward the Jews was the emphasis made in the Assembly's deliberations on the obvious fact that the rights of the citizen granted to the Jews appertain to the Jew *qua* individual and not to the Jews *qua* nation (see document 2). Presumably, it is the Jew *qua* member of the Jewish nation who bears all the egregious qualities that evoke the Frenchman's fears.

The difference between legal emancipation and the basic acceptance of the Jew is

1. In Jewish historiography and social philosophy the term *emancipation* is generally used to designate the legal process, which began in Europe with the French Revolution, of granting to the Jews equal civic rights in the countries in which they reside. The term *emancipation,* however, is somewhat of a linguistic anachronism, for it first emerged with specific reference to the Jewish struggle for civic rights only in 1828. The term was borrowed from the great debate of that year regarding the Catholics' accession to Parliament in England. (See Jacob Katz, "The Term *Jewish Emancipation:* Its Origin and Historical Impact," in Alexander Altmann, ed., *Studies in Nineteenth-Century Jewish Intellectual History* [Cambridge: Harvard University Press, 1964], pp. 1–25.) Some historians use the term *emancipation* to describe the whole cultural and social movement promoting directly and indirectly Jewish integration; here the historical anachronism of the term is even greater.

underscored by the manner in which the Jews were emancipated in the rest of French-"liberated" continental Europe. Here citizenship was granted the Jews by the decree or suasion of the conquering armies of revolutionary France (see documents 7–9). The French emperor Napoleon, who fancied himself the custodian of the French Revolution, pointed to this disparity when he called 112 Jewish "notables" to the plush Hôtel de Ville in Paris on July 29, 1806 (see document 10). Through a series of pointed questions he requested that this Assembly of Jewish Notables affirm that Judaism—the *national* religion of the Jews—does not undermine the civic morality and responsibility expected of the Jew as citizen (see documents 11, 12 and 14). In their carefully worded reply the notables indicated that Judaism does not interfere with the obligations of citizenship (see document 13). The reply of the notables was given the sanctity of binding religious law by Napoleon's revival of the Sanhedrin—the supreme political, religious and judicial body in Palestine during the Roman period until the fifth century C.E. (According to Jewish lore, the reconstitution of the Sanhedrin is associated with the coming of the Messiah; Napoleon was well aware of this.) Meeting from February to March 1807, the Sanhedrin endorsed the answers of the notables (see document 15).

As Napoleon marched east to Poland and to Russia he had undoubtedly hoped that this dramatic, "messianic" gesture of convening the Sanhedrin would earn him the enthusiastic support of the millions of traditional Jews of the region. Indeed many greeted him as a latter-day Cyrus, as an eschatological liberator; others thought that he covertly sought to subvert traditional Judaism (see document 17).

The Congress of Vienna, held in 1814 and 1815 for the reorganization of Europe after the defeat of Napoleon at Waterloo, marked the return of the conservatives (see document 19). For the lands formerly under French influence, the *Vormaerz,* the period between the Congress of Vienna and the liberal revolutions that began in March 1830, witnessed the erosion of the reforms inspired by the French Revolution. In France, however, the legal and economic achievements of the Revolution were respected. The revolutions of 1830 renewed the process of liberalization throughout Europe, redounding to more favorable legislation on behalf of the Jews. The liberal-democratic mood was rekindled more forcefully with the revolutions of 1848. The struggle for liberal and democratic government was accompanied by a demand for the full emancipation of the Jews (see document 21). The revolutions were soon suppressed and much of the legislation that they inspired was repealed. What the liberals were unable to achieve at the barricades was attained through the economic and social revolution that was slowly affecting Europe. This socio-economic transformation of Europe led to a greater support of the "bourgeois" principle of legal equality, to which the remaining or renewed disabilities were an offence. The process of legal emancipation of the Jews in Central Europe was completed only with the unification of Germany from 1869 to 1871, and even then was not truly consummated until after the First World War (see documents 24 and 25).

THE FRENCH NATIONAL ASSEMBLY
1. Declaration of the Rights of Man and of the Citizen (August 26, 1789)[1]

Article I. All men are born, and remain, free and equal in rights: social distinctions cannot be found but on common utility. . . .

10. No person shall be molested for his opinions, even such as are religious, provided that the manifestation of these opinions does not disturb the public order established by the law.

NOTE

1. After the fall of the Bastille on July 14, 1789, a revolutionary National Assembly set out to dismantle France's feudal monarchy and to establish a constitutional democracy. With the Declaration of the Rights of Man and of the Citizen, inspired by the Declaration of Independence of the United States, the National Assembly transcribed the slogan of the French Revolution—"liberty, equality and fraternity"—into law. It became the basic law of the French constitution.

Source: Benjamin Flower, ed. and trans., *The French Constitution* (London, 1792), pp. 17–18.

THE FRENCH NATIONAL ASSEMBLY
2. Debate on the Eligibility of Jews for Citizenship[1]

MONSIEUR THE COUNT OF CLERMONT-TONNERRE: You have, by the Declaration of Rights, secured the rights of men and of citizens. You have irrevocably established the conditions of eligibility for the administrative assemblies. It seemed that there was nothing further to do in this regard. One honorable member has in the meantime informed us that non-Catholic inhabitants of several parts of the provinces have been seeing their rights challenged by motives drawn from the very laws made in their behalf. Another has called your attention to citizens who find in their professions obstacles to their enjoyment of the same rights. I have thus two issues to examine: exclusion related to profession and exclusion related to religion. . . .

I will deal now with religion. You have already addressed this point in stating in the Declaration of Rights that no one shall be persecuted for his religious beliefs. Is it not profound persecution of the citizen to want to deprive him of his dearest right because of his opinions? The law cannot affect the religion of a man. It can take no hold over his soul; it can affect only his actions, and it must protect those actions when they do no harm to society. God wanted us to reach agreement

Source: Achille-Edmond Halphen, *Recueil des Lois, Décrets, ordonnances, avis du conseil d'état, Arrêtés et Règlements concernant les Israélites depuis la Révolution de 1789* (Paris, 1851), pp. 184–89. Trans. here by J. Rubin.

among ourselves on issues of morality, and he has permitted us to make moral laws, but he has given to no one but himself the right to legislate dogmas and to rule over [religious] conscience. So leave man's conscience free, that sentiments or thoughts guided in one manner or another toward the heavens will not be crimes that society punishes by the loss of social rights. Or else create a national religion, arm yourself with a sword, and tear up your Declaration of Rights. [But] there is justice, there is reason. . . .

Every religion must prove but one thing—that it is moral. If there is a religion that commands theft and arson, it is necessary not only to refuse eligibility to those who profess it, but further to outlaw them. This consideration cannot be applied to the Jews. The reproaches that one makes of them are many. The gravest are unjust, the others are merely wrong. Usury, one says, is permitted them. This assertion is founded on nothing but a false interpretation of a principle of charity and brotherhood which forbids them to lend at interest among themselves. . . . Men who possess nothing but money cannot live but by making that money valuable, and you have always prevented them from possessing anything else. . . . This people is insatiable, one says. This insatiability is [however] not certain.

The Jews should be denied everything as a nation, but granted everything as individuals.[3] They must be citizens. It is claimed that they do not want to be citizens, that they say this and that they are [thus] excluded; there cannot be one nation within another nation. . . . It is intolerable that the Jews should become a separate political formation or class in the country. Every one of them must individually become a citizen; if they do not want this, they must inform us and we shall then be compelled to expel them. The existence of a nation within a nation is unacceptable to our country. . . . The emperor admitted the Jews to all ranks, to all duties. They exercised in France the most important public functions. One of our colleagues has authorized me to say that several Jews contributed to his election. They are admitted to the military corps; when I was chairman, a patriotic gift was brought to me by a Jew, a national soldier. . . .

The Jews must be assumed to be citizens as long as it is not proven that they are not citizens, as long as they do not refuse to be citizens. By their petition,[4] they demand to be considered as such; the law must recognize a right that prejudice alone refuses. But, one says, the law does not rule over prejudice. That was true when the law was the work of one man only; when it is the work of all, that is false.

It is necessary to explain oneself clearly on the position of the Jews. For you to keep silent would be the worst of evils. It would be to have seen the good and not to have wanted to do it; to have known the truth and not to have dared to speak it; finally, it would be to place on the same throne prejudice and law, error and reason. . . .

MONSIEUR DE LA FARE, bishop of Nancy:[5] My arguments and my evidence could not add anything to what M. l'abbé Maury[6] has said. Placed close to a great number of Jews by the functions with which I am honored, I must present to you my observations of them, and I will limit myself to that.

The Jews certainly have grievances which require redress. Rights enacted by this legislature should be revoked without forgetting that the Jews are men and are unhappy. It is necessary to grant them protection, security, liberty; but must one admit into the family a tribe that is a stranger to oneself, that constantly turns its eyes toward [another] homeland, that aspires to abandon the land that supports it; a tribe that, to be faithful to its law, must forbid to the individuals who constitute it its entrance into armies, the mechanical and the liberal arts, and into the employ of the civil courts and municipalities; a tribe that, in obeying both its own law and the national law, has 108 valueless days in the year?

In all fairness, I must say that the Jews have rendered great service to Lorraine, and especially to the city of Nancy; but we are faced with a pressing situation. My evaluation [of the situation] obliges me to stand against the motion that has been put before you.

The interest of the Jews themselves demands this stance. The people detest them; in Alsace the Jews are often the victims of popular uprisings. In Nancy, four months ago, people wanted to pillage their homes. I went to the site of the agitation and I asked what complaint they had to make. Some claimed that the Jews had cornered the wheat market; others, that the Jews banded together too much, that they bought the most beautiful houses and that soon they would own the whole city. One of the protesters added: "Yes, Monsieur, if we were to lose you, we would see a Jew become our bishop, they are so clever at taking possession of everything."

A decree that would give the Jews the rights of citizenship could spark an enormous fire. Once they obtained a similar favor from the Parliament of England, but immediately the bakers refused them bread, and these unfortunate Jews very soon demanded the repeal of the bill.

I propose to establish a committee which will be charged with the revision of all the legislation concerning the Jews.

NOTES

1. It would have been logical for the Declaration of the Rights of Man and of the Citizen to have embraced all the denizens of France regardless of religion. Abbé Grégoire, for one, assumed that it would be sufficient to assure equal rights for the Jews and that no special legislation would thus be necessary. But the Assembly hesitated, continually postponing the decision as to whether the Jews of France were indeed included within the purview of the declaration. The issue of Jewish citizenship was immediately prompted by reports from the province of Alsace that the peasants, riding on the crest of revolutionary enthusiasm, had rioted against the Jews. The Jews of Alsace and of the neighboring province of Lorraine, numbering about 30,000 (or eighty percent of the Jewish population of France), were Yiddish speaking and traditional. With few exceptions they earned their livelihood through peddling, grain and cattle trading and petty money lending—pursuits that recurrently brought them into conflict with the local peasantry. The speeches in this document are from the debate in the Assembly on December 23, 1789. On the following day the debate was adjourned, and as was typical no decision had been made.

2. Count Stanislas de Clermont-Tonnerre (1752–1792), French revolutionary, deputy to the National Assembly and consistent advocate of equal rights for the Jews.

3. I.e., citizenship requires that the Jews relinquish their national distinctiveness and judicial autonomy or separateness.

4. The count is referring either to the address of the Jews of Paris to the Assembly or to that of the community of Alsace and Lorraine in which they petitioned for full citizenship. (See *Adresse présentée a l'Assemblée Nationale le 26 Août 1789, par les Juifs résidant à Paris* [près 1789]; *Adresse présentée à l'Assemblée Nationale, 31 Août 1789, par les députés réunis des Juifs établis à Metz, dans les Trois Evêchés, en Alsace et en Lorraine* [1789].) He may also be referring to Berr Isaac Berr's speech before the Assembly on behalf of the Jews of Alsace-Lorraine on October 14, 1789.

5. Anne-Lois Henry de la Fare (1752–1829), bishop of Nancy, Lorraine, and vigorous opponent of Jewish civil rights. His speech before the Assembly was reprinted and widely read. See *Opinion de M. l'êvêque de Nancy, député de Lorraine sur l'admissibilité de Juifs à la plénitude de l'état civil et des droits de citoyens actifs* (Paris, 1790).

6. Abbé Jean Sieflein Maury (1746–1817), delegate from Peronne near Lyons. In opposing an increase of Jewish rights, he argued that by virtue of their religion the Jews were alien to France, and that, moreover, their malevolence was incorrigible.

THE FRENCH NATIONAL ASSEMBLY

3. Decree Recognizing the Jews of Avignon and the Sephardim as Citizens (January 28, 1790)

All of the Jews known in France, under the name of Portuguese, Spanish, and Avignonese Jews, shall continue to enjoy the same rights they have hitherto enjoyed, and which have been granted to them by letters of patent.

In consequence thereof, they shall enjoy the rights of active citizens, if they possess the other requisite qualifications, as enumerated in the decrees of that national assembly.

NOTE

1. The equivocation of the Assembly regarding Jewish civil equality especially aggrieved the Sephardim (Jews of Spanish and Portuguese origin) of Bordeaux and Bayonne. Residing in France (initially as "New Christians") from the sixteenth century, these Jews were highly acculturated Frenchmen. Moreover, by virtue of letters of patent issued by several French monarchs these Jews had tacitly enjoyed extensive civil rights for some two hundred years. They thus argued that their eligibility for citizenship was not to be considered in connection with the Ashkenazim of Alsace and Lorraine. The Sephardim emphasized that the two communities were quite distinct socially, culturally and legally. This argument prevailed, and together with the Jews of Avignon, who had also obtained letters of patent from the *ancien régime,* their "civil rights" were confirmed by the Assembly. This recognition of Jews, even if only a specific category of Jews, served as an important precedent.

Source: M. Diogene Tama, *Transactions of the Parisian Sanhedrin,* trans. F. D. Kirwan (London, 1807), pp. 3–4.

THE FRENCH NATIONAL ASSEMBLY

4. The Constitution of France (September 3, 1791)

Title 1. Fundamental Regulations Guaranteed by the Constitution. The Constitution guarantees, as national and civil rights, (1) That all the citizens are admissible to places and employments, without any other distinction than that of *virtue* and talents.... (3) Liberty to every man to... exercise the religious worship to which he is attached.

NOTE

1. These provisions of the new constitution set the stage for the extension of rights of the citizen to all Jewish residents of France.

Source: Benjamin Flower, ed. and trans., *The French Constitution* (London, 1792), pp. 20–23.

THE FRENCH NATIONAL ASSEMBLY

5. The Emancipation of the Jews of France (September 28, 1791)[1]

The National Assembly, considering that the conditions requisite to be a French citizen, and to become an active citizen, are fixed by the constitution, and that every man who, being duly qualified, takes the civic oath, and engages to fulfil all the duties prescribed by the constitution, has a right to all the advantages it insures;

Annuls all adjournments, restrictions, and exceptions, contained in the preceding decrees, affecting individuals of the Jewish persuasion, who shall take the civic oath, which shall be considered as a renunciation of all privileges in their favor.[2]

NOTES

1. All remaining reservations regarding the applicability of the Declaration of the Rights of Man and of the Citizen to the Jews were removed in this resolution of the National Assembly which explicitly recognized the Jews as full citizens of France. Adrien Duport, a member of the Jacobin Club, who presented the resolution for adoption by the Assembly, argued that the inviolability of the principle of religious freedom, and indirectly all the principles of the constitution, would be assured only if it were consistently applied. "I believe that freedom of worship," he concluded, "does not permit any distinction in the political rights of citizens on account of their creed. The question of the political existence of the Jews has been [repeatedly] postponed. Still the Muslims and the men of all sects are admitted to enjoy political rights in France. I demand that the motion of postponement be withdrawn, and a decree passed that the Jews in France enjoy the privileges of full citizens [*citizens actifs*]" (Achille-Edmond Halphen, *Recueil des Louis,* p. 229).

2. The reference is to the communal autonomy that the European Jews enjoyed in the Middle Ages. Such autonomy was deemed to be incompatible with the principles of the modern state.

Source: M. Diogene Tama, *Transactions of the Parisian Sanhedrin,* trans. F. D. Kirwan (London, 1807), pp. 6–7.

BERR ISAAC BERR

6. Letter of a Citizen to His Fellow Jews[1]

Gentlemen and dear brethren,

At length the day has come when the veil, by which we were kept in a state of humiliation, is rent; at length we recover those rights which have been taken from us more than eighteen centuries ago. How much are we at this moment indebted to the clemency of the God of our forefathers!

We are now, thanks to the Supreme Being, and to the sovereignty of the nation, not only

Source: Berr Isaac Berr, "Lettre d'un Citoyen" (Nancy, 1791), M. Diogene Tama, *Transactions of the Parisian Sanhedrin*, trans. F. D. Kirwan (London, 1807), pp. 11–29.

Men and Citizens, but we are Frenchmen! What a happy change thou hast worked in us, merciful God! So late as the twenty-seventh of September last, we were the only inhabitants of this vast empire who seemed doomed to remain forever in bondage and abasement; and on the following day, on the twenty-eighth, a day for ever sacred among us, thou inspirest the immortal legislators of France. They pronounce, and more than sixty thousand unfortunate beings, mourning over their sad fate, are awakened to a sense of their happiness by the liveliest emotions of the purest joy. Let it be acknowledged, dearest brethren, that we have not deserved this wonderful change by our repentence, or by the reformation of our manners: we can attribute it to nothing but to the everlasting goodness of God: He never forsook us entirely: but, finding that we were not yet worthy of seeing the accomplishment of his promises of a perfect and lasting redemption, he has not, however thought proper still to aggravate our sufferings: and surely our chains had become the more galling from the contemplation of the rights of man, so sublimely held forth to public view. Therefore, our God, who reads the heart of man, seeing that all our resignation would have proved unequal to the task, and that supernatural strength was wanting to enable us to support these new torments, has thought of applying the remedy: He has chosen the generous French nation to reinstate us in our rights, and to effect our regeneration, as, in other times, he had chosen Antiochus, Pompey, and others, to humiliate and enslave us. How glorious it is for that nation, who have, in so short a time, made so many people happy! And surely, if Frenchmen are become so themselves, by the additional rights and the additional liberty they have just acquired, how much the more are we, in particular, gainers by the change! And what bounds can there be to our gratitude for the happy event. From being vile slaves, mere serfs, a species of men merely tolerated and suffered in the empire, liable to heavy and arbitrary taxes, we are, of a sudden, become the children of the country, to bear its common charges, and share in its common rights.

What orator could presume to express to the French nation and to its king, all the extent of our gratitude, and of our unalterable submission? But neither the king nor the representatives of the nation seek for praises or acknowledgments; their only wish is to behold people happy. In that they expect and they will find their reward. Let us then, dear brethren, let us conform to their wishes; let us examine with attention what remains to be done, on our part, to become truly happy, and how we may be able to show, in some measure, our grateful sense for all the favors heaped upon us. On this subject, gentlemen and dear brethren, give me leave to submit to your judgment the result of some reflections, which our change of condition has suggested to me.

The name of active citizen, which we have just obtained, is, without a doubt, the most precious title a man can possess in a free empire; but this title alone is not sufficient; we should possess also the necessary qualifications to fulfil the duties annexed to it: we know ourselves how very deficient we are in that respect; we have been in a manner compelled to abandon the pursuit of all moral and physical sciences, of all sciences, in short, which tend to the improvement of the mind, in order to give ourselves up entirely to commerce, to be enabled to gather as much money as would insure protection, and satisfy the rapacity of our persecutors. . . .

I cannot too often repeat to you how absolutely necessary it is for us to divest ourselves entirely of that narrow spirit, of Corporation and Congregation, in all civil and political matters, not immediately connected with our spiritual laws; in these things we must absolutely appear simply as individuals, as Frenchmen, guided only by a true patriotism and by the general good of the nation; to know how to risk our lives and fortunes for the defence of the country, to make ourselves useful to our fellow citizens, to deserve their esteem and their friendship, to join our efforts to theirs in maintaining public tranquility, on which that of individuals depends.

Let us do for the present what is within our power, let us take the civic oath of being faithful to the nation, to the law and to the king. This oath contains only the sentiments we have always professed. We have never been accused of being breakers of the law, or of having rebelled even against those who domineered over us; we have always respected and obeyed even those by whom we were ill-treated: we shall then, upon much stronger grounds, remain faithful to laws which reinstate us in our rights, and place us, on the same footing with all Frenchmen, leaving us at the same time, at full liberty to profess our religion, and to follow our mode of worship. This oath, I say, which, on our side, is nothing but a renunciation of those presented privileges and immunities which we enjoyed, cannot, under any point of view, wound the conscience of the most orthodox and the most scrupulous of our brethren; our privileges and our immunities were only relative to our state of slavery.

This oath once taken, let us exert ourselves to fulfil the duties within our reach, but let us avoid grasping at our rights; let us not rush headlong against the opinions of some of our fellow citizens who, rendered callous by prejudice, will reject the idea of Jews being fellow men, fellow creatures. Let it be sufficient for us, at present, to have acquired the invaluable right of assisting at all assemblies of French citizens; but let us not attend them, till we have acquired knowledge sufficient to make ourselves useful members; till we know how to discuss and defend the interests of the country; in short, till our most bitter enemies are convinced, and acknowledge the gross misconceptions they had entertained of us. . . .

Our education has been defective in many points of view. Already the famous Rabbi Hartwig Wessely, of Berlin, has rendered us an eminent service, by publishing several works in Hebrew on this subject. One of his productions, entitled [*Words of Peace and Truth*][2] has been translated into French, in the year 1782. It details the causes of our present ignorance, and the means by which we may deserve once more the appellation of the learned and intelligent nation, which God himself gave us. I shall not repeat here what you find in these useful publications; but I entreat you, dear brethren, to follow this author in his meditations; and you will easily remark that our fate, and the fate of our posterity, depends solely on the change we shall effect in our mode of education. . . .

French ought to be the Jews' mother tongue, since they are reared with and among Frenchmen; it has always been the language in which they have made the least proficiency, and which very often they scarcely understand. It is only when compelled by necessity to speak to and to be understood by their neighbours that they begin to blunder some inarticulate words; from hence proceeds this other inconvenience, that those among us who have felt early enough the usefulness of the French language, and have acquired the habit of speaking it with facility, cannot, however, get rid of a German or other foreign accents. Their diction, too, is generally incorrect. I even must say myself, that while I am thus addressing you in French, I feel my want of experience and of proficiency in that language, which I have however chosen in preference, to prove to you, that Jews may commune together and confer with one another in that language, on all topics even on religious matters, and that it is entirely in our powers to avoid encumbering the minds of our youth with the useless study of foreign languages. Have we not the example of the Jews of Asia, the most devout and the most scrupulous of our brethren, who read and write only Hebrew and the language of their country? Why should we continue to bear the name of German or Polish Jews, while we are happily French Jews?. . .

Let us establish charitable houses of industry, in which the children of poor people and those who are not born to a higher rank, shall learn all the trades and mechanical occupations necessary to society. Let us form among us carpenters, smiths, tailors, etc. And if we can succeed in having a man in each profession, able to work as a master, he will soon form apprentices; and gradually we shall see Jewish workmen who will strive to deserve esteem by earning honourably their livelihood. Thus shall we banish sloth and indolence, occasioned by the idleness of our youth. . . .

If we have been reproached at one time with want of industry, indolence and aversion to labour, let us now avoid such reproaches, which might be unjust formerly, but which we should now deserve. Let us exert all our influence to accustom our poor, who, till now, have been fed by our alms, to prefer the gains of labour, even at the sweat of their brows.

In thus imparting to you my humble ideas on our present situation, I am, dear brethren, fulfilling a duty the most congenial to my feelings. My thoughts, as you may see, are presented to you in a crude state: it is by your attention and by your meditations, should you deem [my thoughts] worthy, that they are to be matured and quickened into action. Whatever success may attend them, I hope, at least, that you shall do justice to the fraternal sentiments, which unmixed with any other motives, have urged me to exhort and press you, dear brethren, not to lose one moment in taking our situation into your consideration.

I have the honour to be most fraternally, your most obedient and very humble servant,

Berr Isaac Berr

NOTES

1. Berr Isaac Berr (1744–1828), a successful merchant and banker from Nancy. He was prominent in efforts against the defamation of Jewry and in the Jewish struggle for civil equality. In 1789, he was one of six delegated by the Jewish community of Alsace and Lorraine to present their case for civil protection and rights before the National Assembly. He later served successively as a member of the Assembly of Jewish Notables and the Parisian Sanhedrin. Among his literary works is a translation into French of Naphtali Herz Wessely's *Words of Peace and Truth* (see chapter 2, document 8) under the title *Instructions Salutaires Adressées aux Communautés Juives de l'Empire de Joseph II* (Paris, 1790).

On the morning of the resolution of the National Assembly emancipating all the Jews of France, Berr dispatched this letter to the Jewish congregations of Alsace and Lorraine.

2. See chapter 2, document 8.

THE ROMAN REPUBLIC
7. First Emancipation in Rome (February 1799)[1]

Whereas in accordance with the principles sanctified by the Constitutional Act of the Roman Republic all laws must be common and equal for all Roman citizens, the following Law is hereby decreed: Jews who meet all conditions prescribed for the acquisition of Roman citizenship shall be subject solely to the laws common to all citizens of the Roman Republic. Accordingly, all laws and particular regulations concerning Jews shall be null and void forthwith.

Source: Raphael Mahler, ed. and trans., *Jewish Emancipation, A Selection of Documents,* Pamphlet Series, Jews and the Post-War World, no. 1 (New York: The American Jewish Committee, 1941), p. 28. Reprinted by permission of the American Jewish Committee.

NOTE

1. France's armies, fighting under the banner of the principles of the Revolution, introduced democratic government and Jewish emancipation to the lands of their conquest (e.g., Belgium, the Netherlands, southern Germany, Italy).

THE CENTRAL GOVERNMENT OF PADUA
8. Abolition of the Ghetto in Padua (August 28, 1797)

Liberty Equality

In the Name
Of the French Republic
One and Indivisible

The Central Government of the Paduan Delta Districts of Rovigo and Adria, having heard the reports of the Department of Justice and the Chief of Police, decrees:

First, that the Hebrews are at liberty to live in any street they please;

Second, that the barbarous and meaningless name of Ghetto, which designates the street which they have been inhabiting hitherto, shall be substituted by that of Via Libera.

A copy of these present decisions shall be sent to all the district municipalities so that they may be executed by the respective police departments in the most congenient manner.

Padua, Fruttidoro 11, year V of the French Republic and year I of Italian Liberty.

Source: Raphael Mahler, ed. and trans., *Jewish Emancipation, A Selection of Documents,* Pamphlet Series, Jews and the Post-War World, no. 1 (New York: The American Jewish Committee, 1941), pp. 28–29. Reprinted by permission of the American Jewish Committee.

THE CENTRAL GOVERNMENT OF PADUA
9. Destruction of the Ghetto Walls in Padua (September 15, 1797)

Liberty Equality

In the Name
Of the French Republic
One and Indivisible

The Central Government of the Paduan Delta Districts of Rovigo and Adria, having heard the report of Department III for Legislation and Chief of Police about the proposed levelling to the ground of the Gates, Arches and simple precinct Walls of the former Ghetto, and whereas it is necessary to remove all vestiges of a separation which is contrary to the rights of free Men, and whereas the said levelling is consistent with the new title of Via Libera given to that residential section, and as following the Government Decree of Fruttidoro 11, decrees:

Source: Raphael Mahler, ed. and trans., *Jewish Emancipation, A Selection of Documents,* Pamphlet Series, Jews and the Post-War World, no.1 (New York: The American Jewish Committee, 1941), p. 29. Reprinted by permission of the American Jewish Committee.

First, that the municipal police committee shall carry out the solemn levelling to the ground of the Gates, Arches and simple precinct Walls of the ex-Ghetto in such a manner that no vestige shall remain of the ancient separation from other neighboring streets.

Second, [that] this performance shall take place in all the communities of the department where Ghettos did exist.

Padua, Fruttidoro 29, year V of the French Republic and year I of Italian Liberty.

NAPOLEON BONAPARTE, EMPEROR OF THE FRENCH, KING OF ITALY

10. Imperial Decree Calling for an Assembly of Jewish Notables (May 30, 1806)[1]

On the report which has been made to us, that in many of the northern departments of our empire, certain Jews, following no other profession than that of usurers, have, by the accumulation of the most enormous interests, reduced many husbandmen of these districts to the greatest distress:

We have thought it incumbent on us to lend our assistance to those of our subjects whom rapacity may have reduced to these hard extremities.

These circumstances have, at the same time, pointed out to us the urgent necessity of reviving, among individuals of the Jewish persuasion residing in our dominions, sentiments of civil morality, which, unfortunately, have been stifled in many of them by the abject state in which they have long languished, and which it is not our intention either to maintain, or to renew.

To carry this design into execution, we have determined to call together an assembly of the principal Jews, and to make our intentions known to them by commissioners whom we shall name for that purpose, and who shall, at the same time, collect their opinions as to the means they deem the fittest, to re-establish among their brethren the exercise of mechanical acts and useful professions, in order to replace, by an honest industry, the shameful resources to which many of them resorted, from generation to generation, these many centuries.

To this end, on the report of our Grand Judge, Minister of Justice, of our Minister for the Interior, our Council of State being heard, we have decreed, and do decree as follows:

1. There is a suspension for a year, from the date of the present decree, of all executions of judgment and bond-obligations, except so far as to prevent limitation, obtained against husbandmen, not traders, of the departments of La Sarre, La Roer, Mon Terrible, Upper and Lower Rhine, Rhine and Moselle, and Vosges whenever the bonds entered into by these husbandmen are in favour of Jews.

2. There shall be formed, on the fifteenth of July next, in our good city of Paris, an assembly of individuals professing the Jewish religion and residing in the French territory.[2]

3. The members of this assembly, of the number fixed in the annexed List, shall be chosen in the departments therein named, and nominated by the prefects from among

Source: M. Diogene Tama, *Transactions of the Parisian Sanhedrin*, trans. F. D. Kirwan (London, 1807), pp. 105–8.

the rabbis, the land-holders, and other Jews, the most distinguished by their integrity and their knowledge.[3]

4. In all the other departments of our empire, not mentioned in the aforesaid table, and where men of the Jewish persuasion should reside to the number of one hundred, and less than five hundred, the prefect may name a deputy for every five hundred, and for a higher number, up to one thousand, he may name four deputies, and so on.

5. The deputies thus named shall be in Paris before the tenth of July, and shall send notice of their arrival, and of their place of residence, to the secretary's office of our Minister for the Interior, who shall acquaint them of the place, day, and hour of the meeting.

6. Our Minister for the Interior is charged with the execution of the present decree.

NOTES

1. In January 1806, on his return from the victory at Austerlitz, Napoleon stopped at Strasbourg and received several local delegations' complaints about the "usurious" activities of Jewish moneylenders in Alsace and Lorraine. Inclined to believe these complaints, Napoleon brought the issue before his Council of State, and his imperial decree is the result of these consultations.

2. The Assembly actually was convened on July 29, 1806.

3. The Assembly of Jewish Notables was comprised of 112 prominent businessmen, financiers, rabbis and scholars—all handpicked by the prefects of various government departments of France and Italy.

COUNT MOLÉ[1]

11. Napoleon's Instructions to the Assembly of Jewish Notables (July 29, 1806)

His Majesty, the Emperor and King, having named us Commissioners to transact whatever relates to you, has this day sent us to this assembly to acquaint you with his intentions. Called together from the extremities of this vast empire, no one among you is ignorant of the object for which His Majesty has convened this assembly. You know it. The conduct of many among those of your persuasion has excited complaints, which have found their way to the foot of the throne: these complaints were founded on truth; and nevertheless, His Majesty has been satisfied with stopping the progress of the evil, and he has wished to hear you on the means of providing a remedy. You will, no doubt, prove worthy of so tender, so paternal a conduct, and you will feel all the importance of the trust, thus reposed in you. Far from considering the government under which you live as a power against which you should be on your guard, you will assist it with your experience and cooperate with it in all the good it intends; thus you will prove that, following the example of all Frenchmen, you do not seclude yourselves from the rest of mankind.

The laws which have been imposed on

Source: M. Diogene Tama, *Transactions of the Parisian Sanhedrin*, trans. F. D. Kirwan (London, 1807), pp. 130–34.

individuals of your religion have been different in the several parts of the world: often they have been dictated by the interest of the day. But, as an assembly like the present, has no precedent in the annals of Christianity, so will you be judged, for the first time, with justice, and you will see your fate irrevocably fixed by a Christian Prince. The wish of His Majesty is, that you should be Frenchmen; it remains with you to accept the proffered title, without forgetting that, to prove unworthy of it, would be renouncing it altogether.

You will hear the questions submitted to you, your duty is to answer the whole truth on every one of them. Attend, and never lose sight of that which we are going to tell you; that, when a monarch equally firm and just, who knows every thing, and who punishes or recompenses every action, puts questions to his subjects, these would be equally guilty and blind to their true interests, if they were to disguise the truth in the least.

The intention of His Majesty is, Gentlemen, that you should enjoy the greatest freedom in your deliberations, your answers will be transmitted to us by your President, when they have been put in regular form.

As to us, our most ardent wish is to be able to report to the Emperor, that, among individuals of the Jewish persuasion, he can reckon as many faithful subjects, determined to conform in every thing to the laws and to the morality, which ought to regulate the conduct of all Frenchmen.

One of the secretaries [proceeded to read the following] questions proposed to the Assembly of the Jews by the Commissioners named by His Majesty the Emperor and King. . . .

Is it lawful for Jews to marry more than one wife?

Is divorce allowed by the Jewish religion? Is divorce valid, when not pronounced by courts of justice, and by virtue of laws in contradiction with the French code?

Can a Jewess marry a Christian, or a Jew a Christian woman? Or has the law ordered that the Jews should only intermarry among themselves?

In the eyes of Jews are Frenchmen considered as brethren or as strangers?

In either case what conduct does their law prescribe towards Frenchmen not of their religion?

Do the Jews born in France, and treated by the law as French citizens, consider France as their country? Are they bound to defend it?[2] Are they bound to obey the laws, and to follow the directions of the civil code?

What kind of police-jurisdiction have the Rabbis among the Jews? What judicial power do they exercise among them?[3]

Are the forms of the elections of the Rabbis and their police-jurisdiction regulated by the law, or are they only sanctioned by custom?

Are there professions from which the Jews are excluded by their law?

Does the law forbid the Jews from taking usury from their brethren?

Does it forbid or does it allow usury toward strangers? . . .

NOTES

1. Count Louis Mathieu Molé (1781–1855), a member of the Council of State, he served as one of Napoleon's three commissioners to the Assembly of Notables. As Napoleon's informal advisor on Jewish affairs, he advocated the recision of Jewish emancipation.

2. According to the protocol of this session of the Assembly, the delegates were "not able to conceal the emotions caused by [this] question. . . . The whole Assembly unanimously exclaimed—Even to death" (M. Diogene Tama, *Transactions of the Parisian Sanhedrin,* trans. F. D. Kirwan [London, 1807], pp. 134ff.).

3. The seventh question, "Who names the rabbis?" is missing in M. Diogene Tama's text, *Transactions of the Parisian Sanhedrin.*

ABRAHAM FURTADO

12. Reply on Behalf of the Assembly to Count Molé[1]

Gentlemen Commissioners,

We have listened with all the attention we could command to the intentions of His Majesty the Emperor, which you have just communicated to us.

Chosen by this assembly as the interpreter of its sentiments, I must assure you, in the name of all those who compose it, that, when His Majesty determined to call us together in his capital, in order to further the accomplishment of his glorious designs, we saw, with inexpressible joy, [the] occasion of doing away [with] many errors and putting an end to many prejudices.

The benevolent intentions of His Majesty have offered us an opportunity, most fervently desired this great while, by all honest and enlightened men of the Jewish persuasion, residing in France.

We had, however, but a distant prospect of the epoch which would completely reform habits occasioned by a long state of oppression. Now the moment seems almost at hand, and we owe this precious advantage to the paternal goodness of His Majesty. It was impossible that his exalted mind could, even for an instant, entertain a thought on our situation, without its being materially improved.

We shared, in common with all Frenchmen, the sentiments inspired by that protecting genius which had saved this empire from the rage of party spirit, from the horrors of a bloody anarchy, and from the ambitious designs of its exterior enemies.

We could not suppose that after so many benefits, it could be still possible for him to acquire new rights to our gratitude, or to increase our love for his sacred person. Times of ignorance and of anarchy had always been, for us, days of trials and of misfortune. His Majesty had freed us from any apprehension as to the return of the first of these scourges, the other was chained by his powerful hand. His laws, the establishment of his dynasty, and the return of order, had calmed all the fears we might have entertained of a retrograde motion in the progress of the great science of social economy in France; we flattered ourselves with the hope of progressively enjoying the sweets of so many blessings. The slow but sure regenerations of some of our brethren would have been the result of our new condition. His Majesty wishes to hasten the precious moments, and, through his protecting goodness, we shall enjoy, under his reign, social advantages, which we could expect only from centuries of perseverance.

It is thus that the greatest of heroes becomes the common father of all his subjects; whatever religion they follow, he only sees in them children of the same family.

The enterprise His Majesty undertakes is such as might have been expected from the most astonishing man whose deeds were ever recorded by history. Methinks I see the muse holding her immortal burin, and tracing on her adamant tables, amidst so many deeds, which make this reign so conspicuous, that which the hero of the age has done to destroy utterly the barrier raised between nations and the scattered remains of the most ancient people.

Such is, Gentlemen Commissioners, the point of view under which we consider, with complacency, the communications we have received from you. It confirms us in the idea that no practicable good escapes the penetration of His Majesty, which can be equalled

Source: M. Diogene Tama, *Transactions of the Parisian Sanhedrin,* trans. F. D. Kirwan (London, 1807), pp. 135–38.

only by his goodness, and by the generosity of his heart.

The choice which His Majesty has been pleased to make of you, Gentlemen Commissioners, to convey to us his intentions, adds a new value to the favour he intends for the Jews. The most unlimited confidence will reign between us, in the course of our communications.

While this confidence pleads some excuse for our involuntary errors, it will be a pledge of the purity of our intentions.

Have the goodness, Gentlemen Commissioners, to convey our sentiments to His Majesty, and to assure him that he does not reign over subjects more faithful, or more devoted to his sacred person, than we are.[2]

NOTES

1. Abraham Furtado (1756–1817), a member of the Portuguese-Jewish community of France. He was elected president of the Assembly of Notables; later he served as secretary of the Parisian Sanhedrin. In his capacity as president of the Assembly, Furtado delivered these remarks in response to Count Molé's address (document 11 in this chapter).

2. According to the records of the Assembly, upon the conclusion of Furtado's speech "the hall resounded with repeated cries of 'Long Live the Emperor!'... The Commissioners of His Majesty requested an official receipt for the questions they laid on the table. It was given by the President. Many members manifested their intention of delivering their sentiments [personally] before the Commissioners. But they left the assembly amidst the cries of 'Long Live the Emperor!' " (M. Diogene Tama, *Transactions of the Parisian Sanhedrin,* trans. F. D. Kirwan [London, 1807], p. 138).

THE ASSEMBLY OF JEWISH NOTABLES
13. Answers to Napoleon[1]

Resolved, by the French deputies professing the religion of Moses, that the following Declaration shall precede the answers returned to the questions proposed by the Commissioners of His Imperial and Royal Majesty.

The assembly, impressed with a deep sense of gratitude, love, respect, and admiration, for the sacred person of His Imperial and Royal Majesty, declares, in the name of all Frenchmen professing the religion of Moses, that they are fully determined to prove worthy of the favours His Majesty intends for them, by scrupulously conforming to his paternal intentions; that their religion makes it their duty to consider the law of the prince as the supreme law in civil and political matters; that consequently, should their religious code, or its various interpretations, contain civil or political commands, at variance with those of the French code, those commands would, of course, cease to influence and govern them, since they must, above all, acknowledge and obey the laws of the prince.

That, in consequence of this principle, the Jews have, at all times, considered it their duty to obey the laws of the state, and that, since the revolution, they, like all Frenchmen, have acknowledged no others.

First Question: *Is it lawful for Jews to marry more than one wife?*

Answer: It is not lawful for Jews to marry

Source: M. Diogene Tama, *Transactions of the Parisian Sanhedrin,* trans. F. D. Kirwan (London, 1807) pp. 149–56, 176–95, 201–7.

more than one wife: in all European countries they conform to the general practice marrying only one.

Moses does not command expressly to take several, but he does not forbid it. He seems even to adopt that custom as generally prevailing, since he settles the rights of inheritance between children of different wives. Although this practice still prevails in the East, yet their ancient doctors have enjoined them to restrain from taking more than one wife, except when the man is enabled by his fortune to maintain several.

The case has been different in the West; the wish of adopting the customs of the inhabitants of this part of the world has induced the Jews to renounce polygamy. But as several individuals still indulged in that practice, a synod was convened at Worms in the eleventh century, composed of one hundred Rabbis, with Gershom at their head.[2] This assembly pronounced an anathema against every Israelite who should, in future, take more than one wife.

Although this prohibition was not to last for ever, the influence of European manners has universally prevailed.

Second Question: *Is divorce allowed by the Jewish Religion? Is divorce valid when not pronounced by courts of justice by virtue of laws in contradiction with those of the French Code?*

Answer: Repudiation is allowed by the law of Moses; but it is not valid if not previously pronounced by the French code.

In the eyes of every Israelite, without exception, submission to the prince is the first of duties. It is a principle generally acknowledged among them, that, in every thing relating to civil or political interests, the law of the state is the supreme law. Before they were admitted in France to share the rights of all citizens, and when they lived under a particular legislation which set them at liberty to follow their religious customs, they had the ability to divorce their wives; but it was extremely rare to see it put into practice.

Since the revolution, they have acknowledged no other laws on this head but those of the empire. At the epoch when they were admitted to the rank of citizens, the Rabbis and the principal Jews appeared before the municipalities of their respective places of abode, and took an oath to conform, in every thing to the laws, and to acknowledge no other rules in all civil matters. . . .

Third Question: *Can a Jewess marry a Christian, and a Jew a Christian woman? Or does the law allow the Jews to marry only among themselves?*

Answer: The law does not say that a Jewess cannot marry a Christian, nor a Jew a Christian woman; nor does it state that the Jews can only marry among themselves.

The only marriages expressly forbidden by the law, are those with the seven Canaanite nations, with Amon and Moab, and with the Egyptians. The prohibition is absolute concerning the seven Canaanite nations: with regard to Amon and Moab, it is limited, according to many Talmudists, to the men of those nations, and does not extend to the women; it is even thought that these last would have embraced the Jewish religion. As to Egyptians, the prohibition is limited to the third generation. The prohibition in general applies only to nations in idolatry. The Talmud declares formally that modern nations are not to be considered as such, since they worship, like us, the God of heaven and earth. And, accordingly, there have been, at several periods, intermarriages between Jews and Christians in France, in Spain, and in Germany: these marriages were sometimes tolerated, and sometimes forbidden by the laws of those sovereigns, who had received Jews into their dominions.

Unions of this kind are still found in France; but we cannot deny that the opinion of the Rabbis is against these marriages. According to their doctrine, although the religion of Moses has not forbidden the Jews from intermarrying with nations not of their religion, yet, as marriage, according to the Talmud, requires religious ceremonies called Kiduschim, with the benediction used in such cases, no marriage can be religiously valid unless these ceremonies have been performed. This could not be done towards persons who would not both of them consider these ceremonies as sacred; and in that case the married couple could separate without the religious divorce; they would then be considered as married civilly but not religiously.

Such is the opinion of the Rabbis, members of this assembly. In general they would be no more inclined to bless the union of a Jewess with a Christian, or of a Jew with a Christian woman, than Catholic priests themselves would be disposed to sanction unions of this kind. The Rabbis acknowledge, however, that a Jew, who marries a Christian woman, does not cease on that account, to be considered as a Jew by his brethren, any more than if he had married a Jewess civilly and not religiously.

Fourth Question: *In the eyes of Jews, are Frenchmen considered as their brethren? Or are they considered as strangers?*

Answer: In the eyes of Jews Frenchmen are their brethren, and are not strangers.

The true spirit of the law of Moses is consonant with this mode of considering Frenchmen.

When the Israelites formed a settled and independent nation, their law made it a rule for them to consider strangers as their brethren.

With the most tender care for their welfare, their lawgiver commands to love them, "Love ye therefore the strangers," says he to the Israelites, "for ye were strangers in the land of Egypt."[3] Respect and benevolence towards strangers are enforced by Moses, not as an exhortation to the practice of social morality only, but as an obligation imposed by God himself.[4]

A religion whose fundamental maxims are such—a religion which makes a duty of loving the stranger—which enforces the practice of social virtues, must surely require that its followers should consider their fellow-citizens as brethren.

And how could they consider them otherwise when they inhabit the same land, when they are ruled and protected by the same government, and by the same laws? When they enjoy the same rights, and have the same duties to fulfil? There exists, even between the Jew and Christian, a tie which abundantly compensates for religion—it is the tie of gratitude. This sentiment was at first excited in us by the mere grant of toleration. It has been increased, these eighteen years, by new favours from government, to such a degree of energy, that now our fate is irrevocably linked with the common fate of all Frenchmen. Yes, France is our country; all Frenchmen are our brethren, and this glorious title, by raising us our own esteem, becomes a sure pledge that we shall never cease to be worthy of it.

Fifth Question: *In either case, what line of conduct does their law prescribe towards Frenchmen not of their religion?*

Answer: The line of conduct prescribed towards Frenchmen not of our religion, is the same as that prescribed between Jews themselves; we admit of no difference but that of worshipping the Supreme Being, every one in his own way.

The answer to the preceding question has explained the line of conduct which the law of Moses and the Talmud prescribe towards Frenchmen not of our religion. At the present time, when the Jews no longer form a separate people, but enjoy the advantage of being incorporated with the Great Nation (which privilege they consider as a kind of political redemption), it is impossible that a Jew should treat a Frenchman, not of his religion, in any other manner than he would treat one of his Israelite brethren.

Sixth Question: *Do Jews born in France, and treated by the laws as French citizens, consider France their country? Are they bound to defend it? Are they bound to obey the laws and to conform to the dispositions of the civil code?*

Answer: Men who have adopted a country, who have resided in it these many generations—who, even under the restraint of particular laws which abridged their civil rights, were so attached to it that they preferred being debarred from the advantages common to all other citizens, rather than leave it—cannot but consider themselves as Frenchmen in France; and they consider as equally sacred and honourable the bounden duty of defending their country.

Jeremiah (chapter 29) exhorts the Jews to

consider Babylon as their country, although they were to remain in it only for seventy years. He exhorts them to till the ground, to build houses, to sow, and to plant. His recommendation was so much attended to, that Ezra (chapter 2) says, that when Cyrus allowed them to return to Jerusalem to rebuild the Temple, 42,360 only, left Babylon; and that this number was mostly composed of the poor people, the wealthy having remained in that city.

The love of the country is in the heart of Jews a sentiment so natural, so powerful, and so consonant to their religious opinions, that a French Jew considers himself in England, as among strangers, although he may be among Jews; and the case is the same with English Jews in France.

To such a pitch is this sentiment carried among them, that during the last war, French Jews have been seen fighting desperately against other Jews, the subjects of countries then at war with France.

Many of them are covered with honourable wounds, and others have obtained, in the field of honour, the noble rewards of bravery.

Seventh Question: *Who names the Rabbis?*

Answer: Since the revolution, the majority of the chiefs of families names the Rabbi, wherever there is a sufficient number of Jews to maintain one, after previous inquiries as to the morality and learning of the candidate. This mode of election is not, however, uniform: it varies according to place, and, to this day, whatever concerns the elections of Rabbis is still in a state of uncertainty.

Eighth Question: *What police jurisdiction do Rabbis exercise among the Jews? What judicial power do they enjoy among them?*

Answer: The Rabbis exercise no manner of Police Jurisdiction among the Jews.

It is only in the Mishnah and in the Talmud that the word Rabbi is found for the first time applied to a doctor in the law; and he was commonly indebted for this qualification to his reputation, and to the opinion generally entertained of his learning.

When the Israelites were totally dispersed, they formed small communities in those places where they were allowed to settle in certain numbers.

Sometimes, in these circumstances, a Rabbi and two other doctors formed a kind of tribunal, named Beth Din, that is, House of Justice; the Rabbi fulfilled the functions of judge, and the other two those of his assessors.

The attributes, and even the existence of these tribunals, have, to this day, always depended on the will of governments under which the Jews have lived, and on the degree of tolerance they have enjoyed. Since the revolution those rabbinical tribunals are totally suppressed in France, and in Italy. The Jews, raised to the rank of citizens, have conformed in every thing to the laws of the state; and, accordingly, the functions of Rabbis, wherever any are established, are limited to preaching morality in the temples, blessing marriages, and pronouncing divorces. . . .

Ninth Question: *Are these forms of Election, and that police-jurisdiction, regulated by law, or are they only sanctioned by custom?*

Answer: The answer to the preceding questions makes it useless to say much on this, only it may be remarked, that, even supposing that Rabbis should have, to this day, preserved some kind of police-judicial-jurisdiction among us, which is not the case, neither such jurisdiction, nor the forms of the elections, could be said to be sanctioned by the law; they should be attributed solely to custom.

Tenth Question: *Are there professions which the law of the Jews forbids them from exercising?*

Answer: There are none: on the contrary, the Talmud (vide Kiduschim, chapter 1) expressly declares that "the father who does not teach a profession to his child, rears him up to be a villain."

Eleventh Question: *Does the law forbid the Jews from taking usury from their brethren?*

Answer: Deuteronomy says, "thou shalt not lend upon interest to thy brother, interest of money, interest of victuals, interest of any thing that is lent upon interest."[5]

The Hebrew word *neshekh* has been improperly translated by the word usury: in the Hebrew language it means interest of any kind, and not usurious interest. It cannot then be taken in the meaning now given the word usury.

Twelfth Question: *Does it forbid or does it allow to take usury from strangers?*

Answer: We have seen, in the answer to the foregoing question, that the prohibition of usury, considered as the smallest interest, was a maxim of charity and of benevolence, rather than a commercial regulation. In this point of view it is equally condemned by the law of Moses and by the Talmud: we are generally forbidden, always on the score of charity, to lend upon interest to our fellow-citizens of different persuasions, as well as to our fellow-Jews.

The disposition of the law, which allows to take interest from the stranger, evidently refers only to nations in commercial intercourse with us; otherwise there would be an evident contradiction between this passage and twenty others of the sacred writings.[6]

Thus the prohibition extended to the stranger who dwelt in Israel; the Holy Writ places them under the safe-guard of God; he is a sacred guest, and God orders us to treat him like the widow and like the orphan.

Can Moses be considered as the lawgiver of the universe, because he was the lawgiver of the Jews? Were the laws he gave to the people, which God had entrusted to his care, likely to become the general laws of mankind? Thou shalt not lend upon interest to thy brother. What security had he, that, in the intercourse which would be naturally established between the Jews and foreign nations, these last would renounce customs generally prevailing in trade, and lend to the Jews without requiring any interest? Was he then bound to sacrifice the interest of his people, and to impoverish the Jews to enrich foreign nations? Is it not absolutely absurd to reproach him with having put a restriction to the precept contained in Deuteronomy? What lawgiver but would have considered such a restriction as a natural principle of reciprocity?

How far superior in simplicity, generosity, justice, and humanity, is the law of Moses, on this matter, to those of the Greeks and of the Romans! Can we find, in the history of the ancient Israelites, those scandalous scenes of rebellion excited by the harshness of creditors towards their debtors, those frequent abolitions of debts to prevent the multitude, impoverished by the extortions of lenders, from being driven to despair?

The law of Moses and its interpreters have distinguished, with a praiseworthy humanity, the different uses of borrowed money. Is it to maintain a family? Interest is forbidden. Is it to undertake a commercial speculation, by which the principal is adventured? Interest is allowed, even between Jews. Lend to the Poor, says Moses. Here the tribute of gratitude is the only kind of interest allowed; the satisfaction of obliging is the sole recompense of the conferred benefit. The case is different in regard to capitals employed in extensive commerce: there, Moses allows the lender to come in for a share of the profits of the borrower; and as commerce was scarcely known among the Israelites, who were exclusively addicted to agricultural pursuits, and as it was carried on only with strangers, that is with neighbouring nations, it was allowed to share its profits with them. . . .

It is an incontrovertible point, according to the Talmud, that interest, even among Israelites, is lawful in commercial operations, where the lender, running some of the risk of the borrower, becomes a sharer in his profits. This is the opinion of all Jewish doctors.

It is evident that opinions, teeming with absurdities, and contrary to all rules of social morality, although advanced by a Rabbi, can no more be imputed to the general doctrine of the Jews, than similar notions, if advanced by Catholic theologians, could be attributed to the evangelical doctrine. The same may be said of the general charge made against the Hebrews, that they are naturally inclined to usury: it cannot be denied that some of them are to be found, though not so many as is generally supposed, who follow that nefarious traffic condemned by their religion.

But if there are some not over-nice in this particular, is it just to accuse one hundred thousand individuals of this vice? Would it not be deemed an injustice to lay the same imputation on all Christians because some of them are guilty of usury?[7]

NOTES

1. The committee's answers were adopted by the Assembly at three successive sittings, on the fourth, the seventh and the twelfth of August 1806.

2. Although theoretically permissible, polygamy was discouraged by the sages of the Talmud and it was explicitly prohibited among Ashkenazi Jewry by a ban popularly attributed to Rabbi (Rabbenu) Gershom ben Jehuda (c. 960–1028), German talmudic scholar and spiritual leader.

3. Deut. 10:19.

4. The following passages from Scripture are cited: Exod. 22:21 and 23:9; Lev. 19:34 and 23:22; Deut. 10:18–19 and 24:19; Psalms 145:9; and several talmudic texts.

5. Deut. 23:19.

6. The following passages from Scripture are cited: Exod. 12:49ff.; Deut. 1:16 and 10:18–19; Lev. 19:33; Exod. 22:21; Lev. 25:15.

7. The Assembly, after concluding the adoption of the answers to the questions posed by Napoleon, declared the fifteenth of August, the Emperor's birthday, as a day Jewry would celebrate with "prayers, thanksgiving, and all the demonstrations of a pure and lively joy" (M. Diogene Tama, *Transactions of the Parisian Sanhedrin*, trans. F. D. Kirwan [London, 1807], p. 212).

COUNT MOLÉ
14. Summons for Convening the Parisian Sanhedrin (September 18, 1806)[1]

His Majesty the Emperor and King is satisfied with your answers; we are commanded by him to say, that he has approved the sense in which they are written; but the communication we are going to make in his name will prove, much better than our words, to what extent this assembly may depend on his powerful protection.

In entering this hall for the second time, Gentlemen, we are impressed with the same sentiments, and the same ideas which occurred to us when we were first admitted into it. And who could behold without astonishment such a society of enlightened men, chosen among the descendants of the most ancient people the world? If one of those, who lived in former years, could again visit this world, and were to be introduced into such an assembly, would he not think himself brought into the middle of the Holy City, or would he not suppose that a terrible revolution had renewed, from the very foundations, the state of all human things? In this he would not be mistaken, Gentlemen. It is after a revolution which threatened to swallow up all nations, thrones, and empires, that altars and thrones are raised everywhere from their ruins to protect the earth; a furious multitude attempted to destroy everything: a man has appeared, and has restored everything; his eye embraces the whole world and past centuries even to their very origin; he has the wandering remnants of a nation, rendered as famous by its fall as others are by

Source: M. Diogene Tama, *Transactions of the Parisian Sanhedrin*, trans. F. D. Kirwan (London, 1807), pp. 242–47.

their greatness, scattered over the face of the earth: it was just that he should consider their situation, and it was right to expect that these same Jews, who hold such a distinguished place in the memory of mankind, should fix the attention of the man who is to occupy it eternally.

The Jews, exposed to the contempt of nations, and not unfrequently to the avarice of princes, have never, as yet, been treated with Justice. Their customs and their practices kept them afar from society, by which they were rejected in their turn; they have always attributed the ill-conduct and the vices, laid to their charge, to the humiliating laws which oppressed them. Even to this day they attribute the backwardness for agricultural pursuits and useful employments, manifested by some of them to the little reliance which they can place on futurity, after having been, for so many centuries, the sport of circumstances, and seeing their very existence depend on the whim of men in power: they will have no cause to complain in future, and this ground of defence will be taken from them.

His Majesty's intention is, that no plea shall be left to those who may refuse to become citizens; the free exercise of your religious worship and the full enjoyment of your political rights, are secured to you. But, in return for his gracious protection, His Majesty requires a religious pledge for the strict adherence to the principles contained in your answers. This assembly, constituted as it is now, could not of itself give such a security. Its answers, converted into decisions by another assembly, of a nature still more dignified and more religious, must find a place near the Talmud, and thus acquire, in the eyes of the Jews of all countries and of all ages, the greatest possible authority. It is also the only means left to you to meet the grand and generous views of His Majesty, and to impart, to all of your persuasion, the blessings of this new era.

The purity of your law has, no doubt, been altered by the crowd of commentators, and the diversity of their opinions must have thrown doubts in the minds of those who read them. It will be then a most important service, conferred on the whole Jewish community, to fix their belief on those points which have been submitted to you. To find in the history of Israel, an assembly capable of attaining the object now in view, we must go back to the Great Sanhedrin,[2] and it is the Great Sanhedrin, which His Majesty this day intends to convene. This senate, destroyed together with the temple, will rise again to enlighten the people it formerly governed: although dispersed throughout the whole world, it will bring back the Jews to the true meaning of the law, by giving interpretations, which shall set aside the corrupted glosses of commentators; it will teach them to love and to defend the country they inhabit; but will convince them that the land, where, for the first time since their dispersion, they have been able to raise their voice, is entitled to all those sentiments which rendered their ancient country so dear to them.

Lastly, the Great Sanhedrin, according to ancient custom, will be composed of seventy members, exclusive of the President. Two thirds, or thereabout, shall be Rabbis, and among them, in the first place, those who sit among you, and who have approved the answers. The other third shall be chosen, by this assembly itself, among its members, by ballot. The duties of the Great Sanhedrin shall be to convert into religious doctrines the answers already given by this assembly, and likewise those which may result from the continuation of your sittings.

For you will observe, Gentlemen, your mission is not yet fulfilled; it will last as long as that of the Great Sanhedrin, which will only ratify your answers and give them a greater weight; His Majesty is, besides, too well satisfied with your zeal and with the purity of your intentions, to dissolve this assembly before the accomplishment of the great work in which you were called to assist.

In the first instance it is fit that you should name by ballot a committee of nine members to prepare, with us, the ground-work of your future discussions and of the decisions of the Sanhedrin. You will observe that the Portuguese, German, and Italian Jews, are equally represented in this committee. We also invite you to acquaint the several Synagogues of Europe of the meeting of the Great Sanhedrin, without delay, that they may send deputies able to give the government additional information, and worthy of communicating with you.

NOTES

1. This statement was read before the Assembly of Notables.

2. The Great Sanhedrin in Palestine was the supreme religious and juridical body of Jewry during the Roman period, both before and after the destruction of the Temple, until the abolishment of the patriarchate (c. 425 C.E.). No institution in Judaism has since possessed its authority. The announcement of the revival of this ancient symbol of Jewish sovereignty naturally evoked, as Napoleon intended, awe, messianic presentiments and spontaneous feelings of gratitude toward the French emperor.

THE PARISIAN SANHEDRIN
15. Doctrinal Decisions[1]

Blessed for ever be the name of the Lord, God of Israel, who has placed upon the thrones of France and of the Kingdom of Italy a prince after His heart. God has seen the humiliation of the descendants of Jacob of old, and He has chosen Napoleon the Great as the instrument of His compassion. The Lord judges the thoughts of men, and He alone commands their conscience, and His anointed one permits all men to worship Him according to their belief and faith. Under the shadow of his name security has come into our hearts and our dwellings and from this time on we are permitted to build, to sow, to reap, to cultivate all human knowledge, to be one with the great family of the State, to serve him and to be glorified in his lofty destiny. His high wisdom permits this assembly, which shall be illustrious in our annals, and the wisdom and virtue of which shall dictate decisions, to reconvene after the lapse of fifteen centuries, and to contribute to the welfare of Israel. Gathered this day under his mighty protection, in the good city of Paris, we, learned men and leaders of Israel, to the number of seventy-one, constitute ourselves the Grand Sanhedrin to the end that we may find the means and the strength to promulgate religious decrees which shall conform to the principles of our sacred laws and which shall serve as a standard to all Israelites. These decrees shall teach the nations that our dogmas are in keeping with the civil laws under which we live, and that we are in no wise separated from the society of men.

We therefore declare that the divine Law, the precious heritage of our ancestors, contains within itself dispositions which are political and dispositions which are religious: that the religious dispositions are, by their nature, absolute and independent of circumstances and of the age; that this does not hold true of the political dispositions, that is to say, of the dispositions which were taken for the government of the people of Israel in Palestine when it possessed its own kings, pontiffs

Source: Edmond Fleg, ed., *The Jewish Anthology,* trans. M. Samuel (New York: Harcourt, Brace and Co., 1925), pp. 255–56. Reprinted by permission of Behrman House.

and magistrates; that these political dispositions are no longer applicable, since Israel no longer forms a nation; that in consecrating a distinction which has already been established by tradition, the Grand Sanhedrin lays down an incontestible truth; that an assembly of Doctors of the Law, convened as a Grand Sanhedrin, is alone competent to determine the results of this distinction: that, if the Sanhedrin of old did not establish this distinction, it is because the political situation did not at that time call for it, and that, since the dispersion of Israel, no Sanhedrin has ever been assembled until the present one.

Engaged in this holy enterprise, we invoke the divine light, from which all good emanates, and we feel ourselves called upon to contribute, as far as in our power lies, to the completion of the moral regeneration of Israel. Thus, by virtue of the right vested in us by our ancient usage and by our sacred laws, which have determined that the assembly of the learned of the age shall possess the inalienable right to legislate according to the needs of the situation, and which impose upon Israel the observance of these laws—be they written or contained in tradition—we hereby religiously enjoin on all obedience to the State in all matters civil and political.

NOTE

1. The Sanhedrin met in Paris from February to April 1807. It solemnly endorsed the decisions of the Assembly of Notables, giving them the "spiritual" sanction that Napoleon desired.

RABBI GERSHOM MENDES SEIXAS
16. An American Rabbi's Sermon on the Convening of the Parisian Sanhedrin[1]

Among the many events, predicted by the Prophets, to take place, previous to the restoration of Israel, to their former glory and pre-eminence, the Convention of our brethren in Zarephath,[2] may be viewed, as one of not the least extraordinary, for under the auspices of the most powerful potentate of Europe, [Napoleon Bonaparte] after the lapse of seventeen Centuries since our Captivity, he has collected the most learned of our Rabbonim, who reside in his dominions, and invited every one, who incline to attend from other countries, to assemble in his metropolis, to form a Sanhedrin, for what purpose, or what their business will be, we can not pretend to say. Many things are conjectured, but none to be depended on, from what motives they were convened, we have no more knowledge of, than what is published to the whole world. At present every thing appears in a favorable train, but no one can say with precision, how it will terminate; let us pray that the God of Israel may so direct them, that they may not be involved in difficulty, and may be able to avert every possible evil; that they may find favor in the sight of their Emperor, that he under the influence of divine grace, may be a means to accomplish our reestablishment if not as a nation in our former territory, let it only be as a particular

Source: "Minutes of the Spanish and Portuguese Congregation of New York—J. J. Lyons Collection," *Publications of the American Jewish Historical Society,* 2, no. 27 (1920), pp. 140ff. Reprinted by permission of the American Jewish Historical Society.

society, with equal rights and privileges of all other religious societies. This circumstance alone calls forth our gratitude to God, for His benignity, in having preserved us a distinct body, among all nations....

NOTES

1. Rabbi Gershom Mendes Seixas (1746–1816), first native-born rabbi in the United States and prominent in Jewish and national affairs. The sermon was delivered on the second Shevat 5567, i.e., January 11, 1807.

2. The Hebrew name for France.

THE HASIDIM OF POLAND
17. Reaction to Napoleon[1]

In the time of Napoleon's campaign against the Czar Rabbi Menahem Mendel of Rymanov[2] sought to see the war as the messianic struggle of Gog and Magog,[3] and in order to hasten the redemption he prayed that Napoleon should be victorious. Should the battle, he contended, entail the spilling of the blood of Israel until one would wade in it up to the knees from Przytyk[4] to Rymanov it would be good so long as the end of days would come and thus our redemption. The Zaddikim of Koznitz[5] and Lublin[6] did not agree with him, however. They prayed that Napoleon would fall in battle, for in their revelations the end of days had not yet come. The story is told that when passing through the town of Koznitz, Napoleon disguised himself as a simple man and went to the house of the Zaddik. But the Zaddik recognized him, and raising the Scroll of Esther, uttered: "You will surely fall Napoleon, you will surely fall!"[7]

The saintly Rabbi of Ropshits[8]—who was at the time still in his youth and lived in the town of Dukla[9]—agreed with the Zaddikim of Koznitz and Lublin. He thus journeyed to Rymanov in order to persuade Rabbi Mendel to withdraw his support of Napoleon. He arrived in Koznitz on the eve of Passover—a day when a great and fierce battle was taking place, Rabbi Mendel was in his house, standing before the oven holding *matzos* ready to be baked, and repeatedly saying, "another five hundred Russians will fall." And so it was in battle.... And suddenly the Rabbi of Ropshits entered Rabbi Mendel's house and shouted, "But Rabbi, Napoleon is ritually unclean, and the unclean must defer the celebration of the Jews' redemption from bondage!"[10] Then he fled from the house. Rabbi Mendel commanded that the Rabbi of Ropshits be brought before him, but he was not to be found, for he had already escaped on a wagon which had been waiting to take him home to Dukla.

At the beginning of the year 5574 (1813), on the Day of Atonement before the afternoon prayer, Rabbi Mendel of Rymanov told the

Source: Naphtali Horowitz of Ropshits, *Ohel Naphtali*, ed. Avraham Haim Simha Bunam (Lemberg, 1912), p. 13b; and Rabbi Menahem Mendel of Rymanov, *Ateret Menahem*, ed. Avraham Haim Simha Bunam (Lublin, 1910), p. 38b. Trans. here by P. Mendes-Flohr. The first two paragraphs of the document are from the former volume, the last paragraph is from the latter. Both these volumes are collections of talks, stories and teachings by and about Hasidic masters (*Zaddikim*).

Rabbi of Ropshits, who was the cantor, to pray that Napoleon might be victorious. But the Rabbi of Ropshits of Blessed Memory did not wish for Napoleon's victory, and after the Day of Atonement he travelled to the Seer of Lublin to learn how he might work for Napoleon's defeat. The Seer of Lublin refused to assist him, declaring [he was no longer opposed to Napoleon]![11] The Rabbi of Ropshits then travelled to Koznitz, arriving for the Holy Sabbath on which the portion of the Scripture concerning Jethro are read.[12] The Rabbi of Koznitz was at the time in the *mikveh* [ritual bath], so that the Rabbi of Ropshits went and lay on his bed. When the Rabbi of Koznitz came home from the *mikveh* and desired to lie on his bed, the Rabbi of Ropshits did not allow him to do so until he, the Rabbi of Koznitz, promised [to entreat God against Napoleon]. On the eve of the Holy Sabbath, when the hymn for the Sabbath was recited the Rabbi of Koznitz uttered a prayer: "It is said that the French have retreated from Moscow to the river Berezina.[13] We beseech Thee that they may be destroyed for ever and ever. Thou art above the world, O Lord. . . ." The next day, at the reading of the Torah he cried: "You will wither, Napoleon, you will fall." And thus the Rabbi of Ropshits forced the Rabbi of Koznitz to adopt his view [concerning Napoleon], although he initially held the opinion of Rabbi Mendel of Rymanov.

NOTES

1. As Napoleon's armies moved eastward, the vast traditional Jewish community of East Europe was undecided as to whether to regard Napoleon as a latter-day Cyrus, as an agent of divine redemption, or as a diabolical source of secularism.

2. Rabbi Menahem Mendel of Rymanov (d. 1815), a leading Hasidic master in Galicia. Rymanov is a town in the Rzeszow province of southeast Poland; Galicia embraces what is today southeastern Poland and northwestern Ukrainian S.S.R. With the various partitions of Poland at the end of the eighteenth century, Galicia became a province within the Hapsburg Empire.

3. See Ezek. 38 and 39, in which the prophet relates his vision that the end of days will be heralded by a war of the Lord against "Gog of the land of Magog." In rabbinic literature, Gog and Magog are parallel names for the enemies of Israel who are to be vanquished at the end of days.

4. Town in east central Poland where Rabbi Mendel was born.

5. Rabbi Israel ben Shabbetai Hapstein (1733–1814). Because of his eloquence he was also known as the Maggid (the preacher) of Koznitz. Koznitz (Koznienicie, Kozenitsy) is a town in Kielce province, of east central Poland.

6. Rabbi Jacob Isaac, the "Seer" of Lublin (1745–1815). A renowned Zaddik and master of theurgic mysticism, he was one of the founders of Hasidim in Poland and Galicia. Lublin is a city in eastern Poland. Although like many Zaddikim he saw the Napoleonic wars in a messianic perspective, he initially withheld his "support" for Napoleon. In 1813, after the retreat of the French army from Moscow, he reversed his position and began to employ his theurgic powers on behalf of Napoleon.

7. The incantation is from Esther 6:13.

8. Rabbi Naphtali Horowitz of Ropshits (1760–1827), a disciple of both Rabbi Menahem Mendel of Rymanov and the Maggid of Koznitz. According to legend, the Rabbi of Ropshits feared that Napoleon would bring evil upon the Jews of Poland, viz., he would conscript the Jews into military service, oblige their attendance at Gentile schools and induce unbelief. Ropshits (Ropezye) is a town in Rzeszow province, southeast Poland.

9. Town near Rymanov in the province of Rzeszow, of southeast Poland.

10. "And there were certain men who were unclean through touching the dead body of a man, so they would not keep the Passover on that day. . . . The Lord said to Moses, 'Say to the people of Israel, if any man of you or of your descendants is unclean through the touching of a dead body . . . he shall keep the Passover to the Lord a month later'" (Num. 9:6ff.). By referring to this injunction, the Rabbi of Ropshits sought to indicate that Napoleon did not fulfill the religious prescriptions required of a messianic agent.

11. See note 6, above. On the Feast of Tabernacles 5475 (1814) the Seer met with the Maggid of

Koznitz and the Zaddik of Rymanov in order to hasten the war of Gog and Magog by the means of prayer. All three of these Zaddikim died that very year. According to Hasidic legend, it was the hand of God that brought their death as punishment for their endeavor "to force the end."

12. Exod. 18–20. The passage is read in the Hebrew month Shevat, which falls in early winter.

13. A tributary of the river Dnieper in Belorussia. At Borisov, a major town on the Berezina, Napoleon incurred heavy casualties during his 1812 retreat from Moscow when he was forced to cross the river.

FREDERICK WILLIAM III
18. Emancipation in Prussia (March 11, 1812)[1]

We, Frederick William, by the Grace of God, King of Prussia, etc., have resolved to grant the adherents of the Jewish faith in Our monarchy a new constitution suitable to the general welfare, and declare all laws and regulations concerning Jews (issued) hitherto, which are not confirmed by the present Edict as abolished, and decree as follows:

1. Jews and their families domiciled at present in Our States, provided with general privileges, patent letters of naturalization, letters of protection and concessions, are to be considered as natives [*Einlaender*] and as Prussian state citizens.

2. The continuance of this qualification as natives and state citizens conferred upon them shall however be permitted only under the following obligation: that they bear strictly fixed family names, and that they use German or another living language not only in keeping their commercial books but also upon drawing their contracts and declaratory acts, and that they should use no other than German or Latin characters for their signatures. . . .

4. After having declared and determined his family name, everyone shall receive a certificate from the Provincial Government of his domicile that he is a native and a citizen of the state, which certificate shall be used in the future for himself and his descendants in place of the letter of protection. . . .

7. Jews considered as natives . . . shall enjoy equal civil rights and liberties with Christians, in so far as this Order does not contain anything to the contrary.

8. They may therefore administer academic school teaching and municipal offices for which they qualified themselves.

9. As far as the admission of Jews to other public services and government offices is concerned, We leave to Ourselves its regulation by law in course of time.

10. They are at liberty to settle in the towns as well as in the open country.

11. They may acquire real estate of any kind same as the Christian inhabitants and they may carry on any permitted trade, with the provision that they observe the general legal regulations.

12. Freedom of trade ensuing from the right of state citizenship also includes commerce. . . .

14. Native Jews as such must not be burdened with special taxes.

15. They are, however, bound to fulfill all civic duties towards the State and the community of their domicile which Christians are obliged [to carry out] and to bear imposts

Source: Raphael Mahler, ed. and trans., *Jewish Emancipation, A Selection of Documents,* Pamphlet Series, Jews and the Post-War World, no. 1 (New York: The American Jewish Committee, 1941), pp. 32–35. Reprinted by permission of the American Jewish Committee.

equal to those of other citizens, with the exception of surplice fees.[2]

16. Native Jews are also subject to military conscription or to the duty of serving in their cantons as well as to all other special regulations in connection therewith. The way and manner in which this obligation shall be applied to them, shall be determined in a more detailed manner by the regulation on military conscription.

17. Native Jews may contract marriages among themselves without a special permit for it, or without having to take out a marriage license in so far as no previous consent or permission to contract a marriage depending on others is at all required under the general rules. . . .

20. The civil legal relations of Jews shall be judged by the same laws which serve as the rule for other Prussian state citizens. . . .

29. With regard to competence of a court and to administration by guardianship connected therewith, likewise no difference between Christians and Jews shall take place. Only in Berlin shall the special competence of a court assigned to Jews remain in force for the time being.

30. Under no conditions are Rabbis or Jewish Elders permitted to assume any court jurisdiction nor to institute or direct guardianship proceedings.

31. Foreign Jews are not permitted to take up residence in these States as long as they have not acquired Prussian state citizenship. . . .

36. Foreign Jews may enter the country in transit or for the purpose of carrying on permissible commerce and other business. The Police authorities will be provided with a special instruction concerning the procedure to be observed by them and against them.

37. Concerning the prohibition of peddling in general, Police laws shall remain the same also with respect to Jews.

38. In Koenigsberg, in Prussia, Breslau and Frankfurt on the Oder, foreign Jews may stay for the duration of the fairs with the permission of the authorities.

39. The necessary regulations concerning the church conditions and the improvement in the education of Jews shall be reserved [for later issue], and when these will be considered, men of the Jewish persuasion who enjoy public confidence because of their knowledge and righteousness shall be called in and their judgment consulted.

All Our Government authorities and subjects shall be guided accordingly.

NOTES

1. The establishment of constitutional governments after the French model in the countries conquered by Napoleon induced those states, e.g., Prussia, which remained free of French rule, to consider liberal reforms. This decree, signed by the Prussian monarch, grants the Jews full civil rights; paragraphs 8 and 9 of the decree, however, were sufficiently vague to exclude Jews from judgeships, the officer corps and administrative positions. In 1822, an amendment to the decree explicitly repealed paragraph 8. After the fall of Napoleon, this decree was the most liberal legislation concerning the Jews in a German state until the stillborn constitutions of 1848. The states of southern Germany (e.g., Wuerttemberg, Baden and Bavaria) did not grant their Jews full civil rights; noticeably excluded were the rights to full freedom of trade and to free movement and residence. In the Kingdom of Saxony the Jews did not enjoy equality of rights in trade and industry; they were also forbidden to worship in public.

2. Payment to clergy for marriage and funeral services.

THE CONGRESS OF VIENNA

19. Article 16 (June 8, 1815)[1]

In the Name of the Most Holy and Indivisible Trinity.

The difference among Christian religious parties shall not form the basis of any distinction in the enjoyment of civil and political rights in the lands and areas of the German Confederation.

The Diet of the Confederation shall take into consideration the means of effecting, in the most uniform manner, an amelioration in the civil states of the confessor of the Jewish faith in Germany, as well as the means for providing and guaranteeing for the same the enjoyment of civil rights in the Confederated States in return for their assumption of all the obligations of citizens. Until then, however, the rights of the adherents of this creed already granted to them by the individual Confederated States shall be maintained.

NOTE

1. The Congress of Vienna (from September 1814 to June 1815), a conference of European leaders that was called to discuss the political structure of Europe after the defeat of Napoleon; the congress also gave witness to the formation of the German Confederation. Although the defunct Holy Roman Empire's several hundred principalities were replaced by a thirty-six-state Confederation, the states were hardly more interested in a strong centralized Germany than were the principalities. They jealously guarded their sovereignty and their local institutions and practices. Thus the firm rejection of Prussia's proposal (suggested by Austria and Hanover) that the Prussian decree of 1812 concerning the Jews serve as the basis of policy toward the Jews throughout the Confederation. Federal legislation concerning the Jews was postponed to the envisaged Federal Diet, which, in turn, ignored the matter. The only immediately effective measure was a guarantee of the rights accorded the Jews previously "*by* the individual Confederated States." At the last moment, the latter phrase was hastily substituted for the original formula: "*in* the individual Confederated States." The individual states were thus obliged to affirm only legislation enacted *by* their sovereign institutions and, accordingly, they were permitted to rescind the emancipation of the Jews decreed by foreign powers. As finally adopted, Article 16 constituted a serious setback in the struggle for Jewish emancipation in Central Europe.

Source: The Confederate Acts of the Fundamental Agreement of the German Confederation, in Raphael Mahler, ed. and trans., *Jewish Emancipation, A Selection of Documents,* Pamphlet Series, Jews and the Post-War World, no. 1 (New York: The American Jewish Committee, 1941), p. 38. Reprinted by permission of the American Jewish Committee.

HEINRICH PAULUS AND GABRIEL RIESSER

20. The Paulus-Riesser Debate[1]

PROFESSOR HEINRICH PAULUS:[2] The main point is this. . . . As long as the Jews believe that their continued existence as Jews must be in accordance with the Rabbinic-Mosaic spirit [*Gesinnung*], no nation could grant them civil rights. Civil rights [are to be denied the Jews] because they apparently wish to remain a nation apart, for they conceive of their religious objectives in such a way that they perforce remain a nation apart from those nations which have provided them with shelter. . . . One cannot seek or obtain civil rights from any nation if one wishes to continue to belong to a different nation and believes one should persist in theis adherence. Clearly, granting civil rights presupposes that [the recipient] belongs to the nation which grants these rights and not to any other nation. Jewry, however, dispersed over the entire earth, aspires to preserve through [endogamous] marriage customs and its many particularistic and exclusive laws its nationhood and apartness.

Therefore, it is only possible to grant the Jews (as one specific association in our society) no more than the status of "tolerated residents" [*Untertanenschutz*] or at best that of "protected residents" [*Schutzbuergerschaft*]. And notwithstanding their egregious religion, they should have no reason or desire to insist upon their own national identity. This renunciation must be emphatic and tangible. The Jews must demonstrate that they belong solely to the country of their residence and accept the national identity of that country. They must demonstrate that they no longer consider themselves as members of a necessarily separate, self-sufficient people of God.

DR. GABRIEL RIESSER:[3] To be sure, the Jews were once a nation. But they ceased to be one some two thousand years ago as have most other nations whose descendants constitute the states of present-day Europe. [When the Jews ceased to be a nation], they were dispersed throughout all the provinces of the Roman Empire and were subject to the same legal provisions that applied to other peoples subjugated by the Romans. After the Peregrinic reforms[4] they enjoyed equal rights as Roman citizens. Their creed was not an obstacle here. Although Roman law did preserve the purity of the Roman cult, it is known that the rule of conduct in and out of Rome allowed non-Romans the rights to preserve their own cult, and did not see this as a basis for the exclusion of non-Romans from civil rights.

The charge that our forefathers immigrated here centuries or millennia ago is as fiendish as it is absurd. We are not immigrants; we are native born. And, since that is the case, we have no claim to a home someplace else. We are either German or we are homeless. Does someone seriously wish to use our original, foreign descent against us? Does someone with that civilized status revert back to the barbarous principle of indigenous rights? . . .

Religion has its creed; the state its laws. The confession of a creed constitutes a religious affiliation; obedience to laws determines citizenship in a state. The confusion of these principles leads to misunderstanding,

Source: H. E. G. Paulus, *Die juedische Nationalabsonderung nach Ursprung, Folgen und Besserungsmitteln, oder ueber Pflichten, Rechte und Verordungen zur Verbesserung der juedischen Schutzbuergerschaft in Deutschland* (Heidelberg, 1831), pp. 2–3; and Gabriel Riesser, "Verteidigung der buergerlichen Glueckstellung der Juden gegen die Einwuerke des Herrn Dr. H. E. G. Paulus" (May 1831), in Gabriel Riesser, *Gesammelte Schriften*, published for Das Comite der Riesser-Stiftung, ed. Z. Isler (Leipzig, 1867), vol. 2, pp. 131, 133, 150, 152, 183ff. Trans. here by M. Gelber and P. Mendes-Flohr.

thoughtlessness and falsehood. . . . There is only one baptism that can initiate one into a nationality, and that is the baptism of blood in the common struggle for a fatherland and for freedom. "Your blood was mixed with ours on the battlefield," this was that cry which put an end to the last feeble stirrings of intolerance and antipathy in France.[5] The German Jews also have earned this valid claim to nationality. The Jews in Germany fulfill their military obligations in all instances. They did so even before the Wars of Liberation. They have fought both as conscripts and volunteers in proportionate numbers within the ranks of the German forces. . . .

We the Jews of Germany might indeed enjoy a degree of freedom. But we conceive of freedom differently. We struggle and strive with all of our might to obtain a higher freedom than that which we presently enjoy; we are committed to struggle and to strive [to obtain this freedom] until the very last breath of our lives—this is what we believe makes us worthy to be *German* and to be called *German*. The vigorous tones of the German language and the songs of German poets ignite and nurture the holy fire of freedom in our breast. The breath of freedom which wafts over Germany awakens our dormant hopes for freedom, of which many happy prospects have already been fulfilled. We wish to belong to the German fatherland. We can, and should, and may be required by the German state [to do] all that it justly requires of its citizens. We will readily sacrifice everything for this state: not, however, belief and loyalty, truth and honor, for Germany's heroes and Germany's sages have not taught us that one becomes a German through such sacrifices.

NOTES

1. After the Congress of Vienna the Jewish question became a major issue in Germany. The debate between Professor Heinrich E. G. Paulus and the young Jewish jurist Gabriel Riesser gave a particularly poignant focus to the issues of the debate.

2. Heinrich Paulus (1761–1851), professor of Oriental languages and theology at the University of Heidelberg.

3. Gabriel Riesser (1806–1863). After trying in vain to secure a university lectureship in jurisprudence and after being barred from practice as a notary in his native Hamburg because of his Judaism, Riesser devoted his life to the struggle for Jewish emancipation. He propagated his views in the journal *Der Jude: Periodische Blaetter der Religion und Gewissensfreiheit,* which he founded in 1831 and published until 1833.

4. The reference is to the *Constitutio Antoniniana* of 212 C.E.. This decree extended Roman citizenship to all free inhabitants of the empire, thus obliterating the distinction between Romans and provincials, between conquerors and conquered, between urban and rural dwellers, and between those who possessed Graeco-Roman culture and those who did not. Promulgated by Caracalla, emperor from 211 to 217 C.E., this legislation culminated a process initiated by Julius Caesar.

5. Even prior to their emancipation, the Jews of France—especially in Bordeaux and Paris—volunteered for the various militias formed during the revolution. This fact was raised and regarded favorably during the debates in the National Assembly concerning the eligibility of Jews for citizenship.

THOMAS MACAULAY[1]

21. Civil Disabilities of the Jews

In order to contribute our share to the success of just principles, we propose to pass in review, as rapidly as possible, some of the arguments, or phrases claiming to be arguments, which have been employed to vindicate a system full of absurdity and injustice.

The constitution—it is said—is essentially Christian; and therefore to admit Jews to office is to destroy the constitution. Nor is the Jew injured by being excluded from political power. For no man has any right to power. A man has a right to his property; a man has a right to be protected from personal injury. These rights the law allows to the Jew, and with these rights it would be atrocious to interfere. But it is a mere matter of favour to admit any man to political power; and no man can justly complain that he is shut out from it.

We cannot but admire the ingenuity of this contrivance for shifting the burden of the proof from off those to whom it properly belongs, and who would, we suspect, find it rather cumbersome. Surely no Christian can deny that every human being has a right to be allowed every gratification which produces no harm to others, and to be spared every mortification which produces no good to others. Is it not a source of mortification to any class of men that they are excluded from political power? They have on Christian principles, a right to be freed from that mortification, unless it can be shown that their exclusion is necessary for the averting of some greater evil. The presumption is evidently in favour of toleration. It is for the persecutor to make out his case. . . .

It is because men are not in the habit of considering what the end of government is, that Catholic disabilities and Jewish disabilities have been suffered to exist so long. We hear of essentially Protestant governments and essentially Christian governments —words which mean just as much as essentially Protestant cookery, or essentially Christian horsemanship. Government exists for the purpose of keeping the peace, for the purpose of compelling us to settle our disputes by arbitration, instead of settling them by blows, for the purpose of compelling us to supply our wants by industry, instead of supplying them by rapine. This is the only operation for which the machinery of government is fit, the only operation which wise governments ever attempt to perform. If there is any class of people who are not interested, or who do not think themselves interested, in the security of property and the maintenance of order, that class ought to have no share of the powers which exist for the purpose of securing property and maintaining order. But why a man should be less fit to exercise that power because he wears a beard, because he does not eat ham, because he goes to the synagogue on Saturdays instead of going to the church on Sundays, we cannot conceive.

The points of difference between Christianity and Judaism have very much to do with a man's fitness to be a bishop or a rabbi. But they have no more to do with his fitness to be a magistrate, a legislator, or a minister of finance, than with his fitness to be a cobbler. Nobody has ever thought of compelling cobblers to make any declaration on the true faith of a Christian. Any man would rather have his shoes mended by a heretical cobbler, than by a person who had subscribed to all the thirty-nine articles, but had never han-

Source: Maurice Cross, ed., *Selections from the Edinburgh Review* (London: Longman, 1833), vol. 3, pp. 667–75.

dled an awl. Men act thus, not because they are indifferent to religion, but because they do not see what religion has to do with the mending of their shoes. Yet religion has as much to do with the mending of shoes, as with the budget and the army estimates. . . .

But it would be monstrous, say the persecutors, that a Jew should legislate for a Christian community. This is a palpable misrepresentation. What is proposed is not that Jews should legislate for a Christian community, but that a legislature composed of Christians and Jews should legislate for a community composed of Christians and Jews. On nine hundred and ninety-nine questions out of a thousand, on all questions of police, of finance, of civil and criminal law, of foreign policy, the Jew, as a Jew, has no interest hostile to that of the Christian, or even of the Churchman. On questions relating to the ecclesiastical establishment, the Jew and the Churchman may differ. But they cannot differ more widely than the Catholic and the Churchman, or the Independent and the Churchman. The principle, that Churchmen ought to monopolise the whole power of the state, would at least have an intelligible meaning. The principle, that Christians ought to monopolise it, has no meaning at all. For no question connected with the ecclesiastical institutions of the country can possibly come before Parliament, with respect to which there will not be as wide a difference between Christians as there can be between any Christian and any Jew.

In fact, the Jews are not now excluded from political power. They possess it; and as long as they are allowed to accumulate property, they must possess it. The distinction which is sometimes made between civil privileges and political power, is a distinction without a difference. Privileges are power.

That a Jew should be a judge in a Christian country, would be most shocking. But he may be a juryman. He may try issues of fact; and no harm is done. But if he should be suffered to try issues of law, there is an end of the constitution. . . .

What power in civilised society is so great as that of the creditor over the debtor? If we take this away from the Jew, we take away from him the security of his property. If we leave it to him, we leave to him a power more despotic by far, than that of the King and all his cabinet.

It would be impious to let a Jew sit in Parliament. But a Jew may make money, and money may make members of Parliament. . . .

That a Jew should be privy-councillor to a Christian king, would be an eternal disgrace to the nation. But the Jew may govern the money market, and the money market may govern the world. . . . A congress of sovereigns may be forced to summon the Jew to their assistance. The scrawl of the Jew on the back of a piece of paper may be worth more than the royal word of three kings, or the national faith of three new American republics. But that he should put Right Honourable before his name, would be the most frightful of national calamities. . . .

It is our duty as Christians to exclude the Jews from political power, it must be our duty to treat them as our ancestors treated them—to murder them, and banish them, and rob them. For in that way, and in that way alone, can we really deprive them of political power. If we do not adopt this course, we may take away the shadow, but we must leave them the substance. We may do enough to pain and irritate them; but we shall not do enough to secure ourselves from danger, if danger really exists. Where wealth is, there power must inevitably be.

The English Jews, we are told, are not Englishmen. They are a separate people, living locally in this island, but living morally and politically in communion with their brethren, who are scattered over all the world. An English Jew looks on a Dutch or a Portuguese Jew as his countryman, and on an English Christian as a stranger. This want of patriotic feeling, it is said, renders a Jew unfit to exercise political functions.

The argument has in it something plausible; but a close examination shows it to be quite unsound. Even if the alleged facts are admitted, still the Jews are not the only people who have preferred their sect to their country. The feeling of patriotism, when society is in a healthful state, springs up, by a natural and inevitable association, in the minds of citizens who know that they owe all their comforts and pleasures to the bond which unites them in one community. But under partial and oppressive governments, these associations cannot acquire that strength which they have in a better state of things. Men are compelled to seek from their party that protection which they ought to receive from their country, and they, by a natural consequence, transfer to their party that affection which they would otherwise have felt for their country. . . . It has always been the trick of bigots to make their subjects miserable at home, and then complain that they look for relief abroad; to divide society, and to wonder that it is not united; to govern as if a section of the state were the whole, and to censure the other sections of the state for their want of patriotic spirit. If the Jews have not felt towards England like children, it is because she has treated them like a stepmother.

Rulers must not be suffered thus to absolve themselves of their solemn responsibility. It does not lie in their mouths to say that a sect is not patriotic: it is their business to make it patriotic. History and reason clearly indicate the means. The English Jews are, as far as we can see, precisely what our government has made them. They are precisely what any sect—what any class of men selected on any principle from the community, and treated as they have been treated—would have been. If all the red-haired people in Europe had, for centuries, been outraged and oppressed, banished from this place, imprisoned in that, deprived of their money, deprived of their teeth, convicted of the most improbable crimes on the feeblest evidence, dragged at horses' tails, hanged, tortured, burned alive, if, when manners became milder, they had still remained subject to debasing restrictions, and exposed to vulgar insults, locked up in particular streets, in some countries, pelted and ducked by the rabble in others, excluded everywhere from magistracies and honours, what would be the patriotism of gentlemen with red hair? And if, under such circumstances, a proposition were made for admitting red-haired men to office, how striking a speech might an eloquent admirer of our old institutions deliver against so revolutionary a measure! "These men," he might say, "scarcely consider themselves as Englishmen. They think a red-haired Frenchman or a red-haired German more closely connected with them than a man with brown hair born in their own parish. If a foreign sovereign patronises red hair, they love him better than their own native king. They are not Englishmen—they cannot be Englishmen—nature has forbidden it—experience proves it to be impossible. Right to political power they have none; for no man has a right to political power. Let them enjoy personal security; let their property be under the protection of the law. But if they ask for leave to exercise power over a community of which they are only half members—a community, the constitution of which is essentially dark-haired—let us answer them in the words of our wise ancestors, *Nolumus leges Angliae mutari.*" [We are not willing to change the laws of England.]

But, it is said, the Scriptures declare that the Jews are to be restored to their own country; and the whole nation looks forward to that restoration. They are, therefore, not so deeply interested as others in the prosperity of England. It is not their home, but merely the place of their sojourn—the house of their bondage. . . .

A man who should act, for one day, on the supposition that all the people about him were influenced by the religion which they professed, would find himself ruined before night: and no man ever does act on that supposition, in any of the ordinary concerns of life, in borrowing, in lending, in buying, or in selling. But when any of our fellow-creatures are to be oppressed, the case is different. Then we represent those motives which we know to be so feeble for good as omnipotent for evil. Then we lay to the charge of our victims all the vices and follies to which their doctrines, however remotely, seem to tend. . . .

People are now reasoning about the Jews, as our fathers reasoned about the Papists. The law which is inscribed on the walls of the synagogues prohibits covetousness. But if we were to say that a Jew mortgagee would not foreclose because God had commanded him not to covet his neighbour's house, everybody would think us out of our wits. Yet it passes for an argument to say, that a Jew will take no interest in the prosperity of the country in which he lives, that he will not care how bad its laws and police may be, how heavily it may be taxed, how often it may be conquered and given up to spoil, because God has pronounced, that by some unknown means, and at some undetermined time, perhaps a thousand years hence, the Jews shall migrate to Palestine. Is not this the most profound ignorance of human nature? Do we not know that what is remote and indefinite affects men far less than what is near and certain? Besides, the argument applies to Christians as strongly as to Jews. The Christian believes, as well as the Jew, that at some future period the present order of things will come to an end. Nay, many Christians believe that the Messiah will shortly establish a kingdom on the earth, and reign visibly over all its inhabitants. Whether this doctrine be orthodox or not, we shall not here enquire. The number of people who hold it is very much greater than the number of Jews residing in England. Many of those who hold it are distinguished by rank, wealth, and talent. It is preached from pulpits, both of the Scottish and of the English Church. Noblemen and members of Parliament have written in defence of it. Now, wherein does this doctrine differ, as far as its political tendency is concerned, from the doctrine of the Jews? If a Jew is unfit to legislate for us, because he believes that he or his remote descendants will be removed to Palestine, can we safely open the House of Commons to a fifth-monarchy man, who expects that, before this generation shall pass away, all the kingdoms of the earth will be swallowed up in one divine empire?

Does a Jew engage less eagerly than a Christian in any competition which the law leaves open to him? Is he less active and regular in business than his neighbors? Does he furnish his house meanly, because he is a pilgrim and sojourner in the land? Does the expectation of being restored to the country of his fathers render him insensible to the fluctuations of the Stock Exchange? Does he, in arranging his private affairs, ever take into account the chance of his returning to Palestine? If not, why are we to suppose that feelings which never influence his dealings as a merchant, or his dispositions as a testator, will acquire a boundless influence over him as soon as he becomes a magistrate or a legislator?

There is another argument which we would not willingly treat with levity, and which yet we scarcely know how to treat seriously. The Scriptures, it is said, are full of terrible denunciations against the Jews. It is foretold, that they are to be wanderers. Is it, then, right to give them a home? It is foretold, that they are to be oppressed. Can we with propriety suffer them to be rulers? To admit them too the rights of citizens, is manifestly to insult the Divine oracles.

We allow, that to falsify a prophecy inspired by Divine Wisdom would be a most atrocious crime. It is, therefore, a happy circumstance for our frail species, that it is a crime which no man can possibly commit. If we admit the Jews to seats in Parliament, we shall, by so doing, prove that the prophecies in question, whatever they may mean, do not mean that the Jews shall be excluded from Parliament. . . .

But we protest altogether against the practice of confounding prophecy with precept —of setting up predictions which are often obscure against a morality which is always clear. If actions are to be considered as just and good merely because they have been predicted, what action was ever more laudable than that crime which our bigots are now, at the end of eighteen centuries, urging us to avenge on the Jews—that crime which made the earth shake, and blotted out the sun from heaven? If this argument justifies the laws now existing against the Jews, it justifies equally all the cruelties which have ever been committed against them—the sweeping edicts of banishment and confiscation, the dungeon, the rack, and the slow fire, . . .

We have not so learned the doctrines of Him who commanded us to love our neighbour as ourselves, and who, when He was called upon to explain what He meant by a neighbour, selected as an example a heretic and an alien. Last year, we remember, it was represented by a pious writer in the *John Bull* newspaper, and by some other equally fervid Christians, as a monstrous indecency, that the measure for the relief of the Jews should be brought forward in Passion week. One of these humourists ironically recommended, that it should be read a second time on Good Friday. We should have had no objection; nor do we believe that the day could be commemorated in a more worthy manner. We know of no day fitter for terminating long hostilities, and repairing cruel wrongs, than the day on which the religion of mercy was founded. We know of no day fitter for blotting out from the statute book the last traces of intolerance, than the day on which the spirit of intolerance produced the foulest of all judicial murderers; the day on which the list of victims of intolerance—that noble list in which Socrates and more are enrolled—was glorified by a yet more awful and sacred name.

NOTE

1. Thomas Macaulay (1800–1859), English historian, essayist and politician. Elected to Parliament in 1830, he made his first speech at the second reading of the bill for the Removal of Jewish Disabilities in April of that year. In an article in the *Edinburgh Review* of January 1831, excerpts of which appear here, he argued the same cause. This support expressed by one of England's leading men of letters had a significant effect on public opinion.

THE FRANKFURT PARLIAMENT
22. Religious Equality (December 27, 1848)[1]

The Imperial Regent [*Reichsverwesser*] in execution of the resolution of the National Assembly of December 21, 1848, proclaims as law:

I. The Fundamental Rights of the German People. The following rights shall be granted to the German people. They shall serve as a norm for the Constitution of the individual German states and no constitution or legislation of an individual German state may abolish or restrict them. . . .

Article 5. . . . Paragraph 14. Every German has full freedom of faith and conscience. Nobody shall be forced to disclose his religious creed. . . .

Paragraph 16. The enjoyment of civil or political rights shall be neither conditioned nor limited by religious confession.

Source: "Law Concerning the Fundamental Rights of the German People," in Raphael Mahler, ed. and trans., *Jewish Emancipation, A Selection of Documents,* Pamphlet Series, Jews and the Post-War World, no. 1 (New York: The American Jewish Committee, 1941), p. 49. Reprinted by permission of the American Jewish Committee.

The same religious confession should not impair civil duties.

Paragraph 17. . . . No religious association shall benefit from any state prerogatives before others. No state church shall exist henceforth.

NOTE

1. The revolutions of 1848 that spread throughout Europe were inspired by liberal democratic principles, among them full civil and political equality for the Jews. The Frankfurt National Parliament, which superceded the Diet of the Germanic Confederation, established a provisional government, headed by Archduke John of Austria. Lacking material power (e.g., an army), this government never established its authority, and the attempt to unite Germany under a liberal, parliamentary system soon failed. The constitution, promulgated by the Assembly in March 1849 and incorporating the Fundamental Rights, became obsolete in a few months. Nonetheless, it established important moral and legislative precedents that made it difficult to return to the pre-revolutionary situation. Aside from southern Germany where Jewish civil disabilities generally persisted, the right to vote and to be elected, although frequently questioned, was preserved. Moreover, the cause of Jewish emancipation won the strong support of liberals. Until 1869 the Jews were still restricted by law from administrative and juridical positions.

THE HOUSES OF PARLIAMENT
23. The Jewish Relief Act (July 23, 1858)[1]

Be it enacted by the Queen's Most Excellent Majesty, by and with the Advice and Consent of the Lords Spiritual and Temporal, and Commons, in this present Parliament assembled, and by the Authority of the same, as follows:

1. Where it shall appear to either House of Parliament that a Person professing the Jewish Religion, otherwise entitled to sit and vote in such House, is prevented from so sitting and voting by his conscientious objection to take the Oath which by an Act passed or [is] to be passed in the present Session of Parliament has been or may be substituted for the Oaths of Allegiance, Supremacy, and Abjuration in the Form therein required, such House if it think fit, may resolve that thenceforth any Person professing the Jewish Religion, in taking the said oath to entitle him to sit and vote as aforesaid, may omit the words "and I make this Declaration upon the true Faith of a Christian," and so long as such Resolution shall continue in force the said Oath, when taken and subscribed by any Person professing the Jewish Religion to entitle him to sit and vote in that House of Parliament may be modified accordingly, and the taking and subscribing by any Person professing the Jewish Religion of the Oath so modified shall, so far as respects the Title to sit and vote in such House, have the same Force and Effect as the taking and subscribing by other Persons of the said Oath in the Form required by the said Act.

2. In all other Cases, except for sitting in Parliament as aforesaid, or in qualifying to exercise the Right of Presentation to any Ecclesiastical Benefice in Scotland, whenever any of Her Majesty's Subjects professing the Jewish Religion shall be required to take the

Source: A Collection of the Public General Statutes (London, 1858), pp. 258–59.

said Oath, the words "and I make this Declaration upon the true Faith of a Christian" shall be omitted.

3. Nothing herein contained shall extend or be construed to extend to enable any Person or Persons professing the Jewish Religion to hold or exercise the Office of Guardians and Justices of the United Kingdom, or of Regent of the United Kingdom, under whatever Name, Style, or Title such office may be constituted, or of Lord High Chancellor, Lord Keeper or Lord Commissioner of the Great Seal of Great Britain, or Ireland, or the office of Lord Lieutenant or Deputy or other Chief Governor or Governors of Ireland, or Her Majesty's High Commissioner to the General Assembly of the Church of Scotland.

4. Where any Right of Presentation to any Ecclesiastical Benefice shall belong to any office in the Gift or Appointment of Her Majesty, Her Heirs or Successors, and such office shall be held by a Person professing the Jewish Religion, the Right of Presentation shall devolve upon and be exercised by the Archbishop of Canterbury for the time being and it shall not be lawful for any Person professing the Jewish Religion, directly or indirectly, to advise Her Majesty, Her Heirs or Successors, or any Person or Persons holding or exercising the Office of Guardians of the United Kingdom, or of Regent of the United Kingdom, under whatever Name, Style, or Title such office may be constituted or the Lord Lieutenant or Lord Deputy, or any other Chief Governor or Governors of Ireland, touching or concerning the Appointment to or Disposal of any Office or Preferment in the United Church of England and Ireland, or in the Church of Scotland, and if such Person shall offend in the Premises, he shall, being thereof convicted by due course of Law, be deemed guilty of a high Misdemeanor, and disabled for ever from holding any Office, Civil or Military under the Crown.

NOTE

1. In Great Britain the process of emancipation occurred gradually through a series of separate legislative acts. The elimination of the Christian oath as a prerequisite for legislative office removed a serious obstacle in the attainment of political rights for Jews.

WILHELM I
24. North German Confederation and Jewish Emancipation (July 3, 1869)[1]

We, Wilhelm, by the Grace of God, King of Prussia, etc. with the approval of the Bundesrath and of the Reichstag decree in the name of the North German Confederation as follows:

All still existent restrictions on civil and

Source: "Law Concerning the Equality of All Confessions in Respect to Civil Rights and Political Rights," in Raphael Mahler, ed. and trans., *Jewish Emancipation, A Selection of Documents,* Pamphlet Series, Jews and the Post-War World, no. 1 (New York: The American Jewish Committee, 1941), pp. 57–58. Reprinted by permission of the American Jewish Committee.

political rights derived from the difference in religious confession are hereby repealed. In particular, the qualification for participation in communal and provincial representative bodies and for holding public offices shall be independent of religious confession.

Authentically under Our Most High Signature and with the Seal of the Confederation affixed.

Done at the Castle of Babelsberg, July 3, 1869.

NOTE

1. Under the leadership of Chancellor Otto von Bismarck (1815–1898), Prussia led the fragmented states of Germany to a genuine unification. To facilitate this program, Bismarck sought the cooperation of the National Liberal party and, in turn, made economic and political concessions to liberalism, including the removal of all remaining civil and political disabilities due to differences of religious affiliation.

WILHELM I
25. Emancipation in Bavaria (April 22, 1871)[1]

We, Wilhelm, by the grace of God, German Emperor, King of Prussia, etc., Decree, in the name of the German Reich, following the approval of the Bundesrath and the Reichstag, as follows:

1. The laws of the North German Confederation cited in the following paragraphs shall be introduced in the Kingdom of Bavaria as laws of the Reich, according to the detailed stipulations contained in these paragraphs.

2. From the day on which the present law goes into effect the following shall be in force: . . . (10) the law of July 3, 1869, concerning the equality of confessions with respect to civil and political rights.

Authentically under Our Most High Signature and with the Imperial Seal affixed.

Done in Berlin, April 22, 1871.

NOTE

1. The three South German states of Baden, Wuerttemberg and Bavaria joined the North German Confederation in 1871, establishing the Second German Reich. Baden and Wuerttemberg had already accorded full rights to the Jews in 1861 and 1864, respectively. These rights were extended to the Jews in Bavaria through this act. Legally the process of emancipation in Germany was thereby completed. In practice, however, Jews remained with few exceptions excluded from the officer corps, administrative posts with prestige and authority, foreign service and teaching positions below the university.

Source: "Law Concerning the Introduction in Bavaria of the Laws of the North German Confederation," in Raphael Mahler, ed. and trans., *Jewish Emancipation, A Selection of Documents,* Pamphlet Series, Jews and the Post-War World, no. 1 (New York: The American Jewish Committee, 1941), pp. 58–59. Reprinted by permission of the American Jewish Committee.

IV

Emerging Patterns of Religious Adjustment: Reform, Conservative and Neo-Orthodox Judaism

Emancipation, or at least the promise of emancipation, stimulated a process of acculturation among the Jews. Emancipation implied the breakdown of the Jews' millennial social and cultural isolation; indeed, this was often the explicit expectation of the Gentile advocates of Jewish emancipation. Traditionally, the adoption of non-Jewish culture was frowned upon by Jews as a dangerous act, necessarily involving, especially in the Christian world, religious apostasy. But the "Gentile" culture sponsored by the liberal votaries of the Enlightenment was presumably different. This culture, it was emphasized, was predicated on a resolve to create both a universe of discourse and a structure of social bonds that are open to all men regardless of class, national origin, or religious affiliation. It was said that for the first time in European history the Jews could participate in non-Jewish culture without the stigma of apostasy.

Observant Jews such as Moses Mendelssohn, Naphtali Herz Wessely and other *maskilim* (enlightened Jews) evinced little hesitation in appropriating the philosophical, aesthetic, educational and political values of the Enlightenment. They vigorously maintained that the integrity of traditional Judaism was not compromised by their adoption of the "neutral" culture of the Enlightenment. To be sure, there were many Jews who were not as sanguine, for they perceived that the cultural and social integration recommended by the *maskilim* would inexorably weaken the bonds of the Jew to his ancestral faith. Raising a Cassandran cry, they warned that under the aegis of the Enlightenment Judaism would lose its exclusive claim on the soul and the mind of the Jew and would thus cease to be the bedrock of the Jew's social and spiritual identity, and, moreover, social integration would lead to a relaxation of religious observance. These premonitions were confirmed by the increasingly lax observance of many "enlightened" Jews and the concomitant call to legitimate this "laxity" by the reform of the traditional ritual practices of Judaism.

The ritual practices of traditional Judaism are comprehensive, and, as is often said, they involve the whole life of the Jew. These practices are supported by unique customs, language, memories, hopes and, until the modern period, legal autonomy. Jewry thus enjoyed a distinctive way of life. Theologically, the divine authority sanctioning this way of life was derived from the Oral Law (*Torah she-ba'al peh*) given to Moses along with the written Torah. The Oral Law provided the hermeneutics to interpret God's Word, both ritual and juridical, as found in the written Torah and thus served to guide Jewry in its observance of the divine Will in the ever protean situations and circumstances of life. The Oral Law was eventually recorded in the second century C.E. in the Mishnah and later elaborated upon in the Gemara (Talmud) and in on-going commentaries: the consensus regarding the norms of Jewish behavior that emerges from the Oral Law and the commentaries is known as the Halakha. Sociologically, the way of life of halakhic Judaism vouchsafed Jewry to an unambiguously distinct ethnic, indeed national, identity—an identity that was a source of profound discomfort to those Jews who sought cultural, social and political integration in the Gentile community in which they lived.

The reformation of Judaism sought by the enlightened Jews was not simply a diminution of the ritual burdens of the Jew but also an elimination or, at least, a blurring of the ethnic and national features of traditional Judaism. For these Jews, the urgent issue was to challenge the preeminence in Jewish life of the Halakha (or "rabbinism," as it was disparagingly called by both Jew and non-Jew alike). The Halakha, it was felt, prevented the necessary adaptations facilitating the Jew's integration in the non-Jewish world. Hence, it was concluded that the Halakha would have to be replaced as the supreme authority governing Jewish life. But this demand presented enormous theological and practical problems. Halakha, after all, derived its authority as the Word of God. Moreover, Halakha provided the dispersed nation of Israel with a common religious framework that assured an enduring commonality and continuity to Jewish life despite the disparity of geography and of culture among the respective communities of the nation. What authority other than Halakha would both command the universal fidelity of all Jews and ensure the institutional consensus within the Jewish world?

Aside from Saul Ascher's purely academic exercise to redefine Judaism as a religion of dogma as opposed to a religion of revealed law, i.e., Halakha (see chapter 2, document 20), early Reform in Germany made little more than desultory aesthetic innovations in Jewish ritual, innovations that were intended to make Jewish liturgical services more decorous and becoming. Undoubtedly, these early Reformers (who were almost exclusively laymen) had in mind such comments as those made by J. H. Campe. In his much acclaimed *Dictionary of the German Language* (1808), he urged that German be expunged of foreignisms and that *inter alia* the term *Synagogue,* borrowed from the Greek, be replaced by the German word *Judenschule* ("Jew School"), for like a school of unruly pupils the Jews' house of worship is "a place where people gather and mumble in an unlovely manner."[1]

The first comprehensive, systematic reform of Judaism was instituted by the New Israelite Temple Association founded in Hamburg in December 1817. The Hamburg Temple incorporated the aesthetic innovations of earlier Reformers: strict decorum; emphasis on the Saturday morning service (with the implied neglect of the thrice daily prayers of the weekdays); an abbreviated liturgy and the inclusion of prayers in German; choral and organ music; the abolition of the "oriental" cantillation traditionally employed in the reading of the weekly Torah portion; and sermons in German on edificatory themes as opposed to the traditional homily (*drashah*) on the weekly Torah portion. For this service the Hamburg Reformers also prepared a new prayerbook. Based on the traditional liturgy, the main innovations of this prayerbook were the inclusion of German prayers and the omission or modification of traditional prayers for the coming of the personal Messiah and "national" prayers that expressed the Jews' longing to be redeemed from Exile and to be restored to their ancestral homeland in Zion. In anticipation of rabbinic objection to these reforms, albeit relatively moderate, the Reformers solicited the service of a talmudic scholar, Eliezer Liebermann, to prepare a halakhic defense of Reform.[2] Liebermann issued two volumes: the first, *Nogah ha-Tzedek* ([The light of righteousness], 1818) contained the approbations of four rabbis—two Italian and two Hungarian—of the reforms. The second, *Or Nogah* ([The light of splendor], 1818), an appendix to the first volume but also published separately, presented his detailed apologia for the Hamburg reforms based on Halakha and classical rabbinic opinion (see document 2).

In response the rabbinic court of Hamburg published a volume entitled *Eleh Divrei ha-Brit* ([These are the words of the covenant], 1819). The publication presented statements by twenty-two of Europe's leading rabbis condemning the Hamburg reforms as based on a specious reading of Halakha and as constituting a schismatic threat to the unity of the Jewish people (see document 3). They conspicuously ignored the Reformers' contention that halakhic Judaism itself was in effect schismatic by its failure to acknowledge and adapt to the fact that an ever-increasing number of Jews were abandoning Judaism because they found it incompatible with their new sensibilities and priorities.

The advocates of Reform Judaism had difficulty in determining those principles that would hold an authority similar to that of Halakha. The quest for such principles gained momentum as a new generation of secularly educated rabbis desiring to accommodate Judaism to the "spirit of the age" emerged in the 1830s and 1840s in Germany. These rabbis gathered at various conferences (Brunswick, 1844; Frankfurt,

1. Joachim Heinrich Campe, *Woerterbuch der deutschen Sprache* (Braunschweig, 1808, 1811), vol. 2, p. 852.

2. "Reform" is used here and throughout this chapter anachronistically. This term, as well as the term "Liberal," emerged as a designation only as the movement crystallized.

1845; and Breslau, 1846) to deliberate and to effect a consensus among the attending rabbis regarding the authoritative principles of Reform. Rabbi Samuel Holdheim spoke for the majority of these rabbis when he unequivocally stated that these principles could no longer be based on "rabbinism" as were the earlier lame attempts of Liebermann.

> All the talk about a Talmudical Judaism is an illusion. Science has decided that the Talmud has no authority dogmatically or practically. Even those who will not acknowledge this go beyond the Talmud. The question is, who gives us the right to change the liturgy? This question requires an unequivocal answer. [The rabbis who during the Second Temple period established the traditional liturgy] have authority only in their age; what they ordained was timely, and on this the sanction of their ordinances rested. We have the same authority for our age, [but] even though the Talmud is not authoritative for us we do not wish to disregard the intellectual activity of two thousand years. We say merely this: Anything which upon unbiased, careful criticism contradicts the religious consciousness of the present age has no authority for us.[3]

In their search for an alternative to the talmudic-halakhic tradition as an authoritative basis for Judaism, Holdheim and his colleagues were rather eclectic, basing their arguments on selective philosophical, biblical and, when deemed appropriate, even talmudic references (see documents 5–9).

This apparent "lack of principles" alarmed Rabbi Zecharias Frankel, who was aligned with the minority advocating moderate reforms. In an address before the Frankfurt conference of 1845, Frankel held that in their enthusiasm for Reform his more radical colleagues brazenly and irresponsibly sponsored an abstract ideal of Reform that was perhaps compatible with the needs and wishes of some acculturated German Jews, but an ideal that ignored the existent needs and wishes of the Jewish people as a whole. Frankel, however, agreed with the radical Reformers that Halakha was no longer unquestionably the sole basis of Judaism. As an alternative to both radical Reform and to halakhic Judaism, Frankel presented his conception of a "positive, historical Judaism" that was based on a respect of the patterns of religious community and ritual established by Halakha not as law but as an intrinsic part of the people's evolving historical experience. This conception of Judaism, Frankel maintained, provided the guidelines for reforms that were "organically" part of the nation's experience and thus should be able to command wide adherence (see document 11). Frankel's conception of Judaism constituted the platform for what later became known in the United States as Conservative Judaism.

3. Protocol of the Brunswick conference of 1844, cited in David Philipson, *The Reform Movement in Judaism*, ed. S. B. Freehof, rev. ed. (New York: Ktav Publishing House, 1967), p. 145. Holdheim, the principal exponent of the most radical wing of Reform in Germany, set forth to demonstrate the time-bound qualities of the Talmud and the Halakha: "The Talmud speaks with the standpoint of its time [*Zeitbewusstsein*], and for that time it was right. I speak from the higher level of consciousness of my time, and for this age I am right" (*Ceremonialgesetz im Gottesreich*, trans. D. Philipson [Schwerin, 1845], p. 50).

Traditional or, as they were now called, Orthodox Jews who followed the Reform conferences condemned the deliberations as heretical, and they reasserted that the Halakha is the unimpeachable standard for Israel as the people of God (see document 10). While assuredly endorsing this position, Samson Raphael Hirsch, the founder of the movement of Neo-Orthodoxy, held that halakhic Judaism need not be totally unresponsive to the "spirit of the times." *Torah im derekh eretz* was his slogan: Torah, Jewish law, should be accommodated to *derekh eretz,* the general norms of the non-Jewish world. In practice, this meant that the halakhic Jew was able to pursue a secular education, to adopt the dress and language of the country in which he resided and to institute some revisions in the external trappings of ritual. These revisions, interestingly, were similar to those aesthetic changes introduced by early Reform: decorum; a choir under the direction of a professional musical director; the participation of the congregation in the singing; and a sermon in the vernacular. In opposition to Reform, however, Hirsch defended the traditional liturgy as sacrosanct and the use of Hebrew as the sole language of prayer (see document 12). According to Hirsch, while appreciating modern secular culture, the Jews had to maintain their apartness and distinctiveness as the servants of God and the guardians of His Torah. To justify this distinction, Hirsch ironically turned to Reform Judaism, which viewed Jewry's abiding singularity with even greater ambivalence, and he borrowed its concept of "mission." Israel's particularity, Reformers affirmed, does not imply indifference and withdrawal from the community of men, but a divine "mission" of universal significance (see documents 8 and 12).

Enlightenment and emancipation created new social and cultural conditions for Judaism. The documents presented in this chapter adumbrate the emerging institutional patterns of religious adjustments to these new conditions: Reform, Conservative and Neo-Orthodox Judaism.

THE NEW ISRAELITE TEMPLE ASSOCIATION
1. Constitution of the Hamburg Temple (December 11, 1817)[1]

... Since public worship has for some time been neglected by so many, because of the ever decreasing knowledge of the language in which alone it has until now been conducted, and also because of many other shortcomings which have crept in at the same time—the undersigned, convinced of the necessity to restore public worship to its deserving dignity and importance, have joined together to follow the example of several Israelite congregations, especially the one in Berlin.[2] They plan to arrange in this city also, for themselves as well as others who think as they do, a dignified and well-ordered ritual according to which the worship service shall be conducted on Sabbath and holy days and on other solemn occasions, and which shall be observed in their own temple, to be erected especially for this purpose. Specifically, there shall be introduced at such services a German sermon, and choral singing to the accompaniment of an organ.

Incidentally, the above-mentioned ritual shall not be confined to services in the temple; rather it shall apply to all those religious customs and acts of daily life which are sanctified by the church[3] or by their own nature. Outstanding amongst these are the entrance of the newly-born into the covenant of the fathers, weddings, and the like. Also, a religious ceremony shall be introduced in which the children of both sexes, after having received adequate schooling in the teachings of the faith, shall be accepted as confirmants of the Mosaic religion.

NOTES

1. The New Israelite Temple Association of Hamburg instituted the first systematic Reform worship services; it was founded by sixty-six Jews, led by Eduard Kley (1789–1867), Meyer Israel Bresselau (1785–1839) and Seckel Isaak Fraenkel (1765–1835)—all of them laymen. The Hamburg Temple was dedicated on October 18, 1818, the anniversary of the Battle of Leipzig, which marked the liberation of Germany from Napoleonic rule. Some historians see an ideological motive not only in this gesture but also behind the Reformers' naming their synagogue a "temple." That is, that by adopting the designation traditionally reserved for the fallen Temple of Jerusalem, the Reformers symbolically relinquished the hope of Israel's restoration and they declared Hamburg their Jerusalem. Other historians ascribe to the Reformers the more innocent motive of simply wishing to distinguish their house of worship from the traditional synagogue of Hamburg.

2. On the Feast of Weeks in the year 1815, Israel Jacobson (1768–1828)—the father of German Reform, the founder of a Reform temple in Sessen, Westphalia—inaugurated a "private" Reform worship service in his Berlin home. Later the services moved to the home of Jacob Herz-Beer, a wealthy Berlin banker. Due to the opposition of the conservative Prussian government the Reform synagogue of Berlin was closed down in 1817. Eduard Kley had served as a preacher in Beer's synagogue.

3. This word was intended to underscore the purely religious character of the Hamburg Temple.

Source: W. Gunther Plaut, *The Rise of Reform Judaism: A Sourcebook of Its European Origins* (New York: World Union for Progressive Judaism, 1963), pp. 31ff. Reprinted by permission of the World Union for Progressive Judaism.

ELIEZER LIEBERMANN[1]

2. The Light of Splendor

. . . Why should we not draw a lesson from the peoples among whom we live? Look at the Gentiles and see how they stand in awe and reverence and with good manners in their house of prayer. No one utters a word, no one moves a limb. Their ears and all their senses are directed to the words of the preacher and to [the recitation of] their prayers. Now judge please, you blessed of God, people of the Lord, seedlings of the faithful, how very much more there is for us to do. Are we not obligated to be most discreet and to guard our steps and the utterances of our lips when we go to the House of God? Will someone say that it is prohibited [to learn from our neighbors] for "ye shall not abide by their statutes?"[2] Will it occur to a man of intelligence that we should distance ourselves from a good and righteous act because we do not esteem he who performs it or that a just cause should be invalidated because of the ill-repute of its votaries? Indeed, such opinion is shallow and fatuous. Such an opinion could but evoke derisive laughter.

Pay heed my brethren and my people [so that you might understand]: Who among us is as great in wisdom and works as King Solomon, may he rest in peace, and did he not charge us to receive instruction from animals of a low order of creation when he said: "Go to the ant, thou sluggard, consider her ways and be wise."[3] [In a similar fashion] Job said: "But ask now the beasts and they shall teach thee, the birds of the sky and they shall tell thee . . . and the fishes of the sea shall declare to thee."[4] And our sages of blessed memory have said: "If the Torah had not been given we could have learned modesty from the cat, manners from the cock, honesty [literally, the (objection) to robbery] from the ant and chastity [literally, forbidden intercourse] from the dove."[5] It is also written: The Lord teaches us by the beasts of the earth and makes us wiser by the birds of the sky."[6]

Understand this, all ye of upright heart: If our holy sages of blessed memory have obligated us to receive moral instruction concerning justice and the straight path from the lowliest orders of creation, how can we avoid receiving edification from the very work of God's hands, blessed be He, [that is] from men possessing reason just as we do. Why should we not learn from them and from their correct actions that which is also good and becoming for us, the children of Israel, and which is proper according to our holy Torah? Regarding this matter the prophet has already admonished: "Has a nation exchanged its gods . . . ?"[7] It is also said: "In every place incense is burnt and sacrifices are offered to my name, and a pure offering."[8] And these are the words of the learned Rabbenu Tam, of blessed memory, in the *Book of Righteousness:*

> One should be envious of the pious and more than these of the penitents, and more than these of those who are younger [than oneself] and who from their youth have been diligent in the service of the Lord, blessed be He. . . . And one should be envious of the nations of the world who serve God in awe, fear and submission. How much more must he who serves the Lord of the world do. Should he not envy them and do all in his power to surpass their works many times over?[9]

Source: Eliezer Liebermann, *Or Nogah* (Dessau, 1818), pp. 22–25. Trans. here by S. Fischer and S. Weinstein. The language, style and format of this treatise in defense of Reform are typical of traditional rabbinic literature.

[We may also cite] the words of the pious rabbi [Bahya ibn Pakuda], who in the introduction to his book, *Duties of the Heart,* states:

> I added [as support for my arguments] Scriptural texts and maxims culled from the writings of our teachers of blessed memory. I quoted also the saints and sages of other nations whose words have come to us, hoping that my readers' hearts would incline to them, and give heed to their wisdom. I quote for example the dicta of the philosophers, the ethical teachings of the ascetics and their praiseworthy customs. In this connection our Rabbis of blessed memory already remarked (Sanhedrin 39b): In one verse it is said "After the ordinances of the nations that are round about you, have ye done" (Ezek. 11:12); while in another, it is said "After the ordinances of the nations that are round about you, ye have not done" (Ezek. 5:7). How is this contradiction to be reconciled? As follows: "Their good ordinances ye have not copied; their evil ones ye have followed." The Rabbis further said (*Megillah* 16a): "Whoever utters a wise word, even if he belongs to the gentiles, is called a sage."[10]

And here are the words of Maimonides, of blessed memory:

> As regards the logic for all these calculations [concerning the position of the moon at the time of the new crescent]—why we have to add a particular figure or deduct it, how all these rules originated, and how they were discovered and proved—all this is a part of the science of astronomy and mathematics, about which many books have been composed by Greek sages—books that are still available to the scholars of our time. But the books which had been composed by the Sages of Israel, of the tribe of Issachar, who lived in the time of the Prophets, have not come down to us. But since all these rules have been established by sound and clear proofs, free from any flaw and irrefutable, we need not be concerned about the identity of their authors, whether they were Hebrew Prophets or gentile sages. For when we have to do with rules and propositions which have been demonstrated by sound and flawless proofs, we rely upon the author who has discovered them or has transmitted them only because of his demonstrated proofs and verified reasoning.[11]

All the passages mentioned here are in addition to that which can be found [concerning this matter] in the rest of the books of the great among our ancestors, may they rest in paradise. Space does not permit us to include these texts, which are known to all the educated and learned men of our people, may they be granted long life. . . .

Behold, my brethren, my people know that the Lord has opened the eyes of our brothers [the founders of the Hamburg Temple] men of understanding who are devoted to God, blessed be He. They have cleared the path of stumbling blocks and hailstones and have removed all obstacles from the way of our people by establishing a house of prayer in which they can pour out their hearts before His Great Name, blessed be He. They utter their prayers in an intelligible and lucid manner. They have chosen for an advocate between them and their Father in heaven an upright man, a rabbi eminent in Torah and wisdom and an accomplished orator.[12] His prayer is pleasant and becoming to every one that hears it. All join together with him to praise and glorify in a pleasant and becoming fashion, verse by verse and word by word. No one speaks nor are any words exchanged; the irreverent voices of frivolous conversation are not heard. Would that this be the case in all our houses of worship. For this [manner of prayer] would not dishonor us among the Gentiles, as we have indicated in the passage from Maimonides quoted above. [The present situation] in several of our synagogues is truly a matter of jest and ridicule, fulfilling the words of the prophet: "Has this house become a den of robbers?"[13] Alas for the eyes that witness this.

How much good has [the Hamburg Temple] done by setting up men of wisdom, who walk the upright path and seek the good of their people. These men preach the word of God every Sabbath and festival.[14] They inform the congregation of the ways of the Lord and His statutes according to the righteous law of our holy Torah, so that they may fulfill all that is contained in the Written and Oral Torahs. The preachers inflame their hearts with the fear of God, blessed be He, so that they may observe His commandments, laws and statutes and befriend the poor, have mercy upon the destitute and revive the downhearted. The preachers even instruct them regarding the unity of His name, blessed be He, and also teach that there is no unity comparable to His. They implant the faith of our God in the hearts of small and great, women and children, so that all know the Lord, from their great unto their small. Regarding other righteous matters, my heart rejoiced and I was filled with exultation to hear worthy, straightforward and sincere words flowing from their lips like sap, words which are sweeter to my palate than honey or the choicest nectar. Who will not acknowledge that these are the words of the living God, restoring the soul and strengthening the faith of the weak?

The preacher firmly implants the love of our Creator, blessed be His name, in the heart of every man. They even arouse love of His Majesty, our pious and merciful king, as well as love of the king's household, a delightful offshoot, and of his loyal ministers and counselors. Similarly they inflame the hearts [of their listeners] with the love of our brethren, the children of Israel, including those who oppose [our views]. For we have one God and one Torah; their portion is our portion, their inheritance is our inheritance. They also arouse the love of our brethren, the inhabitants of our land, even if they not be Jewish, and instill love of the land of our birth, so that we should give our lives for it and always pray for its safety. For the prayer for the land of our birth precedes in time the prayer for the land of our fathers, the land of Israel.[15] . . .

These are the words of the Talmud [regarding this subject]:

> Rabbi Jose says, "I was once travelling on the road, and I entered into one of the ruins of Jerusalem in order to pray. Elijah of blessed memory appeared and waited for me at the door till I finished my prayer. After I finished my prayer, he said to me: 'Peace be with you, my master!' and I replied: 'Peace be with you, my master and teacher!' And he said to me: 'My son, why did you go into the ruin?' I replied: 'To pray.' He said to me: 'You ought to have prayed on the road.' I replied: 'I feared lest passers-by interrupt me.' He said to me: 'You ought to have said an abbreviated prayer.' Thus I then learned from him three things: one must not go into a ruin; one may say the prayer on the road; and if one does say his prayer on the road, he recites an abbreviated prayer" [*Berakhot* 3a].

This has been interpreted as follows: It is known that Rabbi Jose lived after the destruction of the Temple. He once entered into prayer to enquire concerning the destruction of Jerusalem. Elijah, who exemplifies the attributes of thought and comprehension, came to him and said: "My son, why did you go into this ruin," that is to say, why do you complain about the destruction of the Temple? Rabbi Jose replied that he was not complaining, but only praying for the Temple to be rebuilt. Elijah said to him: "You ought to have prayed on the road," that is to say, you ought to have prayed for the preservation and survival of Israel in every place where they may be. Rabbi Jose replied: "I feared lest passers-by interrupt me," that is to say, I am grieved by those who oppress us in the Exile. Elijah replied: "You ought to have said an abbreviated prayer," that is to say, the essence of the prayer is for the present salvation of Israel from the nations. This is what Rabbi Jose then said: "Then I learned three things: One must not go into a ruin," that is to say, one must not make the essence of one's prayer the destruction of the Temple; "one may say the prayer on the road," that is to say, [pray] that God render good upon our people in the Exile. Concerning this the man of the Great Assembly[16] established the benediction [beginning] "Look upon our affliction" and concluding [with the words] "Redeemer of Israel." What is referred to here is not actual redemption, but merely our deliverance from the troubles of Exile. The commentators have offered a similar explanation in the tractate *Megillah* of the Talmud.

To be sure, my brethren and compatriots, tears well up in the eyes of every man of feeling when he remembers that our holy city is burnt and its gates desolate, and we must say along with the exiles, "If I forget thee, O Jerusalem."[17] Nevertheless, the prayer for the land of our birth, our present dwelling place, must take precedence in time and we should always pray for its safety and for the well-being of its people. . . .

O that it would be in the hearts of our brethren, the children of Israel, to appoint for themselves in every city men such as these [preachers of the Hamburg Temple], who seek the good of their people and teach the upright way. Were this come to pass, I know that we would glory in the stock of the Lord and [our] sons would be the blessed of God, faithful in spirit to God and to their king. If in former times there had been teachers of righteousness to our people, the children of Israel, who had illuminated the good and beneficial path as contained in our holy Torah and had preached the word of God mingled with sap and nectar, then we would not be an object of ridicule and scorn for the peoples and a figure of strife and contention among the nations. Moreover, many of our people who have left our religion in this generation because of our numerous iniquities would not have done so. For what profit have the people from the sermons of preachers who build fortresses for them, hewn stones and columns, which they ascend by means of homiletics to the heights of sharp-wittedness and erudition. Through casuistry they weave complicated and finespun embroideries. All the people (including the women and children) hear the voices, but they do not understand one word uttered by the man standing on the pulpit. When the ministers and sages [of the Gentiles] come to our places of worship to observe our customs and to hear the words of our teachers, who instruct the people regarding the path they are to follow, they hear merely the sound of noise in the camp of the Hebrews and do not understand anything. Instead of saying, "They are a wise and understanding nation,"[18] they say "They are a misguided and confused people, an impetuous nation." [On this point] my brethren and friends, consult Maimonides' *Commentary on the Mishnah,* Sanhedrin, chapter 8. My pleasant brethren, may you enjoy long life, listen to my upright words and be preserved.

NOTES

1. Little is known about Eliezer Liebermann, other than he was the son of Ze'ev Wolf, rabbi of Hennegau (probably Hagenau, Alsace). Liebermann's services were solicited on behalf of the New Israelite Temple Association of Hamburg by Israel Jacobson (1768–1828), the father of Reform in Germany. According to the historian Heinrich Graetz, Liebermann converted to Catholicism, but this assertion has not been corroborated by subsequent research.
2. Lev. 18:3.
3. Prov. 6:6.
4. Job 12:7–8.
5. Talmud, tractate *Erubin* 100b.
6. Job 35:11.
7. Jer. 2:11. The full passage reads: "Has a nation exchanged its gods which are yet no gods? and still my people has exchanged its glory for that which can not profit." By implication each nation has its own way to the truth.
8. Mal. 1:11.
9. Jacob ben Meir (c.1100–1171), a leading rabbinic scholar from France known as Rabbenu Tam, "our perfect rabbi." He was one of the principal compilers of the *Tosafot,* commentaries on the Babylonian Talmud. *The Book of Righteousness* (*Sefer ha-Yashar*) consists of two parts, the first containing responses and the second, novellas on the Talmud.

10. Bahya ben Joseph ibn Pakuda (second half of eleventh century), moral philosopher who lived in Muslim Spain. *Duties of the Heart* (*Hovot ha-Levavot*), which greatly influenced all subsequent Jewish pietistic literature, contains directions for the development of man's inner life. It is a complement to halakhic books, which concentrate on "the duties of the members of the body," i.e., on religious actions. This passage is found in *Duties of the Heart,* Hebrew-English texts, trans. Moses Hyamson (Jerusalem: Boys Town, 1962), vol. 1, pp. 43–44.

11. "Sanctification of the New Moon," *The Code of Maimonides,* book 3, treatise 8, trans. Solomon Grandz (New Haven: Yale University Press, 1956), ch. 18, par. 25, p. 73.

12. Liebermann apparently is referring to Rabbi Gotthold Salomon (1789–1862), who was appointed preacher of the Hamburg Temple in October 1818. Of the early leaders of the temple, he was the only one to hold a rabbinic title, which at the time meant halakhic ordination. Salomon was an editor of *Sulamith* and evinced even before his appointment to the Hamburg Temple interest in Reform. He was renowned for his eloquence as a preacher; he had studied the sermons and style of famous contemporary Christian preachers for many years.

13. Jer. 7:11.

14. As a preacher Salomon was assisted by Eduard Kley (1789–1867), a disciple of Israel Jacobson and the founding spirit behind the Hamburg Temple. The sermon (*Predigt*) became one of the distinctive features of German Reform. "The nineteenth century saw the rise and development of a new type of Jewish preaching, replacing the traditional *drashah.* The changes involved in this innovation concerned not only the outward form and structure of the sermon but also its substance. The very concept of the purpose of preaching as well as the theology behind it underwent a radical transformation. Obviously, the impact of contemporary trends in the Christian pulpit and in the philosophical thinking of the period accounts for a great deal in this connection" (Alexander Altmann, "The New Style of Preaching in Nineteenth-Century German Jewry," in *Studies in Nineteenth-Century Jewish Intellectual History,* ed. A. Altmann, Philip W. Lown Institute of Advanced Judaic Studies, Brandeis University [Cambridge: Harvard University Press, 1964], vol. 2, p. 65).

15. The author supports this position by citing a long passage from the Babylonian Talmud, tractate *Berakhot* 3a.

16. The Great Assembly is the Knesset ha-Gedolah—the institution which embodied the spiritual leadership of the Jewish people at the beginning of the Second Temple period. Constituting the supreme authority in matters of religious practice and law, it was considered the link between the prophets and the first of the rabbis. This body is said to have established the main text of the traditional liturgy.

17. Psalms 137:5.

18. Deut. 4:6.

THE HAMBURG RABBINICAL COURT
3. These Are the Words of the Covenant[1]

These are the words of the covenant with Jacob, a law unto Israel, an eternal covenant; the word of God is one forever and ever. [These words are uttered] in accordance with the Torah and by judgment of the court of justice of the holy community of Hamburg—may the Lord bless it well—with the support of the leading men of learning in Germany, Poland, France, Italy, Bohemia, Moravia and Hungary. All of them join together, in an edict decreed by the angels and a judgment proclaimed by the holy ones, to abolish a *new law* (which was fabricated by several ignorant individuals unversed in the Torah) instituting practices which are not in keeping with the Law of Moses and of Israel.

Source: Eleh Divrei ha-Brit (Altona, 1819), pp. 1, 3–5. Trans. here by S. Fischer and S. Weinstein.

Therefore these pious, learned, holy and distinguished rabbis have risen to render the Law secure [against such infractions]. They have discoverd a breach [of the Law] and have sought to contain it with prescriptions forbidding the three cardinal sins [of Reform]:

1. It is forbidden to change the worship that is customary in Israel from Morning Benedictions to "It is our duty to praise [the Lord of all]";[2] and all the more so [is it prohibited] to make any deletions in the traditional liturgy.

2. It is forbidden to pray in any language other than the Holy Tongue. Every prayerbook that is printed improperly and not in accordance with our [traditional] practice is invalid, and it is forbidden to pray from it.

3. It is prohibited to play a musical instrument in the synagogue on the Sabbath and on the festivals even when it is played by a non-Jew.

Happy is the man who heeds the decree of the sages of the court of justice and the words of the learned, pious and holy. Happy is the man who does not remove himself from the congregation, in order that he may walk in the way of the good. He who desires the integrity of his soul will take utmost care lest he transgress, Heaven forbid, the words of the learned contained in this volume, as the sages of the Talmud, may their memory be blessed, said: "Pay heed to their legacy." Who is the man who fears the Lord and will not fear the words of the forty pious, exalted and holy men who have affixed their signatures to this book, sparing [thereby] himself and his household.

By Order of the Court of Justice of the Holy Community of Hamburg.

. . . Behold, we had hoped that these men [who have introduced Reform] would have attended to our words and listened to the voice of their teachers, who alone are fit to express an opinion on matters concerning what is permitted and what is prohibited. In former times the men of our proud city have listened to the voice of their teachers, who told them the path they were to take. We had thought that our judgment would be honored and that they would not dare to disobey our utterance, for our strength now is as it was formerly.

But we hoped in vain, for these men disobeyed the counsel [of their teachers] and sank into sin. They quickly built for themselves a house of prayer, which they called a temple, and published a prayerbook for Sabbaths and festivals, which has caused great sorrow and brought tears to our eyes over the destruction of our people. For they have added to and deleted from the text of the prayers according to their hearts' desires. They have eliminated the Morning Benedictions and the blessings for the Torah and have discarded Psalm 145, as well as other psalms from the morning prayers. They have set their hands upon the text of the recitation of "Hear, O Israel," and in the wickedness of their hearts have deleted the texts of "To God who rested," "God the Lord," "True and firm" and "There is none to be compared to Thee."[3] Moreover, they have printed most of the prayers in German rather than in Hebrew. Worst of all, they have perpetrated a sore evil by removing all references to the belief in the Ingathering of the Exiles. [Their deletions include] the text "Lead us with an upright bearing to our land" in the benediction "With great love,"[4] the text "Who will raise us up in joy to our land?" in the Additional Service [*Musaf*] for the Sabbath and the texts "Bring us in jubilation to Zion your city" and "Gather our scattered ones from among the nations" in the Additional Service for festivals. They have thereby testified concerning themselves that they do not believe at all in the promise of our teacher Moses, may he rest in peace: "If any of thine that are dispersed be in the uttermost parts of heaven, from thence will the Lord thy God gather thee, and from thence will He fetch thee."[5] This belief is one of the major tenets of our holy Torah. All the prophets have been unanimous in affirming that the God of our fathers would gather our scattered ones, and this is our hope throughout our Exile. This belief in no way detracts from the honor of Their Majesties the kings and ministers under whom we find protection, for it is common knowledge that we believe in the Coming of the messiah and the Ingathering of the Exiles. No one has ever dared to object to this belief of ours, because they know that we are obligated to seek the well-being of the peoples who have brought us under their protection. They have bestowed much good and kindness upon us, may God grant them success in all their actions and works. Our opinion here corresponds to that which the learned men of our time, may their light shine, have elaborated in their letters. He who rejects this belief denies [one of] the fundamental tenets of our religion. Woe to the ears that have heard that men have arisen in Israel to do violence to the foundations of our holy faith.

Yet with all this they are not content, for their hands are still outstretched and they continue to do evil. At the dedication of their house of prayer men and women sang together at the opening of the ark, in contradiction to the law set out in the Talmud and in the Codes: "a woman's voice is indecent."[6] Such [an abomination] is not done in our house of prayer, which has replaced the Temple, throughout the entire Diaspora of the sanctified ones of Israel. Who has heard or seen such a thing? In addition, they play a musical instrument (an organ) on the holy Sabbath and have abolished the silent prayer. They have even abolished the reading of a selection from the Prophets on the Sabbath [after the reading of the weekly portion from the Pentateuch] as well as the reading of the four portions [of the Pentateuch read in addition to the weekly portion on the four Sabbaths preceding Passover]. On Purim the congregation recited the prayer "Grant us discernment" instead of the Eighteen Benedictions, and in the evening they read the Book of Esther in German from a printed text [rather than from a handwritten Hebrew scroll]. Lack of space prevents the inclusion of all their pernicious customs and practices by means of which they have chosen to disobey the Holy One of Israel and to defy the holy sages of blessed memory, the court of their city and the vast majority of our community who are God-fearing and faithful and fulfill the commandments of God.

Thus we have resolved that this is not the time to place our hands over our mouths and to be silent. Were we to remain silent we would be commiting a sin, for [the Reformers] would say the rabbis are silent and [their] silence [is to be construed] as consent. With honeyed words they would lead astray the God-fearing and the faithful who in their innocence would follow them. [The Reformers] would say to them: "Behold, the path upon which we walk is good. Come, let us join together and be one people." And so the Torah, Heaven forbid, would disappear. Brethren, the children of Israel, it shall not be; Israel has not yet been abandoned. There are still judges in the land who are zealous for God's sake and who will rend the arm, and even crack the skull, of him who pursues the sin [of Reformers]. To these judges we shall hasten for aid. They will rise up and help us abolish the [wicked] counsel [of the Reformers] and strengthen our religion. Accordingly, we have girded our loins and written to the famous learned men of the holy communities of Germany, Poland, Bohemia, Moravia and Italy. We have sent them our legal judgment, which we mentioned above, and we asked them if after close and careful study by means of their clear and pure reason they would confirm all that is in our judgment as being proper. In this way we can make public the abomination that has been committed in Israel. Every pious man who fears the word of God will pay heed to the words of the learned men of our time, may their light shine, and to our words. He shall not follow the counsels of the perverse who walk upon a crooked path.

NOTES

1. In response to Liebermann's *Nogah ha-Tzedek* and *Or Nogah*, the rabbinic court of Hamburg published this volume of *responsa* (halakhic opinions) on the admissibility of Reform, solicited from

Europe's foremost rabbis, including *inter alios* Rabbi Eger of Posen, Prussia (1761–1837), Moses Sofer of Pressburg, Hungary (1763–1839) and Mordecai Benet, chief rabbi of Moravia (1753–1829). The appearance of this volume, which was comprised of twenty-two *responsa*, "may be said to mark the beginning coalescence of an Orthodox party opposed to all tampering with tradition" (W. Gunther Plaut, *The Rise of Reform Judaism: A Sourcebook of Its European Origins* [New York: World Union for Progressive Judaism, 1963], p. 34).

2. Prayer appearing at the end of the evening services as well as the morning services.

3. These prayers are part of the morning service for Sabbaths and festivals.

4. Prayer appearing before the recitation of "Hear, O Israel . . . " in the morning service for weekdays, Sabbaths and festivals.

5. Deut. 30:4.

6. Talmud, tractate *Berakhot* 24a and tractate *Kiddushin* 70a.

MOSES SOFER[1]
4. A Reply Concerning the Question of Reform

Letter from the Rabbi of Great Learning and Renown, Our Venerable Teacher Rabbi Moses Sofer, May God preserve him, President of the [Rabbinic] Court of Pressburg to the [Rabbinic] Court of the Holy Community of Hamburg.

Your [letter] has reached me and has shocked and overwhelmed me with its bitter tidings. For it brings the news that men who do not submit to the yoke of heaven have lately appeared, seeking to nullify the covenant through devious schemes against the religion of our forefathers. One of their innovations is that their house of prayer should be tightly closed on weekdays and only open on the Sabbath. Would that even then its doors would be closed, for they have altered the text of the prayers which we have received from the men of the Great Assembly,[2] the sages of the Talmud, and our hallowed fathers. They have added to and deleted from the prayers, substituting texts of their own invention. [For example,] they have eliminated the Morning Benedictions, which are explained in chapter 3 of the tractate *Berakhot*, and they have also discarded [the benediction for] the flourishing of the House of David, our Messiah, and for the rebuilding of Jerusalem the Holy City. Moreover, they have appointed a non-Jew to play a musical instrument in their presence on the holy Sabbath, [a matter] which is forbidden us, and significantly the majority of their prayers are in German.

This is a concise summary of the letter which I have received this evening from your glorious excellencies. You have requested me to affiliate myself with the lions, the learned men of our time, who repair the breaches of our generation, and to express my opinion whether the truth is with you or not. What shall I reply? Is it not well known that in exile the delightful Daniel "kneeled upon his knees three times a day, and prayed, and gave thanks before his God, as he did aforetime."[3] From this it is explained that even "aforetime," [that is to say] before the Chaldeans decreed their edict [forbidding Jewish prayer], he would pray three times daily and not only on the Sabbath.[4] In the talmudic tractate *Berakhot* our sages of blessed memory interpreted "aforetime" to mean even when the Temple was in existence, as is stated there, "Was it only in captivity [that this began]?"[5]

. . . It is known that in the days of the Second Commonwealth Israel dwelt in its land, wielding the ruler's scepter with great-

Source: Eleh Divrei ha-Brit (Altona, 1819), pp. 32ff. Trans. here by S. Fischer and S. Weinstein.

ness and honor for several hundred years. [During that period] there were among them great sages, whose sole occupation was with the Torah. They and their students numbered tens of thousands. They had great and excellent academies similar to [universities] now being established by all the rulers in their big cities. They also had a Sanhedrin[6] which set up protective fences [around the Law], enacted decrees and maintained everything in good order. After them came tens of thousands of their disciples and the disciples of their disciples, who preceded our hallowed rabbi [Judah ha-Nasi], the compiler of the Mishnah.[7] Not one of these sages is mentioned either in the Mishnah or in the Beraita.[8] Only a very few of them were mentioned in Maimonides' introduction to his commentary on the tractate *Zera'im* of the Talmud.[9] Moreover, out of all their sayings only a small number of the shorter ones have been mentioned. Without doubt it would have been possible to make a great book out of the sayings of each of the sages and their disciples, in comparison with which the Mishnah as well as both the Babylonian and Jerusalem Talmuds would appear to be minor works containing only a small amount of wisdom. The reason [for the limited number of extant sayings] is that the sages winnowed and sifted their words to extract the choicest wheat. Concerning this Rabbi Simon stated at the end of chapter 6 of the talmudic tractate *Gittin:* "My sons, learn my rules [literally "measures"], for they are the cream of the cream of Rabbi Akiba."[10] Afterwards, the choicest statements were set down in the Mishnah and the Talmud.

Now these statements issued from the mouths of wise and discerning men, whose minds were full of knowledge and ideas and who possessed a profound understanding of all the sciences. Over the centuries these ideas have been recurrently clarified by thousands of sages. For nearly two thousand years they have been established in Israel and no one has dared to open his mouth to protest [against them]. But now insignificant foxes have risen up to breach the walls and destroy the fence [that has been erected around the Law]. They seek to change the texts [of the prayers] and the benedictions and to alter the hours and times that have been appointed [for their recitation].

Regarding matters of judgment, one court cannot abolish the ruling of another court unless it is greater in numbers and wisdom. Even if the reason [for the ruling] is invalid the regulation is not voided. This is especially so in the case of the liturgy that is in usage throughout Israel. Even though variant texts exist in several places, [the liturgy] is nevertheless considered to be widespread throughout Israel, since from the beginning one version was established solely for the Ashkenazim, and disseminated among them without dissent, while another version was established among the Sephardim and disseminated among them without dissent. . . .

Therefore let them [the Reformers] stand up and be counted with the sages of our generation; may the grace of the Lord be upon them! These men cannot make the choice to remove themselves from the congregation. If they will say: ". . . we do not accept the sages of the Talmud and their authority," they shall bear the burden of the words of Maimonides: "He who repudiates the Oral Law . . . is classed with atheists [whom any person has a right to put to death]."[11] Nothing more [need be said].

[What] if someone will claim that the reason for praying for the flourishing of the glory of the Messiah Son of David and for the restoration of worship [in the Temple] is in any case invalid, since we are dwelling in peace and tranquility among Their Majesties the kings of the nations? This is not so, for as I have already written above, even in the days of the kings of the Second Commonwealth prayers were recited for the rule of the House of David, for when that comes to pass we [all mankind] will all be around to behold the goodness of the Lord. We do not need to eat the fruits and be sated with the goodness [of an easy and tranquil life among the nations. Were this so] one could then make the blasphemous claim: "Have we not found tranquility and goodness among the Gentiles, sc what need have we for the land of Israel?'

Heaven forbid! We do not pour out our hearts and wait in anticipation all our days for an illusory material tranquility. Rather our hope is to dwell in the presence of God there [in the land of Israel], the place designated for His service and for the observance of His Torah. This does not deprecate the king and ministers under whose protection we live. Nehemia the son of Hakhaliyah was viceroy to the king, enjoying honor and riches. [Yet] he was saddened by the fact that the city, the place of the tombs of his fathers [Jerusalem], lay in waste, its gates consumed with fire.[12] The king [granted his request to return to Jerusalem] and did not do evil by replying, "Have you not riches and all good things in my service? Why do you make this request?" for each people follows the service of its God.

Behold, we are as prisoners of the war of the destruction [of the Second Temple]. In the abundance of His mercy and the righteousness of our dispersion, the Lord had us find favor in the eyes of the kings and ministers of the nations, for whose well-being we are obligated to entreat and for whose safety we are to pray. [We do so] not that we might repay them with evil, Heaven forbid, for they have bestowed many great kindnesses upon us in the past two thousand years. Their reward will surely be great, for the Lord repays with kindness those who do good. Nevertheless, no harm is done if we long to return to our patrimony. From this good that the Lord bestows upon us the nations of the world will also benefit. . . .

The nations [knew all this regarding our beliefs] and were never vexed. But perhaps these men [the Reformers] neither anticipate nor believe at all in the words of our prophets concerning the building of the Third Temple and the coming of the Messiah. Nor do they seem to believe all that is said by our sages of blessed memory regarding these matters. If this is so, then return to the words of Maimonides mentioned above. . . .

With respect to the fact that [the Reformers'] communal prayer is [conducted] in a language other than the Holy Tongue, this is completely reprehensible. . . . If the reason for this [practice] is that the common people do not understand the Holy Tongue, it would be better if it were arranged to have each one learn the meaning of the prayers and recite them in Hebrew than to arrange for them to pray in another language. One does act in such a fashion before a king of flesh and blood. He who speaks with the king must speak the language of the king; it is not proper that the king speak the language of the [common] people, even though he understands it. Nachmanides writes in the beginning of his commentary to the portion *Ki Tisah*[13] that the Holy One, Blessed be He, speaks with His prophets in Hebrew. Our sages of blessed memory said that the world was created in Hebrew. . . .

If this is so, then this is the language of the Holy One, Blessed be He, in which He gave us His Torah and it is inconceivable to speak before Him in our everyday language. Rather, we should speak the special language befitting His holy words. This is the opinion of the men of the Great Assembly who established the texts of the prayers and benedictions in the Holy Tongue. He who deviates [from this practice] is in the wrong, while he who upholds the words of our sages of blessed memory and the customs of our forefathers, has the advantage. He shall perform the will of his Creator and be blessed by God.

Therefore you have acted in accordance with the Torah when you declared in your holy synagogue that it is forbidden to pray from the German prayerbooks of the Reformers and that one may pray [only] in Hebrew according to the versions contained in traditional prayerbooks. Your prohibition of the playing of a musical instrument (organ) in the holy synagogue, especially on the holy Sabbath, is also proper. May our hands be strengthened and may God be with you. There is no doubt that all the learned men, the sages of our time, will concur with this prohibition. They agree and I agree in forbidding every soul in Israel to change even one detail of all that is said above. We will thus be saved from all evil and so merit the rebuilding of the Temple.

Tuesday, Second day of the New Moon of the month of Tevet, Hannukah 1819 (5579).

NOTES

1. Moses Sofer (1762–1839). Popularly known as Hatam Sofer, he was born in Frankfurt. In 1806 he was appointed rabbi of Pressburg, at the time the most important Jewish community in Hungary, where he remained for the rest of his life. Celebrated for his talmudic erudition and religious virtue, he was the recognized leader of traditional Jewry in Central Europe. His famed talmudic academy (*yeshivah*) served as the center of Orthodoxy's struggle against the Reform movement. His obstinate opposition to modernism in any form is eloquently expressed in his ethical testament, published numerous times and still popular among the ultra-Orthodox. It reads in part:

> ... May your mind not turn to evil and never engage in corruptible partnership with those fond of innovations, who, as a penalty for our many sins, have strayed from the Almighty and His law! Do not touch the books of Rabbi Moses [Mendelssohn] from Dessau, and your foot will never slip!... Should hunger and misery lead you into temptation, then the Almighty will protect you; resist temptation and do not turn to the idols or to some god of your own making! The daughters may read German books, but only those which have been written in our own way, according to the interpretations of our teachers (may they rest in peace), and absolutely no others! Be warned not to change your Jewish names, speech, and clothing—God forbid.... Never say: "Times have changed!" We have an old Father—praised be His name—who has never changed and never will change.... The order of prayer and synagogue shall remain forever as it has been up to now, and no one may presume to change anything of its structure

(cited in W. Gunther Plaut, *The Growth of Reform Judaism: A Sourcebook of Its European Origins* [New York: World Union for Progressive Judaism, 1965], pp. 256ff.).

2. See document 2, note 16 in this chapter.

3. Dan. 6:11.

4. In the Book of Daniel, chapter 6, it is related that the plotters against Daniel persuaded the Chaldean king to promulgate a decree forbidding anyone to address a petition to anyone but himself for thirty days, thus effectively, they thought, proscribing Jewish prayer.

5. See Talmud, tractate *Berakhot* 31a.

6. An assembly of seventy-one ordained rabbinic sages functioning both as supreme court and legislature.

7. Collection of oral laws compiled by Judah ha-Nasi in the third century C.E. These laws, together with commentaries on them, the Gemara, form the Talmud.

8. "External teaching"; oral laws of the Mishnaic period which were not included in the Mishnah.

9. In this introduction, the famed philosopher and scholar Maimonides (1135–1204) actually presents a history of the Oral Law from Moses until his own day.

10. Talmud, tractate *Gittin* 67a.

11. "Book of Judges," *The Code of Maimonides*, book 14, trans. Abraham Hershman (New Haven: Yale University Press, 1949), ch. 3, par. 1, p. 143.

12. See Neh. 2:5.

13. The reference is Exod. 31. Nachmanides or Moses ben Nachman (1194–1270), a Spanish rabbi *inter alia* noted for his halakhic and biblical commentaries.

THE REFORM RABBINICAL CONFERENCE AT BRUNSWICK
5. The Question of Patriotism[1]

Tenth Session, June 18, 1844. Continuation of the committee report regarding Philippson's[2] proposal [to endorse the position of the French Sanhedrin on Jewish patriotism].

Source: Protokolle der ersten Rabbiner-Versammlung ... (Braunschweig, 1844), pp. 74–76. Trans. here by J. Hessing.

Question 4 [addressed to the Sanhedrin]: Do the Jews consider Frenchmen as their brethren or as strangers? Answer [of the Sanhedrin]: French Jews are the brethren of Frenchmen.

The committee recommends that [the present assembly adopt the following statement]: The Jew considers members of the people with whom he lives his brethren.

Plenum discussion. A. ADLER:[3] He wants it to be said that the Jews consider not only the people with whom they live as brethren, but all mankind. Do not all men, according to the prophets, have but one Father? . . .

FRANKFURTER:[4] This is quite right. It is, however, not a question of ethics, but of politics. For Judaism, the principle of human dignity is cosmopolitan, but I would like to put proper emphasis on the love for the particular people [among whom we live] and its individual members. As men, we love all mankind, but as Germans, we love the Germans as the children of our fatherland. We are, and ought to be, patriots, not merely cosmopolitans. . . .

HIRSCH:[5] Differentiating between love for the fatherland and love for mankind, he proposes an answer analogous to that of the Parisian notables.

HOLDHEIM:[6] He traces the commandment of recognition and love for fellow countrymen back to the Pentateuch, where the love of the Israelite for the Israelite does not refer to their common religion, but to their common peoplehood. What was once a commandment for the Israelite *with regard to his fellow Israelite,* must also oblige us with regard to our contemporary compatriots—to the Germans. The doctrine of Judaism is thus, first your compatriots [*Vaterlandsgenosse*] then your co-religionists [*Glaubensgenosse*].

A. ADLER, therefore, suggests the following proposal: *The Jew acknowledges every man as his brother.* But he acknowledges *his fellow countryman to be one with whom he is connected by a particular bond,* a bond forged by the effort to realize common political purposes [*Staatszwecke*]. . . .

NOTES

1. It was gradually realized that unless the nascent movement of Reform cease to be merely the desultory effort of isolated congregations it would never obtain the authority to challenge the supremacy of Orthodox Judaism. Abraham Geiger, the most eminent figure in early Reform, argued that the necessary authority could be obtained only if rabbis supporting religious change would confer and establish common principles and a common program for Reform. In August 1837 Geiger attended a largely stillborn conference of like-minded rabbis in Wiesbaden, Germany. The first organizationally successful rabbinical conference on Reform took place from the twelfth to the nineteenth of June 1844. Twenty-five rabbis from throughout Germany attended. The above document is extracted from the protocol of the conference.

At the session of June fourteenth, Ludwig Philippson moved that the conference endorse the patriotism expressed by the Parisian Sanhedrin in response to the fourth question posed by Napoleon regarding the Jews' sentiments toward their fellow countrymen. Philippson's motion was referred to a committee, which, at the session of June eighteenth, submitted its recommendation to accept the motion. "By basing upon the French Sanhedrin, the first gathering of Jewish representatives resulting from the changes superinduced by the political emancipation of the Jews . . ., the conference, whether consciously or unconsciously, declared itself the official voice of the modern spirit" (D. Philipson, *The Reform Movement in Judaism,* rev. ed. [New York: Ktav Publishing House, 1967], pp. 159ff.).

2. Ludwig Philippson (1811–1889), rabbi and preacher at Magdeburg. Supporting a program of moderate Reform, he tried to steer a middle course between radical Reform and Orthodoxy. He was founder and editor of the most widely circulated Jewish publication of the time, *Allgemeine Zeitung des Judentums;* the newspaper was prominent in the struggle for Jewish emancipation and in the fight against anti-Semitism.

3. Abraham Jacob Adler (1813–1856), rabbi at Worms; he was an exponent of radical Reform.

4. Naphtali Frankfurter (1810–1866), from 1840 to 1866 preacher at the Reform temple in Hamburg; identified with the most radical wing of Reform.

5. Samuel Hirsch (1815–1889), chief rabbi in Luxemburg from 1843 to 1866; he then emigrated to the United States, where he was rabbi of Congregation Kennesseth Israel in Philadelphia until 1888. Opposed to the unsystematic reforms by radical lay groups, he upheld the rite of circumcision and the use of Hebrew in the public prayer service; yet, he was the first rabbi to advocate the transfer of the Sabbath to Sunday and he carried this out in the United States.

6. Samuel Holdheim (1806–1860), rabbi of the province of Mecklenburg-Schwerin from 1840 to 1846. In 1847 he accepted an invitation to serve as the rabbi of the newly founded Reform congregation of Berlin, which under his guidance became a center of radical Reform.

THE REFORM RABBINICAL CONFERENCE AT FRANKFURT
6. Hebrew as the Language of Jewish Prayer[1]

Third Session, morning, July 16, 1845. . . .The President moves that it would seem desirable to discuss the report [of the Commission on Liturgy] immediately.

Question 1: To what degree is the Hebrew language necessary for the public prayer service and, if not necessary, is its retention advisable for the time being?

Report of the committee: With respect to question one, the Hebrew language is not in every instance *objectively* necessary for the service, nor does the Talmud, with very minor exceptions, prescribe it. But since a large part of the Israelites in contemporary Germany seem to feel a subjective necessity for it, the committee considers the use of the Hebrew language advisable for typical parts of the liturgy: the *barechu,*[2] the *parshat shema,*[3] the three first and three last benedictions of the liturgy and the blessings upon reading of the Torah, should be recited in Hebrew; all other parts of the liturgy may be recited in a German adaptation.

The *President,* in accordance with the proposal of the committee, now poses the question: Is praying in the Hebrew language *objectively, legally necessary* [*objektiv gesetzlich notwendig*]?

Frankel[4] takes the floor. He deems the occasion important enough to begin with a few general observations. This rabbinical conference consists of the guides and teachers of the people. They are familiar with the people's needs and sorrow; it is their duty to satisfy these needs, to alleviate these sorrows, and to prevent any discord [among the people]. It is the duty of the rabbinical conference to show and to attest that it is moved by serious and sacred aspirations. Its spokesmen, therefore, have to begin by stating their *principles.* It is the pride of Judaism that no person, and no social class, may presume authority, but that every decision must evolve organically from principles and derive its validity therefrom. Points of view may be stated and put to the vote, but without principles they are merely private opinions. First of all, therefore, the people are entitled to an exposition of our principles. . . .

The speaker now explains his principles: He stands for a positive, historical Judaism. [This approach posits that] in order to under-

Source: Protokolle und Aktenstuecke der zweiten Rabbiner-Versammlung . . . (Frankfurt am Main, 1845), pp. 18ff., 32ff. Trans. here by J. Hessing.

stand Judaism in the present one must look back and investigate its past.

The positive forms of Judaism are deeply rooted within its innermost being and must not be discarded coldly and heartlessly. Where would we be if we were to tear apart our inner life and let a new life spring forth from our head as Minerva sprang forth from the head of Jupiter. We cannot return to the *letter of Scripture*. The gap [between it and us] is too wide to be bridged. Even a new exegesis of the Bible is subject to changing phases of scholarship and could not serve as a foundation of a firm edifice. Should we allow any influence on the *Zeitgeist*, on the spirit of the time? But the *Zeitgeist* is as fickle as the times. Besides, it is cold. It may seem reasonable, but it will never satisfy, console and calm the soul; Judaism, on the other hand, always inspires and fills the soul with bliss.

The reform of Judaism, moreover, is not a reform of faith, but one of religious commandments. These still live within the people and exert their influence. We are not called upon to weaken, but rather to strengthen this influence. We must not consider the individuals who do not abide by them; we are not a party and must therefore take care of the whole. Now it is necessary to conserve the things which are truly sacred to the entire people, to prevent any schism in Israel. Rather than creating new parties, we must make peace between the existing ones. . . .

Fourth Session, afternoon, July 16, 1845. . . . *Geiger*[5] demands a strict adherence to the expression of the problem as consisting of the following two questions:

1. Is the complete exclusion of the Hebrew language from the liturgy in general desirable?

2. Are there momentary considerations in favour of a provisional solution?

Both questions, however, overlap and cannot be strictly separated in the debate. The speaker considers it desirable to pray in the mother tongue, which is the language of the soul. Our deepest emotions and feelings, our most sacred relationships, our most sublime thoughts find their expression in it. He feels compelled to admit that as regards himself—although Hebrew is his first mother tongue which he has learnt before other languages, and a language he knows thoroughly—a German prayer strikes a deeper chord than a Hebrew prayer.

The Hebrew language, he continues, has ceased to be alive for the people, and the language of [Jewish] prayer is certainly not the language of the Scripture any more. It is obvious, moreover, that even a reading from the Torah tires a large part of the community.

The introduction of the vernacular into the service, it is claimed, effects the disappearance of the Hebrew language and thus undermines the foundations of Judaism. To this objection the speaker replies that anyone who imagines Judaism to be walking on the crutches of a language deeply offends it. By considering Hebrew as being of central importance to Judaism, moreover, one would define it as a national religion, because a separate language is a characteristic element of a separate nation. But no member of this conference, the speaker concluded would wish to link Judaism to a particular nation. . . .

Fifth Session, morning, July 17, 1845. . . . *Frankel* [takes the floor]. The ongoing debate, far from offering new ideas, has rather confirmed [Frankel's] point of view. Geiger considers a language to be the mark of a separate nationality and claims that the retention of Hebrew would testify to our national aspirations; this point, however, is not essential to the question under consideration. The cause of emancipation has nothing to do with religion, and no religious aspect should be sacrificed for it. Everything pertaining to religion must be retained, and if our nationality were religious, then we should openly confess to it.

In countries [that have granted the Jews full] emancipation,[6] such as Holland and France, he continues, experience has fortunately shown that the Hebrew language does not prevent the Jews from being genuine patriots and from fulfilling all duties towards the state. One has to be very careful with such expressions; our meetings are public, therefore "O Sages, be careful with your words."[7]

If Geiger goes on to claim that a German prayer strikes a deeper chord in him than a Hebrew one, he makes a purely subjective statement. Most speakers of Hebrew will feel differently, because this language is a stronger expression of religious emotions; as witnesses, the speaker calls upon the majority of Rabbis assembled here, who are familiar with the Hebrew language.

Hebrew, the speaker argues, is the language of our Scripture which contains every ingredient of our religion. Religion must provide not only an abstract but also an external bond between us and the deity, this being the reason for precepts such as the *tephillin*[8] and the *mezuzah*[9]; in like manner, the use of Hebrew in the prayers serves as an external bond. The language of the Scripture is a constant reminder of our Covenant with God. These various bonds and reminders resemble the sheaf of arrows in the following parable: As long as they remain bound together a sheaf of arrows is unbreakable, but as soon as single arrows are removed from the sheaf it will quickly fall apart. Many characteristic elements of Judaism have been effaced by now, it is time to halt the process.

There is another aspect to be considered as well. The Bible has been given to the Jews as a pledge to be safeguarded; they were called upon to carry it through the world for thousands of years. Mind you, not the priests of Israel alone were called upon to do so, but all of Israel. Samuel already, by establishing schools for prophets, undermined the hierarchy; it is therefor written of him, "Moses and Aaron among His priests, and Samuel among them that call upon His name . . . " [Ps. 99:6; cited in Hebrew], and the Talmud rightly remarks, "Samuel is equivalent to Moses and Aaron."[10] If the original texts of the Scripture were to become the exclusive property of a separate class of rabbis we should soon have a separation of priests and laymen again. But all of us object to the establishment of a caste of priests and wish to obliterate all memory of it. That is why our youth has to be instructed in the Hebrew language so that it may understand the service and the Scripture.

The speaker adds, however, that it is necessary to conduct part of the service in German; but Hebrew must prevail. The language of revelation, in which God has spoken to Moses, must act as an edifying stimulus. Hebrew, in fact, is so essential to our service *that its use should have been secured by* [halakhic] *law;* had anyone ever thought of abandoning the Hebrew language, such a law would certainly have been passed. The sages allowed another language besides Hebrew in the service [i.e., Aramaic][11] merely out of consideration for the weak who could not find their peace of mind in a Hebrew prayer. They never thought of excluding the Hebrew language from the Temple. . . .

PHILIPPSON: All extremes are to be avoided, and according to the general consensus neither Hebrew nor German should be excluded from the service. The question, then, is one of proportions. We do not work for the moment and for individual communities; we work for the future and for the whole [of Jewry]. The Hebrew and the German elements must be organically melted into one another.

We shall have to distinguish between *prayer* and public *services.* A prayer is the expression of the particular states and emotions of the soul, of happiness and unhappiness, of joy and of suffering, of sorrow, repentance and penance; here, a full understanding is necessary, and a foreign language utterly useless. The public prayer services, on the other hand, do not refer to the individual [*per se*]; public prayer is intended to stimulate, to teach and to express the confession.

The Hebrew language certainly serves as a stimulus. In it, for the first time, the *shema* ["Hear, O Israel," Deut. 6:4], the *unity of God* was expressed; the principle of pure love for mankind, "Thou shalt love thy neighbor as thyself" [Lev. 19:18; cited in Hebrew]; the sentence of the equality of all men before the law, "one law and one ordinance" [Num. 15:16; cited in Hebrew]; Moses spoke to God in Hebrew, "O Lord God, Thou has begun to show Thy servant Thy greatness . . . " [Deut. 3:24]. God had *begun* to reveal Himself to him. By using the original expressions, therefore, the public prayer service acts as a powerful stimulus.

When the Torah is read the Hebrew language will also act as a teacher. This reading must not be abolished, otherwise the people would lose all contact with the Scripture. . . .

As a *center of the confessions* the Hebrew language is indispensable. The German Jews are Germans, they feel and think in German and wish to live and act as patriots. But *Judaism* is not German, it is universal. The Diaspora of the Jews is not tantamount to the Diaspora of Judaism; the latter, on the contrary, must keep its unified character. The content of this character is the *confession;* its form is represented in the *Hebrew language.*

As citizens, we all strive towards *unity* with our fellow countrymen; as members of a religion, however, we are allowed, and even obliged, to retain that which distinguishes us. Facing an immense majority, the minority needs some distinguishing features. The Hebrew language fulfills this purpose.

The Hebrew language, moreover, is neither *poor* nor *dead,* as it is claimed. Masterpieces of unperishable value have been written in it, and as a language of religion it has remained fully alive. To repeat, the Hebrew language must be retained, but at the same time it must be organically united with the German element.

KAHN:[12] I am only speaking from an objective point of view. I certainly wish to retain the Hebrew language for the time being, but we must gratefully acknowledge that its use for our prayers is nowhere prescribed. Our ideal, therefore, should be the establishment of a purely *German* service, because language by itself does not constitute a religious element.

Our *school* ought to teach in Hebrew; the service, however, aims at edification, elevation, instruction; it should not be turned into a means for the preservation of the Hebrew language.

It is claimed that the Hebrew expression *Adonai* (i.e.,God) sounds more solemn than the German word *Gott.* To this differentiation I must seriously object, because it would cast a heavy doubt on our civil oath.[13] The name *Gott* is as sacred to me as *Adonai,* and I hope that everybody here will agree with me on this. (*General and loud consent.*)

We should not have any religious element wrested from us. Granted. But we must first concur regarding the nature of religious elements. Language is not one of them. The *shema* ["Hear, O Israel"] sounds much more religious to the German when spoken in German, and much more edifying to the Englishman when spoken in English, than when spoken in unintelligible Hebrew. With the elimination of the Hebrew language [from the liturgy], then, nothing would really be lost. . . . I vote for the introduction of a purely German service. . . .

LOEWENGARD:[14] It was said: "We are Germans and want to be Germans!" If this statement has any political implications I should like to remind you that we are not yet emancipated. (*Disapproval from all sides. The speaker explains that he merely wants to keep all political aspects out of the debate, because their introduction only causes misunderstanding.*) From the religious point of view, a distinction was made between prayer and service; this was correct. The reading from the Torah, for instance, is meant to demonstrate the unity of Israel established by the Torah, as it is expressed in "And this is the law which Moses set before the children of Israel."[15] Instruction [in the Torah] could be managed without this public reading, because [printed] Bibles are available in sufficient numbers now. As a demonstration [of Jewish unity], however, it should be sufficient to read selections from the Hebrew Pentateuch [at the public service and not also the traditional passages from the prophets].

NOTES

1. With thirty rabbis in attendance, this conference took place in Frankfurt am Main from the fifteenth to the eighteenth of July 1845. The Frankfurt conference was devoted to the consider-

ation of the report of the Commission on Liturgy established at the previous conference at Brunswick.

As a consequence of the new cultural and political situation of the Jews, two distinct problems emerged with regard to the continued use of Hebrew as the language of Jewish public worship: First with the neglect of traditional Jewish learning, Hebrew was increasingly unintelligible to many Jews, and second it was feared that the use of the "national language of the ancient commonwealth of Israel" would seem to vitiate the Jews' patriotic affiliation to the country of their residence. Accordingly, the Commission on Liturgy was requested to reevaluate the place of Hebrew in the liturgy.

2. Part of the daily service, the *barechu* ("Praise the Lord who is to be praised . . . ") calls the congregation to prayer, and affirms the belief in Creation as divine providence. It is followed by *parshat shema.*

3. Consisting of the *shema* (Deut. 6:4–9) and accompanying blessings (largely drawn from Deut. 11:13–21, and Num. 15:37–41), the *parshat shema,* recited daily, proclaims Israel's acceptance of God's sovereignty and the yoke of His Commandments; it links this proclamation with the doctrines of Creation, Revelation and Redemption.

4. Zecharias Frankel (1801–1875). At the time of the conference he was the chief rabbi of Dresden and the founding editor of the *Zeitschrift fuer die religioesen Interessen des Judenthums* [Journal for the religious interests of Judaism], published from 1844 to 1847. An exponent of "moderate Reform," as he put it, Frankel criticized the Brunswick conference (which he declined to attend) for appropriating the authority of an ecclesiastical synod, when in fact it was no more than a consultative body. Further, he charged that the conference demonstrated a single lack of deference to the regnant sentiments of the Jewish people. He decided to attend the Frankfurt conference in order to assure that his colleagues would not exceed their prerogatives.

5. Abraham Geiger (1810–1874). At the time of the conference he was chief rabbi of Breslau and the founding editor of the *Wissenschaftliche Zeitschrift fuer juedische Theologie* [Scientific journal for Jewish theology], 6 vols., 1835–1847. Considered the guiding spirit of the first rabbinical conferences, Geiger emerged as the leading theoretician and spokesman of Reform in Germany. He sought to ground the study of Judaism in a scholarly, historical approach (see chapter 5) that would validate Reform's conception of Judaism as an ongoing evolutionary process.

6. The Jews of Germany, of course, did not at this time enjoy full civil and political rights.

7. Mishnah, Ethics of the Fathers 1:11; cited in Hebrew.

8. Phylacteries, two small black boxes fastened to leather straps, containing four portions of the Pentateuch written on parchment (Exod. 13:1–16; Deut. 6:4–9 and 11:13–21). They are bound ("laid") on the arm and the head of the male Jew during the morning prayers.

9. Parchment scroll placed in a container and fixed to the doorpost of the Jew's abode. On the scroll are inscribed portions from Deut. 6:4–9 and 11:13–21.

10. Talmud, tractate *Berakhot* 31b; cited in Hebrew.

11. Aramaic is a cognate of Hebrew that was for many centuries the vernacular of Palestine. Biblical readings were translated into Aramaic in the synagogue for the benefit of congregants who did not understand Hebrew. Some of the prayers of the traditional liturgy are still in Aramaic, most notably the doxology known as the *kaddish*.

12. Joseph Kahn (1809–1875). He was the chief rabbi of Treves (Trier), where he officiated for more than thirty years.

13. In the Middle Ages a practice was instituted that required the Jews to make a special oath (*more Judaico*) when testifying before a non-Jewish court. Assuming that the Jews did not respect Christian jurisprudence, these oaths bound the Jew's testimony under rabbinic law. The oaths were accompanied by self-imposed curses, delineating the punishment, often in gruesome detail, if the testimony was falsely made; sometimes they were accompanied by humiliating rites, such as standing on a sow's skin. In France the *more Judaico* was abolished only in 1846, in parts of Germany not until the second half of the nineteenth century; it was still administered in Rumania as late as 1904. The Duchy of Brunswick abrogated the practice in 1845.

14. Joseph Loewengard, rabbi of Lehren-Steinfels.

15. Deut. 4:44; cited in Hebrew.

THE REFORM RABBINICAL CONFERENCE AT FRANKFURT

7. The Question of Messianism[1]

Eighth Session, July 20, 1845. Agenda: Discussion of questions pertaining to cult. Question 2: To what degree must the dogma of the Messiah, and anything pertaining to it, be taken into consideration in the liturgy?

Before opening the debate, the President[2] considers it necessary to remark that we are not concerned with the establishment of a certain doctrine of the Messiah, and that such doctrines will not be put to the vote; we are only concerned with how the existing liturgy should be evaluated in this respect, or perhaps conveniently changed. Points of view may differ subjectively, but it is hoped that a version acceptable to all will emerge. The numerous speakers, especially those who are ardent believers in traditional messianism, should beware of creating any doubt concerning their allegiance to the state. Such contrasts and seeming contradictions are easily resolved within the mind of the believer. Here we are only concerned with the demands of truthfulness, lest we pray for something that does not coincide with our convictions.

The committee report reads as follows: The concept of the Messiah must continue to occupy a prominent place in the liturgy, but all political and national implications should be avoided.

EINHORN:[3] The concept of the Messiah is closely linked to the entire ceremonial law. The believer in the Talmud finds his salvation only in the reconstruction of the state, the return of the people, the resumption of sacrifices, etc. Here lies the cause for all our lamentations over the destruction of the Temple, and our yearnings for the ruins of the altar. Ardent belief and unshakable courage were expressed in these hopes, uttered forth from the dark caves of our miserable streets.

But now our concepts have changed. There is no need any more for an extended ceremonial law. The earlier approach restricted divine guidance to the land [of Israel] and the people; the deity, it was believed, enjoyed bloody sacrifices, and priests were needed for penance. With increasing zeal, the prophets spoke up against this restricted view. Everybody knows the passage: "It hath been told thee, O man, what is good, and what the Lord doth require of thee; only to do justly, and to love mercy, and to walk humbly with thy God" [Mic. 6:8, cited in Hebrew]. The decline of Israel's political independence was at one time deplored, but in reality it was not a misfortune, but a mark of progress; not a degradation, but an elevation of our religion, through which Israel has come closer to fulfilling its vocation. The place of the sacrifices has been taken by sacred devotion. From Israel, the word of God had to be carried to the four corners of the earth, and new religions have helped in carrying out the task. Only the Talmud moves in circles; we, however, favor progress.

At one time I took the concept of the Messiah to be a substitute for the idea of immortality, but now I no longer think so. I rather consider it as a hope of both worldly and heavenly salvation. Neither this idea nor the concept of the Chosen People contain anything reprehensible. The concept of the Chosen People, in fact, offers the undeniable advantage, for it creates a beneficial selfconciousness in the face of the ruling church.

I vote for the renunciation of all petitions

Source: *Protokolle und Aktenstuecke der zweiten Rabbiner-Versammlung . . .* (Frankfurt am Main, 1845), pp. 37–77, 81ff. Trans. here by J. Hessing.

for the restoration of the sacrifices and our political independence. I should prefer our prayers for the Messiah to express a hope for a *spiritual renaissance and the unification of all men* in faith and in love through the agency of Israel.

HESS:[4] In discussing the concept of the Messiah we run the greatest risk of losing ourselves in diffuse theories. The question is simply whether one wishes to interpret the Scripture in spirit, or literally; whether one conceives of messianism as an ideal, or as the idea of our religious independence, unattainable without the full political equality of the Israelites; whether, moreover, one sees it as a bond with our brethren living under oppressive rulers. Let us therefore hold on to the fact that the concept of a personal and political Messiah is dead for German Jewry, and that we must not petition God for that which we no longer believe. . . .

HOLDHEIM:[5] Two points of misunderstanding must be clarified:

1. The hope for a national restoration contradicts our feeling for the fatherland; some speakers have claimed, on the other hand, that the two may coexist.

2. We are warned not to emphasize the national element, lest there be misinterpretations; but it was rightly remarked, on the other hand, that we should not pay attention to misinterpretations.

The main point, however, is this: We merely represent the religious, not the political interest of the community. The latter is sufficiently represented by other spokesmen. Our nationality is now only expressed in religious concepts and institutions. It is said: Our original nationality has developed towards religion. But this is erroneous; such a development is unnatural. One must not mistake a national for a religious phenomenon, otherwise many abuses could be justified.

The wish to return to Palestine in order to create there a political empire for those who are still oppressed because of their religion is superfluous. The wish should rather be for a termination of the oppression, which would improve their lot as it has improved ours. The wish, moreover, is inadmissible. It turns the messianic hope from a religious into a secular one, which is gladly given up as soon as the political situation changes for the better. But messianic hope, truly understood, is religious. It expresses either a hope for redemption and liberation from spiritual deprivation and the realization of a Kingdom of God on earth, or for a political restoration of the Mosaic theocracy where Jews could live according to the Law of Moses. This latter religious hope can be renounced only by those who have a more sublime conception of Judaism, and who believe that the fulfillment of Judaism's mission is not dependent on the establishment of a Jewish state, but rather by a merging of Jewry into the political constellations of the fatherland. Only an enlightened conception of religion can displace a dulled one. Those, however, who believe that religion demands a political restoration must not renounce this belief even under the best of circumstances [in the Diaspora], because religion will content itself with nothing less than the complete satisfaction of its demands. This is the difference between strict Orthodoxy and Reform: Both approach Judaism from a religious standpoint; but while the former aims at a restoration of the old political order [in the interest of religion], the latter aims at the closest possible union with the political and national constellations of their times [as the demand of religion]. . . .

WECHSLER:[6] As soon as we try to pin down the "how" of our hope, the hope immediately disappears. We ought not to vivisect our messianism, but to shape the existing prayers in accordance with our consciousness. We must not disregard the masses. If we had to compose new prayers, the situation would be different.

Therefore, everything already in existence should be admitted as long as it does not run counter to commonly accepted truth. *Political* and *national* do not seem to be the right expressions, anyway. Is the *People of Israel* a national or a political term? If it were so the word *People* should not be used, and all passages in the liturgy containing the word should be deleted.

The question only concerns the prayer for our return to Palestine and all its consequences.

In all contemporary additions to the prayerbook our modern conception of the Messiah may clearly be stated, including the confession that our newly gained status as citizens constitutes a partial fulfillment of our messianic hopes. . . .

Resolution adopted by the majority: The messianic idea should receive prominent mention in the prayers, but all petitions for our return to the land of our fathers and for the restoration of a Jewish state should be eliminated from the liturgy. . . .[7]

NOTES

1. The traditional Jewish liturgy gives prominent expression to the millennial yearning for a personal Messiah from the royal House of David who will herald "the ingathering of the exiles" of Israel to their ancestral homeland. The national sentiments of these prayers were considered by some reformers to cast doubt on the Jews' identification with the country of their residence and citizenship. The Commission on Liturgy was charged with reevaluating the place of messianism within the prayerbook.

2. Leopold Stein (1810–1882). From 1844 to 1862 he was a rabbi at Frankfurt am Main.

3. David Einhorn (1809–1879). In 1842 he was appointed rabbi of Hoppstaedten and chief rabbi of the principality of Birkenfeld. In 1855 he emigrated to the United States, where he became a leader of the radical wing of the Reform movement there.

4. Michael Hess (1782–1860). An advocate of thoroughgoing reform, from 1806 to 1855 he served as head-master of the Philanthropin in Frankfurt, a Jewish elementary and high school fashioned in the spirit of the Haskalah.

5. Samuel Holdheim, see documents 5 and 8 in this chapter.

6. Bernhard Wechsler (d. 1874). In 1841 he succeeded Samson Raphael Hirsch as chief rabbi of Oldenburg.

7. The conference unanimously approved the removal of the traditional petitions for the restoration of the sacrificial cult from the liturgy. The majority of the conference, however, voted that provided they were recited only in Hebrew the Torah passages concerning the sacrifice should remain in the liturgy.

SAMUEL HOLDHEIM
8. This Is Our Task[1]

It is the destiny of Judaism to pour the light of its thoughts, the fire of its sentiments, the fervor of its feelings upon all souls and hearts on earth. Then all of these peoples and nations, each according to its soil and historic characteristics, will, by accepting our teachings, kindle their own lights, which will then shine independently and warm their souls. Judaism shall be the seed-bed of the nations filled with the blessing and promise, but not a fully grown matured tree with roots and trunk, crowned with branches and twigs, with blossoms and fruit—a tree which is merely to be transplanted into a foreign soil.

Source: W. Gunther Plaut, *The Rise of Reform Judaism: A Sourcebook of Its European Origins* (New York: World Union for Progressive Judaism, 1963), pp. 138ff. Reprinted by permission of the World Union for Progressive Judaism.

Already 2000 years ago Judaism began to face its historic task and in this manner it must continue to face it. All these unnumbered peoples and nations which were once governed by paganism were converted to ways of thinking which are based—who can deny it—upon the principles of ancient Judaism, which gave them their singular color and form. A forced egalitarianism, which desires that all peoples of the earth should express their innermost thoughts and feelings with the same words, is neither the task nor the content of Judaism. From the beginning it expressed its decisive disapproval of the building of the tower of Babel, that is to say, of the desire to bind men to a single tongue and a single mode of speech and to extinguish their individuality and singularity. Judaism wants to purify the languages of the nations, but leave to each people its own tongue. It wishes for one heart and one soul, but not for one sound and one tone. It does not desire to destroy the particular characteristics of the nations. It does not wish to stultify the directions of spirit and sentiment which their history has brought forth. It does not wish that all should be absorbed and encompassed by the characteristics of the Jewish people. Least of all does it wish to extinguish the characteristics of the Jewish people and to eliminate those expressions of the living spirit which were created through the union and spirit of the Jewish faith.

As a mere philosophical idea, denuded of its historic characteristics and forms, Judaism can never become the common property of mankind. Our ancient Jewish sages correctly understood this important question of the relationship of Judaism to mankind and expressed it felicitously, even though they had a much more limited view concerning that which should be the norm for the internal aspects of our faith. Regarding the peoples of the earth, they spoke of the seven *Noachide* duties,[2] the fundamental rules of faith and morals, but reserved the whole Mosaic law for Israel exclusively. We must spread the *Noachide* laws to all nations, but we must safeguard the Torah as our exclusive possession. To be sure, we do not follow the letter of our sages' pronouncements slavishly, yet we must not fail to acknowledge their spiritual meaning and substance. Translating their words into our more purified expression, we would say: "It is the Messianic task of Israel to make the pure knowledge of God and the pure law of morality of Judaism the common possession of blessing of all the peoples of the earth. We do not expect of the nations that, by accepting these teachings, they would give up their historic characteristics in order to accept those of our people; and, similarly, we shall not permit the Jewish people to give up its innate holy powers and sentiments so that it might be assimilated amongst the nations."

Thus, my friends, we shall safeguard our position internally and externally. What the ancient sages called the seven *Noachide* duties in their universal human application, we now call the Jewish idea of God and the Jewish ethical *Weltanschauung*. When they considered the whole Mosaic ceremonial law as the eternal and exclusive heritage of Israel, we call it the inextinguishable historic characteristic of the Jewish people, the singular spiritual life of Judaism.

This, then, is our task: to maintain Judaism within the Jewish people and at the same time to spread Judaism amongst the nations; to protect the sense of Jewish unity and life and faith without diminishing the sense of unity with all men; to nourish the love for Judaism without diminishing the love of man. We pray that God may give us further strength to search out the way of truth and not to stray from the path of love!

NOTES

1. Samuel Holdheim (1806–1860). This sermon is from 1853. The national, particularistic aspects of traditional Judaism, as we have noticed, were problematic to the Reform movement. To soften these aspects the universal task or mission of Israel was emphasized; here inspiration was drawn from

prophets like Isaiah (42:6–7): "I the Lord have called thee in righteousness. . . . For a light of the nations . . . ." The "mission theory" viewed the Diaspora not as a tragic exile but rather as a sublime occasion to transcend the concerns of political existence and thereby illumine spiritual and moral ideals relevant to all mankind. Israel, according to this theory, was a faith community defined mainly by this universal mission. See also document 5, note 6.

2. The Seven Commandments of the Sons of Noah, which the Talmud holds to be binding upon all mankind, are derived from the early chapters of Genesis (e.g., 9:4–7). Six of these Commandments are negative: the prohibition of idolatry, blasphemy, murder, adultery, robbery and the eating of flesh taken from a living animal. The establishment of courts of justice is the only positive Commandment. Maimonides gave these Commandments a decidedly liberal emphasis when he related them to the Talmudic dictum that the "righteous people of all nations [Gentiles] have a part in the world to come" (*Hilkhoth Melakhim* 8:11). This interpretation, which became the authoritative view of Judaism, was frequently cited by Mendelssohn and other Jewish thinkers in the modern period, as evidence of a tolerant and benign attitude toward non-Jews.

AARON CHORIN
9. The Rationale of Reform[1]

. . . The permanent elements of religion must be expressed in terms that appeal to the people and are consonant with the needs of life. If our religion and life appear to conflict with one another this is due either to the defacement of the sanctuary by foreign additions or to the license of the sinning will which desires to make its unbridled greed and its false tendency authoritative guides for life. If we show ourselves as ready to strip off these unessential additions which often forced themselves upon our noble faith as the spawn of obscure and dark ages, as we are determined to sacrifice our very lives for the upholding of the essential, we will be able to resist successfully with the help of God all wanton, thoughtless and presumptuous attacks which license or ignorance may direct against our sacred cause; the seeming conflict will then disappear and we will have accomplished something lasting for God. I need not tell you that of all the external institutions the public service demands our immediate and undivided attention. He who is faithful to his God, and is earnestly concerned for the welfare of his religion, must exert himself to rescue our service from the ruin into which it has fallen and to give it once again that inspiring form which is worthy of a pious and devout worship of the one true God. For it is not only the excrescences of dark ages which cover it with disgrace, but thoughtlessness, lack of taste, absence of devotion, and caprice that have disfigured its noble outlines.

NOTE

1. Aaron Chorin (1766–1844). From 1789 until his death Chorin was the rabbi in Arad, Hungary. The first traditional rabbi to write on behalf of Reform. In his congregation he abolished the *Kol Nidrei* prayer. *Kol Nidrei* is Aramaic for "all vows"; the prayer opens the Evening Service commencing

Source: David Philipson, *The Reform Movement in Judaism*, ed. S. B. Freehov, rev. ed. (New York: Ktav Publishing House, 1967), p. 442, n. 112.

the Day of Atonement. He also permitted prayer in the vernacular with an uncovered head, approved of the use of an organ on the Sabbath, curtailed the seven-day period of mourning, and allowed riding and writing on the Sabbath. Chorin was one of the four rabbis who contributed to Liebermann's *Nogah ha-Tzedek.*

In July 1844, during the last weeks of his life, Chorin wrote from his sick-bed a declaration expressing his full accord with the prevailing spirit of the deliberations at the Rabbinical Conference at Brunswick. "The Rationale of Reform" is a similar statement addressed to a conference of Hungarian rabbis that met in August 1844. It is presented here as a concise summary of the rationale of early Reform.

SALOMON JEHUDA LEIB RAPPOPORT
10. Open Rebuke[1]

. . . Under what circumstances did Luther seek to renew the foundations of his religion? [Luther initiated the Reformation] as a result of his dispute with the Christian hierarchy over several serious matters [regarding abuse of power]. But what have the rabbis, the religious leaders in Israel done at present? What harm have they done and to whom have they sought to do evil? Are there still to be found in their houses ram's horns [to pronounce excommunication] or whips [to flog transgressors]? Were they even to have such authority would they desire to make use of it? What has led [the Reformers] to rise up suddenly against congregation and community? Nothing but malice. They are instigating strife and contention in Israel and stirring up immense hatred and animosity, of the kind we have seen with the growth of sects in the Second Temple period and later in the rift with the Karaites[2] and the followers of Shabbetai Zevi.[3]

. . . He who says that some small benefit will nonetheless sprout from the actions of these men of destruction is wrong; even were there to be some benefit it would be nothing compared to the great damage [caused by their reforms]. But in truth there is not the smallest trace of benefit. Were there some matter among our customs or laws that stood in need of reform or renewal, it would be reformed or renewed with [the passing of] time. Should the process of Reform proceed gradually and its consummation be delayed, we could not accelerate the process by force. [In the meantime] that which remains [unchanged] will continue to be firmly established. This is part of the ways of the wondrous Providence governing the people of God, and there are many passages in the Talmud attesting to this. . . . [Mere] mortals, however, even were they to number a hundred rabbis and a thousand philosophers, cannot alter that which has become widespread throughout Israel, even if the matter in question were of little value. No one will heed these reforms [elsewhere] in the Jewish Diaspora, for one quarter or even one half of the Jews in Germany does not constitute the entire [Jewish] world. The obstinate rabbis [who support Reform] are not even as one against a hundred when compared to the rabbis throughout the world who are loyal to the tradition. . . . Neither will they succeed in reforming themselves, for they have abandoned the Torah and discarded [its] laws long before they gathered together for selfish reasons in their conference [in Frankfurt]. And if they pretend that they are acting for the sake of their descen-

Source: Tokhahat Megulah (Frankfurt am Main, 1845), pp. 1–4, 6, 8, 12, 21, 26–28. Trans. here by S. Weinstein.

dants, they are either committing an error or are deceitful. We have no doubt that their descendants will prefer to embrace the religions of the gentiles rather than to remain members of an inferior, emasculated religion which contains no trace of feeling or spirit—of a religion which can neither inspire nor direct them heavenwards. . . .Moreover, it is not in the power of such an empty and impoverished religion to resist the worldly pleasures that will surely entice their descendants. The women of the gentile will help them leave the Valley of Tears [i.e., the exile] and to mingle with the merry and prosperous gentiles. [Moreover,] the rulers and the gentiles will not be tempted to allow them political liberty in their countries simply because they have abandoned the religious customs and beliefs of their ancestors. The intention and aim of the gentiles, and of the missionary societies that have been established in Rome, Britain and Prussia to convert us,[4] is not to reform our religion but to have us embrace their religion. As long as we do not do so, we are contemptible in their eyes, and perhaps the more despicable are those among us who put on wise airs and stand in our midst, "neither Jewish nor Aramean."[5] . . . The hostility and the vengefulness [showered upon us] by the gentiles during the Middle Ages was not really due to our observance of the Sabbath and the festivals, or to our recitation of lamentations on the Ninth of Av.[6] Rather, it was due to their burning resentment of us for remaining steadfast to our beliefs, refusing to follow their ways, against which we had been cautioned by the words of our living God. For this reason, hatred has not yet disappeared from the [hearts of the] resentful among them. They are merely too embarrassed to act against us now, as they did in the days of darkness and obscurity. . . .After the anxieties and fears aroused by the oppressive and destructive wrath have passed, and after we have withstood this wrath through all the evil times without relinquishing our faith, are we now suddenly to abandon this faith for the sake of imaginary honor and fabricated pleasures?

Are we to flatter the gentiles, thinking that we can thereby move closer and closer to them until, heaven forbid, there will be no difference between us, when [in reality] they are as distant from us now as they have always been? Woe to such a disgrace! . . .

To be sure, we have heard more than once the claim made in our generation that the ancient sages, the guardians of the tradition, permitted themselves on several occasions to make some innovations and changes in the Halakha with regard to what was written or accepted as tradition, such as the *prosbul*[7] enacted by Hillel. . . . Let us briefly examine this claim:

. . . [In the time of the *geonim*[8]] there was one law and one Torah for the entire community, from Egypt to Persia, from one end of the world to the other. The judgments regarding God's Word contained in the Talmud as well as in the words of the *geonim* were thus treated with esteem and respect, for their teachings and rulings were received and propagated through all the borders of Israel and their words were accepted without dispute. It is not surprising therefore that with the passing of time the presidents [of the rabbinic courts] and the heads of the academies [*yeshivot*] allowed themselves on occasion to enact some religious reform when they perceived that this was necessary for the strengthening and the preservation of the Torah. . . . But even in such cases they did not allow themselves to make even the smallest correction of any part of the Written or Oral Law. They introduced changes only in matters between man and his fellow, . . . or in matters between man and his Maker relating to negative proscriptions, so that no commandment would be transgressed. . . .

These changes were possible only because there was one great and well-established rabbinic court, to which all the courts in the remaining countries were subordinate, accepting all of its statutes, regulations and teachings. From the time that such a court no longer existed, that is, since the end of the rule of the *geonim* and their *yeshivot*, the nation has ceased to have leaders.[9] The teachers have multiplied and departed to their countries and cities in Asia Minor, Egypt and Cyrene, in the Greek Isles and Italy, in Spain, France and Germany. With the multiplication of communities, each appointed its own teachers and rabbis, and not one of them seeks to raise himself above the others saying, I and my court will rule and from us will come forth Torah. From that time on not one of them dared to alter the teachings and customs of our rabbis of blessed memory—the *tannaim*[10] and the *amoraim*[11] as well as the *geonim*. They did not enact any restrictions or preventive measures, for they could not prohibit for the entire nation what had been explicitly permitted by our rabbis of blessed memory and so much the more did they refrain from permitting even for one state or community that which had been explicitly prohibited. Where [in our day] is the rabbinic court that can say it is greater in wisdom and in the number of people obeying its promulgations than the great court that existed in the times of the Talmud and the *geonim*, a court which was heeded by all the people? . . . Moreover, it is inconceivable that [the rabbis of the great court] would have made any changes that would divide Israel into factions. Otherwise, that which was held to be prohibited in one place would be held to be permitted in another place and *vice versa*. Jews would not be able to eat the bread and meat of other Jews, for what was fit for some would be an abomination for others. That which was called a house of prayer in one place would not be considered so by those who came from another place, for many would refuse [to acknowledge] alterations in the order and text of the prayers made in opposition to the regulations and customs of the men of the Great Assembly. Differences would also arise among the men of the Great Assembly. Differences would also arise in the laws of marriage and divorce, and families would be separated one from another, so that the nation of Jeshurun[12] would cease to be whole and united as it was in the past.

. . . If you will say that you no longer wish to follow in the path of the Talmud but rather to free yourselves from its yoke, because this is the only way you can make any reforms in keeping with your views, and if you claim to be able to strengthen the Jewish religion, as you call it, by means of the written Torah alone, then I shall ask you, what you have accomplished by this? . . . We shall turn our attention not only to the long existence [of the Talmud] but also to the mighty and wondrous divine power that is visible in the Torah and in those who have sustained and transmitted the tradition from generation to generation. Know that it is this power which has carried us on the broad wings of time [through good periods and bad]. . . . How, I ask you, could we have continued to be a nation until the present, and how could we have been able to walk such a great distance along the path of history without losing our unity or having our provisions run out, if we did not have the support to sustain us on the path and to breathe a pure and refreshing spirit into the weary. This support comes from the Sabbaths and holy festivals, the *tzitzit*[13] and the phylacteries, the house of prayer and the houses of religious study and together with all these the hope and solace of a better future. And so they have preserved us, guarding us from the danger that we might become too lazy to proceed forward, preferring instead to lie with our mouths open, becoming drunk upon the wine of the time and its pleasures and upon the delicacies of the land and its people. The guardians [of our unity] have isolated us and placed restrictions on all matters of food and marriage, militating against our assimilation among the peoples of the world. . . . All this you wish suddenly to annul and cast aside, and [yet you] still imagine that the name of Jeshurun will endure? These [customs and laws] that have sustained and guarded us have been tried out and have passed the test of time immemorial. Do you think that you can proceed without them and try a new course, without knowing what results it will bring? . . .

What has brought you to deny Israel the comfort of the hope for a future redemption?

This is due merely to the cry of a few reformers who, like a willing slave,[14] say "I love my master, I will not go free." The negation of the hope for redemption has, in turn, led you to seek to change the texts of the blessings, a matter which, in any event, is not within your authority. [Besides] such a step can be of no benefit with regard either to our temporal welfare or to the strengthening of the spirit of Israel. Those among the gentiles who have considered the sons of Jacob to be loyal servants and lovers of their present homeland have done so knowing of [the Jews'] yearning for the holy land of their forefathers. They never rejected, nor will they ever reject, the Jews for seeking comfort in their prayers and pouring out their hearts over past troubles and future good fortune. In contrast, those who have hated Israel in the past will not change their attitudes to the Jews now and love or respect them because they have made themselves desperate and forlorn, without any hope for the future. . . .

Consider also the claim of the reformers that the Jewish nation or Judaism is sick and requires new counsel to make it healthy and to breathe into its midst a new spirit that will cure and sustain it. Let us assume that there is an element of truth in this claim. Even so, the remedy that some of you wish to offer far exceeds the disease. We may compare this matter to a man who received written instructions from distinguished and experienced doctors concerning how he is to behave regarding his diet, bodily activity and repose, bathing and all other similar matters. This man repeatedly ignored the directions of the doctors, eating that which they had warned him not to eat, and in general doing the opposite of what they had suggested. As a result his body grew weaker and weaker and he lost more and more weight, becoming so sick that he had to be confined to bed. [Nevertheless] he did not change his mind and continued to do that which he had been cautioned against doing. In his sickness he thought that it was simply his first doctors who had caused him all this trouble by always deterring him from that which he craved, [for] although he violated their instructions he did so in fear and sorrow. Therefore he sought new doctors, and his first demand from them was to give him the opposite advice of all that the first doctors had prescribed, namely, to make permissible every food and activity that formerly had been forbidden, so that he no longer needed to be grieved in all his actions. The new doctors listened to this fool, flattering him and allowing him everything. As a result they nearly brought him to the gates of death. This is the situation at present among a small number of our brethren. They shout, Judaism is weak and sick. What is the sickness and what caused it? It is due to the fact that many have transgressed the advice of the ancient doctors, the counsellors of the nation; [consequently] the youth have no religion for they no longer know the Torah. . . . You flatter the sick and wish to permit that which the distinguished doctors have cautioned against. Instead of strengthening and preserving our religion, as you seek to do, you will cause it to grow weaker and weaker.

. . . In my humble opinion, this should be our answer [to the reformers]: Our brethren, children of Abraham, Isaac and Jacob, you are demanding from us things that we cannot give you. . . . We teachers have been charged to instruct the people according to all that which has been written and transmitted to us for thousands of years. If you have made for yourself a new way either in thought or action we [nevertheless] will not separate you from our midst as long as you do not cease to consider yourselves as one of us and do not cleave to others. In our opinion, if your actions and thoughts will be in accordance with what you say, you will transgress some of the commandments of the Torah. But we will not on this account cease to consider you as being part of our nation. . . . We are all the children of one father; we share one Torah and even if you do not observe it in a proper and fitting fashion we cannot, nor do we wish to, compel you to accept our view. There is no domination in religion and no compulsion in faith. But from our side, neither can we, nor do we wish to, break down long-lasting barriers and permit you [to do] anything that has been prohibited by our ancient sages or free you from any principle of faith regarding either the past or the future. . . .

[When it becomes time to determine who is responsible for the decline in observance of the customs of our fathers and for the destructive split among our people] all the rhetorical language and visionary dreams which you repeatedly employ, words of untruth, such as "a step forward," "a new spirit in dry bones," and "a fresh wind over still waters," will be of no avail. The coming generation will know how to make a judgment that is exactly the opposite. The people of Israel have always followed the Oral Law, which gave, and will [continue to] give their religion a new and increasingly life-preserving spirit. The wearing of *tzitzit* and the laying of phylacteries every day, [the observance of] the Sabbath and sacred festivals, especially the Day of Atonement, as they have been traditionally celebrated by the God-fearing in Jeshurun, [the devotion to] the Torah and prayer and the sanctification of the soul every day, the abstinence from the food and all the lusts of the gentiles, the hope for future redemption—these are what have renewed, and will always renew, at every time and on every occasion, the spirit of life within our nation. These have been the life of the people and the source of its long life, in former times and forever more. The small sect of reformers will remain with their abbreviated Sabbaths and festivals. Their labor and endeavors on the Sabbath and festivals will be no different from what it is on weekdays. They shall exist without the hope for good times, without the Torah and without feeling. Their life will become like a flat plain and desolate wilderness, lacking flowers and all traces of beauty that could arouse the spirit. Their worship, with the ensemble of singers, will quickly become habitual and insipid, and the house of prayer will appear to the few who visit it as a theatrical stage. Every Sabbath the youth will sing without inner feeling what has already been written down for them. The preacher will demonstrate his proficiency in the movement of his eyes and the twisting of his lips. His eyes will be directed upward and his heart downward; he will set his mouth heavenward and his tongue will crawl along the earth. The few who hear the singers and the preacher will laugh to themselves, and from the house of prayer they will quickly proceed to [pursue] the cravings of their heart or to resume their labors. . . . [This folly will continue] until those Israelites who within their souls feel attached to heaven shall abhor them. . . . Not even all of your current expertise in language will enable you to avoid the names that will be given you by future generations, who will recognize you to be sinners, tempters, men who fan the flame of strife in Israel, men who love material things and hate matters of the spirit.

NOTES

1. Salomon Jehuda Leib Rappoport (1790–1867), also known by his acronym *Shir*. In 1840 he was appointed chief rabbi of Prague. Notwithstanding his commitment to Halakha, he had a broad interest in secular learning. Indeed, he was a pioneer in the critical, historical approach to the study of Judaism known as *Wissenschaft des Judentums* (see chapter 5). In this endeavor he cooperated with leading exponents of Reform, for example, Leopold Zunz, Abraham Geiger and Zecharias Frankel.

The title is taken from Prov. 27:5: "Better open rebuke than hidden love." This pamphlet was written in response to the Frankfurt rabbinical conference of 1845.

2. A still extant sect that first appeared in the eighth century C.E. Rejecting the Oral Law and the talmudic–rabbinical tradition, the Karaites rely on the Bible as the sole source of creed and law, claiming that they thus represent the pristine Mosaic faith.

3. Shabbetai Zevi (1626–1676), central figure in the messianic movement that swept through the Jewish world of the period. In spite of certain

excesses of behavior, Shabbetai Zevi, couching his claims in the symbolism of the Kabbalah, appealed to the people's deeply rooted longings for redemption. Although his apostasy to Islam in 1666 created a profound crisis, the movement continued to have adherents until well into the eighteenth century.

4. In the early nineteenth century missionary efforts directed toward the Jews were intensified; it was assumed that the increasing acculturation of the Jews rendered them susceptible to conversion. Rappoport is apparently referring to the following organizations: House of Catechumens in Rome, London Society for Promoting Christianity among the Jews, Berlin Society for Promoting Christianity among the Jews.

5. Palestinian Talmud, tractate *Sheviit,* ch. 4, 35b. The passage actually reads: "If you are a Jew be a Jew, if you are an Aramean [i.e., a Gentile] be an Aramean."

6. Ninth of Av, day of mourning and fasting commemorating the destruction of the First and Second Temples, both on approximately this date. It is also the traditional anniversary of the fall of Betar in 135 C.E., the expulsion from Spain in 1492 and other national calamities.

7. A legal formula whereby a creditor could still claim his debts after the Sabbatical Year despite the biblical injunction against doing so. Rabbi Hillel (first century B.C.E.) instituted the *prosbul* when he saw that people refrained from giving loans to one another before the Sabbatical Year.

8. *Geonim,* formal title of the heads of the talmudical academies of Sura and Pumbedita in Babylonia. These academies were recognized by the Jews as the highest authority of instruction from the end of the sixth century C.E. to the middle of the eleventh. In the tenth and eleventh centuries the title was also used by the heads of academies in Palestine.

9. The Great Sanhedrin retained its position as the central ecclesiastical authority in Jewry until the middle of the third century C.E., when the talmudical academies of Babylonia became the center of halakhic scholarship. For the greater part of the period between the sixth and eleventh centuries, the preeminence of the Babylonian academies, with authority alternating between the *geonim* of Sura and of Pumbedita, was acknowledged by Jewry throughout the world.

10. *Tannaim,* the Aramaic word for "teacher." Designation for the sages from the period of Hillel to the compilation of the Mishnah, i.e., from the first and second centuries C.E.

11. *Amoraim,* the Aramaic word for "spokesman." Originally used for the "interpreter" who communicated audibly to the assembled pupils, the term was used generically from the post-Mishnaic period to the compilation of the Talmud (i.e., from the second to fifth centuries C.E.) to designate the rabbis.

12. Jeshurun, symbolic name for Israel (Deut. 13:25; 33:5, 26).

13. *Tzitzit,* the Hebrew word for "fringes." According to the biblical injunction fringes are to be appended to each of the four corners of a garment (see Deut. 22:12). To fulfill this commandment the observant Jew wears a small four-cornered prayer shawl beneath his outer clothing.

14. Literally a "pierced slave." According to biblical law Hebrew slaves are to be freed after six years of service. If the slave refuses to go free and wishes to stay in his master's service, then the master pierces his ear with an awl and in this way the slave is bonded to him forever (see Exod. 21:5–6 and Deut. 15:16–17). The master here, of course, is temporal life and its pleasures.

ZECHARIAS FRANKEL
11. On Changes in Judaism[1]

. . . Maintaining the integrity of Judaism simultaneously with progress, this is the essential problem of the present. Can we deny the difficulty of a satisfactory solution? Where is

Source: "Die Symptome der Zeit," *Zeitschrift fuer juedische religioese Interessen,* 2 (1845), pp. 1–21. Mordecai Waxman, ed. and trans., *Tradition and Change: The Development of Conservative Judaism* (New York: The Burning Bush Press, 1958), pp. 44, 46–50.

the point where the two apparent contraries can meet? What ought to be our point of departure in the attempt to reconcile essential Judaism and progress and what type of opposition may we expect to encounter? How can we assure rest for the soul so that it shall not be torn apart or be numbed by severe doubts while searching for the warm ray of faith, and yet allot to reason its right, and enable it to lend strength and lucidity to the religious feeling which springs from the emotions? The opposing elements which so seldom are in balance must be united and this is our task. . . .

Judaism is a religion which has a direct influence on life's activity. It is a religion of action, demanding the performance of precepts which either directly aim at ennobling man or, by reminding man of the divine, strengthen his feelings of dependence on God. And because of this trait neither pure abstract contemplation nor dark mysticism could ever strike root in Judaism. This, in turn, guaranteed that the lofty religious ideas were maintained in their purity, with the result that even today the divine light shines in Judaism.

By emphasizing religious activity, Judaism is completely tied to life and becomes the property of every individual Jew. A religion of pure ideas belongs primarily to the theologians; the masses who are not adapted to such conceptions concern themselves little with the particulars of such religions because they have little relationship to life. On the other hand, a religion of action is always present, demanding practice in activity and an expression of will, and its demands are reflected in the manifold life of the individual, with the result that the faith becomes the common property of every follower.

Thus we have reached the starting point for the consideration of the current parties in Judaism. The viewpoint of the Orthodox party is clear. It has grown up in pious activity; to it the performance of precepts is inseparable from faith, for to it, the two are closely and inwardly connected. Were it to tear itself away from observance and give up the precepts, then it would find itself estranged from its own self and feel as though plunged into an abyss. Given this viewpoint, the direction and emphasis of the Orthodox party is clear. Where else, save in the combination of faith and meticulous observance of the precepts, can it find that complete satisfaction which it has enjoyed in the heritage of the fathers? When it will reject that which it has so long kept holy and inviolable? No—that is unthinkable.

Against this party there has arisen of late another one [Reform] which finds its aim in the opposite direction. This party sees salvation in overcoming the past, in carrying progress to the limit, in rejecting religious forms and returning merely to the simple original idea. In fact, we can hardly call it a party in Judaism, though its adherents still bear the name Jew, and are considered as such in social and political life, and do not belong to another faith. They do not, however, belong wholly to Judaism, for by limiting Judaism to some principles of faith, they place themselves partly outside the limits of Judaism.

We will now turn to a third party which has arisen from the first party, and not only stands within the bound of Judaism, but is also filled with real zeal for its preservation and endeavours to hand it over to the descendants and make it the common good of all times.

This party bases itself upon rational faith and recognizes that the task of Judaism is religious action, but it demands that this action shall not be empty of spirit and that it shall not become merely mechanical, expressing itself mainly in the form. It has also reached the view that religious activity itself must be brought up to a higher level through giving weight to the many meanings with which it should be endowed. Furthermore, it holds that we must omit certain unimportant actions which are not inherently connected either with the high ideas or with the religious forms delineated by the revealed laws. We must, it feels, take into consideration the opposition between faith and conditions of the time. True faith, due to its divine nature, is above time, and just as the nobler part of man is not subjected to time, so does faith rise above all time, and the word which issued from the mouth of God is rooted in eternity. But time has a force and might which must be taken account of. There is then created a dualism in which faith and time face each other, and man chooses either to live beyond time or to be subjected to it. It is in this situation that the Jew finds himself today; he cannot escape the influence of the conditions of the time and yet when the demands of faith bring him to opposition with the spirit of the time, it is hoped that he will heed its call—find the power to resist the blandishments of the times. This third party, then, declares that Judaism must be saved for all time. It affirms both the divine value and historical basis of Judaism and, therefore, believes that by introducing some changes it may achieve some agreement with the concepts and conditions of the time.

In order to have a conception of what changes should and can be introduced, we must ask ourselves the question—does Judaism allow any changes in any of its religious forms? Does it consider all of them immutable, or can they be altered? Without entering into the citation of authorities pro and con, we may point out that Judaism does indeed allow changes. The early teachers, by interpretation, changed the literal meaning of the Scriptures; later scholars that of the Mishnah, and the post-talmudic scholars that of the Talmud. All these interpretations were not intended as speculation. They addressed themselves to life precepts. Thanks to such studies, Judaism achieved stabilization and avoided estrangement from the conditions of the time in various periods. . . . [The rabbis] established a rule which was intended as a guardian and protector against undue changes. It reads as follows: That which was adopted by the entire community of Israel and was accepted by the people and became a part of its life, can not be changed by any authority.[2]

In this fundamental statement there lies a living truth. Through it there speaks a profound view of Judaism which can serve for all times as a formula for needed changes and can be employed both against destructive reform and against stagnation.

This fundamental statement helps to make clear to us what changes in Judaism are justified and how they can be realized. True, Judaism demands religious activity, but the people is not altogether mere clay to be molded by the will of theologians and scholars. In religious activities, as in those of ordinary life, it decides for itself. This right was conceded by Judaism to the people. At such times as an earlier religious ordinance was not accepted by the entire community of Israel, it was given up. Consequently, when a new ordinance was about to be enacted it was necessary to see whether it would find acceptance by the people. When the people allows certain practices to fall into disuse, then the practices cease to exist. There is in such cases no danger for faith. A people used to activity will not hurt itself and will not destroy its practices. Its own sense of religiosity warns against it. Only those practices from which it is entirely estranged and which yield it no satisfaction will be abandoned and will thus die of themselves. On the whole there is always a great fund of faith and religious activity to afford security against negation and destruction.

We have, then, reached a decisive point in regard to moderate changes, namely, that they must come from the people and that the will of the entire community must decide. Still, this rule alone may accomplish little. The whole community is a heavy unharmonious body and its will is difficult to recognize. It comes to expression only after many years. We must find a way to carry on such changes in the proper manner, and this can be done by the help of the scholars.[3] Judaism has no priests as representatives of faith nor does it require special spiritual sanctimoniousness in its spokesmen. The power to represent it is not the share of any one family, nor does it pass from father to son. Knowledge and mastery of the law supply the sanctity, and these can be attained by everybody. In Jewish life, spiritual and intellectual ability ultimately took the place of the former priesthood which, even in early times, was limited in its function primarily to the sacrificial cult. Even in early days, Judaism recognized the will of the people as a great force and because of this recognition a great religious activity came into being. But this activity, in turn was translated into a living force by the teachers of the people through the use of original ordinances and through interpretation of the Scriptures. At times these actions of the sages lightened the amount of observance; at times they increased it. That the results of the studies and research of the teachers found acceptance among the people proves, on the one hand, that the teachers knew the character of their time, and, on the other hand, that the people had confidence in them and that they considered them true representatives of their faith.

Should Jewish theologians and scholars of our time succeed in acquiring such a confidence, then they will attain influence with the introduction of whatever changes may be necessary. The will of the community of Israel will then find its representatives and knowledge will be its proper exercise.

The scholars thus have an important duty in order to make their work effective. It is to guard the sense of piety of the people and to raise their spirit to the height of the great ideas. For this they need the confidence of the people. Opposition to the views of the people, such as some reformers display, is unholy and fruitless. The teacher thereby loses the power to make the essence of faith effective, for in place of that confidence which is the basis in correct relations between teacher and community there comes mistrust and an unwillingness to follow. The truths of faith must be brought nearer to the people so that they may learn to understand the divine content within them and thus come to understand the spiritual nature and inner worth of the forms which embody these truths. Once the people are saturated with an awareness of the essential truths and the forms which embody them, a firm ground will have been established for adhering to Jewish practices. And if the people then cease to practice some unimportant customs and forms of observances it will not be a matter of great concern. And it will not, as recent changes have, lead some Jews into shock and hopelessness. They will no longer see all such changes as leading to the disappearance of our faith and language, as their pusillanimity leads them to believe, the end of the existence of Judaism.

NOTES

1. Zecharias Frankel (1801–1875). He attended the Reform Rabbinical Conference at Frankfurt with grave doubts regarding his colleagues' commitment to the place of Hebrew in the liturgy. On the third day of the deliberations he submitted a letter of resignation from the conference in which he stated: "The preservation of Judaism is the innermost core of my life and the aim of all my endeavors. I am ready to make any sacrifice for this cause and shall always resist any tendency to the contrary." To his profound distress the attitude of the conference to Hebrew was indicative of such a tendency. Subsequently, he endeavored without success to call a conference of all rabbis committed both to the adjustment of Judaism to the spirit of the times and to the preservation of "positive historical Judaism." In his attempt to develop a middle position—articulated in the essay presented here—Frankel was opposed from both Reform and Orthodox quarters. The pain at this failure was assuaged when in 1854 he was named the director of the Juedisch-Theologisches Seminar at Breslau; a position that Geiger, who was instrumental in establishing the institution, desired. Under Frankel's directorship the seminar became the prototype of the modern rabbinical seminary. The seminar's curriculum aimed to teach a "positive historical Judaism," which in this context meant a positive attitude to the practical precepts of Judaism and a critical "historical" inquiry into the Jewish past, including biblical criticism.

2. Talmud, tractate *Avodah Zarah* 3b.

3. Here Frankel means the scholar of the modern mode to be developed at the Breslau seminary.

SAMSON RAPHAEL HIRSCH

12. Religion Allied to Progress[1]

. . . "Religion allied to progress": [the leaders of Reform have] with undaunted courage embroidered [this slogan] in scintillating colours on to the banner of our present-day religious struggles, that the educated "progressive" sons and daughters of the new age might rally to this new flag of the prophet and advance with it unhindered. How leaderless was this new congregation of prophets before this new messenger with this new message of salvation appeared among them! Since the beginning of the century the ancient religion had been to them—ancient; it no longer fitted into the society of the sons and daughters of the new age with their frock coats and evening dresses. In club and fraternity, at the ball and supper party, at concerts and in salons—everywhere the old Judaism was in the way and seemed so completely out of place. And even in the counting-house and in the office, in the courtroom and at the easel, on board ship and in the train—throughout the stream-driven lightning activity of the new age the old Judaism acted as a brake on the hurrying march of progress. Above all it seemed to be the only obstacle in the race for emancipation. No wonder then that without hesitation they shook off the old obstructive religion and hurried into the arms of "progress." And in the political market-place where emancipation was to be purchased, the modern sons of Judah could be seen in every corner offering to exchange the old Judaism for something else, since in any case it had lost all its value for their own use.

For many a decade modern Jewry thus soared aloft like dust on the wings of a butterfly and tasted freedom in the unwonted airy heights; and yet they felt a pain in their hearts where the absence of religion had left a void, and at the end they were ashamed while enjoying the brilliance of modern life to be walking the earth without religion; they felt restless and miserable.

But behold! The prophet of the new message came into their midst with the cry of "religion allied to progress"; he filled the blank, pacified their conscience and wiped out their shame. With this magic word he turned irreligion into Godliness, apostasy into priesthood, sin into merit, frivolity into virtue, weakness into strength, thoughtlessness into profundity. By this one magic phrase he distilled the ancient world-ranging spirit of the Torah into a single aromatic drop of perfume so fragrant that in the most elegant party dress they could carry it round with them in their waistcoat pockets without being ashamed. By means of it, he carved out of the ponderous old rock-hewn Tablets of the Law ornamental figures so tiny that people gladly found room for them on smart dressing tables, in drawing-rooms and ballrooms. By means of this one magic phrase he so skilfully loosened the rigid bonds of the old law with its 613 locks and chains[2] that the Divine Word which until then had inflexibly prohibited many a desire and demanded many a sacrifice, henceforth became the heavenly manna which merely reflected everybody's own desires, echoed their own thoughts, sanctified their own aspirations and said to each one: "Be what you are, enjoy what you fancy, aspire to what you will, whatever you may be you are always religious, whatever you may do—all is religion; continue to progress, for the more you progress the further you move from the ancient

Source: Samson Raphael Hirsch, "Die Religion im Bunde mit dem Fortschritt" (1854). *Judaism Eternal: Selected Essays from the Writings of Rabbi Samson Raphael Hirsch*, ed. and trans. I. Grunfeld (London: Soncino, 1956), vol. 2, pp. 224–38.

way, and the more you cast off old Jewish customs the more religious and acceptable to God will you be. . . .

All this would of itself worry us who are of different mind very little. We allow everyone his own peace and bliss and also his fame, if only he would be fair enough to leave us—not indeed our "fame" (to which we lay no claim), nor indeed our "bliss" (which cannot be impaired by human opinion)—but at least our peace and quiet.

But the eulogist of "religion allied to progress" and its prophet has found it necessary to enhance the brightness of his cause by painting its opposite in the blackest colours. He therefore describes us, [we the so-called proponents of Orthodoxy] who do not believe in the mission of the new prophet, as the "black opponents of progress and civilisation.". . .

May one of these "fools and obscurantists" be permitted in the face of such provocation, a few carefully considered and objective remarks, for the purpose of stating fully and placing in their true light the facts which certain people are so glad to call "religious confusions" (because they fear lest they might be cleared up) and so taking the first step towards resolving them?. . .

[First] a point of fact, it was not "Orthodox" Jews who introduced the word "orthodoxy" into Jewish discussion. It was the modern "progressive" Jews who first applied this name to "old," "backward" Jews as a derogatory term. This name was at first resented by "old" Jews. And rightly so. "Orthodox" Judaism does not know any varieties of Judaism. It conceives Judaism as one and indivisible. It does not know a Mosaic, Prophetic and Rabbinic Judaism, nor Orthodox and Liberal Judaism. It only knows Judaism and non-Judaism. It does not know Orthodox and Liberal Jews. It does indeed know conscientious and indifferent Jews, good Jews, bad Jews or baptised Jews; all, nevertheless, Jews with a mission which they cannot cast off. They are only distinguished accordingly as they fulfil or reject their mission. . . .

Now what about the principle, the much-vaunted, world-redeeming principle of "religion allied to progress"? If it is to be a principle—something more than an empty phrase meant for show—it must have a definable content and we must be permitted to try to clarify it. In the expression "religion allied to progress," progress is evidently intended to qualify religion. Indeed, this is the very essence of the "idea," not religion by itself, but religion only to the extent and in so far as it can co-exist with progress, in so far as one does not have to sacrifice progress to religion. The claim of religion is therefore not absolute but is valid only by permission of "progress." What, then, is this higher authority to which religion is therefore not absolute but is valid only by permission of "progress"? What, then, is this higher authority to which religion has to appeal in order to gain admission? What is this "progress"? Evidently not progress in the sphere of religion, for then the expression would amount to "religion allied to itself" which is nonsense. It means, then, progress in every sphere other than religion. Speaking frankly, therefore, it means: religion as long as it does not hinder progress, religion as long as it is not onerous or inconvenient. . . .

The subordination of religion to any other factor means the denial of religion: for if the Torah is to you the Law of God how dare you place another law above it and go along with God and His Law only as long as you thereby "progress" in other respects at the same time? You must admit it: it is only because "religion" does not mean to you the word of God, because in your heart you deny Divine Revelation, because you believe not in Revelation given *to* man but in Revelation *from* man, that you can give man the right to lay down conditions to religion.

"Religion allied to progress"—do you know, dear reader, what that means? Virtue allied to sensual enjoyment, rectitude allied to advancement, uprightness allied to success. It means a religion and a morality which can be preached also in the haunts of vice and iniquity. It means sacrificing religion and morality to every man's momentary whim. It allows every man to fix his own goal and progress in any direction he pleases and to accept from religion only that part which does not hinder his "progress" or even assist it. It is the cardinal sin which Moses of old described as "a casual walking with God."[3]

Civilisation and culture—we all treasure those glorious and inalienable possessions of mankind. We all desire that the good and the true, all that is attainable by human thought and human will-power, should be the common heritage of all men. But to make religion—which is the mother and father of all civilisation and culture—dependent upon the progress of this same civilisation and culture would mean throwing it into the melting-pot of civilisation; it would mean turning the root into the blossom; it would mean crowning the human edifice with that which should be its foundation and cornerstone. . . .

Now what is it that *we* want? Are the only alternatives either to abandon religion or to renounce all progress with all the glorious and noble gifts which civilisation and education offer mankind? Is the Jewish religion really of such a nature that its faithful adherents must be the enemies of civilisation and progress? . . . We declare before heaven and earth that if our religion demanded that we should renounce what is called civilisation and progress we would obey unquestioningly, because our religion is for us truly religion, the word of God before which every other consideration has to give way. We declare, equally, that we would prefer to be branded as fools and do without all the honour and glory that civilisation and progress might confer on us rather than be guilty of the conceited mock-wisdom which the spokesman of a religion allied to progress here displays.

For behold whither a religion allied to progress leads! Behold how void it is of all piety and humanity and into what blunders the conceited, Torah-criticising spirit leads. Here you have a protagonist of this religion of progress. See how he dances on the graves of your forefathers, how he drags out their corpses from their graves, laughs in their faces and exclaims to you: "Your fathers were crude and uncivilised; they deserved the contempt in which they were held. Follow me, so that you may become civilised and deserve respect!"

Such is the craziness which grows on the tree of knowledge of this "religion allied to progress"!

If our choice were only between such craziness and simple ignorance, again we say we would remain ignorant all our life-long rather than be thus godlessly educated even for one moment.

There is, however, no such dilemma. Judaism never remained aloof from true civilisation and progress; in almost every era its adherents were fully abreast of contemporary learning and very often excelled their contemporaries. If in recent centuries German Jews remained more or less aloof from European civilisation the fault lay not in their religion but in the tyranny which confined them by force within the walls of their ghettoes and denied them intercourse with the outside world. And, thank goodness, even now our sons and daughters can compare favourably in cultural and moral worth with the children of those families who have forsaken the religion of their forefathers for the sake of imagined progress. They need not shun the light of publicity or the critical eye of their contemporaries. They have lost nothing in culture or refinement, even though they do not smoke their cigars on the Sabbath, even though they do not seek the pleasures of the table in foods forbidden by God, even though they do not desecrate the Sabbath for the sake of profit and enjoyment.

Indeed, we are short-sighted enough to believe that the Jew who remains steadfast amidst the scoffing and the enticements of the easy-going world around him, who remains strong enough to sacrifice to God's will profit, inclination and the respect and applause of his fellows, displays far greater moral strength and thus a higher degree of real culture than the frivolous "modern Jew" whose principles melt away before the first contemptuous glance or at the slightest prospect of profit, and who is unfaithful to the word of God and the teachings of his fathers in order to satisfy the whim of the moment. . . .

Our aims also include the conscientious promotion of education and culture, and we have clearly expressed this in the motto of our Congregation: An excellent thing is the study of the Torah combined with the ways of the world [*Yafeh talmud torah im derekh eretz*][4]—thereby building on the same foundations as those which were laid by our sages of old—[then] what is it that separates us from the adherents of "religion allied to progress"?

A mere trifle! They aim at religion allied to progress—and we have seen that this principle negates the truth of what they call religion—while we aim at progress allied to religion. To them, progress is the absolute and religion is governed by it; to us, religion is the absolute. For them, religion is valid only to the extent that it does not interfere with progress; for us, progress is valid only to the extent that it does not interfere with religion. That is all the difference. But this difference is abysmal.

Judaism as it has come down to us from our forefathers is for us the gift and the word of God, an untouchable sanctuary which must not be subjected to human judgment nor subordinated to human considerations. It is the ideal given by God to all the generations of the House of Jacob, never yet attained and to be striven for unto the distant future. It is the great edifice for which all Jews and Jewesses are born to live and die, at all times and in every situation. It is the great Divine revelation which should infuse all our sentiments, justify all our resolutions and give all our actions their strength and stability, foundation and direction.

Comparisons are futile. Judaism is not a religion, the synagogue is not a church, and the Rabbi is not a priest. Judaism is not a mere adjunct to life: it comprises all of life. To be a Jew is not a mere part, it is the sum total of our task in life. To be a Jew in the synagogue and the kitchen, in the field and the warehouse, in the office and the pulpit, as father and mother, as servant and master, as man and as citizen, with one's thoughts, in word and in deed, in enjoyment and privation, with the needle and the graving-tool, with the pen and the chisel—that is what it means to be a Jew. An entire life supported by the Divine idea and lived and brought to fulfilment according to the Divine will.

It is foolish, therefore, to believe—or to pretend to believe—that it is the wording of a prayer, the notes of a synagogue tune, or the order of a special service, which form the abyss between us. It is not the so-called Divine Service which separates us. It is the theory—"the principle" as you call it—which throws Judaism into a corner for use only on Sabbaths and Festivals, and by removing from Jewish souls that have strayed from their Divine destiny the consciousness of their guilt robs them also of their last hope of penitence.

The more, indeed, Judaism comprises the whole of man and extends its declared mission to the salvation of the whole of mankind,[5] the less it is possible to confine its outlook to the four cubits of a synagogue and the four walls of a study. The more the Jew is a Jew, the more universalist will his views and aspirations be, the less aloof will he be from anything that is noble and good, true and upright, in art or science, in culture or education; the more joyfully will he applaud whenever he sees truth and justice and peace and the ennoblement of man prevail and become dominant in human society: the more joyfully will he seize every opportunity to give proof of his mission as a Jew, the task of his Judaism, on new and untrodden ground; the more joyfully will he devote himself to all true progress in civilisation and culture—provided, that is, that he will not only not have to sacrifice his Judaism but will also be able to bring it to more perfect fulfilment. He will ever desire progress, but only in alliance with religion. He will not want to accomplish anything that he cannot accomplish as a Jew. Any step which takes him away from Judaism is not for him a step forward, is not progress. He exercises this self-control without a pang, for he does not wish to accomplish his own will on earth but labours in the service of God. He knows that wherever the Ark of his God does not march ahead of him he is not accompanied by the pillar of the fire of His light or the pillar of the cloud of His grace.

In truth, if only most Jews were truly Jews, most of the factors would disappear which to-day bar many an avenue of activity to them.

If only all Jews who travel or who are engaged in business observed their Jewish duties, the need would—as always—produce its own remedy. The Jew would everywhere find the food demanded by his religion; it would be but little sacrifice for him to refrain from business on the Sabbath; and even in the regulations laid down by State and public bodies enlightened governments would gladly pay respect to a display of conscientiousness which would in itself be a not inconsiderable contribution made by Jewish citizens to the society in which they live.

It is only through unfaithfulness of the majority that the loyalty of the minority becomes a duty demanding so much sacrifice, though the crown which it wins is all the more glorious for the thorns which our brethren strew in our path. . . .

NOTES

1. Samson Raphael Hirsch (1808–1888). Hirsch was born in Hamburg where his family belonged to the traditionalist opponents of the Reform temple of that city. After completing his rabbinic studies he attended the University of Bonn where he befriended his future adversary, Abraham Geiger. From 1830 to 1841 he served as the chief rabbi of the principality of Oldenburg. During this period he published his two most famous works: *Nineteen Letters on Judaism* (1836) and *Horeb: Essays on Israel's Duties in the Diaspora* (1837). Addressed to the perplexed Jewry of his day, both these works seek to demonstrate the viability of traditional Judaism in the modern world. Hirsch did, however, recognize the need to revise certain "external" aspects of Judaism—viz., aesthetic forms of the public worship service—in order to facilitate the Jew's adjustment to the modern sensibility. On the other hand, he emphatically rejected Reform and any changes affecting the principles and content of halakhic Judaism. Hirsch's response to Reform may be summarized as agreeing to revision of the externals but allowing no reform of the principles of Judaism. He added to this formula an endorsement of secular education and patriotic affection to the country of one's citizenship. In 1851 he was called to serve as the rabbi of the traditional congregation of Frankfurt am Main, Adass Yeshurun—a position he held for thirty-seven years. Under Hirsch's guidance this congregation and its allied educational institutions became the paradigm of his vision of a "Neo-Orthodox Judaism," or halakhic Judaism in harmony with the modern world.

This essay was prompted by the argument of Reform that the rabbinic tradition prevents Jews from finding their place in contemporary German society, not only because of the traditional Jew's distinctive dress and manner of prayer—which Hirsch agreed must be revised—but also because of the practical precepts of Halakha which were allegedly difficult to perform in a secular environment.

2. According to the Talmud (tractate *Makkot* 23b), there are 613 divine *mitzvoth* or precepts in the Pentateuch. Popularly, obedience to the "613 *mitzvoth*" refers to adherence to the Halakha.

3. In his interpretation of Lev. 26:21ff.—"and if ye walk contrary unto Me . . ." —Hirsch substitutes "casually" for "contrary."

4. Mishnah, Ethics of the Fathers 2:2

5. This mission, which has become more urgent in modern times, is concisely stated in a previous work by Hirsch:

> Because men had eliminated God from life, nay, even from nature, and found the basis of life in possessions and its aim in enjoyment, deeming life the product of the multitude of human desires, just as they looked upon nature as the product of a multitude of gods, therefore it became necessary that a people be introduced into the ranks of the nations which, through its history and life, should declare God the only creative cause of existence, fulfillment of His will the only aim of life; and which should bear the revelation of His will, rejuvenated and renewed for its sake, unto all parts of the world as the motive and incentive of its coherence (*The Nineteen Letters on Judaism*, trans. S. Drachman [New York, 1899], seventh letter, pp. 66–67).

V

The Science of Judaism

One of the distinctive features of the modern sensibility is a critical historical consciousness, or what may be briefly defined as the heuristic assumption that social and cultural reality can be adequately explained in terms of its historical antecedents. This assumption, according to the German social historian Ernst Troeltsch (1866–1923), constituted a veritable revolution in the consciousness of Western man.[1] To be sure, a sense of history is not entirely modern; it can be traced to classical antiquity. What is innovative in the modern approach to history is the comprehensiveness of its purview, the emphasis on critical methods and the proposition that the historical perspective demonstrates the irrefragable nature of man's cultural and social diversity.[2] Beginning with the seventeenth century,[3] the historian understands that his task is, in the words of Leopold von Ranke (1795–1886), to record "what really happened" ("*wie es eigentlich gewesen ist*"[4]): to isolate fact from fiction. So conceived, historiography was deemed an important supplement to the Enlightenment and the liberation of man from prejudice.[5] Ignorance and misinformation were held to be

1. Ernst Troeltsch, *Die Absolutheit des Christentums* (Tuebingen: J.C.B. Mohr, 1902), p. 1.

2. See Johann Gottfried von Herder, *Reflections on the Philosophy of the History of Mankind*, trans. T. O. Churchill, abridged and ed. Frank E. Manuel (Chicago: The University of Chicago Press, 1968), pp. 3–78; see also Georg G. Iggers, *The German Conception of History* (Middletown, Conn.: Wesleyan University Press, 1968), pp. 5, 29–43, 289ff.

3. See Friedrich Meinecke, *Historicism: The Rise of a New Historical Outlook*, trans. J. E. Anderson (London: Routledge & Kegan Paul, 1972), pp. 3ff. Meinecke correlates the beginnings of the new historiography with the breakdown of "natural law and its belief in the unvariability of the highest human ideals and an unchanging human nature" (ibid., p. 3).

4. Leopold von Ranke, *Geschichte der romanischen und germanischen Voelker, von 1494 bis 1535* (Leipzig, Berlin, 1823), p. x.

5. Van Austin Harvey, *The Historian and the Believer: The Morality of Historical Knowledge and Christian Belief* (New York: Macmillan, 1966), pp. 38–44. Paradoxically, as it developed in the nineteenth century,

primary sources of prejudice: in the face of fact all prejudice would dissipate. It is the sublime and urgent task of the historian, August Wilhelm Schlegel (1767–1845) wrote, to discern "whether or not something actually happened; whether it happened in the way it is told or in some other way. . . ."[6] To facilitate the isolation of fact from fiction it was incumbent upon the historian to assume a strictly scientific (*wissenschaftlich*) method of utter objectivity and detachment.[7] This emphasis on the scientific method required not only the suspension of all preconceptions, but also the suspension of one's metaphysical and religious belief systems, namely, those values and ideas one holds to be eternal and absolute. This latter requirement, in turn, reinforced the new historiography's initial assumption that all human institutions—be they social, cultural or religious—are time-bound and occupy a relative position in the context of history. From this perspective, the alleged absolute status of religious norms and values is radically challenged. The critical historical consciousness, thus, leads to relativism. For the historian confronting his own cultural and religious tradition, the relativistic premise of the new historiography is especially problematic. In his implicit questioning of the epistemological and ontological status of his subject matter, he courts the danger of attenuating his fidelity to the norms and values of his tradition.[8] On the other hand, a historical consciousness may deepen one's identification with and affection for a given facet of human culture, for as the Italian philosopher of history, Benedetto Croce (1866–1952) observed, the study of history may have a synthetic function, molding the sensibilities and personal values of the historian. Refracted and re-animated through the consciousness and writings of the historian, history, as Croce put it, is rendered contemporary.[9]

This contradictory tendency of the new historiography is manifest from the very beginning of modern Jewish scholarship, or, as it is called in German, *Wissenschaft des Judentums* (the Science of Judaism). This contradiction was reinforced by ideological motives—independent of the methodological premises of the new historiography—that initially prompted the introduction of modern historical methods into the study of Judaism.

---

historicism, the most common term for the new historiography, can also be viewed as an aspect of a European-wide "reaction and revolt of national traditions against the French Revolution and the Age of Reason" (Carlo Antoni, *L'Historisme* [Geneva: Librairie D'roz, 1963], p. 9).

6. Cited in Ernst Cassirer, *The Problem of Knowledge*, trans. William H. Woglom and Charles W. Hendel (New Haven: Yale University Press, 1950), p. 228.

7. On the ideal of *Wissenschaft*, see Fritz K. Ringer, *The Decline of the German Mandarins: The German Academic Community, 1890–1933* (Cambridge: Harvard University Press, 1969), pp. 102–13; see also L. Wallach, "The Beginnings of the Science of Judaism," *Historia Judaica*, 8 (1946), pp. 33–60.

8. Nathan Rotenstreich, *Tradition and Reality: The Impact of History on Modern Jewish Thought* (New York: Random House, 1972), pp. 24–35. Troeltsch contended that historicism presented Christianity (and all positive religions) with a grave challenge, for "once the historical method is applied to biblical science and church history it is leaven that alters everything, and finally, bursts apart the entire structure of theological methods employed until the present" (cited in Harvey, op. cit., p. 5).

9. Benedetto Croce, *History as the Story of Liberty*, trans. Sylvia Sprigge (London: George Allen and Unwin, 1941), pp. 19–22.

In 1819 the Verein fuer Cultur und Wissenschaft der Juden (the Jewish student circle in Berlin responsible for the beginnings of the Science of Judaism) was founded. At this time in Germany, mounting anti-Semitism, endorsed by many supposed liberals, followed in the wake of Napoleon's defeat and gained violent expression in the "Hep! Hep!" anti-Jewish riots of 1819. In response, Jewish university students, largely assimilated, joined with a few older *maskilim* of Mendelssohn's generation to establish a sort of anti-defamation project. The new historiography—based on the respectable and objective methodology of *Wissenschaft*—would be their principal weapon to battle the venomous calumny against Judaism. The "scientific" correction of misinformation regarding the Jews, it was believed, would dispel prejudice. Moreover, this information would restore the acculturated Jews' self-respect and pride undermined by regnant misinformation and anti-Semitic accusation. The overarching desire of the Verein, which was reflected in its program and in the scholarship that it sponsored, was to justify the Jews' membership in European culture and politics. *Wissenschaft des Judentums*, in other words, would facilitate Jewry's integration and honorable assimilation into Europe. After the dissolution of the Verein in 1825, this objective would remain a dominant feature of modern Jewish scholarship, at least in its first generation.

Concomitant to this objective were subsidiary motives, such as the cause of religious reform and political emancipation, which revealed the contradiction between the desire for a neutral *Wissenschaft* and the ideological motive for a reform of the Jews' place in society. This contradiction engendered a basic tension within nineteenth-century Science of Judaism, which is traced in the selections presented in this chapter. The selections also illuminate the methodological tension—the dialectic between relativism and the synthetic function—inherent within the new historiography.[10]

A word about the term *Wissenschaft des Judentums*, which we have translated as "the Science of Judaism." It has been argued by several scholars that "science" is an inappropriate, misleading translation of the German term *Wissenschaft* when it is applied to humanistic studies. Accordingly, *Wissenschaft des Judentums* has been rendered as "modern Jewish studies," "Jewish research," "Judaica" and "Judaistica." These translations, however, obscure the methodological and philosophical nuance that the term originally bore in German. *Wissenschaft* unambiguously meant "science" in the fullest sense of the term: a devotion to factual accuracy, normative neutrality and the quest for truth. To be sure, German scholars were aware of the difference in subject matter and epistemological status between the humanistic and social sciences on the one hand and the natural sciences on the other. This awareness is witnessed by the protracted debates in Germany regarding the differences between

10. For an appraisal of the *Wissenschaft des Judentums*, both in terms of its methodology and ideology, see the illuminating essay by Gershom Scholem, "The Science of Judaism—Then and Now," trans. Michael A. Meyer, *The Messianic Idea in Judaism* (New York: Schocken, 1971), pp. 304–13.

the so-called *Geisteswissenschaften* (literally, "the sciences of the spirit") and the *Naturwissenschaften* ("the sciences of nature").[11] It is significant that proponents of the former, while acknowledging that their respective disciplines do not possess the precision and measurability of the natural sciences, nonetheless insisted on viewing their effort as *Wissenschaft*: as value-free, rigorous research. This was particularly true in the nineteenth century, when it was held that *Wissenschaft* would be the basis of high culture and the bedrock of true humanity. Thus, at least at its inception, "the esoteric purpose" of *Wissenschaft des Judentums* was, as Heinrich Heine, a member of the Verein, noted, "none other than the reconciliation of historical Judaism with the modern science which, one supposed, in the course of time would gain world dominion."[12]

11. See Ringer, op. cit., *passim*.

12. Cited in Michael A. Meyer, *The Origins of the Modern Jew* (Detroit: Wayne State University Press, 1967), p. 173. Ismar Elbogen has highlighted an interesting anomaly concerning *Wissenschaft des Judentums*, which underscores its "esoteric motive," by noting that parallel disciplines did not use *Wissenschaft* as a designation: one did not speak of a *Wissenschaft des Christentums*, but rather *christliche Theologie*; nor was there a *Wissenschaft des Deutschtums*, but *Germanistik*. See Ismar Elbogen, "Ein Jahrhundert Wissenschaft des Judentums," *Festschrift zum 50-jaehrigen Bestehen der Hochschule fuer die Wissenschaft des Judentums* (Berlin, 1922), p. 139.

JOEL ABRAHAM LIST

1. A Society for the Preservation of the Jewish People[1]

Behind our decision to found a society for Jews seems to have been an apprehensiveness that in the future we, as individuals, will not be able to continue to live as Jews, or at least not in the way we would like to. Assuming that this is indeed our concern, the immediate question should be: How, then, have we Jews survived until now? To this question, it would be difficult to answer anything but that, even after our banishment from our ancestral home we continue to be a united people—that is, until recent times when a process of dissolution set in. The analysis of what has hitherto constituted the bond and unity of our nation should therefore be our first and foremost priority. There were three reasons for our former unity, which I shall state as generally and as briefly as possible:

1. The avoidance of everything which was likely to undermine our unity. We stuck together like a huddled flock.

2. The instinct for community, a purely human element, which develops when people are faced with a common plight. We clung together like people in a besieged fortress.

3. Religion. We all looked toward a common Heaven and did not lose ourselves in the multifarious activities of earthly life.

If it is evident from all this that we have never been a unity held together by some idea, and even less so, a society dedicated to the achievement of a common goal, we must at least admit that we have had a single-heartedness of sorts. . . . Even this singleness of purpose, however, is now profoundly shaken. Jews one after another are detaching themselves from the community. Jewry is on the verge of complete disintegration. We no longer isolate ourselves [from non-Jews], nor are we excluded to the degree we were formerly. Our personal affiliations, once mainly restricted to our fellow Jews, have greatly expanded, partly as a result of the Enlightenment which generally tends to distinguish human rights from matters of confession, partly because of natural sympathies developing on closer acquaintance with friendly Gentiles, and partly because of an obvious decrease in pressures and oppression from the outside. Increasingly, we are dedicating ourselves to the needy masses of society in general, rather than exclusively to the needs of our fellow Jews. Our humanity no longer recognizes external boundaries, and therefore it does not wish to be internally restricted to merely national objectives. . . .

Our venerable religion must cease to constitute the bond of our nation, not only because of its aforementioned mistaken goal—which it shares with all other religions—but also because of the severity of its [heteronomous] laws.[2] For many years now, a single-minded adherence to the law on the one hand, and a frivolous indifference to the law on the other, have brought about a division within the nation and even the defection of many, which in time is bound to grow and reach quite dangerous proportions. The divine, which the daughter of Heaven carries inside her breasts, does not feed us any more, and we are the victims of either hunger or surfeit. Everywhere, then, Israel rushes toward its decline which, other things being equal, sooner or later will inevitably have to occur. I say "other things being equal," meaning "things" created by time; everything born of time, however, carries

Source: J. A. List, Unpublished Lecture of November 7, 1819, in S. Ucko, "Geistesgeschichtliche Grundlagen der Wissenschaft des Judenthums," *Zeitschrift fuer Geschichte der Juden in Deutschland*, 5 (1934), pp., 10–12. Trans. here by J. Hessing and P. Mendes-Flohr.

within itself the germ of its own destruction. And yet my friends, we feel and realize that that which is unique to our nation, our natural essence,[3] is not merely a product of time, not merely a passing phenomenon. The ephemeral features of our external life can by no means vitiate the eternal values we bear deeply within us, and of which we are acutely conscious. We are aware of a substance within us, an essence of timeless existence. In that we are conscious of our existence as Jews, we wish to preserve our Jewishness, and since we *wish* to preserve our Jewishness, we *must* preserve it. We therefore have a clear conception of our being, of our common being, for otherwise we would no longer be ourselves and hence nothing at all. It is the most characteristic feature of an idea, however, that that which is necessary within it is at the same time possible, and the possible, at the same time, necessary. If we feel an inner necessity of our continued existence [as Jews], then we cannot deny its inherent feasibility. And, my dear friends, do we not ourselves constitute the most irrefutable proof of this truth? What is true for us who have convened here must be true for thousands of our brethren as well. And thus we have perceived a true idea of our inner unity. The dissemination of this perception and the realization [of this unity] should be the ultimate objective of our society. We should never lose sight of this objective, even though we may at times stray from it. The intellectual, vocational and civic improvement of the Jews, although it will be beneficial in itself, can therefore be nothing but a necessary consequence and a by-product of this wider objective. The amelioration of Jewish life in these areas is and should be a matter of concern for all mankind and the duty of the governments under which the Jews happen to be living. For us, however, there must be no greater concern than the integrity of our nation, and we must not shy away from any sacrifice to preserve it. With respect to the Jewish nation, we should regard as meritorious only those deeds which further the realization of this goal. All other deeds, from a Jewish point of view, would be unimportant, because I could just as well do them for any needy Gentile. As Jews, however, our national value must be more important to us than anything else, otherwise it would not be worth twopence that we be called Jews. Why then, this stubborn adherence to something we do not esteem and on account of which we suffer so much?...

If we are convinced of the truth [of these observations] and if it is in the name of our essential nationality that we feel called upon to form a society, then its purpose must be national—otherwise it would be something outlandish.... This task, surely, is the most difficult one that we can set for ourselves as Jews. It demands a great devotion to the community, both extensively and intensively. After having formed a society for the aforementioned purpose it should therefore be our first concern (a) to give it the widest possible scope, and (b) to do everything in our power to restore to our nationality all its dignity, a first step in this direction being the complete abolition of rabbinism which has disfigured and debased our nation....

NOTES

1. Joel Abraham List (1780–c.1848). One of the seven founding members of the Society for the Culture and Science of the Jews, he served as its president from March 1820 to March 1821. He was the founder and director of a private elementary school for Jews.

On November 7, 1819 six Jews—Joseph Hilmar, Isaac Levin Auerbach, Isaac Marcus Jost, Leopold Zunz, Eduard Gans and Moses Moser—accepted List's invitation to meet at his Berlin home. At this meeting they founded the society from which the Society for the Culture and Science of the Jews emerged in 1821. Aside from the desire to work for "the improvement of the situation of the Jews in the German federated states," the initial aims of the society were unclear. In this lecture, given at the first meeting, List sought to outline his understanding of what the society's purpose should be.

2. The members of the society—many of whom were associated with the nascent Reform movement—shared a hostility to rabbinism, or the dominance of talmudic Judaism in Jewish life.

3. This definition of the essence of Judaism as nationality, as opposed to religion, was novel for the time.

THE SOCIETY FOR THE CULTURE AND SCIENCE OF THE JEWS
2. Statutes[1]

Introduction: Paragraph 1. The discrepancy between the inner state of the Jews and their outward position among the nations has existed for many centuries. In modern times, however, this contradiction has become more apparent than before. A powerful change in intellectual orientation, among Jews as well as other peoples, has engendered new [cultural and social] patterns which daily enhance the anguish generated by this contradiction. This situation necessitates a complete reform of the peculiar education and self-definition thus far prevalent among the Jews; they will have to be brought to the same point of development reached by the rest of Europe.

Paragraph 2. If this reform can essentially be undertaken only by the Jews themselves, it nevertheless cannot be the work of all of them but solely that of an intellectually congenial elite of educated Jews. To work toward the realization of these goals, in accordance with these statutes, is the purpose of this society, namely: the society is an association of individuals who feel they have the ability and the calling to harmonize, by way of educational work, the Jews with the present age and with the states wherever they live.

Paragraph 3. . . . In order to fulfill its aims, the society should work from above by promoting significant and rigorous projects, assuring their accessibility and interest to the largest possible audience. Moreover, the society must not fail to secure a firm basis for [Jews] of the lower social strata who may have elevated themselves to the ranks of the educated. At the same time, working from below, the society should endeavor to influence the world-view of different social classes [among the Jews] through the dissemination of a clear, objective knowledge. On the one hand, then, everything that can serve to enlarge the intellect will be made use of, such as the establishment of schools, seminaries, academies and the active encouragement of literary and other public activities of every description; on the other hand, the young generation [of Jews] will be directed to crafts, agriculture and practical sciences, in order to suppress the one-sided preference [of the Jews] for petty-trade and to improve the general tone of their social intercourse [with non-Jews]. Thus, gradually, every peculiarity that distinguishes [the Jews] from the rest of the population will be overcome.

Paragraph 4. . . . In view of the fact that the society, in its nascent stages, will have limited resources at its disposal; in view of the fact that groping about in all directions may dissipate its energies and endanger its future existence; in view of these facts the society feels obliged, albeit in keeping with its basic concepts, to narrow the scope of its activities for the near future. The scope of these activi-

Source: Entwurf von Statuten des Vereins fuer Cultur und Wissenschaft der Juden (Berlin, 1822), Zunz Archives, Jewish National and University Library, Jerusalem. Trans. here by J. Hessing and P. Mendes-Flohr.

ties will be detailed in the following statutes; the broadening of this scope will depend on the degree to which the society manages to increase its strength.

First Section: Activities of the Society. . . . Paragraph 2. The society limits its activities for the time being to the purely scholarly [*wissenschaftliche*] aspects of its objectives, and to the practical matters immediately arising therefrom.

Paragraph 3. To achieve its objectives, the society will establish several institutes, the central one being: (a) A scientific institute. . . .

Paragraph 4. In order to provide this institute with all the necessary means and in order to increase as much as possible its effectiveness the society will establish: (b) Archives. . . .

Paragraph 5. In order to bring the more important results obtained through the activities of these institutes to the knowledge of the public, as well as to increase the general interest in the society's endeavors, the society will initiate: (c) The publication of a journal. . . . [2]

Paragraph 6. Finally, the society will seek to promote and to supervise in a more direct fashion the scientific development of the Jews in general. Accordingly, the society will oblige its members to help the more gifted individuals of the Jewish religion by giving lessons, in accordance with a general plan, in the society's: (d) School.

Paragraph 7. All institutes named above will be maintained by the society, which delegates the special supervision thereof to commissions appointed by it for this purpose; the commissions will keep the society regularly informed about the current affairs of the respective institutes under their supervision. . . .

NOTES

1. Although the society was founded in November 1819, the formulation of the statutes began only at the end of 1820. Drafted by Eduard Gans, Moses Moser and Leopold Zunz, they were passed by the society's membership—which numbered some fifteen at the time—on August 19, 1821. The official name of the society was suggested by Gans and was adopted the previous month. Gans explained that the concept of "the Science of the Jews" in the name connoted the goal of "rendering the Jewish world [i.e., history] part of one's consciousness." "The culture of the Jews" conveyed, according to Immanuel Wolf, who shared Gans' intellectual perspective, "the essence of all circumstances, characteristics, and achievements of the Jews in relation to religion, philosophy, history, law, literature in general, civil life and all the affairs of man" (cited in H. G. Reissner, *Eduard Gans: Ein Leben im Vormaerz* [Tuebingen: J.C.B. Mohr, 1965], pp. 64ff.). The name of the society should be read as having a double meaning, namely, Society for Culture and Science *among/of* the Jews; for as Gans emphasized, "the Jews were to be both the scholars and objects of their scholarship" (cited in Michael A. Meyer, *The Origins of the Modern Jew* [Detroit: Wayne State University Press, 1967], p. 217, n. 69).

2. The journal, entitled *Zeitschrift fuer die Wissenschaft des Judentums* (Periodical for the Science of Judaism) edited by Leopold Zunz, appeared for one year only. The phrase *Wissenschaft des Judentums* occurred for the first time during the course of the debate on the statutes (see Meyer, op. cit., p. 165). The first volume of the journal contained *inter alia* the following articles: "Legislation Concerning the Jews in Rome, According to the Sources of Roman Law," by Eduard Gans; "On the Belief of the Jews in the Coming of the Messiah," by Lazarus Bendavid; "Solomon ben Isaac, called Rashi," by Leopold Zunz; "On the Natural Aspect of the Jewish State," by Ludwig Marcus; "Basic Outlines of a Future Statistic [i.e., sociology] of the Jews," by Leopold Zunz.

EDUARD GANS
3. A Society to Further Jewish Integration[1]

. . . If the idea of our society is to be successfully realized, one must go back to the more profound preliminary questions, without which the basis for our future effectiveness cannot be assured. The preliminary questions, then, are two. What is today's Europe? And what are the Jews? *What* are they I am asking deliberately. Those who have previously dealt with the subject tried to answer the question: *how* are they? Their question was false, and so, by necessity, were their solutions. Who among you, gentlemen and friends, does not remember the stale "pro" and "con" with which, during the last five years—since the end of the War of Liberation—one-sided rationalizers have played their games. They labored under the delusion that all wisdom was to be found in one of the two. . . . While wrath and impetuosity were the mainstay of the opponents [of Jewish emancipation], the supporters indulged in exaggerated circumspection and attempted, with calculating exactitude, to spell out the alleged virtues of the Jewish race; large tables were prepared in which the advantages of the Jews over the rest of mankind were conveniently listed. The fallacy underlying both tendencies stems from the idea that world history moves as freely as the individual, and that it too must perform good and avoid evil—the fallacy of common sense which cannot be convinced that there may be another form of judgment, which involves neither approval nor disapproval. . . .

This is the situation: today's Europe, in our view, is not the work or the outcome of chance which could have been different, better or worse, but the inevitable result of the effort made, through many millennia, by that Spirit of Reason which manifests itself in world history. The meaning of this process, abstractly speaking, lies within the plurality whose unity can only be found in the whole. This we shall now have to work out in detail. As we behold the particular structure of today's Europe, we shall discern it mainly in the blossoming wealth of its many-limbed organism. There is no thought in this organism which has not yet come into being or found its shape; there is no tendency in this organism, and no activity, which has not yet bloomed into fullness. Everywhere one finds the most fertile variety of social classes and conditions, the work of the Spirit which gradually achieves its perfection. Each of these classes is a self-contained unit, complete in itself, and yet it does not gain its meaning from within, but only from another class; each limb has its own particular life, and yet it only lives in the organic whole. The essence of one social class is determined by all; the essence of all social classes is determined by the whole. Therefore no social class, and no social condition, is divided from any of the others by sharply drawn lines, but rather by a series of smooth transitions which bespeak difference and unity at one and the same time. To this totality, the Orient has contributed monotheism; Hellas the ideal of beauty and freedom; the Roman world the import of the state vis-à-vis the individual; Christianity the concept of the preciousness of human existence as a whole; the Middle Ages contributed the sharp delineation of the states and other groups; and the modern world has added its philosophical efforts, so

Source: Eduard Gans, "Halbjaehriger Bericht im Verein fuer Cultur und Wissenschaft der Juden (April 28, 1822)," in S. Rubaschoff, "Erstlinge der Entjudung. Drei Reden von Eduard Gans im 'Kulturverein,'" *Der juedische Wille*, 2 (1919), pp. 109–15. Trans. here by J. Hessing.

that all these contributions may reappear as moving forces after they have abdicated their temporary single rule. Today, Europe has given to the other [Western] hemisphere, as its legacy, the total product of its life of many thousands of years, without the scaffold of its history, however, and while in Asia the contrast [between the classes] ripens into perfection, Europe, a happy old man, may once again remember its cradle. This is the happiness, and the greatness, of the European: that he may freely choose among the manifold classes [*Staende*] of his bourgeois society and yet, within his chosen class, remain in touch with all other classes of society. Take this freedom away from him, and you have deprived him of his foundations and of his meaning. Thus is the [significance of] European life.

In contrast, let us now consider the Jews and the Jewish life. If one defines Europe as the plurality whose unity can only be found in the whole, one may now define the Jews as follows: they are the unity which has not yet become a plurality. In their earliest days, they were appointed to guard the idea of the oneness of God; but even without this idea, state, ethics, law and religion appeared as one indivisible substance. In this, the Jews did not differ from any other people in the Orient. What set them apart was their fertile creativity by which they gave birth to a new world without being themselves part of this world. When their state went down in ruins they wanted to cling to their concept of unity and therefore took hold of one single social class, the class of the merchants. This class granted the Jews their coveted unity, but at the same time it should have allowed their integration with all other social classes. That such development had been delayed for thousands of years may in part be explained by the fact that society itself had not yet completely developed; as long as numerous groups had not been integrated into a totality, this one particularity—Jewry—hardly seemed to be exceptional. Kept apart, and keeping themselves apart, the Jews lived their own history side by side with world history, held together by the artful convergence of their domestic, political and religious life on the one hand and by the disunion of the other classes [*Staende*] of society on the other.

In recent times, however, the Jews' particularity has become problematic due to the previously described developments in contemporary Europe. We have found Europe's strength and vitality to reside within its luxurious wealth of [socio-cultural] particularities and formations, which nevertheless find their unity in the harmony of the whole. The fewer the remaining number of unintegrated details, however, the more disturbing these details will seem; the pressure of the age to integrate these remnants cannot be rebuffed any longer. Where the organism wants a wavy line, the straight line becomes a horror. This, then, is the demand of present-day Europe: the Jews must completely incorporate themselves into [the social and cultural fabric of Europe]. This demand, the logical consequence of the European principle, must be put to the Jews. Europe would be untrue to itself and to its essential nature if it did not put forth this demand. Now the time for this demand, and its fulfilment, has come. What to many observers, who do not go beyond the surface of daily phenomena, may look like an age of recurrent, incomprehensible hatred and reawakened barbarism,[2] is nothing but the symptom of the struggle which must precede unification. For precisely this struggle is the full triumph of world history's necessary development: those who think that they can stand in its way, or even destroy it, serve the inevitable progress of events no less than its so-called supporters. . . .

The way in which the Jewish world will merge into the European follows from the above-mentioned principle. To merge does not mean to perish [*aufgehen ist nicht untergehen*].[3] Only the obstinate, self-centered independence of the Jews will be destroyed, not that element which becomes a part of the whole; serving the totality, this element shall lose nothing of its independence or substance. The larger entity [which will embrace all Judaism] shall be the richer for the new ingredient, not the poorer for the lost contrast.[4]

... The wealth of its particularities is the very source of Europe's strength, and it can neither scorn it nor ever have too much of it. No particularity will ever harm Europe; only the single [autonomous] rule of this particularity, its exclusive self-righteousness, must be abolished; it must become a dependent particle among the many. They who see no third alternative between destruction and conspicuous distinction; who consider the eternal substrate of the idea to be its transitory rather than its material [embodiment]; who do not recognize the truth of the whole in every particularity and the truth of every particularity in the whole; who accept their respective viewpoint as the absolute, and reject another as a lie: they have neither understood their age nor the question at hand. This, however, is the consoling lesson of history properly understood: that everything passes without perishing, and yet persists, although it has long been consigned to the past. That is why neither the Jews will perish nor Judaism dissolve; in the larger movement of the whole they will seem to have disappeared, and yet they will live on as the river lives on in the ocean. Remember, gentlemen and friends, remember on this occasion the words of one of the most noble men of the German fatherland, one of its greatest theologians and poets. His words express the intention of my thoughts more concisely: "There will be a time when no one in Europe will ask any longer, who is a Jew and who is a Christian?"[5]

To hasten the coming of this day, to bring it about with all the power at our disposal, and by concentrated effort: this is the task, gentlemen, which we have set for ourselves in establishing our society. What I have said thus far is nothing but an elaboration upon the first paragraph of our statutes. To recapitulate: we wish to help in pulling down the barrier which still exists between the Jew and the Christian, between the Jewish world and Europe; we want to reconcile that which, for thousands of years, has been moving along side by side without so much as touching each other....

We met for the first time toward the end of the year 1819. In many places of the German fatherland those horrible acts had occurred which to many seemed as the harbinger of an unforeseen return of the darkest Middle Ages.[6] We met with a view to help where it was necessary, and in order to consult with one another as to the means by which the deeply rooted malignancy could best be eradicated. At that time we did not have a more detailed purpose. We were then at the beginning of our efforts, sharing in all the wealth and all the poverty which every beginning offers simultaneously: wealth, because all further developments lay still before us, and poverty, because none of these developments had yet come into being. As befits all periods of childhood, a long time of contemplation had to pass before we could begin to work. We should have gladly encompassed all aspects of life; it hurt us to concentrate on a given detail, because in doing so we seemed to be missing so much. Only deeper insight taught us that he who cares for a detail is the most powerful protagonist of the whole. But as soon as we restricted ourselves we gained the certainty which hitherto eluded us. Only through this restriction did our society come into being.

In this restriction, however, we have been guided by a truly philosophical conception. Although we felt that, with the limited strength and means at our disposal, we could, for the time being, only deal with the scientific aspects of our project, we nevertheless did not yield to any one-sidedness, forgetting the many other directions of life. We have never failed to cling to the totality of all phenomena of life as our constant basis. No landowner will turn over a part of his ground just because he cannot be at all parts at one and the same time; in like manner, we have never neglected any single activity just because we could not start with all of them simultaneously. Here I am only recapitulating what has been laid down in the introduction to our statutes. May I now proceed to develop the major themes of our scientific activity in their natural order, and briefly characterize each one of them.

The scientific study of Jewish religion, history and philosophy has so far been either bereft of freedom or of independence. The studies of ignorant, prejudiced rabbis, who conceived of Judaism not as a part of the whole, but as exclusive and isolated from other branches of knowledge, did not produce any faithful or credible results—nor could they have done so, innocent as they were of any knowledge beyond their own narrow field. Any credible results [in the field of Jewish scholarship] are mainly due to the efforts of Christian scholars. But while the rabbis lacked the necessary freedom in their studies, the Christian approach to Judaism lacked independence: much too often it was turned it into a discipline secondary, and merely ancillary, to Christian theology. Our first priority, therefore, ought to be the establishment of an unbiased and completely independent study of the Science of Judaism which will be integrated into the whole of human knowledge. . . .

NOTES

1. Eduard Gans (1798–1839), a descendant of court Jews. Gans was a jurist and historian. One of the seven founding members of the Society for the Culture and Science of the Jews, he served as its president from March 1821 until November 1823. Some four years earlier, on December 9, 1819, a month after the inaugural meeting of the society, Gans submitted an application to the Prussian minister of education for an academic appointment at the Law Faculty of the University of Berlin. The minister unabashedly indicated his doubts as to whether a professing Jew, no matter how qualified, possessed the requisite spiritual aptitude to serve as a custodian of the German-Christian heritage, especially of such a subject as jurisprudence. Chagrined, Gans wrote to the minister: "I belong to that unfortunate class of human beings, which is hated because it is uneducated, and persecuted because it tries to educate itself." After repeated appeals, in August 1822, the Prussian cabinet responded by explicitly amending the law to ban members of the Jewish faith from academic teaching positions. Gans subsequently went to Belgium, England and France in search of a possible appointment. He was unsuccessful. In exasperation, he was baptized in Paris on December 12, 1825. As a Christian he returned to Berlin and was immediately granted the position he was previously refused as a Jew.

In this semi-annual presidential address, delivered before the society in April 1822, Gans seeks to clarify the philosophical basis of the society. An outstanding student of Hegel, he was naturally influenced by his master.

2. Gans is referring to the 1819 outbreak of anti-Jewish literature and riots.

3. Cf. Hegel's use of the term *Aufhebung*—connoting both abrogation and preservation—to designate the dialectic process in which a lower stage of history is both cancelled and preserved in a higher one.

4. Cf. "Philosophy, as occupying itself with the True, has to do with the *eternally present*. Nothing in the past is lost for it, for the Idea is ever present; Spirit is immortal; with it there is no past, no future, but an essential *now*. This necessarily implies that the present form of Spirit comprehends within it all earlier steps. The grades which Spirit seems to have left behind it, it still possesses in the depths of its present" (Georg Wilhelm Friedrich Hegel, *The Philosophy of History*, trans. J. Sibree [New York: Dover Publications, 1956], p. 79). This book, based on Hegel's lectures, was first edited and published by Gans.

5. The citation is from Johann Gottfried von Herder, *Reflections on the Philosophy of the History of Mankind*, trans. T. O. Churchill, abridged and ed. Frank E. Manuel (Chicago: The University of Chicago Press, 1968), p. 15.

6. Gans is referring to the anti-Jewish riots—the so-called Hep! Hep! riots—that broke out in August 1819 in Germany and spread to Denmark. The authorities exploited the riots to argue against the wisdom of emancipation since it obviously engendered untoward social tensions. In light of Gans' and his friends' concern about the riots, it should be noted that the Jewish establishment sought to belittle the riots' significance.

"Hep! Hep!" was an anti-Jewish slogan used during the riots of 1819. The cry was then said to be of Crusader origin, formed from the initials of the words *Hierosolyma est perdita* ("Jerusalem is lost").

IMMANUEL WOLF

4. On the Concept of a Science of Judaism[1]

Judaism, based on its own inner principle and embodied, on the one hand, in a comprehensive literature, and, on the other, in the life of a large number of human beings, both can be and needs to be treated scientifically. Hitherto, however, it has never been described scientifically and comprehensively from a wholly independent standpoint. What Jewish scholars have achieved, especially in earlier times, is mostly theological in character. In particular, they have almost completely neglected the study of history. But Christian scholars, however great their merit in the development of individual aspects of Judaism, have almost always treated Judaism for the sake of a historical understanding of Christian theology, even if it was not their intention to place Judaism itself in a hateful light, or, as they put it, to confute Judaism. Even though some important scholarly works written from a general literary standpoint and interest have emerged, not merely as vehicles or propaedeutics for Christian theology (which is admittedly difficult to separate from Jewish theology), these achievements apply only to individual aspects of the whole. But if Judaism is to become an object of science in its own right and if a science of Judaism is to be formed, then it is obvious that quite a different method of treatment is under discussion. But any object, no matter of what type, that in its essence is of interest to the human spirit, and comprehensive in its diverse formation and development, can become the object of a special science.

The content of this special science is the systematic unfolding and representation of its object in its whole sweep, for its own sake and not for any ulterior purpose. If we apply this to the science of Judaism, then the following characteristics emerge:

1. The science of Judaism comprehends Judaism in its fullest scope;

2. It unfolds Judaism in accordance with its essence and describes it systematically, always relating individual features back to the fundamental principle of the whole;

3. It treats the object of study in and for itself, for its own sake, and not for any special purpose or definite intention. It begins without any preconceived opinion and is not concerned with the final result. Its aim is neither to put its object in a favorable, nor in an unfavorable light, in relation to prevailing views, but to show it as it is. Science is self-sufficient and is in itself an essential need of the human spirit. It, therefore, needs to serve no other purpose than its own. But it is for that reason no less true that each science not only exercises its most important influence on other sciences but also on life. This can easily be shown to be true of the science of Judaism. . . .

The aim will be to depict Judaism, first from a historical standpoint, as it has gradually developed and taken shape, and then philosophically, according to its inner essence and idea. The textual knowledge of the literature of Judaism must precede both methods of study. Thus we have, first, the textual study of Judaism; second, a history of Judaism; third, a philosophy of Judaism. . . .

This would be, in general outline, the framework of the science of Judaism. A vast field embracing literary researches, compilations, and developments. But if the object, as such, is important in science and the human

Source: Immanuel Wolf, "Ueber den Begriff einer Wissenschaft des Judentums," *Zeitschrift fuer die Wissenschaft des Judentums*, 1, no. 1 (1822), pp. 1ff. trans. Lionel E. Kochan, *Leo Baeck Institute Year Book*, 2 (1957), pp. 201–3. Reprinted by permission of the Leo Baeck Institute.

spirit in general, its progressive development is bound to follow. The truly scientific spirit, therefore, cannot on account of the multifariousness and the vast scope of the field doubt the possibility that such a science might be established. The essence of science is universality, infinity; and therein lies the spur and the attraction which it has for the human spirit whose nobler nature rejects any limitations, any rest, any standing still. . . .

It remains to indicate in a few words that aspect in the light of which establishment of a science of Judaism seems to be a necessity of our age. This is the inner world of the Jews themselves. This world, too, has in many ways been disturbed and shaken by the unrelenting progress of the spirit and the associated changes in the life of the nations. It is manifest everywhere that the fundamental principle of Judaism is again in a state of inner ferment, striving to assume a shape in harmony with the spirit of the times. But in accordance with the age, this development can only take place through the medium of science. For the scientific attitude is the characteristic attitude of our time. But as the formation of a science of Judaism is an *essential need* of the Jews themselves, it is clear that, although the field of science is open to all men, it is primarily the Jews who are called upon to devote themselves to it. The Jews must once again show their mettle as doughty fellow workers in a common task of mankind. They must raise themselves and their principle to the level of a science, for this is the attitude of the European world. On this level the relationship of strangeness in which Jews and Judaism have hitherto stood to the outside world must vanish. And if one day a bond is to join the whole of humanity, then it is *the bond of science, the bond of pure rationality, the bond of truth.*[2]

NOTES

1. Immanuel Wohlwill (pseudonym, *Immanuel Wolf,* 1799–1829). A student of philosophy at the University of Berlin, he served as secretary of the Society for the Culture and Science of the Jews from 1821 to 1822. This essay served to introduce the society's journal and to define the concept of the Science of Judaism. Like that of his friend Gans, Wolf's thought has a strong Hegelian bent.

2. This dogmatic valuation of science betrays a basic flaw in the society's ideology. "Though the leaders [of the society] were concerned with giving expression to their consciousness of themselves as Jews, they failed to develop a rationale for a continued Jewish identification. Their conception of the future did not provide any incentive for the Jew to remain a Jew. The goal was integration into Europe without specification as to how it was to differ from total absorption. Their primary concern was the Jew as human being, not as Jew; they wanted only to lift him to a higher level of self-understanding" (Michael Meyer, *The Origins of the Modern Jew* [Detroit: Wayne State University Press, 1967], p. 180). This ideological flaw may explain why the society so quickly collapsed in the wake of the resignation of its president, Gans. After a Royal Cabinet Order of August 1822 legally proscribed Jews from teaching in Prussia, Gans, in dire economic straits, accepted a government travel grant as "compensation." This act of acquiescence to the powers of reaction irreparably undermined Gans' moral authority within the society, obliging him to withdraw. Dispirited, the society formally dissolved in May 1824. Gans' baptism in December 1825 only added an ironic and tragic coda to the story of a society that was to restore Jewish pride. Gans was not the only member of the society to permit the dictates of career to compromise his integrity and accept baptism. It is, however, an exaggeration to speak of a mass conversion of the society's members. Of a total of eighty-one regular and honorary members only six converted (see H.G. Reissner, *Eduard Gans: Ein Leben im Vormaerz* [Tuebingen: J.C.B. Mohr, 1965], pp. 174–85). In addition to the loss of their president and driving spirit, the demise of the society can be attributed to the lack of support from the Jewish community. Yet, in the last analysis, the society was not a total debacle, for emerging from its ruins was the Science of Judaism, thanks largely to the Promethean efforts of its vice-president and the editor of its journal, Leopold Zunz.

LEOPOLD ZUNZ

5. On Rabbinic Literature[1]

"Anyone can praise," says Nuschirvan, "but well-reasoned censure in a spirit of humility is much more difficult." Now since I esteem this essay above self-love, and science [*Wissenschaft*] above both, I trust that one who truly knows will tell me in his review in what way, my review—for so I see this essay—may be lacking.

The use of the first person "I" in this foreword and of the plural "we" in the essay proper is not intended to satisfy [simultaneously] the captious partisans of both forms. I am of the opinion that an author appears personally only in documents, travelogues, on checks, in prefaces, law suits, laundry slips, receipts, replies to critics, restaurant bills and the like. In humorous pieces the author may use the first person singular but nonetheless, he goes beyond himself; in theoretical speculations he prefers the more modest "we" since he is then part of an entire battalion doing battle for mute science. . . . *"Primum hoc statuo esse virtutis conciliare animos hominum"* ["The conciliation of the minds of men is deemed the highest virtue"] (Cicero). . . .

Beyond the interest they arouse, their antiquity and their content, the venerable literary remains from the efflorescence of the ancient Hebrews owe their importance to chance. The revolutions which began among the Jewish people, and which influenced them no less than the entire world, cast these ruins, called the Hebrew canon, as the foundation of Christian states; the constant advance of science [*Wissenschaft*], adding its own embellishments, transformed these several books into a structure of spiritual industry more wondrous even than the Greek, for its richness was created from scantier matter.

Such an appreciation was never granted to the later productions of the Hebrew nation. One had the impression that after Israel's intellectual and political decline her creative energies had been lost for some considerable time and she was content with exegesis, now more now less successful, of the few works remaining from better days. When the shades of barbarism began to recede slowly from the darkened earth and the light from Jews dispersed everywhere, perforce struck everywhere, a new and alien learning [*Bildung*] intermingled with the remains of the ancient Hebrew and was molded by minds and centuries into a literature we call rabbinic.*

With the Reformation, a necessary consequence of the flourishing of classical learning, great interest was aroused in the study of biblical literature, complemented by what we may call a curious zeal to ransack the Orient. As a result, just as the fatherland's richest and most endearing spiritual creations began to occupy and exhilarate us, we have witnessed this last century a heated assault on rabbinical wisdom which itself had collapsed and had, perhaps, been extinguished forever. But as rabbinic literature was on the decline, European literature was on the rise and Jews began to be drawn to it. What remains of the former in these last fifty years is nothing but a language borrowed as an accessible and familiar garment for clothing

*Accordingly, one should include under this rubric only those writings which are either by content or by authorship rabbinic. But actually, the title *rabbi* is but a polite honorific and its significance is less than the title *Dr.* Why not then talk of neo-Hebrew or simply Jewish literature?

Source: Leopold Zunz, "Etwas ueber die rabbinische Literatur," *Gesammelte Schriften*, (Berlin, 1875), vol. 1, pp. 1–31. Trans. here by A. Schwartz.

ideas which are to prepare the way for the utter disappearance of rabbinic literature.

Precisely because Jews in our times—limiting our attention to the Jews of Germany—are seizing upon German language and German learning [*Bildung*] with such earnestness and are thus, perhaps unwittingly, carrying the neo-Hebraic literature [i.e., rabbinic literature] to its grave, science steps in demanding an account of what has already been sealed away.[2] Now, when no new significant development is likely to disturb our survey, when we have access to tools greater than those available to scholars of the sixteenth and seventeenth centuries, when a higher culture permits a more illuminating treatment, when Hebrew books are more readily available than they will likely be in 1919—now, so we think, the development of our science in a grand style is a duty, one whose weight increases because of the fact that the complex problem of the fate of the Jews may derive a solution, if only in part, from this science. External legal and religious pressures are insufficient to bring forth harmony if one does not know the nature of the instrument or how to handle it. A theoretical—or legal, theological and economic—knowledge of today's Jew is necessarily one-sided; Spirit [*Geist*] can be apprehended only with determinate ideas and by knowledge of customs and of will.[3] An improper point of departure will avenge what goes by the name of amelioration [*Verbesserung*]; hasty innovations grant the old, and what is worse the outworn, too great a value. In order to recognize and distinguish among the old and useful, the obsolete and harmful, the new and desirable, we must embark upon a considered study of the people and its political and moral history. But herein there is a serious problem that Jewish affairs will be dealt with in the same manner that Jewish literature, if highly esteemed or not, is treated—in the heat of bias.

We have not digressed from literature to the civil existence of the Jews in order to leave behind a tangled skein which more adroit fingers may attempt to unravel. We have traced their mutual influence in broad strokes in order to return to an examination of literature, its origins, its contents, its relations with its elder and contemporary sisters, its current stock, its unique qualities. Here and there we do encounter occasional small lamps but their oil is often poor and insufficient; a search for genuine sunlight would be in vain. How is it possible, one may ask, that at a time when all science and all of man's doings have been illumined in brilliant rays, when the most remote corners of the earth have been reached, the most obscure languages studied and nothing seems too insignificant to assist in the construction of wisdom, how is it possible that our science [i.e., the academic study of rabbinic literature] alone lies neglected? What hinders us from fully knowing the contents of rabbinic literature, from understanding it, from properly interpreting it, from estimating its proper worth, from surveying it at ease? (We who have no fear of being misunderstood in this matter. The entire literature of the Jews, in its widest scope, is presented here as the object of scholarly research; in this context it is not at all our concern whether the context of this entire literature should, or could, also be the *norm for our own judgment*.)[4]

We will reach this height only with the aid of sundry and good preliminary works. The question, therefore, recurs: why are they lacking? In response we must clarify what we understand by preliminary literary works and establish that at present they are in fact lacking. After our attempt to account for this phenomenon it will be apparent that as long as this lack persists we will achieve neither clarity nor completeness in our subject.

By preliminary literary works we mean either studies which deal partially with an entire subject or exhaustively with a limited aspect of a specific subject. In the latter type, each individual subject, each scientific problem—even if it does not admit of a total solution—every noteworthy discovery for the advance of knowledge should be illuminated in a critical light. Critical editions of manuscripts, good translations, accurate reference works, biographies and the like, all can properly make claim to the title of preliminary literary works.

Ranking higher in our estimation are those works which encompass an entire science, enriching knowledge with important discoveries or transforming outlooks with new ideas, which take upon themselves to describe the literature of hundreds, even thousands, of years, leaving behind traces broad enough for another century to follow. These include accounts of philosophical systems, histories of individual doctrines, parallels, literary collections, etc.

However laudable and useful these efforts, they will never be able singly to attain to the loftier goal if their authors, in wrapping the small stone they have taken for polishing, disregard the mighty alabaster mountain from whence it came, and having completed their labors fold their arms, content with themselves and their fine work, another gem among the wonders of nature. Only by considering the literature of a nation as a gateway to a comprehensive knowledge of the course of its culture throughout the ages, by noting how at every moment the essence of the given and the supplementary, i.e., the inner and the external, array themsleves; how fate, climate, customs, religion and chance seize one another in friendly or hostile spirit; how, finally, the present is the necessary result of all that preceded it—only thus will one tread with true reverence before this divine temple and humbly enter this hallway, later to regard the panorama spread out below with deserving pleasure.

This honor will be attained only by one who has takén upon himself the pain of scaling this mountain, but even he will be able to give a satisfactory accounting of the entire prospect only if he grasps each part with the perceptive eye of art. In this lofty view our science is transformed into a series of sciences, each of which in all its parts is to be cultivated, lest the whole be distorted by substantial error. If we now turn attention to the vast quantity of material to be investigated, sorted and worked under the aegis of critical scholarship we will discover a three-part path which will assist us in discerning and assessing the given idea [under investigation] as well as our way of knowing it. Theoretically then, we divide critical scholarship into three aspects: ideational, philological and historical analysis. The latter considers the history of ideas from the time of their transmission to the present in which we have arrived at our knowledge.

Proceeding now to the literary products of the Jewish people, the first question to be asked is: What do they include? . . .

Beginning with theology, it must immediately be acknowledged that the Jews have never fully nor clearly set out their theological system; nevertheless in worthy fragments they are expressed more clearly than by Bartolocci[5] who from myths and legends has concocted the "contradiction of rabbinical blasphemies." Concerning the mythology of the Jews, with the exception of several valuable works on ancient mythology, we still lag far behind—this is all the more surprising when we recall that like dogmatology the mythology of the Jews is related to the Christians', as Roeder claims.[6] In the realm of religion the sin has been perpetrated intentionally and systematically! Nothing more distorted, more damaging, more dishonest has ever anywhere been written than that which has been written on the religion of Israel. The art of inciting malice has here reached its pinnacle. No distinctions have been made between custom and liturgy, nor between these and fundamental religious principles; in this manner ten blameless matters have shared in the condemnation of one deserving of scorn. To embark on a history of synagogue ritual based on the sources*

*This research, it seems to us, should be conducted according to the following topics: (a) The nature of Jewish worship and its position in the Halakhah; its influence on the consciousness (*Gesinnung*) and character of the Jews. (b) The form and content of the liturgy; the writings of Jewish authors on this subject. . . . (c) The manner of Jewish prayer; the opinion of non-Jewish authors on this subject. Should the research on this subject, would at the present time be a worthwhile, although a difficult, undertaking.

Leaving behind the ecclesiastical realm and turning to the political we come upon the field of legislation and jurisprudence in which several important works by Jews are available for our scholarly scrutiny. Works on the subject of state constitution are interesting, if only in having been written under conditions of subjugation. Nor would it be unrewarding to study the *Poskim*, halakhic decisions in which the rabbis established the authority of their decisions by citing the words of eminent sages as proof-texts. Even more interesting is the task of systematically comparing criminal theory (*culpa*), so acutely presented in the three talmudic *Babbot*,[7] with Roman law. Hebrew legal terminology will certainly gain clarity from being set parallel to the Roman and Greek. The gradual change of Jewish law and its ultimate submergence in the European could be described only after much arduous preliminary work of this sort.

Religion, legal principles and also ethics should be examined essentially within the context of the sources; and it is high time to present matter-of-factly† the splendid writings on these subjects found in the Talmud and in the writings of later sages. Similarly, whatever in the works of well-known authors is or appears to be in conflict with these writings should be illuminated—a conflict which could have kept Eisenmenger[8] from publishing his [denunciations of the Talmud]. . . .

We should [now] examine man as a denizen of Earth: how he, from the vantage point of this planet, is an investigator of nature, an astronomer measuring the heavenly bodies, a geographer sailing the seas. If we give attention for a moment to the common basis of these sciences, mathematics, we will note the large number of [Hebrew] works in this field. It will thus seem worthwhile to prepare an explanatory dictionary [of Hebrew mathematical terms], especially since each mathematician frequently employs his own terminology. We would also welcome a presentation of the first traces of mathematics in the Talmud, as well as a history of Hebrew mathematical writings to recent times. A still greater yield awaits the student of Jewish astronomy. Beginning with an etymological study of the most ancient [Hebrew astronomical] terms and a collection of relevant sections from some eighty Hebrew books, it would then be possible to approach this literature proper which first appears around the year 1100. It also seems to us necessary to add to the foregoing an inventory of Hebrew chronological studies. . . . Jewish travel and geographic works are less numerous and less interesting, nevertheless it is possible to extract language-enriching topographical notes from them. . . .

The stock of natural science knowledge in the Talmud and in later works is a field which has been completely overlooked. A treasure-house of information addressed specifically to this subject is to be found here. Secular rabbinic literature includes no hiero-botany, hiero-zoology, sacred physics or sacred medical theory, even though it would have been easy to oppose superstition without calling upon its rival, physics. Close by is the theory of medicine, based on a knowledge of nature and man (i.e., psychology, anthropology and physiology and the proper application of this knowledge). Until now no learned physician has taken upon himself the trouble to describe and discuss schools of medical knowledge, discoveries,

---

which will, of course, take into cognizance the differences of country and time, be conducted by the right individuals it will be a source of joy. Moreover, much of pragmatic value will be derived from this research, such as the correction of errors that fell into the liturgy and the identification of patterns of change in the liturgy [as a result of the interests of the Reform movement].

†A basic moral sensibility exists in every individual and despite the great variation man is man [*bleibt der Mensch—Mensch*]. The latest innovation in ethical literature is thus but a renewal of the old, pristine Mosaic ethics. It seems to us then that a compendium of the cardinal moral teachings of the Old Testament would be a worthwhile project, one that a beginning scholar could undertake.

the biographies and works of ancient Jewish physicians, while Imbonati's[9] catalog of Latin translations from Hebrew mentions only three medical works.

Only one step separates the knowledge of nature from the utilization of this knowledge. But rarely have scholars taken the trouble to penetrate the thickets of technology and industrial arts, nor have the authorities taken the trouble to initiate archeological digs in Palestine and Babylonia. Many references to these matters in the Mishnah, therefore, especially in the sixth order, still remain to be clarified. Industry and commerce also belong here. The study of the ancient histories of [Jewish] industry and commerce compared to the opinions of esteemed authors would be an important work bringing to light significant findings. This field, it is true, is somewhat foreign to us but it seems possible that aspects of the paper money system have been developed by Jews. We have several works concerning not only the use of materials but also their embellishment by art. . . . Excepting poetry, about which something will be said later, it seems that only [Jewish] architecture has attracted any attention. For some reason we are unable to recall any Hebrew work on the art of printing among the Jews. And why have [Hebrew] calligraphic masterpieces never been collected? Works on [Jewish] music have for the most part yet to be published. The chapter on [Jewish] inventions is still rather thin, but it is hoped that in an age when we enjoy greater liberty and freer activity, something will be done to enrich it.

We have now arrived at the universal life of the nation in which we will have to distinguish between the ephemeral and the lasting, that is, between history and archeology. But from whence will we bring to Jewish history its impartial Paul Sarpi?[10] For a full account of the fate of the Jews in all the lands in which they dwelled, the Hebrew works do not suffice (they have already been drained dry) nor do the well-known studies of modern scholars such as Basnage,[11] Holberg,[12] Prideaux[13] and others. The most neglected books are a possible source of some fragmentary information; just as the Jewish people are dispersed so is their history. . . .

Turning now to the lever for lifting this mass of material we come upon language which will remain adamantly obscure to whomever does not wholeheartedly devote himself to the lofty treasures . . . of this the most dispersed and abject of peoples. For language is the first friend leading us unto the road to science and the last to which we shall long to return. It alone is capable of removing the veil of the past; it alone can prepare minds for the future; the researcher, therefore, must bear its obstinacy—for what has taken hundreds of years to be produced requires hundreds of years to be refined.

Of the entire linguistic creation we begin first with poetry. Whereas the ancient has been the subject of some clarification, the more recent has been totally neglected. There are problems which have not at all been raised. For example: Did the ancient Jews not write any drama? What poetry was produced during the first thousand years of the Christian era? When were the *piyyutim*[14] composed? What is their relation to Chaldean poetry and the like? The situation of rhetorics, or rather the art of style, is worse yet. As Hebrew works on this subject are rare, its rules should be bared with greater diligence, especially in light of the fact that for a hundred years or so Hebrew style has achieved pure and beautiful form. Many special studies can be undertaken in this as yet untended field, such as on the generally misunderstood nature of hyperbole, the use of *remez*[15] in the Talmud, later philosophical style, the differences between prosaic poetry and poetic prose, satiric literature, etc. A twofold task is called for regarding grammar: to fill in lacunae in the neglected historical account of Jewish grammarians and to establish a system for the structure of modern Hebrew [i.e., post-Biblical Hebrew]. This must be preceded, however, by a learned study of the Chaldean language; only afterwards would it be possible to make any claims for a basic history of the Hebrew language, followed by an examination of philosophical parallels between biblical and rabbinic Hebrew. The required auxiliary tools for that, however, are still in short supply; there is as yet no lexicon, like Forcellini's,[16] nor will there be except as a result of the combined efforts of many, each of whom will prepare lists, or rather, concordances of single works. That the old Hebrew dictionaries stuck in the libraries are of no lexicological use as long as they remain in isolation needs no proof. The state of synonymy is even worse: there are hardly any studies of synonyms found which treat the Jewish authors, even less those which concern ancient Hebrew. Meanwhile, etymology is impoverished by the fact that most of our rabbis neglect Oriental studies, and that the Orientalists neglect Hebrew.

And so we are finally presented with a survey of the large stock of writings about which much useful and excellent, even great things, are to be found in the works of scholars; much, however, yet remains to be done. The account of Jewish diplomacy can be completed; once signatures are confirmed, the chronological order of facsimiles can be established, and the order of undated manuscripts be fixed. To this can be added a history of manuscripts, as well as a long-awaited historical account of Hebrew typography. We will still be lacking good catalogs of public and private library holdings, like the Dibdin Catalog of the Spencer Library,[17] without which the necessary listing of Hebrew literature cannot be completed, and with which we can proceed with greater passion to the critical examination of currently, and formerly, available works.

If we want to comprehend the reasons for the absence of research in rabbinic literature, we must first encounter those [representatives of traditional Judaism] who charge us with degrading what took place in "rabbinic obscurity," to use Schickard's[18] expression. To us it appears that the assaults on and dismissals [such as Schickard's] of the glorious and useful work of our ancestors and contemporaries are signs of a fashionable ignorance, or in more refined language, lack of understanding. We have only sought to point out gaps, to encourage a renewal of study which previously had flourished, not always in the proper direction perhaps, but more vigorously than today when this field is neglected by all. Bearing down on our science is the misfortune common to all science—the misfortune of human fallibility; here, however, further damage has been caused as a consequence of those defects [viz., lack of objectivity] which have brought about this decline of scholarship.

The indifference to rabbinic literature is of two sorts. Either it is directed against all scholarship, in which case it is without remedy, or it is directed exclusively against rabbinic scholarship—on the assumption perhaps that it is not useful, or that it contains no wisdom, or that it is damaging to good taste, or that it is not possible to make much of it, or that it is godless, or because it is nowhere well received. Usually this indifference dissolves into contempt, and not infrequently men of science line up against our science rather than against its authors. More objectionable than the indifference, more shocking than the contempt is the partisanship, not of love but of hatred, with which this study is approached. Anything in it which can be used against the Jews or Judaism has been a welcome find. These scholars have gathered half-understood expressions from every corner in order with their aid to pillory their eternal rival; up until a hundred years ago there was not a single case of a learned doctor taking upon himself to collect the good and beautiful in Jewish writings so that for once the Jews be described in a charitable light.

Thank you, Eternal God! Those times are past. Daring and honest pens spread enlightened learning among the people while greater rulers support the work of those pens with their own honor and might.

Today, when many Jews are lost to the study of rabbinic literature, it is simply because of ignorance, the consequence of an ever-increasing decline in the study of the

Hebrew language. This, in turn, is a consequence in part of the poor prospects for advancement in the profession of Jewish scholarship, the easier paths leading to other sciences, the praiseworthy move into arts, crafts, agriculture and military service, but also in part because of the contemporary coldness toward religion in general and toward our ancestral literature in particular, and because of the foolish notion that this history of Judaism does not befit the honor of an educated man and finally because of an amiable modern superficiality about which we will want to say more.

True, there are inherent obstacles which repel even Hebraists from the profession—the scarcity of manuscripts, the small hope for advancement and livelihood, the difficulties of the Jewish book trade and certainly the need to acquire skill in various allied disciplines when the mastery of Hebrew alone is often difficult enough to achieve. But the contrary error is also widespread, that a few glances in German books can make one learned, not to mention the concomitant writing fury rampant today. A type of person has been created occupying a middling position, hesitant, going about his studies without zeal, analyzing Hebrew works without sufficient preparation, damaging the science and piling up useless material. One sins against interpretation, criticism and particularly against method; another treats his subject cursorily, without due respect, with so little regard for truth and thoroughness that a contempt for both science and reader is revealed. A third makes his work easier still, knowing in advance what he wants to, and will, find, and then swelling with delight when he finds it; yet another recoils from even putting his hand to the task, since his predecessors did not pave a way for him. And so the words of the fathers are confirmed: one error leads to another.

In light of these phenomena it is obvious why we have not had satisfactory studies of Hebrew literature until now, nor can we expect any in the near future. Even if we be equipped with all the requisite tools, with knowledge and auxiliary aids, we will ourselves, by working the ideas, be creating new ideas and material; thus is bibliography, criticism and the history not only of the science but of history itself produced. The material we weave into the fabric of objective science, but which originates in the subjective treatment of a preconceived idea, is converted by the art by which we acquire science into new matter to be worked by us and by future generations.

Above all these realms of science, above all this tumult of human activity, ruling in exclusive majesty, is philosophy, omnipresent but invisible, devoted with unassailable independence to all human cognition. Therefore, we preferred not to see it as a special science nor as the essence of Jewish wisdom. It is as well the higher historical knowledge which this wisdom has traversed over hundreds of years, and which has been set out properly and poorly, in Jewish and non-Jewish works. When we take upon ourselves to learn and transmit the intellectual greatness of this people, it is, therefore, the supreme guide. In this way every historical datum which diligence has uncovered, equity has deciphered, philosophy has utilized and good taste has put in its proper place will be a contribution to human knowledge, the only worthwhile goal of all research. Only this higher view suits a science elevated above human pettiness, lands and nations; it alone can lead us to a true history of Jewish philosophy in which mental processes can be presented and understood while pursuing with all historical rigor the parallel learning embracing the world.

Let not philosophical subalterns hinder this flight to the kingdom of hope by their questions of utility. To whomever does not grasp the highest relations of science, its most estimable greatness, to whomever does not see every detail as an integral part of spiritual creation—to him we have nothing to say. Better that we turn to finer feelings, to noble souls who know that man never ceases his forward motion—those who pay less heed to what has already been done but look instead to what remains to be done. Many fields still covered with thistle and thorn promise a rich harvest to whoever will tend them; many noxious seeds will yet be sown, damaging the fit crop nearby. Much ripened crop will be laid low by the hail of passion, malice and pigheadedness; but much good fruit has been spared lying somewhere in the ground or has been crushed callously by haughtiness.

We conclude this survey of universals with a note on a single unknown and unpublished Hebrew work, on which we are now working. . . . It is entitled *Sefer ha-Ma'alot*[19] by Shemtov ben Joseph ibn Falaquera, a famous rabbi of the thirteenth century. In part because of the solid thoughtfulness of the author it unfolds in a lucid, concise and fluent style a theory of the degrees of intellectual perfection. This work establishes its author as a praiseworthy thinker, a wide reader whose ideas though sometimes daring are presented with restraint. . . .

In accord with the rigor with which we recommend that science be treated generally, we have in the present case attempted to set the task which this work is to fulfill: to present in this critique not only the theoretical skeleton but also to impart all in pleasing form such that nothing, not even what is veiled, is overlooked. But beyond this desired completeness we hope that our effort will beckon others, more worthy of the subject and closer to the goal, to follow in our footsteps. Our intention has not been only to snatch from oblivion a work venerable by virtue of its age, outstanding by virtue of its content and because of its rarity destined for oblivion. More pleasing hopes have sweetened our labors! The hope that it will awake the passion for more thorough and fruitful studies, with gaze ever fixed on completeness, of the outstanding creations of the Jewish nation; the hope that the light so cast on the better parts of rabbinic literature will assist in dispelling the prejudices usually held against it. Truly, when we so boldly break into the midst of the author's world, it is not our talents but our burning desire to strive for the good and the beautiful which will justify us in the critical and indulgent eyes of the reader.

NOTES

1. Leopold Zunz (1794–1886). Among the active members of the Society for the Culture and Science of the Jews, he was the only one to maintain a commitment to Jewish studies. This is partly explained by the fact that he considered the Science of Judaism to be his professional calling; even before the establishment of the society he engaged in Jewish scholarship. He was uniquely equipped to do so, having received a sound traditional education and possessing the disposition for assiduous and meticulous scholarship. As the Science of Judaism was not recognized as a legitimate and autonomous academic discipline and therefore not included in the university curriculum, Zunz pursued his research in this field as a "private scholar." He made his living variously as a preacher in Reform synagogues, as an editor of a Berlin newspaper, as a headmaster of a primary school and as a director of a Jewish teachers' seminary. He refused to support the establishment of an independent institute of Jewish studies for fear that this would sever the discipline from general academic and cultural life. His scholarship was prodigious, the larger portion being devoted to research in synagogal liturgy and practices. Modern Jewish studies are immeasurably indebted to his pioneering effort.

In this essay, published in 1818, a year prior to the founding of the Society for the Culture and Science of the Jews, Zunz presented a program for the scientific study of Judaism. The essay is permeated with a youthful enthusiasm for the ideal of *Wissenschaft*. Specifically, it provided a new, indeed secular, definition of Jewish intellectual activity. Aside from Scripture, Zunz observed, Jewish literature was almost totally neglected by modern scholarship. This neglect he ascribed to Christian bias against post-biblical Jewish spirituality. As a bias this attitude was by definition unscientific, and it had led to a total ignorance of the wide range of Jewish intellectual activity in the post-biblical period. This activity, he maintained, was not confined to scriptual exegesis and talmudic legalism, but embraced all aspects of human culture. Zunz felt that it would thus be more proper to place *all* post-biblical Jewish literature under the rubric of "neo-Hebrew" literature. He preferred this term because it underscored the methodological necessity to expand the conception of Jewish literature from a specific genre of religious literature, bearing as it did great stigma, to a broad chronological designation for all post-biblical Jewish literary endeavor.

2. Hegel summarized this historicist premise when he epigrammatically said that the owl of Minerva—the goddess of the sciences—only takes flight at dusk. Contemplation—philosophy and *Wissenschaft*—is after the event.

3. The language here is Hegelian. Hegel—whose *Phenomenology of Spirit* (1807) was widely discussed at that time in Berlin academic circles—traces the spiritual history of man, namely the historical development of man's consciousness and rational self-awareness of himself and of his position in the universe. Language, art, religion and philosophy—which develop as man's rational consciousness of himself grows—are man's vehicles for understanding *Geist*, that is, the cosmic spirit which is the source of truth and rationality and which underlies and manifests itself in all reality. *Geist* is manifest in the world in accordance with a rational and historical plan. In that man's rational consciousness of himself is also the consciousness of *Geist*, man's cultural history is also the history of *Geist*. The rational plan by which *Geist* unfolds itself is "the universal and one Idea" that determines the inner reason of all external reality. The expression of the idea relevant to an aspect of reality is "the determinate Idea," which is made conscious through conceptual thought. Thus, as Zunz wishes to argue, the essence of a particular cultural group, such as the Jews, is ascertained by its determinate ideas and modes of consciousness. The influence of Hegel is not otherwise marked in Zunz's thought. See A. Altmann, "Zur Fruehgeschichte der juedischen Predigt in Deutschland: Leopold Zunz als Prediger," *Leo Baeck Institute Year Book*, 6 (1961), pp. 21, 25.

4. In the original text this parenthetical statement appears in a footnote.

5. Giulio Bartolocci (1613–1687), Italian Christian Hebraist and bibliographer. He taught Hebrew and rabbinic literature at the Collegium Neophytorum (for Jewish converts) in Rome. His four-volume *Bibliotheca Magna Rabbinica* . . . (1657–1693) was the first systematic, comprehensive bibliography of Jewish literature.

6. Johann Ulrich Roeder, *Archaeologie der Kirchendogmen* (1812).

7. Reference is to *Baba Kama*, *Baba Meztia* and *Baba Batra*—three sections of the Mishnaic tractate *Nezikin*.

8. Johann Andreas Eisenmenger (1654–1704), author of a pseudo-scholarly work, *Entdecktes Judenthum* [Judaism unmasked], denouncing talmudic Judaism.

9. Carlo Guiseppe Imbonati(-tus) (1650?–1696), Italian Hebraist.

10. Paolo Sarpi (pseudonym, *Pietro Soave Polano*, 1552–1623), Venetian patriot, church reformer and scholar. His chief literary work, the *History of the Popes* (1615)—a critique of the papal attempt at a Counter-Reformation—was considered in Zunz's day to be a milestone in scholarly archival research. Leopold von Ranke was later to demonstrate Sarpi's tendentious reading of manuscripts. See Ranke, *History of the Popes* . . . (Berlin, 1834–1836), appendix three.

11. Jacques Christian Basnage (1653–1725), French Protestant and historian. His five-volume *L'histoire et la religion des Juifs depuis Jésus Christ jusqu' à present* . . . (1706–1711) marks the first attempt to understand Judaism in terms of history.

12. Ludvig Holberg (1684–1754), Danish writer and dramatist. He published a sympathetic history of the Jews, *Den jødiske historie* (1742).

13. Humphrey Prideaux (1648–1724), English orientalist. He lectured in Hebrew at Christ Church College, the University of Oxford.

14. As a genre the term *piyyutim* ("synagogal poetry") refers specifically to those liturgical poems added to the statutory prayers.

15. Hebrew *remez* ("veiled allusion") is a type of scriptural exegesis.

16. Egidio Forcellini (1688–1768), Italian lexicographer. His monumental *Totius latinitatis lexicon* appeared posthumously in 1771.

17. The Spencer Library was founded by the English bibliophile George John Spencer, earl of Wimbledon (1758–1834). His priceless library of over 40,000 volumes is today part of the John Rylands Library in Manchester. Spencer's librarian was Thomas Frognall Dibdin, who prepared the four-volume catalog, *Bibliotheca Spenceriana* (London, 1814).

18. Wilhelm Schickard (also Schickhardt, 1592–1635), professor of biblical languages at the University of Tuebingen.

19. Zunz later wrote a Latin dissertation on this book, for which he was awarded a doctorate from the University of Halle in 1821.

MORITZ STEINSCHNEIDER
6. The Future of Jewish Science[1]

. . . During the last half century, greater and lesser results have been achieved by Jewish science. For a long time, this endeavor was influenced, externally, by the so-called "question of Jewish emancipation," and, internally, by the various attempts at religious reform. Jewish science has gained from both, and—where it has deepened and clarified the understanding [of Judaism]—it, in turn, has had a salutary influence on the external position of the Jews and on their religious situation as well. [But the findings of science can only serve pragmatic ends; they cannot solve questions of principle.] And the question of Jewish civil equality is no longer a matter of expedience, nor, indeed, merely a *Jewish* question. The religious question, too, is now one of more general interest and its determination no longer depends on the opinions of a narrow circle; religious reform is now a question of principles which perforce demand a broader framework.

At first, the schismatic process [implied by the Science of Judaism and Reform] prompted an opposition to the official representatives of Judaism, namely, the rabbis. A number of scholars refused to accept an office which necessitated considerations extraneous to science. But a new generation of rabbis adopted the new science, and a need was soon felt for institutions in which Jewish clergy [*Cultusbeamten*] could be trained. Halfway through the period under consideration, the establishment of a Jewish theological faculty at a German university was discussed, but this project had to be dropped for a lack of funds.[2] Moreover, it was by no means sure that German universities at the time would not have interfered with the independent work of lecturers and Jewish science. Since 1848, however, Germany has been working toward the implementation of the postulate: "Science and instruction must enjoy freedom." Yet Jewish history and literature can almost nowhere be studied at the universities.

In the meantime, due to a generous legacy, a rabbinical seminary had been founded. Its curriculum includes a general, preliminary education and is thus especially suited for students without such a background.[3] Aside from this element of secular studies, the seminary has maintained at least the outer appearance of a certain religious direction. Upon graduation, the younger rabbis take up their practical tasks, especially those of giving sermons and religious instruction. The few Jewish talmudic scholars, who in the big cities make their living from various occupations, are gradually dying out. Most candidates for a rabbinate in Germany attend universities. The majority have graduated from the traditional talmudic academies of East Europe, where they had no formal secular education. Without these students, the classes on Semitic literature would be almost empty. As a rule, the students base their claim to a doctorate—an indispensable title, in their eyes—on a knowledge of "Semitic literature." The examiners, meanwhile, have to face all kinds of embarrassments.

These students condescendingly still attend the old-style lessons on the Talmud and *Shulkhan Arukh*,[4] mainly because of the scholarships that go along with them, or because of the ordination certificate, which can rather easily be attained from the rabbis who conduct these lessons. A talent to preach has become the main requirement of a rabbi, *everything* else has become secondary. Now and again, an attempt is made to give one of these traditional talmudic academies—the

Source: Moritz Steinschneider, "Die Zukunft der juedischen Wissenschaft," *Hebraeische Bibliographie*, 9 (1869), pp. 76–78. Trans. here by J. Hessing and P. Mendes-Flohr.

yeshivot—a more modern character. Universally, the amorphous situation with regard to organization and pedagogy that prevails in the *yeshivot* arouses the desire to revamp their methods totally; on the other hand, there is an inhibiting fear that such changes would undermine the inalienable liberties of the traditional manner of talmudic study.

First and foremost, the debates over the establishment of new, modern institutes refer to the training of *rabbis* and teachers of religion; opinions differ according to religious affiliations. In this context, the Science of Judaism is largely considered in terms of its pertinence to [religious] cult and pedagogy. This practical point of view is certainly justified, but is it the only feasible approach? What about Jewish history as a link and source of cultural history in general? Is the Science of Judaism a part of theology? What will become of it if the universities, according to the Dutch example, leave theology, as a practical science, to the care of the various religious communities?[5]

It could be argued that the Jews, as a religious community, have no particular reason to take care of a science which goes beyond their religious needs, unless this science is created by Jews and can thus only be transmitted by Jews. The state and its scientific institutions must undertake and foster scientific investigations of the Jewish works contained in their libraries, just as they are investigating the pyramids, the ruins of Pompeii and of Nineveh. They should do this all the more so since the spirit which has created these works has not yet died out, but is still alive in citizens of their state! If the Jews, so would the argument go, take over this task which rightfully belongs to the state, they would perpetuate the old mistake that Jewish literature is nothing but a subsidiary science to theology. Jewish institutions would also fail to carry their science beyond a narrow circle and thus miss their target—a mistake which could not be easily remedied, even if the Jews restricted themselves to their own theology and consigned everything else to oblivion. But oblivion will be the inescapable future of the new-born science, if it is not soon given the appropriate spiritual nourishment to assure its prosperous growth. . . .

These are some of the questions and doubts concerning the conditions and tendencies of the Science of Judaism as pursued in *Germany*. If our description has been one-sided or false, we would gladly accept corrections and additions. In Eastern Europe, they are already shouting: German Jewry no longer represents authentic Judaism, as Alexandrian Jewry did not in ancient times . . . . Are not then the German Jews at least [authentic] representatives of the Jewish science? Can the most urgent needs of this science only be fulfilled at the expense of the Jewish religion or vice versa? . . .

NOTES

1. Moritz Steinschneider (1816–1907). Having a thorough grounding in traditional Jewish learning, he was introduced to the academic study of Jewish sources by several non-Jewish scholars. Like Zunz, he pursued Jewish science as a "private scholar," supporting himself by officiating as a rabbi at weddings, delivering sermons, teaching, translating and writing textbooks for the study of elementary Hebrew. In 1869 he was named to the important post of assistant in the Royal Library of Berlin. Steinschneider's approach to Jewish studies is usually cited as an extreme example of historicism, of a cold, objective scholarship that posited the demise of Judaism as living faith and creative culture. His attitude to Judaism, however, was more complex. Although favoring religious reform, he was actually quite conservative in religious matters, particularly in the earlier part of his career. He insisted, for instance, upon the use of Hebrew in the service as necessary for the integrity of Judaism and Jewry. Also indicative of his attitude was his consistent treatment of the Jews as a nation, and not simply as a religious confession. He was equally concerned with the integrity of Jewish sci-

ence, and believed that the Science of Judaism, to be credible and true to its calling, must maintain a jealous regard for the standards of objectivity. Thus it must eschew all extraneous concerns, such as religious reform or political emancipation. To be sure, he recognized that these issues were legitimate and exigent, but they could not become the charge of the Science of Judaism, for such concerns inevitably rendered scholarship selective and tendentious. Moreover, although recognizing the desire for a synoptic treatment and presentation of Judaism—a desire related to the drive for religious reform and political emancipation—Steinschneider emphatically opposed such projects. At this early stage of scholarship, such summary treatment of Judaism would perforce be based on hasty, superficial research, which would at best be platitudinous, at worst fraudulent. At this juncture, Jewish science must suffice with laborious, patient groundwork, particularly in philology and bibliography. His scholarship became a paradigm of this type of research, devoted to a thorough and scientific recording of all available printed and manuscript materials in Judaica—work he deemed to be indispensable before scholarship could proceed. He applied himself to this type of research, devoting his efforts to cataloging, with annotations of awe-inspiring erudition, the Judaica collections of Europe's leading libraries: the Bodleian Library in Oxford and the libraries in Leiden, Munich, Hamburg and Berlin. In these catalogs, which represented many years of research, he disclosed hitherto unknown treasures of Jewish literature and culture. The "father of Jewish bibliography," as he is now reverently called, also contributed studies on Jewish literature, especially on the interaction between Hebrew and Arabic literature in the Middle Ages. The bibliography of his own writings, containing more than 1400 items, constitutes a veritable library. This article was first published in *Hebraeische Bibliographie,* a journal edited by Steinschneider from 1858 to 1882.

2. In 1838 a committee and fund were created to promote the establishment of a Jewish theological faculty at a German university. Steinschneider opposed the idea of such a faculty. He consistently strove, however, to have Jewish science included within the curriculum of German universities. At the height of the Revolution of 1848 he submitted a memorandum to the University of Berlin, suggesting that the triumph of liberalism made it imperative to introduce Jewish science into the curriculum. His proposal was rejected. It was not until after the First World War that a place was allocated in a German university for the Science of Judaism.

3. The reference is to the Juedisch-Theologisches Seminar in Breslau, Germany, established in 1854 with funds bequeathed by Jonas Fraenkel, a prominent Breslau businessman. The seminary, headed for its first twenty years by Zecharias Frankel, was the first institution that made it possible for scholars to devote themselves entirely to the Science of Judaism. The seminary's principal objective, however, was to train rabbis along the lines of "positive historical Judaism." The seminary, which functioned until 1939, served as a model for similar institutions (e.g., Hochschule fuer die Wissenschaft des Judentums, founded by Abraham Geiger in 1871) and was associated with the Reform movement.

4. The standard code of Jewish law and practice compiled by Joseph Karo and first published in 1565. Joseph Karo (1488–1575), codifier and kabbalist. In 1536 he went to Palestine and settled in Safed where he was acknowledged as a distinguished scholar and mystic.

5. In Germany, sectarian theological faculties were part of the university structure.

SAMSON RAPHAEL HIRSCH
7. A Sermon on the Science of Judaism[1]

. . . We who have fully imbibed the spirit of modern Judaism, we do not fast, do not pray *Selichot*[2], do not say *Kinot*[3] on *Tisha b'Av* [the Day of Zion] anymore. We would be

Source: Samson Raphael Hirsch, "Die Trauer des 9. Av," *Gesammelte Schriften* (Frankfurt am Main, 1902), vol. 1, pp. 130–31. Trans. here by J. Hessing.

ashamed of the tear in our eye or the sigh in our breast for the fallen Temple; we would be ashamed to feel the slightest longing for this scene of "bloody sacrificial rites." For us, alas, all this has become a myth. With our feelings "refined" by a cool reality, and with our unbiased scientific insights, we understand and evaluate all this very differently. Moses and Hesiod, David and Sappho, Deborah and Tyrtaeus, Isaiah and Homer, Delphi and Jerusalem, the Pythian tripod and the Sanctuary of the Cherubim, prophets and oracle, psalm and elegy—for us, all this has been peacefully encased and buried in our mind, reduced to one and the same human origin. For us, all this has received an identical meaning, human and transitory and of a by-gone age. The fog has lifted; the tears and sighs of our fathers do not fill our breasts anymore. They fill our libraries. The warmly pulsating heart of our fathers has become our national literature, their ardent life-breath has turned into the dust of letters. On *Tisha b'Av*, we let the old Jews pray *Selichot* and cry *Kinot*; we, however, know much better than they do in which centuries these "poets" flourished, in what meter they wrote their "verse," at whose breast they fed when they were sucklings. We adore Jewish antiquity so much that we raise all the dust in the libraries and collections in order to verify the dates of birth and death of these authors and to register correctly the inscriptions on their tombstones. We take care that now, as the old Judaism is carried to its grave, at least its memory is kept alive in histories of literature, and that now and then the evergreen around its grave sheds a few of its leaves upon our scholarly temple. Our simple-minded fathers did not believe in the death of these authors at all. They—their song, their lamentation, their solace, their prayer—lived on in the breasts of thousands of Jews. While their weather-worn tombstones were crumbling in the graveyards, every Jewish heart was their mausoleum and ensured them the only kind of immortality they desired, that the song might obliterate the poet, the prayer its author and the thought the man who had given expression to it. What they had thought and felt and sung and lamented became the living property of the nation; its origin—the mortal individual, the accidental organ by which these national feelings and thoughts had been voiced—could now step back into the shadow of oblivion.

Will these deceased spirits delight in the literary gratitude of our generation? Whom will they recognize as their true inheritors? Those who prayed their prayers and forgot their names, or those who forget their prayers, but remember their names?

NOTES

1. Samson Raphael Hirsch (1808–1888), foremost exponent of Neo-Orthodoxy in Germany. He looked askance at the Science of Judaism which, because of its historicism, failed, in his view, to contribute to the preservation and strengthening of Jewish life. On Hirsch's concept of Judaism, see chapter 4, document 12. This selection is taken from a sermon Hirsch delivered on *Tisha b'Av* (fast-day commemorating the destruction of the Temple) in 1855.

2. Penitential prayers recited on the days of fast in the Jewish liturgical calendar, especially in the month preceding the Day of Atonement.

3. "Dirges" in talmudic designation of the biblical book of Lamentations which is read in the synagogue during the evening and morning services of *Tisha b'Av*.

SAMUEL DAVID LUZZATTO[1]

8. Learning Based on Faith

Padua, Sivan 15, 5620

To the glory of the rabbis and the crown of the priests, preeminent among scholars and leader among wise men, [Rabbi Rappoport, chief rabbi of Prague].[2]

May the Lord who has brought you to ripe old age prolong your life in goodness and serenity, and may you continue to be a light unto the Diaspora . . . may you strengthen the righteous . . . may the wicked bow down before you and bite the dust of your feet, Amen.

I am like a mouse, half flesh, half earth; half rotten and worn out like a garment that has been eaten by moths and worms, and half strengthened in the Lord and in the labor of the Torah, to bring its mysteries to the light and to silence those who speak evil.

And now, friend of my soul, hearken and let your servant speak a word before you. . . . Why do you refrain from spreading your wisdom in Israel?

And why should two or three wicked men prevent you from doing justice and goodness with the Torah and with the many who love the Torah and love you, who honor the Torah and honor you? By your silence you give pleasure to your enemies and the enemies of the Torah, for their one aim is to silence a righteous man and slacken the hand of a valiant warrior, that they may behave arrogantly and entrap souls. . . .

For surely you know that a people living in its own country can exist even without faith, but the Sons of Israel, dispersed to the four corners of the earth, have survived to this day only because they have adhered to their faith. And if, God forbid! they should one day cease to believe in the Heavenly Torah, then they will necessarily cease to be a people, the name of Israel will be forgotten, and they will suffer the fate of the streams that run into the sea.[3] For some this would be the final salvation; such men call it fusion. The Wisdom of Israel[4] as it is studied in Germany by several Jewish scholars of this generation cannot continue to exist. It is not studied for its own sake; in the last analysis these scholars respect Goethe and Schiller more than all the prophets and the *Tanaim*[5] and *Amoraim*.[6] They study ancient Israel the way other scholars study ancient Egypt, Assyria, Babylon and Persia—that is, for the love of science or the love of fame. And they intend, in addition, to increase the honor of Israel in the eyes of the Gentiles; they exalt the role of some of our ancient sages in order to hasten the first step toward salvation which is, in their eyes, emancipation. But this kind of wisdom cannot endure; it will cease to exist as soon as salvation is achieved or when those men die who learned Torah as children and who believed in God and Moses before they went to study with Professor so-and-so and his pupils.

But the Wisdom of Israel which will endure forever is learning grounded in faith;[7] it is the wisdom that seeks to understand the Torah and the prophets as the Word of God, that attempts to understand the unique history of our unique people. This Wisdom strives to comprehend how, throughout our history, the spirit of God, which is our nation's inheritance, warred with the human spirit . . . and how in each generation the divine aspect prevailed over the human. For if at any time the human aspect should prevail in Israel (as some think it now does) then our people would cease to exist and be utterly lost.

This true Wisdom of Israel, which, like the

Source: Samuel David Luzzatto to Salomon J. Rappoport, June 5, 1860, in *Iggrot Shadal* (Premsl, 1882), pp. 1366–67. Trans. here by L. Sachs.

stars, will stand forever, is the very Wisdom you study. It will immortalize those who master it and will make your name blessed unto the furthest generations.

Therefore be strong and of good courage, my dear and illustrious friend! Be not frightened, neither be you dismayed.[8] Do not hasten to the call of the foxes, the small and the great. Collect your ideas and thoughts and make of them a profound little book. You will then carry your head high.[9] Righteous men will revere and praise you, and the honest man will rejoice and exalt your name, and injustice will be utterly silenced.

And now may God bless you and your house and all that belongs to you. As you have arrived at old age may you continue to live long in full health and happiness.

Your honored friend and servant,
Shadal

NOTES

1. Samuel David Luzzatto (1800–1865). Often referred to by his acronym, *Shadal,* he was an Italian-Jewish scholar, philosopher, Bible commentator and translator. He was the only member of the first generation of the Science of Judaism to earn his livelihood as a scholar. In 1829 he was appointed a professor in the modern, albeit traditionalist, rabbinical college of Padua. His scholarship had a wide scope, including Scripture, Hebrew philosophy, medieval Hebrew poetry and philosophy. His most significant contribution to Jewish science is probably the discovery and publication of numerous Hebrew manuscripts found in Italian archives and libraries. He shared many of the fruits of his research in his voluminous correspondence with his fellow scholars in the fledgling discipline of Jewish science. For him critical research was a way of deepening his understanding and commitment to traditional Judaism. He therefore was profoundly disturbed by the detached scholarship and the historical relativism of his German colleagues.

2. Salomon J. Rappoport (acronym, *Shir,* 1790–1867), an Orthodox rabbi and one of the founders of the Science of Judaism. Within his native Galicia he was esteemed as a brilliant talmudist, and served as the rabbi of Tarnopol; in 1840 he was appointed the chief rabbi of Prague. Although he lacked a university education, he acquired a knowledge of classical, Semitic and modern languages. He published critical, scholarly articles in various Hebrew journals sponsored by the *maskilim*. Known as the father of modern Jewish historiography, Rappoport was the first to reveal the value of using traditional Jewish sources to reconstruct Jewish history. Like Luzzatto, Rappoport exercised self-restraint and avoided issues that were liable to affect the essential beliefs of the Jewish people; thus, for example, the Pentateuch was considered too sacred to be profaned by the irreverent scrutiny of critical scholarship.

3. An apparent allusion to Eduard Gans' famous simile regarding the type of integration of Jewry into Europe to be fostered by Jewish science. See document 3 in this chapter.

4. In Hebrew the Science of Judaism is referred to as *Hokhmat Yisrael,* "the Wisdom of Israel."

5. Rabbinic teachers mentioned in the Mishnah.

6. Interpreters of the Mishnah noted in the Gemara, the second part of the Talmud.

7. *Ha-hokhmah ha-meyusedet 'al ha-emunah.*

8. See Josh. 1:7.

9. See Lev. 26:13.

MARTIN BUBER[1]
9. Jewish Science: New Perspectives

. . . What is Jewish science? To what purpose, and how, does one engage in it? Where does it exist? What does it have to do with Zionism? And what about the questions concerning the spiritual furtherance of the Jewish people? All this is not self-evident. We must try to clarify the meaning of a Jewish science and its pertinence to our endeavors.

A Jewish science may fulfill a threefold purpose. According to its point of departure, it may either be the Science of Judaism, the Science of the Jewish question, or the Science of Zionism. In the first case, its point of departure would be the historical and present reality of the Jewish people; it would aim to describe and to explain the actual situation; it would pursue no other practical aspect than that of tracing consistent developments through a maze of complex phenomena. In the second case, it would have to deal with an eminently practical problem, with the "pathology" of contemporary Jewry and the anomaly of its relations to other peoples; this science would find it more difficult to remain objective than the science of the Jewish people, for even the choice of its material would already be determined by its purpose. The Science of Zionism, finally, could hardly be objective at all; its point of departure would not be a question, but an answer, which in most cases was not found by a scientific method, but by intuition, or in any case subjectively, and must now be justified; the purpose would thus not merely determine the choice of the factual material, but also its arrangement, its interpretation and evaluation. . . .

In truth, there can only be *one* Jewish science: The Science of Judaism [*Wissenschaft des Judentums*]. It would partly result in a scientific treatment of the Jewish question and of Zionism (since it would adumbrate a historical and sociological explanation of contemporary conditions), and would partly be complemented by them, just as the theory of political economy is complemented by economic policy. But where is this Science of Judaism?

One might answer: It does not exist. . . .

This is true. It does not exist. And it cannot be created. It does not exist, because no circumscribed field belongs to it, nor does it have one specific methodology which it systematically pursues. And it cannot be created because no proper science evolves from plans, schemes and programs, however well-intentioned they might be, but from the far-sighted and yet narrowly circumscribed research by the man of knowledge. Plans and programs can never be its foundation, but only its roof.

And yet, we not only speak of a scientifically pursued Zionism, but also of a Jewish science. Admittedly, this expression is not quite correct; it is to be retained for merely practical reasons. But if one accepts our definition of it (I shall presently try to prove its relative justification), then the answers to the questions as to where this science might be found will turn out not to be quite correct, either.

For, if you wish, the science does exist: Its smaller part is embodied in what is presently called the Science of Judaism; its greater part is in various other disciplines. And it is not a matter of creating, but one of tracing and

Source: Martin Buber, "Juedische Wissenschaft," *Die Welt*, nos. 41–43 (October 11 and 25, 1901); reprinted in Buber, *Die juedische Bewegung: Gesammelte Aufsaetze und Ansprachen, 1900–1915* (Berlin: Juedischer Verlag, 1916), pp. 45–51. Reprinted by permission of Mr. Rafael Buber. Trans. here by J. Hessing.

linkage. This process of tracing and linkage, however, does not take place in order to create an independent science, valid according to the principles of the philosophy of science—no independent subject matter without a valid methodology will suffice to establish a particular science—but in order to collect that which belongs to us, to build up a continuously developing inventory of Judaism, to see what we are, what we have and what we are able to do. This, too, like the other disciplines I have mentioned above may possess a practical aspect, but it does not diminish the objectivity and completeness of the scientific complex under consideration.

The parts pertaining to Judaism should therefore be traced in the relevant disciplines and then linked to the so-called Science of Judaism. It is to be hoped that through these efforts and the consequent organizational work, as well as through the development and deepening of the Jewish national movement, the interest in the new material will be enhanced, and that Jewish scholars will study the relevant problems in their respective fields.

But what about the so-called Science of Judaism, around which the nascent complex is to crystallize?

It is not entitled to its proud name. That much is certain. It is true that outstanding men have always been dedicated to it. It is true that it has developed its method with critical finesse and heuristic acumen. It is also true that it has researched and analyzed with utmost zeal. But inevitably, it has always remained what it was from the beginning: A species of philology. Its object was ancient Jewish literature; its method of research was philological. It is not entitled to the name Science of Judaism, much less so than German philology to the name Science of Germanism.

Laymen may have grouped other scientific creations under this heading as well. But the history of the Jewish people is certainly a part of the science of history, the legislation in Bible or Talmud part of a general history of law, studies of Jewish legends and customs part of folklore, the research of ancient Jewish monuments part of archeology and the history of art. The studies of the Jewish people as an ethnic group, of their alleged psychophysical attributes, of ancient Jewish economy, of our social stratification, of the evolution of specific customs and morals, of Jewish spirit and Jewish culture—all these studies, which we are looking forward to, will not belong to that science which depends on the philological method, but to anthropology, ethnology and economic, social, moral and cultural history—disciplines of different purposes and, therefore, of different methods.[2] . . .

I have tried to prove that there can be no valid Jewish science in a strictly methodological sense, but merely a scientific complex of Jewish matters. It could be organized by tracing the areas pertaining to Judaism in the various disciplines and by linking them to philological Judaica of a modern type. It is this complex which I shall now, for reasons of expediency, call Jewish science.

This largely answers our first question, "What is Jewish science?" And therefore we already know its purpose as well. We ought to engage in Jewish science in order to learn about the Jewish people—its origins, development and present conditions. This would serve a double purpose. To understand, first of all, what one loves. But then we should go further and learn from the given situation what is needed for our people, and what may be expected from it; in other words, our people's requirements and possibilities. The former and the latter are needed in order to create the scientific foundation for the grand design of a Jewish policy, i.e., in order to approach that which we have called the science of the Jewish question. The purpose is then, at one and the same time theoretical and practical. . . .

NOTES

1. Martin Buber (1878–1965), German-Jewish social and religious philosopher. After the publication of his book *I and Thou* in 1923, he was best known for his philosophy of dialog. While a student at the University of Berlin he joined the Zionist movement. He was appointed by Theodor Herzl in 1901 to edit the central weekly organ of the movement, *Die Welt*, in which Buber called for a renaissance of Jewish cultural activity. In this essay, which first appeared in *Die Welt*, Buber criticized nineteenth-century Jewish science precisely because it lacked, in his view, a commitment to Judaism as a living cultural reality. In this criticism—and in the related demand that Jewish science expand its thematic horizons from an antiquarian interest in Jewish literature to include all aspects of Jewish life—Buber anticipated the new scope and conception that would characterize Jewish science in the twentieth century. While perhaps not fully overcoming the historicist bias, the Jewish scholar no longer feels that scientific objectivity is compromised by recognizing, in the words of Julius Gutmann, "the creative energies of present-day Judaism." Methodologically, Jewish scholarship is no longer restricted to philosophy and the scientific exegesis of texts, but employs broad conceptual and phenomenological tools for the study of Jewish literature and, moreover, incorporates the focus and methods of various disciplines to facilitate the effort, as Buber said, "to explore and know what one loves."

2. In consonance with such considerations, it is now customary to underscore the multidisciplinary character of academic Jewish scholarship by speaking of the sciences of Judaism or, more felicitiously, Jewish studies.

VI

Jewish Identity Challenged and Redefined

In the accelerated process of acculturation and assimilation that characterized the Jews' entrance into modernity, a large number of Jews were estranged over time from their primordial community. Their bonds—social, cultural, spiritual and psychological—with the community of their fathers were weakened, while at the same time Jewish self-identity became problematic. The readings in this chapter represent various types of response to the problems of Jewish identity in the modern period: estrangement (Solomon Maimon, Karl Emil Franzos, Franz Kafka); conversion (Joseph Michael Edler von Arnsteiner, Abraham Mendelssohn, Heinrich Heine); cosmopolitanism (Ludwig Boerne, Rosa Luxemburg, Rahel Levin Varnhagen, Eduard Bernstein, Isaac Deutscher); Jewish self-hatred (Walter Rathenau, Otto Weininger, Theodor Lessing). In contradistinction to these responses, from the midst of assimilation, there is a dialectical affirmation of Jewish identity and Judaism. Four varieties of this affirmation are represented here: national-Zionist affirmation (Moses Hess); affirmation of Jewishness *qua* unique sensibility (Gustav Landauer, Daniel Bell); *Trotzjudentum* ("defiant Jewry"), an affirmation of Jewish identity in defiance of the anti-Semites and as an expression of solidarity with one's oppressed brethren (Arthur Koestler); and the affirmation of Jewish religious faith (Franz Rosenzweig, Jeri M. Langer).

SOLOMON MAIMON

1. My Emergence from Talmudic Darkness[1]

. . . The subjects of the Talmud, with the exception of those relating to jurisprudence, are dry and mostly unintelligible to a child—the laws of sacrifice, of purification, of forbidden meats, of feasts and so forth—in which the oddest rabbinical conceits are elaborated through many volumes with the finest dialectic, and the most far-fetched questions are discussed with the highest efforts of intellectual power; for example, how many white hairs a red cow may have, and yet remain a *red cow;* what sorts of scabs require this or that sort of purification; whether a louse or a flea may be killed on the Sabbath—the first being allowed, while the second is a deadly sin—whether an animal should be slaughtered at the neck or tail; whether the high priest puts on his shirt or his socks first; whether the *Jabam,* that is, the brother of a man who dies childless, being required by law to marry the widow, is relieved of his obligation if he falls off a roof and sticks in the mire. *Ohe jam satis est:* ["Alas, it is enough already!"] Compare these glorious disputations, which are served up to young people and forced on them even to their disgust, with history, in which natural events are related in an instructive and agreeable manner, and with a knowledge of the world's structure, by which the outlook into nature is widened, and the vast whole is brought into a well-ordered system; surely my preference will be justified. . . .

I must now say something of the condition of the Jewish schools in general. The school is commonly a small smoky hut, and the children are scattered, some on benches, some on the bare earth. The master, in a dirty blouse sitting on the table, holds between his knees a bowl, in which he grinds tobacco into snuff with a huge pestle like the club of Hercules, while at the same time he wields his authority. The ushers give lessons, each in his own corner, and rule those under their charge quite as despotically as the master himself. Of the breakfast, lunch and other food sent to the school for the children, these gentlemen keep the largest share for themselves. Sometimes the poor youngsters get nothing at all; and yet they dare not make any complaint on the subject, if they will not expose themselves to the vengeance of these tyrants. Here the children are imprisoned from morning to night, and have not an hour to themselves, except on Friday and a half-holiday at the New Moon.

As far as study is concerned, the reading of Hebrew is regularly taught. On the other hand, very seldom is any progress made towards the mastery of the Hebrew language. Grammar is not taught in the school at all, but has to be learnt by translation of the Holy Scriptures, very much as the ordinary man learns imperfectly the grammar of his mother-tongue by social intercourse. Moreover, there is no dictionary of the Hebrew language. The children therefore begin at once with the explanation of the Bible. This is divided into as many sections as there are weeks in the year, in order that the Books of Moses, which are read in the synagogue every Saturday, may be read through in a year. Accordingly, every week some verses from the beginning of the section of the week are explained in school, and those with every possible grammatical blunder. Nor can it well be otherwise. For the Hebrew must be explained by means of the vernacular. But the vernacular of the Polish Jews is itself full of defects and grammatical inaccuracies; and so

Source: The Autobiography of Solomon Maimon, trans. J. Clark Murray (London: The East and West Library, 1954), pp. 28, 31–33, 68–70, 126–28. Reprinted by permission of the East and West Library.

the Hebrew language, which is learned by its means, must be of the same stamp. The pupil thus acquires just as little knowledge of the language, as of the contents of the Bible.

In addition to this the Talmudists have attached all sorts of curious fancies to the Bible. The ignorant teacher believes with confidence, that the Bible cannot in reality have any other meaning than that which these expositions ascribe to it; and the pupil must follow his teacher's faith, and so the right understanding of words necessarily becomes lost. . . .

Thanks to the instruction received from my father, but still more to my own industry, I had got on so well, that in my eleventh year I was able to pass as a full rabbi. In addition I possessed some disconnected knowledge in history, astronomy and other mathematical sciences. I burned with desire to acquire more knowledge, but how was this to be accomplished, lacking guidance, scientific books and all other means for the purpose? I was obliged therefore to content myself with making use of any help that I could by chance obtain, without plan or method.

In order to gratify my desire for scientific knowledge, there were no means available but that of learning foreign languages. But how was I to begin? To learn Polish or Latin with a Catholic teacher was for me impossible, on the one hand because the prejudices of my own people prohibited all languages but Hebrew, and all sciences but the Talmud and the vast array of its commentators; on the other hand because the prejudices of Catholics would not allow them to give instruction in those matters to a Jew. I was obliged to support a whole family by teaching, by correcting proofs of the Holy Scriptures, and by other work of a similar kind. For a long time therefore I had to sigh in vain for the satisfaction of my natural inclination.

At last a fortunate accident came to my aid. I observed in some stout Hebrew volumes, that they contained several alphabets, and that the number of their sheets was indicated not merely by Hebrew letters, but that for this purpose the characters of a second and a third alphabet had also been employed, these being Latin and German letters. . . . [I] gradually learnt the Latin and German characters.

By a kind of deciphering I began to combine various German letters into words; but as the characters used along with the Hebrew letters might be quite different from these, I remained doubtful whether the whole of my labour would not be in vain, till fortunately some leaves of an old German book fell into my hands. I began to read. How great were my joy and surprise, when I saw from the connection, that the words completely corresponded with those which I had learnt. . . .

I still felt a want I was not able to fill. I could not completely satisfy my desire for scientific knowledge. Up to this time the study of the Talmud was still my chief occupation. With this, however, I found pleasure merely because of its form, for this calls into action the higher powers of the mind; but I took no interest in its matter. It affords exercise in deducing the remotest consequences from their principles, in discovering the most hidden contradiction, in hunting out the finest distinctions, and so forth. But as the principles themselves have merely an imaginary reality, they cannot by any means satisfy a soul thirsting after knowledge. . . .

[Maimon eventually obtained some old German books on the natural sciences.] I pocketed the few books, and returned home in rapture. After I had studied these books thoroughly, my eyes were opened. I believed that I had found a key to all the secrets of nature, as I now knew the origin of storms, of dew, of rain, and such phenomena. I looked down with pride on all others who did not yet know these things, laughed at their prejudices and superstitions, and proposed to clear up their ideas on these subjects and to enlighten their understanding. But this did not always succeed. I laboured once to teach a Talmudist that the earth is round. . . .

[Having made his way to the centers of the Enlightenment in Germany, and after great travail, Maimon acquired the rudiments of German secular culture.] I had received too much education to return to Poland, to spend my life in misery without rational occupation or society, and to sink back into the darkness of superstition and ignorance, from which I had delivered myself with so much labour. On the other hand, I could not reckon to succeed in Germany owing to my ignorance of the language, as well as of the manners and customs of the people to which I had never been able to adapt myself properly. I had learnt no particular profession. I had not distinguished myself in any special science, I was not even master of any language in which I could make myself perfectly intelligible. It occurred to me, therefore, that there was no alternative left but to embrace the Christian religion and get myself baptised in Hamburg. Accordingly I resolved to go to the first clergyman I should come across and inform him of my resolution, as well as of my motives for it, without any hypocrisy in a truthful and honest fashion. But as I could not express myself well orally, I put my thoughts into writing in German with Hebrew characters, went to a schoolmaster, and got him to copy it in German characters. The purport of my letter was in brief as follows:

> I am a native of Poland, belonging to the Jewish nation, destined by my education and studies to be a rabbi; but in the thickest darkness I have perceived some light. This has induced me to search further after light and truth and to free myself completely from the darkness of superstition and ignorance. As this could not be attained in my native place, I went to Berlin, where through the support of some enlightened men of our nation I studied for some years—not indeed with any plan, but merely to satisfy my thirst for knowledge. But as our nation is unable to use, not only such planless studies, but even those based on the most perfect plan, it cannot be blamed for becoming tired of them, and pronouncing their encouragement to be useless. I have therefore resolved, in order to secure temporal as well as eternal happiness, which depends on the attainment of perfection, and in order to become useful to myself as well as to others, to embrace the Christian religion. The Jewish religion, it is true, comes in its articles of faith, nearer to reason than Christianity. But in practical use the latter has an advantage over the former; and since morality, which consists not in opinions but in actions, is the aim of all religion, clearly the latter comes nearer than the former to this aim. Moreover I esteem the mysteries of the Christian religion for that which they are, that is, allegorical representations of the truths that are most important for man. Thus I make my faith in them harmonise with reason, but I cannot believe them literally. I beg therefore most respectfully an answer to the question, whether after this confession I am worthy of the Christian religion or not. If I am, I am prepared to carry my proposal into effect; but if not, I must give up all claim to a religion which enjoins me to lies, that is, to deliver a confession of faith which contradicts my reason. . . .

I went then to a prominent clergyman, delivered my letter, and asked for a reply. He read it with great attention, was equally astonished, and on finishing began to converse with me.

"So," he said, "your intention is to embrace the Christian religion merely in order to improve your temporal circumstances."

"Excuse me, Herr Pastor," I replied, "I think I have made it clear enough in my letter that my object is the attainment of perfection. For this, it is true, the removal of all hindrances and the improvement of my external circumstances are an indispensable condition. But this condition is not the chief end."

"But," said the pastor, "do you not feel any inclination to the Christian religion without reference to any external motives?"

"I should be telling a lie if I were to give you an affirmative answer."

"You are too much of a philosopher," replied the pastor, "to be able to become a Christian. Reason has taken the upper hand with you, and faith must accommodate itself to reason. You hold the mysteries of the

Christian religion to be mere fables, and its commands to be mere laws of reason. For the present I cannot be satisfied with your confession of faith. You should therefore pray to God, that He may enlighten you with His grace and endow you with the spirit of true Christianity; and then come to me again."

"If that is the case," I said, "then I must confess, Herr Pastor, that I am not qualified for Christianity. Whatever light I may receive, I shall always make it luminous with the light of reason. I shall never believe that I have fallen upon new truths, if it is impossible to see their connection with the truths already known to me. I must therefore remain what I am—a stiff-necked Jew. My religion enjoins me to *believe* nothing, but to *think* the truth and to *practise* goodness. If I find any hindrance in this from external circumstances, it is not my fault. I do all that lies in my power."

With this I bade the pastor goodbye. . . .

NOTES

1. Solomon Maimon (c.1753–1800). Born in Sukoviboeg, Poland, he received a traditional talmudic education. In search of secular learning, Maimon abandoned his family and rabbinic office, and went to Germany, where he gradually acquired a profound knowledge of German culture and philosophy. Kant noted that of all his critics nobody understood his work as well as Maimon. In his autobiography, published in German in 1793, Maimon describes his estrangement from traditional Judaism. Although he presents it as process immanent to his experience of Judaism, his estrangement undoubtedly gained articulation and self-consciousness from his contact with non-Jewish culture. His autobiography was widely read by German intellectuals—non-Jewish and Jewish—throughout the nineteenth and twentieth centuries, who derived their concepts of Orthodox Judaism from it.

KARL EMIL FRANZOS
2. Every Country Has the Jews that It Deserves[1]

When I took up my pen four years ago, I strongly felt the necessity of making my work as artistic as possible. I wished to write stories, and strove to give them poetic value. For this very reason, it seemed necessary that I should describe the kind of life with which I was best acquainted. This was essentially the case with regard to that of the Podolian Jews. I therefore became the historian of the Podolian Ghetto, and it was my great desire to give these stories an artistic form; but not at the cost of truth. I have never permitted my love of the beautiful to lead me into the sin of falsifying the facts and conditions of life, and am confident that I have described this strange and outlandish mode of existence precisely as it appeared to me. If in my first published volume my efforts to portray men and manners needed the assistance of my powers as a novelist, so in this book my knowledge of men and manners has to help me in my labors as a novelist. Sometimes the one side of my character takes the upper hand, and sometimes the other; but still they are at bottom inseparable, and it has always been my endeavor to describe facts artisti-

Source: Karl Emil Franzos, "Preface," *The Jews of Barnow,* trans. M. W. Macdowall (New York: D. Appleton & Co., 1883), pp. xix–xxi.

cally. However the novelist may be judged, the portrayer of men and manners demands that his words should be believed.

This request is not superfluous, for it is a very strange mode of life on which I am about to introduce the reader. . . . I have kept before my eyes, while penning these stories, that I am writing for a Western reader. If he will only trust to my love of truth, and regard the separate stories in combination with each other, he will gain a clear idea of the kind of life I describe without any further particulars. Every country has the Jews that it deserves—and it is not the fault of the Polish Jews that they are less civilized than their brethren in the faith in England, Germany, and France. At least, it is not entirely their fault. . . .

NOTE

1. Karl Emil Franzos (1848–1904), Austrian-Jewish novelist and journalist. He was born in Czortkow, Galicia, which he later fictionalized as Barnow. His collections of sketches and tales about life in the Podolian Ghetto—most notably *Halb-Asien* [Semi-Asia] (1876) and *The Jews of Barnow* (1877)—reveal Franzos' ambivalent feelings. On the one hand he is compassionate, on the other he is self-consciously critical about the superstitions and backward, "Asiatic" ways of the ghetto. Franzos' popular stories did much to disseminate a negative image of the "unassimilated" Jews of Eastern Europe.

FRANZ KAFKA
3. My Father's Bourgeois Judaism[1]

I found little means of escape from you in Judaism. Here some escape would, in principle, have been thinkable, but more than that, it would have been thinkable that we might both have found each other in Judiasm or even that we might have begun from there in harmony. But what sort of Judaism was it I got from you? In the course of the years I have taken roughly three different attitudes to it.

As a child I reproached myself, in accord with you, for not going to the synagogue enough, for not fasting, and so on. I thought that in this way I was doing a wrong not to myself but to you, and I was penetrated by a sense of guilt, which was, of course, always ready to hand.

Later, as a young man, I could not understand how, with the insignificant scrap of Judaism you yourself possessed, you could reproach me for not (if for no more than the sake of piety, as you put it) making an effort to cling to a similar insignificant scrap. It was indeed really, so far as I could see, a mere scrap, a joke, not even a joke. On four days in the year you went to the synagogue, where you were, to say the least, closer to the indifferent than to those who took it seriously, [you] patiently went through the prayers by way of formality, [you] sometimes amazed me by being able to show me in the prayer book the passage that was being said at the moment, and for the rest, so long as I was in the synagogue (and this was the main thing) I was allowed to hang about wherever I liked.

Source: Franz Kafka, *Dearest Father: Stories and Other Writings,* trans. E. Kaiser and E. Wilkins (New York: Schocken Books, 1954), pp. 171–72.

And so I yawned and dozed through the many hours (I don't think I was ever again so bored, except later at dancing lessons) and did my best to enjoy the few little bits of variety there were, as, for instance, when the Ark of the Covenant was opened, which always reminded me of the shooting galleries where a cupboard door would open in the same way whenever one got a bull's eye, only with the difference that there something interesting always came out and here it was always just the same old dolls with no heads. Incidentally, it was also very frightening for me there, not only, as goes without saying, because of all the people one came into close contact with, but also because you once mentioned, by the way, that I too might be called up to read the Torah. That was something I went in dread of for years. But otherwise I was not fundamentally disturbed in my state of boredom, unless it was by the *bar mitzvah*, but that meant no more than some ridiculous learning by heart, in other words, led to nothing but something like the ridiculous passing of an examination, and then, as far as you were concerned, by little, not very significant incidents, as when you were called up to read the Torah and came well out of the affair, which to my way of feeling was purely social, or when you stayed on in the synagogue for the prayers for the dead, and I was sent away, which for a long time, obviously because of being sent away and lacking, as I did, any deeper interest, aroused in me the more or less unconscious feeling that what was about to take place was something indecent.—That was how it was in the synagogue, and at home it was, if possible, even more poverty-stricken, being confined to the first evening of Passover which more and more developed into a farce, with fits of hysterical laughter, admittedly under the influence of the growing children. (Why did you have to give way to that influence? Because you brought it about in the first place.) And so there was the religious material that was handed on to me, to which may be added at most the outstretched hand pointing to "the sons of the millionaire Fuchs," who were in the synagogue with their father at high holidays. How one could do anything better with this material than get rid of it as fast as possible was something I could not understand; precisely getting rid of it seemed to me the most effective act of "piety" one could perform. . . .

NOTE

1. Franz Kafka (1883–1924), Czech-born German-Jewish novelist. Although estranged from the bourgeois Judaism of his father, Kafka identified positively with Judaism, shown by his interest in secular Jewish culture and Zionism, which provided a counter-Jewish identity for many middle-class Jewish youths of his day. Kafka wrote this autobiographical letter to his father in 1919, at the age of thirty-six.

JOSEPH MICHAEL EDLER VON ARNSTEINER

4. I Have Converted[1]

My venerable Parents!

Believe me, dearest Parents, since I have last opened my heart to you I was ready for the daring step a hundred times; now, fi-

Source: Hilde Spiel, *Fanny von Arnstein oder die Emanzipation ein Frauenleben an der Zeitwende, 1758–1818* (Frankfurt am Main: S. Fischer Verlag, 1962), pp. 86–89. Trans. here by J. Hessing.

nally, I am going to take it. [I herewith inform you that I have adopted the Catholic faith.]

Only respect—and fear, lest you look harshly upon my [decision]—have kept me from writing to you. I wanted first to prove to you . . . that your son is not unworthy of you. I wanted to show you that neither ulterior motives, nor desire for the easy life, nor innate licentiousness have led me to forgo your religion, but rather a conviction that I will find salvation and peace of mind on a different road. Ever since [my conversion], I have tried everything, and have used every means, to gain your permission to meet with you and to kiss the hand of my venerable parents; but, alas, all these efforts were in vain! Either my entreaties have not reached your ears or, even worse, have not reached your heart. I am your son, dearest father! I—formerly, your most beloved son—challenge anybody to point out one single fact by which I have [deservedly] forfeited the love and the affection of my parents; were it so, were I conscious of any offence against you, I would be able to bear my predicament more easily; I would patiently wait for the softening of your heart; I would seek to expiate my crimes, and [deem it proper] that an appropriate punishment precede our reconciliation. But mine, unfortunately, is the case of the melancholic individual who is most depressed because he cannot find an objective reason for his depression, for I do not know of any personal defect for which I should deserve such painful chastisement.

I certainly appreciate, dearest parents, the attitudes usually inculcated by upbringing and a misconceived religion, but are you really capable of hating your son just because he adheres to principles of belief other than your own? In our age of enlightenment, under the government of our most gracious monarch, whose every action creates a singular example of general tolerance for each of his subjects, who lets everyone *believe* in whatever he wishes as long as he *acts* as he should? Under such a government which grants you, who abide by Jewish law, the same protection, and the same rights, as every other fellow citizen? Where you can collect your riches and live off them without the slightest fear of pressure and coercion? Under a tolerant government such as ours, could you really be capable of hating an innocent, blameless son, and of rejecting his request for permission to meet with you and to receive your blessing, only because he does not share your religious principles? Could you banish your grandchild from your countenance, an innocent minor who could do nothing but follow the well-meant advice of his father? In this case, may I refer to my brother and sister-in-law who are still Jewish and who, on their many excursions into the world, are met with all due love and respect by the members of the numerically dominant religion, while you, out of religious hatred, banish an erstwhile beloved son from your eyes! Your very religion, dearest parents, does not condemn anybody forever, and yet even in our temporal life, you have chosen to be inexorably severe!

Once again, therefore, venerable parents, I implore you to accept my entreaties which do not stem from my self-interest and do not pursue any secondary object: allow me and my dear child, your grandchild, to approach you and even to come and see you daily, so that we may kiss your hands and receive your blessing. We are human beings, dearest parents! Human beings who are flourishing today and may fade away tomorrow! It is a dreadful thought to me—and, I daresay, should be one to you, as well—that one of us might leave this temporal world without having achieved a complete and cordial reconciliation and reunification. I therefore implore you to think all this over once more, and to take the words of wise Solomon into consideration: *He who lives within the boundaries of the laws is the son of a wise man; but he who follows the squanderer brings disgrace upon his father.*

Please fix an hour when I and my child shall be allowed to appear before you, our parents. Believe me that I shall remain until the final breath of my life,

Your dearest son, . . .

NOTE

1. Joseph von Arnsteiner (d. 1811), son of Adam Isaac Arnsteiner (1721–1785), purveyor to the court of Austrian Empress Maria Theresa. Joseph Michael converted to Catholicism in 1778; he was ennobled in 1783 after his second marriage into Austrian aristocracy. Despite his impassioned plea for parental forebearance, his father disowned him for having abandoned Judaism.

ABRAHAM MENDELSSOHN
5. Why I Have Raised You as a Christian: A Letter to His Daughter[1]

My dear Daughter,

You have taken an important step, and in sending you my best wishes for the day and for your future happiness, I have it at heart to speak seriously to you on subjects hitherto not touched upon.

Does God exist? What is God? Is He a part of ourselves, and does He continue to live after the other part has ceased to be? And where? And how? All this I do not know, and therefore I have never taught you anything about it. But I know that there exists in me and in you and in all human beings an everlasting inclination towards all that is good, true, and right, and a conscience which warns and guides us when we go astray. I know it, I believe it, I live in this faith, and this is my religion. This I could not teach you, and nobody can learn it; but everybody has it who does not intentionally and knowingly cast it away. The example of your mother, the best and noblest of mothers, whose whole life is devotion, love and charity, is like a bond to me that you will *not* cast it away. You have grown up under her guidance, ever intuitively receiving and adopting what alone gives real worth to mankind. Your mother has been, and is, and I trust will long remain to you, to your sister and brothers, and to all of us, a providential leading star on our path of life. When you look at her and turn over in your thoughts all the immeasurable good she has lavished upon you by her constant self-sacrificing devotion as long as you live, and when that reflection makes your heart and eyes overflow with gratitude, love, and veneration, then you feel God and are godly.

This is all I can tell you about religion, all I know about it; but this will remain true, as long as one man will exist in the creation, as it has been true since the first man was created.

The outward form of religion your teacher has given you is historical, and changeable like all human ordinances. Some thousands of years ago the Jewish form was the reigning one, then the heathen form, and now it is the Christian. We, your mother and I, were born and brought up by our parents as Jews, and without being obliged to change the form of our religion have been able to follow the divine instinct in us and in our conscience. We have educated you and your brothers and sister in the Christian faith, because it is the creed of most civilized people, and contains

Source: Abraham Mendelssohn to Fanny Mendelssohn, c. July 1820, in S. Hensel, *The Mendelssohn Family (1729–1847): From Letters and Journals*, 2nd rev. ed., trans. C. Klingemann (New York, 1882), vol. 1, pp. 79–80.

nothing that can lead you away from what is good, and much that guides you to love, obedience, tolerance, and resignation, even if it offered nothing but the example of its Founder, understood by so few, and followed by still fewer.

By pronouncing your confession of faith you have fulfilled the claims of *society* on you, and obtained the *name* of a Christian. Now *be* what your duty as a human being demands of you, *true, faithful, good;* obedient and devoted till death to your mother, and I may also say to your father, unremittingly attentive to the voice of your conscience, which may be suppressed but never silenced, and you will gain the highest happiness that is to be found on earth, harmony and contentedness with yourself.

I embrace you with fatherly tenderness, and hope always to find in you a daughter worthy of your, of our, mother. Farewell, and remember my words.

NOTE

1. Abraham Mendelssohn (1776–1835), son of Moses Mendelssohn. A deist and a rationalist by conviction, Abraham brought up his children—Fanny and Felix—as Protestants in order to improve their social opportunities. In 1822 he and his wife also embraced Christianity "because it is the religious form acceptable to the majority of civilized human beings." He wrote this letter to his daughter Fanny (1805–1847) upon her confirmation into the Lutheran church.

HEINRICH HEINE[1]
6. A Ticket of Admission to European Culture

From the nature of my thinking you can deduce that baptism is a matter of indifference to me, that I do not regard it as important even symbolically, and that in the circumstances in which it will be carried out in my case it will have little significance for others likewise. For me perhaps its significance will be that I can better devote myself to championing the rights of my unfortunate brethren. And yet I hold it beneath my dignity and a stain on my honor to undergo conversion in order to obtain a position in Prussia. Dear old Prussia! I really do not know what course to take in this bad situation. I'll turn Catholic yet for spite, and hang myself.... We are living in sad times. Scoundrels become our "best," and the best must turn scoundrel. I understand well the words of the psalmist: "Lord, give us our daily bread, that we blaspheme not Thy name...."

The baptismal certificate is the ticket of admission to European culture....

My becoming a Christian is the fault of those Saxons who suddenly changed saddles at Leipzig,[2] or of Napoleon, who really did not have to go to Russia, or of his teacher of geography at Brienne, who did not tell him that Moscow winters are very cold.

Source: Hugo Bieber, *Heinrich Heine: A Biographical Anthology,* trans. M. Hadas (Philadelphia: The Jewish Publication Society of America, 1956), pp. 157, 196. Reprinted by permission of the Jewish Publication Society of America.

NOTES

1. Heinrich Heine (1797–1856), German-Jewish poet and essayist. In 1825 he was baptized a Lutheran, with the hope that his conversion would facilitate the gaining of a doctorate and the pursuit of a career as a civil servant or academic. His repeated attempts to secure a position were, however, futile. Finally, after having failed to obtain a promised chair at the University of Munich and fearing police action against himself because of his political satire, he left Germany for Paris in 1831. He spent the remainder of his life in exile. His attitude to Judaism was complex. He deemed it "a misfortune," but he also wrote warmly and proudly of Judaism. To a friend he once declared, "I make no secret of my Judaism, to which I have not returned, because I never left it."

2. At the battle of Leipzig, October 1813, the Saxon troops fighting with the French defected to the allies, and thus ensured the defeat of Napoleon.

LUDWIG BOERNE

7. Because I Am a Jew I Love Freedom[1]

My well-meaning friend in the *Deutsche Allgemeine Zeitung* says: no one should forget that I am a Jew. Unlike others, however, he does not mean this as a reproach; on the contrary, he recalls the fact as an excuse for me, or even in praise of me. He says: I am justified in being resentful of the Germans who have oppressed and disgraced my people; not hatred, but love has distorted my view. . . . It is miraculous! I have experienced it a thousand times, and yet it is always new to me. Certain people object to my being a Jew; others forgive me; still others even praise me for it; but everybody remembers it. The Jewish mystique seems to have cast its spell on them, they are unable to free themselves from it. And I know fairly well where this evil spell comes from. The poor Germans! Living on the first floor, and oppressed by the seven stories of the higher classes, it relieves them of their anxiety to speak of people who live even further down, in the basement. That they are not Jews consoles them for the fact that they are not even court counselors. No, that I was born a Jew has never made me bitter against the Germans and has never distorted my perspective. I would not be worthy of the sunlight if I repaid with base ingratitude the grace which God has bestowed upon me by making me a German and a Jew at the same time—just because of the scorn which I have always despised, or because of the pain which I have long since forgotten. No, I know how to value the undeserved fortune of being a German and also a Jew, thus being able to strive for all virtues of a German without having to share any of his faults. Yes, because I was born a slave I love freedom more than you do. Yes, because I have learnt all about servitude, I understand more about freedom than you do. Yes, because I was born to no fatherland, I yearn for a fatherland more fervently than you. And because my birthplace was no bigger than the *Judengasse* and beyond its locked gate foreign territory began for me, neither city nor even country or province will suffice me as a fatherland. . . . I have built the house of my freedom on strong foundations; do as I have done, do not content yourselves with putting new tiles on the roof of the dilapidated building of your state. I beg you, do not

Source: Ludwig Boerne, *Briefe aus Paris,* in *Gesammelte Schriften,* ed. Alfred Klaar (Leipzig, 1899), vol. 6, pp. 62–64. Trans. here by J. Hessing.

despise my Jews. If you were as they are you would be better off; were they as many as you are they would be better than you. You are thirty million Germans and you count only as thirty in the world; were there thirty million Jews, the world would count as nothing in comparison. You have deprived Jews of air but this saved them from decay. You have strewn their hearts with the salt of hatred; but this has kept their hearts fresh. During the entire long winter you have shut them up in a deep cellar and stuffed the cellar hole with dung; but you yourself, exposed to the cold, are half frozen to death. When spring comes we shall see who blossoms earlier, the Jew or the Christian.

NOTE

1. Ludwig Boerne (1786–1837), German-Jewish political essayist, born into a prominent banking family and raised in the Frankfurt ghetto. After the defeat of France at Waterloo in 1815, the anti-Jewish restrictions of the pre-Napoleonic era were re-imposed in Germany. As a result Boerne lost his position as an official in the Frankfurt police department. He converted to Lutheranism so that he could reassume the position, but then decided to become a political journalist instead. Because of his radical views, he was obliged to leave Germany in 1830; he fled to Paris, where he was regarded as the leader of the political émigrés. His *Briefe aus Paris* [Letters from Paris] (1830–1833), from which the above is taken, were a milestone in the struggle for liberalism and democracy in Germany. Although he was greatly concerned with the Jewish question, he insisted that the cause of Jewish emancipation should not be divorced from that of the freedom of mankind as a whole.

ROSA LUXEMBURG
8. No Room in My Heart for Jewish Suffering[1]

. . . But look, girl, if you so rarely find the opportunity to take a book into your hand, at least make a point of reading *good* books, not such *kitsch* as the Spinoza novel you have just sent me. Why do you come with your particular Jewish sorrows? I feel equally close to the wretched victims of the rubber plantations in Putumayo, or to the Negroes in Africa with whose bodies the Europeans are playing catch-ball. Do you remember the words elicited by the General Staff's work on Trotha's campaign in the Kalahari desert: ". . . The rattling in the throats of the dying, and the mad screams of those who were withering from thirst, faded away into the sublime stillness of the infinite." Oh, this "sublime stillness of the infinite" in which so many screams fade away unheard—it reverberates within me so strongly that I have no separate corner in my heart for the ghetto: I feel at home in the entire world wherever there are clouds and birds and human tears.

NOTE

1. Rosa Luxemburg (1871–1919), Marxist theoretician and politician. Born into a Jewish family in Zamosc, Russian Poland, she helped found the Social Democratic party of Poland and

Source: Rosa Luxemburg to Mathilda Wurm, February 16, 1916, in Rosa Luxemburg, *Briefe an Freunde,* ed. B. Kautsky (Hamburg: Europaeische Verlagsanstalt GmbH, 1950), pp. 48–49. Reprinted by permission of the Europaeische Verlagsanstalt GmbH. Trans. here by J. Hessing.

Lithuania. In 1898, she immigrated from Switzerland to Germany, where she became a leading figure in the revolutionary left wing of the German Socialist movement. With Franz Mehring and Karl Liebknecht she founded the Spartakusbund (the Spartacus party), which at the end of 1918 was transformed into the Communist party of Germany. She and Liebknecht were arrested in Berlin on January 15, 1919 for their involvement in the Spartacist uprising. While they were being transported to prison both were murdered by army officers. A consistent internationalist, she found national particularism inimical to socialism—an attitude that is reflected in the letter presented here, in which she rebuked her friend for her Jewish national sentiments.

RAHEL LEVIN VARNHAGEN[1]
9. O How Painful To Have Been Born a Jewess!

I imagine that just as I was thrust into this world some supermundane being plunged these words into my heart with a dagger: "Yes, have sensibility, see the world as only a few see it, be great, noble; nor can I free you of incessant, eternal thought. But I add one thing more: Be a Jewess!" And now my whole life is a slow bleeding to death. By keeping still I can prolong it. Every attempt to stop the bleeding is to die anew, and immobility is only possible for me in death itself. . . . I can ascribe every evil, every misfortune, every vexation that has befallen me from *that.*

"What a history!" she exclaimed with deep emotion. "Here I am, a fugitive from Egypt and Palestine, who has found your help, love, attention! Divine guidance has led me to you, dear August, and you to me! With sublime rapture I am contemplating my origins and this fateful nexus between the oldest memories of mankind and the latest developments linking poles far apart in time and space. What for a long period of my life has been the source of my greatest shame, my most bitter grief and misfortune—to be born a Jewess—I would not at any price now wish to miss. Will it be the same with my illness, shall I once find delight in it, never wanting to miss it again? O dear August, what consoling insight, what a meaningful parable! Let us continue on this way!" And then, weeping, she went on: "Dear August, my heart is refreshed in its innermost depths; I thought of Jesus and cried over his passion. I have felt, for the first time in my life, that he is my brother. And Mary, how she must have suffered! She witnessed the pain of her beloved son, and did not succumb, but kept standing at the cross! I could not have been able to do that; I would not have been strong enough. May God forgive me, I confess how weak I am."

NOTE

1. Rahel Levin Varnhagen (1771–1833). Born into a prosperous Jewish merchant family in Berlin, she was raised in Orthodox Jewish surroundings. She was noted for her scintillating intelligence, and her home became the informal center of literary, social and political luminaries of her day. In 1819,

Source: Rahel Levin to David Veit, 1795, in *Briefwechsel zwischen Rahel und David Veit,* ed. Ludmilla Assing (Leipzig, 1861), vol. 2, pp. 79–80. Trans. here by P. Mendes-Flohr. Statement by Rahel on her death bed as recorded by Karl August Varnhagen von Ense, in *Rahel, Ein Buch des Andenkens fuer Ihre Freunde* (Berlin, 1834), vol. 1, p. 34. Trans. here by J. Hessing.

after repeated romantic disappointments, she married a man fourteen years her junior, a minor Prussian diplomat named Karl August Varnhagen von Ense and she converted to his religion, Protestantism.

EDUARD BERNSTEIN
10. How I Grew Up as a Jew in the Diaspora[1]

. . . My parents were Reform Jews, but Jews nevertheless. To which degree my father believed in God I cannot tell; we have never discussed the question in depth. He approached the Bible as a rationalist, and I can still remember his critical remarks about it. This critical thinking, to be sure, accounts for the fact that my surname is not David. According to Jewish family tradition I should have been named thus. But my father held David in particular disdain, for as a king, David was a villain, and, therefore, my father was not going to have his son bear the name of such a man. My father, in any case, was not a pious man. But he knew much about Judaism, he could explain the Jewish customs and knew all the old songs by heart, which he recited at times. My mother, on the other hand, although not religious by the letter, was of a more pious nature and would have preferred, had the situation allowed it, to keep a Jewish household. She did not actually contradict my father, but did not share his rationalistic aloofness. During the High Holy Days, both my parents liked to attend the service at the Reform congregation in Berlin. . . .

Upon leaving my parents' home [for boarding school] I entered a house, a street, and a school of completely Gentile character. This Gentile world seemed to me the normal, the Jewish world the anomalous one, and children, more gregarious than adults, tend to respect greatly what seems normal to them. Moreover, the Gentiles I met were Protestants, which made them very sympathetic to me. Which childish soul is not touched by the stories of Jesus, his mother, his suffering, and his great love of mankind? I heard of this in the dormitory and read of it in the spelling-book while I attended the first grades of boys' school. For a while, although as a Jew I was not obliged to do so, I even attended religious classes and enjoyed them more than the majority of my Christian schoolmates.

I still remember quite a few Christian chorals; some of them arouse feelings in me as strong as those associated with the ardent Jewish songs I heard in my parents' home, and later in the Reform temple. Emotionally, I accepted Judaism and Christianity, too, as long as Christian dogma was not discussed. My father praised Christ's Sermon on the Mount, and my mother used to say that Jesus, although he was not God's son, surely was a very noble human being. Nor did they mind when we children—on Christmas Eve, while father, in the living room, was spreading out the gifts under the Christmas tree—sat down in the dark adjoining room and sang assorted Christmas chorals to our edification. . . . Christmas actually was the main feast in my parents' home, my father's favorite holiday. Always short of money, he gladly put in a bit of work in order to transform a young, unhewn, cheaply bought conifer into a beautiful Christmas tree and, being a plumber by training, to prepare many a

Source: Eduard Bernstein, "Wie Ich als Jude in der Diaspora aufwuchs," *Der Jude,* 2 (1917–18), pp. 186–95. Trans. here by J. Hessing.

present for us children with his own hands. . . .

[At the age of eleven] I decided to be a proper Jew, at least. Accordingly, in my opinion, I had to refrain first of all from eating pork. Whereupon I revealed to my parents one day that, in the name of Judaism, I would touch pork no more. Surprisingly, there was no opposition. "If you don't want to, my son, don't eat pork," replied my father. This absolute tolerance was poison to my intention. A bit of opposition would certainly have strengthened it, but now it lacked the attraction of a conquered right and consequently did not last very long. Without pork, to be sure, I could have done for quite a while. But since the law also prohibited all food prepared with lard, my decision was actually much more far-reaching than I had thought. I soon found out, moreover, that even a strict adherence to my decision would be of little avail, because to an Orthodox Jew many other things besides the eating of pork were forbidden. After a few weeks I gave in and admitted that observance of the dietary laws did not yet make a Jew.

When I was fifteen, a fatal illness befell a beloved member of my family, and I remember the prayer I sent to heaven: "If you exist, good Lord, please help my cousin." This help, however, was not extended. To be brief, my belief in the world to come finally broke down three years later, the night after the death of my mother, whom I had loved very much. I wondered for a long while whether I might hope to meet my dear mother again in the next world. The longer I thought about it, the more clearly I felt that it was impossible that I should ever meet my mother again as I had known and loved her, with all her virtues and weaknesses, with all her human attributes; she would live on for me only as long as I could keep her image in my mind. With the loss of my belief in the world to come, however, I lost the last vestige of my belief in a personal God as well.

There was no trace of Jewish faith in me, and for the Jewish ritual I only felt the contempt of the rationalist who was not influenced by any tradition. And yet, not all Jewish interest had died within me. I had a certain, albeit not pronounced, concern for the Jewish people. On the Sunday after my confirmation, walking home from the temple, I told my father that I would like to study the history of Judaism after the advent of Christianity, and especially during the Middle Ages. I was interested in finding out how the Jewish people had survived and developed throughout centuries of strife and suffering. But the vicissitudes of life never allowed me to realize my plan. There was no relevant literature in my home, and my evenings belonged to endeavors which led me into very different fields.

My formative years, moreover, overlapped the time when liberalism seemed to dominate the public scene in Germany and Jews played an ever-growing part in politics. To be sure, the Jews had enemies, but there was [as yet] no anti-Semitic movement; civil service was not yet quite open to the Jews, but it was gradually opening up to them. Even in countries where the Jews had not yet gained equality, a spreading liberalism tended to improve their lot. In short, there was nothing to involve me, who had broken with the Jewish faith, in any way with the Jewish cause.

I felt thoroughly German, although a German of the liberal-democratic school. As many others, the national movement for German unification in the sixties held me in its spell. Black-Red-Gold, the democratic tricolor of German unity, was my flag: at times I even carried it on my breast, in the shape of an artfully designed heart of pasteboard. I bemoaned the suffering of the Schleswig-Holsteiners under Danish rule, whose situation was idyllic, compared to the life of Jews in Russia and Poland to whom I remained indifferent. I composed jubilant verses when the Danes were defeated in 1864 and later, with young people of my age, I secretly sang the "Wacht am Rhein" and "Deutschland ueber Alles," which at the time were officially forbidden in Prussia. When war broke out between Germany and France in 1870, I decided that if Germany was going to suffer defeat I would volunteer, despite my weak health. "Napoleon, who has in cold blood provoked this war, must not be victorious," I wrote to my best friend, who was vacationing with relatives at a village in the March. But he, a "pure" German, wrote back that I should not exaggerate, that no one really knew what was going on in the world of diplomacy. At the end of the war, neither he nor I were flushed by the victory, and when, after the battle at Sedan, the capture of Napoleon III did not bring the coveted peace, I lost all interest in the war. A year and a half later my friend and I joined the Social-Democratic party, which sided with the International.

The early years after the establishment of the new German Empire were ill-suited to awaken my Jewish sympathies. The part played by Jewish capital on the stock-exchange; Jewish wheeling and dealing with billions in the period known as the "foundation era"; the [opportunistic] participation of Jewish liberal newspapers in the struggle against the Catholic Church; the shallow opposition of these papers to socialism—all this repelled me, a socialist and a democrat, so much that at times it aroused anti-Jewish feelings within me. The first signs of anti-Semitism, which appeared in Germany during the second half of the seventies, seemed to me to be a logical reaction against the improper intrusion of the Jews and it did not greatly excite me. It was my mistake not to realize that these obtrusive Jews were but a small minority compared with the large numbers of Jews who quietly pursued their livelihood. Only as anti-Semitism turned from accusation to persecution, my attitude gradually changed. But in fighting against it, I always considered the question in terms of democratic equality. I have never thought of the Jewish question as one in which Jewish national rights or interests were involved.

In the light of my personal development, could it have been different? I do not want to make too much of the fact that until a very advanced age all of my more intimate friends were Gentiles. In this, chance has played no small part. I very much loved most of my Jewish relatives, felt attracted to a number of my Jewish fellow-students in high school, and met many a Jew whom I esteemed for his personal qualities and admired for his intellect. Circumstance, not prejudice, prevented an intimacy with Jewish contemporaries. I had no inherent affinity for a Jew *qua* Jew in favor of a Gentile. Eight years after the Franco-German war I once used the words "we Jews" in a conversation with a friend, who was completely taken aback. "Never before," he said, "have you drawn a line between yourself as a Jew and the rest of us. Do you really want to start doing this now?" I had never intended anything of the sort. I had used the phrase as one might say "we traders," or "we non-smokers." But it made a strong impression on me that he should have taken offense at the phrase.

With this friend, as I have said already, I had joined the International in 1872, enthusiastically embraced its principles and program. As much as I felt myself a German, I was never possessed by national prejudices. In 1864, during the Prusso-Danish War, a high school teacher forbade the recitation of a poem by Simrock, "Half the Bottle," because its protagonist was a Dane; this, my patriotism and respect for the teacher notwithstanding, seemed rather tasteless to me. On two occasions in 1870, in the early stages of the [Franco-German] war, I barely escaped lynching when I publicly rebuked individuals who had insulted the French people. Now at last my thoughts—which a pure feeling for humanity had bred within me, and whose roots surely go back to my upbringing, free as it was of all religious prejudice—had found political expression. And when the Jewish question began to take on a more aggressive character, I believed that the solution would be found in the Socialist International. To this belief I still adhere, and it is more important to me than any separatist movement. After the experience of this World War more than ever before, I wish to work for this belief with undivided devotion.

NOTE

1. Eduard Bernstein (1850–1932), German-Jewish socialist theoretician, identified with the so-called revisionist school within Marxism. In his book, *The Task of Jewry during the World War (Die Aufgabe der Juden im Weltkrieg,* 1917), he argued that because of their dispersion and universalist values, the Jews were uniquely qualified to lead the world to internationalism which would unite nations and put an end to war. Toward the end of his life, Bernstein lent Zionism his moral support through his participation in the International Socialist Pro-Palestine Committee.

After the publication of his book of 1917, the Zionist journal, *Der Jude,* edited by Martin Buber, invited Bernstein to set forth his views on Zionism. Rather than give an ideological statement he offered this autobiographical explanation of his attitude toward Judaism and Jewish identity.

ISAAC DEUTSCHER[1]
11. The Non-Jewish Jew

There is an old Talmudic saying: "A Jew who has sinned still remains a Jew." My own thinking is, of course, beyond the idea of "sin" or "no sin"; but this saying has brought to my mind a memory from childhood which may not be irrelevant to my theme.

I remember that when as a child I read the Midrash, I came across a story and a description of a scene which gripped my imagination. It was the story of Rabbi Meir, the great saint and sage, the pillar of Mosaic orthodoxy, and co-author of the Mishnah, who took lessons in theology from a heretic, Elisha ben Abuyah, called Akher (The Stranger). Once on a Sabbath Rabbi Meir was with his teacher, and as usual they became engaged in a deep argument. The heretic was riding a donkey, and Rabbi Meir, as he could not ride on a Sabbath, walked by his side and listened so intently to the words of wisdom falling from his heretical lips that he failed to notice that he and his teacher had reached the ritual boundary which Jews were not allowed to cross on a Sabbath. The great heretic turned to his orthodox pupil and said: "Look, we have reached the boundary—we must part now; you must not accompany me any farther—go back!" Rabbi Meir went back to the Jewish community, while the heretic rode on—beyond the boundaries of Jewry.

There was enough in this scene to puzzle an orthodox Jewish child. Why, I wondered, did Rabbi Meir, that leading light of orthodoxy, take his lessons from the heretic? Why did he show him so much affection? Why did he defend him against other rabbis? My heart, it seems, was with the heretic. Who was he? He appeared to be in Jewry and yet out of it. He showed a curious respect for his pupil's orthodoxy, when he sent him back to the Jews on the Holy Sabbath; but he himself, disregarding canon and ritual, rode beyond the boundaries. When I was thirteen, or perhaps fourteen, I began to write a play about Akher and Rabbi Meir and I tried to find out more about Akher's character. What made him transcend Judaism? Was he a Gnostic? Was he an adherent of some other school of Greek or Roman philosophy? I could not find the answers, and did not manage to get beyond the first act.

The Jewish heretic who transcends Jewry belongs to a Jewish tradition. You may, if you like, see Akher as a prototype of those great

Source: Isaac Deutscher, *The Non-Jewish Jew and Other Essays* (London: Oxford University Press, 1968), pp. 25–27. Reprinted by permission of Mrs. Tamara Deutscher and Mr. Robert Harben.

revolutionaries of modern thought: Spinoza, Heine, Marx, Rosa Luxemburg, Trotsky, and Freud. You may, if you wish to, place them within a Jewish tradition. They all went beyond the boundaries of Jewry. They all found Jewry too narrow, too archaic, and too constricting. They all looked for ideals and fulfillment beyond it, and they represent the sum and substance of much that is greatest in modern thought, the sum and substance of the most profound upheavals that have taken place in philosophy, sociology, economics, and politics in the last three centuries.

Did they have anything in common with one another? Have they perhaps impressed mankind's thought so greatly because of their special "Jewish genius"? I do not believe in the exclusive genius of any race. Yet I think that in some ways they were very Jewish indeed. They had in themselves something of the quintessence of Jewish life and of the Jewish intellect. They were *a priori* exceptional in that as Jews they dwelt on the borderlines of various civilizations, religions, and national cultures. They were born and brought up on the borderlines of various epochs. Their minds matured where the most diverse cultural influences crossed and fertilized each other. They lived on the margins or in the nooks and crannies of their respective nations. Each of them was in society and yet not in it, of it and yet not of it. It was this that enabled them to rise in thought above their societies, above their nations, above their times and generations, and to strike out mentally into wide new horizons and far into the future.

NOTE

1. Isaac Deutscher (1907–1967). Marxist theoretician and historian, born in Cracow, Poland, he was raised in the strictly Orthodox tradition of Hasidism. In his youth he was renowned for his mastery of the Talmud and of the Hebrew language. In 1926 he became a member of the illegal Communist party of Poland. However, because of his Trotskyite sympathies, he was expelled from the party in 1932. In 1939 he emigrated to London, where he devoted himself to journalism and historical research. His political biographies of Stalin and Trotsky earned him wide acclaim. His tender feelings for the Jewish masses of Eastern Europe and the Yiddish and Hebrew languages did not compromise his commitment to internationalism.

WALTER RATHENAU
12. Hear, O Israel![1]

Let me confess at the outset that I am a Jew. Need I any justification for not writing in defence of the Jews? Many members of my tribe know themselves only as Germans, not as Jews. A few, especially those who by profession and inclination meet with native Germans [*Stammesdeutsche*] more often than with one another, and whose external features, therefore, have ceased to differ greatly from those of the Germans, are frank enough not to follow the flag of their philo-Semitic protectors any longer. I am gladly joining their ranks. . . .

You may ask if I am trying to convert you

Source: Walter Hartenau [pseud.], "Hoere, Israel!" *Zukunft,* 18 (March 16, 1897), pp. 454–62. Trans. here by J. Hessing.

[my fellow Jews] to Christianity. Certainly not.

Baptism will certainly not bring an end to the Jewish question. The individual, perhaps, could improve his conditions by dissociation; the Jewish entity could not. Were half of Israel converted, nothing would come of it but an impassioned "anti-Semitism against the baptized," full of spying and snooping on the one hand, and mendacity and hatred against renegades on the other. This new anti-Semitism would be even less healthy, and less moral, than the contemporary movement.

What, then, ought to be done? Something without historical precedent: the conscious self-education and adaptation of the Jews to the expectations of the Gentiles. Adaptation not as "mimicry" in the Darwinian sense—namely, the art of certain insects to take on the coloration of their environment—but a shedding of tribal attributes which, whether they be good or bad in themselves, are known to be odious to our countrymen, and a replacement of these attributes by more appropriate ones. If such a metamorphosis also brought about an improvement in the balance of our moral values, this would be all for the better. The final result of the process should not be Germans by imitation, but Jews of German character and education. At first both sides will act as a dividing and connecting link between the Germans and the incorrigible Jews: Jewish patricians, not of property, but of spiritual and physical culture. From below, this class will imbibe up more and more nourishment through its roots, until in due time all material capable of transformation has been digested.

Few outsiders may know that there are already such Jewish patricians who because of the conservatism inherent in the Jewish people are readily accepted. Far less than it is generally believed can the traditional concept of the "good family" be blurred by either old or new wealth. While many very poor families are highly esteemed, many extremely wealthy families are fairly detested despite their contacts with the genuine gentry. The intermediary class, experienced in the task of radical self-education, would exert a greater influence on the masses below, were it not for [the apostasy] of individuals from this class. But fortunately, even among the masses a new self-awareness can now be detected which is beginning to be cognizant of certain attitudes and traits as typically "Jewish." I overheard a conversation about a man who, for reasons of his career, had himself baptized. It was a Jew who pronounced the verdict: "Lord, how Jewish!" . . .

Look at yourselves in the mirror! This is the first step toward self-criticism. Nothing, unfortunately, can be done about the fact that all of you look frighteningly alike and that your individual vices, therefore, are attributed to all of you. Neither will it console you that in the first place your east Mediterranean appearance is not very well appreciated by the northern tribes. You should therefore be the more careful not to walk about in a loose and lethargic manner, and thus become the laughingstock of a race brought up in a strictly military fashion. As soon as you have recognized your unathletic build, your narrow shoulders, your clumsy feet, your sloppy roundish shape, you will resolve to dedicate a few generations to the renewal of your outer appearance. During that time you will refrain from donning the costumes of the lean Anglo-Saxons, in which you look like a dachshund dressed up like a greyhound. You will not offend nature by wearing a sailor's dress on the beach, or half-stockings in the Alps. I do not know what the people of Israel looked like in Palestine—their contemporaries do not seem to share their beauty—but two thousand years of misery cannot but leave marks too deep to be washed away by eau de cologne. During all this time your women have forgotten their smile; their laughter has become shrill and unhappy, and their beauty has become melancholy. If you understood their strange and exotic beauty you would never choke it under bales of satin, clouds of lace, and nests of diamonds. . . .

You rarely find a middle course between

wheedling subservience and vile arrogance. Self-confidence without presumption cannot be learned, of course; only he who feels himself to be neither creditor nor debtor to anyone will gain it. Furthermore, all of you labor under the extreme obligation to keep up appearances. If you could only observe yourselves through the eyes of others, you sportsmen on the coach-box, you patrons of the studios, you directors of the board, standing on your platforms! You masters of observation and sarcasm—what striking analogies you would find! But, surely, dear reader and fellow Jew! all this may be true for the others, but the two of us are completely different, aren't we?! . . .

NOTE

1. Walter Rathenau (1886–1922), German-Jewish writer, industrialist and statesman. In February 1922 he became foreign minister of Germany, the first Jew to hold this position. A target of anti-Semitic attacks, he was assassinated by extreme right-wing youth on June 24, 1922.

"Hear, O Israel!" was first published pseudonymously in Maximilian Harden's influential journal *Zukunft*. When it later became apparent that his essay, with its severe critique of his fellow Jews, abetted the cause of anti-Semitism, Rathenau withdrew from circulation the volume of his collected writings in which the essay was reprinted. Moreover, he did not include the essay in later editions of his works. The Nazis, however, made "Hear, O Israel!" required reading in German schools. Although he did not rescind his view favoring complete assimilation, toward the end of his life Rathenau expressed pride in the intellectual, ethical and economic achievements of Jewry.

OTTO WEININGER
13. The Jew Must Free Himself from Jewishness[1]

. . . I must make clear what I mean by Judaism; I mean neither a race nor a people nor a recognised creed. I think of it as a tendency of the mind, as a psychological constitution which is a possibility for all mankind, but which has become actual in the most conspicuous fashion only amongst the Jews. Anti-Semitism itself will confirm my point of view.

The purest Aryans by descent and disposition are seldom anti-Semites, although they are often unpleasantly moved by some of the peculiar Jewish traits; they cannot in the least understand the anti-Semite movement, and are, in consequence of their defence of the Jews, often called philo-Semites; and yet these persons writing on the subject of the hatred of Jews, have been guilty of the most profound misunderstanding of the Jewish character. The aggressive anti-Semites, on the other hand, nearly always display certain Jewish characteristics, sometimes apparent in their faces, although they may have no real admixture of Jewish blood.

The explanation is simple. People love in others the qualities they would like to have but do not actually have in any great degree; so also we hate in others only what we do not wish to be, and what notwithstanding we are partly. We hate only qualities to which we

Source: Otto Weininger, *Sex and Character,* translator not noted (London: William Heinemann, 1906), pp. 303–12.

approximate, but which we realise first in other persons.

Thus the fact is explained that the bitterest anti-Semites are to be found amongst the Jews themselves. For only the quite Jewish Jews, like the completely Aryan Aryans, are not at all anti-Semitically disposed; amongst the remainder only the commoner natures are actively anti-Semitic and pass sentence on others without having once sat in judgment on themselves in these matters; and very few exercise their anti-Semitism first on themselves. This one thing, however, remains none the less certain: whoever detests the Jewish disposition detests it first of all in himself; that he should persecute it in others is merely his endeavour to separate himself in this way from Jewishness; he strives to shake it off and to localise it in his fellow-creatures, and so for a moment to dream himself free of it. Hatred, like love, is a projected phenomenon; that person alone is hated who reminds one unpleasantly of oneself.

The anti-Semitism of the Jews bears testimony to the fact that no one who has had experience of them considers them loveable—not even the Jew himself; the anti-Semitism of the Aryans grants us an insight no less full of significance; it is that the Jew and the Jewish race must not be confounded. . . .

That these researches should be included in a work devoted to the characterology of the sexes may seem an undue extension of my subject. But some reflection will lead to the surprising result that Judaism is saturated with femininity, with precisely those qualities the essence of which I have shown to be in the strongest opposition to the male nature. It would not be difficult to make a case for the view that the Jew is more saturated with femininity than the Aryan, to such an extent that the most manly Jew is more feminine than the least manly Aryan.

This interpretation would be erroneous. It is most important to lay stress on the agreements and differences simply because so many points that become obvious in dissecting woman reappear in the Jew.

Let me begin with the analogies. It is notable that the Jews, even now when at least a relative security of tenure is possible, prefer moveable property, and, in spite of their acquisitiveness, have little real sense of personal property, especially in its most characteristic form, landed property. Property is indissolubly connected with the self, with individuality. It is in harmony with the foregoing that the Jew is so readily disposed to communism. Communism must be distinguished clearly from socialism, the former being based on a community of good, an absence of individual property, the latter meaning, in the first place a co-operation of individual with individual, of worker with worker, and a recognition of human individuality in every one. Socialism is Aryan (Owen, Carlyle, Ruskin, Fichte). Communism is Jewish (Marx). Modern social democracy has moved far apart from the earlier socialism, precisely because Jews have taken so large a share in developing it. In spite of the associative element in it, the Marxian doctrine does not lead in any way towards the State as a union of all the separate individual aims, as the higher unit combining the purposes of the lower units. Such a conception is as foreign to the Jew as it is to the woman.

For these reasons Zionism must remain an impracticable ideal, notwithstanding the fashion in which it has brought together some of the noblest qualities of the Jews. Zionism is the negation of Judaism, for the conception of Judaism involves a world-wide distribution of the Jews. Citizenship is an un-Jewish thing, and there has never been and never will be a true Jewish State. The State involves the aggregation of individual aims, the formation of and obedience to self-imposed laws; and the symbol of the State, if nothing more, is its head chosen by free election. The opposite conception is that of anarchy, with which present-day communism is closely allied. The ideal State has never been historically realised, but in every case there is at least a minimum of this higher unit, this conception of an ideal power which distinguishes the State from the mere collection of human beings in barracks. Rousseau's much-despised theory of the conscious co-operation of individuals to form a State deserves more attention than it now receives. Some ethical notion of free combination must always be included.

The true conception of the State is foreign to the Jew, because he, like the woman, is wanting in personality; his failure to grasp the idea of true society is due to his lack of a free intelligible ego. Like women, Jews tend to adhere together, but they do not associate as free independent individuals mutually respecting each other's individuality.

As there is no real dignity in women, so what is meant by the word *gentleman* does not exist amongst the Jews. The genuine Jew fails in this innate good breeding by which alone individuals honour their own individuality and respect that of others. There is no Jewish nobility, and this is the more surprising as Jewish pedigrees can be traced back for thousands of years.

The familiar Jewish arrogance has a similar explanation; it springs from want of true knowledge of himself and the consequent overpowering need he feels to enhance his own personality by depreciating that of his fellow-creatures. And so, although his descent is incomparably longer than that of the members of Aryan aristocracies, he has an inordinate love for titles. The Aryan respect for his ancestors is rooted in the conception that they were *his* ancestors; it depends on his valuation of his own personality, and, in spite of the communal strength and antiquity of the Jewish traditions, this individual sense of ancestry is lacking.

The faults of the Jewish race have often been attributed to the repression of that race by Aryans, and many Christians are still disposed to blame themselves in this respect. But the self-reproach is not justified. Outward circumstances do not mould a race in one direction, unless there is in the race the innate tendency to respond to the moulding forces; the total result comes at least as much from the natural disposition as from the modifying circumstances. We know now that the proof of the inheritance of acquired characteristics has broken down, and, in the human race still more than the lower forms of life, it is certain that individual and racial characteristics persist in spite of all adaptive moulding. When men change, it is from within, outwards, unless the change, as in the case of women, is a mere superficial imitation of real change, and is not rooted in their natures. . . .

Orthodox or unorthodox, the modern Jew does not concern himself with God and the Devil, with Heaven and Hell. If he does not reach the heights of the Aryan, he is also less inclined to commit murder or other crimes of violence. So also in the case of the woman; it is easier for her defenders to point to the infrequency of her commission of serious crimes than to prove her intrinsic morality. The homology of Jew and woman becomes closer the further examination goes. There is no female devil, and no female angel; only love, with its blind aversion from actuality, sees in woman a heavenly nature, and only hate sees in her a prodigy of wickedness. Greatness is absent from the nature of the woman and the Jew, the greatness of morality, or the greatness of evil. In the Aryan man, the good and bad principles of Kant's religious philosophy are ever present, ever in strife. In the Jew and the woman, good and evil are not distinct from one another.

Jews, then, do not live as free, self-governing individuals, choosing between virtue and vice in the Aryan fashion. They are a mere collection of similar individuals each cast in the same mould, the whole forming as it were a continuous plasmodium. The anti-Semite has often thought of this as a defensive and aggressive union, and has formulated the conception of a Jewish "solidarity." There is a deep confusion here. When some accusation is made against some unknown member of the Jewish race, all Jews secretly take the part of the accused, and wish, hope for, and seek to establish his innocence. But it must not be thought that they are interesting themselves more in the fate of the individual Jew than they would do in the case of an individual Christian. It is the menace to Judaism in general, the fear that the shameful shadow may do harm to Judaism as a whole, which is the origin of the apparent feeling of sympathy. In the same way, women are delighted when a member of their sex is depreciated, and will themselves assist, until the proceeding seems to throw a disadvantageous light over the sex in general, so frightening men from marriage. The race or sex alone is defended, not the individual. . . .

I desire at this point again to lay stress on the fact, although it should be self-evident, that, in spite of my low estimate of the Jew, nothing could be further from my intention than to lend the faintest support to any practical or theoretical persecution of Jews. I am dealing with Judaism, in the Platonic sense, as an idea. There is no more an absolute Jew than an absolute Christian. I am not speaking against the individual, whom, indeed, if that had been so, I should have wounded grossly and unnecessarily. Watchwords, such as "Buy only from Christians," have in reality a Jewish taint; they have a meaning only for those who regard the race and not the individual, and what is to be compared with them is the Jewish use of the word "Goy," which is now almost obsolete. I have no wish to boycott the Jew, or by any such immoral means to attempt to solve the Jewish question. Nor will Zionism solve that question; as H. S. Chamberlain has pointed out, since the destruction of the Temple of Jerusalem, Judaism has ceased to be a nation, and has become a spreading parasite, straggling all over the earth and finding true root nowhere. Before Zionism is possible, the Jew must first conquer Judaism.

To defeat Judaism, the Jew must first understand himself and war against himself. So far, the Jew has reached no further than to make and enjoy jokes against his own peculiarities. Unconsciously he respects the Aryan more than himself. Only steady resolution, united to the highest self-respect, can free the Jew from Jewishness. This resolution, be it ever so strong, ever so honourable, can only be understood and carried out by the individual, not by the group. Therefore the Jewish question can only be solved individually; every single Jew must try to solve it in his proper person.

NOTE

1. Otto Weininger (1880–1903), Austrian-Jewish psychologist and philosopher. On the day he received his Ph.D. he converted to Protestantism—an expression of his desire to become a "non-Jew." His major work *Sex and Character (Geschlecht und Charakter,* 1903) was a very popular book, enjoying some thirty editions. It advances the thesis of a fundamental relationship between sex and character. Man, a Platonic typology, is a positive, productive, logical, conceptual, ethical and spiritual force; Woman is a negative force, incapable of any of these virtues. Woman is either interested purely in sexual pleasure (the Prostitute) or in procreation (the Mother). Accordingly, Woman depends on Man, on the Phallus, and Man's emancipation as well as his spiritual progress is contingent upon the ending of coitus. Judaism is a force that is even more deleterious than Woman; the Jew believes in nothing and thus is drawn to the spiritual vacuities of communism, anarchism, naturalism, empiricism and atheism. Every individual is a combination of Male and Female elements. As a Platonic idea, Judaism is also a tendency of the mind to which every individual is subject in varying degrees. There are thus Germans who are more Jewish than Jews and *vice versa.* This conception of Judaism provided Weininger with the mechanism to transcend the "tragedy" of his Jewish birth. However, a few months after the publication of *Sex and Character,* he rented a room in the house in which Beethoven had died and solemnly put a bullet in his heart. It was surmised by his friends that this desperate act was prompted by his failure to convince the world that he had overcome the Judaism within himself and had become an authentic Aryan.

THEODOR LESSING

14. Jewish Self-Hatred[1]

I should like to . . . put a few questions to the non-Jewish world:

Do you know how it feels to curse the soil on which one lives? To draw poison from one's roots instead of nourishment? Do you know what it means to be ill-born, begotten in the nuptial bed of calculation and superficial selfishness? To be ill-protected, neglected, pampered, effeminate and thrashed? And now to hate, senselessly and for an entire lifetime, your father, your mother, your teachers and all those others who have bred and shaped you in their own disgusting image? . . .

If it is true that most individuals of all peoples have to suffer an unhappy fate and that the perfect and successful only come about in rare cases, it is also true that a *people* resembles a large stream which can absorb all dark tributaries and yet, finally, carry them into the clear and pure surge.

Thus even the most wretched individual breathes like a leaf in a verdant forest. His national identity [*Volkstum*] supported him. A revered history receives him. A legitimate culture accepts his voice into the choir of a great community.

With the Jew, alas, it is otherwise. For centuries, his national identity has been like a small and calm pond, constantly endangered by an underlying swamp. He has had only the company of his dead, and he has forgotten their language. No soil has supported him, no history relieved him of his sins, no cultural heritage [*Bildung*] has been *his own;* his hero is the sufferer.

We all love to use the beautiful phrase: "Happy is he who gladly remembers his forefathers." But what is left for a child who must turn away in shame from his forefathers because they have played their irresponsible games with the energies peculiar to their race and have thrown him, the grandchild, into the world as though he were an *accident?* Such a child, surrounded by a base and unsatisfactory environment, spends his feeble answers on a hateful tearing against unbreakable chains.

We are always taught about "community." One should teach about loneliness. The community, in one way or another, is sought by everyone. Loneliness is a matter for the few. It is possible for a man to *hate* deeply the community into which he was born, in which he was reared, and in which he spends his entire lifetime. But he will nevertheless not be able to separate his individual fate from that of the community.

There are countless Jews who constantly quarrel with community and family [*kille und mishpoche*] and yet live according to the awful proverb: "Bind my hand and bind my feet, and throw me into the family." How can this be explained?

What could they who are uprooted expect when they find themselves in another community? Secretly, he would have to live with the humiliating consciousness: "I do not belong here, actually. They may be no better than I am, and they may not achieve more than I do. But they have something which I, obviously, lack: *They love themselves.*" . . .

What alternatives are left to him who hears this? I discern three:

First: It is possible that he who was born with a defect will become a judge of the world. He becomes a castigator, a zealot, a moralist who delivers penitential sermons.

Source: Theodor Lessing, *Der juedischer Selbsthass* (Berlin: Juedischer Verlag, 1930), pp. 45–51. Trans. here by J. Hessing.

There is an ethical power which can arise only from corrupt blood. This moralism torments those who are nearest (and, at the same time, the farthest away) with sublime demands which cannot be fulfilled; and, in most cases, are not even fulfilled by the prophet himself. His spirit carries him beyond himself and beyond the unloved world. This is possible as long as he lives in his *spirit.* But woe! should he fall. He is nothing but a moving ball, thrown about by fate. The more often he touches earth, the weaker he becomes until he remains grounded on the most hated spot. His spirit is used up, and he is full of doubt and despair. And then he discovers what he never wanted to see: "I have no innate equilibrium, I have merely kept myself balanced. I am a priest who has turned his fault into a virtue. A liar who has covered up his empty holes with ideals. A broken man who has turned his own discontent against others. A fraud who has been living in the air because he did not know of any place on earth whose people and soil did not disgust him."

This way, then, leads to the death of the *soul.*

Second: A greater and more noble way than the way of the prophet and the judge of the world—he directs his torment exclusively against himself. He exempts all others. He is his own judge and hangman. He loves others more than himself. He dedicates himself completely and selflessly to his friend, to his lover. . . . Woe to him!

He has made himself into a footstool to be stepped upon by anyone. The more he gives the more surely he will be abused. . . . Be a tormentor of men, and men will adore you. Be truculent, and they will honestly love you. But turn yourself into a lamb, and the wolves will devour you.

Offer yourself up for sacrifice—good and well! They will kiss your hands and then proceed to celebrate the feast of immolation. Those whom you have loved the most will butcher you. And they will never realize what they are doing. And never repent. . . . They will always find reasons to bless themselves. They sacrifice you in good faith. He who does not love himself sufficiently is not loved by anyone. And no one will have mercy on him.

This is the end of the second way, worse than the death of the soul.

Third: Now the great transformation succeeds, all mimicry succeeds. You become "one of the others" and look marvelously genuine. Perhaps a little too German in order to be completely German. Perhaps a little too Russian to be completely Russian. And precisely because Christianity is a little new to you, you tend to over-emphasize it a bit. But still: Now you are protected. Really?

Your corpse is protected. You are dead. Your duality has died, and so have you. You went the way of suicide in order to gain happiness and fame. But deep down in your soul a million dead are crying, and the dead are more powerful than your happiness and fame.

All ways, then, seem to be useless. What ought to be done?

. . . Be whatever you *are,* and bring to perfection whatever potential you find within yourself. But do not forget that by tomorrow, you and this entire world of human beings will have wasted away. Fight, yes—fight incessantly. But do not forget that *every* life, even the defective one, even the criminal one, is in need of love. . . .

We all tend to take our existence much too seriously.

Who you *are*? The son of the slovenly Jewish pedlar Nathan, would you think, and of lazy Sarah whom he had accidentally slept with because she had brought enough money into their marriage? No! Judah Maccabee was your father, Queen Esther your mother. From you, and you alone, the chain goes back—*via* defective links, to be sure—to Saul and David and Moses. They are present in every one of you. They have been there all the time and tomorrow their spirit could be revived.

You carry an oppressive legacy. So what! Free yourself from it. Your children will forgive you that you were the child of your parents. Do not betray your fate. Love it.

Accept it. Accept it even unto death. Be firm! You will surely endure your personal hell and attain deliverance in your true self in your eternal people.

NOTE

1. Theodor Lessing (1872–1933), German-Jewish philosopher. As a student he converted to Lutheranism. He later, however, embraced Zionism and returned to Judaism. His *Der juedische Selbsthass* [Jewish self-hatred] is a psychological analysis of Jewish intellectuals who suffered self-hatred, a malady that had once afflicted Lessing himself. He viewed the Jews as an exiled Asiatic people forced to live an unnatural life in Europe. Once a peasant people, the Jews were cut off from the soil and became overspiritualized. Their return to the land of Israel promised the renewal of both the land and the people. In 1933, he was assassinated by Nazi agents in Marienbad, Czechoslovakia.

MOSES HESS
15. Returning Home[1]

After an estrangement of twenty years, I am back with my people. I have come to be one of them again, to participate in the celebration of the holy days, to share the memories and hopes of the nation, to take part in the spiritual and intellectual warfare going on within the House of Israel, on the one hand, and between our people and the surrounding civilized nations, on the other; for though the Jews have lived among the nations for almost two thousand years, they cannot, after all, become a mere part of the organic whole.

A thought, which I believed to be forever buried in my heart, has been revived in me anew. It is the thought of my nationality, which is inseparably connected with the ancestral heritage and the memories of the Holy Land, the Eternal City, the birthplace of the belief in the divine unity of life, as well as the hope in the future brotherhood of men.

For a number of years this half-strangled thought stirred within my breast and clamored for expression. I lacked the strength to swerve suddenly from my beaten track, which seemed to be so far from the road of Judaism, to a new path which had unfolded itself before me in the hazy distance, in vague and dim outline. . . .

It was only when I saw you* [the Jewess, symbol of our nation's piety] in anguish and sorrow that my heart opened and the cover of my slumbering, national feeling was thrown off. I have discovered the fountain whence flows your belief in the eternity of the spirit.

Your infinite soul-sorrow, expressed on the death of one dear to you, brought about my decision to step forth as a champion of the national renaissance of our people. Such love

*The Talmud, as well as the Midrash, ascribes the redemption of Israel from Egypt to the chastity of the Jewish women and their faithfulness to the Jewish nationality. It is especially emphasized that the Jews in Egypt retained their national names and language and did not adopt the names and language of the Egyptians and were thus more worthy of redemption than the exiles of later generations, when this form of assimilation was a frequent phenomenon. . . .

Source: Moses Hess, *Rome and Jerusalem: A Study in Jewish Nationalism,* trans. Meyer Waxman (New York: Bloch Publishing Company, 1945), pp. 40–41. Reprinted by permission of Bloch Publishing Company.

which, like maternal love, flows out of the very lifeblood and yet is as pure as the divine spirit; such infinite love for family can have its seat only in a Jewish heart. And this love is the natural source whence springs the higher, intellectual love of God which, according to Spinoza, is the highest point to which the spirit can rise. Out of this inexhaustible fountain of family love have the redeemers of humanity drawn their inspiration.

"In thee," says the divine genius of the Jewish family, "shall all the families of the earth be blessed."[2] Every Jew has within him the potentiality of a Messiah and every Jewess that of a Mater dolorosa.

NOTES

1. Moses Hess (1812–1875), German-Jewish socialist and precursor of Zionism. Until the age of fourteen, Hess was raised in the Orthodox Jewish home of his grandfather. During his student days he was fervently commited to socialism and cosmopolitan values. He is said to have won Friedrich Engles to communism and to have exercised a seminal influence on Karl Marx's thought. In his twenties he declared that the Jews have already accomplished their mission in history and should therefore assimilate into more historically relevant nations, such as Germany. In this respect, he claimed himself to be thoroughly German. Although the suffering of his fellow Jews occasionally did affect him, it was not until the publication of *Rome and Jerusalem* in 1862 that he evinced a genuine identification with Jewry. This *volte-face* was effected, he claimed, by the Austro-Italian War of 1859 which witnessed the emergence of the movement of Italian national liberation as a vigorous, democratic, progressive force. He now viewed the struggle of oppressed peoples as of equal significance to the class struggle. In *Rome and Jerusalem* he developed the thesis that the regeneration of these peoples would be an essential component of the ultimate liberation of humanity that socialism strives for, and he focused on the exigent need for the national and political rehabilitation of the Jewish people.

2. Gen. 12:8.

GUSTAV LANDAUER
16. Jewishness Is an Inalienable Spiritual Sensibility[1]

No true human being can consider himself merely as a bridge for coming generations, as a preface, as seed and fertilizer. He wants to be somebody and to accomplish something. The mother tongue of some of my offspring will perhaps be Hebrew, perhaps; it does not affect me. My language and the language of my children is German. I feel my Judaism in the expressions of my face, in my gait, in my facial features, and all these signs assure me that Judaism is alive in everything that I am and do. But much more than the Frenchman Chamisso was a German poet—if there can be a "more" in such matters—am I, the Jew, a German. The expressions "German Jew" or "Russian Jew" sound odd to me, just as would the terms "Jewish German" or "Jewish Russian." The relationship indicated

Source: Gustav Landauer, "Sind das Ketzergedanken?" in *Vom Judentum: Ein Sammelbuch,* ed. Verein Juedischer Hochschueler Bar Kochba in Prag (Leipzig, 1913). Trans. here by J. Hessing. Gustav Landauer [Review of Martin Buber], *Die Legende des Baal Schem,* in *Das Literarische Echo* (Berlin, October 1, 1910), pp. 148–49. Trans. here by J. Hessing.

by these terms is not one of dependency and cannot be described by means of an adjective modifying a noun. I take my fate as it is, and live accordingly: My being a Jew and a German at the same time does not do me any harm, but actually a lot of good, just as two brothers, a first-born and a Benjamin, are loved by their mother—not in the same way but with equal intensity. And just as these two brothers can live in peace with one another whenever their paths cross and whenever they go their different ways—just so I experience this strange and yet intimate unity in duality within myself as something precious and do not distinguish one element of this relationship within myself as primary, and the other, secondary. I have never felt the need to simplify myself or to create an artificial unity by way of denial; I accept my complexity and hope to be an even more multifarious unity than I was aware of.

But since it is now that I am alive and active, now that I exist and act as a Jew, I cannot inwardly prepare for a thing, cannot find the will within me for a new decision that would extinguish part of my being, or at least hinder it. . . .

Only that is alive which has developed through time and is still in the process of developing. Only he who, in his own time and reality, simultaneously recognizes his past and his future, and only he who takes himself, his true and complete self, on the journey to his promised land—only he, it seems to me, cherishes his Judaism as a living possession. The [Gentile] nations have drawn political boundaries around themselves and have neighbours beyond their borders who are their enemies; the Jewish nation has its neighbours in its own breast; and this friendly neighbourliness creates peace and unity within anyone who is complete within himself, and who acknowledges this unity. Is not this a sign of the mission which Judaism ought to fulfill in relation to humanity and within humanity?

In the thought and poetry of Martin Buber more than anywhere else, a Jew can learn what many nowadays no longer learn in their homes, but often find within themselves by way of an impulse from the outside: That Judaism is not an external contingency, but an inalienable inner property which transforms a number of individuals into a single community. This is the common ground on which the reviewer and the author of the book meet one another—a common spiritual sensibility [*Seelensituation*] which cannot *a priori* be assumed to be existent in other readers [of Martin Buber]. And yet, many among the Germans do perceive the authenticity and beauty, the depth and truth in the poetry, fairy tales and legends of the Greeks, Indians, Chinese, and Finns. In like manner, the myth of the Jews . . . has become part of popular culture in Germany, and this latest product of Jewish myth [viz., Hasidim], reborn in the spirit of the German language, must therefore sound familiar to many. . . .

Everywhere [in Martin Buber's *The Legend of the Baal Schem*] we are faced with the struggle of the soul to grasp the incomprehensible and ultimate, the experience beyond the life of the senses, . . . the realization of God. . . . At the same time, however, this God is the Messiah who will raise the poor and persecuted Jews in the Diaspora out of their agony and oppression. Here more than anywhere else the legend, the fairy tale of God [*Gottesmaerchen*], is steeped in a melancholy made of earthly depression and heavenly yearning. . . .

NOTE

1. Gustav Landauer (1870–1919), German-Jewish philosopher, literary critic, novelist and anarchist. Like many other Jewish intellectuals of his day who sought to identify themselves as Jews, Landauer was estranged from the Jewish religion and communal institutions on the one hand, and

yet was not satisfied with merely ethnic identification on the other. He was inspired by Martin Buber (1878–1965) and his concept of a primal Jewish religiosity or spiritual sensibility that is independent of doctrine and ritual prescriptions. His indebtedness to Buber is indicated in two complimentary articles presented here. The first is an essay Landauer published in a volume sponsored by the Bar Kochba Society of Prague, a Zionist student circle close to Buber; the second is a review of Buber's *The Legend of the Baal Schem* (1908).

When the Bavarian Soviet Republic was proclaimed in 1919, Landauer became the minister of public instruction. In May of that year he was bludgeoned to death by anti-revolutionary troops. Buber, whom he named in his will the executor of his literary estate, compiled his scattered articles into several volumes and edited his voluminous correspondence. During their friendship Landauer exercised a seminal influence on Buber's social philosophy.

DANIEL BELL[1]
17. Jewishness As Memory

. . . What is left, then, for one who feels himself to be a Jew, emotionally rather than rationally—who has not lost his sense of identification with the Jewish past and wants to understand the nature of that tie? A Jew, we are told by one existentialist thinker (Emil Fackenheim), is "anyone who by his descent is subject to Jewish fate"—the covenant; one who by *fate* is urged to *faith*.[2] The ground here is still faith, though the ground is "absurd," in that the compulsions to belief are beyond one's control, shaped by descent and, therefore, by history. But this is an attempt to defend faith, not fate. Lacking faith, I myself can only "choose" fate. For me, therefore, to be a Jew is to be part of community woven by memory—the memory whose knots are tied by the *Yizkor Elohim nishmas aboh mori,* "May God remember the name of. . . ."[3]

The *yizkor* is the tie to the dead, the link to the past, the continuity with those who have suffered and, through suffering, have made us witnesses to cruelty and given us the strength of courage over pride. However much, as moderns, we reject the utterances of authority and the injunctions of ritual, the religious link with our fellows is not the search for immortality or other consolatory formulas against the fear of extinction—but is the link of memory and its articulation.

All societies have memorial occasions, a day that commemorates an event of the past, a day of mourning for the dead. A memorial day, a holy day, often becomes, in secular terms, a holiday and an escape from the past. The *yizkor* is different. It is recited not just on one day, but on a set of days whose occasions form the wheel of life. For the *yizkor* is said on four days: Passover, Shevuoth, Succoth, and Yom Kippur—the escape from bondage, the giving of the Law, the ingathering of the harvest and the day of atonement, which is also the day of "at-one-ment."

One lives, therefore, as a Jew, through the meaning of the *yizkor,* through the act of commemoration, through the saying of a common prayer—but singling out in that prayer a specific name of one's own dead. In the *minyan* of my fellows, I am linked to my own parent. In the *yizkor,* through memory, I am identified as a Jew. . . .

Source: Daniel Bell, "Reflections on Jewish Identity," *Commentary* (June 1961), pp. 473–74. Reprinted by permission of *Commentary Magazine.*

NOTES

1. Daniel Bell, born in New York City in 1919. Bell has been a professor of sociology at Harvard University since 1969.

2. Emil L. Fackenheim, "Can We Believe in Judaism Religiously?" *Commentary* (December 1948), p. 527.

3. The opening line of the Hebrew prayer in commemoration of the dead. This prayer is popularly known as the *yizkor*.

ARTHUR KOESTLER
18. A Valedictory Message to the Jewish People[1]

In the Proclamation of Independence of the new State [of Israel] there is a paragraph which says:

> Exiled from the Land of Israel, the Jewish people remained faithful to it in all the countries of their dispersion, never ceasing to pray and hope for their return and the restoration of their national freedom.

It is the kind of phrase which has been so often said before that one hardly realizes what momentous implications it carried on that specific occasion for the seven or eight million Jews outside Palestine. For it was the occasion on which their prayer had been fulfilled; and the logical consequence of the fulfillment of a prayer is that one ceases to repeat it. But if prayers of this kind are no longer repeated, if the mystic yearning for the return to Palestine is eliminated from the Jewish faith, its very foundations and essence will have gone.

Towards the end of the Passover meal which commemorates the Exodus from Egypt, Jews all over the world lift their glasses and exclaim: "To next year in Jerusalem." For nearly twenty centuries this was a moving ritual symbol. Now that no obstacles bar any longer the fulfillment of the wish, the alternative before the faithful is either to be next year in Jerusalem, or to cease repeating a vow which has become mere lip-service.

In fact, the greater part of the formulae and vocabulary of Jewish ritual has become meaningless since May 15, 1948. The Proclamation of Independence affirms that "the State of Israel will be open to Jews from all the countries of their dispersion." In the future, Jews can no longer refer to themselves with the ritual stock phrase of living in the Diaspora, or in Exile—unless they mean a self-imposed exile, which has nothing to do with religion or tradition.

The existence of the Hebrew State—that is, a State whose language and culture are Hebrew, not Yiddish, Polish or American—puts every Jew outside Israel before a dilemma which will become increasingly acute. It is the choice between becoming a citizen of the Hebrew nation and renouncing any conscious or implicit claim to separate nationhood.

This dilemma is not derived from abstract speculation, nor from the claims of logical consistency; it is imposed by hard historical circumstances. Anti-Semitism is once more on the increase. In his address to the Anglo-

Source: Arthur Koestler, "Epilogue," *Promise and Fulfillment: Palestine, 1917–1949* (London: Macmillan Co., 1949), pp. 332–35. Copyright 1949 by Arthur Koestler, renewed 1977 by Arthur Koestler and reprinted by permission of Macmillan Publishing Company Inc. Also reprinted by permission of A. D. Peters & Co., Ltd.

American Committee of Enquiry, the aged leader of Zionism, Dr. Chaim Weizmann, summed up a lifetime of experience:

> I am worried, but I don't see how I can stop it or what can be done. [Anti-Semitism] is a sort of disease that spreads apparently according to its own laws. I only hope that it will never reach the terrible dimensions which it reached in Europe. In fact, I somehow think that the Anglo-Saxon countries may be immune from it. But that is a hope, a pious wish—and when I look at Canada, South Africa, even Great Britain, even America, I sometimes lose my freedom from fear. . . . I believe the only fundamental cause of anti-Semitism—it may seem tautological—is that the Jew exists. We seem to carry anti-Semitism in our knapsacks wherever we go. . . .

It is the twenty-first installment of a twenty-century-old story. To expect that it will come to a spontaneous end is to go against historical and psychological evidence. It can only be brought to an end by Jewry itself.

Before the prayer was fulfilled by the rebirth of Israel this was difficult if not impossible. To renounce being a Jew meant in most cases to deny solidarity with the persecuted, and seemed a cowardly capitulation. Apart from pride, there was the consciousness of an old heritage which one had no right to discard, of a mission uncompleted, a promise unfulfilled. Jewry could not vanish from the scene of history in an anti-climax.

Now the climax is reached, the circle closed. It is no longer a question of capitulation, but of a free choice. The proclamation of the Hebrew State is a signal to Jewry to pause on its long journey, review its situation with sincerity towards itself, and face facts which some time ago it was excusable and even honourable to shun.

The dilemma would not arise if being a Jew were merely a matter of religion like being a Protestant, or merely a matter of racial descent like being a French-Canadian. But both these comparisons are fallacious. The Jewish religion is not merely a system of faith and worship, but implies membership of a definite race and potential nation. The greater part of the sacred texts is national history. To be a good Catholic or Protestant it is enough to accept certain doctrines and moral values which transcend frontiers and nations; to be a good Jew one must profess to belong to a chosen race, which was promised Canaan, suffered various exiles and will return one day to its true home. The "Englishman of Jewish faith" is a contradiction in terms. His faith compels him to regard himself as one with a different past and future from the Gentile. He sets himself apart and invites being set apart. His subjective conviction creates the objective fact that he is not an English Jew, but a Jew living in England. . . .

The conclusion is that since the foundation of the Hebrew State the attitude of Jews who are unwilling to go there, yet insist on remaining a community in some way apart from their fellow-citizens, has become an untenable anachronism. The true orthodox believer must draw the consequences, now that the opportunity is offered to him, otherwise his creed will become lip-service. But orthodox Jewry is a vanishing minority. It is the well-meaning but confused majority which, through inertia, perpetuates the anachronism by clinging to a tradition in which it no longer really believes, to a mission which is fulfilled, a pride which may become inverted cowardice. Such honest sentimentalists should stop to think whether they have the right to place the burden of the ominous knapsack, now void of contents, on their children who have not asked for it.

To break the vicious circle of being persecuted for being "different," and being "different" by force of persecution, they must arrive at a clear decision, however difficult this may be. They must either follow the imperative of their religion, the return to the Promised Land—or recognize that that faith is no longer theirs. To renounce the Jewish faith does not mean to jettison the perennial values of Judaic tradition. Its essential teachings have passed long ago into the mainstream of the Judeo-Christian heritage. If a Judaic religion is to survive outside Israel, without inflicting the stigma of separateness on its followers and laying them open to the charge of divided loyalty, it would have to be a system of faith and cosmopolitan ethics freed from all racial presumption and national exclusivity. But a Jewish religion thus reformed would be stripped of all its specifically Jewish content.

These conclusions, reached by one who has been a supporter of the Zionist movement for a quarter-century, while his cultural allegiance belonged to Western Europe, are mainly addressed to the many others in a similar situation. They have done what they could to help to secure a haven for the homeless in the teeth of prejudice, violence and political treachery. Now that the State of Israel is firmly established, they are at last free to do what they could not do before: to wish it good luck and go their own way, with an occasional friendly glance back and a helpful gesture. But, nevertheless, to go their own way, with the nation whose life and culture they share, without reservations or split loyalties.

Now that the mission of the Wandering Jew is completed, he must discard the knapsack and cease to be an accomplice in his own destruction. If not for his own sake, then for that of his children and his children's children. The fumes of the death chambers still linger over Europe; there must be an end to every calvary.

NOTE

1. Arthur Koestler (b. 1905), British author. Born into an assimilated Jewish family in Budapest, Hungary, Koestler joined the Zionist movement at the age of nineteen, and from 1926 to 1929 he lived in Palestine. In 1931 he became a Communist, but the Stalinist purges of the later thirties and the Stalin-Hitler pact disillusioned him and he left the party. With the spectre of Nazi anti-Semitism over Europe, he once again passionately devoted himself to the Zionist cause and the establishment of a Jewish state as a refuge for European Jewry. However, when this objective was realized, he withdrew—as he explains in the above epilogue to his history of the Zionist struggle for Palestine—from the Zionist movement and the Jewish community.

FRANZ ROSENZWEIG
19. Jewish Learning and the Return to Judaism[1]

. . . Learning—there are by now, I should say, very few among you unable to catch the curious note the word sounds, even today, when it is used in a Jewish context. It is to a book, the Book, that we owe our survival—that Book which we use, not by accident, in the very form in which it has existed for millennia: it is the only book of antiquity that is still in living use as a scroll. The learning of this Book became an affair of the people, filling the bounds of Jewish life, completely. Everything was really within this learning of the Book.

Then came the Emancipation. At one blow

Source: Franz Rosenzweig: His Life and Thought, ed. Nahum N. Glatzer (New York: Schocken Books, 1953), pp. 228–29, 231–32, 234.

it vastly enlarged the intellectual horizons of thought and soon, very soon, afterwards, of actual living. Jewish "studying" or "learning" has not been able to keep pace with this rapid extension. What is new is not so much the collapse of the outer barriers, even previously, while the ghetto had certainly sheltered the Jew, it had not shut him off. He moved beyond its bounds, and what the ghetto gave him was only peace, home, a home for his spirit. What is new is not that the Jew's feet could now take him farther than ever before—in the Middle Ages the Jew was not an especially sedentary, but rather a comparatively mobile element of medieval society. The new feature is that the wanderer no longer returns at dusk. The gates of the ghetto no longer close behind him, allowing him to spend the night in solitary learning. To abandon the figure of speech—he finds his spiritual and intellectual home outside the Jewish world.

The old style of learning is helpless before this spiritual emigration. In vain have both Orthodoxy and Liberalism tried to expand into and fill the new domains. No matter how much Jewish law was stretched, it lacked the power to encompass and assimilate the life of the intellect and the spirit. The *mezuzah* may have still greeted one at the door, but the bookcase had, at best, a single Jewish corner. And Liberalism fared no better, even though it availed itself of the nimble air squadron of ideas rather than trying to master life by engaging it in hand-to-hand combat with the Law. There was nothing to be done apparently, except dilute the spirit of Judaism (or what passed for it) as much as possible in order to stake off the whole area of intellectual life; to fill it in the true sense was out of the question. . . .

There is no one today who is not alienated, or who does not contain within himself some small fraction of alienation. All of us to whom Judaism, to whom being a Jew, has again become the pivot of our lives—and I know that in saying this here I am not speaking for myself alone—we all know that in being Jews we must not give up anything, not renounce anything, but lead everything back to Judaism. From the periphery back to the center, from the outside, in. . . .

It is not a matter of apologetics, but rather of finding the way back into the heart of our life. And of being confident that this heart is a Jewish heart. For we are Jews.

That sounds very simple. And so it is. It is really enough to gather together people of all sorts as teachers and students. Just glance at our prospectus. You will find, listed among others, a chemist, a physician, a historian, an artist, a politician. Two-thirds of the teachers are persons who, twenty or thirty years ago, in the only century when Jewish learning had become the monopoly of specialists, would have been denied the right of teaching in a Jewish House of Study. They have come together here as Jews. They have come together in order to "learn"—for Jewish "learning" includes Jewish "teaching." Whoever teaches here—and I believe I may say this in the name of all who are teaching here—knows that in teaching here he need sacrifice nothing of what he is. Whoever gathers—and all of us are "gatherers"—must seize upon that which is to be gathered wherever he finds it. And more than this: he must seize upon himself as well, wherever he may find himself. Were we to do otherwise, we should continue in the errors of a century and perpetuate the failure of that century: the most we could do would be to adorn life with a few "pearls of thought" from the Talmud or some other source, and—for the rest—leave it just as un-Jewish as we found it. But no: we take life as we find it. Our own life and the life of our students; and gradually (or at times, suddenly) we carry this life from the periphery where we found it to the center. And we ourselves are carried only by a faith which certainly cannot be proved, the faith that this center can be nothing but a Jewish center.

This faith must remain without proof. It carries further than our word. For we hail from the periphery. The oneness of the center is not something that we possess clearly and unambiguously, not something we can be articulate about. Our fathers were better off in that respect. We are not so well off today. We must search for this oneness and have faith that we shall find it. . . .

It is in this sense that now, at the opening of the new term in this hall, I bid you welcome. May the hours you spend here become hours of remembrance, but not in the stale sense of a dead piety that is so frequently the attitude toward Jewish matters. I mean hours of another kind of remembrance, an inner remembering, a turning from externals to that which is within, a turning that, believe me, will and must become for you a returning home. Turn into yourself, return home to your innermost self.

NOTE

1. Franz Rosenzweig (1886–1929), German-Jewish philosopher and theologian. Overcoming a philosophical agnosticism, Rosenzweig affirmed a faith in the traditional God of Creation, Revelation and Redemption. Initially, he felt that this faith could only be realized within the Church. But on the threshold of the baptismal font, he returned to Judaism and discovered therein the possibility of a living faith. Thereafter he devoted himself totally to the study and practice of Judaism. This approach was expressed in the Juedisches Lehrhaus, a house of Jewish study, which he founded in 1920 in Frankfurt am Main. The Lehrhaus became the center and source of inspiration for a growing number of Jews, many from assimilated backgrounds, seeking to rediscover Jewish religious spirituality. The above statement is taken from Rosenzweig's inaugural address at the Lehrhaus.

JERI LANGER

20. From Prague to Belz[1]

It is an impassable road to the empire of the Chassidim.[2] The traveller who pushes his way through the thick undergrowth of virgin forests, inexperienced and inadequately armed, is not more daring than the man who resolves to penetrate the world of the Chassidim, mean in appearance, even repellent in its eccentricity.

Only a few children of the West have accomplished this journey, hardly as many—when I come to think of it—as there are fingers on the hand that writes these lines.

One summer's day in 1913, a nineteen-year-old youth, brought up like all the youth of his time in the dying traditions of the pre-war generation, left Prague inspired by a secret longing which even now after the passage of so many years he still cannot explain to himself, and set out for the east, for strange countries.

Had he a foreboding of what he was losing on that day?

European civilization with its comforts and achievements, its living successes called careers? Had he a foreboding that his soul would no longer be capable of feeling poetry which up to that time he had been so fond of quoting, that, from the first moment when he heard the rhythms of the Chassidic songs, all the magic charms of music would be

Source: Jeri Langer, *Nine Gates to the Chassidic Mysteries,* trans. Stephen Jolly (New York: James Clarke & Co. Ltd., 1961), pp. 3–5, 12ff., 18.

swamped once and for all, and all beautiful things which his eye had ever conceived would in the future be half hidden by the mystic veil of the knowledge of good and evil?

He hardly suspected that, at the very moment when he believed he had reached his goal, the most impassable part of his journey was only beginning. For the gate to the empire of the Chassidim never opens suddenly for anyone. It is closed by a long chain of physical and spiritual suffering. But he who has once looked inside will never forget the riches he has seen.

The rulers of this empire are hidden from the eyes of the world. Their miraculous deeds and all-powerful words are only, as it were, of secondary importance—they are merely the hem of the veil in which their being is wrapped, while their faces are turned away from us towards the distant calm of the Absolute. Only a faint reflection of their souls falls on our too material shadows. Yet, even today, years afterwards, these shapes haunt me one after the other. Not only those I knew personally but also those I have heard so much about and read about in the old Hebrew books; they rise again before me in all their greatness and strength. I feel overcome. Something compels me to take up my pen and faithfully write down everything as best I can.

It is a Friday afternoon. The small town of Belz, the Jewish Rome, is preparing to welcome the Sabbath.

Small towns in eastern Galicia have all had the same character for centuries. Misery and dirt are their characteristic outward signs. Poorly clad Ukrainian peasant men and women, Jews wearing side-whiskers, in torn caftans, rows of cattle and horses, geese and large pigs grazing undisturbed on the square. Belz is distinguished from other places only by its famous synagogue, its no less famous House of Study and the large house belonging to the town rabbi. These three buildings enclose the square on three sides. They are simply constructed. But in this poor, out-of-the-way region of the world they are truly memorable. Belz has somewhat more than three thousand inhabitants, half of whom are Jews.

It is a long summer afternoon. There are still six or seven hours before dusk, when the Sabbath begins and even the lightest work is strictly forbidden. In spite of this, the shops are already shut, the tailors are putting away their needles, and the casual labourers—wearing side-whiskers like the rest—their hoes and spades. The housewives in the cottages are adding the last touches to their preparations for the festival.

The men hasten to the baths. After a steam bath we dive—always several of us at the same time—into a small muddy swimming-pool, a *mikve,* or special ritual bath. As though in mockery of all the rules of hygiene, a hundred bodies are "purged" from the spirit of the working day. The water, like all the water in Belz, smells of sulphur and petroleum. . . .

Although everybody is in a tearing hurry on this day, the whole community already knows that a *bocher,* or young lad, has come to Belz all the way from Prague. A hundred questions are fired at me from every side. I am embarrassed because I do not understand a single word. I have never heard "Yiddish" spoken before, that bizarre mixture of mediaeval German and Hebrew, Polish and Russian. It was only later that I gradually began to learn it. . . .

From the window of the [House of Study's] entrance hall to the saint's apartment one can see far out across the Ukrainian steppe. For miles round there is nothing but a flat plain, without a single tree or hill to be seen. It is a fen with a narrow path made of boards running across it. In the distance a small bridge leads into a barren little field; then the path leads on across the bog into the unknown. When I am weary of the House of Study, I cross this bridge and lie down in the little field. This is the only bit of nature where one can find spiritual refreshment in all this wilderness!

I can endure it no longer. This life of isolation from the rest of the world is intolerable. I feel disgusted with this puritanism, this ignorance, this backwardness and dirt. I escape, I travel back to my parents in Prague. But not for long. I must perforce return to my Chassidim.

[In Prague] one night I cannot sleep. I am lying down, facing the kitchen door, which looks towards the East. I have left the door ajar. I have just been reading some holy Hebrew book in the kitchen. The kitchen windows are open, open towards the East, the East where Belz lies at the end of a train journey of a few hours more than a day and a night. . . . It is useless for me to close my eyes to induce sleep. Suddenly I am dazzled by a bright light penetrating into my dark bedroom through the half-open door. What is it?—I know that I have put out the lamp, and there is no one in the kitchen. I stare at the light, and in the middle of it a few steps in front of me, I can see quite clearly through the half-open door—*the saint of Belz!* He is sitting in his room at Belz looking fixedly at me. On his expressive countenance shines that barely recognizable, sublime smile of his, full of wisdom. I have no idea how long the apparition lasts, but it is long enough to shake me.

So I travel to Belz a second time, this time firmly resolved. I am no longer alone as on my first pilgrimage. This time I have a companion, a Prague lad like myself, who has also decided for Chassidism.

My vision of the saint of Belz that night was a great favour. So the Chassidim said when I told them about it. To behold a living saint from far away and, moreover, while still awake, is not indeed an absolutely isolated phenomenon among the Chassidim, but it is a greater expression of God's favour than, for instance, a conversation with someone who is dead or with the prophet Elijah. . . .

I am still a foreigner. People are very polite and full of respect when they talk to me, but they are mistrustful. The mere fulfillment of religious injunctions, however precise and conscientious, is as little adequate to inspire confidence here as is the utmost zeal over one's study. Excessive religiosity is not welcomed. But now that my beard and side-whiskers are well grown, now that I am able to speak some Yiddish and have begun wearing a long *shipits* [an overcoat similar to a caftan] instead of a short coat, and ever since I have started wearing a black velvet hat on weekdays, as all the other Chassidim do, this ice-wall of mistrust has gradually begun to thaw. But why even now am I not completely like the others? For example, why am I not gay, all the time, as a true Chassid ought to be? . . .

At last, when my face is pallid from undernourishment and illness, and my emaciated body has acquired a stoop, it is clear to nearly all of them that "I am really in earnest." No longer will the gates of Chassidism be closed in front of the youth from Prague.

NOTES

1. Jeri Mordecai Langer (1894–1943), Czech poet and writer. Raised in an acculturated upper middle-class Jewish family, in 1913, prompted by vague mystical longings, he left his native Prague for the Hasidic (in this text "Chassidic") community of Belz. In Belz, the center of Galician Hasidism, he discovered his spiritual roots and calling, and adopted the Hasidic mode of Jewish piety. Langer eventually returned to Prague, but he retained his loyalty to Hasidism. He wrote extensively in Czech and German on Hasidism and kabbalah. His Freudian interpretations of Jewish mystical literature and piety in particular generated great excitement among students of religion. A friend of Kafka, whom he taught Hebrew, Langer displayed his literary interests in two volumes of Hebrew poetry and in his rendition of Hasidic tales into Czech, *Nine Gates to the Chassidic Mysteries* (1937), from whose introduction this excerpt is taken. Upon the Nazi invasion of Czechoslovakia, Langer fled to Palestine.

2. Chassidim (the common spelling is "Hasidim"), members of a religious and mystical revival movement that originated in southern Poland and the Ukraine in the eighteenth century and spread to other parts of Eastern Europe (Poland, Rumania, Hungary). Hasidism is now found mainly in the State of Israel and the United States.

VII

Political and Racial Anti-Semitism

Modern anti-Semitism, as distinct from Christian medieval contempt toward Jewry, is prompted, at least at the ideological level, by secular motives. As already indicated in our discussion of emancipation, the civil and socio-economic integration of the Jews into a modern state was not a simple legal process. Emancipation of the Jews met much opposition. We have seen that emancipation was an intrinsic feature in the formation of a modern democratic, liberal state. Correspondingly the antagonism toward the modern, "emancipated" Jew is related to the tensions and ideological responses that surrounded the formation of a modern state. A thematic delineation of modern anti-Semitism readily illustrates this correlation.

1. The modern state requires cultural and national integration. The Jews, possessing distinct cultural and national aspirations of their own, are hence fundamentally incompatible with the modern state that hosts them. Indeed, they form "a state within a state." (See document 4 by Johann Gottlieb Fichte.)

2. The modern state has witnessed the emergence of an aggressive capitalism; its most egregious features, variously defined, of course, were frequently attributed to Jewry. (See the following: document 5 by Jakob Friedrich Fries; document 6 by K.B.A. Sessa; document 10 by Karl Marx; document 14 by Alphonse Toussenel; and document 15 by Edouard-Adolphe Drumont.)

3. The democratic, parliamentary character of the modern state permitted the politicization of anti-Semitism. Anti-Semitism became an aspect of political propaganda, either instrumentally—pandering to popular anti-Semitic attitudes in order to strengthen a political party's electoral support—or intrinsically, the party's principal motive being to check what was perceived to be the excesses of Jewish influence in certain areas of public life. (See document 16 by Adolf Stoecker.)

4. The rise of the modern state wrought many social and economic dislocations,

which engendered a profound discontentment with the very fabric and texture of modern life. Those who were discontented with modernity frequently directed their anger at the Jews who seemed to be the most obvious beneficiaries of—and thus somehow responsible for—modernity. (See the following: document 11 by Richard Wagner; document 12 by Wilhelm Marr; and document 20 by Houston Stewart Chamberlain.)

5. Anti-modernity developed into a comprehensive Weltanschauung. Joined by anti-Semitism it fostered the view that Jewry was secretly conspiring through the manipulation of the various forces of modernity—from capitalism to socialism—to subvert the idyllic world of the Gentiles. (See the following: document 12 by Wilhelm Marr; document 15 by Edouard-Adolphe Drumont; and document 22, the *Protocols.)*

6. The conspiratorial view of the world led to a Manichaean bifurcation of humanity into the opposing forces of good and evil. Racial theories, which associated specific moral and intellectual characteristics with somatic, anatomical and chromosomal factors of a given "race," helped "explain" the moral and spiritual division of humanity. Peoples, such as the Jews, affiliated with the forces of evil were members of a distinct race. Hence, the Jews were incorrigibly Jewish. The sublime program (viz., tolerance and education) of the liberals and democrats for the moral "betterment" of the Jews was not only platitudinous, but would dangerously mislead the Gentile world. Hence, the warning that appeared on the title page of the *Protocols of the Elders of Zion*, "Gentiles, Beware! The Jews are an alien bacillus that must be urgently contained and isolated." (See the following: document 8 by Dominicus Haman Epiphanes; document 13 by Karl Eugen Duehring; and document 20 by Houston Stewart Chamberlain.)

Whether the political and racial anti-Semitism which evolved in nineteenth-century Europe led ineluctably to the Holocaust, or even contributed to it, is a complex methodological and historical question. What is certain is that Nazi anti-Semitism did not arise *ex nihilo*.

FRANÇOIS-MARIE AROUET DE VOLTAIRE

1. Jews[1]

You order me to draw you a faithful picture of the spirit of the Jews, and of their history, and—without entering into the ineffable ways of Providence, which are not our ways—you seek in the manners of this people the source of the events which that Providence prepared.

It is certain that the Jewish nation is the most singular that the world has ever seen; and although, in a political view, the most contemptible of all, yet in the eyes of a philosopher, it is on various accounts, worthy of consideration.

The Guebers, the Banyans and the Jews are the only nations which exist dispersed, having no alliance with any people, are perpetuated among foreign nations, and continue apart from the rest of the world.... From [a] short summary of their history it results that the Hebrews have ever been vagrants or robbers, or slaves, or seditious. They are still vagabonds upon the earth, abhorred by men....

It is commonly said that the abhorrence in which the Jews held other nations proceeded from their horror of idolatry; but it is much more likely that the manner in which they at the first exterminated some of the tribes of Canaan, and the hatred which the neighboring nation conceived for them, was the cause of this invincible aversion. As they knew no nations but their neighbors, they thought that in abhorring them they detested the whole earth, and thus accustomed themselves to be the enemies of all men.

One proof that this hatred was not caused by the idolatry of the nations is that we find in the history of the Jews that they were very often idolaters. Solomon himself sacrificed to strange gods. After him, we find scarcely any king in the little province of Judah that does not permit the worship of these gods and offer them incense. The province of Israel kept its two calves and its sacred groves, or adored other divinities....

You ask, what was the philosophy of the Hebrews? The answer will be a short one—they had none. You then ask whether the ancient philosophers and law-givers borrowed from the Jews, or the Jews from them? We must refer the question to Philo,[2] he admits that before the translation of the Septuagint[3] the books of his nation were unknown to the Gentiles. A great people cannot have received their laws and their knowledge from a small, obscure and enslaved people. In the time of Osias,[4] indeed, the Jews had no books; in his reign was accidentally found the only copy of the law then in existence. This people, after their captivity at Babylon, had no other alphabet than the Chaldean; they were not famed for any art, any manufacture whatsoever; and even in the time of Solomon they were obliged to pay dear for foreign artisans. To say that the Egyptians, the Persians and the Greeks were instructed by the Jews is as if one were to say that the Romans learned the crafts from the people of Brittany. The Jews never were natural philosophers, nor geometricians, nor astronomers. So far were they from having public schools for the instruction of youth, that they had not even a term in their language to express such an institution. The people of Peru and Mexico measured their year much better than the Jews. Their stay in Babylon and in Alexandria during which individuals might acquire wisdom and knowledge trained the [Jewish] people as a whole in no art save that of usury.... In short, we find in them only an

Source: The Works of Voltaire, trans. William F. Fleming (Akron, Ohio: The Werner Co., 1904), vol. 10, pp. 266, 278, 280, 281, 283–84.

ignorant and barbarous people, who have long united the most sordid avarice with the most detestable superstition and the most invincible hatred for every people by whom they are tolerated and enriched. Still, we ought not to burn them.

NOTES

1. François-Marie Arouet de Voltaire (1694–1778), perhaps France's most popular and ardent advocate of free thought and of political as well as religious liberty. In his attack on the church—an institution which he deemed to be a major source of man's intellectual and spiritual bondage—Voltaire preferred to concentrate his criticism on the precursors of the church, the Old Testament and its protagonists, the Jews. Scholars debate whether Voltaire's venemous comments on Judaism and Jewry were merely a tactical strategem to attack the church or an uncritical hatred of the Jews that contradicted his teaching of tolerance and brotherhood. In any event, in the anti-Semitic campaigns of the following centuries he was used as an authority and frequently cited. Thus, paradoxically, he both helped prepare the mental climate that led to the emancipation of the Jews and contributed to the formation of the ideology of modern secular anti-Semitism. This article first appeared in the fifth edition of Voltaire's *Oeuvres Complètes* (Geneva, 1756), vol. 7, ch. 1; it later appeared in his *Dictionnaire Philosophique* (Basle, 1764), vol. 14, from which it is most frequently quoted.

2. Philo Judaeus (c.20 B.C.E.–c.40 C.E.), Jewish philosopher in Alexandria, Egypt, who used a wide, but eclectic knowledge of Hellenistic philosophy and culture to illuminate the teachings of Judaism.

3. A Greek translation of the Hebrew Bible, so named because its oldest part, the Pentateuch, was—according to legend—translated at the command of Ptolemy II (d. 246 B.C.E.) by seventy (septuagint is Latin for "the seventy") Jewish scholars, each working independently, whose translations agreed in every word.

4. Osias refers to Josiah, king of Judah (640–609 B.C.E.). It is widely believed by scholars that during Josiah's reign the book of Deuteronomy—the fifth and last book of the Pentateuch—was found by the prophet Hilkiah in the Temple in 621 B.C.E. This discovery provided an impetus for religious reform in Judah (see Kings 2:22–23).

ISAAC DE PINTO
2. An Apology for the Jewish Nation[1]

. . . Are there any imputations which can be laid on a people in general? Can a whole nation be accessory to a crime? Can the murder of Charles I, be with justice imputed to the whole English nation? Or the massacre of St. Bartholomew to the French in the reign of Charles IX? Every universal proposition is suspicious and liable to error, more especially when we speak of the general character of a nation, the shades of which are always much diversified, according to the station, rank, temper, and profession of every individual. Each province of an empire is as different from the next, as either of these differ from the capital, and the capital from the court, where also each family has a particular tint by

Source: Isaac de Pinto, *Apologie pour la nation juive, ou reflexions critiques sur le premier chapitre du VIIe tome des oeuvres de M. De Voltaire au sujet des Juifs* (Amsterdam, 1762), in *Letters of Certain Jews to Monsieur Voltaire, Concerning an Apology for Their Own People and for the Old Testament,* 2nd ed., trans. Philip Lefanu (Covington, Kentucky, 1845), pp. 23–35, 37–42.

which the individuals of it are divided into various characters. If in a wood there are not two leaves which bear a strict resemblance, in the world there are not two faces perfectly alike, nor two men exactly of the same way of thinking on every subject, how is it possible to give the moral picture of a nation with one dash of the pen?

If this be true with regard to nations in general, it is much more so with respect to the Jews in particular. They have been scattered through so many nations, that they have, we may say, adopted in each country, after a certain time, the characters of the inhabitants; a Jew in London bears as little resemblance to a Jew in Constantinople, as this last resembles a Chinese Mandarin! A Portuguese Jew of Bordeaux and a German Jew of Metz appear two beings of a different nature! It is therefore impossible to speak of the manners of the Jews in general without entering into very long detail, and into particular distinctions; the Jew is a chameleon that assumes all the colors of the different climates he inhabits, of the different peoples he frequents, and of the different governments under which he lives.

Notwithstanding this, M. Voltaire has melted them all down to the same substance, and has given us a shocking picture of them which bears no resemblance....

If M. Voltaire had acted according to that principle of sound reason which he affects to do, he would have begun by distinguishing from the other Jews the Spanish and the Portuguese, who never have been mixed or incorporated with the crowd of the other sons of Jacob; he would have made this great distinction evident. I am sensible that it is little known in France, and that the want of proper information on this head has been detrimental on many occasions to the Portuguese [Jewish] nation of Bordeaux. M. Voltaire cannot be ignorant of the scrupulous exactness of the Portuguese and Spanish Jews not to intermix in marriage, alliance, or any other way, with the Jews of other nations. He has been in Holland, and knows that they have separate synagogues, and that, although they profess the same religion and the same articles of faith, yet their ceremonies have often no resemblance. The manners of the Portuguese Jews are also very different from those of the rest: the former have no beards, nor anything peculiar in their dress. The rich among them vie with the other nations of Europe in refinement, elegance and show, and differ from them in worship only. Their variance with their other brethren is at such a height that if a Portuguese Jew in England or Holland married a German Jewess, he would of course lose all his prerogatives, be no longer reckoned a member of their Synagogue, forfeit all civil and ecclesiastical preferments, be absolutely divorced from the body of the nation and not even buried with his Portuguese brethren. They think, in general that they are descended from the tribe of Judah, and they hold that the chief families of it were sent into Spain at the time of Babylonian captivity. This is the cause of those distinctions and of that elevation of mind which is observed among them, and which even their brethren of other nations seem to acknowledge.

By this wise policy they have preserved purer morals, and have acquired a certain importance, which helps even Christians to distinguish them from the other Jews. They do not, then, deserve those epithets which M. Voltaire lavishes on them. The Jews of Holland brought thither great riches at the end of the fifteenth century; and with manners irreproachable, greatly improved the trade of that commonwealth. Their Synagogue was like an assembly of senators, and, when German noblemen went into it, they could not be persuaded that those there present were of the same nation with those of Germany. They have been of greater use to Holland, at the beginning of the seventeenth century, than the French refugees were at the end of it. These latter, after the repeal of the edict of Nantes[2] brought into Holland much industry and little wealth, [however] the Portuguese, besides much wealth, drew into Holland the trade of Spain, and excited the industry [of Holland]. Their descendants have been rather dupes than knaves; they have often been the prey of usurers; rarely, if ever, usurers themselves. Scarcely can one instance be given of a Portuguese Jew executed at Amsterdam or the Hague, during two centuries. It would be hard to find in the annals of mankind so numerous a body of people as that of the Portuguese and Spanish Jews settled in Holland and England, among whom so few crimes punishable by law have been committed; and to this I call to witness all well-informed Christians of those nations. . . .

Let us say a word of the German and Polish Jews. Is it surprising that a people who are deprived of all the privileges of society, who increase and multiply by the laws of nature and religion, who are despised and reviled on all sides, who are often persecuted, always insulted, is it surprising, I say, that among them human nature, debased and degraded, should seem to have no acquaintance with any thing but worldly want? The sharp stings of want inspire these martyrs to it with every means of banishing or lessening it. That contempt which is heaped on them chokes up all the seeds of virtue and honour; there can be no sense of shame, where undeserved contempt precedes guilt; to cover the innocent with ignominy is to pave the way to it. And is it wrong to continue firmly attached to a religion which was formerly looked on as sacred by these very persons who now condemn it? We ought to pity them if they err; but it would be ungenerous not to admire the constancy, resolution, courage, steadiness, and disinterestedness with which they give up so many worldly advantages. Who would not praise a son who gives up his right to a great estate, because he thinks, perhaps without just grounds, that he cannot take possession of it without acting in opposition to his father's will by the act required of him? Ought so delicate, so praise-worthy, so noble and so uncommon a feeling to draw on him from his younger brothers, who enjoy the estate, contempt, insults and abuse? It is not sufficient to abstain from burning people with faggots; they may be burned with the pen; and this fire is so much more to be dreaded, because it lasts to future generations. What can be expected from the ignorant, savage [and] vulgar, when the destruction of an unfortunate nation is determined [as by Voltaire], if these horrid prejudices are authorized by the greatest genius of the most enlightened age? Let him consult his reason and his heart, and I am confident he will employ all his talents in recanting his errors: he will show in a masterly way that the mean characters of certain Polish and German Jews are not to be laid to the charge of that ancient, divine, and sacred religion.

NOTES

1. Isaac de Pinto (1717–1787), philosopher and economist of Portuguese-Jewish origin who spent most of his life in Holland. De Pinto earned his reputation as a genuine innovator in economic theory by opposing the Physiocrats and advocating the economically productive role of the national debt as well as of modern credit and commerce.

In this refutation of Voltaire, de Pinto anticipates a new genre of Jewish apologetic literature. In this literature self-consciously acculturated Jews seek to parry the accusations of anti-Semites by claiming that the criticism levelled is only true of those Jews who have yet to leave the ghetto. Anti-Semites would often use such statements as evidence corroborating their charges. De Pinto sent his pamphlet to Voltaire, whose reply is presented in document 3.

2. Edict of Nantes. The law was promulgated in 1598 by the French king, Henry IV, and it secured a large measure of religious liberty to his Protestant subjects, the Huguenots. It was repealed in 1685.

FRANÇOIS-MARIE AROUET DE VOLTAIRE

3. Reply to de Pinto

The lines you complain of are cruel and unjust. There are among you very learned and respectable persons. Your letter is a sufficient evidence of this. I shall take care to insert a cancel-leaf in the new edition. When a man is in the wrong he should make reparation for it; and I was wrong in attributing to a whole nation the vices of some individuals.

I shall tell you as frankly, that there are many who cannot endure your laws, your books, or your superstitions. They say that your nation has done, in every age, much hurt to itself and to the human race. If you are a philosopher, as you seem to be, you will think as those gentlemen do, but you will not say it. Superstition is the most dreadful scourge of the earth; it is superstition that in every age has caused so many Jews and Christians to be slaughtered; it is superstition that still sends you Jews to the stake among nations praise-worthy in other respects. . . . But perhaps I should provoke you to anger, and you seem to be too worthy a man to deserve provocation. As you are a Jew remain so. But be a philosopher.[1] This is my best wish to you in this short life.

I have the honor of remaining, Sir, with all the sentiments of respect due to you,

Voltaire

Christian gentleman in Ordinary to the most Christian King [Voltaire, chrétien gentilhomme de la chambre du Roi très-chrétien].[2]

NOTES

1. For Voltaire, to be a philosopher meant the adoption of the rational Deistic culture of the Enlightenment and assimilation. On the latter point Voltaire was explicit. With his characteristic sarcasm, he contended that the acceptance of the Jew by enlightened society was contingent on the Jew's rejection of his people's dietary laws and misanthropy. "But what shall I say to my brother the Jew?" he wrote.

> Shall I give him dinner? Yes, provided that during the meal Balaam's ass doesn't take it into its head to bray; that Ezekiel doesn't come to swallow one of the guests and keep him in his belly for three days; that a serpent doesn't mix into the conversation to seduce my wife; that a prophet doesn't take it into his head to sleep with her after dinner, as that good fellow Hoseah did for fifteen francs and a bushel of barley; above all that no Jew make a tour around my house sounding a trumpet, making the walls come down, killing me, my father, my mother, my wife, my children, my cat and my dog, in accord with the former usage of the Jews. [From "Tolerance," *Questions sur l'Encyclopédie,* cited in P. Gay, *The Party of Humanity* (New York: W. W. Norton, 1971), pp. 101ff.]

2. Voltaire ordinarily signed his correspondence, "Down with infamy!"

Source: Letters of Certain Jews to Monsieur Voltaire, Concerning an Apology for Their Own People and for the Old Testament, 2nd ed., trans. Philip Lefanu (Covington, Kentucky, 1845), pp. 54–56.

JOHANN GOTTLIEB FICHTE[1]

4. On the French Revolution

. . . A powerful, hostilely disposed nation is infiltrating almost every country in Europe. This nation is in a state of perpetual war with all these countries, severely afflicting their citizenry. I am referring to the Jewish Nation [*das Judentum*]. I believe, and hope to demonstrate subsequently, that the Jewish Nation is so dreadful not because it is isolated and closely-knit, but rather because it is founded on the hatred of mankind. It is a people whose most humble member elevates his ancestors higher than we exalt our entire history. Jewry sees as its ancestor a patriarch older than itself—a legend we ourselves have incorporated into our creed. It perceives all peoples as the descendants of those it drove out of its fervently loved fatherland. It condemned itself and is condemned to petty trade, which debilitates the body and deadens any tendency for noble feelings. The Jewish nation excluded itself from our meals, from our festive toasts, and from sweet, heart-to-heart exchanges of happiness with us by the most binding element of mankind—religion. It separates itself from all others in its duties and rights, from here until eternity. One would expect something different from such a people than what we see, namely, that in a state where the absolute monarch may not take away my ancestral dwelling and where I retain my rights before the all-powerful minister, the first Jew whom it so pleases pillages that which is mine and goes unpunished. You see all this; it cannot be denied. Yet, you speak sugar-sweet words about toleration and human rights and civic rights, by which you infringe upon our basic human rights. Your loving toleration of those who do not believe in Jesus Christ [expressed] by all the titles, honors and high positions you grant [the Jews], brings no satisfaction, for you are openly denouncing those who believe in Christ just as you do, depriving them of their civic honor and their honestly earned bread. Does this not recall to you the notion of a state within a state? Does the obvious idea not occur to you, that the Jews alone are citizens of a state which is more secure and powerful than any of yours? If you also give them civic rights in your states, will not your other citizens be completely trod under foot?*

*Let the poisonous air of intolerance stay as far from these pages as it is from my heart. The Jew who overcomes the difficult, one may say insurmountable, barriers which lie before him, and attains a love of justice, mankind, and truth—that Jew is a hero and a saint. I do not know whether such Jews ever existed or exist today. I shall believe it as soon as I meet such Jews. But dare you not sell me beautiful appearances for the real thing. Let the Jews never believe in Jesus Christ. Let them never even believe in God. If only they did not believe in a misanthropic God and in a double ethical standard [one applicable to Jews alone, another for their dealings with Gentiles]. They must have human rights, even if they will not grant them to us. For, they *are* human and their malevolence does not justify our becoming like them. Do not force these rights on the Jew against his will—do not allow that to happen when you are present and able to prevent it. . . . If you have eaten yesterday, but are hungry and only have enough bread for today, then give it to the Jew. He hungers for it, since he did not eat yesterday. You will be doing a good deed. Still, I see absolutely no way of giving them civic rights; except perhaps, if one night we chop off all of their heads and replace them with new ones, in which there would not be one single Jewish idea. And then, I see no other way to protect ourselves from the Jews, except if we conquer their promised land for them and send all of them there.

Source: Johann Gottlieb Fichte, "Beitrag zur Berichtung der Urteile des Publicums ueber die Franzoeische Revolution" [1793], in *Saemtliche Werke,* ed. J. H. Fichte (Berlin: Verlag von Veit, 1845), vol. 6, pp. 149–50. Trans. here by M. Gelber.

NOTE

1. Johann Gottlieb Fichte (1762–1814), German philosopher and founder of ethical idealism. Fichte's attitude toward Jews and Judaism was complex. He manifested a reverent attitude toward the Bible, but completely rejected the Jewish religion. He fought against the Jews' citizenship rights, but declared that human rights must be given to the Jews, "for, they *are* human and their malevolence does not justify our becoming like them. . . ."

JAKOB FRIEDRICH FRIES[1]

5. On the Danger to the Well-Being and Character of the Germans Presented by the Jews

. . . For about forty years now Prussian scholars, in particular, have defended the Jews in face of the antipathy shown them by the common people. Some were motivated by friendship for noble individuals belonging to this people; others, by their fervor for enlightenment and against narrow-minded attachment in particular, positive forms of religion; still others, because they had become dependent on rich, individual Jews. Yet, the spirit of this debate was cosmopolitan and characterized by a general love of man, whereby each individual held his fellow to be his equal. But precisely because of this last, very noble motivation, many misunderstandings continue to be debated, two of which we wish to mention here.

The first concerns the prejudice that the Jews were persecuted by us with blind rage and unjust religious zeal during the Middle Ages as well as down to the present. This, Herr Ruehs[2] has incontrovertibly disproved. To be sure, due to the more coarse manners of an earlier age, people alternated between rash, superstitious patronage and cruel excesses in their behavior toward the Jews. Princes almost always favored them too much, while cruelty originated from the common people. This cruelty, however, was not due to an inexplicable hatred for those who lived by deceit—those insidious, second-hand dealers and exploiters of the common people. The idea that the Jews were excessively oppressed in civic matters derives from this [erroneous belief that the Jews were treated with blind hatred]. If they were only to receive more civic rights, it is held, they would thus improve themselves. Ruehs has clearly shown that the opposite is true by using examples from history. Both in Germany and abroad the Jews had free states where they enjoyed every right, and even countries where they reigned—but their sordidness, their mania for deceitful, second-hand dealing always remained the same. They shy away from industrious occupations not because they are hindered from pursuing them but simply because they do not want to.

The second prejudice is the kind that can easily deceive human understanding with regard to the most important things. An abstract, general expression is replaced with the reality of a particular one. In this case, the [terms] Jews, Jewry and Judaism are interchanged. We declare war not against the Jews, our brothers, but against Judaism. Should one we love be stricken by the plague, is it not proper that we wish him deliverance

Source: Jakob Friedrich Fries, *Ueber die Gefaehrdung des Wohlstandes und Charakters der Deutschen durch die Juden* (Heidelberg: Mahr und Winter, 1816), pp. 9–11. Trans. here by M. Gelber.

from it? Should we abuse those who, stricken by the plague, lament its horrors and conjecture how to free themselves from it? Judaism is a residue from the uncultured past, which instead of being restricted should be completely extirpated. In fact, improving the condition of the Jews in society means rooting out Judaism, destroying the whole lot of deceitful, second-hand pedlars and hawkers. Judaism is the sickness of a people who are rapidly multiplying. Jewry will acquire power through money wherever despotism or distress engenders oppressive taxation; wherever oppressive, public ransoms become necessary; wherever the well-being of the citizen is so endangered that indebtedness on a small scale grows ever worse. Finally, the Jews also gain power where many unproductive countries are wasteful. The idle, stagnant capital of these countries is devoured by the Jews like worms gnawing on rotting matter.

NOTES

1. Jakob Friedrich Fries (1773–1843), German philosopher. He lectured in both Jena and Heidelberg and published authoritative works on philosophy and psychology. His popularity with the students contributed to the success of his anti-Jewish writings. Under his influence, the *Burschenschaften* ("students' associations") decided not to accept Jews as members.

2. Christian Friedrich Ruehs (1781–1820), nationalist professor of history in Berlin who opposed Jewish emancipation in a pamphlet entitled *Ueber die Ansprueeche der Juden an das deutsche Buergerrecht* (1815). In this work Ruehs maintained that Jewry already constitutes a nation complete with laws and aristocracy and therefore cannot be granted citizenship in a Christian state. Because of the unbridgeable gap existing between Germans and Jews, stemming from their inherently opposing natures, Jews may be tolerated only as a subject nation and the medieval restrictions must be reapplied.

K.B.A. SESSA
6. Our Visitors[1]

. . . ABRAHAM: A new perzon you'll become! Avay from Egypt, an from da fleshpots of mama, you'll go avay! In da vilderness, you'll look around, vere you'll not get da tiniest zip of water for noting! You'll see der da promized lant of da rich goyim! Your inheritenz you'll take avay from dem however you can, if you'll be a true zon of the children of Izrael! . . .

Geh! Geh! Step on you, let dem! Trow you out, let dem! Sue you in courtz, let dem! You'll go to da dogs, they'll bind you mit rope an chainz. Let dem whip you, martyr you till you're half dead! But (*threateningly) Rich* you *must* become! . . .

My Yankele! My sonnie! Listen t'me, vat I'll tell you. Not from greed do I vant it. It's da pleasure an joy at havin' muney dat's da reazon. Ven I count muney, my heart's ad ease. Ven I count muney, I need no oder pleasure. Ven I count muney, I need no docta, no medecine. I'm totally vell. Sonnie, von't you do just a little somting for da healt of your papa? Von't you give your old papa some relief in his old age? . . .

Source: K.B.A. Sessa, *Unser Verkehr,* Eine Posse in einem Aufzug (Leipzig, 1816), pp. 34ff. Trans. here by M. Gelber.

NOTE

1. Karl Barromaeus Alexander Sessa (1786–1813), physician in Breslau. *Unser Verkehr*, a comedy, was first presented on the Breslau stage (under the title, *Die Judenschule)* in 1813. It was performed in Berlin and elsewhere, until it was banned by the police. However, the play was published anonymously in numerous editions, and it inspired many of the anti-Semitic caricatures found in German literature. Sessa's play emphasizes the putative greed, vulgarity and pernicious immorality of all Jews. The play's great popularity was due to its parody of the poor German spoken by the Jews who had only recently been liberated from the ghetto.

HARTWIG VON HUNDT-RADOWSKY
7. The Jewish Mirror[1]

. . . I do not deny in the least that Jews are able to acquire scholarly knowledge. But such knowledge never ennobles their spirit or feelings. For them, gaining knowledge is like gaining a profit. They deal dishonestly and accumulate their wealth, with no intention of benefiting mankind. . . . The Jew's inherited nature is well disposed to usury and haggling, greed for money, falsehood and deceit, in much the same way that it is disposed to scabies. It is impossible for the Jews to become good. An emperor or king can indeed elevate [a Jew] to nobility, but he can never make him noble, the depravity of this people is too enormous and it increases with every day by its more than one thousand year old hatred and resentment of other peoples. . . .

To be sure, there might be now and then a Jew who seems less wicked than the others. Still, these are highly rare, and singular exceptions can never provide the standard for judging a significant and numerous people. An old coincidence of circumstances and a fortunate occurrence of peculiarities can perhaps cause an exception from time to time. However, this never invalidates the rule. If there are also instances, where white parents give birth to black children, so can one Jew be born accidentally an Israelite, lacking the Jewish facial characteristics, odor and haggler's disposition.

Further, granting civic rights to Jews was an injustice perpetrated by the government against the non-Jewish inhabitants. The latter and their ancestors founded the state, defended and preserved it with their wealth, blood, and lives, against both internal and external enemies. Now, however, a class of morally and spiritually degenerate people (whom we shelter, and who have benefited from the state but never benefit it at all) is treated in exactly the same manner that we are. . . .

Certainly they will gain the upper hand in many European countries very soon unless strict laws are introduced against them and circumcision is replaced by castration. . . .

I claim that the Jew is incapable of becoming a scholar; that is, a man who benefits the world through his spirit and learning, and is instrumental in the further education of his contemporaries for posterity. . . .

[Reflections concerning the betterment, "destruction" (*Ausrottung)* and "expulsion" (*Vertreibung*) of the Jews.] It would not be advisable to gather the Jews together (since

Source: Hartwig von Hundt-Radowsky, *Judenspiegel: Ein Schand- und Sittengemaelde alter und neuer Zeit* (Reutlingen: Ensslin'sche Buchhandlung, 1821), pp. 45–47, 51, 57–58, 78–79, 106, 109. Trans. here by M. Gelber.

they have few admirers left in Germany) and expel them to the promised land, where milk and honey flow and great clusters of grapes grow. Cannot we as easily shove the vermin across Turkey? At any rate, Abraham's other ancestors, the Ishmaelites, would push their circumcised half-brothers, the Israelites, even further on. Then, we will have reconquered Constantinople without spilling a drop of Christian blood.

NOTE

1. Hartwig von Hundt-Radowsky (1759–1835), German political writer and journalist. The title of his anti-Semitic treatise, "The Jewish Mirror," seems to be an allusion to Johannes Pfefferkorn's (1469–1521) similarly entitled pamphlet in which he held that Jewish literature was inimical to Christianity. In a later work, *Neuer Judenspiegel oder Apologie der Kinder Israel* (1828), Hundt-Radowsky executed a complete about-face, acknowledging the moral and social perfectability of the Jews through re-education (albeit after they had repudiated their religion) and recognized the responsibility of the Christian states for what he saw as the Jews' present state of corruption. Not surprisingly, this apology was not as popular as his earlier works.

DOMINICUS HAMAN EPIPHANES[1]
8. A Demonstration of the Necessity of Exterminating the Jews

. . . But since this plan [to relocate the Jews on the moon] presents several difficulties, it seems that the total extermination [*Vertilgung*] of Jewry would be incomparably easier. At the same time, perhaps, we could provide the productive class with several opportunities. Ideas from the time of the French Revolution could again be put forth: turn humans into tallow candles, iron medals, or pretty, milk-white glass. . . . Thereafter, a competition in the field of economics would be announced, whose subject would be according to which principles the total massacre [*Niedermetzelung*] of Jewry could be used to improve the soil. And, after that is determined, the proposal would be fully implemented. . . . It would then be possible to consider the tentative suggestion to exempt young Jewish women from the proposed penal measures. After all Jewish mates have been erased from the face of the earth, there would be no man of that people left for marital purposes. It is generally well-known, how due to our heightened morality, the female sex is thoroughly convinced of its noble duty. Many, therefore, heroically put everything aside in order to achieve the lofty goal of motherhood. Also, from this sense of duty originated the praiseworthy endeavor of many women to acquire a husband through refined and artificial coquetry and many other arts which increase the joys of social life. Now after it has become impossible to marry one of their own people, Jewish women will follow this praiseworthy example of non-Jewish women. If this should not work out, Jewish women could be utilized for another very important end. . . .

Source: Dominicus Haman Epiphanes, *Unumstoesslicher Beweis dass ohne die schleunigste Niedermetzelung aller Juden und den Verkauf der Juedinnen zur Sklaverei, die Welt, die Menschheit, das Christenthum und alle Staaten nothwendig untergehen muessen* (Jerusalem: Herschel, 1833), pp. 32–33. Trans. here by M. Gelber. We should like to thank Mr. Gelber for bringing this essay to our attention.

Many travel books assure us that as soon as white women are seen outside of Europe, they attract crowds of admirers and are preferred above negresses and other indigenous women. Therefore, we could anticipate a huge market for these Jewesses in Asia and Africa. . . . If, however, marketing them in this manner is not entirely feasible, it would have to be decided to sell a large part of them in Turkey and in that way bring a considerable sum of cash into our country. . . .

NOTE

1. Dominicus Haman Epiphanes, a pseudonym, possibly for Friedrich Freiherr von Holzschuher (1796–1861), Franconian assessor and provincial judge and little-known author of popular, satirical anti-Semitic writings.

BRUNO BAUER
9. The Jewish Problem[1]

. . . The advocates of Jewish emancipation are . . . in the strange position that they fight against privilege and at the same time grant to Judaism the privilege of unchangeability, immunity, and irresponsibility. They fight for the Jews with the best of intentions, but lack true enthusiasm, for they treat the Jewish problem as a matter foreign to them. If they are partisans of progress and the higher development of humanity, the Jews are excluded from their party. They demand that the Christians and the Christian state give up prejudices which not only have grown into their hearts but which are an essential part of their heart and being, and yet they demand no such thing from the Jews. The heart of Judaism must not be touched.

The birth of the new epoch which is now emerging will cost the Christian world great pains: are the Jews to suffer no pain, are they to have equal rights with those who fought and suffered for the new world? As if that could be! As if they could feel at home in a world which they did not make, did not help to make, which is contrary to their unchanged nature!

Those people who want to spare them the pains of criticism are the worst enemies of the Jews. Nobody who has not gone through the flames of criticism will be able to enter the new world which will soon come. . . .

Of the Jews it will at least be admitted that they suffered for their law, for their way of life and for their nationality, that they were martyred. They were thus themselves to blame for the oppression they suffered, because they provoked it by their adherence to their law, their language, to their whole way of life. A nothing cannot be oppressed. Wherever there is pressure something must have caused it by its existence, by its nature.

In history nothing stands outside the law of causality, least of all the Jews. With a stubbornness which their advocates themselves praise and admire they have clung to their nationality and resisted the movements and

Source: Bruno Bauer, *The Jewish Problem* [*Die Judenfrage,* 1843], ed. Ellis Rivkin and trans. Helen Lederer (Cincinnati: Hebrew Union College—Jewish Institute of Religion, 1958), pp. 2–3, 5–6, 11–16, 18, 22–26, 39, 41, 45, 57, 61–64. Reprinted by permission of Dr. Ellis Rivkin.

changes of history. The will of history is evolution, new forms, progress, change; the Jews want to stay forever what they are, therefore they fight against the first law of history—does this not prove that by pressing against this mighty spring they provoke counter-pressure? They were oppressed because they first pressed by placing themselves against the wheel of history.

Had the Jews been outside this action of the law of causality, had they been entirely passive, had they not from their side strained against the Christian world, there would not be any tie to connect them with history. They could never have entered into the new development of history and have influenced it. Then their cause would be quite lost.

Therefore, give the Jews the honor that they were to blame for the oppression which they suffered, that the hardening of their character caused by this oppression was their own fault. Then you admit them to a place in a two thousand year old history, although a subordinate one; then you make them members who are capable, and finally have the duty to take part in history's progress. . . .

Instead of praising the tenacity of the Jewish national spirit and regarding it as an advantage, one should ask what its basis is and where it comes from.

Its base is lack of ability to develop with history, it is the reason of the quite unhistorical character of that nation, and this again is due to its oriental nature. Such stationary nations exist in the Orient, because there human liberty and the possibility of progress are still limited. In the Orient and in India, we still find Parsees living in dispersion and worshipping the holy fire of Ormuzd. . . .

The hostility of the Christian world towards the Jews is therefore quite understandable and is caused by the circumstances. Neither of the two parties can acknowledge the other and allow it to remain in existence. The existence of the one excludes the existence of the other; each one believes itself to be the representative of absolute truth. It would mean denying that it is the truth if it were to acknowledge the other.

Jews and Christians can consider each other and treat each other as *men* only when they have given up the special nature which separates them and enjoins them to "eternal segregation"—when they acknowledge the common nature of man and consider humanity as their true nature.

The idea of human rights was discovered for the Christian world in the last century only. It is not innate in man, it has rather been won in battle against historical traditions which determined the education of men until now. So human rights are not a gift of nature or of history, but a prize which was won in the fight against the accident of birth and against privilege which came down through history from generation to generation. Human rights are the result of education, and they can be possessed only by those who acquire and deserve them.

Can the Jew really possess them as long as he lives as a Jew in perpetual segregation from others, as long as he therefore must declare that the others are not really his fellowmen? As long as he is a Jew, his Jewishness must be stronger in him than his humanity, and keep him apart from non-Jews. He declares by this segregation that this, his Jewishness, is his true, highest nature, which has to have precedence over his humanity.

In the same manner the Christian as a Christian cannot grant human rights.

What neither of the two parties possesses it cannot give to or accept from the other.

But surely citizens' rights could be granted the Jews? They cannot be deprived of civil rights.

The question is, rather, whether in a Christian state as such there are such universal rights, whether there are not exclusively special rights, that is a greater or smaller sum of privileges which are a right for some and a non-right, but not as such a wrong, for the other; for the other will have his own special privileges, unless one would want to assert that the sum of special rights is at the same time the sum total of wrongs, or that the lack of universal civil rights is the universal wrong.

Do the Jews want to become "citizens" in the Christian state? Ask first whether this state knows "citizens" or only subjects; whether the Jewish quarter is a contradiction if the subjects are divided into special estates according to privilege; whether it would even be remarkable if the Jews were commanded to wear special attire or special badges, if even the estates when formally represented must wear different clothes. . . .

If the opposition is no longer religious, if it is scientific and has assumed the form of criticism, if the Jew shows the Christian that his religious view is only the historical product of certain factors, then a solution has been given, because now the opposition is really not even scientific anymore. As soon, namely, as the Jew directs scientific, and not merely crude, religious criticism against Christianity, he must have looked critically at Judaism at the same time, because he must conceive of Christianity as a necessary product of Judaism. As soon, however, as both parties direct scientific criticism against each other, therefore also each against itself, there will be no religious hostility any more, and scientific differences of opinion are solved by science itself.

This is the solution of the contrast, that it dissolves into nothing. The Jews cease to be Jews without the necessity of becoming Christians, or rather, they must cease being Jews and must not become Christians. . . .

All right! The Jew wants to see his religion preserved, it is his real nature, his totality. He wants to make the acknowledgment of human rights dependent upon the acknowledgment and preservation of his religion. The Christian state therefore, is only doing what he himself wishes; it acts according to his words. . . . It declares religion as the foundation and essential characteristic of the state; only this religion is Christianity, the successor of Judaism. . . .

The most universal, therefore, also the most exclusive privilege, is faith. . . . Man cannot acquire it by himself, he cannot develop it from reason, he cannot manipulate it according to his will. It is, rather, a gift of grace, given to the chosen. . . .

Like the community of the believers, Israel boasts of a special privilege. Therefore, one privilege confronts another: one excludes the other. The Christian state is under the obligation to respect privileges, to protect them, to base its organization upon them. The Jew regards his special character as a privilege. Therefore, his only possible position in the Christian state is that of a privileged one, the Jews can only exist as a special corporation. . . .

It had to happen, this epoch had to become a time of general suffering. The error had been that one thought emancipation possible while the privileges of the religious barriers remained standing, even acknowledged in the emancipation itself. The Jew received concessions as a Jew, was allowed to continue to exist as a being segregated from all others, and this in itself made true emancipation impossible. Everybody still lacked courage to be simply a human being. Some privileges were sacrificed at that time, but the main privilege, the heavenly, god-given, supernatural privilege remained in force and this in turn must always generate all the others.

The emancipation of the Jews in a thoroughgoing, successful, safe manner will only be possible when they are emancipated not as Jews, that is as forever alien to the Christians, but as human beings who are no longer separated from their fellowmen by barriers which they wrongly consider to be all-important.

Therefore, the emancipation can also not be made dependent upon their conversion to Christianity, for by this they would only exchange one privilege against another. It would remain a privilege, even if expanded to everybody, to all mankind.

The emancipation problem has until now been treated in a basically wrong manner by considering it one-sidedly as the Jewish problem. Neither was it possible to find a theoretical solution in this manner, nor will it be possible to find a practical solution. Without being free oneself, one cannot help another to freedom. The serf cannot emancipate. The minor cannot help another to get rid of his guardians. One privilege can limit another, that is, by the very act [of] limitation [the privilege] recognizes and designates [itself] as a privilege but it can never replace [itself with] universal human rights without abolishing itself.

The problem of emancipation is a general problem, it is *the* problem of our age. Not only the Jews, but we, also, want to be emancipated. Only because nobody was free, because privilege was the ruling power, the Jews could not have freedom either. We all were surrounded by barriers; the Jewish quarter is right next to the police-supervised quarters where all of us are registered.

Not the Jews only, we, too, are no longer content with the chimera. We want to be real nations.

If the Jews want to become real—they cannot achieve it in their chimerical nationality, only in the real nations of our time living in history—then they have to give up the chimerical prerogative which will always alienate them from the other nations and history. They have to sacrifice their disbelief in the other nations and their exclusive belief in their own nationality. Only then will they be able to participate sincerely in national and state affairs.

We, however, have to give up our skepticism regarding the world and the rights of man, the exclusive belief in monopoly, and our immaturity, before we can think of becoming real nations and within the life of the nation, real human beings. . . .

NOTE

1. Bruno Bauer (1809–1882), German Protestant theologian, philosopher and historian who, as a student in Berlin, came under the influence of Hegel. His radical criticism of the New Testament led to his dismissal as a lecturer at Bonn in 1842. Returning to Berlin, he devoted himself to writing historical works and critical studies of the rise of Christianity. He also wrote on contemporary political issues, defending Prussian conservatism and strongly opposing the granting of emancipation to the Jews in Germany. The essay *Die Judenfrage,* from which the above is taken, argues that the Jew's desire to preserve his identity as a Jew is incompatible with the modern spirit and thus also with the requirements of genuine emancipation. The essay sparked a sharp controversy in which Abraham Geiger, Gabriel Riesser, Samuel Hirsch and Karl Marx (see the following) took part.

KARL MARX
10. On the Jewish Problem[1]

. . . Bauer reveals his one-sided conception of the Jewish problem. It is not at all sufficient to investigate: Who shall emancipate? Who shall be emancipated? The critic has to put a third question. He must ask: What kind of emancipation is in question? Which conditions are caused by the nature of the demanded emancipation? The critique of political emancipation itself was the final critique of the Jewish Problem and its true solution, dissolving it into the "general problem of the age." Because Bauer does not raise the problem to this level, he falls into contradictions. He poses conditions which are not founded

Source: Karl Marx, *On the Jewish Problem* [*Zur Judenfrage,* 1844], ed. Ellis Rivkin and trans. Helen Lederer (Cincinnati: Hebrew Union College, n.d.), pp. 6–10, 34–42. Reprinted by permission of Dr. Ellis Rivkin.

in the nature of political emancipation itself. He brings up questions which are not germane to his subject, and he solves problems, the solution of which, leaves his question unanswered. When Bauer says of the enemies of emancipation of the Jews: "Their only mistake was that they presumed the Christian state to be the only true state, and they did not subject it to the same criticism that they applied to Judaism," we hold that Bauer himself makes the mistake of subjecting only the "Christian state" to his criticism, not the "state in itself," that he does not examine the relation of political emancipation to human emancipation, and that he therefore poses conditions which are explicable only by an uncritical confusion of political with universal human emancipation. If Bauer asks the Jews: "Have you, from your point of view, the right to demand political emancipation?," then we rejoin with the question: Has the protagonist of political emancipation the right to demand that the Jew abolish Judaism, that men in general abolish religion? . . .

The political emancipation of the Jew, the Christian, the religious man in general is the emancipation of the state from Judaism, from Christianity, from religion in general. In its own manner, according to its nature, the state emancipates itself from religion, by emancipating itself from the state religion; that means that the state as such does not profess a religion, but professes itself as a state. The political emancipation from religion is not the accomplished, unresisted emancipation from religion for the reason that the political emancipation is not the accomplished, unresisted manner of human emancipation. The limit of political emancipation is revealed by the fact that the state can free itself of an impediment without the individual becoming really free, that the state can be a free state without the citizens being free men.

We have demonstrated now that political emancipation from religion allows religion to stand, although it tolerates no privileged religion. The contradiction in which the adherent of a particular religion finds himself with his status as a citizen, is only a part of the general contradiction between the political state and bourgeois society. The perfection of the Christian state is that state which proclaims itself a state and ignores the religion of its citizens. *The emancipation of the state from religion is not the emancipation of the individual from religion.*

Therefore we do not tell the Jews as Bauer does: You cannot be emancipated politically without emancipating yourselves radically from Judaism. On the contrary, we tell them: Because it is possible to emancipate you politically without your giving up Judaism completely and absolutely, therefore political emancipation itself is not human emancipation. If you Jews want to be emancipated politically without emancipating yourselves as men, the incompleteness and contradiction is not only to you, it is in the nature and category of political emancipation. . . .

The problem of the capability for emancipation of the Jews becomes in our eyes the question of which particular social element has to be abolished in order to abolish Judaism. For the capability of today's Jew to be emancipated is the relationship of Judaism to the emancipation of today's world. This relationship is the logical result of the special position of Judaism in our present world of slavery.

Let us observe the real worldly Jew, not the Sabbath Jew as Bauer does, but the everyday Jew. Let us not look for the mystery of the Jew in his religion, let us look for the mystery of the religion in the actual Jew.

What is the worldly basis of Judaism? Practical necessity, selfishness. What is the worldly culture of the Jew? Commerce. What is his worldly God? Money. All right! The emancipation from commerce and from money, from the practical real Judaism, would be the self-emancipation of our age.

An organization of society which would make commerce impossible by abolishing its presuppositions would have made the existence of the Jew impossible. His religious consciousness would dissolve like a thin vapor in the real life atmosphere of society. On the other hand, if the Jew does recognize this, his real nature, as worthless, and works for its annihilation, then he is working for the emancipation of man and turns against the highest practical expression of human self-estrangement.

We recognize therefore in Judaism a generally present anti-social element which has been raised to its present peak by historical development, in which the Jews eagerly assisted, and now it has of necessity to dissolve itself. *In its final meaning the emancipation of the Jews is the emancipation of humanity from Judaism.*[2]

The Jew has emancipated himself in a Jewish manner not only by gaining financial power, but because through him and without him money has become a world power and the practical Jewish spirit has become the practical spirit of the Christian nations. The self-emancipation of the Jews has gone so far that the Christians have become Jews. . . .

Yes, the practical dominion of Judaism over the Christian world has reached its normal, unambiguous expression in North America. . . .

Judaism has survived alongside Christianity not only as religious criticism of Christianity, but just as much because the practical Jewish spirit has survived within the Christian society and even reached its highest development there. The Jew who stands out as a specific member in civil society is only the specific phenomenon of Judaism within civil society.

Out of its own body civil society creates continuously the Jew.

What was the real basis of the Jewish religion? Practical need, egotism.

Jewish monotheism is therefore in reality the polytheism of the varied needs, a polytheism which makes even the privy an object of divine ordinance. Practical need, egotism, is the principle of civil society and emerges in its pure form as soon as civil society has given birth to the political state. The God of practical need and egotism is money.

Money is the jealous God of Israel before whom no other God may endure. Money debases all gods of men—and transforms them into commodities. Money is the common value of all things constituted for itself. So it robbed the whole universe, the world of men, of nature, of their specific values. Money is the essence of man's labor and existence, alienated from man, and this alien being rules him and he adores it.

The God of the Jews has become the God of the universe. The real God of the Jews is money. Their God is only an illusory bill of exchange. . . .

Judaism reaches its climax in the perfection of bourgeois society; but bourgeois society reaches its perfect development in the Christian world only. Only under the rule of Christianity, which externalizes all national, natural, moral, and theoretical aspects of man, could civil society separate itself completely from the life of the state, tear all ties to the human race and replace them by egotism and self-interest, dissolving the world of man into a world of atomistic individuals regarding each other with hostility. . . .

The Christian egotism of salvation becomes in practice necessarily the personal egotism of the Jew, the longing for heaven becomes earthly desire, the wish for individual salvation becomes self-interest. We explain the tenacity of the Jew not by his religion, but by the human basis of his religion, the practical need, egotism.

Because in bourgeois society the real nature of the Jew has found universal realization, therefore that society cannot convince the Jew of the non-reality of his religion, which is nothing other than the ideal concept of practical need. Not only in the Pentateuch or Talmud, but in our present society we find the nature of the Jew, not in the abstract, but in a highly empirical being, not in the narrow-mindedness of the Jew but in the Jewish narrow-mindedness of society.

As soon as society will succeed in abolishing the empirical nature of Judaism, commerce and its presuppositions, the existence of the Jew will be impossible, because his consciousness will have lost its object, the subjective basis of Judaism, the practical need, will be humanized, the conflict of the individual-material existence with the existence of humanity as a species will have ceased to exist.

The social emancipation of the Jew is the emancipation of society from Judaism.

NOTES

1. Karl Marx (1818–1883), German social philosopher. His parents were Jewish, but his father had converted before his birth and had him baptized at the age of six. Like Bauer, he was a student of Hegel, but unlike Bauer he developed the master's thought in a radical, leftist direction. The above is taken from a review of two of Bauer's essays, "Die Judenfrage," and "Die Faehigkeit der heutigen Juden und Christen, frei zu werden" [The Jewish question and the capacity of the present-day Jews and Christians to become free]. Marx's critique of Bauer's position on Jewish emancipation is a key work in his development toward dialectical materialism and "scientific" socialism. Although it should not be overlooked that in this essay Marx supports Jewish emancipation, he nonetheless unhesitatingly employed derogatory stereotypes of the Jews. The essay has thus been considered by many a *locus classicus* of both Jewish self-hatred and leftist anti-Semitism.

2. Cf. "The German word *Judentum* had, in the language of the time, the secondary meaning of 'commerce,' and in this and other passages Marx exploits the two senses of the word" (T. B. Bottomore, ed., *Karl Marx: Early Writings* [New York: McGraw-Hill, 1963], p. 36, n. 3).

RICHARD WAGNER
11. Jewry in Music[1]

. . . Since it here is merely in respect of art, and specially of music, that we want to explain to ourselves the popular dislike of the Jewish nature, even at the present day, we may completely pass over any dealing with this same phenomenon in the field of religion and politics. When we strove for emancipation of the Jews . . . we virtually were more the champions of *abstract principle,* than of a concrete case: just as all our liberalism was not a very lucid mental sport—since we went for freedom of the folk [*Volk*] without knowledge of that folk itself, nay, with a dislike of any genuine contact with it—so our eagerness to level up the rights of Jews was far rather stimulated by a general idea, than by any real sympathy; for, with all our speaking and writing in favour of the Jews' emancipation, we always felt instinctively repelled by any actual operative contact with them.

Here, then, we touch the point that brings us closer to our main inquiry: we have to explain to ourselves the *involuntary repellence* possessed for us by the nature and personality of the Jews, so as to vindicate that *instinctive dislike* which we plainly recognise as stronger and more overpowering than our conscious zeal to rid ourselves thereof. Even to-day we only purposely belie ourselves, in this regard, when we think it necessary to

Source: Richard Wagner [K. Freigedank], "Das Judenthum in der Musik," *Neue Zeitschrift fuer Musik*, 33, no. 19 (September 3, 1850) and 33, no. 20 (September 6, 1850). William Ashton Ellis, trans., in *Richard Wagner's Prose Works,* ed. W. A. Ellis (London, 1897).

hold immoral and taboo all open proclamation of our natural repugnance against the Jewish nature. . . .

We have no need to first substantiate the be-Jewing of modern art; it springs to the eye, and thrusts upon the senses, of itself. Much too far afield, again, should we have to fare, did we undertake to explain this phenomenon by a demonstration of the character of our art-history itself. But if *emancipation from the yoke of Judaism* appears to us the greatest of necessities, we must hold it weighty above all to prove our forces for this *war of liberation.* Now we shall never win these forces from an abstract definition of that phenomenon per se, but only from an accurate acquaintance with the nature of that involuntary feeling of ours which utters itself as an *instinctive repugnance against* the Jew's prime essence. Through it, through this *unconquerable feeling*—if we avow it quite without ado—must there become plain to us what we hate in that essence; what we then know definitely, we can make head against; nay, through his [the Jew's] very laying bare, may we even hope to rout the demon from the field, whereon he has only been able to maintain his stand beneath the shelter of a twilight darkness—darkness we good-natured humanists ourselves have cast upon him, to make his look less loathsome.

The Jew—who, as everyone knows, has a God all to himself—in ordinary life strikes us primarily by his outward appearance, which, no matter to what European nationality we belong, has something disagreeably foreign to that nationality; instinctively we wish to have nothing in common with a man who looks like that; a man whose appearance we must hold unfitted for artistic treatment—not merely in this or that personality, but according to his kind in general—neither can we hold him capable of any sort of artistic utterance of purely human essence.

The Jew, who is innately incapable of presenting himself to us artistically through either his outward appearance or his speech, and least of all through his singing, has nevertheless been able in the widest-spread of modern art-varieties, to wit in music, to reach the rulership of public taste. To explain to ourselves this phenomenon, let us first consider how it grew possible for the Jew to become a musician.

From that turning-point in our evolution where money, with less and less disguise, was raised to the virtual patent of nobility, the Jews—to whom money-making without actual labour, i.e., usury, had been left as their only trade—not merely could no longer be denied the diploma of a new society that needed naught but gold, but they brought it with them in their pockets. Wherefore our modern culture, accessible to no one but the well-to-do, remained the less a closed book to them, as it had sunk into a venal article of luxury. Henceforward, then, *the cultured Jew appears in our society;* his distinction from the uncultured, the common Jew, we now have closely to observe. The cultured Jew has taken the most meticulous pains to strip off all the obvious tokens of his lower coreligionists; in many a case he has even held it wise to make a Christian baptism wash away the traces of his origin. This zeal, however, has never got so far as to let him reap the hoped-for fruits; it has led him only to his utter isolation, and to making him the most heartless of all human beings; to such a pitch, that we have been bound to lose even our earlier sympathy for the tragic history of his stock. His connexion with the former comrades in his suffering, which he arrogantly tore asunder, it has stayed impossible for him to replace by a new connexion with that society whereto he has soared up. He stands in correlation with none but those who need his money; and never yet has money thriven to the point of knitting a goodly bond twixt man and man. Alien and apathetic stands the educated Jew in the midst of a society he does not understand, with whose tastes and aspirations he does not sympathise, whose history and evolution have always been indifferent to him. . . .

By what example will this all grow clearer to us—ay, wellnigh what other single case could make us so alive to it, as the works of a musician of Jewish birth whom Nature had endowed with specific musical gifts as very few before him? All that offered itself to our gaze, in the inquiry into our antipathy against the Jewish nature; all the contradictoriness of this nature, both in itself and as touching us; all its inability, while outside our footing, to have intercourse with us upon that footing, nay, even to form a wish to further develop the things which had sprung from out of our soil; all these are intensified to a positively tragic conflict in the nature, life, and art-career of the early-taken Felix Mendelssohn Bartholdy.[2] . . .

I said above, the Jews had brought forth no true poet. We here must give a moment's mention, then, to Heinrich Heine.[3] At the time when Goethe and Schiller sang among us, we certainly knew nothing of a poetic Jew; at the time, however, when our poetry became a lie, when every possible thing might flourish from the wholly unpoetic element of our life, but no true poet, then was it the office of a highly-gifted poet-Jew to bare with fascinating taunts that lie, that bottomless aridity and jesuitical hypocrisy of our versifying which still would give itself the airs of true poetry. His famous musical congeners, too, he mercilessly lashed for their pretence to pass as artists; no make-believe could hold its ground before him: by the *remorseless demon of denial* of all that seemed worth denying was he driven on without a rest, through all the mirage of our modern self-deception, till he reached the point where in turn he duped himself into a poet, and was rewarded by his versified lies being set to music by our own composers. He was the conscience of Judaism, just *as Judaism is the evil conscience of our modern civilisation.*

Yet another Jew have we to name, who appeared among us as a writer. From out of his isolation as a Jew, he came among us seeking redemption: he found it not, and had to learn that only with our redemption, too, into genuine manhood, would he ever find it. To become man at once with us, however, means firstly for the Jew as much as ceasing to be Jew. And this had Boerne done.[4] Yet Boerne, of all others, teaches us that this redemption cannot be reached in ease and cold, indifferent complacence, but costs—as cost it must for us—sweat, anguish, want, and all the dregs of suffering and sorrow. Without once looking back, take ye your part in this regenerative work of deliverance through self-annulment; then are we one and undissevered! But bethink ye, that *one only thing* can redeem you from the burden of your curse: the *redemption of Ahasuerus*[5]—*Going under!*

NOTES

1. Richard Wagner (1813–1883), German composer who sought to achieve a union of music and dramatic poetry, utilizing a wide range of symbols, with special emphasis on national and romantic themes. He hoped that his music would give expression to, and foster the rebirth of, what he called the Germanic hero-spirit, a "racial characteristic" he believed to be possessed only by the "pure-bred Germanic branches of the Aryan race." His essay, "Jewry in Music"—first published under a pseudonym and later, in 1869, under his own name—is considered to be one of the first formulations of racial anti-Semitism. Wagner's works, which enjoyed a large audience among the educated class of his day, made anti-Semitism culturally respectable, and generally facilitated the diffusion of racist doctrines. His political essays were greatly admired by Adolf Hitler and his operas were regularly performed at Bayreuth in connection with Nazi party conventions.

2. Jakob Ludwig Felix Mendelssohn-Bartholdy (1809–1847), German composer. A grandson of Moses Mendelssohn, he was baptized early in life.

3. Heinrich Heine (1797–1856), one of the greatest lyric poets in the German language and Germany's most famous Jewish writer. Heine's later poems and especially his prose works established him as a satirist of barbed wit and as an astute critic of romanticism, jingoistic patriotism and current and political affairs.

4. Ludwig Boerne (1786–1837), German liberal political essayist. He used wit and irony to inject subversive political allusions into writings on the most harmless of subjects. Born into a prominent Jewish banking family in Frankfurt, he converted to Lutheranism in 1818. The idea that the freedom of mankind as a whole is inextricably bound up with freedom for the Jews recurs consistently in his writings.

5. Ahasuerus is the name given to the wandering Jew, who, according to legend, is doomed to wander eternally without hope of rest until the millennium as punishment for taunting Jesus on the way to crucifixion. The legend first appeared in a German pamphlet in 1602 and quickly spread in a variety of forms. It also received numerous applications in literary works.

WILHELM MARR
12. The Victory of Judaism over Germandom[1]

There is no stopping them. . . .

Are there no clear signs that the twilight of the Jews [*juedische Goetterdaemmerung*] is setting in?

No.

Jewry's control of society and politics, as well as its practical domination of religious and ecclesiastical thought, is still in the prime of its development, heading toward the realization of Jehovah's promise: "I will hand all peoples over to thee."

By now, a sudden reversal of this process is fundamentally impossible, for if it were, the entire social structure, which has been so thoroughly Judaized, would collapse. And there is no viable alternative to this social structure which could take its place.

Further, we cannot count on the help of the "Christian" state. The Jews are the "best citizens" of this modern, Christian state, as it is in perfect harmony with their interests. . . .

It is not a pretentious prophecy but the deepest inner conviction which I here utter. Your generation will not pass before there will be absolutely no public office, even the highest one, which the Jews will not have usurped.

Yes, through the Jewish nation, Germany will become a world power, a western New Palestine. And this will happen, not through violent revolutions, but through the compliance of the people. . . .

We should not reproach the Jewish nation. It fought against the western world for 1800 years, and finally conquered and subjugated it. We were vanquished and it is entirely proper that the victor shouts "Vae Victis!"[2]

German culture has proved itself ineffective and powerless against this foreign power. This is a fact; a brute inexorable fact. State, Church, Catholicism, Protestantism, Creed and Dogma, all are brought low before the Jewish tribunal, that is, the [irreverent] daily press [which the Jews control].

The Jews were late in their assault on Germany, but once they started there was no stopping them.

Gambetta,[3] Simon,[4] and Crémieux[5] were the dictators of France in 1870–1871. During the war, they drove thousands upon thousands of Frenchmen to their senseless deaths. After Sedan, the whole world believed in peace. But, no! Bismarck was lured by the rhetoric of a Jules Favre.[6] "Blood and Iron" had to continue because of the frivolous, worthless, fanatical action of the Semites in Tours.

Poor, Judaized France!

Source: Wilhelm Marr, *Der Sieg des Judenthums ueber das Germanenthum vom nicht confessionellen Standpunkt ausbetrachtet* (Bern: Rudolph Costenoble, 1879), pp. 30–35, Trans. here by P. Mendes-Flohr and J. Reinharz.

In England, the Semite Disraeli,[7] a German-hater (*comme il faut*), holds in his vest pocket the key to war and peace in the Orient.

Who derived the real benefit at the Congress of Berlin from the spilled blood of the Orient? Jewry. The Alliance Israélite Universelle[8] was first in line. Rumania was forced to open officially its doors and gates to destructive Semitism. Jewry did not yet dare to make the same demand of Russia. But, this demand, too, will soon come.

Dear reader, while you are allowing the German to be skinned alive I bow my head in admiration and amazement before this Semitic people, which has us under heel. Resigned to subjugation to Jewry, I am marshalling my last remaining strength in order to die peacefully, as one who will not surrender and who will not ask forgiveness.

Can we deny the historical fact?

No!

The historical fact, that Israel became the leading social-political superpower in the nineteenth century, lies before us. It is already notorious to what extent we lack the physical and intellectual strength to de-Judaize ourselves. The raw, brutal, but completely unconscious protest against the real Judaization of society was Social Democracy. It sided, however, with the Jews, because Jewry has also infiltrated its ranks. After all, the founder of German Social Democracy, Lassalle,[9] was a Semite.

Why are we so surprised? We have among us a flexible, tenacious, intelligent, foreign tribe that knows how to bring abstract reality into play in many different ways. Not individual Jews, but the Jewish spirit and Jewish consciousness have overpowered the world. . . .

All this is the consequence of a cultural history—so unique in its way, so grand that everyday polemics can achieve nothing against it. With the entire force of its armies, the proud Roman Empire did not achieve that which Semitism has achieved in the West and particularly in Germany.

NOTES

1. Wilhelm Marr (1818–1904), German anti-Semite. His pamphlet, *The Victory of Judaism over Germandom: Regarded from a Non-Demoninational Point of View*—from which excerpts are presented here—reached its twelfth edition by 1879. As is reflected in its title, this influential pamphlet contrasts the Jew not with the Christian, but with the German; the two peoples, Marr holds, are diametrically and irreconcilably opposed to one another. Marr is considered to have introduced in 1879 the word *anti-Semite* into the political lexicon by the founding of the League of Anti-Semites (*Antisemiten-Liga*) which organized lectures and published a short-lived monthly. The league was the first effort at creating a popular political movement based on anti-Semitism.

2. "Woe to the conquered!" This appeared as the motto of the pamphlet.

3. Léon Gambetta (1838–1882), erroneously considered to be a Jew. A leader of the republicans, he was minister of the interior in the new government of national defense after the defeat of the French forces at Sedan in 1870. He organized an unsuccessful resistance to the Germans in 1871. From 1879 to 1882 Gambetta was the president of the chamber of deputies, where he wielded considerable influence.

4. Jules François Simon (1814–1896), born to a Protestant father and Catholic mother. Marr, however, apparently assumed he was a Jew. Simon was minister of instruction in the government of national defense. Though himself an opponent of the monarchy, he forced the resignation of Gambetta after the capitulation of Paris in 1870 in order to avoid German retaliation.

5. Isaac Adolphe Crémieux (1796–1880), French lawyer and statesman and leader of French Jewry. He served several times in the chamber of deputies and in 1870 was minister of justice.

6. Jules Favre (1809–1880), leading republican statesman known for his oratorical powers. As foreign minister he was charged with negotiating peace with Germany. On September 6, 1870, he made the ill-considered statement that he "would not yield to Germany an inch of territory nor a single stone of the fortresses." Otto von Bismarck,

the German chancellor, quickly responded by declaring that the cession of Alsace and Lorraine was the indispensable condition of peace.

7. Benjamin Disraeli, Earl of Beaconsfield (1804–1881), British statesman and novelist. Although baptized at the age of 13, he was proud of his Jewish origins. During his second term as prime minister (1874–1880) he acted to strengthen the British Empire and check Russian penetration into the Mediterranean. He was a moving force at the Congress of Berlin (1878), where Russia was forced to relinquish her acquisitions in the Balkans.

8. Alliance Israélite Universelle, the first modern international Jewish organization, founded in 1860 and centered in Paris. The Jewish community of Berlin, supported by the Alliance and the Zion society of Bucharest, petitioned the chairman of the congress and head of the German delegation, Otto von Bismarck, to raise the question of equal rights for Rumanian Jews at the congress. As a result, the German representatives were instructed to demand equal civil rights for the members of all religions in the Balkan countries and the inclusion in the peace treaty of a special paragraph to this effect explicitly providing for their implementation.

9. Ferdinand Lassalle (1825–1864), German-Jewish socialist leader whose latter years were devoted to organizing a political party of the workers of Germany; his efforts culminated in the establishment of the Allgemeiner Deutscher Arbeiter-Verein in 1863.

KARL EUGEN DUEHRING[1]

13. The Question of the Jew Is a Question of Race

A Jewish question would still exist, even if every Jew were to turn his back on his religion and join one of our major churches. Yes, I maintain that in that case, the struggle between us and the Jews would make itself felt as ever more urgent—although the struggle certainly is felt now even when the Jews have yet to convert [in large numbers]. It is precisely the baptized Jews who infiltrate furthest, unhindered in all sectors of society and political life. It is as though they have provided themselves with an unrestricted passport, advancing their stock to those places where members of the Jewish religion [*Religionsjuden*] are unable to follow. Furthermore, several doors are closed to members of the Jewish religion by our legislation, and more particularly, by the principles of our administration. Through these portals the racial Jew [*Racenjude*], who has forsaken his religion, can enter unhindered. A situation similar to the one involving the baptized Jews results as soon as all civic rights and opportunities become available to members of the Jewish religion. Thereupon, they force themselves into all aspects of social and political life, just like those who have converted to Christianity. And, in this way, their contact with the nation in which they live becomes more pronounced. This takes place despite the fact that in society [as opposed to the state] there is never an instance in which the members of the Jewish religion are made completely equal. . . . I return therefore to the hypothesis that the Jews are to be defined solely on the basis of race, and not on the basis of religion. I dismiss all conclusions hitherto upheld. . . . The Mosaic attempt to locate within the base of our people a Jewish component only makes the Jewish question a more burning issue. The diverse admixture of our modern cultures, or in other words, the sprinkling of racial-Jewry in the cracks and crevices of our national abode, must inevi-

Source: Karl Eugen Duehring, *Die Judenfrage als Racen- Sitten- und Culturfrage* (Karlsruhe and Leipzig: H. Reuther, 1881), pp. 3–4. Trans. here by M. Gelber.

tably lead to a reaction. It is impossible that close contact [between Germans and Jews] will take effect without the concomitant realization that this infusion of Jewish qualities is incompatible with our best impulses.

NOTE

1. Karl Eugen Duehring (1833–1921), German economist and philosopher. One of the initial proponents of modern racial anti-Semitism, he had a seminal influence on the development of German anti-Semitism in the 1880s.

ALPHONSE TOUSSENEL
14. The Jews: Kings of the Epoch[1]

Critical periods arise in the life of a nation, as they do in the life of an individual. At such times, it seems as if the blood is clotting in your heart. They are times of terrible stagnation, when all of the achievements of the past are undone by one mistake; times when [the forces of corruption], encouraged by a general inertia and torpor of the spirit, usurp the government of a degraded society and consolidate their power for centuries to come. The French nation has come to one of these critical periods.

The parliament is powerless and, one might say, chronically so as of recently. The chamber of deputies, an all too faithful representation of the country, is divided; its factions vote for laws piecemeal. The words *system* and *unity* frighten its members. If, by chance, some miserable question concerning a portfolio [of stocks] or secret funds succeeds in galvanizing [the deputies] from [their] torpor, the majority come together for a moment out of fear, but immediately they scatter when the danger is past. And, every representative, taking up again the harness of local interests, goes back to lining his own pockets with renewed zeal. The law, deprived of any grandiose and national character, is nothing other than a financial transaction among greedy and narrow-minded men. Ministers can only receive a parliamentary majority on the condition, set by the parliament, that they do not govern. The purchase of consciences and catering to villainy—this is the edifying task, and almost the exclusive one, which the spirit of the age assigns to its rulers.

The machinery of the central administration has broken down. The prefect can no longer administrate effectively. Rather, it is the deputy who governs and distributes employment. Ministers have become used to paying for the votes delivered to them by appointing their supporters prefectures and granting them shares in tax collection, so that the highest officers of the government have lost all prestige in the people's eyes, and the holders of those offices have lost their former influence. Accusations of bribery against the highest government officials are daily events: a marshal of France admits before the court that he has *compromised the dignity of his command* by falsifying an account of tribute payments imposed on the enemy; a minister of the navy ingenuously confesses in court that the accounts of his department are not without several *irregularities.* Bankruptcy has be-

Source: Alphonse Toussenel, *Les Juifs, rois de l'époque, histoire de la féodalité financière,* 4th ed., 2 vols. (Paris: Libraire de la Sociéte des Gens de Lettres, 1888), vol. 1, pp. 1–6. Trans. here by J. Green.

come as commonplace among the agents as among notaries and stockbrokers. Some are even being arraigned in criminal court for offenses against decency. Twenty-five Algerian public officials were arraigned at the same time, then dismissed, or simply censured for acts of bribery, indiscipline, or incompetence. And, the courts of the mother country are as full as those of Algeria with scandalous cases of bribery and illicit payments. On this topic, one can even say that there is competition between certain military and naval departments. Excisemen participate in the business of the adulteration of beverages. Employees of the mint are accused of having sold the half-marks. Fraud, demoralization, and contempt for honesty are omnipresent.

The judiciary itself, which has for so long been the last safeguard of our liberty and honor, seems to have forgotten the difference between "just" and "unjust" in the general collapse of public morality and equity. Judges have imprisoned and fined poor workers guilty of joining together *in order to live from their work.* It never occurred to those rigorous executors of the law to blame the employers, who are guilty of having joined together *in order to live from the labor of their workers.* Hardly one judge could be found in the courthouses to find that this coalition of employers had an extenuating circumstance in favor of the poor miners of Saint-Étienne. Even less has French justice, so harsh toward the poor, considered accusing the bankers of Judea, London and Geneva of the crime of ransacking the public treasury, those bankers who brazenly unite every day in order to secure a monopoly of public loans and railroads for a low price.

In foreign affairs, France has fallen to the level of a second-rate power. The absolutist states keep her in quarantine, as the poet said. They deal with questions affecting the balance of power in Europe, without French participation. They banish her from their congresses. And, instead of withdrawing nobly in formidable isolation and making them pay a high price for her return of these congresses (where nothing can be decided without her), France begs shamefully for the favor of resuming her place. In order to be forgiven, she makes herself humble and modest. She grants the English navy a monopoly in policing the seas. She allows foreign cruisers to inspect her ships. When public opinion has been stirred by these indignities, the French government deceitfully avoids the issue. . . .

Now, favored by this lack of parliamentary power, political inertia, and torpor of spirit, economic feudalism advances rapidly to the heart of our institutions. Skillfully taking advantage of the divisions between the royalty and the people that are fomented by the press, this feudalism entrenches itself in the soil more deeply each day, pressing with its two feet the throats of the royalty and of the people. Today, [this feudal clique] is not yet completely organized. But, it will be tomorrow. It already has the producer and the consumer at its mercy. The Jew reigns and governs France.

In [this book], I point out the origin, tendencies and successive invasions of financial feudalism. I expose the dangers of the present situation and indicate the means to remove them. I show that it is still possible to check the insolent power of money. I call upon the king and the people to unite in order to rid themselves of the aristocracy of money—as the king and the people did once before under Richelieu in order to overthrow the aristocracy of caste. I prove that the king must only wish to save the people's freedom one more time and thus be transfigured gloriously in their eyes.

And now, to those who are tempted to ask who I am, I answer: I am one of those you could call "men of the hour," as opposed to those you call "men of tomorrow"; I am one of those devoted and inept people you are always sure to meet in the hottest part of the fighting and in stormy circumstances, but who willingly forget to set conditions on the eve of the battle and to claim their share of the booty on the morrow of the victory. For ten years I served the cause of power with an energetic devotion, which the dangers of battle never weakened for a moment.[2] And I would continue to serve the cause of order and authority, if it were possible for an honorable man to support that degrading policy of continual self-abasement, [euphemistically] called modesty. When I saw that the ministers, who had commissioned me to defend them, betrayed their government and sold France to the Jews, I deserted their camp, so as not to go over to the enemy with them.

NOTES

1. Alphonse Toussenel (1803–1885), French publicist and follower of François Marie Charles Fourier, the French utopian socialist. Toussenel was exceedingly popular as a writer on ornithology and wild-life. In these studies, which earned him the title Balzac of the animal world, he celebrated the pristine majesty of the woods and forests of France—which, alas, he charged, were being destroyed by the "Rothschild's railroads." His two volume work, *Les Juifs, rois de l'époque,* was one of the most vehement attacks on the Jews published in France before the appearance of Edouard-Adolphe Drumont's *La France Juive* (see document 15).

In this work, first published in 1845 (second edition 1847; republished in 1886 and 1888), Toussenel paints an apocalyptic picture of France under the July monarchy (1830–1848). He focuses on the parliamentary corruption and social unrest concomitant to the rapid industrial development of this period and on the fact that Jewish financiers were prominent among the ruling oligarchy. In its spiritual and moral torpor, he argues, France had allowed itself to be victimized by "financial feudalism," that is, by usurious Jewry. Toussenel was a pioneer of a literature that linked the medieval image of the Jew as a usurer to the popular contempt for the financier and banker in the age of nascent capitalism: "I wish to point to the popular sense of the word [*Jew*]: banker, usurer" (Toussenel). This dialectic between anti-capitalism and anti-Semitism was encouraged by the tendency of early socialists, especially in France, to identify the essence of capitalism with high finance and the depiction of this activity as a form of usury. As George Lichtheim observed in his study of socialist anti-Semitism, "the anti-capitalism and the anti-Jewish themes were intertwined, it took considerable time and trouble before they could be disentangled" ("Socialism and the Jews," *Dissent* [July-August 1968], p. 316).

2. In the early 1840s Toussenel spent three years in Algeria as a civilian commissioner working with the French army.

EDOUARD-ADOLPHE DRUMONT
15. Jewish France[1]

. . . The Jews possess half of the capital in the world. Now the wealth of France, with a national budget of close to four million francs, is possibly worth one hundred and fifty billion francs, of which the Jews possess at least eighty billion. In my estimation, however, because one must proceed with circumspection and because of the ease with which finances can be juggled, [the expropriation of Jewish wealth] would produce immediately no more than ten to fifteen billion. I take the figure of ten billion as a minimum: five or six billion francs in cash, and certainly one could also expropriate enough factories. [The latter action] would allow the workers to test their social doctrines in optimal condi-

Source: Edouard-Adolphe Drumont, *La France Juive,* 14th ed. (Paris: C. Marpon and E. Flammarion, 1885), vol. 1, pp. 520–23, 526. Trans. here by J. Green.

tions, in that there would be no violent revolution, and no unemployment would be created. All of this, and I do not hestitate to emphasize the point, would be accomplished without violence, without bloodshed; it would, if you will, be accomplished by simple decree, without plunging the country into one of those crises which only benefit the foreigners [viz., the Jews]. The Office of Confiscated Jewish Wealth would function much as the [Revolutionary] Office of National Wealth functioned. And, I do not see very well how anyone could attack the legitimacy of such expropriation, for none of the civics textbooks that are put into the hands of the young dares to condemn revolutionary confiscation.

Actually, the transfer of property which we propose is more legitimate than that which occurred during the revolution. In effect, no one could seriously deny that Jewish wealth has, as we have said, a special character. It is essentially parasitical and usurious. It is not the carefully husbanded fruit of the labor of innumerable generations. Rather, it is the result of speculation and fraud. It is not created by labor, but extracted with marvelous cleverness from the pocket of real workers by financial institutions, which have enriched their founders by ruining their stockholders.

. . . The obstacles [placed before the workers by the Jews] are indeed considerable. Still they are not insurmountable. A man of French origin may yet arise from among the people, harboring the magnificent ambition of attaching his name to the peaceful solution [I have proposed] of the problem of the proletariat, which has already cost the workers so much blood and which will cost them still more if they follow the old path.[2]

Likewise, a brave officer might appear, who would be acutely struck by the degradation of his country and who would risk his life to raise it up. Given the actual situation, with a government scorned by all and falling apart at the seams, five hundred determined men in the suburbs of Paris and a regiment surrounding the Jewish banks would suffice to carry out the most fruitful revolution of modern times. Everything would be over by the end of the day. After seeing posters announcing that the operations of the Office of Confiscated Jewish Wealth were going to begin in two days, people would embrace in the streets.

Thus, the beautiful saying of Pierre the Venerable, Abbot of Cluny, would be realized: *Serviant populis christianis, etiam invitis ipsis, divitiae Judeorum.* "Let the wealth of the Jews even against their will, serve the Christian peoples."

NOTES

1. Edouard-Adolphe Drumont (1844–1917), journalist and leader of the anti-Semitic movement in France. His *La France Juive*—first published in 1886; subsequently more than a hundred editions were issued—was said to be the most widely read book in France. He followed his success by trying to organize anti-Semitism as a political and social force; in this effort he was primarily supported by students and lower echelons of the Catholic clergy. In 1892 he founded the *La Libre Parole,* a daily newspaper which reflected both his anti-Semitism and what has been called his "sentimental socialism," or a paternalistic concern for the poor and a repugnance of capital (as opposed to property), which he defined as wealth illicitly gained through speculation. Property is a Christian value, capital is Jewish.

His two-volume work of over a thousand pages purports to depict the historical clash between Jewry and France. This account is prefaced by an effusive discussion of the racial differences between the Aryans of Gaul—an idealistic, chivalrous Christian people—and the Jews. In contradistinction to the Frenchman, the Jew lacks a creative impulse, and he is correspondingly ugly (a hooked nose, contorted fingers, an unpleasant body odor). The Jews, moreover, are by nature spies, traitors, criminals and carriers of disease. Through their cunning "the Jewish race" has all but subjugated the benign, but careless Aryans of France. The major theme of Drumont's anti-Semitic canard, however, is the contrast between the poverty of the French workers and peasants and the wealth of Jewish bankers and industrialists. His program for liberating a benighted France from the clutches of a predatory Jewry is presented in above excerpt.

2. The advertisement for an illustrated edition of Drumont's work published in 1887 "portrayed Drumont as a second Charles Martel, clad in shining armor and attacking the nineteenth-century Saracens of the bank and stock exchange, while the cover of this edition showed Drumont, carrying a cross, stamping upon an old man who was holding the tablets of Sinai" (R. F. Byrnes, *Anti-Semitism in Modern France* [New Brunswick: Rutgers University Press, 1950], vol. 1, pp. 139ff.).

ADOLF STOECKER

16. What We Demand of Modern Jewry[1]

. . . We do not believe the end of the German spirit to be so near. Peoples as well as individuals can be reborn. Germany, and Berlin too, will recover and rid themselves of the foreign spirit. But there are symptoms of the presence of a disease: our national body is plagued by social abuses, and social hostility never exists without reason. Christians as well as Jews should be seriously concerned lest this enmity turn into hatred. For the rumbling of a far-off thunderstorm can already be heard. It is strange indeed that the Jewish liberal press does not have the courage to answer the charges of its attackers. Usually it invents a scandal, even if there is none. It sharpens its poisonous pen by writing about the sermons in our churches and the discussions in our church meetings; but it hushes up the Jewish question and does everything to prevent its readers from hearing even a whisper from these unpleasant voices. It pretends to despise its enemies and to consider them unworthy of an answer. It would be better to learn from the enemy, to recognize one's own defects, and work together toward the social reconciliation which we need so badly. It is in this light that I intend to deal with the Jewish question, in the spirit of Christian love, but also with complete social truthfulness. . . .

I do indeed consider modern Jewry a great danger to German national life. By this I mean neither the religion of the orthodox nor the enlightenment of the reformed. Orthodox Judaism, this ossification of the Law, the Old Testament without a temple, without priests, without sacrifice, without a Messiah, is neither attractive nor dangerous to the children of the nineteenth century. It is a form of religion which is dead at its very core, a low form of revelation, an outlived spirit, still venerable but set at nought by Christ and no longer holding any truth for the present. Reformed Judaism is of even less religious significance. It is neither Judaism nor Christianity, but a pitiful remnant of the Age of Enlightenment. Its ideas did not originate on Jewish soil but in a wretched period of the Christian church, a period long since overcome by the church itself. Both factions boast, of course, that the Jews are the bearers of the loftiest religious and moral ideals for mankind and the world and that it is the mission of Jewry, now and in the future, to maintain those ideals, to develop and spread them. On this point the Jewish press, from right to left, stands united. . . .

Here we wish to make our request. We ask: *please, be a little more modest!* We do not deny that Israel carried the knowledge of the one

Source: Paul W. Massing, *Rehearsal for Destruction: A Study of Political Anti-Semitism in Imperial Germany* (New York: H. Fertig, 1967), pp. 278–87.

and only God through ancient times like a sacred flame until Christ came and brought the more perfect faith, the richer conception of God, and the higher truth. But it is a historic fact that the people of Israel time and again relapsed into the grossest idolatry, that God was able to suppress apostasy for short periods only by sending outstanding personalities. It is God's grace rather than Israel's merit that the doctrine of the one God has been preserved for mankind. It is just as indubitable that the ideas of freedom of religion, of tolerance in the modern sense, do not fit into the character of the Old Testament. Whoever violated the Sabbath was stoned, the priests of Baal were slaughtered. This was inherent in the Jewish legal institutions and we are far from blaming the Old Testament for it.

But it is quite out of order when Jews claim as their own ideas which were historically altogether unknown to their religion. And furthermore they are quite aware of the fact that they had a caste of priests—certainly the opposite of equality; that they had slavery—certainly the opposite of freedom; that they indulged in polygamy—certainly the opposite of ideal family life. Only Teutonic-Christian life put an end to these abuses. It is true, Israel had an enlightened economic legislation, social forms of property ownership, the prohibition of usury, and the greatest charity toward the poor. But we have only to mention these things to realize the fearful chasm between the Old Testament and modern Jewry. It was German law alone that protected the concept of common property, the Christian church alone that decreed the prohibition of usury; it is precisely here that the faults and sins of modern Jewry are plainly revealed.

Even if we presume for once that this lofty mission really is Israel's permanent task, who, then, are those thinkers and poets, who, inspired by the divine spirit, preach, praise and honor the living God? Perhaps the editors of the *Tageblatt?*[2] Or the scholars of the *Kladderadatsch?*[3] Where is the school of the prophets of the Holy Spirit which trains young men for their world mission? Where are the missionary posts? Where are the missionaries? Perhaps at the stock exchanges of Berlin, Vienna and Paris? Alas, the Jews should not be told such foolishness. For it is their ominous fate that, having failed Christ, they have lost their divine course, have abandoned their sublime mission. Confronted with the Lord's sharp-edged alternative—"Thou canst not serve both God and Mammon"—they now worship the idol of gold, having forsaken the path of God. . . .

And in spite of this truth, in spite of their utter lack of religious creativeness, they stick to their delusion of being a religious power. The truth is that modern Jewry is most certainly a power against religion; a power which bitterly fights Christianity everywhere, uproots Christian faith as well as national feeling in the people, in their stead offering them nothing but the idolatrous admiration of Jewry such as it is, with no other content but its self-admiration. . . .

The question is: What shall be done? We believe that Jews and Christians must try to establish a proper relationship with each other. There is no other way. Hatred of the Jews is already flaring up here and there, and this is repugnant to the Gospels. If modern Jewry continues to use the power of capital and the power of the press to bring misfortune to the nation, a final catastrophe is unavoidable. Israel must renounce its ambition to become the master of Germany. It should renounce its arrogant claim that Judaism is the religion of the future, when it is so clearly that of the past. Let not foolish Christians continue to strengthen the self-conceit of this people. Jewish orthodoxy with its circumcision is decrepit, while reformed Judaism is not a Jewish religion at all. Once Israel has realized this, it will quietly forget its alleged mission and stop trying to rob of their Christianity people who offer it hospitality and civil rights. The Jewish press must become more tolerant—that is the first prerequisite for improving the situation. The social abuses which are caused by Jewry must be eradicated by wise legislation. It will not be easy to curb Jewish capital. Only thoroughgoing legislation can bring it about. The mortgage system in real estate should be abolished and property should be inalienable and unmortgageable; the credit system should be reorganized to protect the businessman against the arbitrary power of big capital. There must be new stock and stock-exchange regulations; reintroduction of the denominational census so as to find out the disproportion between Jewish capital and Christian labor; limitation of appointments of Jewish judges in proportion to the size of the population; removal of Jewish teachers from our grammar schools, and in addition the strengthening of the Christian-Germanic spirit—are the means to put a stop to the encroachment of Jewry on Germanic life, this worst kind of usury.

Either we succeed in this and Germany will rise again, or the cancer from which we suffer will spread further. In that event our whole future is threatened and the German spirit will become Judaized. The German economy will become impoverished. These are our slogans: A return to a Germanic rule in law and business, a return to the Christian faith. May every man do his duty, and God will help us.

NOTES

1. Adolf Stoecker (1835–1909), German anti-Semitic preacher and politician. Imperial court chaplain from 1874, Stoecker was a member of the Prussian diet from 1879 to 1898. In 1881 he was elected to the Reichstag where he served (except from 1893 to 1898) until 1908. In 1878 he founded the Christian Social Workers' party, renamed Christian Social party in 1881. Through his party Stoecker created a right-wing mass movement of discontented artisans and small shop owners, who were later joined by members of the conservative educated classes. He was a powerful demagogue who knew how to channel discontent into anti-Semitism. His inflammatory speeches paved the way for the rampant anti-Semitic movement in Berlin in the early 1880s which spread to provincial cities and the countryside. The above is the text of a speech that was delivered at the Christian Social Workers' party rally of September 19, 1879.

2. *Berliner Tageblatt* was a Berlin daily owned by Jews and had a large proportion of Jews on the staff.

3. *Kladderadatsch* was a weekly of political satire, founded in 1848.

HEINRICH VON TREITSCHKE
17. A Word About Our Jewry[1]

Among the symptoms of a great change in mood in the German nation, none appears so strange as the violent movement against the Jews. Until a few months ago, the notorious *reverse* "Hep-Hep call"[2] was still dominant in Germany. About the national shortcomings of the Germans, the French, and all other nations, everybody could freely say the worst things; but if somebody dared to speak in just and moderate terms about some undeniable weakness of the Jewish character, he was immediately branded as a barbarian and religious persecutor by nearly all of the newspapers. Today we have already come to the

Source: Heinrich von Treitschke, *A Word About Our Jewry,* ed. Ellis Rivkin and trans. Helen Lederer (Cincinnati: Hebrew Union College—Institute of Religion, n.d.), pp. 1–7. Reprinted by permission of Dr. Ellis Rivkin.

point where the majority of the Breslau voters—obviously not in wild excitement but with quiet deliberation—conspired not to elect a Jew to the diet under any circumstances. Anti-Semitic societies are formed, the "Jewish question" is discussed in noisy meetings, a flood of anti-Semitic pamphlets appears on the market. There is only too much of dirt and brutality in these doings, and it is impossible to suppress one's disgust when one notices that some of these incendiary pamphlets obviously come from Jewish pens. It is well known that since Pfefferkorn[3] and Eisenmenger[4] there were always many former Jews among the most fanatical Jew-haters. But is there really nothing but mob brutality and business envy at the bottom of this noisy activity? Are these outbreaks of a deep, long-suppressed anger really only a momentary outburst, as hollow and irrational as the Teutonic anti-Semitism of 1819? No,—the instinct of the masses has in fact clearly recognized a great danger, a serious sore spot of the new German national life; the current expression "the German Jewish question" is more than an empty phrase.

If the English and the French talk with some disdain of the prejudice of the Germans against the Jews we must reply to them: "You don't know us; you live in happier circumstances which make the rise of such prejudices impossible." The number of Jews in Western Europe is so small that they cannot have any noticeable influence upon the morality of the nation. But our country is invaded year after year by multitudes of assiduous pants-selling youths from the inexhaustible cradle of Poland, whose children and grand-children are to be the future rulers of Germany's exchanges and Germany's press. This immigration grows visibly in numbers and the question becomes more and more serious how this alien nation can be assimilated. The Jews of the Western and Southern European countries belong mostly to the Spanish branch which looks back on a comparatively proud history and which always adjusted comparatively easily to the Western way of life. In fact, the great majority of them have become good Frenchmen, Englishmen, Italians, as far as can be expected from a people of such pure blood and such distinct peculiarity. We Germans, however, have to deal with Jews of the Polish branch, which bears the deep scars of centuries of Christian tyranny. According to experience they are incomparably more alien to the European, and especially to the German national character.

What we have to demand from our Jewish fellow-citizens is simple: that they become Germans, regard themselves simply and justly as Germans, without prejudice to their faith and their old sacred past which all of us hold in reverence; for we do not want an era of German-Jewish mixed culture to follow after thousands of years of German civilization. It would be a sin to forget that a great number of Jews, baptized and unbaptized, Felix Mendelssohn,[5] Veit,[6] Riesser[7] and others, not to mention the ones now living, were Germans in the best sense of the word, men in whom we revere the noble and fine traits of the German spirit. At the same time it cannot be denied that there are numerous and powerful groups among our Jews who definitely do not have the good will to become simply Germans. It is painful enough to talk about these things. Even conciliatory words are easily misunderstood here. I think, however, some of my Jewish friends will admit, with deep regret, that recently a dangerous spirit of arrogance has arisen in Jewish circles and that the influence of Jewry upon our national life, which in former times was often beneficial, has recently often been harmful. I refer the reader to *The History of the Jews* by Graetz.[8] What a fanatical fury against the "arch enemy" Christianity, what deadly hatred of the purest and most powerful exponents of German character, from Luther to Goethe and Fichte! And what hollow, offensive self-glorification! Here it is proved with continuous satirical invective that the nation of Kant was really educated to humanity by the Jews only, that the language of Lessing and Goethe became sensitive to beauty, spirit, and wit only through Boerne and

Heine! Is there any English Jew who would dare to slander in such manner the land which guards and protects him? And this stubborn contempt for the German *goyim* is not at all the attitude of a single fanatic. There is no German city which does not count many honest, respectable Jewish firms among its merchants. But it cannot be denied that the Jews have contributed their part to the promoting of business with its dishonesty and bold cupidity, that they share heavily in the guilt for the contemptible materialism of our age which regards every kind of work only as business and threatens to suffocate the old simple pride and joy the German felt in his work. In many thousands of German villages we have the Jewish usurer. Among the leading names of art and science there are not many Jews. The greater is the number of Semitic hustlers among the third rank talents. And how firmly this bunch of literateurs hangs together! How safely this insurance company for immortality works, based on the tested principle of mutuality, so that every Jewish poetaster receives his one-day fame, dealt out by the newspapers immediately and in cash, without delayed interest.

The greatest danger, however, is the unjust influence of the Jews in the press—a fateful consequence of our old narrow-minded laws which kept the Jews out of most learned professions. For ten years public opinion in many German cities was "made" mostly by Jewish pens. It was a misfortune for the Liberals, and one of the reasons of the decline of the party, that their papers gave too much scope to the Jews. The present weakness of the press is the necessary reaction against this unnatural state of things. The little man is firmly convinced now that the Jews write everything in the newspapers and he will not believe anything they say any longer. Our newspapers owe much to the Jewish talent. The acuteness and nimble quickness of the Jewish mind found the arena of the press always a congenial field. But here, too, the effect was two-edged. Boerne was the first to introduce into our journalism the peculiar shameless way of talking about the fatherland [in an] off-hand [manner] and without any reverence, like an outsider, as if mockery of Germany did not cut deeply into the heart of every individual German.[9] To this was added that unfortunate busybody "me-too" attitude, which has to have a hand in everything and does not even refrain from passing judgment on the inner affairs of the Christian churches. What Jewish journalists write in mockery and satirical remarks against Christianity is downright revolting, and such blasphemies are offered to our people as the newest acquisitions of "German" Enlightenment! The moment emancipation was gained the Jews insisted boldly on their "certificate," demanded literal parity in everything, forgetful of the fact that we Germans are, after all, a Christian nation and the Jews are only a minority. It has happened that the removal of Christian pictures was demanded, and even the celebration of the Sabbath in mixed schools.[10]

If we consider all this—and much more could be added—then the noisy agitation of the moment appears only as a brutal and spiteful but natural reaction of the Germanic national consciousness against an alien element which has usurped too much space in our life. It has at least the one involuntary merit of having liberated us from the ban of a tacit falsehood. It is already a gain that an evil which everybody sensed but which nobody wanted to touch is now discussed openly. Let us not deceive ourselves: The movement is deep and strong. A few jokes about the words of wisdom from the mouths of Christian-Socialist soap-box orators will not be sufficient to suppress it. Even in the best educated circles, among men who would reject with horror any thought of Christian fanaticism or national arrogance, we hear today the cry, as from one mouth, "the Jews are our misfortune!"[11]

There can be no talk among the intelligent of an abolition or even of a limitation of the Emancipation. That would be an open injustice, a betrayal of the fine traditions of our state, and would accentuate rather than mitigate the national contrasts. What made the

Jews of France and England harmless and often beneficent members of society was at the bottom nothing but the energy of the national pride and the firmly rooted national way of life of these two nations which look back on centuries of national culture. Ours is a young nation. Our country still lacks national style, instinctive pride, a firmly developed individuality; that is the reason why we were defenseless against alien manners for so long. But we are in the process of acquiring these qualities, and we can only wish that our Jews recognize in time the change which is now occurring in Germany as a necessary consequence of the foundation of the German state. In some places there are Jewish societies against usury which silently do much good. They are the work of intelligent Israelites who have recognized that their fellow-Jews must adjust to the customs and ideas of their Christian fellow-citizens. Much remains to be done in this direction. It is not possible to change the hard German heads into Jewish heads. The only way out therefore is for our Jewish fellow-citizens to make up their minds without reservation to be Germans, as many of them have done already long ago, to their advantage and ours. There will never be a complete solution. There has always been an abyss between Europeans and Semites, since the time when Tacitus complained about the *odium generis humani*. There will always be Jews who are nothing else but German speaking orientals. There will also always be a specifically Jewish education; and, as a cosmopolitan power, it has a historical right to existence. But the contrast can be mitigated if the Jews, who talk so much about tolerance, become truly tolerant themselves and show some respect for the faith, the customs, and the feelings of the German people which has long ago atoned for old injustice and given them human and civil rights. The lack of such respect in many of our Jewish fellow-citizens in commerce and in literature is the basic reason for the passionate anger in our days.

It is not a pleasant sight, this raging and quarrelling, this boiling up of unfinished ideas in our new Germany. But we cannot help our being the most passionate of all nations, although we called ourselves phlegmatics so often. New ideas never broke through in our country other than under bad convulsions. May God grant that we come out of the ferment and unrest of these exciting years with a stricter concept of the state and its obligations and with a more vigorous national consciousness.

NOTES

1. Heinrich von Treitschke (1834–1896). In 1879 and 1880 this renowned German historian published a series of articles in the *Preussische Jahrbuecher*—a prestigious academic journal which he edited. These articles, entitled "Ein Wort ueber unser Judenthum," justified the growing hostility toward the Jews in the wake of the unification of Germany. Treitschke held that the core of the problem was Jewry's contradictory desire to preserve its national identity while simultaneously claiming the right to participate fully in the national life of Germany. Accordingly, he urged the Jews to rid themselves of their frivolous arrogance and to pursue a genuine and rapid assimilation into German culture and society. His articles on the Jewish question generated considerable controversy, particularly in educated circles.

2. "Hep! Hep!" A derogatory rallying cry against the Jews common in Germany. It is also the name given to a series of anti-Jewish riots that broke out in August 1819 in Germany and spread to Denmark.

3. Johannes Pfefferkorn (1469–c.1521), German-Jewish convert to Christianity and writer of anti-Jewish tracts. His knowledge of Jewish sources was minimal, and, as a result of a virulent controversy with the humanist scholar Johannes Reuchlin, his name became proverbial for unprincipled denigrators of their own origin and faith.

4. Johann Andreas Eisenmenger (1654–1704), a German Christian Hebraist who assiduously studied Jewish sources for more than ten years before completing his work denouncing the Jewish religion. Entitled *Entdecktes Judenthum* [Judaism un-

masked], this book, which purports to prove Judaism's intrinsic misanthropy, had a formative influence on modern anti-Semitic polemics.

5. Jakob Ludwig Felix Mendelssohn-Bartholdy (1809–1847), German composer and grandson of Moses Mendelssohn. Of Jewish birth, Felix was baptized and raised as a Protestant. He showed musical talent at an early age and became a brilliant pianist.

6. Moritz Veit (1808–1864), member of a wealthy Jewish banking family in Berlin. He was a prominent publisher, politician and leader of the Berlin Jewish community.

7. Gabriel Riesser (1806–1863), German-Jewish political figure and an indefatigable champion of Jewish civil equality. See chapter 3, document 20.

8. Heinrich Graetz (1817–1891), German-Jewish historian and Bible scholar. His monumental *Geschicte der Juden (History of the Jews,* 11 volumes) was the first comprehensive attempt to write a history of the Jews from a Jewish viewpoint and to regard the Jews as a living people. Treitschke is referring to the eleventh volume of Graetz's work (1868) in which the author's passionate desire to foster Jewish pride is particularly manifest. Graetz exuberantly celebrates the Jewish contribution to German culture and at the same time denounces German national heroes like Luther and Kant for their anti-Semitism. He also unhesitatingly discusses Christianity's role in the suffering of the Jews, and concludes that Christian ethics would be an inadequate basis for a healthy society. Treitschke viewed Graetz's "Jewish nationalism" as parochial and indicative of his unwillingness to identify with the German nation and culture. In the public debate following Treitschke's attack on Graetz, most Jewish writers, while condemning Treitschke's anti-Semitic outbursts, nevertheless dissociated themselves from Graetz's brand of Jewish "national pride."

9. See chapter 6, document 7. Treitschke is apparently referring to Boerne's "Letters from Paris," containing ascerbic and radical criticism of German society. Published in a liberal newspaper in Frankfurt am Main, these letters were widely read and debated.

10. Cf. Treitschke's remarks in this paragraph to Bruno Bauer's argument (document 9 of this chapter) that the demand for Jewish emancipation would only be valid if the Jews were to fight for the de-Christianization—as well as de-Judaization—of the state.

11. This phrase was to become one of the slogans of German anti-Semitism—it was later adopted by the Nazis. Heinrich Class, a student of Treitschke and later the president of the Pan-German League once observed that his teacher's "phrase, 'the Jews are our misfortune,' became part of my body and soul when I was twenty years old; it essentially influenced my later political work" (cited in Paul W. Massing, *Rehearsal for Destruction* [New York: H. Fertig, 1967], p. 246, n. 37).

THEODOR MOMMSEN[1]
18. Another Word About Our Jewry

. . . It is the fate of our generation—an opportunity rarely provided by history—that the great goals we thought lay before us have now been reached by our nation. Anyone who still remembers the assemblies in which the Estates held a consulting vote, and the Germany which showed one lone color on the map, will consider no price too high for our parliament and our imperial flag come what may. But one has to be very steadfast and far-sighted in order to be happy under the existing circumstances. The immediate consequences [of the unification] remind one of the saying that fate punishes him whose wishes have come true. While Germany was still in the making, nobody—as befits those

Source: Theodor Mommsen, *Auch ein Wort ueber unser Judentum* (Berlin: Weidmannische Buchhandlung, 1880), pp. 1–16. Trans. here by J. Hessing.

who are fighting for a common goal—asked about religious or racial differences, about conflicting interests of rural and urban population, of trader and industrialist. . . .

How, then, does the status of the Jews within our people differ from that of the Saxons or Pomeranians? It is true that they are neither the descendants of Istaevo nor of Hermino and Ingaevo;[2] and our common descent from Noah will certainly not suffice if the genealogy is supposed to make the German. Our nation, however, would have to do without a lot more than just the Children of Israel if its current stock were to be corrected according to Tacitus' *Germania*.[3] Years ago, Mr. Quatrefages[4] proved that only the central states are of truly Germanic descent, while *la race prussienne* is a mass actually made up of depraved slaves and other human refuse; it so happened that *la race germanique* and *la race prussienne* later combined to become the trailblazers for the German nation, and that all those who were retreating before them did not seem to notice any difference between them. Anybody who is really familiar with history will know that the transformation of a nationality is a gradual development with numerous and manifold transitions. Historically as well as practically, only he who is alive is in the right; just as the descendants of the French Colony in Berlin are by no means Frenchmen born in Germany, so our Jewish compatriots are nothing less than Germans. . . .

What does it mean that [Treitschke (see preceding document)] demands that our Jewish compatriots become Germans? They are Germans already, just as I am, and just as he is. He may be more virtuous than they are; but do virtues make a German? What gives us the right to remove our compatriots who are of this or that group from our German ranks? Surely this right is not derived from the few defects which we attribute to this group, even if we do so with a certain amount of justification. However harshly we may judge these defects of our compatriots, however strictly we may deny them any mitigating circumstances—in the last resort, we shall merely come to the conclusion, logically as well as practically, that Jews are Germans who have had to carry more than the normal share of original sin. Serious people who have understood this will have no doubt that harmful results of these defects ought to be met by preventive and punitive legislation. The status of German citizens, however, should not be defined by any supposed quantity of original sin on their part.

This insight, however, is not enough. There is a need for a clearer and more refined conception of the inequality between German Occidentals and Semitic blood. With the war of the Jews, we—whose nation has just been unified—enter upon a dangerous path. Our tribes are very unequal among themselves. None of them lacks their own specific defects, and our mutual love is not so old that it would not easily corrode. Today we are concerned with the Jews—whether only with the unbaptized or even with the baptized, and, in the latter case, to what degree, nobody cares to define. The question could soon bring about the breakdown of the cordial understanding reached by the pastoral and the Germanic orthodoxy. Any future regulations concerning the mixture of blood really belongs to the domain of Ernst Dohm.[5] . . .

By no means do I wish to deny that the peculiarities of the Jews living among us are felt more sharply than those of other tribes or even nations. They are more distinct, and the suppression of the Jews—which for thousands of years has been equally harmful to German Jews and German Christians—has led them to adopt an artificial, and at times gruesome, manner. Our historical and literary development bears the marks of this, and no historian can keep quiet about it. From an international point of view, the history of the Rothschild family is more important than the internal history of the state of Saxony, and does it not matter that this is the history of a German Jew? Our century may not have produced a poet more gifted than Heine; and who could understand his intellectual playing with the blood of his own heart and his creative talent, so powerful in sensuality and fantasy, but devoid of all Shakespearean tragedy, without remembering his origin? Certainly, there are differences; and they are of such a nature that the cult of the Jews during a certain period, or the fear of the Jews—this being the shape which the cult tends to take on nowadays—seems to belong to the most simple-minded confusions of which our nation has loved, and still loves, to avail itself. These failures and defects, however, are balanced by talents and advantages which in turn have partly been acquired under the pressure of the very same agitation directed against the Jews. That the purest and most idealistic philosopher lives and suffered as a Jew was no matter of chance;[6] and Jewish philanthropy, toward Christians as well, may serve the latter as an example. Here as elsewhere, the lights and the shadows are mingled, and nobody will dare to determine the precise degree of the mixture, unless he is a court preacher.[7] Just as the Jews were an element of national decomposition in the Roman state,[8] so they doubtlessly are an element of tribal decomposition in Germany. That is why in the German capital, where the tribes mingle more freely than elsewhere, the Jews hold a position for which they are envied in other places. Such processes of decomposition are often necessary, but they are never pleasant. Their consequences are inevitably negative, in Germany less so than in Rome, because our nation is no pale chimera as the nation of the Caesars used to be. I am not so estranged from my homeland, however, that I do not painfully feel the loss of something I used to have and that my children will miss. But the happiness of children and the pride of men do not go together. A certain amount of mutual adjustment on the part of the tribes is necessary, resulting in the formation of a German nationality in which no tribal ingredient will be dominant. The great cities, and first of all Berlin, must become the natural protagonists in this process. I do not consider it at all unfortunate that the Jews have been active in this direction for centuries. It is my opinion that Divine Providence, much more so than Stoecker, has understood very well why a few percent of Israel ought to be added to the Germanic metal. . . .

In conclusion, let me say a word about the way in which the Jews themselves react [to anti-Semitism]. It is self-evident that our nation, by right and honor, must protect the principle of equality before the law and defend itself from open offence as well as from discrimination by the authorities. This duty, which we first of all owe to ourselves, is by no means dependent on the appropriate conduct of the Jews. We cannot, however, protect the Jews from the estrangement and inequality with which the German Christian still tends to treat them. There is danger in this, as the present moment shows, for the Jews as well as for us—the danger of a civil war waged by a majority against a minority; even the possibility of such a war would be a national calamity. This, in part, is the fault of the Jews as well. The word *Christianity,* in our day no longer means what it used to mean; nevertheless it is the only word which still defines the entire international civilization of our day and which numerous millions of people of our highly populated globe accept as their intrinsic link. It is possible to remain outside these boundaries and yet live within the nation, but it is difficult and fraught with danger. He whose conscience—be it for positive or for negative reasons—does not permit him to renounce his Judaism and accept Christianity, will act accordingly, but he should be prepared to bear the consequences; issues of this nature can only be resolved in privacy, not in public. It is a notorious fact, however, that a great number of Jews are prevented from conversion not by their conscience, but by quite different emotions which I can understand but not justify. The numerous specifically Jewish societies which have been founded in Berlin, for instance, do not seem—except where they do not serve purely religious ends—to have any positive purpose at all. I should never join a philanthropic institution whose statutes would oblige me to support nobody but the people of Holstein; and while I respect the endeavors and achievements of these societies, I view their separate existence as nothing more than an anachronistic phenomenon from the days of protected Jews [*Schutzjudenzeit*]. If such anachronistic feudal phenomena are to be abolished on the one side, they will have to disappear on the other side as well; and on both sides there is still much to be done. The admission into a large nation has its price. The people of Hanover, Hessen and Schleswig-Holstein are prepared to pay the price, and we all feel that they are giving up a part of themselves. But we make this sacrifice to our common fatherland. The Jews, too, will not be led by another Moses into the Promised Land; whether they sell trousers or write books, it is their duty to do away with their particularities wherever they can do so without offending their conscience. They must make up their minds and tear down all barriers between themselves and their German compatriots.

NOTES

1. Theodor Mommsen (1817–1903), German classical scholar and historian. A staunch liberal member of the Prussian and German parliaments and a luminary of Berlin University, Mommsen was active on behalf of Russian Jewry and consistently opposed all anti-Semitic manifestations. He was the sole Christian to attack Treitschke publicly. Significantly, Mommsen, despite his liberalism, had no sympathy with the Jews' wish to preserve their cultural identity and religious independence and called upon them to abandon their separateness by assimilating in a more thorough fashion.

2. The three sons of Mannus, son of the god Tuisto, son of Earth, from whom, according to ancient legends, the Germans are descended.

3. Cornelius Tacitus (56 C.E.–c.120 C.E.), Roman orator and historian. His *Germania,* published in 98 C.E., is a valuable source of ethnographical information regarding the origins of the Germans.

4. Jean Louis Armand Quatrefages (1810–1892), French anthropologist who conducted craniological research.

5. Ernst Dohm (1819–1883), German writer and political satirist.

6. Mommsen is apparently referring to Hermann Cohen (1842–1918), the founder of the neo-Kantian school of philosophy at the University of Marburg. On Cohen see chapter 10, document 16, note 1.

7. The reference is to Adolf Stoecker. See document 16 in this chapter.

8. Mommsen first made his assessment of the Jews' historical role in a passage in his *History of Rome* (3 volumes, 1854–1856). Although Mommsen took a positive attitude here to the Jewish role in furthering the breakdown of parochial boundaries, anti-Semites frequently cited this very passage as confirming that the Jews were an alien cosmopolitan element in European history.

THEODOR FRITSCH
19. The Racists' Decalogue[1]

1. Be proud of being a German and strive earnestly and steadily to practice the inherited virtues of our people, courage, faithfulness and veracity, and to inspire and develop these in thy children.

2. Thou shalt know that thou, together

Source: Theodor Fritsch, *Antisemiten-Katechismus* (Leipzig, 1883), pp. 858ff. Reprinted here with permission from *Rehearsal for Destruction: A Study of Political Anti-Semitism in Imperial Germany* by Paul W. Massing (New York: H. Fertig, 1967), pp. 306–7.

with all thy fellow Germans, regardless of faith or creed, hast a common implacable foe. His name is Jew.

3. Thou shalt keep thy blood pure. Consider it a crime to soil the noble Aryan breed of thy people by mingling it with the Jewish breed. For thou must know that Jewish blood is everlasting, putting the Jewish stamp on body and soul unto the farthest generations.

4. Thou shalt be helpful to thy fellow German and further him in all matters not counter to the German conscience, the more so if he be pressed by the Jew. Thou shalt at once take into court any offense or crime committed by the Jew in deed, word or letter, that comes to thy knowledge, lest the Jew abuse the laws of our country with impunity.

5. Thou shalt have no social intercourse with the Jew. Avoid all contact and community with the Jew and keep him away from thyself and thy family, especially thy daughters, lest they suffer injury of body and soul.

6. Thou shalt have no business relations with the Jews. Never choose a Jew as a business partner, nor borrow nor buy from him, and keep your wife, too, from doing so. Thou shalt sell nothing to him, nor use him as an agent in thy transactions, that thou mayest remain free and not become slave unto the Jew nor help to increase his money, which is the power by which he enslaves our people.

7. Thou shalt drive the Jew from thy own breast and take no example from Jewish tricks and Jewish wiles, for thou shalt never match the Jew in trickery but forfeit thy honor and earn the contempt of thy fellow Germans and the punishment of the courts.

8. Thou shalt not entrust thy rights to a Jewish lawyer, nor thy body to a Jewish physician, nor thy children to a Jewish teacher lest thy honor, body and soul suffer harm.

9. Thou shalt not lend ear nor give credence to the Jew. Keep away all Jewish writings from thy German home and hearth lest their lingering poison may unnerve and corrupt thyself and thy family.

10. Thou shalt use no violence against the Jews because it is unworthy of thee and against the law. But if a Jew attack thee, ward off his Semitic insolence with German wrath.

NOTE

1. Theodor Fritsch (1852–1933), German anti-Semitic publicist and politician and one of the leading early racists. In 1883 he founded the Hammer Publishing House whose first production was the *Antisemiten-Katechismus* from which the "Decalogue" is taken. Later renamed *Handbuch der Judenfrage,* it was published in more than forty editions, inspiring the Nazis, who honored Fritsch as their *Altmeister*.

HOUSTON STEWART CHAMBERLAIN
20. The Foundations of the Nineteenth Century[1]

. . . Out of the midst of the chaos towers, like a sharply defined rock amid the formless ocean, one single people, a numerically insignificant people—the Jews. This one race has established as its guiding principle the purity of the blood; it alone possesses, there-

Source: Houston Stewart Chamberlain, *The Foundations of the Nineteenth Century,* trans. John Lees (New York: John Kane Co., 1914), vol. 1, pp. 253–54, 269–73, 330–31.

fore, physiognomy and character. If we contemplate the southern and eastern centers of culture in the world-empire in its downfall, and let no sympathies or antipathies pervert our judgment, we must confess that the Jews were at that time the only people deserving respect. We may well apply to them the words of Goethe, "the faith broad, narrow the thought." In comparison with Rome and still more so with Hellas their intellectual horizon appears so narrow, their mental capacities so limited, that we seem to have before us an entirely new type of being; but the narrowness and want of originality in thought are fully counterbalanced by the power of faith, a faith which might be very simply defined as "faith in self." And since this faith in self included faith in a higher being, it did not lack ethical significance. However poor the Jewish "law" may appear, when compared with the religious creations of the various Indo-European peoples, it possessed a unique advantage in the fallen Roman Empire of that time: it was, in fact, a law; a law which men humbly obeyed, and this very obedience was bound to be of great ethical import in a world of such lawlessness. Here, as everywhere, we shall find that the influence of the Jews—for good and for evil—lies in their character, not in their intellectual achievements. Certain historians of the nineteenth century, even men so intellectually pre-eminent as Count Gobineau,[2] have supported the view that Judaism has always had merely a disintegrating influence upon all peoples. I cannot share this conviction. In truth, where the Jews become very numerous in a strange land, they may make it their object to fulfill the promises of their Prophets and with the best will and conscience to "consume the strange peoples"; did they not say of themselves, even in the lifetime of Moses, that they were "like locusts"? However, we must distinguish between Judaism and the Jews and admit that Judaism as an idea is one of the most conservative ideas in the world. The idea of physical race-unity and race-purity, which is the very essence of Judaism, signified the recognition of a fundamental physiological fact of life; wherever we observe life from the hyphomycetes[3] to the noble horse we see the importance of "race"; Judaism made this law of nature sacred. And this is the reason why it triumphantly prevailed at that critical moment in the history of the world, when a rich legacy was waiting in vain for worthy heirs. It did not further, but rather put a stop to, universal disintegration. The Jewish dogma was like a sharp acid which is poured into a liquid which is being decomposed in order to clear it and keep it from further decomposition. Though this acid may not be to the taste of every one, yet it has played so decisive a part in the history of the epoch of culture to which we belong that we ought to be grateful to the giver; instead of being indignant about it, we shall do better to inform ourselves thoroughly concerning the significance of this "entrance of the Jews into the history of the West," an event which in any case exercised inestimable influence upon our whole culture, and which has not yet reached its full growth.

Nothing is so convincing as the consciousness of the possession of race. The man who belongs to a distinct, pure race, never loses the sense of it. The guardian angel of his lineage is ever at his side, supporting him where he loses his foothold, warning him like the Socratic demon where he is in danger of going astray, compelling obedience, and forcing him to undertakings which, deeming them impossible, he would never have dared to attempt. Weak and erring like all that is human, a man of this stamp recognizes himself, as others recognize him, by the sureness of his character, and by the fact that his actions are marked by a certain simple and peculiar greatness, which finds its explanation in his distinctly typical and superpersonal qualities. Race lifts a man above himself: it endows him with extraordinary—I might almost say supernatural—powers, so entirely does it distinguish him from the individual who springs from the chaotic jumble of peoples drawn from all parts of the world. And should this man of pure origin be perchance gifted above his fellows, then the fact of race strengthens and elevates him on every hand, and he becomes a genius towering over the rest of mankind, not because he has been thrown upon the earth like a flaming meteor by a freak of nature, but because he soars heavenward like some strong and stately tree, nourished by thousands and thousands of roots—no solitary individual, but the living sum of untold souls striving for the same goal. He who has eyes to see at once detects race in animals. It shows itself in the whole habit of the beast, and proclaims itself in a hundred peculiarities which defy analysis; nay more, it proves itself by achievements, for its possession invariably leads to something excessive and out of the common—even to that which is exaggerated and not free from bias. Goethe's dictum, "only that which is extravagant makes greatness," is well known. That is the very quality which a thoroughbred race reared from superior materials bestows upon its individual descendants—something "extravagant"—and, indeed, what we learn from every racehorse, every thoroughbred fox-terrier, every Cochin China fowl, is the very lesson which the history of mankind so eloquently teaches us! Is not the Greek in the fullness of his glory an unparalleled example of this "extravagance"? And do we not see this "extravagance" first make its appearance when immigration from the North has ceased, and the various strong breeds of men, isolated on the peninsula once and for all, begin to fuse into a new race, brighter and more brilliant, where, as in Athens, the racial blood flows from many sources—simpler and more resisting where, as in Lacedaemon,[4] even this mixture of blood had been barred out? Is the race not as it were extinguished, as soon as fate wrests the land from its proud exclusiveness and incorporates it in a greater whole? Does not Rome teach us the same lesson? Has not in this case also a special mixture of blood produced an absolutely new race, similar in qualities and capacities to no later one, endowed with exuberant power? And does not victory in this case effect what disaster did in that, but only much more quickly? Like a cataract the stream of strange blood overflooded the almost depopulated Rome and at once the Romans ceased to be. Would one small tribe from among all the Semites have become a world-embracing power had it not made "purity of race" its inflexible fundamental law? In days when so much nonsense is talked concerning this question, let Disraeli teach us that the whole significance of Judaism lies in its purity of race, that this alone gives it power and duration, and just as it has outlived the people of antiquity, so, thanks to its knowledge of this law of nature, will it outlive the constantly mingling races of today.

What is the use of detailed scientific investigations as to whether there are distinguishable races? whether race has a worth? how this is possible? and so on. We turn the tables and say: it is evident that there are such races; it is a fact of direct experience that the quality of the race is of vital importance; your province is only to find out the how and the wherefore, not to deny the facts themselves in order to indulge your ignorance.

Direct experience, however, offers us a series of quite different observations on race, all of which may gradually contribute to the extension of our knowledge as well as to its definiteness. In contrast to the new, growing, Anglo-Saxon race, look, for instance, at the Sephardim, the so-called "Spanish Jews"; here we find how a genuine race can by purity keep itself noble for centuries and tens of centuries, but at the same time how very necessary it is to distinguish between the nobly reared portions of a nation and the rest. In England, Holland and Italy there are still genuine Sephardim but very few, since they can scarcely any longer avoid crossing with the Ashkenazim (the so-called "German Jews"). Thus, for example, the Montefiores of the present generation have all without exception married German Jewesses. But every one who has travelled in the East of Europe, where the genuine Sephardim still as far as possible avoid all intercourse with German Jews, for whom they have an almost comical repugnance, will agree with me when I say that it is only when one sees these men and has intercourse with them that one begins to comprehend the significance of Judaism in the history of the world. This is nobility in the fullest sense of the word, genuine nobility of race! Beautiful figures, noble heads, dignity in speech and bearing. The type is Semitic in the same sense as that of certain noble Syrians and Arabs. That out of the midst of such people prophets and psalmists could arise—that I understand at the first glance, which I honestly confess that I had never succeeded in doing when I gazed, however carefully, on the many hundred young Jews—"Bochers"—of the Friedrichstrasse in Berlin. . . .

We live today in a "Jewish age"; we may think what we like about the past history of the Jews; their present history actually takes up so much room in our own history that we cannot possibly refuse to notice them. Herder[5] in spite of his outspoken humanism had expressed the opinion that "the Jewish people is and remains in Europe an Asiatic people alien to our part of the world, bound to that old law which it received in a distant climate, and which according to its own confession it cannot do away with." Quite correct. But this alien people, everlastingly alien, because—as Herder well remarks—it is indissolubly bound to an alien law that is hostile to all other peoples—this alien people has become precisely in the course of the nineteenth century a disproportionately important and in many spheres actually dominant constituent of our life. Even a hundred years ago that same witness had sadly to confess that the "ruder nations of Europe" were "willing slaves of Jewish usury"; today he could say the same of by far the greatest part of the civilized world. The possession of money in itself is, however, of least account; our governments, our law, our science, our commerce, our literature, our art . . . practically all branches of our life have become more or less willing slaves of the Jews, and drag the feudal fetter, if not yet on two, at least on one leg. In the meantime the "alien" element emphasized by Herder has become more and more prominent; a hundred years ago it was rather indistinctly and vaguely felt; now it has asserted and proved itself, and so forced itself on the attention of even the most inattentive. The Indo-European, moved by ideal motives, opened the gates in friendship: the Jew rushed in like an enemy, stormed all positions and planted the flag of his, to us, alien nature—I will not say on the ruins, but on the breaches of our genuine individuality.

Are we for that reason to revile the Jews? That would be as ignoble as it is unworthy and senseless. The Jews deserve admiration, for they have acted with absolute consistency according to the logic and truth of their own individuality, and never for a moment have they allowed themselves to forget the sacredness of physical laws because of foolish humanitarian day-dreams which they shared only when such a policy was to their advantage. Consider with what mastery they use the law of blood to extend their power: the principal stem remains spotless, not a drop of strange blood comes in: as it stands in the Torah, "A bastard shall not enter into the congregation of the Lord; even to his tenth generation shall he not enter into the congregation of the Lord";[6] in the meantime, however, thousands of side branches are cut off and employed to infect the Indo-Europeans with Jewish blood. If that were to go on for a few centuries, there would be in Europe only one single people of pure race, that of the Jews, all the rest would be a herd of pseudo-Hebraic mestizos, a people beyond all doubt degenerate physically, mentally and morally.

NOTES

1. Houston Stewart Chamberlain (1855–1927), racist anti-Semitic author. British by birth, he chose to live in Germany after he married a daughter of Richard Wagner. Influenced by the current anti-

Semitic theories of his time, Chamberlain refined the theory of the "Nordic race" as the born leaders of mankind. Chamberlain's *Die Grundlagen des Neunzehnten Jahrhunderts* (1899) became an important guide for the Nazis. He himself was an admirer and friend of Hitler.

2. Joseph Arthur Gobineau (1816–1882), French diplomat, essayist, and author of *Essai sur l'inégalité des races humaines* (1853–1855), in which he argued that the various human races are innately unequal in talent, worth and ability to absorb and create culture. Gobineau placed the white race, in particular its "Aryan" branch, at the top of the hierarchy as the sole possessor of the supreme human values. Gobineau did not, however, associate the Aryans with any particular nation; nor was he an anti-Semite.

3. A group of simple fungi.

4. Sparta.

5. Johann Gottfried Herder (1744–1803), German philosopher and critic.

6. Deut. 23:2.

HERMANN GOEDSCHE
21. The Rabbi's Speech: The Promise of World Domination[1]

Our fathers have bequeathed to the elect of Israel the duty of gathering together once each century around the tomb of the Grand Master Caleb, the holy rabbi Simeon ben Jehuda, whose knowledge gives the elect of each generation power over all the earth and authority over all the descendants of Israel.

For eighteen centuries Israel has been at war with that power which was first promised to Abraham but which was taken from him by the Cross. Trampled underfoot, humiliated by its enemies, living ceaselessly under the threat of death, of persecution, of rape, and of every kind of violation, the people of Israel has not succumbed; and if it is dispersed over the whole earth, that is because it is to inherit the whole earth.

For eighteen centuries our wise men have been fighting the Cross courageously and with a perseverance which nothing can discourage. Gradually our people is rising up and its power increases day by day. Ours is that God of today whom Aaron raised up for us in the desert, that Golden Calf, that universal deity of the age.

The day when we shall have made ourselves the sole possessors of all the gold in the world, the real power will be in our hands, and then the promises which were made to Abraham will be fulfilled.

Gold, the greatest power on earth . . . gold, which is the strength, the recompense, the instrument of every power . . . the sum of everything that man fears and craves . . . *there* is the only mystery, the deepest understanding of the spirit that rules the world. *There* is the future!

Eighteen centuries belonged to our enemies, the present century and future centuries must belong to us, the people of Israel, and they surely will belong to us.

Now for the tenth time, in a thousand years of terrible and ceaseless war against our enemies, the elect of a given generation of the people of Israel are gathered in this cemetery, around the tomb of our Grand Master Caleb, the holy rabbi Simeon ben Jehuda, to take counsel as to how to turn to the advantage of our cause the great errors and sins which our enemies the Christians never cease to commit.

Each time the new Sanhedrin has pro-

Source: Norman Cohn, *Warrant for Genocide: The Myth of the Jewish World Conspiracy and the Protocols of the Elders of Zion* (London: Eyre and Spottiswoode, 1967).

claimed and preached a merciless struggle against the enemies; but in no earlier century were our ancestors able to concentrate in our hands so much gold, and therefore so much power, as the nineteenth century has bestowed on us. We can therefore expect, without any rash illusions, to achieve our aim soon, and we can look with confidence to our future.

Most fortunately, the persecution and the humiliations, those dark and painful days which the people of Israel endured with such heroic patience, are no more with us, thanks to the progress of civilization among the Christians, and that progress is the best shield for us to hide and act behind, so as to cross with firm and rapid strides the space that separates us from our supreme objective.

Let us just look at the material condition of Europe, let us analyse the resources which the Jews have got into their possession since the beginning of the present century simply by concentrating in their hands the huge amount of capital which they control at this moment. Thus, in Paris, London, Vienna, Berlin, Amsterdam, Hamburg, Rome, Naples, etc., and in all the Rothschild branches, everywhere the Jews are the financial masters, simply by possession of so many milliards; not to mention that in every town of second or third magnitude it is the Jews who control the currency in circulation, and that nowhere can any financial operation, any major undertaking be carried through without the direct influence of the children of Israel.

Today all reigning emperors, kings, and princes are burdened with debts contracted in keeping up large standing armies to support their toppling thrones. The stock exchange assesses and regulates those debts, and to a great extent we are masters of the stock exchange everywhere. We must therefore study how to encourage borrowing more and more, so as to make ourselves the regulators of all values and, as security for the capital we lend to countries, take the right to exploit their railways, their mines, their forests, their great ironworks and factories, and other kinds of real estate, even their taxes.

In every country agriculture will always be the greatest source of wealth. The possession of large landed property will always bring honours and much influence to the owners. From this it follows that we must concentrate on ensuring that our brothers in Israel acquire landed property on a large scale. So far as possible we must therefore encourage the splitting-up of large estates, so as to help us acquire it more quickly and more easily.

Under the pretext of helping the working classes, we must place the weight of taxation on the great landed proprietors, and when all properties have come into our hands, all the work of the Gentile proletarians will become a source of huge profits for us.

Since the Christian Church is one of our most dangerous enemies, we must work doggedly to diminish its influence; so far as possible, therefore, we must implant in the minds of those who profess the Christian religion the ideas of free thought, of scepticism, of schism, and provoke the religious disputes which are so naturally productive of divisions and sects within Christendom.

Logically, we must begin by disparaging the ministers of that religion. Let us declare open war on them, let us rouse suspicions about their piety, about their private conduct. So, by ridicule and malicious banter, we shall undermine the respect in which the profession and the cloth are held.

Each war, each revolution, each political or religious upheaval brings nearer the moment when we shall attain the supreme aim of our journey.

Trade and speculation, two branches so fertile in profits, must never leave Jewish hands, and once we have become proprietors we shall be able, thanks to the obsequiousness and the shrewdness of our agents, to penetrate to the first source of real influence and real power. It is understood that we are concerned only with those occupations which bring honours, power, or privileges, for those which demand knowledge, work, and inconvenience can and must be left to the

Gentiles. The magistrature is for us an institution of the first importance. A career at the bar does most to develop the faculty of civilization and to initiate one into the affairs of our natural enemies, the Christians, and it is in this way that we can get them at our mercy. Why should Jews not become ministers of Education, when they have so often had the portfolio of Finance? Jews must also aspire to the rank of legislators, so that they can work to abrogate the laws which those sinners and infidels, the Goyim, have made against the children of Israel, who by their unvarying devotion to the laws of Abraham are the truly faithful. But what must be obtained, what must be the object of our ceaseless efforts, is that the law against bankruptcy should be made less severe. Out of that we shall make ourselves a mine of gold which will be far richer than the mines of California ever were.

The people of Israel must direct its ambition towards that height of power which brings esteem and honours. The surest means of attaining it is to have supreme control over all industrial, financial, and commercial operations, while carefully avoiding every trap and temptation which might expose one to legal proceedings in the country's courts. In its choice of speculation the children of Israel will therefore display the prudence and tact which are the mark of its congenital talent for business.

We must be familiar with everything that earns one a distinguished position in society: philosophy, medicine, law, political economy. In a word all the branches of science, of art, of litérature, are a vast field where our successes must give us a big part and show off our talent.

These vocations are inseparable from speculation. Thus the performance even of a very mediocre musical composition will give our people a plausible excuse to put the Jewish composer on a pedestal and surround him with a radiance of glory. As for the sciences, medicine and philosophy, they too must be incorporated into our intellectual domain.

A doctor is initiated into the most intimate secrets of the family. The health and life of our mortal enemies, the Christians, are in his hands.

We must encourage marriages between Jews and Christians, for the people of Israel loses nothing by the contact and can only gain from these marriages. Our race, chosen by God, cannot be corrupted by the introduction of a certain amount of impure blood, and by these marriages our daughters will secure alliances with Christian families of some influence and power. It is right that, in exchange for the money we give, we should obtain the equivalent in influence over everything around us. To be related to Gentiles does not imply a departure from the path we have chosen to follow; on the contrary, with a little skill it will make us the arbiters of their fate.

It is desirable that Jews should refrain from taking women of our holy religion as their mistresses and that they should choose Christian virgins for that role. It would be a great gain for us to replace the sacrament of marriage in church by a simple contract before some civil authority, for then Gentile women would stream into our camp!

If gold is the first power in this world, the second is undeniably the press. But what can the second achieve without the first? As the aims listed above cannot be attained without the help of the press, our people must become the editors of all daily newspapers in all countries. Our possession of gold, our skill in devising means of exploiting mercenary instincts, will make us the arbiters of public opinion and enable us to dominate the masses.

So advancing step by step in this path, with that perseverance which is our great virtue, we will push the Gentiles back and undo their influence. We shall dictate to the world what it is to have faith, what it is to honour, and what it is to curse. Perhaps some individuals will rise up against us and will hurl insults and anathemas against us, but the docile and ignorant masses will listen to us and take our side. Once we are absolute masters of the press we will be able to transform ideas about honour, about virtue, about uprightness of character; we will be able to deal a blow against that institution which so far has been sacrosanct, the family, and we shall extripate all belief and faith in everything that our enemies the Christians have venerated up to the present and, using the allurements of the passions as our weapon, we shall declare open war on everything that people respect and venerate.

Let all this be understood and noted, let every child of Israel absorb these true principles: Then our might will grow like a gigantic tree whose branches will bear the fruits called wealth, enjoyment, power, as compensation for that hideous condition which for long centuries has been the only lot of the people of Israel. When one of our people takes a step forward, let another follow him closely; if his foot slips, let him be picked up and succoured by his co-religionists. If a Jew is summoned before the courts of the country where he lives, let his brothers in religion hasten to give him aid and assistance; but only if the accused has acted in accordance with the Law of Israel, so strictly observed and kept for so many centuries!

Our people is conservative, faithful to the religious ceremonies and the customs bequeathed to us by our ancestors.

It is in our interest that we should at least make a show of zeal for the social questions of the moment, especially for improving the lot of the workers, but in reality our efforts must be geared to getting control of this movement of public opinion and directing it.

The blindness of the masses, their readiness to surrender to that resounding but empty eloquence that fills the public squares, make them an easy prey and a double instrument, of popularity and of credit. We will have no difficulty in finding as much eloquence among our people for the expression of false sentiments as Christians find in their sincerity and enthusiasm.

So far as possible we must talk to the proletariat, bring it into subjection to those who have the handling of money. By this means we will be able to make the masses rise when we wish. We will drive them to upheavals, to revolutions; and each of these catastrophes marks a big step forward for our particular interests and brings us rapidly nearer to our sole aim—world domination as was promised to our father Abraham.

NOTE

1. "The Rabbi's Speech" has its origin in the novel *Biarritz* (1868) by Hermann Goedsche, published under the pseudonym of Sir John Retcliffe. In a chapter entitled "In the Jewish Cemetery in Prague," Goedsche purports to describe a secret nocturnal meeting among thirteen Jews (representing the twelve tribes of Israel and the Jews of the Exile) who report on their activities during the century that has elapsed since their last meeting and who vow to have conquered all of their enemies by the time of the next meeting. This frankly fictional episode was soon treated as an authentic record, appearing as a pamphlet first in Russia (1872), and later in Paris and Prague. In 1887 Theodor Fritsch published the "Speech" in his "Decalogue" (see document 19 in this chapter), and it received a wide circulation in a number of anti-Semitic publications, enjoying its greatest vogue in post-war Germany. The "Speech" was constantly invoked as proof of the authenticity of the *Protocols of the Elders of Zion* (see the following document).

22. Protocols of the Elders of Zion[1]

Protocol Number 1: Let us put aside phraseology and discuss the inner meaning of every thought; by comparisons and deductions let us illuminate the situation. In this way I will describe our system, both from our own point of view and from that of the *Goys*. . . .

Political freedom is not a fact but an idea. One must know how to employ this idea when it becomes necessary to attract popular forces to one's party by mental allurement if it plans to crush the party in power. The task is made easier if the opponent himself has contradicted the idea of freedom, by embracing liberalism, and thereby yielding his power. It is precisely here that the triumph of our theory becomes apparent; the relinquished reins of power are, according to the laws of nature, immediately seized by a new hand because the blind force of the people cannot remain without a leader even for one day, and the new power merely replaces the old, weakened by liberalism.

In our day the *power of gold* has replaced liberal rulers. There was a time when faith ruled. The idea of freedom cannot be realized because no one knows how to make reasonable use of it. Give the people self-government for a short time and it will become corrupted. From that very moment strife begins and soon develops into social struggles, as a result of which states are set aflame and their authority is reduced to ashes.

Whether the state is exhausted by internal convulsions, or whether civil wars deliver it into the hands of external enemies, in either case it can be regarded as hopelessly lost: it is in our power. The despotism of capital, which is entirely in our hands, holds out to it a straw which the state must grasp, although against its will, or otherwise fall into the abyss. . . .

Politics have nothing in common with morals. The ruler guided by morality is not a skilled politician, and consequently he is not firm on his throne. He who desires to rule must resort to cunning and hypocrisy. The great popular qualities—honesty and frankness—become vices in politics, as they dethrone more surely and more certainly than the most powerful enemy. These qualities must be the attributes of *Goy* countries; but we by no means should be guided by them.

Our right lies in might. The word *right* is an abstract idea, unsusceptible of proof. This word means nothing more than: Give me what I desire so that I may have evidence that I am stronger than you.

Where does right begin? Where does it end? . . . In laying our plans we must turn our attention not so much to the good and moral as to the necessary and useful. Before us lies a plan in which a strategic line is shown, from which we must not deviate on pain of risking the collapse of many centuries of work.

In working out an expedient plan of action it is necessary to take into consideration the meanness, vacillation, changeability of the mob, its inability to appreciate and respect the conditions of its own existence and of its own well-being. It is necessary to realize that the power of the masses is blind, unreasoning, and void of discrimination, prone to listen to right and left. The blind man cannot guide the blind without bringing them to the abyss; consequently, members of the crowd, upstarts from the people, even were they men of genius but incompetent in politics, cannot step forward as leaders of the mob without ruining the entire nation. . . . Our motto is Power and Hypocrisy. Only power can conquer in politics, especially if it is concealed in talents which are necessary to

Source: Protocols of the Meetings of the Zionist Men of Wisdom, translator not indicated (Boston: Small, Maynard & Co., 1920), pp. 11–22.

statesmen. Violence must be the principle; hypocrisy and cunning the rule of those governments which do not wish to lay down their crowns at the feet of the agents of some new power. This evil is the sole means of attaining the good. For this reason we must not hesitate at bribery, fraud, and treason when these can help us to reach our end. In politics it is necessary to seize the property of others without hesitation if in so doing we attain submission and power.

Our government, following the line of peaceful conquest, has the right to substitute for the horrors of war less noticeable and more efficient executions, these being necessary to keep up terror, which induces blind submission. A just but inexorable strictness is the greatest factor of governmental power. We must follow a program of violence and hypocrisy, not only for the sake of profit, but also as a duty and for the sake of victory.

A doctrine based on calculation is as potent as the means employed by it. That is why not only by these very means, but by the severity of our doctrines, we shall triumph and shall enslave all governments under our supergovernment.

Even in olden times we shouted among the people the words *Liberty, Equality, and Fraternity.* These words have been repeated so many times since by unconscious parrots, which, flocking from all sides to the bait, have ruined the prosperity of the world and true individual freedom, formerly so well protected from the pressure of the mob. The would-be clever and intelligent *Goys* did not discern the symbolism of the uttered words; did not notice the contradiction in the meaning and the connection between them; did not notice that there is no equality in nature; that there can be no liberty, since nature herself has established inequality of mind, character, and ability, as well as subjection to her laws. They did not reason that the power of the mob is blind; that the upstarts selected for government are just as blind in politics as is the mob itself, whereas the initiated man, even though a fool, is capable of ruling, while the uninitiated, although a genius, will understand nothing of politics. All this has been overlooked by the *Goys*. . . .

In all parts of the world the words *Liberty, Equality, and Fraternity* have brought whole legions into our ranks through our blind agents, carrying our banners with delight. Meanwhile these words were worms which ruined the prosperity of the *Goys*, everywhere destroying peace, quiet, and solidarity, undermining all the foundations of their states. You will see subsequently that this aided our triumph, *for it also gave us, among other things, the opportunity to grasp the trump card, the abolition of privileges; in other words, the very essence of the aristocracy of the Goys, which was the only protection of peoples and countries against us.*

On the ruins of natural and hereditary aristocracy we have established this new aristocracy on the qualification of wealth, which is dependent upon us, and also upon science which is promoted by our wise men. . . .

Protocol Number 2: It is necessary for us that wars, whenever possible, should bring no territorial advantages; this will shift war to an economic basis and force nations to realize the strength of our predominance; such a situation will put both sides at the mercy of our million-eyed international agency, which will be unhampered by any frontiers. Then our international rights will do away with national rights, in a limited sense, and will rule the peoples in the same way as the civil power of each state regulates the relation of its subjects among themselves.

The administrators chosen by us from among the people in accordance with their capacity for servility will not be experienced in the art of government, and consequently they will easily become pawns in our game, in the hands of our scientists and wise counselors, specialists trained from early childhood for governing the world. As you are aware, these specialists have obtained the knowledge necessary for government from our political plans, from the study of history, and from the observation of every passing event. The *Goys* are not guided by the practice of impartial historical observation, but by theoretical routine without any critical regard for its results. Therefore, we need give them no consideration. Until the time comes let them amuse themselves, or live in the hope of new amusements or in the memories of those past. Let that play the most important part for them which we have induced them to regard as the laws of science (theory). For this purpose, by means of our press, we increase their blind faith in these laws. Intelligent *Goys* will boast of their knowledge, and verifying it logically they will put into practice all scientific information compiled by our agents for the purpose of educating their minds in the direction which we require.

Do not think that our assertions are without foundation: note the successes of Darwinism, Marxism, and Nietzscheism, engineered by us. The demoralizing effects of these doctrines upon the minds of the *Goys* should be already obvious to us. . . .

There is one great force in the hands of modern states which arouses thought movements among the people. That is the press. The role of the press is to indicate necessary demands, to register complaints of the people, and to express and foment dissatisfaction. The triumph of free babbling is incarnated in the press; but governments were unable to profit by this power *and it has fallen into our hands.* Through it we have attained influence, while remaining in the background. Thanks to the press, we have gathered gold in our hands, although we had to take it from rivers of blood and tears.

But it cost us the sacrifice of many of our own people. Every sacrifice on our part is worth a thousand *Goys* before God.

Protocol Number 3: To-day I can tell you that our goal is close at hand. Only a small distance remains, and the cycle of the *Symbolic Serpent*— the symbol of our people—will be complete. When this circle is completed, then all the European states will be enclosed in it as in strong claws. . . .

To induce the lovers of authority to abuse their power, we have placed all the forces in opposition to each other, having developed their liberal tendencies towards independence. We have excited different forms of initiative in that direction; we have armed all the parties; we have made authority the target of all ambitions. We have opened the arenas in different states, where revolts are now occurring, *and disorders and bankruptcy will shortly appear everywhere.*

Unrestrained babbles have converted parliamentary sessions and administrative meetings into oratorical contests. Daring journalists, impudent pamphleteers, make daily attacks on the administrative personnel. The abuse of power is definitely preparing the downfall of all institutions and everything will be overturned by the blows of the infuriated mobs.

The people are shackled by poverty to heavy labor more surely than they were by slavery and serfdom. They could liberate themselves from those in one way or another, whereas they cannot free themselves from misery. We have included in constitutions rights which for the people are fictitious and are not actual rights. All the so-called rights of the people can exist only in the abstract and can never be realized in practice. What difference does it make to the toiling proletarian, bent double by heavy toil, oppressed by his fate, that the babblers receive the right to talk, journalists the right to mix nonsense with reason in their writings, if the proletariat has no other gain from the constitution than the miserable crumbs which we throw from our table in return for his vote to elect our agents. Republican rights are bitter irony to the poor man, for the necessity of almost daily labor prevents him from using them, and at the same time deprives him of his guarantee of a permanent and certain livelihood by making him dependent upon strikes, organized either by his masters or by his comrades.

Under our guidance the people have exterminated aristocracy, which was their natural protector and guardian, for its own interests are inseparably connected with the well-being of the people. Now, however, with the destruction of this aristocracy the masses have fallen under the power of the profiteers and cunning upstarts, who have settled on the workers as a merciless burden.

We will present ourselves in the guise of saviors of the workers from this oppression when we suggest that they enter our army of Socialists, Anarchists, Communists, to whom we always extend our help, under the guise of the rule of brotherhood demanded by the human solidarity of our *social masonry*. The aristocracy which benefited by the labor of the people by right was interested that the workers should be well fed, healthy, and strong.

We, on the contrary, are concerned in the opposite—in the degeneration of the *Goys*. Our power lies in the chronic malnutrition and in the weakness of the worker, because through this he falls under our power and is unable to find either strength or energy to combat it.

Hunger gives to capital greater power over the worker than the legal authority of the sovereign ever gave to the aristocracy. Through misery and the resulting jealous hatred we manipulate the mob and crush those who stand in our way. . . . This hatred will be still more accentuated by the *economic crisis*, which will stop financial transactions and all industrial life. Having organized a general economic crisis by all possible underhand means, and with the help of gold which is all in our hands, we will throw great crowds of workmen into the street, simultaneously, in all countries of Europe. These crowds will gladly shed the blood of those of whom they, in the simplicity of their ignorance, have been jealous since childhood and whose property they will then be able to loot.

They will not harm our people because we will know of the time of the attack and we will take measures to protect them. . . .

Remember the French Revolution, which we have called "great"; the secrets of its preparation are well known to us, for it was the work of our hands. Since then we have carried the masses from one disappointment to another, so that they will renounce even us in favor of *a despot sovereign of Zionist blood, whom we are preparing for the world. . . .*

NOTE

1. The *protocols* or secret meetings of an international conference of "the learned elders of Zion" is an anti-Semitic literary hoax aimed at showing the existence of an international Jewish conspiracy bent on world dominance. As part of this plot the Jews are said to be behind the egregious forces of modernity: liberalism, parliamentary democracy, finance capitalism, Marxism, anarchism, the press. The term *elders of Zion* is apparently an allusion to the First Zionist Congress, which was held at the time the *Protocols* were written. The *Protocols* were almost certainly concocted in Paris in the last decade of the nineteenth century by an unknown author working for the Russian secret police; in all probability this volume was intended to influence the policy of Czar Nicholas II toward the interests of the secret police. For his purposes the anonymous author adapted a political satire written in 1864 by Maurice Joly (d. 1879). It is ironical that Joly's work—which has nothing to do with the Jews and which seeks to illuminate the tensions of modern society that led to the authoritarian regime of Napoleon III—is a defense of liberalism. Although first published in Russia at the beginning of the twentieth century, the *Protocols* only enjoyed wide readership when they were translated into numerous languages after the First World War. In the United States they were principally distributed by Henry Ford I, under the title *The Jewish Peril*.

VIII

The Russian Experience

Modern Russian Jewish history began with the partitions of Poland in 1772, 1793 and 1795; with the incorporation of large numbers of Jews into czarist Russia; and with the incorporation of a smaller, but not insignificant, number into the Austro-Hungarian Empire, particularly in the province of Galicia. Before the partitions of Poland the czars had sought to keep the Jews out of Russia, but suddenly millions of Jews were within the borders of the empire. Rather than expelling the Jews, the czars adopted a threefold policy which restricted them to certain areas, the so-called Pale of Settlement; this promoted their economic utility and fostered their Russification. Until the February Revolution this policy, with various alterations, determined the fate of the Jews in the Russian Empire. The czars attempted to undermine the Jews' traditional way of life, to restructure their communal and social patterns, to direct them into useful "non-Jewish" occupations and to encourage their assimilation. The execution of this policy alternated between enlightened tact and uninhibited ruthlessness.

Slowly the Jewish community began to crumble, witnessed by the break-down of traditional leadership and the weakened bonds to traditional Judaism. This was similar to the experience of Western Jewry. But there are crucial differences. Economically, despite some spectacular gains, czarist Russia was still a stagnant, feudal economy; politically, czarist Russia had made little progress toward liberalism and democracy; demographically, the Jews of Russia were numerous and confined to large concentrations within the Pale of Settlement, which hindered the possibility of a rapid social and cultural assimilation. The Jews of Russia, therefore, experienced modernity differently from their brethren in the West.

Although they borrowed much from the experience of the German Jews (see documents 6 through 9), the Russian Jews, in response to their unique situation, developed cultural and ideological patterns of their own. In the religious sphere, we may mention the modern *yeshivah* movement of Rabbi Haim ben Isaac of Volozhin (see documents 10 and 11) and the Musar movement founded by Rabbi Israel Lipkin Salanter. The religious denominationalism that characterized Jewish life in Germany and America never took root in Russia. In the social sphere, both the deracinated intellectuals and the poor urbanized Jewish masses displayed an affinity to socialism and, in time, developed a socialist ideology specifically adjusted to Jewish needs and aspirations. These needs and aspirations, of course, were variously interpreted. Some felt that the Jewish situation was defined by the oppressive czarist policies and by the *transitional* fact that most Jews still spoke Yiddish and had particular cultural sensibilities. To organize the Jewish masses for the cause of socialism, therefore, it was *tactically* necessary to acknowledge their Jewishness. Others considered the abiding Jewishness of the masses of the Pale to be of an enduring national value, and, accordingly, attributed to Jewish secular culture a role independent of or complementary to socialism (see documents 26, 27 and 28).

Secular Jewish culture, based either on Yiddish or Hebrew, was a living reality for millions of Russian Jews. For the majority of Russian Jews secularization was not accompanied by assimilation, as it often was in the West, or even by acculturation. The challenge faced by Russian Jewry was how to foster secular Jewish culture as a viable, creative expression. Given the multi-ethnic character of czarist Russia—and the neighboring Austro-Hungarian Empire—national cultural autonomy, distinct from political and economic autonomy, seemed to provide the framework for legitimizing a secular Jewish culture without undermining the claim to full civic rights within Russia. The Zionists, although not opposed to cultural autonomy, of course, argued that it would not be sufficient (see document 28).

Another point of contrast between East and West European Jewish history is the nature of the anti-Semitism encountered by the respective communities. In the West, anti-Semitism, until Nazism, remained mostly on the level of public intellectual discourse or propaganda, while in the East it often fell to the level of physical violence. The pogroms of 1880–1881, 1903 and 1905, followed by the Russian Revolution greatly unsettled Russian Jewry. Despair and panic provoked a massive emigration of Russian Jewry. Faith in the czar and Russia waned, and for many Jews the vision of a more dignified and prosperous life was now focused on the West, particularly America, and for some, on Palestine (see documents 23 through 25).

Fearing that the flesh-pots of the West would entice Jewry into assimilation, many Jews remained in Russia (see documents 11, 12 and 15). Still others placed their faith in the revolution. And the Russian Revolution did indeed remove the shackles, granting Jewry full civic rights. "The emancipation of the Jews," Maxim Gorki exclaimed, "is one of the finest achievements of our Revolution. By granting to the Jews the same rights as to Russians, we have erased from our conscience a shameful and bloody stain" (see the articles by Gorki in *Novaya Zhizn,* 1917–1918 and in the French translation in André Pierre, *Écrite de Revolution* [Paris: Stock, 1922]). But to the Bolsheviks, emancipation meant the opportunity to hasten the process of Jewish assimilation, which they viewed as a progressive and desirable solution to the Jewish question. They considered any attempt to foster Jewish identity reactionary. Jewish cultural institutions were merely necessary means to combat clerical and nationalist forces within the Jewish community and to further the cause of communism among Jews (see document 32).

HAROLD FREDERIC
1. A People That Dwells Apart[1]

Once you cross the Russian frontier, you can tell the Jews at railway stations or on the street almost as easily as in America you can distinguish the Negroes. This is more a matter of dress—of hair and beard and cap and caftan—than of physiognomy. But even more still is it a matter of demeanour. They seem never for an instant to lose the consciousness that they are a race apart. It is in their walk, in their sidelong glance, in the carriage of their sloping shoulders, in the curious gesture with the uplifted palm. [Czar] Nicholas [the First]... solidified [the Jews] into a dense, hardbaked and endlessly resistant mass.

NOTE

1. Harold Frederic (1856–1898), London representative of the *New York Times*. Frederic traveled in Russia in the 1880s on an assignment. A book on the plight of the Jews under the czars, *The New Exodus*, from which this excerpt is taken, emerged from that journey. The title we have given to this selection refers to Num. 23:9: "There is a people that dwells apart. Not reckoned among the nations."

Source: Harold Frederic, *The New Exodus: Israel in Russia* (London, 1892), pp. 79–80.

ALEXANDER I
2. Statutes Concerning the Organization of Jews (December 9, 1804)[1]

Numerous complaints have been submitted to us regarding the abuse and exploitation of native farmers and laborers in those provinces in which the Jews are permitted to reside.... The following regulations are in accord both with our concern with the true happiness of the Jews and with the needs of the principal inhabitants of those provinces....

I. Education and Language.

1. Jewish children may study in all the public schools, secondary schools and universities in Russia, on equal terms with other children.

2. Jewish pupils will neither be required to renounce their religion nor will they be compelled to study subjects which are contrary to their religion....

Source: P. Levanda, *Polnyi khronologicheskii sbornik zakonov i polozhenii kasaiuschikhksia evreev* [Complete chronological collection of laws and ordinances relating to Jews] (St. Petersburg, 1874), pp. 53–59. Trans. here by R. Weiss.

6. If the Jews refuse, despite all these encouragements, to send their children to public schools, special schools must be built at their expense. For this purpose a special tax will be levied. The study of either Polish, Russian or German *must* be included in the curriculum. . . .

8. All the Jews residing in the Russian Empire, although free to use their native language in all their religious and domestic affairs, are obliged, as of January 1807, to use the Russian, Polish or German language in all public documents, contracts, and bills of sale. Otherwise these documents will not be registered. . . .

In accordance with these regulations, Jews who are elected as members of the municipal councils in the former Polish province, shall, for the sake of order and uniformity, dress in the Russian or Polish fashion; whereas Jews elected to the municipal councils in those Russian provinces in which they are permitted to reside permanently, shall dress in the German fashion. As of the year 1808, a Jew who cannot read and write either Russian, German or Polish, may not be elected to the municipal councils. . . .

10. As of the year 1812, a person who is not literate in one of the previously mentioned languages, may not be appointed to a communal position or to the rabbinate.

II. The Status, Occupations and Rights of the Jews.

11. All the Jews are divided into four classes: (a) farmers, (b) manufacturers and craftsmen, (c) merchants and (d) city dwellers. . . .

13. Jews who are farmers, as well as those who are manufacturers, craftsmen, merchants and city dwellers, are allowed to purchase and own property in the unpopulated areas of the provinces of Lithuania, Belorussia, Little Russia, Kiev, Minsk, Volhynia, Podolia, Astrakhan, Caucasus, Ekaterinoslav, Kherson and Tsabaria. They may sell the land, lease it, bequeath it or bestow it as a gift. . . .

18. No Jew will be compelled to engage in agriculture in the aforementioned provinces, but those who do, shall be exempt from payment of taxes for a period of ten years. This exemption, however, does not extend to debts related to the purchase of land. They will receive loans which will be repayable after a few years, on terms under which similar loans are given to settlers from abroad. . . .

20. Jews are permitted to establish factories of all kinds, in those provinces in which they are permitted to settle, with the same freedom and on the same basis as that granted to all subjects of Russia. . . .

23. In the aforementioned provinces, Jewish craftsmen may engage in any craft not prohibited by law. Managers of workshops, or organizations of craftsmen may not interfere in their rights. They [i.e., Jews] are permitted to register as members of a craftsmen's association if it is not in conflict with local regulations. . . .

29. When all the Jews shall evince diligence and industry in agriculture, commerce and manufacturing, the government will take steps to equalize their taxes to those of other Russian citizens.

III. The Duties of the Jews According to Their Aforementioned Class.

30. If he is not registered in one of these classes, a Jew will not be tolerated anywhere in Russia. Jews who will not present a written document in standard legal form, certifying their membership in a class will be regarded as vagrants and will be treated according to the full severity of the law. . . .

34. As of January 1, 1807, in Astrakhan, the Caucasus, Little Russia and New Russia, and the other provinces mentioned, no Jew is permitted to hold rented property in any village or settlement. They may not own taverns, pubs or inns, either in their own name or in that of a monitor. . . .

IV. The Legal Status of Jews.

44. . . . No persons may coerce [the Jews], or disturb them in matters of their religious practice, and in civilian life generally, either in word or in deed. Their complaints, what-

ever they may be, will be heard before the courts and will be satisfied according to the strict letter of the law as it applies to all the citizens of Russia. . . .

NOTE

1. From the sixteenth century on, the czars sought to expel and bar the Jews from Russia. As a result of the various partitions of Poland, by which Russia inherited a Jewish population of some nine hundred thousand, this policy was no longer realistic. The czars felt that their new subjects presented a grave problem that required a radical solution. Catherine II, who ascended the throne in 1762, was the first to tackle the "Jewish Problem." In 1772 the czarina enacted legislation that limited the exercise of the rights granted the Jews under Polish rule to the areas in which they lived prior to the partitions; Polish Gentiles were specifically permitted, by the same legislation, to exercise their former rights throughout the Russian Empire. A decree of 1791 barred the Jews from specific areas in the empire. Thus the Pale of Jewish Settlement began to take shape. Alexander I, who reigned from 1801 to 1825, resolved to find a "humane" solution to the Jewish problem. In 1802 he ordered the creation of a Committee for the Amelioration of the Jews, to consider all aspects of the problem. In their deliberations the committee assumed that the Jews were a parasitic element and that the non-Jewish population, especially the peasants of the territories that formerly belonged to Poland, had to be protected from the already rapacious Jews. The committee's proposals—a mixture of restrictions and "liberal" inducements to Jewish self-improvement—were accepted by the czar and embodied in the above legislation, enacted on December 9, 1804. It was the first comprehensive Russian legislation dealing with the Jewish problem.

NICHOLAS I
3. Statutes Regarding the Military Service of Jews (August 26, 1827)[1]

I. General Rules Applying to the Jewish People.

1. Upon being called to military service, Jews shall fulfill their obligation in a manner identical to that of other citizens who are members of that class which is required to serve in the armed forces. . . .

II. Manner of Fulfilling Military Draft Obligations.

6. If, at the time of the call to service, it is generally permitted to substitute a sum of money for a recruit, this privilege shall be extended to Jews under the following conditions: (a) The Jewish community owes no back taxes to the government; (b) The community is not in debt to other communities or individuals. . . .

8. Jews presented by the community for the purpose of military service must be no younger than twelve and no older than twenty-five years of age. . . .

[III.] 13. The Jews of each province must fill their quota of recruits independently of the Gentile population thereof. . . .

Source: P. Levanda, *Polnyi khronologicheskii sbornik zakonov i polozhenii, kasaiuschikhksia evreev* [Complete chronological collection of laws and ordinances relating to Jews] (St. Petersburg, 1874), pp. 193–200. Trans. here by R. Weiss.

[V.] 24. The responsibility for fulfilling the military obligations falls upon the Jewish communities themselves. They shall follow the dictates of the appropriate provincial authority. . . .

Exemptions:

58. In addition to merchants, rabbis also are exempt from military service. They must show proper documents proving their title. . . .

62. Jewish youths who are enrolled in general schools for a minimum of three years and who perform adequately and those apprenticed to Gentile artisans are exempt from military service for the duration of their studies. . . .

64. Jews who have settled and who work upon land designated for agricultural purposes are exempt. . . .

X. The Assignment of Jews to Various Branches of the Military.

74. Jewish minors—those under 18—shall be sent to preparatory institutions for military training [i.e., cantonist units].

75. Jews from the age of eighteen and upwards shall be assigned to active military duty according to their physical condition, as ordered by the military command.

XI. Jews Evading the Draft.

87. Whoever discloses the names of those who hide a Jew escaping the draft, shall receive a reward in the sum of one hundred rubles from the treasury. . . .

90. For the purpose of release from the draft, only time spent in active duty after the age of eighteen shall be taken into account.

91. Jews in active military duty are permitted to observe their religious customs during their *spare time*. This is in accordance with the law of the land concerning accepted religions. Commanding officers shall protect the Jews from disturbances or abuses which may be caused by their religious affiliation.

NOTE

1. The reign of Czar Nicholas I (1825–1855) is a dark chapter in the history of Russian Jewry. The above legislation is indicative of his policy to solve the Jewish problem through coerced assimilation or Russification. In addition to a general conscription of Jewish adult males, who served for a period of twenty-five years, the legislation decreed the recruitment of Jewish boys from the ages of twelve to eighteen as cantonists (the Russian term for *juvenile conscripts*). The cantonists underwent a tough regime of military drill and Russian education; at the age of eighteen they were drafted to the regular army where they served the full twenty-five-year term. The objective of this system was to alienate the Jewish youth from their families and religion; they were forbidden to practice Judaism, speak their native Yiddish and were obliged to attend classes in Christian dogma and ritual. The government imposed on the Jewish communal leaders the task of supplying a quota of cantonists. To meet this quota the leaders—often rabbis—were obliged to dispatch *khapers* (Yiddish for "kidnappers") to seize Jewish children, often as young as eight, from their parents. Needless to say, this institution weakened the moral authority of the traditional leadership—precisely what the government desired. Before the law was rescinded in 1859, it is estimated that between forty and fifty thousand Jewish minors were conscripted into cantonist units.

NICHOLAS I

4. Delineation of the Pale of Settlement (April 1835)[1]

. . . 3. A permanent residence is permitted to the Jews: (a) In the provinces: Grodno, Vilna, Volhynia, Podolia, Minsk, Ekaterinoslav. (b) In the districts: Bessarabia, Bialystok.

4. In addition to the provinces and districts listed in the preceding section, a permanent residence is permitted to the Jews, with the following restrictions: (a) in Kiev province, with the exception of the provincial capital, Kiev; (b) in Kherson province, with the exception of the city of Nikolaev; (c) in Tavaria province, with the exception of the city of Sebastopol; (d) in Mogilev and Vitebsk provinces, except in the villages; (e) in Chernigov and Poltava provinces, but not within the government and Cossack villages, where the expulsion of the Jews has already been completed; (f) in Courland province permanent residence is permitted only to those Jews who have been registered until the present date with their families in census lists. Entry for the purpose of settlement is forbidden to the Jews from other provinces; (g) in Lithland province, in the city of Riga and the suburb Shlok, with the same restrictions as those applying in Courland province. . . .

11. Jews who have gone abroad without a legal exit-permit are deprived of Russian citizenship and not permitted to return to Russia.

12. Within the general area of settlement and in every place where the Jews are permitted permanent residence, they are allowed not only to move from place to place and to settle in accordance with the general regulations, but also to acquire real estate of all kinds with the exception of inhabited estates, the ownership of which is strictly forbidden to Jews. . . .

23. Every Jew must be registered according to the law in one of the legal estates of the realm. Any Jew not complying with this regulation will be treated as a vagrant.

NOTE

1. The above legislation clearly defined the boundaries of the Pale of Settlement; it included regions beyond those of Poland only in such instances where the Jews could serve as a colonizing element. From time to time its boundaries were modified, but on the average the area of the Pale covered one million square kilometers (386,100 square miles), extending from the Baltic Sea to the Black Sea. By 1897, according to an official census, 4,899,300 Jews lived there, forming 11.6 percent of the general population of the area; 82 percent of the Jews lived in towns and villages. They formed 36.9 percent of the urban population. After the February Revolution (1917), the provisional government abolished the Pale of Settlement.

Source: P. Levanda, *Polnyi khronologicheskii sbornik zakonov i polozhenii kasaiuschikhksia evreev* [Complete chronological collection of laws and ordinances relating to Jews] (St. Petersburg, 1874), pp. 360–63. Trans. here by L. Sachs.

The Jewish Pale of Settlement in Russia, 1835–1917
SWEDEN
Baltic Sea
St. Petersburg
Moscow
KOVNO
VITEBSK
Vitebsk
Vilna
VILNA
GERMANY
MOGILEV
Minsk
Bialystok
GRODNO
MINSK
Warsaw
Lodz
POLAND
Pinsk
R U S S I A
Lublin
VOLHYNIA
CHERNIGOV
Berdichev
Kiev
KIEV
POLTAVA
AUSTRIA-HUNGARY
PODOLIA
EKATERINOSLAV
BESSARABIA
Kishinev
KHERSON
Odessa
TAURIDA
RUMANIA
Black Sea
BULGARIA
Pale of Settlement. The boundaries of the Pale of Settlement were intermittently altered.
Adapted from a map drawn by F. Inoue.

ALEXANDER III

5. The May Laws (May 3, 1882)[1]

The Council of Ministers, having heard the presentation made by the Minister of Internal Affairs, regarding the execution of the Temporary Regulations regarding the Jews has concluded as follows:

1. As a temporary measure, and until a general re-examination of the laws pertaining to the Jews takes place by set order, it is henceforth forbidden for Jews to settle outside the cities and townships. Existing Jewish settlements which are engaged in agricultural work are exempted [from this ban].

2. The registration of property and mortgages in the name of Jews is to be halted temporarily; the approval of the leasing by Jews of real estate beyond the precincts of the cities and townships is also to be halted temporarily. Jews are also prohibited from administering such properties.

3. It is forbidden for Jews to engage in commerce on Sundays and Christian holidays. . . .

4. The regulations contained in paragraphs one through three apply to those provinces in which the Jews permanently reside.

NOTE

1. Alexander II, who reigned from 1855 to 1881, adopted a milder Jewish policy than his father, pursuing the Russification of the Jews in a more liberal fashion. He abolished the cantonist system and offered special rewards for "useful" Jews, namely, allowing them to reside outside of the Pale of Settlement. This right was extended to wealthy merchants in 1859, university graduates in 1861, and certified craftsmen and all medical personnel in 1865. The Jewish communities outside of the Pale, which developed in this period, particularly in Moscow and St. Petersburg, became a major factor in Russian Jewish life. Moreover, a great number of Jews now began to participate in Russian intellectual and cultural life. The assassination of Alexander II by revolutionaries in March 1881 led to a sudden shift in Jewish fortunes. In the period of political unrest that followed, widespread pogroms against the Jews broke out. Czar Alexander III set up a commission to investigate the cause of the disturbances. In its report the commission underscored the alleged failure of the liberal policies of Alexander II and pointed to "Jewish exploitation" as the principal cause of the pogroms. Based on this report, the Temporary Laws were promulgated in May 1882. Excerpts from these so-called May Laws are presented above. In effect they constituted a contraction of the Pale of Settlement. They were repealed in March 1917 by the revolutionary provisional government.

Source: Nedelnaya kronica voskhoda, no. 20 (May 15, 1882), pp. 534–35. Trans. here by R. Weiss.

S. J. FUENN

6. The Need for Enlightenment[1]

You asked, dear friend, for my opinion on the current news and for my judgment on the questions being asked by the governmental commissions with regard to the children of Israel. Now that the good graces of the Czar have appeared among us to lighten our darkness and he has descended from his lofty throne to lower his gaze on our poverty, to improve our condition, to heal Jacob's misfortune and the bruises of thousands of years—bruises without hope of cure; now that he has ordered that faithful men, lovers of truth, be selected into whose hands and hearts the supervision of our bad situation and station is to be entrusted, so that the source of the evil and the reasons for our fall in wisdom and ethics be known, and the cure and remedy for every fault and fracture be known also; now this question of yours has come my way, and I find myself duty-bound to pour out my thoughts before you. Perhaps they will reach high places, for I dwell among my people, see and know well their station, and have secretly shed not one nor two heartfelt tears for their misfortune. I will, therefore, explain most clearly to you, dear friend, their present condition in all its aspects, good and bad, and the aids and cures which will benefit them, and provide for them a much needed success. After the government has acquired the wisdom to set a good end, to find the general remedy "for improving the station of the leaders of the nation and its rabbis," I too will labor to portray for you details of our brethren's situation, with regard to the teachers and rabbis, for it appears that for the success or ruin of the people we can rely only on them. And I say: The congregation of Israel in this land today compared to the Gentiles of the Christian countries and our brethren in other countries still stands on the lowest rung of the ladder of political and ethical enlightenment. They produce foul fruit but not for a lack of knowledge and readiness to receive the good and useful seed, nor because the soil of their soul is barren rock do they sprout nought but thorns and briar. No, it is because they lack farmer and plowman for land they have not had, and do not have even today, nor have they had bounteous dew, for several hundred years, not until the days of the good Czars of Russia, may the Lord bless them. The Jew is far from the threshold of the world's ways for he has not yet been granted the right of all men to nourish himself by visiting the halls of wisdom and enlightenment, and because his customs and garments (which he wears not for religious reasons) are a great dividing screen. Because the Christian heads of the country estrange themselves from these Jews, whom they have hostilely rejected, [the Jews] have become the poorest of men, without any land or source of livelihood to support themselves and the members of their household. They have been pushed into one small circle of activity—petty commerce—which tends to be deceitful, and which is based on scheming and contriving that sometimes clashes with the general good of society. Commerce alone is their allotted work; they are far from all that can induce rapprochement with the Christians, far from the spirit of the time which is daily changing, each year growing glorious with wisdom and the splendor of knowledge. They remain at the level of enlightenment where they were hundreds of years ago. Their value diminishes like the house that, having neither

Source: S. J. Fuenn to Bezalel Stern, Summer 1840, in *Pardes* (Odessa, 1897), vol. 3, pp. 149–56. Trans. here by A. Schwartz.

prop nor support, grows shaky and collapses. They have not known the language of the people among whom they dwell, except for what is needed for their trade. Wisdom and science cannot take root among them, for these will find neither passage nor currency among men depressed in spirit and soul. What can inculcate itself into [the Jews'] broken-heartedness is hatred of the religions of other nations. Several generations have passed thus and the Jews of these lands are thought by their neighbors to be harmful members of society. How then can we now amend this sin? What will they do, these impoverished, wretched, depressed exiles who so often have stood before their shearers like mute lambs—not only was their wool shorn but their flesh and skin cut and stripped from them! How many rivers of their blood were spilled as nought throughout history for a libel now known everywhere, as God is in heaven and earth, as an empty lie? How many years of poverty rife with scorn and contempt for the near success of their work in the land of their neighbors? How could they have approached the enemies of their soul, associate with the devourers of their flesh and blood? Does the love of man penetrate the hearts of oppressed and downtrodden Christians? But blessed be you, O Lord, who sees into every broken heart, who rules this world with His mercy, who has placed goodness for a downtrodden people in the heart of our pious king and in the hearts of his advisors. Blessed too be our lord the Czar who has voiced ideas beneficial to us. We now can hope that the light of deliverance will also fall on the dwellers in darkness, that the iron-bound prisoners chained to slavery and humiliation will also breathe the spirit of freedom, like every man. Now it has begun to be seen that Jacob is man not stone, that his flesh is flesh not wood, that his blood is the blood of mortals not of snakes and scorpions. Our lord the Czar has now taken upon himself to be farmer and plowman for us; he will uproot each root of ours which sprouts wormwood, will purify the hearts of the children of Israel of every evil scheme, will sprinkle blessed dew on parched thirsty land, and will sow it with the seed of righteousness, wisdom, and mercy. How good and dear is the sentiment that will come to the aid of thousands and thousands of dejected and humiliated people; how fortunate will be the man who raises his hand or engages his mind and soul to consider their welfare; how blessed will be the pen which will inscribe for posterity the remembrance of mercy and truth.

Having spoken about a bit of the corruption of order among the people of Israel, we may add that the government has done well in advising that the leadership of our nation be handed over to several individuals, and that all parts of the leadership be united toward one end. The rabbis to be chosen for this task will be the sailors of Israel's ship lashed by the seas of poverty and woe. Their way should first be cleared of stumbling blocks and then these sailors should be instructed in honest and new leadership, that they may bring the storm-tossed ship to port, to the good port desired by the government.

It is apparent to whoever has eyes that the foremost cause of the distance and enmity between the children of Israel and the Christians in our state is the difference of dress. Since the Jew is unwilling to change his dress and is recognizable wherever he goes, this distance will be increased in the heart both of the Jew and the Christian. Before the government takes one step for our welfare it is fitting that we call its attention to having this obstacle removed. The division and difference in dress derive not from reasons of religion, but rather from a corrupted source, the hatred of the nations during the Middle Ages toward Israel. Wanting not to mingle with the children of Israel they placed a seal on the brow of the Jew which established his religion. . . . In the course of time this became a distinguishing mark among the children of Israel, setting them off from their oppressors. From this isolation they took comfort—as do all those who suffer the prohibitions of insolent masters. In the course of time, when the original reason had been forgotten, they claimed it was for their benefit and was freely chosen. Why then should the children of Israel not want to remove their filthy garments which set them off from their neighbors to this very day? Why should they not be willing to erase all traces of the hatred of the forefathers of our present neighbors which they bear on their persons?...

Having set its eyes in particular on the rabbis at the forefront of the people as a means to improve the station of the nation as a whole, the government would be well advised to achieve its goal not only by improving but by thoroughly changing the rabbis' status. Today the rabbi is but a single man standing alone among the assembly of his people, for the most part instructing them with the aid of talmudic hairsplitting to abandon difficult prohibitions concerning forbidden foods, status of women and the like. He closets himself in his room, has, except for his public lessons on the Talmud, intercourse with no man. The more hallowed among them may also preach on the exalted matters contained in the kabbalah, for in laws of property they have no legal power to give rulings. Today money matters are brought before the government courts, unless the rabbi is chosen by the disputants of their own accord to bring them to compromise. Even then he has no power—not to enforce his decisions, nor to influence the nation's education, nor to guide them toward the government's aim. The nation's leaders are [surely not the rabbis].[2] ...

NOTES

1. Samuel Joseph Fuenn (1818–1890), Hebrew writer and educator. Fuenn, an observant Jew, was a respected spokesman of early Haskalah in Russia. Haskalah, the Hebrew term for the enlightenment movement and ideology that began within Jewish society in the 1770s, was introduced into Russia from Western Europe, particularly Germany. Fuenn served as an inspector of the government schools for Jews in his native district of Vilna. He later published and edited the Hebrew periodical *Ha-Karmel* (1860–1881), which included a supplement in German and Russian.

In 1837 Czar Nicholas I visited a modern Jewish school established by *maskilim* in Odessa. He was greatly impressed and was inspired to consider the creation of a government network of "modern" schools for the Jews. Upon receiving the report of a special study commission in 1844, the government issued a decree establishing a system of modern Jewish schools. The *maskilim* were delighted by the czar's "enlightened policy." They surely did not know of the secret instructions accompanying the decree which declared that the purpose of the schools "is to bring the Jews nearer to the Christians and to uproot their harmful beliefs which are influenced by the Talmud." In the above letter, written during the public debates preceding the governmental decree of 1844, to Bezalel Stern (1798–1853), the director of the Jewish school in Odessa, Fuenn summarizes the concerns and program of the early Haskalah.

2. Fuenn proceeds to outline a detailed plan for the reform of the rabbinate and its functions.

JUDAH LEIB GORDON
7. Awake My People![1]

Awake, my people! How long will you slumber?
The night has passed, the sun shines bright.

Source: Judah Leib Gordon, "Hakiza Ammi," *Ha-Karmel*, 7, no. 1 (1866). Trans. here by D. Goldman.

Awake, lift up your eyes, look around you—
Acknowledge, I pray you, your time and your place. . . .

The land in which now we live and are born—
Is it not thought to be part of Europe?
Europe—the smallest of Earth's regions,
Yet the greatest of all in wisdom and reason.

This land of Eden [Russia] now opens its gates to you,
Her sons now call you "brother"!
How long will you dwell among them as a guest,
And why do you now affront them?

Already they have removed the weight of suffering from your shoulder,
They have lifted off the yoke from your neck,
They have erased from their hearts gratuitous hatred and folly,
They give you their hand, they greet you with peace.

Raise your head high, straighten your back,
And gaze with loving eyes upon them.
Open your heart to wisdom and knowledge,
Become an enlightened people, and speak their language.

Every man of understanding should try to gain knowledge;
Let others learn all manner of arts and crafts;
Those who are brave should serve in the army;
The farmers should buy ploughs and fields.

To the treasury of the state bring your strength,
Take your share of its possessions, its bounty.
Be a man abroad and a Jew in your tent,
A brother to your countrymen and a servant to your king. . . .

NOTE

1. Judah Leib Gordon (1831–1892). The foremost Russian Hebrew poet of the Haskalah, Gordon at first believed that the Jews' isolation was at the root of all the troubles that plagued them. "Be a man abroad and a Jew in your tent"—a line from his poem "Hakiza Ammi"—became the motto for a whole generation of *maskilim*. This poem was composed in 1863, after the liberation of the serfs by Czar Alexander II. It expressed Gordon's belief in the dawn of a new era for Russian Jewry. For his subsequent beliefs, see document 9 in this chapter.

MASKILIM TO GOVERNORS OF THE PALE
8. A Jewish Program for Russification (1841)[1]

The Russian government's objectives in the encouragement of enlightenment among the Jewish people [should be]:

1. To establish special schools for Jews in every city and town where Jews live, without, however, preventing any Jew from receiving an education in the general school system.

2. To give greater emphasis to the moral as opposed to the academic aspect in the education of the Jews. To pay special attention to the teaching of Russian history and language, for there is nothing which unites diverse ethnic groups with the dominant nation better than the dissemination of information concerning that nation's history and literature.

3. In order to thwart the harmful influence of the Talmud, without, at this stage, destroying the book which the Jews regard as the Word of God, the rabbis should be empowered to prepare a short religious textbook, to be approved by the director of the General School System. This text should teach the fundamentals of their religion—in accordance with the accepted principles regarding civic responsibilities to the Czar and the motherland—and guide the students to respectable and useful labor in all branches of the crafts, commerce and agriculture, as is being done in the Jewish schools in Odessa and Uman.[2]

4. The teachers in the Jewish schools shall be selected from among the Jews by the school's governing board. Some of the teachers must be chosen from among those Jews educated in Prussia and Austria. The school at Uman has already demonstrated the success of this method. There, despite opposition from the Jewish community, the teachers trained in Austria have successfully taught the Jewish religion in the spirit of universal principles.

5. Education in the "cottage schools"[3] is to be permitted only where the teachers have passed examinations based on the general requirements for all teachers and instructors [*melamdim*]. Any educational activity outside this approved framework will incur severe punishment. . . .

8. Inasmuch as Jewish dress has no relation whatsoever to religious law, the Jews must be ordered to change their dress for the clothing commonly worn throughout the country, according to the social class to which they belong.

NOTES

1. This document articulates the tendency, typical of the early Haskalah in Russia, to view the government's Jewish policy favorably and to cooperate with the reform of the social and cultural structure of Jewish life.

2. See document 2 in this chapter.

3. The reference is to the traditional Jewish primary school, the *heder* ("the room").

Source: [Memorandum on the organization of the Jewish people in Russia sent by a group of *maskilim* to district governors in the Pale of Settlement (1841)] *Voskhod* Library Pamphlet, no. 5 (1901), pp. 4–5. Trans. here by R. Weiss.

JUDAH LEIB GORDON
9. For Whom Do I Toil?[1]

My enlightened brothers have acquired worldly wisdom,
And are but loosely bound to the language [i.e., Hebrew] of their people;
They scorn the aged mother holding her spindle.
"Abandon that language whose hour has passed;
Abandon its literature, so tasteless, so bland;
Leave it, and let each one use the language of the land."
And our sons? The generation to follow us?
From their youth on they will be strangers to us.
—My heart bleeds for them—
They make progress, year by year they forge ahead:
Who knows where they will reach, how far they will go?
Perhaps to that place whence they shall never return. . . .
Still the Muse visits by night,
Still the heart listens, the hand writes—
Fashioning songs in a tongue forsaken.
What will I, what hope? To what end travail?
For whom do I toil? To what avail?
The good years wasted, . . .
Oh, who can foresee the future, who can foretell?
Perhaps I am the last of Zion's poets;
And you, the last readers?

NOTE

1. Judah Leib Gordon, see document 7, note 1, in this chapter. By the 1870s the enthusiasm of the early votaries of the Hebrew Haskalah began to wane. They showed signs of despair of the possibilities of reforming Jewish culture and life in Russia. They were also disappointed with the young *maskilim*, who exaggerated, in their view, the need to assimilate, and who impetuously abandoned Jewish values and the Hebrew language. In the poem presented here Gordon gives bitter protest to the assimilationist trend.

Source: Judah Leib Gordon, "Lemi Ani Amel?," *Ha-Shahar*, 2 (Vienna, 1871), pp. 353–54. Trans. here by D. Goldman.

RABBI DAVID MOSES JOSEPH OF KRYNKI

10. The Volozhin Yeshivah[1]

An important announcement concerning the Torah:[2] I have seen with my own eyes that the honor of the holy *yeshivah* of Volozhin—which was founded by our holy master, Rabbi Haim Volozhin through prayer and entreaty, and even the shedding of tears—has been brought down and made low. There are those who say: What in fact is the importance of the *yeshivah*, are there not other *yeshivot* in the world? There are others who say that with respect to curricula, the *yeshivot* in other cities are superior to the *yeshivah* of Volozhin. Everyone seems to feel that there have always been *yeshivot* in the big cities. I know that this is not the case and that the truth is that the *yeshivah* of Volozhin is the mother and source of all the *yeshivot* and Talmud Torahs[3] in the world. The latter are as pipes which come from the source and thus in the blessing of the source they too will be blessed. . . .

Therefore I see it as my duty to proclaim the truth to the world, words of truth for he who wants to know as it is written (Deut. 32:7), "ask your father and he will tell you, your elders and they will say to you." Today I am, with God's help, seventy-eight years old and when our holy rabbi founded the *yeshivah* I was about fifteen or sixteen years old. I was familiar with the ways of the world and I noted that before our holy rabbi founded the "house of God" the world was empty, literally without form; it was void, for even the term *yeshivah* was unknown, let alone what activities took place in one. The term *public study of Torah* was also unknown to a world void of Torah. Holy books, such as volumes of the Talmud, were rare and to be found only in homes of exceptional individuals, such as famous patrons. Even in the communal study halls [*batei midrash*] of large towns, a complete set of the Talmud was not to be found. This was the case because there was no need for these books. When our holy rabbi founded the *yeshivah*, an appeal was made for volumes of the Talmud and it was necessary to send to the large towns for books. When the rabbi of Slavuta[4] saw that there was a need for volumes of the Talmud, he printed a few hundred sets, in large and small formats, and as a result of their popularity, they spread all over the world. In the first year of the *yeshivah* I noted that many merchants made it their business to travel by way of Volozhin in order to see what this thing called a *yeshivah* was and what was done there. At the sight of dozens of Torah scholars sitting and studying day and night with a wonderful diligence, they were astonished and amazed for they had never seen or even imagined anything like it. Many merchants remained for days and did not want to leave.

After a number of years, one of the students of our holy rabbi went to Minsk—this was Rabbi Mordechai Minsker. He studied with awesome discipline and the sons of the great patroness Bluma of that city became attached to him. He inspired them and together with their mother they founded a small prayer room and study hall [*kloiz*].[5] She supported all the students of the *kloiz* at her own expense and covered the other expenses of the *kloiz* out of her own pocket as well. This was the very first *kloiz* in the world, for there was no other. A few years later another patron, I think it was Rabbi Haim Michvantzer, founded another and after him Rabbi Samuel Rofe and others. Meanwhile in Vilna there was still no *yeshivah*. I once asked our holy rabbi for permission to give a daily lecture [*shiur*] to students as was done in the

Source: Moshe Shmuel Schmuckler [The history of the rabbi of Volozhin] (Vilna, 1909), pp. 32–34. Trans. here by S. Stampler.

yeshivah [of Volozhin]. He replied with these words: I get more satisfaction and gratification from the *yeshivot* of Minsk than from my own *yeshivah*. With regard to the latter I am troubled by all the details necessary for the running of the *yeshivah*, whereas at the *yeshivot* of Minsk I have no worries at all and all [the pleasure] is mine! After a few years Mordechai Minsker settled in Vilna and founded a *yeshivah* in the old *kloiz*. Then, with the help of Rabbi Judah Kliatsky he set up a *yeshivah* in the new *kloiz* and after that *yeshivot* and Talmud Torahs multiplied in a number of towns. Were it not for the fact that our holy rabbi founded his *yeshivah*, the Torah would have—God forbid—been forgotten in Israel. This I often say about our teacher and holy rabbi, "How great are the deeds of your life." My eyes saw all that is written here and it is not from hearsay. . . .

NOTES

1. Traditional Judaism in Russia was not as desiccated and petrified as the *maskilim* tended to portray it. Throughout the nineteenth century, the leaders of traditional Judaism, aware of the growing disaffection of Russian Jewry, especially of the youth, with the regnant patterns of Jewish life, sought to renew Orthodox Judaism. One of the first signs of this renewal was the establishment in 1803 by Rabbi Haim ben Isaac (1749–1821) of the *yeshivah* at Volozhin, a village in Lithuania. Alarmed by the decline of Torah learning among East European Jewry, a process that began in the seventeenth century, Rabbi Haim reintroduced Lithuanian Jewry to the joys of rigorous Torah and talmudic study, both in terms of method and routine. For six days a week, the more enthusiastic students would commence their studies at 3 A.M., with a break at 8 A.M. for the morning prayers and meal; they would return to the study halls at 10 A.M., continuing to study until 1 P.M.; after a midday recess, study would resume from 4 P.M. until 10 P.M.; some would stay until midnight. The Volozhin *yeshivah* became the prototype and inspiration for the great talmudic academies of Eastern Europe of the nineteenth and twentieth centuries. The *yeshivah* of Volozhin, which the poet H. N. Bialik was to call "the place where the soul of the nation was molded," profoundly affected the whole intellectual and spiritual character of Lithuanian Jewry. The *yeshivah*, renamed *Etz Haim* ("the Tree of Life") in honor of its founder, was closed by the czarist government in 1879 and was reopened in 1881; it was closed again in 1892 for its refusal to introduce secular studies. In 1899 it was refounded but did not retain its previous position of eminence. The above selection is from a letter, dated Tammuz 25, 5625 (i.e., 1865), by Rabbi David Moses Joseph of Krynki, a former student of the Volozhin *yeshivah*. In the letter he solicits support for a fund-raising campaign on behalf of the Volozhin *yeshivah*, whose building had burned down the previous year.

2. A play of words on a passage in the Babylonian Talmud 88a.

3. Hebrew for "a place for the study of Torah"—a preparatory school for study in the *yeshivah*.

4. Slavuta is a city in the province of Volhynia. During the late eighteenth and the first half of the nineteenth centuries, the Jewish community of Slavuta became renowned for its printing press, founded in 1791 by Rabbi Moses Shapira.

5. "Blumke's *kloiz*" became the largest *yeshivah* in Minsk.

HIRSCH LEIB GORDON
11. The Musar Yeshivah—A Memoir[1]

A visitor entering the large hall of the Musar *yeshivah* in Slobodka—and there was only one hall—could see the supervisor [*mashgiah*] moving like a shadow among the diligent

Source: Hirsch Leib Gordon [On the banks of the Vilija and the Neman], *Ha-Doar*, 40, no. 8 (1968), p. 207. Reprinted by permission of *Ha-Doar*. Trans. here by L. Sachs.

students. But everyone knew that he and his authority were not of the essence there. The authority of Musar, and the edifier [*mashpia*] who wielded the authority, played the essential role. Rabbi Netta Hirsch Finkel,[2] who at the time of my studies in Slobodka was not yet called "the Grandfather," would go about the *yeshivah* in seeming humility. But all knew that the power and rule were vested in him. The aristocratic figure of the head of the *yeshivah*, Rabbi Moshe Mordecai Epstein,[3] would appear occasionally but it was obvious that he felt a little strange in the spacious hall, where not the Torah held sway but rather "the Method," the special Musar method beside which the Torah was unimportant.

Rabbi Netta Hirsch would look around constantly as if searching for something in the behavior of the students that was not to his liking or taste. Sometimes he would stop beside the desk of a *yeshivah* youth and examine his comportment—his chanting, his movements, his reactions to what was going on around him. The youth upon whom Rabbi Netta Hirsch fixed his stare would shake with fear before the penetrating gaze, uncertain as to whether he had found favor and approval in the eyes of his examiner. Rabbi Netta Hirsch stood in the center of all that went on in the *yeshivah*, and yet stood above it all.

The power and authority of Rabbi Netta Hirsch were at their peak on Sabbath night between *Minchah*[4] and *Ma'ariv*.[5] Then the hall would be enveloped in shadows and the crowd would surround the chair in the center of the hall on which sat the great *mashpia* like a king in his court. No member of the *yeshivah* would dare be absent from this session. From the day of the great scandal involving the books of the Musar which had been thrown into the public toilet, the relations between the Musar movement and its opponents in Lithuania became increasingly strained; both friend and foe saw in Rabbi Netta Hirsch the chief protagonist in the battle, and my child's heart went out in devotion to this majestic figure.

I began to visit the great *yeshivah* in the evenings, especially at dusk on the Sabbath, when the Grandfather would speak in a low and pleasant voice that dropped sometimes to a secret whisper. Hundreds of youths swarmed around him like bees. Most seemed moved by the preaching and the somber voice, although here and there I could detect an expression of doubt, or a secret smile. On one occasion the Grandfather happened to look at me, and wondering at my relative youth he asked me:

"Who are you, little man?"

"I am the son of Rabbi Komay, and I am studying in the *yeshivah* of Rabbi Hirschel."

"And what are you doing here?"

"I come here in the evenings, that I may gain in piety." (I realized that in my eagerness I was exaggerating a bit.)

The Grandfather smiled and stroked my face affectionately. And whenever he exhorted us in the evenings he would embrace me and hold me in his arms.

The Grandfather would speak in broken phrases, in isolated words and fragments of sentences. I can recall one sermon which he gave in the month of Elul:[6]

> . . . repentance . . . repentance and good deeds . . . difficult to accomplish them . . . but one must try anyway . . . nothing can stand in the way of true penitents . . . the Mouth of Hell [*Gehenna*]. . . . He that talks inordinately with women shall inherit Gehenna[7] . . . anyone who swears obscenely . . . anyone who gets angry . . . a flatterer . . . vulgarities . . . one who leaves the path of Torah will fall into Gehenna . . . but one who recites the *Shema*[8] and observes it faithfully, for him Gehenna is cooled . . . as long as a man lives he has hope . . . today there is still time, but who can know about tomorrow . . . anyone who cries in the night, his voice is heard. . . .

At this point the crowd would burst out weeping. And anyone passing in front of the Holy Ark [in which the Torah scrolls are kept] during the evening prayer after the sermon was like a cantor chanting *Kol Nidrei*.[9]

NOTES

1. The Musar movement was a pietistic movement, deriving its name from the Hebrew word for moral instruction (*musar*), which advocated moral earnestness as a necessary supplement to the observance of *mitzvoth* and talmudic learning. The movement arose in mid-nineteenth-century Lithuania, becoming by the turn of the century a dominant trend within its *yeshivot*. Founded by Rabbi Israel Lipkin Salanter (1810–1883), the Musar movement was a response to the increasing laxity in the observance of the Halakha that resulted from the secular influences on Lithuanian Jewry. The problem, as Rabbi Salanter and his disciples understood it, was how to instill a spiritual vitality into the practice of Judaism without attenuating the values of punctilious observance of traditional Judaism. Eventually, the movement developed a distinctive pattern of spiritual and intellectual exercises designed to effect the moral and religious edification of the individual. This program of Musar, directed especially at the young *yeshivah* student, included the reading of classical ethical literature of Judaism, select verses from the Bible, Talmud and Midrash. These passages would be recited, preferably in twilight or subdued lighting, to a melody suitable for evoking a pensive mood of isolation and emotional openness to God and His Commandments. The student was also encouraged to continual self-examination; some Musar rabbis recommended that a notebook be kept in which the student would record his moral and personal failings. The Musar *yeshivah* would have a special *mashgiah* or supervisor, who served as a sort of spiritual mentor guiding the moral and religious development of the students. At least once a week the *mashgiah* would hold a *shmuse* (Yiddish for "talk"), with all the *yeshivah* students, on either a general moral topic or on a specific incident. In addition to punctilious observance of the *mitzvoth*, the need for mutual spiritual support, purity of the mind and intention, humility and regard for one's fellow human beings were stressed. The first Musar society was founded by Rabbi Salanter in Vilna in 1842; he later moved to Kovno. After his death, the movement was led by Rabbi Isaac Blaser (1837–1907) known as Rabbi Itzelle Peterburger, who transformed the *yeshivah* of Slobodka (a suburb of Kovno) into a center of Musar, which influenced the *yeshivot* throughout Lithuania. The Musar movement—its pride, fraternity and spiritual intensity—helped Lithuanian Jewry resist the secularizing influence of Haskalah, the Bund and other forms of socialism and of Zionism. The above selection is from the memoirs of one who studied at the *yeshivah* of Slobodka in the first decade of the twentieth century.

2. Rabbi Nathan Zevi ben Moses Finkel (1849–1927), founder (with the help of Rabbi Isaac Blaser) of the Musar *yeshivah* in Slobodka. As a mark of the deep respect his students had for him, they affectionately called him the Sabba ["grandfather"] from Slobodka.

3. Rabbi Mordecai Epstein (1866–1933) was appointed by Rabbi Finkel as the *rosh yeshivah* ("headmaster") of the *yeshivah* of Slobodka, a position he filled from 1893 until his death.

4. Hebrew term for daily afternoon prayer service.

5. Hebrew term for daily evening prayer service.

6. The twelfth month of the Hebrew calendar, corresponding to August-September. Preceding the "Days of Awe" (Rosh Hashanah and Yom Kippur), Elul is traditionally a period devoted to preparation for penitence.

7. See Ethics of the Fathers.

8. Hebrew designation for the confession of faith, "Hear, O Israel, the Lord our God, the Lord is One."

9. Opening prayer of the Yom Kippur evening service, which is recited in a very solemn manner.

RABBI ISAAC JACOB REINES
12. The Modern Yeshivah of Lida[1]

Upon examining the state of Torah learning and Judaism among the people of Israel in Russia today we see before us a heart-rending spectacle. The houses of learning, where once flocks of pupils eagerly pursued knowledge of the Torah, now stand vacant and desolate. Instead of young men imbued with the knowledge of God and schooled in the ways of Judaism, we encounter everywhere youths who deny their God and their nation, youths innocent of Torah learning who are as far removed from us in spirit as the moon is from the earth. Our ears are daily assaulted with the sounds of new knowledge and modern opinion such as our forefathers could not have fathomed. In vain do we strain to hear the sweet voice of Jacob. Judaism and tradition, the love of God and Torah learning have grown scarce. We stand besieged by alien thoughts and foreign views. The scholars among us grow fewer and fewer. They are no longer well respected and our sons have ceased to turn to them in their pursuit of knowledge.

Upon the ruins of our world a strange, new world is rising; where once our vineyards flourished we now plant strange fruits. The day is near when not a single scholar will be found among us, and the honor, glory and genius of Judaism will turn to dust. Soon, the vital and vivid Judaism we still find among the Jews of Russia will suffer a fate like that which befell her in France. A dreadful disaster is imminent!

Most regretably, the fathers, even those who have remained faithful to their God and to the ways of Judaism, are bringing, with their very hands, this disaster upon themselves and upon their sons. They send their sons out at a tender age to face the temptations of the world, to be educated in the secular schools, to earn a living in industry and commerce. What are we to expect then from our offspring who are nurtured upon foreign soil, who are not nourished by a proper study of Judaism? The future awaiting us is grim, indeed. A horrible fate awaits Judaism, the very Judaism which has so valiantly fought for her survival these thousands of years.

Our wise men took this situation to heart, and gathered together to contemplate a solution to the crisis. They understood that the new situation demands a new outlook, that it would be a crime before God and the nation to sit idly while the crisis grows and worsens. They agreed that the present day realities must be reckoned with and may not be ignored, and that one must take into account the changing needs of the people. To this end, they decided to establish a new *yeshivah*, a *yeshivah* which will permit our sons to remain in the temple of the Torah and yet acquire the sort of knowledge and understanding that would assure their future well-being. The *yeshivah* will grant its pupils the moral authority to be rabbis and equip them with enough worldly knowledge to assure their acceptance as leaders of their generation. The *yeshivah* will not only educate talmudic scholars, but will seek to give a rich Jewish education to those who will find their future in practical, mundane spheres. The *yeshivah* is intended for the good of the Jewish people and for the preservation of Torah learning.

The *yeshivah* is established along the following guidelines: (1) The *yeshivah* will give the students a thorough education in those disciplines required of a rabbi. A special

Source: Isaac Jacob Reines [The mission of the holy *yeshivah* of Lida] (Vilna, 1907), pp. 6–7. Trans. here by R. Weiss.

committee will plan the course of studies. The method of study will be based on common sense and intellectual honesty. (2) The *yeshivah* will give the students an adequate education in biblical studies, Hebrew language and its grammar. Jewish history will be taught from the traditional and correct point of view. The pupils will also become familiar with Jewish literature and its bibliography. (3) The *yeshivah* will provide its students with a secular education equal to that of the public schools. They will be taught to speak and write Russian fluently, and will study as well Russian and world history, geography of the five continents, arithmetic, geometry, algebra, and some of the natural sciences. (4) The *yeshivah* will have six grades for the course of studies extending over a period of six years. In order to advance from one form to the next a student will have to pass an examination. Those who fail the examination will repeat the year's study. (5) Four committees shall be in charge of the *yeshivah*. One committee of rabbis will supervise the religious scholars, a second committee will supervise secular studies, a committee of home owners will supervise financial matters and a committee of pupils will concern itself with matters pertaining to the daily life of the pupils. . . . (6) In matters of scholarship and conduct each student will be supervised individually. The students will be educated to be faithful to God, loyal to their nation and observant of the *mitzvoth*. They will be expected to be well behaved and civilized. (7) Students of the *yeshivah* will receive financial support which will be increased with each year of study. Students in the upper grades will receive a stipend large enough to support them entirely. . . .

NOTE

1. Rabbi Isaac Jacob Reines (1839–1915). One of the first rabbis to join the Zionist movement, he founded the religious Zionist Mizrahi movement in 1902. In 1905 he established (after an earlier abortive attempt in the 1880s) the first modern *yeshivah* in Eastern Europe. At the *yeshivah* (founded in Lida, a town in the province of Grodno), secular studies—with an emphasis on the pragmatic—were taught side by side with traditional studies. As is indicated in Reines' statement, the founding of the *yeshivah* of Lida was guided by a desire to strengthen traditional Jewry in the face of the crisis presented by various secular trends. Reines "explained the increase of influence of the *maskilim* as the result of the fact that they were fighting with 'material and practical weapons,' while the leaders of traditional Judaism confined themselves to moral ones. In other words, the *maskilim* provided the needs of this world while [the rabbis] provided only for the next world" (Joseph Salmon, "The *Yeshivah* of Lida: A Unique Institution of Higher Learning," *YIVO Annual*, 15 [1974], p. 111). Hence, in light of the pressing economic plight of the Jewish masses, Reines held that the youth should be provided with an education that would equip them with the tools to earn a livelihood.

> Despite Reines' emphasis on the economic factor in the crisis, he did not wholly overlook the weakening of individual faith in the tradition and its proponents. This clearly implies a process of transformation of values within the [traditional] community. Haskalah is not seen merely as vocational preparation, but as the road to social esteem. A scholar lacking general knowledge was subject [in Reines' words] to "indifference and contempt," on the part of the rank-and-file. . . . Reines did not see his program as revolutionizing values, but rather as an attempt to find new means to strengthen the basis of traditional society within new social conditions (J. Salmon, op. cit., pp. 113ff.).

O. RABINOWICH
13. Russian Must Be Our Mother Tongue[1]

In other European countries the Jews speak the pure language of their Christian brothers, and that fact does not hinder them from being good Jews. We in Russia, however, instead of learning the glorious Russian language, persist in speaking our corrupted jargon (i.e., Yiddish), that grates on the ears and distorts. This jargon is incapable in fact of expressing sublime thoughts. . . . It is our obligation to cast off these old rags, a heritage of the dark Middle Ages. . . . We believe the time has come for the Russian language to become the Jews' guide on the road to enlightenment and to the widening of their spiritual and material sphere of activity. . . . The Russian language must serve as the primary force animating the masses, because, apart from divine providence, language is the constitutive factor of humanity. Our homeland is Russia—just as its air is ours, so its language must become ours.

NOTE

1. The *maskilim* were divided regarding which language—Russian, Hebrew or Yiddish—should be the vehicle to promote social and cultural progress among the Jewish masses. Opinion on this issue reflected differences of generation and ideology. The representatives of the early Haskalah and the Zionists on the whole favored Hebrew. The socialists by and large preferred Yiddish. Liberals who believed in the eventual liberalization of the Russian polity and the civil emancipation of the Jews, urged the adoption of Russian. According to a government census of 1897, 96.7 percent of the Jews of the Pale spoke Yiddish as their first language; only 1.3 percent spoke either Russian, Ukrainian or Belorussian as their mother tongue. Outside of the Pale, the latter figure was 72 percent. Hebrew as a written language was known to those Jews who had received a thorough traditional education. The number of Jews who knew Hebrew, although difficult to ascertain, was far greater than the number of those literate in Russian.

The above selection is from the first Russian Jewish weekly, *Razsvet* [Dawn]. The purpose of this weekly, founded in 1860, was "to assist our government in its constant and sincere efforts to improve the conditions of our people and raise its moral and cultural level." To further this end, *Razsvet* would interpret government decrees for its readers, preach patriotism, genuine piety and morality, and disseminate "useful" knowledge. In the dispute over which language should be used by the "modern" Jew, *Razsvet* advocated the adoption of Russian. Its foremost aim, however, was to champion the cause of Jewish civil rights. This latter position brought the paper into conflict with the government censor and it was forced to fold within a year of its first issue.

Source: O. Rabinowich [Russia—our native land: just as we breathe its air we must speak its language], *Razsvet,* no. 16 (Odessa, 1861), pp. 200–205. Trans. here by R. Weiss.

SOCIETY FOR THE PROMOTION OF CULTURE AMONG JEWS

14. Program[1]

. . . 1. Regarding the dissemination of the Russian language. In accordance with the request of the Deputy Minister of Education we shall endeavor: (a) to publish a new edition of the books originally published by the government in 1857 to teach the Jews to read the Russian language, and to publish an inexpensive Russian primer adapted for the Jewish reader; (b) to print Jewish history texts in Russian, because the contents will surely touch the heart of every Jew; (c) to encourage our brethren who have literary talent and Russian language skills to write material in Russian, by awarding them grants and financial assistance, and to publish their compositions in books, pamphlets and periodicals. This material should deal with Jewish history, literature and other topics of relevance and use to us. This project will have two beneficial results. On the one hand, in the course of time, there will be many Jewish writers of Russian and, on the other hand, such compositions will provide a powerful incentive for the Jewish public to learn Russian. Furthermore, since the books will be published with the help of the Society, it will be possible to sell them at low enough prices to enable all Jews to buy them.

2. Regarding the dissemination of useful knowledge among our brethren. Since the aim of our Society is to care for the masses of our people and their educational needs, to motivate them to acquire an education and to persuade them that enlightenment is not opposed to our faith, it is necessary to distribute among the people books which contain nothing touching on faith and religion. Accordingly, we shall promote only those books dealing with scientific matters which have been edited with good taste and present the material in an appropriate way. Since, as is now the case, the masses of the people do not yet know Russian, the only way to bring this material to their attention is to publish it in Hebrew and in the traditional rabbinic style of the Talmud, which is most widely understood by the people. Therefore the executive committee of the Society has decided as follows: (a) to attempt to edit for our brethren books written in the aforementioned style and language, dealing with the natural sciences, mathematics, geography and history—especially Jewish history—and other works that the committee will find useful; (b) in order to disseminate information on the natural sciences and mathematics in particular, the committee shall empower [one of its members to speak to the authorities] about renewing the publication of *Ha-Zefirah*,[2] under the conditions approved by the committee; (c) so that Jewish youth shall be informed of all that goes on in the world of Jewry and be acquainted, in addition, with the works of German scholars in the area of the Science of Judaism, the committee will send the relevant German Jewish periodicals to the talmudic academies, the *yeshivot*, and to some of the middle-level schools, to libraries and to the *heders* [traditional primary schools]; (d) to attempt to implement the idea of establishing libraries and reading rooms for the Jews in every city, with the assistance of the Society's members in each city.

After looking into the matter of allotting certain sums to some of the projects deemed appropriate to the goals of the Society as

Source: [Decisions of the Executive Committee of the Society for the Promotion of Culture among Jews, February 8, 1864], in Leon Rosenthal, *Toldot hevrat marbei haskalah be-yisrael be-eretz Rusyah* (St. Petersburg, 1885), vol. 1, pp. 4–5. Trans. here by D. Goldman.

specified in its statutes, the committee has decided to set aside three-eighths of the Society's income this year, for support of needy Jewish students in the institutions of higher learning; and one-eighth of the Society's income for the promotion of the Russian language and useful books among the Jews. . . .

Further, we will increase the stipends given to students in the colleges in St. Petersburg, Moscow, Kiev, Cracow and Derpt, in the St. Petersburg Medical School, the Technical Institute, the Art School and the Music Conservatory.

NOTES

1. The Society for the Promotion of Culture among Jews was founded in St. Petersburg in 1863 by members of the Jewish upper bourgeoisie; the society was under the supervision of the Ministry of Education. The principal reason for the founding of the society, according to Leon Rosenthal (1817–1887), its first treasurer, was to address a charge made by the government: "whenever Jewish leaders broached the question of civic rights to government representatives, the latter countered by charging them with the task of educating the masses of Jewry" (Rosenthal, *Toldot hevrat marbei haskalah be-yisrael be-eretz Rusyah*, p. vii). The society accordingly set as its task, as its program reflects, the preparation of its brethren for emancipation and integration into Russian society and culture.

2. Hebrew periodical appearing intermittently in Warsaw from 1862 to 1931. The initial object of the periodical—until 1879 when Nahum Sokolow (1860–1936) joined its editorial staff and changed its direction to emphasize Hebrew literature and Zionist ideology—was to disseminate a knowledge of the natural sciences and mathematics among the Jews of the Pale.

ISAAC DOV LEVINSOHN
15. Yiddish Is a Corrupt Jargon[1]

This language which we speak here in this country, which we borrowed from the Germans and which is called Judeo-German—this language is completely corrupted. This corruption is a consequence of the eclectic nature of the language, a mixture of corrupted words taken from Hebrew, Russian, French, Polish, as well as from German, and even the German words are mispronounced and slurred. Moreover, this, our language, cannot serve us except for popular usage and simple conversations. If we wish to formulate concepts about higher things, Judeo-German will not suffice. . . .

Why Judeo-German?—From these observations [concerning the shortcomings of Judeo-German] you will readily acknowledge the need to study at least one pure language and know it well. And there is no need to add that the language of the country we live in is doubtlessly the one we are obligated to learn correctly. Thus we can ask: in this country, why speak Judeo-German? Either pure German or Russian. Not only is Russian the language of the country, it is also an especially pure and rich language. It is not lacking in pleasant tones or aesthetic form and it contains all the elements considered necessary for the perfect language (as I have explained at length in the introduction to my book in Hebrew, *The Elements of the Russian Language*, which I wrote for the benefit of

Source: Isaac Dov Levinsohn, *Teudah be-Yisrael* (Vilna, 1828), pp. 34–36. Trans. here by D. Goldman.

Jewish youth and which I hope to publish soon, if God grant me life). We may conclude from our discussion so far that it is a great obligation and necessity to know one of the foreign languages well, especially the language of the country where we live, and that we should know it perfectly so that we can articulate our thoughts in a correct manner.

NOTE

1. Isaac Dov Levinsohn (1788–1860) was the first great protagonist of Haskalah in Russia. He was hailed by his contemporaries as the Russian Moses Mendelssohn. His works are mainly polemical, excoriating traditional Jewish leadership, particularly Hasidic, and advocating educational reform and the transition to a life of labor and agriculture. This selection is taken from his most influential work, *Teudah be-Yisrael* [Testimony in Israel], written in 1823, but due to fierce Orthodox opposition it was not published until 1828. The Russian government gave him an award for this work.

PEREZ SMOLENSKIN[1]
16. Hebrew—Our National Fortress

. . . When people ask what the renewal of the Hebrew language will give us I shall answer: It will give us self-respect and courage, it will bind us indissolubly to the name Israel. Other peoples may erect stone monuments . . . and spill their blood like water in order to perpetuate their own name and language. . . . We have no monument, country or name, and the only memory remaining to us from the destruction of the Temple is the Hebrew language. Many [Jews] despise and scorn it, and those who do, denigrate our entire people . . . they are traitors to their name and faith. They exhort us: "Let us be like all the other nations." I answer: Let us, like other nations, pursue knowledge and reject evil, let us, like other nations, take pride in our origins and acknowledge our language and national honor. Our faith must not be a source of shame to us. . . . We are secure if we hold fast to the ancient language which has accompanied us from country to country, to the tongue in which our poets and prophets spoke, in which our forefathers cried aloud with their dying breath. . . . Our language is our national fortress; if it disappears into oblivion the memory of our people will vanish from the face of the earth.

NOTE

1. Perez Smolenskin (1840–1885), Russian Hebrew novelist and publicist. In 1868 he founded the Hebrew monthly *Ha-Shahar* [The dawn], which, under his dedicated editorship, became the most significant Hebrew literary platform of the Haskalah in its late period. Smolenskin sought to steer a path between what he held to be the Scylla of the Orthodox obscurantism and the Charybdis of assimilation. He found this path in Jewish nationalism. And accordingly, he was a passionate advocate of the Hebrew language and literature, which he deemed to be the ground of Jewish nationhood and the surrogate for a national territory.

Source: Perez Smolenskin [Foreword], *Ha-Shahar*, 1 (1868), pp. v–vii. Trans. here by L. Sachs.

MENDELE MOYKHER SFORIM[1]

17. My Soul Desired Yiddish

. . . Here I am, observing the ways of our people and attempting to write for them stories from Jewish sources in the holy tongue, yet most of them do not even know this tongue. Their language is Yiddish. And what life is there for a writer, what profit in his labor, if he is of no use to his people? The question—"for whom do I toil?"[2]—has not ceased to trouble me. . . . The Yiddish language in my day was an empty vessel, containing nothing but slang and trite, meaningless phrases. . . . The women and the poor would read Yiddish without understanding it, while the rest of the people, even if they didn't know how to read in another language, were ashamed to be caught reading Yiddish, lest this private folly of theirs become public knowledge. And if one of them gave in to temptation and read a Yiddish book and, enjoying it, laughed over it, he immediately justified his deed by saying to himself it was unintentional. Indeed he would justify his reaction by dismissing the book as women's literature, capable of provoking laughter but not thought. Those of our writers who know Hebrew, our holy tongue, and continue to write in it, do not care whether or not the people understand it. These writers look down on Yiddish and greatly scorn it. And if one out of many occasionally remembered the cursed jargon and wrote a few lines in it, he kept his works hidden, so as to escape criticism and ridicule. How perplexed I was then, when I thought of writing in Yiddish, for I feared it would entail the ruin of my reputation—so my friends in the Hebrew literature movement had warned me. But my love for the useful defeated false pride, and I decided to take pity on the much-scorned language and do what I could for my people. One of my friends [Shiye-Mordkhe Lifshits[3]] joined me in persuading the publisher of *Ha-Melitz*[4] to publish a periodical in Yiddish, the language of our people. The publisher agreed and *Kol Mevasser*[5] began to appear with great success. I was soon inspired to write my first story in Yiddish: "Das kleine Menshele, oder a lebens beshraybung fun Avrom Yitzhok Takif," gedrukt b'hishtadlus Mendele Moykher Sforim.[6] . . . And other stories and books followed.

My first story made a big impact on the Jewish masses and was soon published in a third edition . . . and then in a fourth edition. . . . That story laid the cornerstone of modern Yiddish literature. From then on, my soul desired only Yiddish, and I dedicated myself entirely to it. . . .

NOTES

1. Mendele Moykher Sforim is the pen name of Russian, Hebrew and Yiddish author Shalom Jacob Abramowitsch (c. 1836–1917). Beloved for his affectionate descriptions and satires of the Jewish masses of Russia in the later nineteenth century, he was an innovator in artistic prose style in both Hebrew and Yiddish literature; his influence on the latter was particularly marked.

2. Title of poem by Judah Leib Gordon, see document 9, in this chapter.

3. Shiye-Mordkhe Lifshits (1829–1878) was one of the pioneers of Yiddish literature.

Source: Mendele Moykher Sforim [Autobiographical notes, The complete works of Mendele Moykher Sforim] (Tel Aviv: Devir, 1947), pp. 4–5. Reprinted by permission. Trans. here by D. Goldman.

4. *Ha-Melitz* [The advocate] was a Hebrew periodical which appeared from 1860 to 1904; from 1886 to 1904 it appeared as a daily. Considered the central organ of Russian Jewry, it was moderately conservative and very influential.

5. A Yiddish supplement of *Ha-Melitz*.

6. ["The little man, or the life of Abraham Isaac Takif," printed with the assistance of Mendele Moykher Sforim] (Odessa: *Kol Mevasser*, 1864).

AARON LIEBERMANN
18. The Jewish Question in Eastern Europe[1]

In all countries about to acknowledge the dignity of every child of man, the question of Jewish civil rights has, in the context of normal social life, become increasingly important. As of now, however, this question is still out of place in the countries of the East where it has not yet occurred to anyone to consider someone not of his tribe or allegiance as human. [This question has not yet occurred to the] barbaric peoples nor to their yet more barbaric rulers. In America and Western Europe, on the other hand, the question has already been forgotten, for there the concept "man" has dispelled the concepts of nation and faith—at least among the enlightened. Only in those countries bordering the East and the West—the settlements of the Slavic tribes—will some still parley over the Jewish question without resolving the "unsolvable riddle." . . .

[In Eastern Europe] the Jews and their supporters have been compelled to fight for their lives in a defensive war against enemies waging a war of offense, and their stratagems greatly vary depending on the features of the battlefield. In Rumania the Jews seek refuge from persecution and oppression in the protection of the powerful kings. And sometimes they gain satisfaction by hurling insult and abuse back at those who vilify them. It is understandable that they then completely overstep bounds, and seizing upon the doings of their opponents heap scorn and contempt on the entire Rumanian people. For the misdeeds of some, they defame an entire nation with curses of the marketplace. . . . These stratagems may help, but woe to the member of the household who seeks the protection of strangers to defend him from the blows of his father or brother! On most occasions they will manage to break all his bones before his protectors rush to his aid. In the land of Galicia, the Jews are strong enough to defend themselves without outside help. Those Jews with sidelocks as twisted and as long as our exile, who wear cloth pants, stockings, and all the other old Polish garb—now called "Jewish clothing"—those men are politicians and diplomats! Positioned between the Germans and the Poles, they always lean toward that faction whose way seems right to their sight. There, in Galicia, the Jews truly stand on one footing with the other national tribes as far as politics are concerned, and in a time of need they will come here to Vienna with their shoes and stockings, their sidecurls and *zjupitse*[2] to stand before the Kaiser. The Jews of Russia are not like that. Only rarely may their voices be heard speaking of their enemies in the Russian journals. It is not a voice of jubilation but—whoever hears may laugh—a voice of supplication spoken halfheartedly, gravely and in a spirit of utter defeat. We know that

Source: Aaron Liebermann, "She'elat ha-Yehudim," *Ha-Emet*, 1 (Summer 1877), pp. 1–5. Trans. here by A. Schwartz.

our brethren in Russia apologize that they have not been permitted to respond to their enemies as they would like, and we can believe them. . . . But in fact it is all the same to us if they respond in a tone of jubilation, like the Jews of Rumania, or in a tone of entreaty as they now do. For as we have said from the outset, this is a war of might and guile, lie and deceit—and it is indeed a war! At one end are those who will bring all Jews to trial for every offense committed by individual Jews. The Jews, for their part, will make every effort to drag out their rights and show them off in the bright light of day declaring: Here is the Jewish people! Both will place individuals in the stead of the collective as a whole. However much the Jew-haters increase their search among us for evil doings, the Jews will strive wherever they can to conceal the blemishes of their brothers from the "desecration of God's name," or they will produce their righteous brothers as having been maligned as sinners. This will sometimes be successful, but most of the time it will fail. For how is it possible to show that all of Israel is a righteous nation or that in all of Jacob's flock there is not even one leprous lamb?

This war over the Jewish question could continue forever, for while both sides are correct concerning details, they have both relied in their arguments on sophistry, both have emphasized *quid pro quo* and both have missed the larger truth. How will it come to an end? When will the fate of the Jews and of the Slavs be joined together in peace? When will each side acknowledge the other's humanity and join hands for the ascent to human perfection? . . .

NOTES

1. Aaron Liebermann (1845–1880), pioneer of Jewish socialism and a Hebrew writer. In 1875 he fled his native Russia in order to avoid arrest for his socialist activities. In London he began to develop a program for a revolutionary socialist organization among the Jews of Russia. He was inspired by the Narodnik principle of "going to the masses," which he interpreted as going to the Jewish masses. In 1877 he settled in Vienna and began to publish *Ha-Emet* [The truth]—the first Hebrew socialist periodical. Only three issues of the periodical appeared; its quick demise was caused by financial difficulties and the need to smuggle the periodical into Russia. Liebermann wrote most of the articles and in them he criticized organized Jewish life, the exploitation of the poor by the rich Jews and the unthoughtful hostility of Jewish socialists to Jewish tradition. This selection is taken from the inaugural article of *Ha-Emet*. It describes the plight of various East European Jewish communities.

2. A black overcoat, similar to a caftan.

19. Awaiting a Pogrom[1]

. . . We expected a pogrom during the Christmas holidays and the city was in a state of siege. Before the holidays we went to the governor and asked for protection. The Cossacks were called and the stores closed for three days. And now, although the holidays have passed quietly (i.e., there were no riots), our fears have not been allayed and we expect a pogrom at any minute. In brief, we see no end to our anxiety. For ahead of us are the

Source: [Letter to the editor from a Jew in Vilna], *Nedelnaya kronika voskhroda,* no. 1 (February 1882), p. 3. Trans. here by L. Sachs.

civil New Year, the "Week of Butter," the Holiday of Baptism and Easter. How many threats and curses we heard before the holidays! If someone gets into an argument with a Christian the latter immediately says: "Just wait, soon we'll settle all the scores," or something similar or even worse. What kind of life is this? If I had the courage I would kill all those close to me and then myself, and the farce would be over. If I do not, some drunken riff-raff will come along, ravish my wife and daughter and throw my infant Sonia from the third-floor window. Would it not be better for me to kill everyone? What a miserable creature is the Jew! Even when the advantage is clear to him he cannot summon the courage to do a good thing. Death awaits us in any case, so why should we wait?

NOTE

1. *Pogrom* is a Russian word for a violent riot, accompanied by pillage and murder, perpetrated by one group against another. Throughout Russian history pogroms occurred between various communities in the multinational empire. In the international lexicon *pogrom* is now a technical term designating the type of attack carried out by the non-Jewish population of Russia—and Eastern Europe in general—against the Jews between 1881 and 1921. Rarely did the police or the army intervene; indeed, they often lent their support to the rioters. The pogroms occurred during periods of severe political crisis and Christian holidays. Three major waves of pogroms took place: in 1881–1884, 1903–1906 and 1917–1921. The first began in the period of political unrest and confusion that followed the assassination of Czar Alexander II in March 1881. Starting at the end of April 1881 in a Ukrainian town, pogroms spread quickly throughout the region and then erupted in Warsaw, Belorussia and Lithuania. The pogroms of the 1880s had a profound influence on the history of Russian Jewry. The radicalization of Jewish youth, the development of the nationalist and Zionist movement in Russia and the mass emigration of Russian Jewry were all to a great extent prompted by the pogroms. This selection is from a letter to the editor of a Russian-language Jewish periodical published in St. Petersburg. The periodical served as the organ of the Russian Jewish intelligentsia, who maintained both a commitment to Judaism and a confidence in the ultimate triumph of liberalism in Russia.

20. The Massacre of Jews at Kishinev[1]

Shortly before Easter, when the Bishop of the Greek Church in the Kishinev province was asked to contradict the absurd rumor that the Jews murdered a young man for their ritual [at Passover], . . . this high priest publicly stated that he himself believed the story of Jews using Christian blood for ritualistic purposes.

The semi-official paper . . . openly preached the extermination of Jews for months . . . All applications for permission to publish a more impartial paper having been repeatedly refused. . . .

And still, when the actual massacres began, the Governor—it is said now—failed for two days to obtain orders from the Ministry and the Czar at St. Petersburg to use military force against the housebreakers and murderers. Moreover, he refused in the course of those two days any communication with the suffering Jewish population, never left his private quarters, closed all the telephones in

Source: Free Russia: Organ of the Friends of Russian Freedom, vol. 14, no. 5, (May 1903).

the town to the public, and prohibited [the sending of] any private telegrams from Kishinev to St. Petersburg.

The police of the town not only refused to render any efficient protection and assistance to the . . . attacked and murdered Jewish population, but deliberately prevented by force any assistance being rendered to them by those private persons who were willing to do so. The police actually pointed out Jewish houses to the rioters. Whenever Jews themselves attempted to gather to show armed resistance, the police and military instantly attacked, disarmed, and dispersed them.

The results of this terrible circumstance are awful: 118 Jews, men, women and children, have already been buried; over 200 cases of serious injuries are still in the hospitals; and over 1000 cases of lighter injuries [have been] attended [to] in infirmaries; 800 Jewish houses destroyed and demolished; 600 shops and stores broken into and looted; over 4000 Jewish families have been rendered homeless and destitute. . . .

It has been learned that there were about 12,000 troops in Kishinev at the time, against 200 to 300 active rioters and housebreakers. And as soon as the Government chose to proclaim martial law, after two days of delay, all disorders instantly stopped. . . .

NOTE

1. Kishinev, today the capital of Moldavia, USSR, was formerly the capital of Bessarabia. At the turn of the century some 50,000 Jews lived there, constituting 46 percent of the population. The pogrom, described in this document, took place during Easter on April 6 and 7, 1903. Agents of the Ministry of the Interior and high officials of the Bessarabian administration were apparently involved in the preparation of the pogrom. The pogrom was preceded by a venomous anti-Jewish campaign led by an editor of a local newspaper, who incited the population through a constant barrage of hateful articles. The immediate cause of the pogrom was the death of a Christian child whom the Jews were accused of killing, for the use of his blood in their religious rites. The pogrom caused a public outcry throughout the world and led to establishment of Jewish self-defense units.

HAIM NAHMAN BIALIK
21. The City of Slaughter[1]

Arise and go now to the city of slaughter;
Into its courtyard wind thy way;
There with thine own hand touch, and with the eyes of thine head,
Behold on tree, on stone, on fence, on mural clay,
The spattered blood and dried brains of the dead.
Proceed thence to the ruins, the split walls reach,
Where wider grows the hollow, and greater grows the breach;
Pass over the shattered hearth, attain the broken wall
Whose burnt and barren brick, whose charred stones reveal
The open mouths of such wounds, that no mending
Shall ever mend, nor healing ever heal.

Source: Haim Nahman Bialik, "City of Slaughter," trans. Abraham M. Klein, in *The Complete Works of Hayyim Nahman Bialik,* ed. Israel Efros (New York: The Histadruth Ivrith of America, 1948), vol. 1, pp. 129, 133–34.

There will thy feet in feathers sink, and stumble
On wreckage doubly wrecked, scroll heaped on manuscript,
Fragments against fragmented—
Pause not upon this havoc; go thy way. . . .

Descend then, to the cellars of the town,
There where the virginal daughters of thy folk were fouled,
Where seven heathen flung a woman down,
The daughter in the presence of her mother,
The mother in the presence of her daughter,
Before slaughter, during slaughter, and after slaughter!
Touch with thy hand the cushion stained, touch
The pillow incarnadined;
This is the place the wild ones of the wood, the beasts of the field
With bloody axes in their paws compelled thy daughters yield;
Beasted and swined!
Note also, do not fail to note,
In that dark corner, and behind that cask
Crouched husbands, bridegrooms, brothers, peering from the cracks,
Watching the sacred bodies struggling underneath
The bestial breath,
Stifled in filth, and swallowing their blood!
The lecherous rabble portioning for booty
Their kindred and their flesh!
Crushed in their shame, they saw it all;
They did not stir nor move;
They did not pluck their eyes out; they
Beat not their brains against the wall!
Perhaps, perhaps, each watcher had it in his heart to pray:
A miracle, O Lord,—and spare my skin this day!
Those who survived this foulness, who from their blood awoke,
Beheld their life polluted, the light of their world gone out—
How did their menfolk bear it, how did they bear this yoke?
They crawled forth from their holes, they fled to the house of the Lord,
They offered thanks to Him, the sweet benedictory word.
The *Cohanim* [descendants of priestly families] sallied forth, to the Rabbi's house they flitted:
Tell me, O Rabbi, tell, is my own wife permitted?[2]
The matter ends; and nothing more.
And all is as it was before. . . .

Come, now, and I will bring thee to their lairs
The privies, jakes and pigpens where the heirs
Of Hasmoneans lay, with trembling knees,
Concealed and cowering, —the sons of the Maccabees!
The seed of saints, the scions of the lions!
Who, crammed by scores in all the sanctuaries of their shame,
So sanctified My name!
It was the flight of mice they fled,
The scurrying of roaches was their flight;
They died like dogs, and they were dead!

NOTE

1. Haim Nahman Bialik (1873–1934). Considered the poet laureate of modern Hebrew, Bialik exercised a profound influence on modern Jewish culture. Raised in the Pale of Settlement, he broke with traditional Judaism at the age of eighteen, and he devoted himself to the creation of a national, secular Jewish culture. His attitude to traditional Judaism, however, was ambivalent. On the one hand, he was angered at what he felt to be the moribund state of traditional Jewish society, on the other hand, he was painfully aware of the dilemma of the modern Jew whose struggle for the right to determine his own destiny seemed to require a desperate rejection of divine law.

Bialik was sent to Kishinev on behalf of the Jewish Historical Commission in Odessa in order to interview survivors of the pogrom and to prepare a report on the atrocities. After his visit to Kishinev he wrote this poem, denouncing neither God nor the Russian mobs, but the Jews themselves. This poem became a symbol of the Zionist revolt against traditional Judaism's supine acceptance of Exile and the millennial humiliation of Jewry.

2. The Cohanim are subject to strict laws of purity.

22. The Beilis Trial[1]

In Kiev, Russia yesterday, there was placed on trial behind closed doors, one Mendel Beilis, charged with the murder of a Russian lad, Yuschinsky, in 1911. Beilis is a Jew, and is accused of "ritual murder," that is to say of having killed a boy to get his blood for alleged use in the rites of the Jewish religion. There are two elements in this case which make it of great importance and interest to right-thinking persons in all parts of the world.

One is the clear presumption, on all available official Russian testimony, of the entire innocence of the accused. Immediately after the murder of the boy, M. Minschuk, Chief of the Detective Service in Kiev, with several assistants, investigated the case and reported, first, that there was no evidence against Beilis, the accused, and second, that the boy was murdered by a gang of criminals whom he was suspected of betraying. For this report M. Minschuk was accused of manufacturing evidence to hinder the prosecution and to protect Jews, and though acquitted on one trial, was retried and condemned to prison for a year, with his assistants receiving lighter sentences. That fact clearly discredits the whole case of the prosecution.

The second significant fact in the case is the nature of the accusation, the allegation of murder for Jewish ritual purposes. The crime does not and cannot exist. It has been shown over and over again, and long ago, that there is nothing in the religious belief or practice of the Jews that remotely requires or sanctions or suggests the thing charged. Strict and searching inquiry by eminent men of science, theologians, historians, physicians, not Jews, in Great Britain, in Germany, in France, has resulted in the distinct and unqualified verdict that the belief in this crime has not the slightest foundation in fact, and that it is a foolish, blind superstition bred of prejudice upon ignorance.

It has so been held and denounced by the Pope, by the head of the Orthodox Church, by living Bishops of that Church, and by a Czar of Russia, Alexander I, in 1817, confirmed by Nicholas I in 1835. What renders this base and baseless accusation more revolting at this late day, and by the officials of a Government professedly Christian, is the

Source: Editorial, "The Czar on Trial," *New York Times,* October 9, 1913, p. 12.

fact that it is in the twentieth century the revival of a service used by the pagans in the first century to justify the oppression and slaughter of Christians. The Government of Russia, and especially the Czar of Russia, the authoritative head of a great branch of the Christian Church, in the mad, stupid war on the Jews, is 2000 years behind the times.

For the Russian peasants who are the helpless victims of this superstition, and who accept it as a like superstition was accepted by the savage crowds of the Roman Arena, we can have pity, and even with the brutal action inspired by it we can have patience. But for educated men, particularly for Russian officials who deliberately appeal to the superstitious and incite to brutal action, we can have only indignant detestation. And that feeling is in no wise affected by the fact that this outrage is directed to those of one or another race, one or another religion. The outrage is upon humanity.

Every human, every decently human instinct condemns it; it is true that the offense is one that cannot be dealt with in the ordinary ways of international communication, though it is by no means wholly beyond them, as was very properly shown in the case of Rumania as conducted by the late Secretary Hay. But in the court of public opinion such an offense can and must be dealt with. Fortunately there is a large number of educated and fair-minded Russians who not only will recognize the jurisdiction of that court and respect its verdict, but will contribute to it. And this element in Russia is bound to gain in strength and influence. If the second trial at Kiev results in the conviction of the hapless Beilis, and that is followed by the disorders it is calculated to produce, this element will be not weakened, but reinforced. In view of this fact and of the general protest that has been aroused it may be said the Czar and the autocracy are now on trial.

NOTE

1. On March 20, 1911, the mutilated body of a twelve-year-old Gentile boy, Andre Yushchinsky, was found in a cave on the outskirts of Kiev. The right-wing press immediately accused the Jews of killing the child in order to use his blood for ritual purposes. Although the police possessed incontrovertible evidence that a gang of thieves was responsible, the chief district attorney, pressured by anti-Semitic interests, disregarded the police report and instead insisted on pursuing the blood libel against the Jews. Finally a Jew, Menahem Mendel Beilis (1874–1934), on the basis of circumstantial evidence, was accused of killing the Russian child. On July 21, 1911 Beilis was arrested and sent to prison, where he languished for over two years before being brought to trial. The case attracted universal attention. Liberal-minded people throughout the world were shocked that the baseless blood libel, rooted in medieval folklore, still had credence in Russia. An editorial from the *New York Times* is presented here as an example of this protest. The trial of Beilis took place in Kiev in 1913 from the twenty-fifth of September through the twenty-fifth of October. Beilis was acquitted.

JUDAH LEIB LEVIN
23. To America or to the Land of Israel[1]

. . . It is clear that if there were no other proposal for saving tens of thousands of our brothers from their hard and bitter sufferings, if there were no other way in which our

Source: Judah Leib Levin, in *Ha-Maggid*, 25, no. 39 (October 6, 1881), pp. 321–22. Trans. here by L. Sachs.

people could be reborn and fulfill their destiny, then it would be easier to reconcile ourselves to a thousand sacrifices and to the European spiritual abominations in order to live in tranquility without fear of the wrath of tyrants who threaten to disperse and destroy us, without fear that at any moment our lives and property may be pillaged and plundered. But before us lies the prospect of deliverance from evil and national rebirth in the land of America. The intelligent man will, therefore, choose this path, arguing that . . . although the ancient memories of our souls are not bound up with the American soil, it is nonetheless a suitable land in which to raise up the remnants of Israel, for it is a country settled by enlightened peoples of culture and civilized behavior. Further, there the Jews, unconstrained by the commandments enjoined upon them concerning their own soil, would be able to lead a good life. And America has a further advantage in connection with the rebirth of our nation and that is: In the Holy Land our dream would be far from realized; there we would be slaves to the Sultan and the Pashas; there, as here, we would bear a heavy burden in the midst of a wild desert people, sustaining ourselves with the distant hope that if our numbers increase sufficiently we might perhaps, after many years, become another small principality that will, finally, in some ultimate utopia, . . . achieve its destiny. But in America our dream is closer to fulfillment, for the constitution of that country provides that when the number of colonists reaches sixty thousand they have the right to establish a separate state with a governor, ministers, and a constitution, and to determine their own laws, and our hope of attaining our independence and leading our lives in accordance with our beliefs and inclinations would not be long deferred.

Kindly note, my friend, that I speak not only of the advantages in regard to spiritual rebirth; I have not mentioned the material advantages of America, as they are obvious and require no proof. . . . Our brethren beg for relief from oppression. . . . They must find a safe haven. Our rich and generous must . . . rescue the lost flock of Israel from the dwellings of lions. . . . Let [the rich] find any place which suits them if only they save our wretched brethren.

The eloquence of the Bible, the piteous spectacle of the bereaved daughter of Zion, the emotion aroused by our ancient memories, all these speak for the Land of Israel. The good life recommends America. You know, my friend, that many will yearn for the Holy Land, and I know that even more will stream to America. Let there be no quarrel! Let the writers sharpen their pens, but in the meantime the generous must rise up to rescue their oppressed and persecuted brethren in any way they may choose.

NOTE

1. Judah Leib Levin (acronym, *Yehalel,* 1844–1925). Ḥebrew poet and socialist, he assisted Aaron S. Liebermann in the publication of *Ha-Emet.* His poems were the first to introduce socialist themes into Hebrew literature. After the pogroms of 1881 he despaired of a solution to the Jewish problem in Russia and advocated emigration to the United States. He presented his position in a letter to David Gordon (1831–1886), editor of the Hebrew weekly *Ha-Maggid* (which was at the time published in Lyck, East Prussia). Excerpts of the letter are presented here. Soon after writing this letter Levin joined the Hovevei Zion in his native Kiev and became a fervent supporter of emigration to Palestine.

The Jewish masses of the Pale responded to the pogroms with a panicked, spontaneous flight across the borders of Russia. Within a decade perhaps 200,000 Jews emigrated. Most were penniless. The Jewish leadership was divided on the question as to whether or not to organize, encourage and regulate the emigration from Russia. The Jewish upper bourgeoisie felt that such endorsement of emigration would be construed as unpatriotic and endanger the cause of Jewish emancipation in Russia. Many rabbinic leaders felt that emigration to the West, especially "materialistic" America, would increase the threat of secularization, a danger worse in their eyes than intermittent pogroms. Only a minority of Jewish leaders favored emigration. The issue was debated in the Jewish press for several years. An estimated 70 to 80 percent of those who emigrated went to the United States; between 1881 and 1890 the number of Russian Jews to enter the United States totaled 135,003 (S. Joseph, *Jewish Immigration to the United States from 1881–1910* [New York, 1914], p. 93). For the Jewish intellectuals who favored emigration the main issue was: America or Palestine?

24. On the Latest Wave of Emigration (1891)[1]

With respect to the exodus of Jews from Russia—which has recently gained in momentum—the following letter appeared in the journal *Novoe Vremya:*

Since the spring of this year almost all the Jews living in the southern provinces of Russia have been seized by the urge to leave for abroad. The success of some few Jews who went to America; the false tales spread among the Jews by shipowners' agents about the success and happiness awaiting those who go; and the rumors circulated in anti-Jewish periodicals about the harsh laws soon to be promulgated against them—all these have strengthened the desire of the Jews to leave Russia and go to Palestine or America, with no heed to the danger of this step and no fear of the evil into which they may fall. . . .

Those Jews who wish to go to America make every effort to find the money for the journey, and in anticipation of the success and happiness to come they sell all of their movable possessions. When they are unable to take their families with them, as is frequently the case, they go without them, leaving their wives and children to be a burden on the Jewish community. In most cases the fate of these abandoned wretches is miserable and bitter, for the charity of the Jewish community rarely suffices to meet their needs. And from the husbands and fathers in America come letters full of moans and wails about *their* bitter lot in the new country, for they soon realize there is no chance of success, it is difficult to find work and their pay is sufficient only to buy themselves a few crusts of bread. How then could they save even a penny to send home to their families? Those who leave yearn with all their hearts to return to their homeland, but are unable to find the money for the journey. Many of the refugees who went to America last year are in this miserable state. . . .

[An appeal from a Jewish immigration relief committee in Memel.] May it please you, dear Sir, to publish this letter to all the residents of this city cautioning them against leaving their homes for England or America without sufficient funds to cover the entire cost of the journey and assuming that help will be forthcoming from the committee in this city or in Hamburg. We feel compelled to issue a solemn warning that anyone doing so is bringing a grave disaster upon himself. We are unable to offer any monetary help whatsoever, and the police may seize him and expel him across the border back to his point of origin. . . . His blood is upon his own head, for we must abide by our warning. . . .

Source: Ha-Zefirah, no. 135 (June-July 1891), pp. 548–49. Trans. here by L. Sachs.

NOTE

1. In 1891 the emigration of Jews from Russia suddenly increased twofold and more. They were spurred by rumors about discriminatory laws, the expulsion of Jews from Moscow and other cities of the interior, and the economic depression that severely affected the Pale. A U.S. commission appointed in 1891 to investigate the causes prompting the wave of emigration to the United States from Europe visited Russia. With regard to the remnants of the Moscow Jewish community it reported, "Homes are destroyed, businesses ruined, families separated, all claiming that they are not criminal except that they are charged with being Jews; all expressing a willingness and an anxiety to work, begging the opportunity to begin life [anew] somewhere, where they do not know nor do they care.... We found," the commissioners added with reference to the general situation of Russian Jewry, "that America was by no means an unknown country to them, and that many of the families have relatives and friends in the United States" (cited in L. Greenberg, *The Jews in Russia: The Struggle for Emancipation* [New Haven: Yale University Press, 1951], vol. 2, pp. 74–75). It is estimated that by 1914 some two million Jews left Russia. This selection is from the Warsaw newspaper *Ha-Zefirah;* it cites, as a warning against precipitous emigration, a letter to the editor of *Novoe Vremya,* a daily newspaper in St. Petersburg. To strengthen the point of this letter, *Ha-Zefirah* published an accompanying appeal for caution from a Jewish immigration relief committee in Memel, a port city in East Prussia. However, the threat of pogroms exceeded that of poverty as seen by the following figures.

> The yearly average of the Russian Jews going to the United States alone was 12,856 for 1881–1886; it reached 28,509 in the next five-year period, rose to 44,829 during 1891–1895 and declined (perhaps affected by an economic slump in America) to 31,278 from 1896 to 1900. The average yearly figures were 58,625 for 1901–1905; 82,223 for 1906–1910 and 75,144 for 1911–1914. Altogether nearly two million Jews left Russia from 1880 to 1914 (Hans Rogger, "Tsarist Policy on Jewish Emigration," *Soviet Jewish Affairs,* 3, no. 1 [1973], p. 28. See also W. W. Kaplun-Kogan, *Die juedischen Wanderbewegungen in der neuesten Zeit* (Bonn, 1919), especially pp. 19–25).

BARON MAURICE DE HIRSCH
25. Appeal to the Jews in Russia[1]

To my coreligionists in Russia: You know that I am endeavouring to better your lot. It is, therefore, my duty to speak plainly to you and to tell you that which it is necessary you should know.

I am aware of the reasons which oblige many of you to emigrate, and I will gladly do all in my power to assist you in your hour of distress. But you must make this possible for me. Your emigration must not resemble a headlong, reckless flight, by which the endeavour to escape from one danger ends in destruction.

You know that properly organised committees are shortly to be established in Russia, with the consent and under the supervision of the Imperial Russian Government. The duty of these committees will be to organise the emigration in a business-like way. All persons desirous of emigrating will have to apply to the local committees, who alone will be authorised to give you the necessary facilities.

Only those persons who have been selected by the committees can have the advantage of the assistance of myself and of those who are working with me. Anyone who leaves the country without the concur-

Source: The Jewish Chronicle (London), September 18, 1891, p. 13.

rence of the committees will do so at his own risk, and must not count on any aid from me.

It is obvious that in the beginning the number of emigrants cannot be large; for not only must places of refuge be found for those who first depart, but necessary preparations be made for those who follow. Later on the emigration will be able to assume larger proportions.

Remember that I can do nothing for you without the benevolent and gracious support of the Imperial Russian Government.

In conclusion, I appeal to you. You are the inheritors of your fathers, who for centuries, have suffered so much. Bear this inheritance yet awhile with equal resignation.

Have also further patience, and thus render it possible for those to help you who are anxious to do so.

I send you these words of warning and of encouragement in my own name and in the name of thousands of your coreligionists. Take them to heart and understand them.

May the good God help you and me, and also the many who work with us for your benefit with so much devotion.

NOTE

1. Baron de Hirsch (1831–1896), one of the wealthiest individuals of his time. A German Jewish financier, he devoted the larger portion of his life and vast fortune to philanthropy. He was the benefactor of a variety of Jewish causes, e.g., the Alliance Israélite Universelle; the Baron de Hirsch Fund in New York City, established to assist Jewish immigrants in the United States; and the Jewish Colonization Association, established in 1891 to facilitate and organize the mass emigration of Jews from Russia and to encourage their rehabilitation in agricultural colonies, particularly in Argentina and Brazil. He chose these countries because they contained an abundance of unpopulated land suitable for agriculture and because their governments were eager to receive immigrants. The Baron hoped to divert the flow of Jewish immigration to these areas, for he felt the crowding of hundreds of thousands of pauperized Jews into the cities of North America was bound to lead to anti-Semitism. A life of farming, even with the Baron de Hirsch's generous assistance, in an unknown distant land, appealed to relatively few immigrants. America continued to be the main destination. The above letter, which originally appeared in Russian and Yiddish, was addressed to the prospective emigrants from Russia, appealing to them to cooperate with the Jewish Colonization Association.

SIMON DUBNOW
26. Autonomism[1]

. . . Autonomy as a historic claim is thus the firm and inalienable right of each national individuality; only its forms depend on the status which a nationality has within a multinational state. . . . In view of its condition in the Diaspora, Jewish nationality cannot strive for territorial or political isolation, but only for social and cultural autonomy. The Jew says: "As a citizen of my country I participate in its civic and political life, but as a member of the Jewish nationality I have, in addition, my own national needs, and in this sphere I

Source: Simon Dubnow, *Nationalism and History, Essays on Old and New Judaism,* ed. Koppel S. Pinson (New York: Atheneum, 1970), pp. 136–39. Copyright 1958 by the Jewish Publication Society. Reprinted by permission.

must be independent to the same degree that any other national minority is autonomous in the state. I have the right to speak my language, to use it in all my social institutions, to make it the language of instruction in my schools, to order my internal life in my communities, and to create institutions serving a variety of national purposes; to join in the common activities with my brethren not only in this country but in all countries of the world and to participate in all the organizations which serve to further the needs of the Jewish nationality and to defend them everywhere."

During the "period of isolation" the Jews enjoyed in great measure the right of national autonomy, although in outmoded forms, but they lacked civic and political rights. During the "period of assimilation" they began to participate in the civic and political life of the countries in which they lived, but many became alienated from the chosen inheritance of the nation, from its internal autonomy, which, in their limited view, did not accord with civic emancipation already granted or about to be granted by law. In this manner old Jewry sacrificed its civic rights for its national rights, and new Jewry its national rights for its political or civic rights. The period of autonomy now approaching does not tend to either of the two extremes of the previous epochs, which had rendered the life of the Jewish people defective and impaired. The new epoch must combine our equal civic and political rights with the social and cultural autonomy enjoyed by other nationalities whose historical conditions resemble our own. The Jews must demand simultaneously all civic, political and national rights, without renouncing one for the other as had been the case in the past.

The chief axiom of Jewish autonomy may thus be formulated as follows: Jews in each and every country who take an active part in civic and political life enjoy all rights given to the citizens, not merely as individuals, but also as members of their national groups.

Now that we have succeeded in establishing the principle of autonomy, we must analyze the problem of how it can be realized under the conditions in which the Jewish nationality finds itself. Here we have to differentiate between two kinds of national minorities in a multi-national state: (1) a territorial minority, which is a minority as compared with the total population of the commonwealth, but which constitutes a majority in its own historical state or province; (2) a non-territorial minority, scattered over various provinces without being a majority in any. Nationalities of the first kind require regional autonomy where they are settled, nationalities of the second kind must have communal and cultural autonomy. . . .

The fiction of the "religious community" was bound to be destroyed together with the fiction of the "religious society," not in the sense of a disruption of the religious service, but of a removal of the religious label from secular institutions. It is necessary to reconstruct the shattered autonomy in forms which are adapted to modern social conditions. In countries of German culture, the nationalist Jews must convert their religious communities into national communities [*Volksgemeinden*]. Even before such a change can be effected officially, with the approval of the government, it is possible on the basis of the existing laws guaranteeing freedom of association, to widen perceptibly the circle of activities of the communities, and, at the same time, to wage a parliamentary battle for the recognition of the fullest measures of secular national communal autonomy. . . . Real and broad autonomy is especially possible in countries in which the principle prevails that the government does not interfere in the private lives of its citizens, and where authoritarian governments or exaggerated concentrations of power do not exist. In such countries, especially in the United States of America, Jews could enjoy a large measure of self-administration even now if they only were willing to advance beyond the confines of the "religious community." . . .

There is no need to demonstrate that national-cultural autonomy is of singular value to the Jewish masses concentrated in eastern Europe. Here the Jews do not yet have full rights as citizens and, therefore, the extension of the autonomy of their communities meets with external difficulties. Over and against this, however, there are strong inner tendencies in that direction among the Jewish masses which are attracted to the modern national movement. . . .

NOTE

1. Simon Dubnow (1860–1941), Russian Jewish historian, author of the monumental *World History of the Jewish People* (10 volumes, written in Russian, but first published in German, 1925–1929; it was published in English in 1967). From 1897 to 1902 he published a series of articles on the Jewish question in the Russian Jewish journal *Voskhod.* In these articles, drawing upon his study of Jewish history, Dubnow developed a conception of the Jewish people as a "spiritual community," which, despite its dispersion throughout the world, enjoys a national cohesion by virtue of historical, cultural and religious bonds. As such, the Jewish people does not require the material framework of a common territory and of political independence to preserve its national existence. Through spiritual nationhood, the Jewish people, according to Dubnow, have entered a higher stage of history, anticipating the future of all nations. Notwithstanding his historical optimism, Dubnow recognized the pressures of assimilation in a secular age, and accordingly held that although the Jews will remain politically and territorially members of the respective states of their dispersion, they should enjoy cultural autonomy. The historical and theoretical bases of the concept of extra-territorial, cultural (as opposed to political!) autonomy were expounded in his fourth article (1901), excerpts of which are presented above. Dubnow sought to realize his program through the political efforts of the Society for Full and Equal Rights of the Jewish People in Russia, an association of non-socialist Jews founded in 1905, and of the Jewish People's Party, which he helped establish in 1906. Although he was not successful in the sphere of practical politics, Dubnow's theory of autonomism exercised a seminal influence on the Bund's nationality policy (see document 27 in this chapter) and on the Helsingfors Program of the Zionists (see document 28 in this chapter).

THE BUND
27. Decisions on the Nationality Question[1]

The Third Party Convention (December 1899):[2] . . . The Bund has inscribed on its banner the demand for equal civil rights for the Jews. At the Convention the opinion was expressed that 'Jewish Social Democracy deals with the needs of the Jewish proletariat in too narrow a manner. Many of the most significant rights to be obtained with the fall of the autocratic regime [of the czar], it was observed, would, as regards the Jewish workers, remain but a dead letter, if complete national emancipation, e.g., freedom to use

Source: [Protocol of third convention of the Bund] (Kovno, December 1899), in *Materialy k istorii yevreiskago rabochago dvizhenii* (St. Petersburg, 1906), vol. 1, pp. 74–76. Trans. here by R. Weiss. [Resolution of fourth convention of the Bund] (Bialystok, May 1901), in *Yiddisher Arbeter,* no. 2 (1901), pp. 97–102. Trans. here by P. Mendes-Flohr. [Resolution of the sixth convention of the Bund] (Zurich, October 1905), in *Der Yiddisher Arbeter,* ed. M. Rafes (Moscow, 1925), vol. 1, p. 321. Trans. here by D. Goldman. [Resolution of eighth conference of the Bund] (Vienna, October 1910), in M. Rafes, *Ocherki po istorii Bunda* (Moscow, 1923), pp. 393–95. Trans. here by R. Weiss.

their own national language, is not also granted them. Accordingly, one comrade[3] insisted that there be a greater emphasis on the national aspect of the Bund's program, for the Jewish proletariat must demand national emancipation as well as equal civil rights. Civil rights, he said, are not enough to enable the Jewish proletariat to protect its own interests. Germany is a prime example of this. Whereas in Germany all citizens enjoy equal civil rights under the law, the Polish workers [residing in Germany and possessing German citizenship] cannot enjoy them to the same extent as the German workers. The Polish worker, like his German comrade, is allowed to convene meetings, but because the commissars who must be present at the meetings do not usually understand Polish, the meetings must be conducted in German. This means that many who are unable to express their thoughts in German or do not understand that language sufficiently, are in practice denied their right to participate in the meetings. If this is the case with regard to the Polish proletariat in Germany, how much more so does this hold for the Jewish workers in Russia. One may ask—what benefit will derive from the Jewish workers' freedom of assembly, if in these meetings they must speak Russian, that is to say, a language neither spoken nor understood by the majority of the Jewish workers? Freedom of assembly is thus revealed to be a fine but empty phrase, at least as regards the Jewish workers, as long as Yiddish does not enjoy a status equal to that of Russian. Thus it is necessary to correct the program of the Bund by supplementing the paragraph on equal civil rights with one on equal national rights. It is possible of course to contest this point, continued that comrade, and say that the question of equal national rights is merely of academic interest to us at this time; that the most important task facing us, the task to which we must now devote ourselves fully, is the achievement of political rights. The question of national rights is not likely to become a burning issue for the Jewish worker nor become his battle-cry until there be a democratic regime in Russia, and then only if the democratic character of the Russian constitution be imperfect. Those who present this argument, the comrade continued, forget that every party includes in its program, alongside its short-term demands, demands which may be realized only in the distant future. The Bund should not be an exception in this regard. It must include in its program demands which in all likelihood will be fought for in the more or less distant future.

The paragraph on equal national rights received little support from the congress and aroused a heated debate, involving many of the delegates. Essentially, the discussions focused on the need to avoid making demands which would divert the worker from his class interests by the pull of [spurious or less urgent] national interests. The danger in having the Bund's program include a demand for comprehensive equality of national rights lies in the possibility that it will blur the Jewish proletariat's class consciousness, and, like every nationalism, it could lead to chauvinism.

After lengthy discussion the following decision was passed: (1) The demand for equal civil rights but not equal national rights should be included among the Bund's political demands. (2) To enable comrades to express their opinions on the national question and help clarify the subject, a special section entitled "Arguments" will be set aside for this purpose in the [party's paper] *Yiddisher Arbeter:*[4] there individual authors may express their opinions, on their own responsibility. . . .

The Fourth Party Convention (May 1901):[5] . . . The Convention recognizes the fact that a state such as Russia, consisting of a great number of disparate nations, will need to be reorganized in the future into a federation of national groups, each enjoying full national autonomy, independent of the territory in which they reside.

The Convention deems that the term "nationality" applies to the Jewish people.[6]

In view of the fact that it is premature

under the present conditions [in Russia] to put forth the demand for national autonomy for the Jews, the Convention finds that at the present time it is sufficient to fight for the abolition of all discriminatory laws directed against the Jews and to protest against all forms of oppression of the Jewish people. At the same time, the Bund will refrain from inflating nationalist feelings among the Jews which can only blur the class consciousness of the Jewish proletariat and lead to chauvinism. . . .

The Convention regards Zionism as a reaction of the bourgeois classes to the phenomenon of anti-Semitism and to the abnormal civil status of the Jewish people in Russia.[7] The Convention views the ultimate goal of political Zionism—i.e., the acquisition of a territory for the Jews—as an objective of little value, because such a territory would be able to contain but a fraction of the whole nation, and thus would be incapable of solving the Jewish question. Hence, to the extent that the Zionists seek to concentrate the whole of the Jewish people, or at least a majority of the Jewish people, in a single land, they pursue a utopian goal.

Furthermore, the Convention believes that Zionist propaganda inflames nationalist feelings and hinders the development of class consciousness among the Jewish proletariat.

The Sixth Party Convention (October 1905):[8] In accordance with the general principles laid down in the Fourth Convention, the Sixth Convention formulated the program of the Bund regarding the Jewish nationality question as follows: (1) Full civil and political equality for the Jews. (2) The right, guaranteed by law, for the Jews to use their own language in all legal and governmental institutions. (3) National-cultural autonomy [on an extra-territorial basis]: the removal of all functions connected with cultural matters (e.g., popular education) from the administrative responsibility of the state and local government and the transference of these functions to the Jewish nation. [Under the autonomous jurisdiction of the Jewish nation] these functions will be organized in the form of central and local institutions whose officials will be elected in general elections by all those who identify themselves as belonging to the Jewish nation by an honest, secret ballot.

The Eighth Party Conference (October 1910):[9] Whereas the legislation regarding linguistic rights currently being considered by the Duma[10] directly opposes the interests of the proletariat and the masses of the Jewish nation; and whereas this question is of special urgency to the Jewish workers, in that Yiddish is a denigrated, persecuted language, the Conference believes that it is necessary to raise and forcefully pursue the following demands: (1) The division of languages [as proposed in the legislations before the Duma] into two categories, dominant and tolerated, is unacceptable. (2) All governmental institutions—central, regional and local—must use the local languages when dealing with the population. (3) This demand must be fulfilled by means of special legislation and legal guarantees. (4) Until the realization of national-cultural autonomy which will transfer responsibility for educational and cultural matters to the nations themselves, it is necessary to work for the establishment of a government school for each national group in the general population in which its own language will be used. (5) All limitations on the use of one's mother tongue in public life, assemblies, the press, business institutions, schools, *et cetera* must be abolished.

In the struggle to achieve these demands, it is necessary to secure the rights of the Yiddish language, which is denied these rights more than any other language and, moreover, is not even officially recognized, while the other non-dominant languages receive at least partial recognition.

While making clear its reservations about those nationalist trends which turn the struggle for Yiddish into an instrument with which to blunt the class consciousness of the proletariat, Jewish Social Democracy, considering the interests and needs of the proletariat, must conduct the struggle against the assimilationists and the Hebraists so that the Yiddish language will acquire in all areas of Jewish public life—especially, in the schools and cultural institutions—the prominent position it merits as the national language of the Jewish people. (*Adopted unanimously.*)

NOTES

1. The Bund is an abbreviation and popular designation for the Algemeyner Arbeter Bund in Polyn un Rusland (General Jewish Workers' Union in Poland and Russia) a Jewish socialist party founded in Russia in 1897. (Lithuania was later added to the party's name.) The Bund was the result of the merger of several local socialist organizations among the Jews in the northwestern region of the Russian Empire, which was formerly the Lithuanian segment of the old Polish-Lithuanian commonwealth. In this region the Jewish proletariat were a predominant factor in the major cities (viz., Vilna, Vitebsk, Bialystok and Minsk); moreover, the Jewish intelligentsia in this region "was subject to weaker assimilationist pressures than were its counterparts in the Ukraine and Russian Poland. This combination of a dominant Jewish proletariat and an intelligentsia more likely than elsewhere to be sensitive to its needs made possible the emergence of a specifically Jewish labor movement" (Ezra Mendelsohn, *Class Struggle in the Pale: The Formative Years of the Jewish Workers' Movement in Tsarist Russia* [London: Cambridge University Press, 1970], pp. x–xi). During the 1880s and 1890s the first socialist circles were formed among the Jewish workers of Lithuania. The leaders of these circles were russified Jews who viewed their task as preparing the Jewish workers for socialism. Initially, these "schools for socialism" concentrated on teaching Yiddish-speaking workers Russian (the language of the vast majority of the empire's proletariat), literature and natural sciences—the modicum of skills and knowledge deemed necessary for a mature class consciousness. Gradually, these circles evolved into trade unions, concerning themselves with the concrete problems faced by the Jewish proletariat. The struggle of the Jewish proletariat inevitably involved the need to remove the disabilities suffered by the Jewish people as a whole, a battle that the Jewish bourgeoisie, because of their limited class interests, were held to be inherently incapable of waging effectively. This focus of political action, together with the need to employ Yiddish to organize the Jewish workers, led to the formation of a socialist-nationalist ideology, in which Yiddish was glorified as the language of the laboring class and national-cultural autonomy for Jewish people was a leading principle. The above documents trace the emergence of this ideology. Although the Bund confined its purview to the Jewish workers of the Russian Empire and opposed collaboration with other Jewish parties (even in matters of self-defense against pogroms), its program was rejected by the Russian Social Democratic Workers' party (RSDWP), of which it was a constituent member. After the final split between the Bolshevik and the Menshevik factions of the RSDWP in 1912, the Bund aligned itself with the Mensheviks, who tended to favor Jewish national-cultural autonomy, while the Bolsheviks stiffened their opposition to this program. By the end of 1917, the Bund had approximately 40,000 members, organized in almost 400 branches. At the twelfth Bund convention held in Moscow in 1920, the majority favored affiliation with the Communists, but on an autonomous basis. Although this condition was rejected by the Communists, the Bund conference of March 1921 decided to join the Communist party. In the parts of Poland not incorporated within the Soviet Union, the Bund remained an independent organization, and it became a major factor in the Jewish life of that country; on the eve of the Nazi invasion of Poland in 1939, the Polish Bund had nearly 100,000 members.

2. At this convention the issue of Jewish national—as opposed to civic and political—rights was broached and debated for the first time in an open forum of the Bund.

3. The reference is to John Mill (1870–1952), one of the founders of the Bund and head of its Committee Abroad. Based in Geneva, the committee served as the party's representative vis-à-vis the international socialist movement, raised funds and printed party literature (which was illegal in Russia). In 1915 Mill emigrated to the United States, where he was active in various Jewish socialist organizations.

4. The Yiddish-language organ of the Committee Abroad of the Bund, which was edited at the time by John Mill.

5. At its fourth convention the Bund went be-

yond its former demand for equal civic and political rights for the Jews and became an advocate of national rights for the Jews of Russia. This was a turning point in Bundist thought; from now on the party's ideology and propaganda would increasingly emphasize the national element. Various factors prompted this change, such as the appeals among the Jewish workers of the positions on Jewish national rights articulated by Simon Dubnow (see document 26), Chaim Zhitlovsky (1865–1943) and Zionism. The Bund drew Marxist "legitimation" for its nationalist program from the multi-national Austrian Social Democratic Party's Marxist conception of extraterritorial autonomy. In contrast to other Jewish national ideologies, the Bund did not consider the Jews as a worldwide people and thus restricted its concern to the Jews of the Russian Empire. Despite the cautious language of the resolutions of the fourth convention, they quickly aroused the opposition of the RSDWP, of which the Bund was a founding member. The opposition was led by those connected with the magazine *Iskra,* of whom Vladimir Lenin was foremost. Rebuffed, the Bund withdrew from the RSDWP in protest.

6. The formulation of this section of the resolution marked a compromise with the opponents of the proposal. At the sixth party convention the limitation was removed.

7. The RSDWP pilloried the Bund members as crypto-Zionists, "who suffered from sea-sickness" as Georgi Valentinovich Plekhanov (1856–1918), the founder and for many years the leading exponent of Russian Marxism, put it. The Bund for its part defined Zionism as reactionary and bourgeois, even including the socialist Zionist parties—which had become in this period a political force in the Pale—in this category.

8. After the failure of the Revolution of 1905 and the new restrictions on political and trade union activities, the Bund was obliged to concentrate on cultural issues. It became a vigorous advocate of a secular, socialist Jewish culture based on Yiddish. Literary and musical societies, evening courses and drama circles were among the varied activities that the Bund organized. The Bund now even took part in some general Jewish cultural activities. To underscore that its devotion to Jewish culture was solely in the interest of the Jewish proletariat and the class struggle, the Bund formulated the concept of "neutralism"—i.e., it had no romantic commitment to Jewish survival, which was a matter for the objective, dialectic laws of history.

9. In addition to conventions, which had full authority to decide party policy, the Bund also held conferences, which had less authority than conventions. The policy outlined by the eighth conference, which included the demand for freedom to rest on the Jewish Sabbath and the establishment of state Yiddish schools, together with the resolutions of the sixth convention, remained the Bund's nationality policy until after the Russian Revolution.

10. The Duma was the Imperial Russian legislature in existence between 1906 and 1917.

ALL-RUSSIAN ZIONIST CONFERENCE

28. The Helsingfors Program[1]

The political program includes the following:

1. Full democratization of the regime according to the principles of parliamentary democracy, autonomy of the national territories and guaranteed legal rights for all minority peoples.

2. Full and unconditional [civic and national] rights to the Jewish population.

3. Representation of all national minorities in federal, regional and local elections that shall be conducted by direct secret ballot. The right to vote shall be extended to women.

4. Recognition of the Jewish people in Russia as a single political entity entitled to govern itself in matters of national culture.

5. A national assembly of Russian Jews

Source: Juedische Rundschau, 22 (June 8, 1917), pp. 190–93. Trans. here by R. Weiss and P. Mendes-Flohr.

shall be convened for the purpose of forming the basic structure of a national organization.

6. Jews shall have the right to use the national language (Hebrew) and the spoken language (Yiddish) in schools, courts and public life.

7. Jews shall have the right to observe the Sabbath on Saturday instead of Sunday. This right shall be guaranteed without regard to geographical location. . . .

NOTE

1. The Third All-Russian Zionist Conference, which included various Zionist groups, met in 1906 from December fourth to December tenth, in Helsingfors (Helsinki), Finland. In the wake of recent events—the Revolution of 1905, pogroms, the death of Theodor Herzl who was the founder of political Zionism, the Seventh Zionist Congress, the growing influence of competing ideologies among the Jewish masses—the conference dealt with fundamental issues facing the Zionist movement in general, and Russian Zionism in particular. Without rejecting the basic Zionist goal of "negating the Diaspora," the conference adopted a program of *Gegenwartsarbeit* or "work in the present," that is, political and cultural activities to be undertaken with regard to the immediate needs of Jewish life in the Diaspora. The ideological formulation of this program, which constituted a major revision in Zionist policy, is presented in chapter 10, document 13. The specific proposals for Russia are presented in the above document.

V. I. LENIN
29. Critical Remarks on the National Question (1913)[1]

. . . Whoever wants to serve the proletariat must unite the workers of all nations and unswervingly fight bourgeois nationalism, *home* and foreign. The place of one who advocates the slogan of national culture is among the nationalist philistines and not among the Marxists.

Take a concrete example. Can a Great-Russian Marxist accept the slogan of national, Great-Russian culture? No. Such a man should be placed among the nationalists and not among the Marxists. . . .

The same applies to the most oppressed and persecuted nation, the Jewish. Jewish national culture is a slogan of the rabbis and the bourgeoisie, a slogan of our enemies. But there are other elements in Jewish culture and in the entire history of the Jews. Of the ten and a half million Jews throughout the world, a little over half live in Galicia and Russia, backward and semi-barbarous countries, which *forcibly* keep the Jews in the position of a caste. The other half live in the civilized world, and there the Jews are not segregated in a caste. There, the great, world-progressive features of Jewish culture have clearly made themselves felt: its internationalism, its responsiveness to the advanced movements of the epoch (the percentage of Jews in the democratic and proletarian movements is everywhere higher than the percentage of Jews in the population as a whole).

Whoever, directly or indirectly, presents

Source: V. I. Lenin, *Critical Remarks on the National Question, 1913,* translator not indicated (Moscow: Foreign Language Publishing House, 1954), pp. 19–24.

the slogan of a Jewish "national culture" is (whatever his good intentions may be) an enemy of the proletariat, a supporter of the *old* and of the *caste* among the Jews, an accomplice of the rabbis and the bourgeoisie. On the other hand, those Jewish Marxists who, in international Marxist organizations amalgamate with the Russian, Lithuanian, Ukrainian, etc., workers, contributing their might (in Russian and in Yiddish) to the creation of the international culture of the working-class movement, such Jews, despite the separatism of the Bund, continue the best traditions of the Jews, fighting the slogan of "national culture."

Bourgeois nationalism and proletarian internationalism—such are the two irreconcilably hostile slogans that correspond to the two great class camps throughout the capitalist world and express the two policies (more than that—two world outlooks) in the national question. By championing the slogan of national culture, building on it an entire plan and practical programme of so-called "cultural-national autonomy," the Bundists *actually* serve as the vehicles of bourgeois nationalism among the workers.

The question of assimilation, i.e., of the loss of national peculiarities, of becoming absorbed by another nation, makes it possible to visualize the consequences of the nationalist vacillations of the Bundists and their like-minded friends. . . .

Developing capitalism knows two historical tendencies in the national question. First: the awakening of national life and national movement, struggle against all national oppression, creation of national states. Second: development and intensification of all kinds of intercourse between nations, break-down of national barriers, creation of the international unity of capital, of economic life in general, of politics, science, etc.

Both tendencies are a world-wide law of capitalism. The first predominates at the beginning of its development, the second characterizes mature capitalism that is moving toward its transformation into socialist society. The national programme of the Marxists takes both tendencies into account, and demands, firstly, equality of nations and languages, prohibition of all *privileges* whatsoever in this respect (and also the right of nations to self-determination, with which we deal separately lower down); and secondly, the principle of internationalism and uncompromising struggle against the contamination of the proletariat with bourgeois nationalism, even of the most refined kind. . . .

Whoever does not recognize and does not champion equality of nations and languages, does not fight against all national oppression or inequality, is not a Marxist, is not even a democrat. This is beyond doubt. But it is equally doubtless that the alleged Marxist who fulminates against a Marxist of another nation as an "assimilator" is simply a *nationalist philistine.* In this little-esteemed category of people are all the Bundists. . . .

Those who shout most about Russian orthodox Marxists being "assimilators" are the Jewish nationalists in Russia in general, and the Bundists in particular. And yet, as is evident from the above-quoted figures, of the ten and a half million Jews in the whole world, *about half* that number live in the *civilized* world, under conditions where there is the *largest* degree of "assimilation," whereas only the unhappy, downtrodden rightless Jews in Russia and Galicia, those who are crushed by the anti-Semites (Russian and Polish), live under conditions where there is the *least* degree of "assimilation," the largest degree of segregation, right up to "Pale of Settlement," "percentage restrictions," and other charms of Purishkevich [the czarist bigots'] rule.

The Jews in the civilized world are not a nation, they have become assimilated most of all, say K. Kautsky[2] and O. Bauer.[3] The Jews in Galicia and in Russia are not a nation, they, unfortunately (*not* due to their own fault, but to the fault of the [anti-Semites]), are here still a *caste.* Such is the indisputable opinion of people who are undoubtedly familiar with the history of the Jews and who take the above-cited facts into consideration.

What do these facts tell us? That only Jewish reactionary philistines who want to turn back the wheel of history, to compel it to go not away from the conditions prevailing in Russia and Galicia toward the conditions prevailing in Paris and New York, but the opposite way, can shout against "assimilation."

The best Jews of world-historic fame who gave the world advanced leaders of democracy and socialism never shouted against assimilation. Only those who with reverential awe contemplate the "backside" of Jewry shout against assimilation. . . .

NOTE

1. Vladimir Ilyich (Ulyanov) Lenin (1870–1924), Russian revolutionary. He was the leader of the Bolshevik faction within the Russian Social Democratic Workers' Party (RSDWP), and, later, the founder of the Soviet Union. He was very concerned with the Jewish question, and particularly with the Bundist nationality policy and demand to reorganize the RSDWP on a federated, national basis. He held this policy to be both an ideological and political threat to the cause of the Russian Revolution. Lenin, as his above essay shows, deemed assimilation as the only progressive solution of the Jewish question. It was incumbent upon the Marxist revolutionaries to oppose anti-Semitism, he held, not only because it was a moral wrong, but because it tended to aggravate Jewish national consciousness and thus inhibit the process of Jewish assimilation. Hence anti-Semitism was reactionary. Accordingly, Lenin was a consistent and vigorous opponent of anti-Semitism in both czarist Russia and later during the founding years of the Soviet Union.

2. Karl Kautsky (1845–1938), the leading Marxist theoretician in the German Social Democratic Party before World War I.

3. Otto Bauer (1881–1938), the leading theoretician of the Austrian Social Democratic Party.

JOSEPH STALIN
30. The Jews Are Not a Nation[1]

What is a nation? . . . *A nation is a historically constituted, stable community of people, formed on the basis of a common language, territory, economic life, and psychological make-up manifested in a common culture.*

It goes without saying that a nation, like every historical phenomenon, is subject to the law of change, has its history, its beginning and end.

It must be emphasized that none of the above characteristics taken separately is sufficient to define a nation. More than that, it is sufficient for a single one of these characteristics to be lacking and the nation ceases to be a nation.

It is possible to conceive of people possessing a common "national character" who, nevertheless, cannot be said to constitute a single nation if they are economically disunited, inhabit different territories, speak different languages, and so forth. Such, for instance, are the Russian, Galician, American, Georgian and Caucasian Highland *Jews*, who, in our opinion, do not constitute a single nation. . . .

The fact of the matter is primarily that among the Jews there is no large and stable stratum connected with the land, which would naturally rivet the nation together, serving not only as its framework but also as a

Source: Joseph Stalin, *Marxism and the National Question*, translator not indicated (Moscow: Foreign Language Publishing House, 1934), pp. 9, 16, 64–67, 73–75.

"national" market. Of the five or six million Russian Jews, only three to four percent are connected with agriculture in any way. The remaining ninety-six percent are employed in trade, industry, in urban institutions, and in general are town dwellers; moreover, they are spread all over Russia and do not constitute a majority in a single *guberniia.*

Thus, interspersed as national minorities in areas inhabited by other nationalities, the Jews as a rule serve "foreign" nations as manufacturers and traders and as members of the liberal professions, naturally adapting themselves to the "foreign nations" in respect to language and so forth. All this, taken together with the increasing re-shuffling of nationalities characteristic of developed forms of capitalism, leads to the assimilation of the Jews. The abolition of the "Pale of Settlement" would only serve to hasten this process of assimilation.

The question of national autonomy for the Russian Jews consequently assumes a somewhat curious character: autonomy is being proposed for a nation whose future is denied and whose existence has still to be proved!

Nevertheless, this was the curious and shaky position taken up by the Bund when at its Sixth Congress (1905) it adopted a "national programme" on the lines of national autonomy.

Two circumstances impelled the Bund to take this step. The first circumstance is the existence of the Bund as an organization of Jewish, and only Jewish, social-democratic workers. Even before 1897 the social-democratic groups active among the Jewish workers set themselves the aim of creating "a special Jewish workers' organization." They founded such an organization in 1897 by uniting to form the Bund. That was at a time when Russian Social-Democracy as an integral body virtually did not yet exist. The Bund steadily grew and spread, and stood out more and more vividly against the background of the bleak days of Russian Social-Democracy. . . . Then came the 1900s. A *mass* labour movement came into being. Polish Social-Democracy grew and drew the Jewish workers into the mass struggle. Russian Social-Democracy grew and attracted the Bund workers. Lacking a territorial basis, the national framework of the Bund became too restrictive. The Bund was faced with the problem of either merging with the general international tide, or of upholding its independent existence as an extra-territorial organization. The Bund chose the latter course.

Thus grew up the "theory" that the Bund is "the sole representative of the Jewish proletariat." . . .

The second circumstance is the peculiar position of the Jews as separate national minorities within compact majorities of other nationalities in integral regions. We have already said that this position is undermining the existence of the Jews as a nation and puts them on the road to assimilation. But this is an objective process. Subjectively, in the minds of the Jews, it provokes a reaction and gives rise to the demand for a guarantee of the rights of a national minority, for a guarantee against assimilation. Preaching as it does the vitality of the Jewish "nationality," the Bund could not avoid being in favour of a "guarantee." And, having taken up this position, it could not but accept national autonomy. For if the Bund could seize upon any autonomy, i.e., *cultural-national* autonomy, there could be no question of territorial-political autonomy for the Jews, since the Jews have no definite integral territory.

Social-Democracy strives to secure for *all nations* the right to use their own language. But that does not satisfy the Bund; it demands that "the rights of the *Jewish language*" . . . be championed with "exceptional persistence" (see *Report of the Eighth Conference of the Bund*), and the Bund itself in the elections to the Fourth Duma declared that it would give "preference to those of them (i.e., electors) who undertake to defend the rights of the Jewish language."

Not the *general* right of all nations to use their own language, but the *particular* right of the Jewish language. Yiddish! Let the workers of the various nationalities fight primarily for their own language; the Jews for Jewish, the Georgians for Georgian, and so forth. The struggle for the general right of all nations is a secondary matter. You do not have to recognize the right of all oppressed nationalities to use their own language; but if you have recognized the right of Yiddish, know that the Bund will vote for you, the Bund will "prefer" you.

But in what way then does the Bund differ from the bourgeois nationalists?

Social-Democracy strives to secure the establishment of a compulsory weekly rest day. But that does not satisfy the Bund; it demands that *by legislative means* "the Jewish proletariat should be guaranteed the right to observe their Sabbath and be relieved of the obligation to observe another day."

It is to be expected that the Bund will take another "step forward" and demand the right to observe all the ancient Hebrew holidays. And if, to the misfortune of the Bund, the Jewish workers have discarded religious prejudices and do not want to observe these holidays, the Bund with its agitation for "the right to the Sabbath," will remind them of the Sabbath, it will, so to speak, cultivate among them "the Sabbatarian spirit." . . .

Quite comprehensible, therefore, are the "passionate speeches" delivered at the Eighth Conference of the Bund demanding "Jewish hospitals," a demand that was based on the argument that "a patient feels more at home among his own people," that "the Jewish worker will not feel at ease among Polish workers, but will feel at ease among Jewish shopkeepers."

Preservation of everything Jewish, conservation of *all* the national peculiarities of the Jews, even those that are patently harmful to the proletariat, isolation of the Jews from everything non-Jewish, even the establishment of special hospitals—that is the level to which the Bund has sunk!

Comrade Plekhanov[2] was right a thousand times over when he said that the Bund "is adapting socialism to nationalism."

NOTES

1. Joseph (Dzhugashvili) Stalin (1879–1953), Bolshevik revolutionary, ruler of the Soviet Union, and leader of the world communist movement. During the early factional disputes within the Russian Social Democratic Workers' Party, he sided with Lenin in his opposition to the Bund. In 1913, with the approbation of Lenin, he published an essay entitled "Social Democracy and the National Question" (later renamed "Marxism and the National Question"), in which *inter alia* the Jewish question and the Bund's "misconceived" policy are analyzed. Excerpts from the essay are presented here. Stalin later became the first commissar of nationalities of the Soviet Union (1917–1923), and, with Lenin, tacitly recognized the Jews of Russia at least as a nationality, whose distinct culture and language would have to be considered if effective revolutionary work were to be performed among them. Stalin, especially through the *Yevsektsiya,* fostered Yiddish culture, administrative institutions and agricultural settlements. In the late thirties, during the great purges of the Communist Party and government, he reversed his attitude toward Jewish national culture. Yiddish schools, publishing houses, theaters, etc., were systematically liquidated. This policy was somewhat suspended during the Second World War. Moreover, in an effort to dislodge Britain from the Near East he became a firm supporter of the establishment of a Jewish state in Palestine. From the end of 1948 until his death, however, Stalin's attitude toward Jews and Jewish culture was hostile in the extreme, obsessively linking any positive expressions of Jewish identity with Zionism and U.S. espionage.

2. Georgi Plekhanov, see document 27, note 7, in this chapter.

THE PROVISIONAL GOVERNMENT
31. Emancipation by the March Revolution (April 2, 1917)[1]

Whereas it is our unshakable conviction that in a free country all citizens should be equal before the law, and that the conscience of the people cannot acquiesce in legal restrictions against particular citizens on account of their religion and race:

The Provisional Government has decreed: All restrictions on the rights of Russian citizens which had been enacted by existing laws on account of their belonging to any creed, confession or nationality, shall be abolished.

In accordance with this: All laws shall be abolished which have been in force both throughout the entire territory of Russia, as well as in any of her particular localities, and which enacted restrictions depending on the adherence of Russian citizens to any creed, confession or nationality, relating to: (1) settlement, (domicile) and freedom of movement; (2) acquisition of the right of ownership and other property rights on all kinds of movable and immovable goods as well as the disposal, use and administration of those goods and the giving or receiving of them as security; . . . (6) entering of government services, civil and military alike, the rules and conditions of promotion therein, participation in elections to local self-government bodies and to all kinds of communal bodies, the occupation of all kinds of posts in government and communal institutions and the fulfillment of all duties attached to such offices; (7) entering educational institutions of all kinds, private, community and government owned alike, the attendance of courses therein and benefits from stipends, as well as engaging in instruction and education; (8) fulfillment of duties of guardians, trustees and jurymen; (9) use of languages and dialects, other than Russian in the management of private associations, in teaching in educational institutions of any kind and in the keeping of commercial books. . . .

NOTE

1. After the March Revolution (1917) and the dismantling of the czarist regime, the Provisional Government of Russia headed by Prince Lvov, issued the above decree abolishing all restriction on rights of Russian subjects, which had been based on national origin and religion.

Source: "Decree of the Provisional Government about the Abolition of Religious and National Restrictions," *Jewish Emancipation, A Selection of Documents,* ed. and trans. Raphael Mahler, Pamphlet Series, Jews and the Post-War World, no. 1 (New York: The American Jewish Committee, 1941), pp. 64–65.

YEVSEKTSIYA

32. The Liquidation of Bourgeois Jewish Institutions[1]

Our Cultural Tasks: Education has always been a powerful means in the hands of the ruling classes. The bourgeoisie claims that schooling and education are beyond class interests and politics. At the same time, however, it makes sure that the broad masses will obtain neither knowledge nor enlightenment.

The Jewish community has hitherto been dominated by the members of the propertied class who want to keep the masses in the dark by superimposing a Hebrew culture upon them. While the upper classes have been sending their own children to public schools, they have provided only dark primary schools [*hadarim*] and synagogues [*shuls*] for the offspring of the proletariat, in which nothing but nonsense is taught.

Only the proletariat, defending the interests of their class, and thus defending the interests of all mankind, will be able to open the treasures of human culture to the broad masses.

Only the proletariat is strong enough to forge the golden chain of human culture, freeing it from the bloody hands of the decadent bourgeoisie.

From now on, the Jewish proletariat will assume the reigns of power in the Jewish community.

Only the Jewish worker and the Jewish laboring masses will create a free Jewish culture for themselves and arm themselves with the strong weaponry of knowledge.

Our Relations with the [Jewish] Community and Other Bourgeois Societies: The First Conference of Jewish Communists and Communist *Yevsektsiya* declares that the various institutions which have so far ruled the traditional communal organization, the so-called *kehile* . . . have no further function in our life.

In the struggle against the organized Jewish community [*kehile*], no compromise can be made with the bourgeoisie. All its institutions are harmful to the interests of the Jewish masses, who are seduced by sweet lullabies of alleged democracy.

Following the proletarian victory in the October Revolution, the Jewish workers have assumed power and have established the dictatorship of the proletariat in the Jewish community. They now call upon the Jewish masses to unite around the Jewish commissariat in order to strengthen its rule.

The first all-Russian conference of Jewish Communists authorizes the members of the Central Commissariat for Jewish Affairs to take steps toward a systematic liquidation of the institutions of the Jewish bourgeoisie. . . .

The Liquidation of the Zionist Party—A Memorandum [Submitted July 4, 1919]: The General Council of the Jewish Communist Union in the Ukraine, in full agreement with the resolution adopted by the conference of Jewish Communist sections of the Russian Communist party in Moscow, has decided to suspend immediately all activities of the Zionist party and its affiliated institutions and organizations.

This decision has been taken for the following reasons: Proclaiming the dictatorship of the proletariat, the Soviet has suspended the activities of all bourgeois parties and organizations and discontinued the publication of all their printed periodicals. The free existence of these organs and institutions would merely have interfered with the creative activity of the proletarian power, for they surely would have been used to support the

Source: S. Agurskii, ed., *Di yidishe komisariatn un di yidishe komunistishe sektsies: Protokoln, rezolutsies un dokumentn, 1918–1921* (Minsk, 1928), pp. 58–60, 178–81. Trans. here by J. Hessing.

counter-revolution which aims at the re-establishment of the old order. Only a misunderstanding deriving from the incomplete organization of the Soviets can explain, but not justify, the exception that is being made of the Zionists. They are still allowed to publish their official organ, *Chronik fun idishen leiben* [Chronicle of Jewish life], and to employ their entire party organization.[2] [But we must not forget that] by its political and social structure, the Zionist party is a Jewish version of the General Russian Cadet party.[3] By forging together the representatives of big and small capital with the Jewish petty bourgeoisie and cementing their union with a nationalistic ideology, this party—in close cooperation with clerical groups—constitutes a natural political center for all Jews who support the counter-revolution and wish to regain their freedom of exploitation and speculation. The pogroms that recently took place in the Ukraine and in Poland[4] have stirred nationalistic tendencies among reactionary Jews and are now being exploited by the Zionist party to strengthen its position. It is natural that in its most recent circular, the central committee of the Zionists in the Ukraine has reported a major increase of its organization, in spite of numerous cases in which local authorities have tried to interfere with this development.

The Zionists often protest their loyalty and pretend to be interested only in their work concerning Palestine. But in reality, their Palestinian agitation is nothing but a nationalistic response to the political events of the day. At the present time when the authorities and the Communist party are trying with all their might to mobilize the laboring masses for the struggle against local and Polish gangs, when they are committing themselves to liberating thousands of Jewish workers from the ideological influence of the petty bourgeoisie and to enlisting them in the revolutionary Red Army—at this time the Zionist agitation, even where it is performed by the Zionist left, is harmful because it hinders the mobilization of the workers just as it had previously interfered with the attempts to make the Jewish masses a part of the revolutionary movement.

It must further be noted that the Palestinian ideal of the Zionists is in its very content a bourgeois one. Moreover, the current international situation has firmly established the Zionist party in the camp of the international imperialistic counter-revolution.

The Zionist party has linked its fate with the powers of the Entente who, upon dividing the Turkish empire, have made certain promises to the Zionists which force them to support their coalition. The Peace of Versailles, forging chains for the enslavement of the proletariat and for entire peoples, is welcomed by the Zionists. This is a logical consequence of their bourgeois nature. Furthermore, the Zionists are directly interested in a victory of the Entente in Eastern Europe. Only a victory of these powers will get them a little closer to the practical realization of their hopes. Under these circumstances, the continued activity of the Zionist party would be harmful to the interests of the Soviet Union and her international policies. Any protestation on the part of the Zionists that they are not interested in the victory of the reactionary forces cannot be taken seriously if one remembers that the Jewish bourgeoisie, and the Zionists among them, were able to accept even Plehve's regime.[5]

Simultaneously with its political activity, the Zionist party is also engaged in cultural and economic activities which interfere with the cultural and economic policies of the Soviet Union. The Zionists endeavor to defend the vested interests of the petty bourgeoisie, of the middle class, and even of the patricians. . . .

The Zionist party puts special emphasis on its cultural and educational institutions. . . . The Zionist cultural and educational programs, however, do not even pretend to share the liberalism adopted by the Cadet party. All they endeavor to achieve is the strengthening of the clerical spirit in the Jewish *shul*. Furthermore, they support the religious instruction in the [traditional Jewish] schools as the mainstay of their nationalistic education. Their energies are directed toward an artificial revival of the Hebrew language, thereby endangering the daily language of the Jewish laboring masses. The cultural and educational activities of the Zionist party persistently undermine—too often successfully—the budding culture of socialism which has been emerging from within the Jewish proletarian movement throughout the last few decades. In this respect, positive action has already been undertaken in Greater Russia where Hebrew schools are now forbidden. . . .

That is why we must urgently proceed to suspend all activities of the Zionist party, not only where its central and local committees are concerned, but also the economic, cultural and professional organizations centered around the party. In doing so we shall only be taking the steps necessary for the propagation of communistic ideas among the Jewish working class and the younger generation of the Jewish petty bourgeoisie.

NOTES

1. *Yevsektsiya* (plural, *Yevsektsii*) was the Jewish section of the propaganda department of the Russian Communist party from 1918 to 1930 (the singular, *Yevsektsiya*, is commonly used even in reference to many sections). Upon taking power in November 1917 the Communist party was faced with the need to integrate the numerous nationalities and distinct ethnic groups of the Russian Empire into the revolution and ideological structure of the new state. In a radical reversal of Bolshevik policy, special "national" sections were established within the party for this purpose. In January 1918 a Jewish Commissariat was created and Jewish sections (*Yevsektsii*) were formed in order to organize within the revolution the millions of Jews in Russia who spoke their own language and maintained their own social and cultural institutions. The first conference of the Jewish *Yevsektsii*, which were established throughout the Soviet Union, took place in Moscow in October 1918. Some of the resolutions of the conference are presented above. At this conference it was repeatedly emphasized that the *Yevsektsiya* had no other goal than to integrate the Yiddish-speaking masses of the Soviet Union into the revolution; the *Yevsektsiya* was on no account to serve national goals. With the full cooperation of the police and other government agencies, the *Yevsektsiya* dismantled the traditional Jewish communal organization, the *kehilot*, expropriated synagogue buildings, closed *yeshivot* and other educational institutions and exercised strict control on the publication of books of Jewish interest. At the same time the *Yevsektsiya* attempted to create a Jewish Communist culture: A Communist Yiddish press, publishing houses, a network of primary and secondary schools, Yiddish theaters and other cultural projects. The *Yevsektsiya* even sponsored Jewish settlement projects, the most significant being the proclamation in 1928 of an autonomous Jewish region in Birobidzhan on the Manchurian border. The *Yevsektsiya* seemed increasingly committed to preserving the identity of Soviet Jewry. "The Communist party [however] saw the Jewish sections as a transient instrument through which the Jewish masses could be socialized, transformed, and integrated into the society as a whole, and if that integration meant the loss of separate ethnic identity so be it, or even, some argued, so much the better" (Zvi Y. Gitelman, *Jewish Nationality and Soviet Politics: The Jewish Sections of The CPSU 1917–1930* [Princeton: Princeton University Press, 1972], p. 11). In 1930 the party decided to liquidate all national sections, including the *Yevsektsiya*. Gradually, the institutions created by the *Yevsektsiya*, along with many of the section's activities, were liquidated, a process that was completed by the late 1940s.

2. For several years after the revolution the Soviets authorized, for tactical reasons, restricted activities of the Zionists and then only in certain regions of the country; by 1928 Zionism was absolutely banned in the Soviet Union. Many leaders of the movement were imprisoned and sent to labor camps, or exiled to outlying districts of Soviet Asia.

3. Popular name of the Constitutional Democratic party, founded in October 1905; it was the principal middle-class party in czarist Russia.

4. Between 1917 and 1920 (a period of protracted revolutions and civil wars), Eastern Europe, especially Poland and the Ukraine, was blighted by devastating pogroms. It has been estimated that

530 communities had been subjected to more than a thousand separate pogroms, in which more than 60,000 Jews were killed and several times that number were wounded. During the pogroms, the Red Army, which adopted strict measures against anti-Semitism, was generally regarded by the Jews as their protector. Nonetheless, the pogroms strengthened the national consciousness of the Jews and the desire for an independent Jewish homeland.

5. Vyacheslav K. Plehve (1846–1904), Russian politician and leader of reactionary circles during the regimes of Alexander III and Nicholas II. In his post as minister of the interior, he was widely suspected of orchestrating the Kishinev pogroms of April 1903. In August of that year, Herzl met with Plehve and other Russian officials, soliciting their support for the Zionist idea of an organized emigration and resettlement of the Jews in a territory of their own.

IX

The American Experience

The Jews of the United States were never legally emancipated. They already enjoyed a large measure of legal equality under the British colonial government (see the Plantation Act of 1740, chapter 1, document 5). In light of the founding ideals of the United States—especially that of the inalienable equality of all men and of the absolute separation of Church and State—the granting of citizenship to the Jews, along with other (white) minorities of the land, was self-evident and was, in contrast to Europe, never a matter of special legislation. From its very inception religious and ethnic pluralism in the United States, although occasionally challenged, was firmly secured in its Constitution and abiding ethos.

The nation thus became a haven for the dissenters and the persecuted minorities of Europe. Significantly, the inspired poem that graces the Statue of Liberty—"Give me your tired, your poor, your huddled masses yearning to breathe free..."—was written by a Jewish poetess, Emma Lazarus (1849–1887). She was a descendant of the so-called first wave of Jewish immigration to America; a group of predominantly Spanish-Portuguese Jews who began to arrive on the shores of America in the 1650s (see document 1). From 1840 to 1880 large numbers of Jews from German-speaking lands arrived, appreciably augmenting the Jewish population of the United States. From only 4,000 in 1820 the Jewish population increased to about 50,000 in the 1840s and to approximately 280,000 in the 1880s. The largest immigration of Jews, however, came in the period from 1880 to the outbreak of the First World War in 1914. Prompted by the pogroms and the increasingly repressive conditions of their native lands, over two million Russian and other East European Jews left for the United States. In 1914 the Jewish population of the United States had reached three million.

With an expanding industrial, urban economy, America was a land of opportunity, *a goldene medine,* as expressed in Yiddish. But the immigrants encountered many difficulties, not the least of which was anti-Semitism. It is crucial to note that the antagonism toward the Jew in America remained largely social in character and that—given America's pluralism of prejudice—the Jews were not the only object of discrimination. The blacks, the Catholics, the Irish, the Chinese and others were often, at different times and places the major focus of group hostility. To be sure, American anti-Semitism was exacerbated by the influx of large numbers of Jews who represented an alien culture and who were concentrated in the centers of socio-economic stress, that is, the large cities. Nonetheless, with few exceptions the hostility never truly became, as it did in Europe, the focus of a political and ideological struggle. America's strong tradition, indeed ethos of tolerance and pluralism, confined anti-Semitism to the social sphere.

Each wave of Jewish immigration developed institutions and patterns of Jewish life that have become distinctive of American Jewry. The German Jews, for instance, founded many of the major national Jewish organizations for charity, mutual aid and welfare, among them the B'nai B'rith (1843), the Young Men's Hebrew Association (1854) and the American Jewish Committee (1906). The German Jews also helped establish Jewish religious denominationalism, which had already begun to emerge in Europe but which crystallized in the more tolerant and innovative United States. Reform Judaism, for instance, was more radical in the United States than it was in its native Germany. Similarly, Conservative Judaism, derivative of Zecharias Frankel's Historical School of Judaism, first took shape in America. Immigrants who arrived after the turn of the century adopted these religious institutions, but they added a vigorous form of "Americanized" Orthodoxy and the Reconstructionism of Mordecai M. Kaplan to the denominational pattern. The East European immigrants also brought with them socialism and various secular Jewish ideologies, for example, Zionism and Yiddishism, which they sought to implant in America. They established a vital ethnic-national Jewish culture based on these ideologies. This orientation contrasted sharply with the purely confessional and philanthropic Judaism of the older community. At first, these differences engendered considerable conflict between the newer, "ethnic" community and the older, "assimilated" community of Jews. In time, the contrast between the two communities of Jews decreased and they adjusted their institutions and conceptions of Judaism to accommodate one another. Zionism, with its unambiguous affirmation of Jewish nationality, became a touchstone of the older community's accommodation. Rabbi Judah L. Magnes' sermon, entitled "A Republic of Nationalities," illustrates this adjustment. The rabbi's topic was the complementary nature of Americanism and ethnic solidarity, or Jewish national consciousness; the sermon was delivered in 1909 before Temple Emanuel of New York City, one of America's oldest Reform congregations. Magnes, like Israel Friedlaender, Solomon Schechter and Mordecai M. Kaplan, used the term *Jewish national consciousness* to express the idea of solidarity with and philanthropic support of one's fellow Jews, especially those who sought to construct a secure future for themselves in their ancestral homeland. Jewish solidarity so conceived does not contradict allegiance to America. For America's pluralism, this school of thought held, is not only religious, but also ethnic, and hence ethnic affections and solidarity are not inimical to American citizenship and patriotism. In a lecture entitled "The Jewish Problem: How to Solve It" given in 1915, Louis D. Brandeis (Supreme Court Justice from 1916 to 1939) summarized this viewpoint when he affirmed that "loyalty to America demands that every Jew become a Zionist" (see document 28). Here ethnic solidarity is extended to include support for those Jews who sought to construct a secure future for themselves in their ancestral homeland. This pro-Zionism, later pro-Israelism, eventually became the factor that bound, some would say defined, most of American Jewry. It was endorsed, so to speak, in the 1950 agreement between Jacob Blaustein, president of the American Jewish Committee, and David Ben Gurion, premier of the State of Israel.

PETER STUYVESANT

1. Petition to Expel the Jews from New Amsterdam (September 22, 1654)[1]

The Jews who have arrived would nearly all like to remain here, but learning that they (with their customary usury and deceitful trading with the Christians) were very repugnant to the inferior magistrates,[2] as also to the people having the most affection for you; the Deaconry also fearing that owing to their present indigence they might become a charge in the coming winter, we have, for the benefit of this weak and newly developing place and the land in general, deemed it useful to require them in a friendly way to depart; praying also most seriously in this connection, for ourselves as also for the general community of your worships, that the deceitful race—such hateful enemies and blasphemers of the name of Christ—be not allowed to further infect and trouble this new colony to the detraction of your worships and the dissatisfaction of your worships' most affectionate subjects.

NOTES

1. Peter Stuyvesant (1592–1672). In May 1645 Stuyvesant was selected by the Dutch West India Company as director of New Netherland; he arrived in New Amsterdam (i.e., New York) on May 11, 1647. A violent and despotic man, he was nonetheless an obedient servant to his employer, the Dutch West India Company, established by the Estates General of the Netherlands as a public company in June 1621. The purpose of the company was to regulate and protect the contraband trade already carried on by the Dutch in the American and African possessions of Spain and Portugal, and to establish colonies on both continents and their islands. By the terms of its charter the company was composed of five boards or chambers, established in Amsterdam, Zeeland, Rotterdam, Friesland and Groningen. The general board was endowed with power to negotiate treaties, and make war and peace with native rulers; to appoint its officials, generals and governors; and to legislate in its possessions subject to the laws of the Netherlands.

In September 1654, twenty-three Jewish refugees arrived in New Amsterdam, after fleeing from Brazil where the Portuguese had recaptured several colonies from the Netherlands. Although Dutch subjects, these Jewish refugees met with unexpected hostility from Stuyvesant, the governor of the New Netherland. Stuyvesant immediately wrote the letter presented here to the directors of the West India Company, requesting permission to ban Jews from the colony.

2. I.e., the sheriff, mayors and aldermen, who constituted the Inferior Court of Justice of the colony.

Source: Peter Stuyvesant to the Directors of the Amsterdam Chamber of the Dutch West India Company, in Samuel Oppenheim, "The Early History of the Jews in New York, 1654–1664," *Publications of the American Jewish Historical Society*, 18 (1909), pp. 4–5. Reprinted by permission of the American Jewish Historical Society.

DUTCH WEST INDIA COMPANY
2. Reply to Stuyvesant's Petition (April 26, 1655)[1]

We would have liked to effectuate and fulfill your wishes and request that the new territories should no more be allowed to be infected by people of the Jewish nation, for we foresee therefrom the same difficulties which you fear, but after having further weighed and considered the matter, we observe that this would be somewhat unreasonable and unfair, especially because of the considerable loss sustained by this nation, with others, in the taking of Brazil, as also because of the large amount of capital which they still have invested in the shares of this company. Therefore after many deliberations we have finally decided and resolved to apostille upon a certain petition presented by said Portuguese Jews that these people may travel and trade to and in New Netherland and live and remain there, provided the poor among them shall not become a burden to the company or to the community, but be supported by their own nation. You will now govern yourself accordingly.

NOTE

1. Three overriding factors seemed to induce the Amsterdam Chamber to reject Stuyvesant's petition to ban Jews from settling in New Amsterdam: the vigorous intercession on the part of Amsterdam Jewry, some of whom had substantial investments in the Dutch West India Company, an appreciation of the loyalty of the Jews in Brazil and the imperatives of mercantilism.

Source: Reply of the Amsterdam Chamber of the West India Company to Peter Stuyvesant, in Samuel Oppenheim, "The Early History of the Jews in New York, 1654–1664," *Publications of the American Jewish Historical Society,* 18 (1909), p. 8. Reprinted by permission of the American Jewish Historical Society.

DUTCH WEST INDIA COMPANY
3. Rights of the Jews of New Amsterdam (March 13, 1656)[1]

The consent given to the Jews to go to New Netherland and there to enjoy the same liberty that is granted them in this country was extended with respect to civil and political liberties, without the said Jews becoming thereby entitled to a license to exercise and carry on their religion in synagogues or gatherings. So long, therefore, as no request is presented to you [Stuyvesant] to allow such a free exercise of religion, any consideration relative thereto is too premature, and when later something shall be presented about it you will be doing well to refer the matter to us in order to await thereon the necessary orders.

Considering the Jewish nation with regard

Source: The Amsterdam Chamber of the West India Company to Peter Stuyvesant, in Samuel Oppenheim, "The Early History of the Jews in New York, 1654–1664," *Publications of the American Jewish Historical Society,* 18 (1909), p. 21. Reprinted by permission of the American Jewish Historical Society.

to trade, they are not hindered, but trade with the same privilege and freedom as other inhabitants. Also, they have many times requested of us the free and public exercise of their abominable religion, but this cannot yet be accorded to them. What they may be able to obtain from your Honors time will tell.

NOTE

1. The above letter was in reply to a letter by Stuyvesant dated October 30, 1655 in which he argued that "to give liberty to the Jews [of New Amsterdam] will be very detrimental, because the Christians there will not be able at the same time to do business. [Moreover], by giving them liberty we cannot refuse the Lutherans and the Papists" (cited in Samuel Oppenheim, "The Early History of the Jews in New York, 1654–1664," *Publications of the American Jewish Historical Society,* 18 [1909], p. 20).

4. The Declaration of Independence (July 4, 1776)[1]

The unanimous declaration of the thirteen United States of America:

When, in the course of human events, it becomes necessary for one people to dissolve the political bands which have connected them with another, and to assume among the powers of the earth the separate and equal station to which the laws of nature and of nature's God entitle them, a decent respect to the opinions of mankind requires that they should declare the causes which impel them to the separation.

We hold these truths to be self-evident, that all men are created equal, that they are endowed by their Creator with certain unalienable rights, that among these are life, liberty, and the pursuit of happiness. That to secure these rights, governments are instituted among men, deriving their just powers from the consent of the governed. That whenever any form of government becomes destructive of these ends, it is the right of the people to alter or to abolish it, and to institute new government, laying its foundation on such principles and organizing its powers in such form, as to them shall seem most likely to effect their safety and happiness. . . .

We, therefore, the representatives of the United States of America, in general congress assembled, appealing to the Supreme Judge of the world for the rectitude of our intentions, do, in the name, and by authority of the good people of these colonies, solemnly publish and declare, that these united colonies are, and of right ought to be free and independent states; that they are absolved from all allegiance to the British Crown, and that all political connection between them and the state of Great Britain is and ought to be totally dissolved: and that as free and independent states they have full power to levy war, conclude peace, contract alliances, establish commerce, and to do all other acts and things which independent states may of right do. And for the support of this declaration, with a firm reliance on the protection of Divine Providence, we mutually pledge to each other our lives, our fortunes, and our sacred honor. . . .

Source: Francis Newton Thorpe, *The Federal and State Constitutions* (Washington, D.C., 1909), vol. 5, pp. 2636–37.

NOTE

1. Declaration by which the thirteen original states of the Union broke their allegiance to Great Britain. Its justificatory preamble, presented here, contains idealistic principles largely based on Locke's theory of natural right. The principles of the Declaration were legally equivalent to promises. Indeed, although translated into law on the federal level in the Constitution of 1789, New Hampshire, for instance, enacted the principle of religious freedom only in 1876–1877.

5. The Virginia Act of 1785[1]

The General Assembly, on the sixteenth day of December, seventeen hundred and eighty-five, passed an act in the words following, to wit:

Whereas, Almighty God has created the mind free; that all attempts to influence it by temporal punishment, or burthens, or by civil incapacitations, tend only to beget habits of hypocrisy and meanness, and are a departure from the plan of the Holy Author of our religion, who, being Lord both of body and mind, yet chose not to propagate it by coercions on either, as was in his Almighty power to do; that the impious presumption of legislators and rulers, civil as well as ecclesiastical, who being themselves but fallible and uninspired men, have assumed dominion over the faith of others, setting up their own opinions and modes of thinking as the only true and infallible, and as such endeavoring to impose them on others, have established and maintained false religions over the greatest part of the world, and through all time, that to compel a man to furnish contributions of money for the propagation of opinions which he disbelieves, is sinful and tyrannical, and even the forcing him to support this or that teacher of his own religious persuasion, is depriving him of the comfortable liberty of giving his contributions to the particular pastor whose morals he would make his pattern, and whose powers he feels most persuasive to righteousness, and is withdrawing from the ministry those temporary rewards which, proceeding from an approbation of their personal conduct, are an additional incitement to earnest and unremitting labors, for the instruction of mankind; that our civil rights have no dependence on our religious opinions any more than our opinions in physics or geometry; that therefore the proscribing any citizen as unworthy the public confidence by laying upon him an incapacity of being called to offices of trust and emolument, unless he profess or renounce this or that religious opinion, is depriving him injuriously of those privileges and advantages to which, in common with his fellow-citizens, he has a natural right; that it tends only to corrupt the principles of that religion it is meant to encourage, by bribing, with a monopoly of worldly honors and emoluments, those who will externally profess and conform to it; that though, indeed, those are criminal who do not withstand such temptation, yet neither are those innocent who lay the bait in their way; that to suffer the civil magistrate to intrude his powers into the field of opinion, and to restrain the profession or propagation of principles on supposition of their ill tendency, is a dangerous fallacy, which at once destroys all religious liberty, because he, being of course judge of that tendency, will make his opinions the rule of judgment, and approve or

Source: Bill for Establishing Religious Freedom, *Code of Virginia* (Richmond, Virginia, 1904), vol. 1, pp. 770–71.

condemn the sentiments of others only as they shall square with or differ from his own; that it is time enough for the rightful purposes of civil government, for its officers to interfere, when principles break out into overt acts against peace and good order; and finally, that truth is great and will prevail, if left to herself; that she is the proper and sufficient antagonist to error, and has nothing to fear from the conflict, unless by human interposition disarmed of her natural weapons, free argument and debate; errors ceasing to be dangerous when it is permitted freely to contradict them:

Be it enacted by the General Assembly, That no man shall be compelled to frequent or support any religious worship, place or ministry whatsoever, nor shall be enforced, restrained, molested or burthened, in his body or goods, nor shall otherwise suffer on account of his religious opinions or belief; but that all men shall be free to profess, and by argument to maintain, their opinions in matters of religion, and that the same shall in no wise diminish, enlarge or affect their civil capacities.

And though we well know that this Assembly elected by the people for the ordinary purposes of legislation only, have no power to restrain the acts of succeeding assemblies constituted with powers equal to our own, and that, therefore, to declare this act to be irrevocable would be of no effect in law; yet we are free to declare, and do declare, that the rights hereby asserted are of the natural rights of mankind; and that if any act shall be hereafter passed to repeal the present, or to narrow its operation, such act will be an infringement of natural right.

NOTE

1. This bill was framed by Thomas Jefferson (1743–1826), the foremost advocate of religious freedom among the founding fathers of the United States. The bill, which was passed by the General Assembly of Virginia on December 16, 1785, served as a precedent for the freedom of religion clause passed by the Federal Constitutional Convention in 1791. The Virginia Act also inspired the votaries of Enlightenment and democracy in Europe. Later, the champions of Jewish emancipation in the French National Assembly also used it as an authoritative precedent for the removal of religious restrictions to citizenship.

6. The Constitution of the United States of America (1789)

We, the people of the United States, in order to form a more perfect union, establish justice, insure domestic tranquility, provide for the common defence, promote the general welfare, and secure the blessings of liberty to ourselves and our posterity, do ordain and establish this constitution for the United States of America. . . .

Article VI. [Freedom of religion as a basic law of the land.[1]] . . . The senators and representatives before mentioned, and the members of the several state legislatures, and all executive and judicial officers, both of the United States and of the several states, shall be bound by oath or affirmation to support this constitution; but no religious test shall ever be required as a qualification to any office or public trust under the United States.

Source: Francis Newton Thorpe, *The Federal and State Constitutions* (Washington, D.C., 1909), vol. 1, p. 19.

Amendment 1. Congress shall make no law respecting an establishment of religion, or prohibiting the free exercise thereof; or abridging the freedom of speech, or of the press; or the right of the people peaceably to assemble, and to petition the government for a redress of grievances.

NOTE

1. The Constitution and its First Amendment guaranteed the legal equality of all citizens of the United States regardless of religion. Although Article VI of the Constitution abolished any religious test "as a qualification to any office," at least two states, Maryland and North Carolina, continued to restrict the right of Jews and Christian dissidents to hold public office, arguing that the Constitution only referred to federal positions. The two states removed these restrictions in 1824 and 1868, respectively.

THE HEBREW CONGREGATION OF NEWPORT, RHODE ISLAND
7. Message of Welcome to George Washington (August 1790)[1]

Sir:

Permit the children of the stock of Abraham to approach you with the most cordial affection and esteem for your person and merits and to join with our fellow-citizens in welcoming you to New Port.

With pleasure we reflect on those days—those days of difficulty and danger—when the God of Israel who delivered David from the peril of the sword shielded your head in the day of battle. And we rejoice to think that the same Spirit, who rested in the bosom of the greatly beloved Daniel, enabling him to preside over the provinces of the Babylonish Empire, rests, and ever will rest upon you, enabling you to discharge the arduous duties of Chief Magistrate in these states.

Deprived as we have hitherto been of the invaluable rights of free citizens, we now, with a deep sense of gratitude to the Almighty Disposer of all events, behold a government, erected by the majesty of the people, a government which to bigotry gives no sanction, to persecution no assistance, but generously affording to all liberty of conscience and immunities of citizenship, deeming every one, of whatever nation, tongue, or language, equal parts of the great governmental machine. This so ample and extensive federal union whose basis is philanthropy, mutual confidence, and public virtue, we cannot but acknowledge to be the work of the Great God, who ruleth in the armies of heaven and among the inhabitants of the earth, doing whatsoever seemeth him good.

For all the blessings of civil and religious liberty which we enjoy under an equal and benign administration, we desire to send up our thanks to the Antient of Days, the great Preserver of Men, beseeching him that the angel who conducted our forefathers through the wilderness into the promised land may graciously conduct you through all the dangers and difficulties of this mortal life. And when like Joshua, full of days and full of

Source: Lewis Abraham, "Correspondence Between Washington and Jewish Citizens," *Proceedings of the American Jewish Historical Society,* 3 (1895), pp. 90–91. Reprinted by permission of the American Jewish Historical Society.

honor, you are gathered to your fathers, may you be admitted into the heavenly paradise to partake of the water of life and the tree of immortality.

Done and signed by order of the Hebrew Congregation in New Port, Rhode Island.

August 17, 1790.

Moses Seixas, Warden

NOTE

1. When George Washington, who was inaugurated the first president of the fledgling Republic in April 1789, visited Newport on August 17, 1790, the warden of the local synagogue addressed the above message of welcome to him. Washington's reply follows in document 8.

GEORGE WASHINGTON
8. A Reply to the Hebrew Congregation of Newport

Gentlemen:

While I receive with much satisfaction your address replete with expressions of affection and esteem, I rejoice in the opportunity of assuring you that I shall always retain a grateful remembrance of the cordial welcome I experienced in my visit to New Port from all classes of citizens.

The reflection on the days of difficulty and danger which are past is rendered the more sweet from a consciousness that they are succeeded by days of uncommon prosperity and security. If we have wisdom to make the best use of the advantages with which we are now favored, we cannot fail, under the just administration of a good government, to become a great and a happy people.

The citizens of the United States of America have a right to applaud themselves for having given to mankind examples of an enlarged and liberal policy, a policy worthy of imitation.

All possess alike liberty of conscience and immunities of citizenship. It is now no more that toleration is spoken of, as if it was by the indulgence of one class of people that another enjoyed the exercise of their inherent natural rights. For happily the government of the United States, which gives to bigotry no sanction, to persecution no assistance, requires only that they who live under its protection should demean themselves as good citizens, in giving it on all occasions their effectual support.

It would be inconsistent with the frankness of my character not to avow that I am pleased with your favorable opinion of my administration and fervent wishes for my felicity.

May the children of the stock of Abraham who dwell in this land continue to merit and enjoy the good will of the other inhabitants, while every one shall sit in safety under his own vine and fig-tree, and there shall be none to make him afraid.

May the Father of all mercies scatter light and not darkness in our paths, and make us all in our several vocations useful here, and, in his own due time and way, everlastingly happy.

G. Washington

Source: Lewis Abraham, "Correspondence Between Washington and Jewish Citizens," *Proceedings of the American Jewish Historical Society*, 3 (1895), pp. 91–92. Reprinted by permission of the American Jewish Historical Society.

MORDECAI MANUEL NOAH

9. Proclamation to the Jews (1825)[1]

Whereas, it has pleased Almighty God to manifest to his chosen people the approach of that period when, in fulfillment of the promises made to the race of Jacob, and as a reward for their pious constancy and triumphant fidelity, they are to be gathered from the four quarters of the globe, and to resume their rank and character among the governments of the earth;

And Whereas, the peace which now prevails among civilized nations, the progress of learning throughout the world, and the general spirit of liberality and toleration which exists together with other changes favorable to light and to liberty, mark in an especial manner the approach of that time, when "peace on earth good will to man" are to prevail with a benign and extended influence, and the ancient people of God, the first to proclaim his unity and omnipotence, are to be restored to their inheritance, and enjoy the rights of a sovereign independent people;

Therefore, I, Mordecai Manuel Noah, citizen of the United States of America, late Consul of the said States to the City and Kingdom of Tunis, High Sheriff of New York, Counsellor at Law, and by the grace of God, Governor and Judge of Israel, have issued this my Proclamation, announcing to the Jews throughout the world, that an asylum is prepared and hereby offered to them, where they can enjoy that peace, comfort and happiness which have been denied them through the intolerance and misgovernment of former ages; an asylum in a free and powerful country remarkable for its vast resources, the richness of its soil, and the salubrity of its climate; where industry is encouraged, education promoted, and good faith rewarded, "a land of milk and honey," where Israel may repose in peace, under his "vine and fig tree," and where our people may so familiarize themselves with the science of government and the lights of learning and civilization, as may qualify them for that great and final restoration to their ancient heritage, which the times so powerfully indicate.

The asylum referred to is in the State of New York, the greatest State in the American confederacy. New York contains forty-three thousand, two hundred and fourteen square miles, divided into fifty-five counties, and having six thousand and eighty-seven post towns and cities, containing one million, five hundred thousand inhabitants, together with six million acres of cultivated land, improvements in agriculture and manufactures, in trade and commerce, which include a valuation of three hundred millions of dollars of taxable property; one hundred and fifty thousand militia, armed and equipped; a constitution founded upon an equality of rights, having no test-oaths, and recognizing no religious distinctions, and seven thousand free schools and colleges, affording the blessings of education to four hundred thousand children. Such is the great and increasing State to which the emigration of the Jews is directed.

The desired spot in the State of New York, to which I hereby invite my beloved people throughout the world, in common with those of every religious denomination, is called Grand Island, and on which I shall lay the foundation of a City of Refuge, to be called Ararat.

Grand Island in the Niagara river is bounded by Ontario on the north, and Erie on the south, and within a few miles of each of these great commercial lakes. The island is

Source: M. J. Kohler, "Some Early American Zionist Projects," *Publications of the American Jewish Historical Society*, 8 (1900), pp. 106–13. Reprinted by permission of the American Jewish Historical Society.

nearly twelve miles in length, and varying from three to seven miles in breadth, and contains upwards of seventeen thousand acres of remarkably rich and fertile land.

Deprived, as our people have been for centuries of a right in the soil, they will learn, with peculiar satisfaction, that here they can till the soil, reap the harvest, and raise the flocks which are unquestionably their own; and, in the full and unmolested enjoyment of their religious rights, and of every civil immunity, together with peace and plenty, they can lift up their voice in gratitude to Him who sustained our fathers in the wilderness, and brought us in triumph out of the land of Egypt; who assigned to us the safekeeping of his oracles, who proclaimed us his people, and who has ever walked before us like a "Cloud by day and a pillar of fire by night."

In His name do I revive, renew and *reestablish* the government of the Jewish Nation, under the auspices and protection of the constitution and laws of the United States of America; confirming and perpetuating all our rights and privileges, our name, our rank, and our power among the nations of the earth, as they existed and were recognized under the government of the Judges. And I hereby enjoin it upon all our pious and venerable Rabbis, our Presidents and Elders of Synagogues, Chiefs of Colleges and brethren in authority throughout the world, to circulate and make known this, my Proclamation, and give it full publicity, credence and effect. . . .

Those of our people who, from age, local attachment, or from any other cause, prefer remaining in the several parts of the world which they now respectively inhabit, and who are treated with liberality by the public authorities, are permitted to do so, and are specially recommended to be faithful to the governments which protect them. It is, however, expected that they will aid and encourage the emigration of the young and enterprising, and endeavor to send to this country such as will add to our national strength and character, by their industry, honor and patriotism.

Those Jews who are in the military employment of the different sovereigns of Europe are enjoined to keep in their ranks until further orders, and conduct themselves with bravery and fidelity.

I command that a strict neutrality be observed in the pending wars between the Greeks and the Turks, enjoined by considerations of safety towards a numerous population of Jews now under the oppressive dominion of the Ottoman Porte.

The annual gifts which, for many centuries, have been afforded to our pious brethren in our holy City of Jerusalem (to which may God speedily restore us) are to continue with unabated liberality; our seminaries of learning and institutions of charity in every part of the world are to be increased, in order that wisdom and virtue may permanently prevail among the chosen people. . . .

The Caraite and Samaritan Jews, together with the black Jews of India and Africa, and likewise those in Cochin, China and the sect on the coast of Malabar, are entitled to an equality of rights and religious privileges, as are all who may partake of the great covenant and obey and respect the Mosaical laws.

The Indians of the American continent, in their admitted Asiatic origin, in their worship of God, in their dialect and language, in their sacrifices, marriages, divorces, burials, fastings, purifications, punishments, cities of refuge, divisions of tribes, in their High Priests, in their wars and in their victories, being in all probability, the descendants of the lost tribes of Israel, which were carried captive by the King of Assyria, measures will be adopted to make them sensible of their condition and finally re-unite them with their brethren, the chosen people.

I recommend peace and union among us; charity and good-will to all; toleration and liberality to our brethren of every religious denomination, enjoined by the mild and just precepts of our holy religion; honor and good faith in the fulfillment of all our contracts, together with temperance, economy, and industry in our habits.

I humbly entreat to be remembered in your

prayers; and lastly and most earnestly I do enjoin you to "keep the charge of the Holy God," to walk His ways, to keep His statutes, and His commandments, and His judgments, and His testimonies, as it is written in the laws of Moses, "That thou mayest prosper in all thou doest, and whithersoever thou turnest thyself."

Given at Buffalo, in the State of New York, this second day Tishri, in the year of the world 5586, corresponding with the fifteenth day of September, 1825, and in the fiftieth year of American independence.

NOTE

1. Mordecai Manuel Noah (1785–1851), editor, politician and playwright. He was probably the most prominent and influential Jew in the United States in the early nineteenth century. After serving as U.S. consul in Tunis from 1813 to 1815, he became active in New York State and national politics. For many years he was intrigued by the idea of Jewish territorial restoration and in 1825 he solicited funds to purchase a tract of land on Grand Island in the Niagara River near Buffalo, New York. He named the territory *Ararat* and declared it the future national home of the Jewish people. The project was a fiasco, but it did elicit much discussion both in America and in Europe on the plight of the Jews. It was also one of the first articulations of the concept of America as a haven for oppressed Jewry.

L. KOMPERT
10. Off to America![1]

"The harvest is past, the summer is ended, and we are not saved" (Jer. 8:20).

The sun of freedom has risen above the fatherland, but for us it is nothing but a bloody northern light. The larks of redemption warble in the sky; for us, however, they are the screaming harbingers of a terrible storm. Shame and rage overcome us when we remember the terrible and hair-raising events of recent weeks! Because slavish hordes and petty merchants have failed to understand the spirit of freedom, *we* Jews must suffer. Can God really want us to hold out our heads to every cudgel and to tremble before every despot, great or small? We have reached the point where at the very hour which has brought freedom into the land, we have no other wish but to avoid *this* kind of freedom!

The [Gentiles] apparently do not want it otherwise, and so be it! It will not be the first time that we shall acquiesce to their whims. For centuries, our history has been nothing but a silent acceptance of every torture, agony and restriction they have chosen to impose on us! But should we always accept, always bow our head? . . . For once, with the permission of the "sovereign people," we want to lose our patience, only once we want to resist—and then we shall move on!

For we shall go to America! Those among you who do not understand the essence of history, should take this as an indication of it—that four centuries ago, at a time when the Jews were persecuted most cruelly, it was a

Source: L. Kompert, "Auf, nach Amerika," *Oesterreichisches Central-Organ fuer Glaubensfreiheit, Cultur, Geschichte und Literatur der Juden,* no. 6 (Vienna, May 6, 1848), p. 77. Trans. here by J. Hessing.

man from Genoa who was haunted by the idea of discovering a new world and did not find peace until Queen Isabella of Spain—whose husband had evoked the dark figure of Torquemada[2] and his thousands of bloodstained Dominican brethren—allowed him [Christopher Columbus] to discover America. It is for this America that we are yearning, thither you shall move! "Off to America!"

We know all your objections and all your answers! . . . Do you not have any other advice for us, you ask, but to take up once again the wanderer's staff and with wife and child seek a far and foreign land? Shall we leave the native soil which has born and fed us, and in which we have buried our dead? I sense in these words something of Egypt's fleshpots; yes, I, too, smell the flavor of the golden soups and juicy roast—but I also see the people who are stirring the flames and who are extracting their daily bread from the fires of hatred, of prejudice, and of narrow-mindedness. By God, may he who has a penchant for these things stay behind and feed himself!

In our time, two sentences may serve us as points of departure. The first one was said by Moses: "Stand fast and still." The second one was said by Jeremiah: "The harvest is past, the summer is ended, and we are not saved." Which of the two sentences do you prefer? To stand still and to wait, to wait patiently, until all who are now opposed to us will make peace with us, until the spirit of humanity is victorious? Or, since "we are not saved," to seek salvation elsewhere—and to move to America?

I think the two sentences can be reconciled easily! May those in our fatherland who wish to "stand fast and still" build their homes upon the sands of the future! We do not want to prevent them from doing so; on the contrary, we shall gladly provide them with bricks for their endeavor. But to all the others, the oppressed and persecuted, those who have been driven from their homes and plundered in the notorious communities, all those who have gained nothing but calamity from this "freedom," all those who feel in their hearts that it will take a long time before there is peace for them in the fatherland . . . to all those we say: we are not saved. Salvation can only be sought in America!

The idea is not new. This we know; but it is practical. . . . The purpose of emigration is the finding of a new fatherland and the gain of immediate freedom! . . .

Thousands before you have taken this step and are still taking it! And only a disproportionate few have regretted it. The God of your forefathers will watch over you. He will guide you safely across the sea and through the first difficulties of your new life! I am not afraid for you! You have all the necessary qualities and virtues: circumspection, sobriety, frugality, discipline and faith; they will help you in the building of a new life and wealth. Others have perished there, but you will prosper and grow; the God of freedom will be with you.

In my spirit I already greet your children there, the children of those who have *become* free. Greetings! [*Shalom Aleichem!*]

A bright glow fills me as I think of the children *born* free, and of their mothers.

Therefore, in light of the horrors of the past weeks . . . I call to you: "Off to America!"

NOTES

1. L. Kompert (1822–1886), German writer celebrated for his descriptions of Bohemian Jewish life. An enthusiastic supporter of the 1848 Revolution, he joined with other Jews in founding a journal (in which the above was published) advocating Jewish rights, or as Kompert prefered to say, Jewish "right, not rights" (*Recht, nicht Rechte*). The *Oesterreichisches Central-Organ fuer Glaubensfreiheit, Cultur, Geschichte und Literatur der Juden* (an Austrian journal for Jewish religious freedom, culture, history and literature), appeared between April and October 1848 in Vienna. In mid-April anti-Jewish riots occurred in Prague, Budapest and Pressburg; the Jews of Alsace were subject to the fury of the

masses in February; and in March, Prussian Poland was the scene of anti-Jewish riots. Kompert was grievously disappointed and responded by urging the Jews to emigrate to the United States. His above article was followed by many similar pleas in the *Oesterreichisches Central-Organ* for organized emigration to the United States. Although the editor of the journal, Isidor Bush, himself heeded the call and emigrated to America, Kompert remained in Vienna, where he was active in Jewish affairs.

2. Tomas De Torquemada (1420?–1498), first head of the Spanish Inquisition. At the age of fourteen he entered the Dominican Order where he became the confessor of Queen Isabella and her husband, King Ferdinand. He helped to establish the Inquisition in Spain and was known for his ferocity and cruelty in dealing with Jews and conversos.

11. The Manhattan Beach Affair (1879) [1]

The war against the Jews, which was carried on at Saratoga two years ago, is apparently to be revived at Coney Island. This time it is in a quarter where the Jewish residents of New York City are particularly aimed at. Several days ago a rumor was circulated to the effect that Austin Corbin, the President of the Manhattan Beach Company, had taken an open stand against admitting Jews to the beach or hotel. This report was on Sunday strengthened by a statement from Mr. P. S. Gilmore, the leader of the Manhattan Beach band, who said that Mr. Corbin told him he was going to oppose the Jews, and that he would rather "sink" the two millions invested in the railway and hotel than have a single Israelite take advantage of its attractions. A representative of the *Herald* called upon Mr. Corbin at his banking establishment in the new Trinity building, No. 115 Broadway, yesterday, to ascertain what foundation there was for these most extraordinary rumors. Mr. Corbin at first exhibited some timidity about talking on the subject, but finally invited the reporter into his private office, where he was joined by his brother and partner, Daniel C. Corbin.

"You see," he began, "I don't want to speak too strongly, as it might be mistaken for something entirely different from its intended sense. Personally I am opposed to Jews. They are a pretentious class, who expect three times as much for their money as other people. They give us more trouble on our road and in our hotel than we can stand. Another thing is, that they are driving away the class of people who are beginning to make Coney Island the most fashionable and magnificent watering place in the world."

"Of course, this must affect business?"

"Why, they are hurting us in every way, and we do not want them. We cannot bring the highest social element to Manhattan Beach if the Jews persist in coming. They won't associate with Jews, and that's all there is about it."

"Do you intend to make an open stand against them?"

"Yes, I do. They are contemptible as a class, and I never knew but one 'white' Jew in my life. The rest I found were not safe people to deal with in business. Now, I feel pretty warm over this matter, and I will write a statement which you can publish."

Mr. Corbin sat down at his desk and wrote a few sentences on a slip of paper, as follows:

Source: Stanley McKenna, "Reviving a Prejudice: Jewish Patronage Not Welcomed at Manhattan Beach . . . ," *New York Herald,* July 22, 1879.

"We do not like the Jews as a class. There are some well behaved people among them, but as a rule they make themselves offensive to the kind of people who principally patronize our road and hotel, and I am satisfied we should be better off without than with their custom."

"There," said he, handing the statement to the reporter, "that is my opinion, and I am prepared to follow up the matter. It is a question that has to be handled without gloves. It stands this way: We must have a good place for society to patronize. I say that we cannot do so and have Jews. They are a detestable and vulgar people. What do you say, eh, Dan?"

This last sentence was addressed to his brother, Mr. Daniel Corbin, who had taken an active part in the conversation. Dan said, with great emphasis, "Vulgar? I can only find one term for them, and that is nasty. It describes the Jews perfectly."

Mr. Austin Corbin then spoke warmly of the loss sustained by the Manhattan Beach Company in consequence of Israelitish patronage.

"Do you mean, Mr. Corbin, that the presence of Jews attracts the element of ruffianism?" asked the reporter.

"Not always. But the thing is this. The Jews drive off the people whose places are filled by a less particular class. The latter are not rich enough to have any preference in the matter. Even they, in my opinion, bear with them only because they can't help it. It is not the Jews' religion I object to; it is the offensiveness which they possess as a sect or nationality. I would not oppose any man because of his creed."

"Will the other members of the Manhattan Beach Company support you in your position?"

"I expect them to. They know just as much about it as I do, and no reasonable man can deny that the Jews will creep in a place just as it is about to become a grand success and spoil everything. They are not wanted at the Beach, and that settles it."

"Have you spoken to any other members about it?"

"No; but I guess they know my opinions."

Mr. Corbin rose from the chair he had been sitting in and paced the floor. "I'll tell you," said he, running his fingers through his hair, "if I had had my way and there was no one to consult in the matter but myself, I would have stopped the Jews from coming long ago. You just publish my statement. It covers the whole ground, and I mean every word of it."

Mr. Corbin concluded the conversation by telling the reporter to be sure and not give the impression that he was warning against the Jewish religion, but he stigmatized the Jews as having no place in first-class society.

NOTE

1. Beginning in the 1870s social anti-Semitism in the United States became increasingly manifest. The much publicized refusal of accommodations to the Jewish financier Joseph Seligman at the Grand Hotel in Saratoga Springs, New York, symbolized the problem. Seligman was informed that the hotel's manager, Henry Hilton, had "given instructions that no Israelites shall be permitted in the future to stop at this hotel." Jews were barred from private resorts, social clubs and private schools—institutions of the upper classes. The older social elite were striving to secure their position and to fend off the intrusions of those individuals who had only recently acquired wealth in the post–Civil War industrial boom. The above article is an interview with Austin Corbin, president of both the Long Island Railroad and the Manhattan Beach Company. Corbin candidly explains why he wishes to bar Jews from Coney Island, a place that he wants to develop into a fashionable resort.

HENRY ADAMS[1]
12. The Jews Make Me Creep

[*To Charles Milnes Gaskell—July 31, 1896.*]

I am myself more than ever at odds with my time. I detest it, and everything that belongs to it, and live only in the wish to see the end of it, with all its infernal Jewry. I want to put every money-lender to death, and to sink Lombard Street and Wall Street under the ocean. Then, perhaps, men of our kind might have some chance of being honorably killed in battle and eaten by our enemies. I want to go to India, and be a Brahmin, and worship a monkey. . . .

We are in the hands of the Jews. They can do what they please with our values. . . .

For three years I have told you that in my opinion there was only one safe and surely profitable investment, and that is gold, locked up in one's private safe. There you have no risk but the burglar. In any other form you have the burglar, the Jew, the Czar, the socialist, and, above all, the total, irremediable, radical rottenness of our whole social, industrial, financial, and political system. . . .

[*To Elizabeth Cameron—August 14, 1901.*]

We arrived here [Warsaw] yesterday afternoon, after a tiresome night and day in what they call an express, through a country flatter than Florida, and less varied. But we had the pleasure of seeing at last the Polish Jew, and he was a startling revelation even to me, who have seen *pas mal de Jew*. The country is not bad; on the contrary, it is a good deal like our plains, more or less sandy, but well-watered. It is the people that make one tired. You would gratify all your worst instincts if you see a dozen women reaping the grain, and one big, clumsy man standing over them, superintending and doing nothing. With what pleasure should I have called your attention to it, knowing your ferocious and evil nature in regard to my sex! While Sister Anne is really so indifferent to masculine crime, wrapped up as she is in the passion for her two hulking boys! I can get very little fun out of her on that account, and she seems to grow worse always. She bore the journey well—better than I expected, for I found it fatiguing; but we've a worse one tomorrow to Moscow, and I shall be glad to see her well over it. Warsaw is a big, bustling city, like all other cities, only mostly Jew, in which it is peculiar to Poland. I see little to remark in the streets; nothing in the shops. The people are uglier than on Pennsylvania Avenue which is otherwise my lowest standard. Like all other cities and places, it is evidently flattened out, and has lost most of its characteristics. The Jews and I are the only curious antiquities in it. My only merit as a curio is antiquity, but the Jew is also a curiosity. He makes me creep. . . .

[*To Charles Milnes Gaskell—February 19, 1914.*]

The winter is nearly over, I am seventy-six years old, and nearly over too. As I go, my thoughts turn to you and I want to know how you are. Of myself, I have almost nothing to tell. It is quite astonishing how the circle narrows. I think that in reality as many people pass by, and I hear as much as I ever did, but it is no longer a part of me. I am inclined to think it not wholly my fault. The atmosphere really has become a Jew atmosphere. It is curious and evidently good for some people, but it isolates me. I do not know the language, and my friends are as ignorant

Source: W. C. Ford, ed., *Letters of Henry Adams, 1892–1918,* (Boston and New York: Houghton Mifflin Company, 1938), vol. 2, pp. 338, 620, 110ff.

as I. We are still in power, after a fashion. Our sway over what we call society is undisputed. We keep Jews far away, and the anti-Jew feeling is quite rabid. We are anti-everything and we are will up-lifters; yet we somehow seem to be more Jewish every day. This is not my own diagnosis. I make none. I care not a straw what happens provided the fabric lasts a few months more; but will it do so? I am uneasy about you. I judge you to be worse than we. At least you are making almost as much howl about it. . . .

NOTE

1. Henry Adams (1838–1918), a grandson of John Quincy Adams, and a distinguished American historian.

CONFERENCE OF REFORM RABBIS
13. The Pittsburgh Platform (1885)[1]

In view of the wide divergence of opinion and of the conflicting ideas prevailing in Judaism today, we, as representatives of Reform Judaism in America, in continuation of the work begun at Philadelphia in 1869, unite upon the following principles:

First: We recognize in every religion an attempt to grasp the Infinite One, and in every mode, source or book of revelation held sacred in any religious system the consciousness of the indwelling of God in man. We hold that Judaism presents the highest conception of the God-idea as taught in our holy Scriptures and developed and spiritualized by the Jewish teachers in accordance with the moral and philosophical progress of their respective ages. We maintain that Judaism preserved and defended amid continual struggles and trials and under enforced isolation this God-idea as the central religious truth for the human race.

Second: We recognize in the Bible the record of the consecration of the Jewish people to its mission as priest of the One God, and value it as the most potent instrument of religious and moral instruction. We hold that the modern discoveries of scientific researches in the domains of nature and history are not antagonistic to the doctrines of Judaism, the Bible reflecting the primitive ideas of its own age and at times clothing its conception of divine providence and justice dealing with man in miraculous narratives.

Third: We recognize in the Mosaic legislation a system of training the Jewish people for its mission during its national life in Palestine, and to-day we accept as binding only the moral laws and maintain only such ceremonies as elevate and sanctify our lives, but reject all such as are not adapted to the views and habits of modern civilization.

Fourth: We hold that all such Mosaic and Rabbinical laws as regulate diet, priestly purity and dress originated in ages and under the influence of ideas altogether foreign to our present mental and spiritual state. They fail to impress the modern Jew with a spirit of priestly holiness; their observance in our

Source: Yearbook of the Central Conference of American Rabbis, 45 (1935), pp. 198–200. Reprinted by permission of the Central Conference of American Rabbis.

days is apt rather to obstruct than to further modern spiritual elevation.

Fifth: We recognize in the modern era of universal culture of heart and intellect the approach of the realization of Israel's great Messianic hope for the establishment of the kingdom of truth, justice and peace among all men. We consider ourselves no longer a nation but a religious community, and therefore expect neither a return to Palestine, nor a sacrificial worship under the administration of the sons of Aaron, nor the restoration of any of the laws concerning the Jewish state.

Sixth: We recognize in Judaism a progressive religion, ever striving to be in accord with the postulates of reason. We are convinced of the utmost necessity of preserving the historical identity with our great past. Christianity and Islam being daughter-religions of Judaism, we appreciate their mission to aid in the spreading of monotheistic and moral truth. We acknowledge that the spirit of broad humanity of our age is our ally in the fulfillment of our mission, and therefore we extend the hand of fellowship to all who cooperate with us in the establishment of the reign of truth and righteousness among men.

Seventh: We reassert the doctrine of Judaism, that the soul of men is immortal, grounding this belief on the divine nature of the human spirit, which forever finds bliss in righteousness and misery in wickedness. We reject as ideas not rooted in Judaism the belief both in bodily resurrection and in Gehenna and Eden (hell and paradise), as abodes for everlasting punishment or reward.

Eighth: In full accordance with the spirit of Mosaic legislation which strives to regulate the relation between rich and poor, we deem it our duty to participate in the great task of modern times, to solve on the basis of justice and righteousness the problems presented by the contrasts and evils of the present organization of society.

NOTE

1. The German Jews who came to the United States in the first half of the nineteenth century brought with them Reform Judaism. By the time of the Civil War several dozens of Reform congregations were established. The tendency in the practice of Judaism was to radical Reform and by 1885, when the Pittsburgh Conference of Reform Rabbis was convened, it was the dominant position, as is expressed in the platform adopted by the conference. At its founding in 1889, the Central Conference of American Rabbis, the principal Reform rabbinical organization, adopted the Pittsburgh Platform without reservation. It remained the basic statement of the tenets of Reform in America until the Columbus Conference in 1937.

KAUFMANN KOHLER
14. The Concordance of Judaism and Americanism[1]

There is no room for Ghetto Judaism in America. Look at any of the creeds and churches in our free land! They are all more tolerant, more liberal, more humane and sympathetic in their mutual relations than those in Europe. Our free institutions, our

Source: Kaufmann Kohler, "American Judaism," *Hebrew Union College and Other Addresses* (Cincinnati: Ark Publishing Co., 1916), pp. 198–99.

common school education, our enlightening press and pulpit, with their appeal to common sense, enlarge the mental and social horizon and render progress the guiding maxim. Least of all could Judaism retain its medieval garb, its alien form, its seclusiveness, in a country that rolled off the shame and the taunt of the centuries from the shoulders of the wandering Jew, to place him, the former Pariah of the nations, alongside of the highest and the best, according to his worth and merit as *man*, and among a people that adopted the very principles of justice and human dignity proclaimed by Israel's lawgivers and prophets, and made them the foundation stones of their commonwealth. No, American Judaism must step forth, the equal of any church in broadness of view and largeness of scope, as a living truth, as an inspiring message to the new humanity that is now in the making, not as a mere memory of the past and a piece of Orientalism in the midst of vigorous, forward-pressing Occidental civilization.

American Judaism! What a power of inspiration lies in these two words! They spell the triumph of the world's two greatest principles and ideals, the consummation of mankind's choicest possessions, the one offered by the oldest, the other by the youngest of the great nations of history, the highest moral and spiritual and the highest political and social aim of humanity; the God of righteousness and holiness to unite and uplift all men and nations, and the Magna Charta of liberty and human equality to endow each individual with God-like sovereignty. Behold America, the land of the future! When the sun sets on the western horizon of Europe, its effulgent rays gild the hills that herald the dawn to the new world. The land of promise for all the persecuted! God hid it, as it were, in His treasure-house to reserve it for the most glorious chapter of human history, when out of the mingling of races and sects, nay, out of the boldest, the most courageous and most independent elements of society, a new, a stronger, healthier and happier type of men and women should emerge, able to cope successfully with the hardships and problems of life, and bring the world nearer to the realization of its highest and holiest dreams and ideals, social, political and religious. And behold Judaism leaving the ark, because the flood of unrighteousness, of cruelty and inhumanity has ceased, and looking out upon a new earth and a new heaven, wherein justice, liberty and peace reign in fulfillment of its seer's visions. Was not the cry "Land! Land!" that resounded on Columbus' ship, the opening up of a new future for the martyr-race at the very time, when its woe and misery had reached their culmination in the land it had enriched by its own toil? Then the voice of God was heard speaking to the fugitive Spanish Jew, as He afterward spoke to the German, the Galician and the Russian Jew: "Go forth and be a blessing to the multitudes of people, and a light to the many nations and classes that settle in the new hemisphere."

NOTE

1. Kaufmann Kohler (1843–1926), American Reform rabbi and president of Hebrew Union College. Born and educated in Germany, Kohler came to the United States in 1869. He was the principal spirit behind the Pittsburgh Platform, and he was a vigorous proponent of the classical Reform point of view, namely, that Judaism is preeminently a religious confession devoted to the mission of leading the world to a genuine, universal faith. Like many Reform leaders, he viewed this mission to be utterly compatible with the ideals of the American Republic, *ergo* there was no contradiction between an abiding loyalty to Judaism and integration into American polity and culture.

The title we have given this excerpt from Kohler is a phrase taken from Emil Gustav Hirsch (1851–1923), another leader of Reform in the United States. The above address was delivered before the Council of American Hebrew Congregations on January 8, 1911.

15. Jewish Immigration into the United States: 1881* –1948

Year	Number	Year	Number	Year	Number	Year	Number
1881	8,193†	1899	37,415‡	1916	15,108	1933	2,372
1882	31,807	1900	60,764	1917	17,342	1934	4,134
1883	6,907	1901	58,098	1918	3,672	1935	6,252
1884	15,122	1902	57,688	1919	3,055	1936	6,252
1885	36,214	1903	76,203	1920	14,292	1937	11,352
1886	46,967	1904	106,236	1921	119,036	1938	19,736
1887	56,412	1905	129,910	1922	53,524	1939	43,450
1888	62,619	1906	153,748	1923	49,989	1940	36,945
1889	55,851	1907	149,182	1924	10,292	1941	23,737
1890	67,450	1908	103,387§	1925	10,267	1942	10,608
1891	111,284	1909	57,551	1926	11,483	1943	4,705‖
1892	136,742	1910	84,260	1927	11,639	July 1943 to Dec. 1945	18,000#
1893	68,569	1911	91,223	1928	11,639	1946	15,535
1894	58,833	1912	80,595	1929	12,479	1947	25,885
1895	65,309	1913	101,330	1930	11,526	1948 (Jan. to Oct.)	12,300
1896	73,255	1914	138,051	1931	5,692		
1897	43,434	1915	26,497	1932	2,755		
1898	54,630						

*We have no, even approximately exact, figures of the Jewish immigration prior to 1881. Some 50,000 German Jews arrived up to 1848. No statistics are available about arrivals from Central Europe after 1848. From 1869, when greater numbers of Jewish emigrants began to arrive from Russia, till 1880, an estimated total of 30,000 landed in the United States. Of smaller contingents of Jews from Austro-Hungary and Rumania who immigrated up to 1880 we have likewise no statistics.

†For 1881 to 1898 statistics are available only for the number of Jews admitted at the ports of New York, Philadelphia and Baltimore.

‡For 1899 to 1907 figures are available for Jewish immigrants at all ports of the United States.

§Since 1908, statistics of departure as well as of arrivals have been kept on record.

‖That is, the fiscal year of July, 1942 to June 30, 1943.

#The figure for July, 1943 to December, 1945, is an estimate.

Source: Mark Wischnitzer, *To Dwell in Safety: The Story of Jewish Migration Since 1800* (Philadelphia: The Jewish Publication Society, 1948), p. 289. Copyright 1948 by the Jewish Publication Society of America. Reprinted by permission.

ABRAHAM CAHAN

16. The Russian Jew in America[1]

... The Jewish population in the United States has grown from a quarter of a million to about one million. Scarcely a large American town but has some Russo-Jewish names

Source: The Atlantic Monthly, July 1898, pp. 130–33.

in its directory, with an educated Russian-speaking minority forming a colony within a Yiddish-speaking colony, while cities like New York, Chicago, Philadelphia, and Boston have each a Ghetto rivaling in extent of population the largest Jewish cities in Russia, Austria, and Roumania. The number of Jewish residents in Manhattan Borough is estimated at two hundred and fifty thousand, making it the largest centre of Hebrew population in the world. The Russian tongue, which twenty years ago was as little used in this country as Persian, has been added to the list of languages spoken by an appreciable portion of the polyglot immigrant population.

Have the newcomers justified the welcome extended to them from Chickering Hall? Have they proved a desirable accession to the American nation?

"Let another man praise thee, and not thine own mouth; a stranger, and not thine own lips," is a proverb current among the people who form the subject of this paper; and being one of them, I feel that it would be better, before citing figures and facts, to let Gentile Americans who have made a study of the New York Ghetto answer the question. Here is what Mr. Jacob A. Riis, an accepted authority on "how the other half lives," has to say of Jewish immigrants:

> They (the Jews) do not rot in their slum, but, rising, pull it up after them. . . . As to their poverty, they brought temperate habits and a redeeming love of home. Their strange customs proved the strongest ally of the Gentile health officer in his warfare upon the slum. The death-rate of poverty-stricken Jewtown, despite its crowding, is lower always than that of the homes of the rich. . . . I am a Christian, and hold that in his belief the Jew is sadly in error. So that he may respect mine I insist on fair play for him all round. I am sure that our city has to-day no better and no more loyal citizen than the Jew, be he poor or rich, and none she has less to be ashamed of. . . .

The question of limiting immigration engages the attention of Congress at frequent intervals, and bills aiming at reform in this direction are brought before the Senate and the House. In its bearings upon the Russian, Austrian, or Roumanian Jew, the case is summed up by the opinions cited. Now let us hear the testimony of facts on the subject. The invasion of foreign illiteracy is one of the principal dangers which laws restricting immigration are meant to allay, and it is with the illiteracy of the New York Ghetto that we shall concern ourselves first.

The last report of the commissioner-general of immigration gives twenty-eight per cent as the proportion of illiterates among the immigrants who came during the past year from Russia. The figure would be much lower, should the computation be confined to immigrants of the Mosaic faith instead of including the mass of Polish and Lithuanian peasants, of whose number only a very small part can read and write. It may not be generally known that every Russian and Polish Jew, without exception, can read his Hebrew Bible as well as a Yiddish newspaper, and that many of the Jewish arrivals at the barge office are versed in rabbinical literature, not to speak of the large number of those who can read and write Russian. When attention is directed to the Russian Jew in America, a state of affairs is found which still further removes him from the illiterate class, and gives him a place among the most ambitious and the quickest to learn both the written and the spoken language of the adopted country, and among the easiest to be assimilated with the population.

The cry raised by the Russian anti-Semites against the backwardness of the Jew in adopting the tongue and the manners of his birthplace, in the same breath in which they urge the government to close the doors of its schools to subjects of the Hebrew faith, reminds one of the hypocritical miser who kept his gate guarded by ferocious dogs, and then reproached his destitute neighbor with holding himself aloof. This country, where the schools and colleges do not discriminate between Jew and Gentile, has quite another tale to tell. The several public evening schools of the New York Ghetto, the evening school supported from the Baron de Hirsch fund, and the two or three private establishments of a similar character are attended by thousands of Jewish immigrants, the great majority of whom come here absolutely ignorant of the language of their native country. Surely nothing can be more inspiring to the public-spirited citizen, nothing worthier of the interest of the student of immigration, than the sight of a gray-haired tailor, a patriarch in appearance, coming, after a hard day's work at a sweat-shop, to spell "cat, mat, rat," and to grapple with the difficulties of "th" and "w." Such a spectacle may be seen in scores of the class-rooms in the schools referred to. Hundreds of educated young Hebrews earn their living, and often pay their way through college, by giving private lessons in English in the tenement houses of the district—a type of young men and women peculiar to the Ghetto. The pupils of these private tutors are the same poor overworked sweat-shop "hands" of whom the public hears so much and knows so little. A tenement house kitchen turned, after a scanty supper, into a class-room, with the head of the family and his boarder bent over an English school reader, may perhaps claim attention as one of the curiosities of life in a great city; in the Jewish quarter, however, it is a common spectacle.

Nor does the tailor or peddler who hires these tutors, as a rule, content himself with an elementary knowledge of the language of his new home. I know many Jewish workmen who before they came here knew not a word of Russian, and were ignorant of any book except the Scriptures, or perhaps the Talmud, but whose range of English reading places them on a level with the average college-bred American.

The grammar schools of the Jewish quarter are overcrowded with children of immigrants, who, for progress and deportment, are rated with the very best in the city. At least 500 of 1677 students at the New York City College, where tuition and books are free, are Jewish boys from the East Side. The poor laborer who will pinch himself to keep his child at college, rather than send him to a factory that he may contribute to the family's income, is another type peculiar to the Ghetto.

The innumerable Yiddish publications with which the quarter is flooded are also a potent civilizing and Americanizing agency. The Russian Jews of New York, Philadelphia, and Chicago have within the last fifteen years created a vast periodical literature which furnishes intellectual food not only to themselves, but also to their brethren in Europe. A feverish literary activity unknown among the Jews in Russia, Roumania, and Austria, but which has arisen here among the immigrants from those countries, educates thousands of ignorant tailors and peddlers, lifts their intelligence, facilitates their study of English, and opens to them the doors of the English library. The five million Jews living under the Czar had not a single Yiddish daily paper even when the government allowed such publications, while their fellow countrymen and co-religionists who have taken up their abode in America publish six dailies (five in New York and one in Chicago), not to mention the countless Yiddish weeklies and monthlies, and the pamphlets and books which to-day make New York the largest Yiddish book market in the world. If much that is contained in these publications is rather crude, they are in this respect as good—or as bad—as a certain class of English novels and periodicals from which they partly derive their inspiration. On the other hand, their readers are sure to find in them a good deal of what would be worthy of a more cultivated language. They have among their contributors some of the best Yiddish writers in the world, men of undeniable talent, and these supply the Jewish slums with popular articles on science, on the history and institutions of the adopted country, translations from the best literatures of Europe and America, as well as original sketches, stories, and poems of decided merit. It is sometimes said (usually by those who know the Ghetto at second hand) that this unnatural development of Yiddish journalism threatens to keep the immigrant from an acquaintance with English. Nothing could be further from the truth. The Yiddish periodicals are so many preparatory schools from which the reader is sooner or later promoted to the English newspaper, just as the several Jewish theatres prepare his way to the Broadway playhouse, or as the Yiddish lecture serves him as a stepping-stone to that English-speaking, self-educational society, composed of working-men who have lived a few years in the country, which is another characteristic feature of life in the Ghetto. Truly, the Jews "do not rot in their slum, but, rising, pull it up after them."

NOTE

1. Abraham Cahan (1860–1953), Russian-born editor, author and socialist leader. Eluding the czarist police who sought his arrest because of his revolutionary activities, Cahan arrived in New York City in 1882. There he became a central figure in the Jewish labor movement. In 1897 he helped found the Yiddish-language socialist newspaper the *Forverts* or the *Jewish Daily Forward,* which he edited from 1903 until 1951. (Although published in Yiddish, the front page of the newspaper indicated its title in both English and Yiddish.) Under his editorship, the *Forverts* became America's largest and most influential foreign-language newspaper.

In the title of Cahan's article, as in American literature in general, the term *Russian Jew* is a generic designation for all Jewish immigrants from Russia, Rumania, Galicia, Poland and other countries of Eastern Europe who entered America after 1880.

THE AM OYLOM MOVEMENT
17. The Bethlehem Judea Colony, South Dakota (1883)[1]

The colony Bethlehem Judea is founded by the first group of the Kremenchug *Bne Horin* (Sons of Freedom) to help the Jewish people in its emancipation from slavery and in its rehabilitation to a new truth, freedom, and peace. The colony shall demonstrate to the enemies of our people the world over that Jews are capable of farming. With this as our main premise, we . . . have adopted the following resolutions:

All members of the colony Bethlehem Judea must engage in farming. Only when all work on the farm is finished may they engage in other productive occupations. Commerical activity is absolutely forbidden. (This point cannot be revised.)

All members of the colony form one family enjoying the same rights and privileges.

Two-thirds of the income of the colony are to be spent on its maintenance and expansion and one-third is to be set aside for a special colonization fund.

The colony considers it its duty to continue the colonization of Russian Jews in America through the establishment of new colonies.

The new colonies thus established form one community with the mother colony and are subject to its regulations.

The scope of the colonization fund is to be determined annually, after the harvest, by the Council of the Colony.

The Council of the Colony, which has also

Source: Abraham Menes, "The Am Oylom Movement," *YIVO Annual of Jewish Social Science,* 4 (1949), pp. 26–27. Reprinted by permission of the Yivo Institute for Jewish Research.

judicial functions, consists of the president, the vice-president, and the judge of the colony.

The Council of the Colony is elected for a period of five years, until such time as the land will become the property of the colony.

The executive powers of the colony are vested in the hands of the president and vice-president. They conclude all agreements in the name of the community, appoint the manager and the agronomist of the community. They bear the responsibility for the financial and social state of the community.

Once a year the president and vice-president shall submit a report to the general assembly of the colony.

The president has the right of veto in all matters pertaining to the colony.

All disputes among members must be brought before the judge of the colony.

Women shall enjoy equal rights with men. . . .

The colony has unanimously elected the following officers: Saul Sokolovski, president; Isidor Geselberg, vice-president; Shlomo Promislovski, judge. This Council of the Colony is elected for a period of five years, that is from January 1, 1883 to January 1, 1888.

NOTE

1. Am Oylom is the name of a Russian Jewish society, founded in Odessa in 1881, that sought to promote the settlement of Jews in the United States in the form of agrarian communes guided by socialist principles. The movement derived its name from Perez Smolenskin's essay of 1872, "Am Olam" (The eternal people), published in the Hebrew monthly, *Ha-Shahar,* in which he called for the national revival of the Jewish people. Between 1881 and 1882 groups were formed in Yelizavetgrad, Kiev, Kremenchug, Vilna and Odessa. Although many members of these groups never made it beyond New York City, four Am Oylom communes were established in 1882: one in Louisiana, two in South Dakota and one in Oregon. Because of debt and other difficulties these communes disbanded within a few years. After a brief attempt to establish urban communes in San Francisco and in New York, the movement dissolved in 1890. Many of its former members continued to play a significant role in the Jewish labor movement.

The Bethlehem Judea commune initially consisted of twelve young people, all unmarried men, except for one married couple. They were from Kremenchug and called themselves Bne Horin ("the sons of freedom"). The aims of the Bne Horin, which eventually totaled thirty-two members, Menes observes, "were rather ambitious. They dreamed of combining the idea of national revival with a new social order. The members of Bethlehem Judea believed that their enterprise would ultimately prove to be a great material and moral success and that large groups of immigrants would emulate them" (Abraham Menes, "The Am Oylom Movement," *YIVO Annual of Jewish Social Science,* 4 [1949], p. 27). But, after eighteen months Bethlehem Judea dissolved.

CHARLES S. BERNHEIMER
18. Sweatshops in Philadelphia (1905)[1]

We enter a sweatshop on Lombard, Bainbridge, Monroe or South Fourth Street. It may be on one of several floors in which similar work is going on. The shop is that of

Source: Charles S. Bernheimer, "The Economic Condition of the Russian Jew in Philadelphia," *The Russian Jew in the United States: Studies of Social Conditions in New York, Philadelphia, and Chicago, with a Description of Rural Settlements,* ed. C. S. Bernheimer (Philadelphia: The John C. Winston Co., 1905), pp. 124–34.

the so-called contractor—one who contracts with the manufacturer to put his garments together after they have been cut by the cutter. The pieces are taken in bundles from the manufacturer's to the contractor's. Each contractor usually undertakes the completion of one sort—pants, coats, vests, knee pants, or children's jackets. There is probably one whole floor devoted to the making of this one kind of garment. It may be that two contractors divide the space of a floor, the one, perhaps, being a pants contractor, and the other a vest contractor, with an entirely distinct set of employees. To his employees the contractor is the "boss," as you find out when you inquire at the shop. Before you have reached the shop, you have probably climbed one, two, or three flights of stairs, littered with debris. You readily recognize the entrance to one of these shops once inside the building. The room is likely to be ill-smelling and badly ventilated: the workers are afraid of draughts. Consequently, an abnormally bad air is breathed which it is difficult for the ordinary person to stand long. Thus result the tubercular and other diseases which the immigrant acquires in his endeavor to work out his economic existence.

There are the operator at the machine, the presser at the ironing table, the baster and the finisher with their needles—the latter young women—all bending their backs and straining their eyes over the garments the people wear, many working long hours in [the] busy season for a compensation that hardly enables them to live, and in [the] dull season, not knowing how they will get along at all.

If we apply our ordinary standards of sanitation to these shops they certainly come below such standards. By frequent visits we may grow accustomed to the sights and smells, and perhaps unconsciously assume that such shops must in the nature of things be in bad condition. But a little reflection will readily show the error of such an assumption.

It is all the more harrowing that the workers have a tenacity of life due to a rich inheritance of vitality, and that through sickness and disease, through squalor and filth, they proceed onward, often managing to pull themselves out of the economic slough, though retaining, perhaps, the defects of bad physical development and surroundings. . . .

The shops are chiefly conducted by the contractors, entirely independent of the manufacturers and the various manufacturers for whom they work assume no liability with reference to them or their employees. They merely agree to pay so much per piece for the garments they give out, and expect the garments to be returned to their establishments as agreed upon by the contractors. Few in this city have "inside" shops, that is, shops in which the entire garment is completed inside the establishment, or in a separate building, under their own supervision. Wherever these inside shops have been established the conditions are very much better; the shop is much cleaner, the light good, the air bearable, and the compensation usually more steady.

The last statement requires elucidation. In one clothing manufacturing establishment, there is in the rear a so-called inside shop with a regular contractor in charge. The firm furnishes its first work to this contractor and thus enables him to give, in turn, steady employment, but claims it could not extend such a shop without adding considerably to the expense, as the rental and the assurance of regularity involve a larger outlay than arranging with contractors who compete on the basis of low rentals and the smallest possible expense.

The contractor is usually an operator or other worker who becomes imbued with the desire to set up for himself. Excessive competition among the small contractors has contributed to the bad economic state of affairs in the garment trades. The contractor is between the upper mill-stone of the manufacturer and the nether mill-stone of the workman, forced to take the prices of the one and trying to make the utmost possible out of the other. Some few have saved enough to become manufacturers themselves. Some of the old established manufacturing firms have retired from business as the result of the competition of this new element.

In actual money gains, the contractors whose earnings have been estimated are better off than their workmen. Many said that if they could get their little capital back they would probably return to their former occupation—at least for a time, for the desire to be a "boss" is strong and would doubtless lead to other attempts. . . .

In [the] busy season the employees are required to work long hours, sometimes as high as fifteen, perhaps eighteen, a day. In [the] slack season they must wait for the work that is doled out to them. Where time enters at all into the measurement of the pay, the employers endeavor to stretch it without giving corresponding pay. There seem to be numerous devices by which the workers can be taken advantage of. The character of the work varies so much in any one trade that it seems difficult to regulate the prices unless by the most iron-clad arrangement, backed by the force of strong organization. But the weakness of the organizations has been apparent in the past. Sometimes they have been affiliated with one general labor organization, sometimes with another. They are now welded together under the United Garment Workers of America, into which they have gone during the past few years. With the exception of the Cutters' Union the membership of these organizations is almost entirely composed of Russian Jews.

NOTE

1. Charles Seligman Bernheimer (1868–1960), Philadelphia-born social worker, who was active in Jewish affairs. He edited the pioneer study *The Russian Jew in the United States,* to which he contributed the essay presented here.

Many immigrants found employment in the garment trade. At the time much of the work in this trade was done on a contractual basis. Contractors—middlemen—received cut goods from the manufacturers or merchants, either rented shop space or used their own apartments, bought or hired sewing machines, and recruited workers. The minute division of labor permitted the employment of relatively unskilled people. These cramped workshops, with their long working days—a seventy-hour week was not uncommon—became known as "sweatshops."

ISAAC M. RUBINOW[1]

19. The Economic Condition of the Russian Jew in New York City (1905)

The Russian Jewish population in New York is far from being the uniform mass that it appears to a superficial observer. It is true that for more than twenty years a uniform stream of poverty-stricken Russian Jews has flowed to New York—but we must not forget that the process began more than twenty years ago and that social differentiation has had time to work upon the early comers. Almost every newly arrived Russian Jew must pay his exorbitant rent to a Russian Jewish landlord. It is almost certain that both have

Source: Isaac M. Rubinow, "The Economic Condition of the Russian Jew in New York City," *The Russian Jew in the United States: Studies of Social Conditions in New York, Philadelphia, and Chicago, with a Description of Rural Settlements,* ed. C. S. Bernheimer (Philadelphia: The John C. Winston Co., 1905), pp. 103–7.

originally come from the same social stratum—for the rich Russian Jewish immigrant was an exception, so rare as to be almost statistically negligible—both at present represent two aspects of the same "economic condition." It is extremely probable that at present the majority of Russian Jewish workers work for Russian Jewish employers. . . .

The years (1898–1903) of unprecedented business activity and "prosperity" for the United States, caused an unusually brisk demand for the products of this Jewish industry; and the growth of Russian Jewish fortunes in New York has been the immediate result of this demand. . . . It certainly is not ready-made clothing and dry goods alone that have brought about this prosperity in a part of the Russian Jewish population. The jewelry business, the liquor business, to a limited extent, and the drug business, to a much greater extent, have all contributed to the same end. New York Jews have come to play a very important part in the theatrical business, but outside of Yiddish theatres and music halls, within the limits of the Ghetto, the Russian Jews have hardly entered this field.

It is a characteristic phenomenon of Russian Jewish life in New York that professions have formed as important a basis of prosperity as business, and perhaps even a larger one. . . .

Medicine has remained one of the favorite professions. . . . Probably from four hundred to six hundred of the seven thousand physicians in greater New York are Russian Jews. Though of late symptoms of over-supply in the market have been noticed, the influx into the profession does not show any signs of abatement. The economic status of the majority is fair—many older members are well-to-do. In the real estate business of the East Side the medical man plays a part by no means unimportant. The dentists, less numerous, are much more prosperous. In the legal profession, on the contrary, the Russians cannot boast of any great success, either financial or otherwise. Pharmacy, on the border line between profession and business, has also attracted a large number of Russian youths, but the returns are far less satisfactory than those of the other occupations.

The teaching profession has probably provided a livelihood for more Jewish families than the others which we have enumerated. For obvious reasons, only the second generation, i.e., those born on the American soil, or those who had emigrated at a very early age, are fit for the profession; but it will certainly be a revelation to many an American to learn how many Russian Jewish young men and girls are doing this work of "Americanization," not only of Jewish, but of Irish, German, and Italian children. There is no doubt that the Jews have supplied a greater proportion of public school teachers than either the Germans or the Italians. The profession has never been a road to fortune; yet with the latest salary schedule, a very comfortable living has been provided for several thousands of families.

The important position which the Russian Jew occupies in the professions of New York City is more significant because he entered them but a short time since. Ten years ago, a Russian Jewish journalist found only a few dozen representatives of his race in medicine and law, a few individuals in dentistry, and hardly any in the teaching profession, or in municipal service. These dozens have grown into hundreds, and even thousands, within the following decade. With a remarkable display of energy and enterprise, the Russian Jew was ready to grasp the opportunity whenever and wherever it presented itself. . . .

While the economic significance of the facts passed under review cannot be denied, it is evident that business and professional classes make up only a small percentage of the Russian Jewish population of New York City—much smaller, indeed, than of the German Jews. . . . The vast majority of the Russian Jews are on a much lower economic level. They belong to the "masses," as against the "classes." . . .

Within these "masses" industrial labor of various kinds is the main source of livelihood. The New York Russian Jew is a wage-worker, notwithstanding the numerous exceptions to the rule. The examples of wage-workers of yesterday changing into employers of labor almost overnight are many. Lately these examples have been rapidly multiplying with the remarkable changes going on within the clothing industry—a process of decentralization, due to the legislative difficulties put in the way of the domestic system, which was the backbone of the clothing industry some years ago. In 1900, New York State had more than 4,000 establishments for [the] manufacture of clothings, most of them in New York City, and a very large proportion in Russian Jewish hands. Yet the number of these proprietors is insignificant in comparison with more than 100,000 workers in this same industry in the same state. The vast majority of the newcomers also join this industrial army in this as well as other branches of manufacturing. The question of the economic condition of the Russian Jew in New York is therefore preeminently the question of wages, hours, and conditions of labor in general.

NOTE

1. Isaac Max Rubinow (1875–1936), Russian-born economist and social worker. He was active in Jewish affairs in New York City.

FORVERTS
20. The International Ladies Garment Workers' Union and the American Labor Movement (1920)[1]

In Chicago a convention of the International Garment Workers' Union opens to-day at which there will be present about three thousand delegates from the entire length and breadth of the country.

For the first time in the history of this powerful labor organization, the most important trade in the general women's clothing industry comes to the convention one hundred per cent organized. The cloak makers have, during the past two years, captured the last stronghold of the employers, who have always been considered invincible. Cleveland fell; the last factories in Canada were captured; cities in the far West were organized; and the cloak trade comes to the convention entirely under the flag of the union.

Of great significance is the recommendation of the executive committee that the union should organize co-operative shops. This plan reflects the spirit of the new tendencies in the union movement of the world, the spirit which leads workers to control industries themselves.

The I.L.G.W.U. stands now in the foremost ranks of the American labor movement, both materially and spiritually. It is one of the most important unions in the country. It has won for its members such conditions that very few of the real American unions may compare with it. Spiritually it is in every

Source: "Editorial, *Forverts,* May 3, 1920," trans. in Mordecai Soltes, *The Yiddish Press: An Americanizing Agency* (New York: Teachers College, Columbia University, 1925), pp. 147–48.

respect one of the most progressive. It responds to every movement for justice, for light. It is always prepared to help the workers in other trades in their struggles to help the oppressed and the suffering.

The International Ladies Garment Workers' Union is a blessing to its members, a pride to the general labor movement, and a hope for the progress of humanity at large.

NOTE

1. The *Forverts* was a Yiddish-language daily founded in New York City in 1897 as a more moderate offshoot of the militantly left-wing *Abendblatt*. The *Forverts* considered itself to be an educator of the immigrant Jewish community in its transition to American culture. At its peak in the 1920s, the newspaper's circulation, encompassing eleven local and regional editions, surpassed a quarter of a million. And the *Forverts* defended the cause of labor, socialism, humanity and distinguished literature; its articles were published both in Yiddish and in other languages.

It has been estimated that in 1916 nearly 40 percent of all gainfully employed Jews in New York City were garment workers. It is thus not surprising that organizing the Jewish garment workers was the primary sphere of trade-union activity among the Jews of New York City. The International Ladies Garment Workers' Union (ILGWU), founded in 1900 in New York City, was the largest and most influential of the "Jewish" unions.

ISRAEL FRIEDLAENDER
21. The Division Between German and Russian Jews[1]

America has, in less than one generation, become the second largest center of the Jewish Diaspora, and bids fair to become the first, instead of the second, within another generation. No other country in the world offers, even approximately, such a favorable combination of opportunities for the development of a Diaspora Judaism, as does America: economic possibilities, vast and sparsely populated territories, freedom of action, liberty of conscience, equality of citizenship, appreciation of the fundamentals of Judaism, variety of population, excluding a rigidly nationalistic state policy, and other similar factors. It is no wonder, therefore, that in no other country did [German] Reform Judaism, as the incarnation of Diaspora Judaism, attain such luxurious growth as it did in America. It discarded, more radically than in Europe, the national elements still clinging to Judaism, and it solemnly proclaimed that Judaism was wholly and exclusively a religious faith, and that America was the Zion and Washington the Jerusalem of American Israel.

On the other hand, the emigrants from Russia brought the antithesis on the scene. They quickly perceived the decomposing effect of American life upon Jewish doctrine and practice, and they became convinced more firmly than ever that Diaspora Judaism was a failure, and that the only antidote was Palestine and nothing but Palestine. The nationalists among them beheld in the very same factors in which the German Jews saw the possibilities of a Diaspora Judaism the

Source: Israel Friedlaender, "The Present Crisis of American Jewry" [1915], *Past and Present: Collected Essays* (Cincinnati: Ark Publishing Co., 1919), pp. 341–43.

chances for organizing Jewry on purely nationalistic lines. Nowhere else, except perhaps in Russia, can be found a greater amount of Palestinian sentiment, as well as a larger manifestation of a one-sided Jewish nationalism, than is to be met with in this country.

This conflict of ideas became extraordinarily aggravated by numerous influences of a personal character. The division between the so-called German Jews and the so-called Russian Jews was not limited to a difference in theory. It was equally nourished by far-reaching differences in economic and social position and in the entire range of mental development. The German Jews were the natives; the Russian Jews were the newcomers. The German Jews were the rich; the Russian Jews were the poor. The German Jews were the dispensers of charity; the Russian Jews were the receivers of it. The German Jews were the employers; the Russian Jews were the employees. The German Jews were deliberate, reserved, practical, sticklers for formalities, with a marked ability for organization; the Russian Jews were quick-tempered, emotional, theorizing, haters of formalities, with a decided bent toward individualism. An enormous amount of explosives had been accumulating between the two sections which if lit by a spark might have wrecked the edifice of American Israel while yet in the process of construction.

NOTE

1. Israel Friedlaender (1876–1920). Polish-born, German- and French-educated, from 1904 until his death he was a professor of Semitics and Bible at the Jewish Theological Seminary of America. In addition to many significant scholarly publications, he wrote extensively on contemporary Jewish affairs. He was celebrated for his uncanny ability to appreciate contrasting perceptions of a problem and to offer a Solomonic reconciliation between them; this was particularly true with regard to the tension between the native American Jews of German origin and the Jewish immigrants from Russia.

The masses of Jewish immigrants that began to reach the shores of the United States in the 1880s were greeted by a native Jewish community of some 280,000. The native Jews, mostly of German origin, were economically successful, and, despite some set-backs, liked to think of themselves as culturally and socially integrated into America. As American anti-immigrant sentiments increased in the 1880s and 1890s the native, class-conscious German Jews were clearly threatened by the influx of Yiddish-speaking, culturally "backward" immigrants (the overwhelming majority of whom came from the poor working classes of East European Jewry). Notwithstanding the antagonism between the "uptown" native Jews and the "downtown" immigrants, the native Jews established an elaborate complex of agencies and philanthropic institutions to aid their co-religionists in their adjustment to the American way of life.

JACOB H. SCHIFF
22. The Galveston Project (1907)[1]

I had a conference yesterday with Messrs. Cyrus Sulzberger,[2] Oscar Straus,[3] and Professor Loeb[4] upon the project about which we have been recently corresponding, and we

Source: Jacob H. Schiff to Israel Zangwill, October 25, 1907, in *Jacob H. Schiff: His Life and Letters,* ed. C. Adler (Garden City: Doubleday, 1928), vol. 2, pp. 98–99.

have reached the conclusion that the Removal Office at New York, with the experience and connections it has already secured, would be well in position to undertake the carrying out of my project, as far as the labor on this side is concerned.

With this in view, it is proposed that the Removal Office create an organization at New Orleans or Galveston, or both, to receive arriving immigrants and at once forward them to their destination, which latter is to be previously arranged for through the New York organization of the Removal Office. To accomplish this properly, it is thought that the Removal Office should have sixty days' previous notice of the initial embarkation of emigrants for New Orleans or Galveston, and that the first shipment should not exceed 500 persons.

It would be left to the ITO [Jewish Territorial Organization], allied in this, as I hope, with Dr. Paul Nathan's Hilfsverein,[5] to father the movement in Russia, to gather the proposed emigrants, to arrange steamship routes, etc., and for any expense attached to this the funds would have to be found in Europe. On the other hand, I shall undertake to place at the disposal of the Removal Office the $500,000 which it is my intention to devote to the initiation of the project. Based upon the cost per head of carrying on the present removal work, which is steadily going forward, half a million dollars should suffice to place from 20,000 to 25,000 people in the American "Hinterland," and I believe, with the successful settlement of such a number, others would readily follow of their own accord, and that then a steady stream of immigration will flow through New Orleans and Galveston into the territory between the Mississippi River on the east, the Pacific Ocean on the west, the Gulf on the south and the Canadian Dominion on the north.

This project is now to a great extent in your own and your friends' hands, and I shall look forward with deep interest to see what can be done with it. . . .

NOTES

1. Jacob H. Schiff (1847–1920), financier and philanthropist. Born in Germany, Schiff came to the United States in 1865; in 1885 he became head of the banking firm of Kuhn, Loeb, and Company. For many years he was deemed the head of American Jewry and actively and generously supported numerous religious and cultural projects within the Jewish community.

The Galveston Project, initiated and financed by Schiff, was a project to divert European Jewish immigration to the United States from the big cities of the East Coast to the southwestern states. Established in 1907, the Jewish Territorial Organization (ITO), headed by Israel Zangwill, undertook to sponsor and supervise the project. The Galveston Project managed to settle 10,000 Jewish immigrants before it ceased operation during the First World War. In addition to genuine humanitarian motives, the Galveston Project was prompted by a desire to break-up the concentration of the Jews in urban ghettoes, which the "uptown" Jews deemed to be an inhibiting factor in the Americanization of the immigrants.

2. Cyrus Leopold Sulzberger (1858–1932), prominent New York merchant, philanthropist and Jewish communal leader.

3. Oscar Solomon Straus (1850–1926), active in Jewish affairs and a U.S. public official. He was a U.S. diplomat and was the first Jew to serve in an American cabinet; he was the secretary of commerce and labor under Theodore Roosevelt from 1906 to 1909.

4. Morris Loeb (1863–1912). Son of Solomon Loeb, the original partner of the banking firm Kuhn, Loeb, and Company, he was a professor of chemistry at New York University and was active in Jewish communal life; he was Schiff's brother-in-law.

5. Hilfsverein der deutschen Juden was the central charitable society of German Jewry to assist Jews in Eastern Europe and oriental countries. Founded in Berlin in 1901, it continued to exist until 1941. Paul Nathan (1857–1927) was a founder of the Hilfsverein and was its general secretary from 1901 to 1914.

LOUIS MARSHALL

23. The American Jewish Committee[1]

. . . What I am trying to accomplish is, to get order out of chaos, and to unite all elements that might possibly seek to father a national movement with the result that discord instead of union would be the rule. Dr. Voorsanger[2] has attempted to organize one movement, Dr. Magnes[3] another, Dr. Mendes[4] a third, the Central Conference[5] a fourth. Mr. Kraus[6] believes that the B'nai B'rith[7] affords a panacea for all ills, and the East Side is bristling with organizations, each national in scope and zero in accomplishment.

It has therefore occurred to me and to my associates, that before any scheme is launched, those who have the welfare of Judaism at heart should come together, merely for the purpose of comparing notes, with a view of ascertaining whether or not there is a possibility of promulgating a plan which will be generally acceptable, and which will accomplish the object which all of us have sincerely at heart.

What I am trying to avoid more than anything else is, the creation of a political organization, one which will be looked upon as indicative of a purpose on the part of the Jews to recognize that they have interests different from those of other American citizens. I conceive that there can be but two tenable theories on which the Jews have the right to organize: firstly, as a religious body, and secondly, as persons interested in the same philanthropic purposes.

Obviously, it will be an absolute impossibility for the Jews of this country to unite as a religious body having ecclesiastical and disciplinary powers. It would be impossible to afford to such an organization the authority and sanction which are essential to successfully carry out such a scheme.

We can, however, all unite for the purpose of aiding all Jews who are persecuted, or who are suffering from discrimination in any part of the world on account of their religious beliefs; and we can at the same time, unite for the purpose of ameliorating the condition of our brethren in faith, who are suffering from the effects of such persecution and discrimination directly or indirectly.

Whether it will be wise to go beyond this, I seriously doubt. Whether, if it were attempted, much harm would result, I strongly believe.

As you will see from some of the names which I have mentioned, it is my idea to bring into this organization, everybody who, if outside of it, would be a freelance, and a power for evil. It is better, therefore, to bring into the organization men of every shade of opinion.

I do not believe it to be feasible to organize upon the basis of existing organizations. There would be much inequality and injustice if such a plan were adopted. We must, in some way or other, go back to the people, and organize on the theory of democracy. While the beginning would be troublesome, I think, in the end, the results accomplished would be most excellent.

NOTES

1. Louis Marshall (1856–1929). U.S. lawyer and Jewish communal leader, Marshall was the chief spokesman of New York City's German Jewish elite. He served as president of the American

Source: Louis Marshall to Rabbi Joseph Stolz, January 12, 1906, in Charles Reznikoff, *Louis Marshall: Champion of Liberty* (Philadelphia: The Jewish Publication Society of America, 1957), vol. 1, pp. 21–22.

Jewish Committee, which he helped establish, from 1912 to 1929. Although non-Zionist, Marshall supported Jewish settlement in Palestine and sought to cooperate with the Zionists. Through his efforts the governing board of the Jewish Agency for Palestine was expanded to include non-Zionists. In the above letter to Rabbi Joseph Stolz, a Reform rabbi in Chicago and one of Marshall's most intimate friends, Marshall broaches his idea to establish an organization later to be known as the American Jewish Committee.

The American Jewish Committee, established in 1906, is the oldest Jewish defense organization in the United States. In addition to Marshall, its founders included some of the most prominent members of the German Jewish elite in the United States. The organization was their response to pogroms in Russia. The committee conducted its affairs in an oligarchic, *noblesse oblige* fashion until the 1940s, limiting membership to a select few.

2. Jacob Voorsanger (1852–1908), Reform rabbi in San Francisco. He was considered the foremost rabbi on the West Coast.

3. Judah Magnes (1877–1948), Marshall's brother-in-law. A Reform rabbi, he was the founder and president of the Kehillah of New York City from its inception in 1908 until its demise in 1922. Adapting the Kehillah of Eastern Europe as a model, the Kehillah in the United States attempted to be the central organization of their respective communities. Most ambitious was the effort of the New York City Kehillah which sought to direct community affairs in the fields of education, sociology, religion, industrial problems and general public relations.

4. Henry Peireira Mendes (1852–1937), English-born rabbi of New York City's Sephardi congregation, Shearith Israel. He was one of the founders of the Union of Orthodox Congregations in America, the Jewish Theological Seminary of America and the Federation of American Zionists.

5. The Central Conference of Rabbis—U.S. association of Reform rabbis founded in 1889.

6. Adolf Kraus (1850–1928). U.S. lawyer and Jewish communal leader, Kraus served as the international president of the B'nai B'rith from 1905 to 1925; he also helped found the Anti-Defamation League in 1913.

7. B'nai B'rith, founded in New York City in 1843, is the world's oldest and largest Jewish service organization.

DAVID PHILIPSON[1]
24. American Judaism Will Not Be Ghettoized (1908)

I hear it said that since the day of the organization of this Conference the face of the American Jewish universe has greatly changed; that, owing to the arrival of masses of immigrants during the past twenty years our religious situation is altogether different from what it was before. Dismay has seized many. The tide of reactionism has swept them off their feet. The optimistic note of the leaders of the nineteenth century has changed in many quarters to a pessimistic wail. The despairers cry that the progressive tendency that this Conference represents cannot possibly hold its own against the overwhelming odds that spell reactionism, ghettoism, romanticism, neo-nationalism and neo-orthodoxy. In spite of many untoward signs I firmly believe that there is no cause for despair, dismay and disheartenment. Ghettoism and reactionism are merely passing phases in the americanization of our most recently arrived brethren. Let us have no fear; American Judaism will not be ghettoized nor russianized, but our Russian brethren under the spell of the spirit of our free institutions will be americanized, and if

Source: David Philipson, "Message of the President," Proceedings of the Nineteenth Annual Convention of the Central Conference of American Rabbis, *Yearbook of the Central Conference of American Rabbis,* 18 (1908), pp. 145–46. Reprinted by permission of the Central Conference of American Rabbis.

not this first generation then their children and their children's children will stand with the descendants of the earlier comers to this land as the representatives of that union of progressive modernity and sane conservatism which this Conference symbolizes. In the process of americanization all the perverted viewpoints that are now distorting the vision of many otherwise excellent people will go the way of all the other extravagant notions wherewith the onward course of civilization has been diverted for a brief spell. Such fads as the glorifying of *Yiddish* as the national language of the Jews, such vain discussions as to whether there is a Jewish art or no, such empty dreams as the political rehabilitation of the Jewish state . . . will all pass as interesting incidents in the strange medley of this period of transition. And that which shall remain will be the great fundamental ideal of the mission of the Jews . . . as a people of religion and of Judaism as a religious force through all the world. . . .

NOTE

1. David Philipson (1862–1949), American Reform rabbi. He was the founder of the Central Conference of American Rabbis, serving as its president from 1907 to 1909. He was regarded as a representative spokesman of "classic" Reform Judaism.

CHAIM ZHITLOVSKY[1]
25. Our Future in America

. . . Firstly, we believe that the basis of our life in America will not be the Jewish religion, but rather our Jewish nationality. Actually, this is already the case, as it has always been. Jews in the Diaspora [*golus*] have always lived as a national minority, indeed everywhere they led *the* struggle to live as a national minority. Until the era of assimilation we never denied the national character of our existence. . . .

To be sure, religion was the chief weapon in our struggle for a separate existence as a national minority. But it was not religion that constituted us as a people; it is not thanks to religion that we have remained a separate people. We created the Jewish religion: Judaism exists by virtue of the existence of the Jews. We elevated religion to a national duty of every Jew because our people needed it and because religion had the power to maintain us as a nation. In these times, however, religion is being transformed into a private matter of individuals alone, for it is now deemed that every individual has the right to believe as he wishes.

Hence, religious Judaism loses its national value and our existence is now to be reconstituted on a purely secular basis, having no relationship to one's religious belief whatsoever. Nowhere is the secular-national character of our people so manifest as here in America. The so-called congregation—the official religious organization [in America]—performs no effective role in our communal life. . . .

What then can unify the Jewish people, if religion is no longer a factor [in the communal

Source: Chaim Zhitlovsky, "Unzer tsukunft dor in land" [1915], *Gezamelte Shriften* (New York: Ferlag Gezelshaft, 1919), vol. 10, pp. 87–91. Trans. here by S. Fuks and P. Mendes-Flohr.

life of the Jew]? What remains, of course, is the national factor: the fact that we are Jews, that we want to live as Jews, that we have national interests. The national Jewish minority in America will therefore have once again to renew its struggle for its national minority existence as it did before the era of assimilation. And if America should not be amenable to our existence as a national minority, we will have to be prepared to bear the sacrifices necessitated by our struggle and to shake off the dust from our feet and once again take the wanderer's staff in our hand.

Fortunately, we have no reason to fear such an eventuality. We are not living in medieval Spain of the Inquisition, nor in contemporary barbaric Poland or Russia. We live in one of the freest countries known in history, a country which will not deny any group the right to live as it wishes, provided, of course, that this group be devoted to the political and social progress of the land, and on the condition that this group love the free nature of America's institutions and laws—provided, of course, that these institutions and laws indeed are free and democratic. We accept these conditions with alacrity, because no other national group appreciates as much as we do political equality and freedom. . . .

We contend that our national cultural existence [in America] will be built on the foundation of the Yiddish language. Through Yiddish we will preserve all the significant treasures of universal culture as well as our own rich Hebrew heritage. We will educate our children in this language. We will establish our own educational institutions, from elementary schools to universities. . . . [These institutions will be the crown of Yiddish culture.]

[In order that the Jewish people be preserved under present circumstances,] we need a power capable of binding all Jews into one entity, while allowing each the freedom of decisions, beliefs, hopes and actions. This power, of course, must be spiritual; it must also be a power that will serve to foster universal human progress. Such a spiritual power can only be the Yiddish language. Hence, our people in America will build its national future on the basis of this language. Nowhere is this being done with such drive and success as here in America.

NOTE

1. Chaim Zhitlovsky (1865–1943), socialist and philosopher of Diaspora (*golus*) nationalism and Yiddishism. In 1893, living in Zurich, he helped found the non-Marxist Russian party of Socialist Revolutionaries in exile and co-edited its journal. At the same time, he founded a Jewish socialist union, which published socialist literature in Yiddish. Although a Jewish nationalist, he opposed Zionism as reactionary and inimical to the interests of the Jewish workers of Eastern Europe. According to Zhitlovsky, the Jews—both as Jews and workers—will be emancipated only under socialism. While continuing the struggle for socialism, the Jewish workers should also seek to develop their own cultural and educational institutions. These opinions were close to those of the Bund, which he joined for a short time. In an article entitled "Farvos davke Yiddish?" (Why Yiddish?), published in 1900, he introduced his notion of Yiddishism, that is, the cultivation of Yiddish culture as the basis of future Jewish life. In 1904 Zhitlovsky came to the United States for a lecture tour on behalf of the Socialist Revolutionary party. On this occasion he attacked the melting-pot theory and advanced the vision of America as a place of harmony and integrity for separate nationalities. After chairing the Czernowitz Yiddish Conference of 1908, which proclaimed Yiddish to be a national language of the Jews, Zhitlovsky returned to the United States, where he became a leading figure in the burgeoning Yiddish culture and socialist movement.

SOLOMON SCHECHTER[1]
26. English and Hebrew Must Be the Languages of American Jewry (1904)

I can quite understand the attachment some of us feel toward the German-jargon, or *patois*—call it what you will—in which for so many centuries Jewish mothers wrote their *Techinoth* (supplications), and which is still spoken by such a large portion of Jewry. But let us beware lest we attach any sacredness to this dialect [Yiddish]. America, someone rightly remarked, is the grave of languages. No foreign language, be it ever so rich in masterpieces of literature, survives a single generation in this country. The children of the immigrant who visit our public schools soon compel their parents to speak English. It would thus be a sin to attach the fortunes of our great literature to the fortunes of this language, which is a mere accident in our history, doomed to die, and is dying before our very eyes. We cannot, we dare not, endanger the Judaism of our children by making a virtue of what may have once been an unfortunate necessity, but at present, thank God, is becoming an impossibility.

On the other hand, it is not necessary to dwell here at length on the vital importance of Hebrew, the Sacred tongue. It is the great depository of all that is best in the soul-life of the Congregation of Israel. Without it we will become a mere sect, without a past, and without a literature, and without a proper Liturgy, and severed from the great Tree which is life unto those that cling to it. Hellenistic Judaism is the only one known to history which dared to make this experiment of dispensing with the Sacred Language. The result was death. It withered away and terminated in total and wholesale apostasy from Judaism. Let us not deceive ourselves. There is no future in this country for a Judaism that resists either the English or the Hebrew language.

NOTE

1. Solomon Schechter (1847–1915). Rumanian-born rabbinic scholar, he served from 1902 until his death as the president of the Jewish Theological Seminary of America. He is considered the chief architect of Conservative Judaism in the United States (see document 29 in this chapter).

Source: Solomon Schechter, "Altar Building in America," *Seminary Addresses and Other Papers* (New York: The Burning Bush Press, 1959), p. 88. Reprinted by permission of the United Synagogue of America.

JUDAH L. MAGNES[1]
27. A Republic of Nationalities

Lincoln believed in freedom. For him an American was a freeman, at liberty to develop his spirit as he chose, so long as he obeyed the law. . . .

Source: Judah L. Magnes, "A Republic of Nationalities," *The Emanuel Pulpit,* February 13, 1909, p. 5.

Since Lincoln's time, however, a strange phrase has become current. We hear much of Americanization. This is applied particularly to the Americanizing of the immigrant. What Lincoln would have thought of such a phrase is, of course, hard to say; but it is not difficult to see that the term Americanization, as all too often used, is not conceived in liberty and dedicated to the proposition that all men are created free and equal.

It must be accepted as almost axiomatic, that every one living in this land should be a citizen of the land. If Americanization means this, that every inhabitant, native born or foreign, assume the obligations of American citizenship, then Americanization is a process that should be aided by us in every legitimate way. It is, in fact, the very rare exception, that a newcomer refuses to renounce allegiance to his former political sovereign. The newcomers of the past generation and more have equalled their predecessors in the avidity with which they have entered into political partnership with their fellow citizens. There is no force, no compulsion about American citizenship. It is a privilege and a duty. A man is attracted to American citizenship just because this nation was conceived in liberty, and dedicated to the proposition that all men are created free and equal. There is hardly an American citizen who does not love this land, its history, its heroes, its literature, its institutions and its ideals of freedom and equality. That process of Americanization that makes clear the privilege and the duty of American citizenship is something for which we may all be grateful.

For some, however, the process of Americanization goes still further. They would demand of a prospective American that in order to become completely an American, he abandon his traditional religion. This view is, perhaps, more widespread than we imagine. . . .

The phrase Americanization is used in still another sense. To become an American, thus many would have it, it is necessary not that one yield his inherited religion, but that he abandon his traditional nationality. You will understand from what I have already said, that I do not use the word nationality in its political sense. Politically a man can be a member of but one nation at one time. When I speak of nationality here I mean, in particular, such elements of nationality as a man can carry with him when he leaves his old home—his national language, his race, his culture, his history, his traditions, his customs, his ideals. It is such things that a man is asked by some to give up in the name of Americanization. It is held that a man must give up his spiritual nationality in order that he may the better become an American; that is, that he may the better learn the language, the spirit, the ways, the institutions, the ideals of this land.

Now, of course, we must, all of us, accommodate ourselves to our surroundings. Even though we have not the will to do it, the force of life itself modifies us more or less in accordance with our environment. Everyone must learn the language of the land, everyone must seek to understand the spirit of its history, its laws, its institutions, its ideals. Everyone must, in greater or in less degree, saturate himself with the dominant culture of the land, which is English. Our language is English, our history, our literature, our laws, our institutions, our ideals are almost entirely English. . . .

This does not, however, by any means, imply that therefore a man's traditional national culture must be abandoned. On the contrary, it is possible and it is desirable that parallel with a high appreciation of, and assimilation to English culture, a man cling with reverence to the national culture of his fathers. Such a parallelism is desirable both from the point of view of the individual and for the sake of the developing culture of this country.

Thus there is no reason why, especially in large centers of population, the various nationalities there quartered should not foster their distinctive national culture parallel with the dominant culture of this land. The Italians, the Germans, the Jews, the Irish, the Slavic peoples and others might do this with advantage to themselves and to the whole country. The advantage to themselves would be their development along natural lines. The hiatus between the traditional national culture and the new surroundings is often so great that it leads to degeneracy of many kinds. The children of minority nationalities are all too often not the equals of their parents in those things that have permanent value, because the chain of tradition has been broken and the accumulated wisdom and beauty of ages is set at nought. A member of a minority nationality is seldom, if ever, caricatured, because he is true to himself, because he speaks his own tongue with love and cherishes his inherited spirit. He is most often caricatured and is despised because of his absurd haste to become as English as have those whose traditions reach back into English ways for many generations.—For this country, too, the fostering of the national cultures in our midst would mean a richness, a picturesqueness, a variety, which, despite our individualism, we sadly lack. Democracy has the tendency to level all distinctions, to create the average type, almost to demand uniformity. If, however, by reason of a variegated national culture, we might be able to overcome this weakness of democracy, that Americanism which is not yet a finished product, but which is in the making might eventually become like a garden of blossoms of many colors, rather than a vast field of flowers of the same size and color.

Indeed, this recognition of the value to this country of national individualities would help us with many of our problems. I would not have you regard it as a mere pleasantry when I say that the negroes, for example, may and do lend color to American culture in the making. They have not, by reason of their unfortunate history, attained the dignity of a national entity. But they have a racial individuality possessed of much of beauty and strength and sweetness, and calculated to lend attractiveness and power to the institutions and ideals of this land. The recognition of the same principle would help us in our relations to the Japanese in our midst. It is essential that all of our inhabitants become American citizens. That once accomplished, every one is free to develop his personality as best he can. Have we reached so far beyond barbarism that we can afford to ignore those elements of culture which the Japanese may bring us? Theirs is an ancient and a noble heritage and it ill becomes us to set our faces against the beauty and the power of a civilization that happens to be oriental. America must, in order to be true to its high conception of liberty and of equality, seek to gather within its borders the representatives of all national cultures and of every civilization.

We Jews in particular, have good reason to take this lesson to heart. With us nationality and religion are so inextricably interwoven that it would be dangerous, particularly from the point of view of our religion, to allow the cultivation of our Jewish nationality to fall into neglect or disrepute. . . .

But the cultivation of Jewish nationality in our midst will be of particular benefit to this country if it becomes an element in the development of the Jewish youth. Unfortunately, our main problem lies in the fact that our youth have lost their traditional religion and have not won for themselves an ideal that can even approximately take its place. The cleavage between parents and children presents a tragedy. The children learn (and are very often taught by us) to despise the spiritual heritage of their parents. We are in danger of rearing a godless generation, not because of any unworthiness inherent in our young, but rather because in the name of a spurious Americanization we shout from the housetops that our people give up their national individuality. . . . American culture, American nationality can be made fruitful and beautiful by contact with the culture of the varied nationalities that are among us. America is not the melting pot. It is not the Moloch demanding the sacrifice of national individuality. America is a land conceived in liberty and dedicated to the principle that all men are created free and equal. And a national soul is as precious and as God-given as is the individual soul. . . .

NOTE

1. Judah L. Magnes (1877–1948), American-born rabbi and communal leader. Upon his ordination as a Reform rabbi by Hebrew Union College in 1900, Magnes went to Germany to study. This occasioned several extended trips to Eastern Europe, where he was profoundly impressed by the richness and vitality of Jewish life there. This strengthened his sympathy for Jewish tradition, peoplehood and Zionism. On his return to the United States in 1904, he served as a rabbi of several Reform congregations, most notably Temple Emanu-El (1906–1910). During that time, he was the secretary of the American Zionist Federation (1905–1908) and later became the president of the organized Jewish community of New York City, the so-called Kehillah, from its founding in 1908 until its demise in 1922. He left for Palestine in the same year, where he became the chancellor and first president of the Hebrew University of Jerusalem.

LOUIS D. BRANDEIS
28. Zionism Is Consistent with American Patriotism[1]

Let no American imagine that Zionism is inconsistent with Patriotism. Multiple loyalties are objectionable only if they are inconsistent. A man is a better citizen of the United States for being also a loyal citizen of his state, and of his city; for being loyal to his family, and to his profession or trade; for being loyal to his college or his lodge. Every Irish American who contributed towards advancing home rule was a better man and a better American for the sacrifice he made. Every American Jew who aids in advancing the Jewish settlement in Palestine, though he feels that neither he nor his descendants will ever live there, will likewise be a better man and a better American for doing so.

Note what Seton-Watson says:

> America is full of nationalities which, while accepting with enthusiasm their new American citizenship, nevertheless look to some centre in the old world as the source and inspiration of their national culture and traditions. The most typical instance is the feeling of the American Jew for Palestine which may well become a focus for his *déclassé* kinsmen in other parts of the world.

There is no inconsistency between loyalty to America and loyalty to Jewry. The Jewish spirit, the product of our religion and experiences, is essentially modern and essentially American. Not since the destruction of the Temple have the Jews in spirit and in ideals been so fully in harmony with the noblest aspirations of the country in which they lived.

America's fundamental law seeks to make real the brotherhood of man. That brotherhood became the Jewish fundamental law more than twenty-five hundred years ago. America's insistent demand in the twentieth century is for social justice. That also has been the Jews' striving for ages. Their affliction as well as their religion has prepared the Jews for effective democracy. Persecution broadened their sympathies. It trained them in patient endurance, in self-control, and in sacrifice. It made them think as well as suffer. It deepened the passion for righteousness.

Source: Louis D. Brandeis, "The Jewish Problem: How to Solve It," *Brandeis on Zionism: A Collection of Addresses and Statements,* foreword by Mr. Justice Felix Frankfurter, ed. Solomon Goldman (Washington, D.C.: Zionist Organization of America, 1942).

Indeed, loyalty to America demands rather that each American Jew become a Zionist. For only through the ennobling effect of its strivings can we develop the best that is in us and give to this country the full benefit of our great inheritance. The Jewish spirit, so long preserved, the character developed by so many centuries of sacrifice, should be preserved and developed further, so that in America as elsewhere the sons of the race may in future live lives and do deeds worthy of their ancestors.

But we have also an immediate and more pressing duty in the performance of which Zionism alone seems capable of affording effective aid. We must protect America and ourselves from demoralization which has to some extent already set in among American Jews. The cause of this demoralization is clear. It results in large part from the fact that in our land of liberty all the restraints by which the Jews were protected in their Ghettos were removed and [the] new generation [is] left without [the] necessary moral and spiritual support. And is it not equally clear what the only possible remedy is? It is the laborious task of inculcating self-respect, a task which can be accomplished only by restoring the ties of the Jew to the noble past of his race, and by making him realize the possibilities of a no less glorious future. The sole bulwark against demoralization is to develop in each new generation of Jews in America the sense of *noblesse oblige*. That spirit can be developed in those who regard their people as destined to live and to live with a bright future. That spirit can best be developed by actively participating in some way in furthering the ideals of the Jewish renaissance; and this can be done effectively only through furthering the Zionist movement.

In the Jewish colonies of Palestine there are no Jewish criminals; because everyone, old and young alike, is led to feel the glory of his people and his obligation to carry forward its ideals. The new Palestinian Jewry produces instead of criminals, scientists like Aaron Aaronsohn,[2] the discoverer of wild wheat; pedagogues like David Yellin;[3] craftsmen like Boris Schatz, the founder of the Bezalel;[4] intrepid *Shomrim*,[5] the Jewish guards of peace, who watch in the night against marauders and doers of violent deeds.

NOTES

1. Louis D. Brandeis (1856–1941), leader of American Zionism, prominent lawyer and first Jew to be appointed Supreme Court justice. His espousal of Zionism and intense involvement in the movement marked a significant rapproachement between the native American Jews and the Russian immigrants. In this address, delivered at the conference of the Eastern Council of Reform Rabbis in June 1915, he spoke to the question of divided loyalties.

2. Aaron Aaronsohn (c.1875–1919), pioneer of scientific agriculture in Palestine. To Brandeis he was the living symbol of the "new Jew."

3. David Yellin (1864–1941), a native of Jerusalem, was an outstanding educator, scholar and communal leader.

4. The Bezalel School for industrial arts was founded in Jerusalem in 1906 by the sculptor Boris Schatz (1866–1933).

5. The *Shomrim* ("guards") were members of Hashomer, a volunteer organization of Jewish workers who defended the Jewish colonies of Palestine against marauders.

SOLOMON SCHECHTER

29. Catholic Israel[1]

It is not the mere revealed Bible that is of first importance to the Jew, but the Bible as it repeats itself in history, in other words, as it is interpreted by Tradition. The Talmud, that wonderful mine of religious ideas from which it would be just as easy to draw up a manual for the most orthodox as to extract a *vade-mecum* for the most sceptical, lends some countenance to this view by certain controversial passages—not to be taken seriously—in which "the words of the scribes" are placed almost above the words of the Torah. Since then the interpretation of Scripture or the Secondary Meaning is mainly a product of changing historical influences, it follows that the centre of authority is actually removed from the Bible and placed in some *living body,* which, by reason of its being in touch with the ideal aspirations and the religious needs of the age, is best able to determine the nature of the Secondary Meaning. This living body, however, is not represented by any section of the nation, or any corporate priesthood, or Rabbi-hood, but by the collective conscience of Catholic Israel as embodied in the Universal Synagogue. The Synagogue "with its long, continuous cry after God for more than twenty-three centuries," with its unremittent activity in teaching and developing the word of God, with its uninterrupted succession of Prophets, Psalmists, Scribes, Assideans, Rabbis, Patriarchs, Interpreters, Elucidators, Eminences, and Teachers, with its glorious record of saints, martyrs, sages, philosophers, scholars, and mystics; this Synagogue, the only true witness to the past, and forming in all ages the sublimest expression of Israel's religious life, must also retain its authority as the sole true guide for the present and the future. And being in communion with this Synagogue, we may also look hopefully for a safe and rational solution of our present theological troubles. For was it not the Synagogue which even in antiquity determined the fate of Scripture? On the one hand, for example, books like Ezekiel, the Song of Songs, and Ecclesiastes, were only declared to be Holy Writ in virtue of the interpretation put upon them by the Rabbis; and, on the other hand, it was the veto of the Rabbis which excluded from the canon the works that now pass under the name of Apocrypha. We may, therefore, safely trust that the Synagogue will again assert its divine right in passing judgment upon the Bible when it feels called upon to exercise that holy office. It is "God who has chosen the Torah, and Moses His servant, and Israel His people." But indeed God's choice invariably coincides with the wishes of Israel; He "performeth all things" upon which the councils of Israel, meeting under promise of the Divine presence and communion, have previously agreed. As the Talmud somewhere expresses itself with regard to the Book of Esther, "They have confirmed above what Israel has accepted below."

Another consequence of this conception of Tradition is that it is neither Scripture nor primitive Judaism, but general custom which forms the real rule of practice. Holy Writ as well as history teaches that the law of Moses was never fully and absolutely put in practice. Liberty was always given to the great teachers of every generation to make modifications and innovations in harmony with the spirit of existing institutions. Hence a return to Mosaism would be illegal, perni-

Source: Solomon Schechter, "Introduction," *Studies in Judaism* (Philadelphia: The Jewish Publication Society of America, 1896), pp. 17–20.

cious, and indeed impossible. The norm as well as the sanction of Judaism is the practice actually in vogue. Its consecration is the consecration of general use—or, in other words, of Catholic Israel. It was probably with a view to this communion that the later mystics introduced a short prayer to be said before the performance of any religious ceremony, in which, among other things, the speaker professes his readiness to act "in the name of all Israel."

NOTE

1. Solomon Schechter (1847–1915), president of the Jewish Theological Seminary of America and one of the architects of Conservative Judaism. In this selection he develops his idea of "catholic Israel," by which he meant the universally accepted sentiments and practices of devoted Jews. This concept exercised a seminal influence on the evolving ideology of Conservative Judaism, the largest single religious movement in American Jewry.

MORDECAI M. KAPLAN

30. The Reconstruction of Judaism[1]

In the first place, we are intensely desirous of having Judaism play an important role in the spiritual life of mankind, and we therefore refuse to view with equanimity the plight in which Judaism finds itself today. We are not deceived by the few sporadic signs of activity and interest in things Jewish, because we know full well that they represent nothing more than the momentum of Jewish life in the past. If a new synagogue is established, the organizers are not men who have been born and brought up in an American environment, but who immigrated to this country from eastern Europe. If, as a result of strenuous endeavor, a few Jewish student organizations spring up in some of our colleges, in nine cases out of ten the initiative is taken by the foreign-born, or by those who were brought up in the Jewish ghettos of our larger cities. Judaism in America has not given the least sign of being able to perpetuate itself. Very few American Jewish homes, if any, have produced rabbis, or teachers of religion, or communal leaders. Our spiritual poverty is so great that we have not in this country a single Hebrew printing establishment for the publication of books that are essential to the preservation of Judaism. We have not a single original edition of the traditional prayer book, to say nothing of the Bible or post-Biblical literature. These and many similar facts go to prove that Judaism under democratic conditions such as obtain in this country has thus far not been able to develop that vitality which could endow it with creative power and make it capable of sustained effort and adaptability. . . .

Secondly we are agreed that the salvation of Judaism cannot come either from Orthodoxy or from Reform. Orthodoxy is altogether out of keeping with the march of human thought. It has no regard for the world view of the contemporary mind. Nothing can be more repugnant to the thinking

Source: Mordecai M. Kaplan, "A Program for the Reconstruction of Judaism," *The Menorah Journal*, 6 (August 4, 1920), pp. 181–93.

man of today than the fundamental doctrine of Orthodoxy, which is that tradition is infallible. Such infallibility could be believed in as long as the human mind thought of God and Revelation in semi-mythological terms. . . .

Our dissent from Reform Judaism is even more pronounced than that from Orthodoxy. If we have been content to put up with much in Orthodoxy that we do not approve of, it is that we might not be classed with the "Reformers." The reason for this attitude of ours toward Reform is that we are emphatically opposed to the negation of Judaism. The principles and practices of Reform Judaism, to our mind, make inevitably for the complete disappearance of Jewish life. Reform Judaism represents to us an absolute break with the Judaism of the past. . . .

The third point on which we concur, and which therefore gives us reason to believe that we may arrive at conclusions acceptable to all of us, is the fact that we are Zionists. We not only share the aspiration to see Israel restored to his homeland, but also subscribe to the principle that such aspiration is synonymous with the revival of Judaism. The very act of translating the longing for the restoration into practical effort has opened up to us a new vista of Jewish thought. It has helped us to discover the reality of the Jewish soul and the Jewish consciousness behind the system of beliefs and practices identified as Judaism. If we profess a Zionism that is more than merely political, we are largely indebted to Ahad Ha-Am, who was the first to give articulate expression to the spiritual significance of the Zionist Movement. Though practically nothing has been done to develop the larger implications of this profounder view of Zionism, there is a broad basis for cooperation in the conviction common to all of us, that the fate of Judaism is bound up with the success of Zionism. . . .

In view of the fact that existing congregational and rabbinic organizations seem to be insensible to the danger which is threatening Judaism, and spend most of their time either perfecting their machinery or listening to speeches full of soothing banalities, it is imperative that something be done immediately apart from those organizations to halt the impending disaster to our religion. . . .

In getting to work upon a program for the reconstruction of Judaism we must take care not to miscalculate the magnitude of the task before us. Unless we are prepared to go to the root of the spiritual ills in Jewish life, we had better not begin at all. We must not be like physicians who are content to treat the symptoms of a disease rather than attack the cause, and who, instead of suggesting a real remedy, recommend some patent medicine or incantation. The real issue is not how to render our ritual in keeping with the requirements of modern life, but how to get our people sufficiently interested in religion to want a ritual. If we are not prepared to do much more for Judaism than revise the prayer book, we should leave the prayer book alone. We are faced with a problem no less than that of transforming the very mind and heart of the Jewish people. Unless its mythological ideas about God give way to the conception of divinity immanent in the workings of the human spirit, unless its static view of authority gives way to the dynamic without succumbing to individualistic lawlessness, and unless it is capable of developing a sense of history without, at the same time, being a slave to the past, the Jewish people has nothing further to contribute to civilization. . . .

The adoption of the social viewpoint is an indispensable prerequisite to a thoroughgoing revision of Jewish belief and practice. That viewpoint will enable us to shift the center of spiritual interest from the realm of abstract dogmas and traditional codes of law to the pulsating life of Israel. We will then realize that our problem is not how to maintain beliefs or uphold laws, but how to enable the Jewish people to function as a highly developed social organism and to fulfill the spiritual powers that are latent in it. This is not the place to elaborate upon the manner in which the social approach to Judaism would revitalize the fundamental ideas of religion. . . .

In fact, our adherence to the Zionist movement has already paved the way for a common acceptance of the social point of view in Judaism, for the main problem of the Zionist movement is how shall the Jewish people live. As Zionists, the problem of Judaism is to us simply the problem of the spiritual life of the Jewish people, and not a problem of abstract creeds and laws. . . .

In view of these considerations, I believe that a program for the reconstruction of Judaism ought to include the following three items: (1) The interpretation of Jewish tradition in terms of present-day thought. (2) The fostering of the social solidarity of the Jewish people through the upbuilding of Palestine, and the establishment of Kehillahs and communal centers in the Diaspora. (3) The formulation of a code of Jewish practice so that every Jew may know definitely what constitutes loyalty to Judaism.

While all of these activities should be instituted as soon as feasible, the order in which they are mentioned represents the degree of emphasis to be laid upon each at the present time. Thus, any attempt on an extensive scale to change the ritual would be entirely premature just now, before we ourselves have become firmly grounded in this newer outlook upon religion and Judaism, and have developed at least some of the most important implications of that outlook. Even then, I believe that the major part of the energy and time at our disposal will have to be devoted to what might be termed an educational campaign for popularizing the social approach to Judaism.

The achievement of our purpose will be facilitated if our initial activities identify us in people's minds as a new school of thought in Judaism, rather than as a new brand of Reform. If, for example, we come out with a new and revitalized conception of the Jewish duty toward the Talmud Torah, in its most comprehensive sense, we are less likely to be misunderstood. We must recognize that it is important not only to do right but to appear right. While we do not want to retard unduly the adoption of the much needed changes in our ceremonial practices, we should by all means avoid such a distortion of issues as that which is responsible for making the question of wearing or not wearing the hat the main line of cleavage between diametrically opposed types of Jewish life. We would no doubt be saved from such a fate if our first efforts were aimed at reinstating Jewish study as a religious duty from which no Jew, whether young or old, should be exempt. . . .

The second line of activity, which should consist of efforts to strengthen the social solidarity of the Jewish people throughout the Diaspora, requires as much attention on our part as the work of transforming the mind of the Jewish people. There is at the present time no organized Jewish group that is qualified to foster Jewish communal life in the Diaspora. Both the Orthodox and the Reform Jews have a tendency to concentrate all their efforts upon one limited aspect of Jewish life, the one upon a decorous service, the other upon a kosher meal. The extreme Zionists, who despair of any spiritual life outside of Palestine, certainly have no patience with any attempt to bring order out of the chaos existing in the communal life in the Diaspora. The very existence of that chaos, they believe, will constitute an additional incentive to those who are intensely Jewish to migrate to Palestine. They would, therefore, do nothing to improve the status of Jewish communal life. In the meantime, there has come to the forefront a class which is only too anxious to take control of some of the Jewish communal affairs, in order to guide them away from Judaism. I refer to the class of Jewish philanthropists who are determined to kill Judaism with charity. They are ready to assist the Jew whenever he is in trouble, to heal him in his sickness, to send him relief if he is in want, to supply his children with social facilities and decent amusement, and, if need be, to distribute him to the four corners of the world. But they systematically oppose anything and everything that might strengthen the Jewish consciousness or promote Jewish solidarity. Their policy has brought into existence a new type of social worker, whose main problem is how to administer an anesthetic to the Jewish people, so as to render its death painless. If, here and there, a social worker is to be found who refuses to contribute towards this solution of the problem, he has a hard time squaring himself with his directorate.

It should be the aim of a movement such as ours to see that the control of Jewish institutions passes over into the hands of those who believe in Judaism and the Jewish future. There is, of course, much more to this second line of activity than merely perfecting the machinery of organization. Jewish organization in the Diaspora must be given a philosophy so as to save it from misunderstanding on the part of either the Jew or the Gentile. Much educational work will have to be done to teach our people to create institutions that are calculated to further Jewish aims. How great an amount of misdirected energy would have been saved if those who have built up synagogues had been shown that the future of many a congregation has been compromised by the failure to provide social and recreational facilities in the synagogue itself. The relation of social and recreational life to spiritual development has only become apparent in recent years, and the truth concerning it is in need of wide diffusion in order that our people may not repeat the mistakes committed in the various Jewish institutions, religious, philanthropic and educational, which they have established. . . .

NOTE

1. Mordecai M. Kaplan (b. 1881), U.S. rabbi and founder of the Reconstructionist movement. Drawing upon traditional Jewish sources, Zionist thought and American philosophical pragmatism, Kaplan developed a program for the creative survival of Judaism in the intellectual, political and social reality of the twentieth century. The sociologist Charles S. Liebman has observed that Reconstructionism is a distinctive "second-generation American Jewish phenomenon" (Charles S. Liebman, "Reconstructionism in American Jewish Life," *American Jewish Year Book*, 71 [1970], p. 4). Reconstructionism, Liebman contends, articulates more authentically than any other religious tendency the consensus of twentieth-century native-born American Jews. In consonance with Kaplan's premises, "American Jews no doubt are more ethnic, or people oriented than religion oriented" (ibid., p. 95). Nonetheless, Reconstructionism has failed to capture the Jewish community, and only a few synagogues identify themselves with the movement. A number of American synagogues, however, have accepted many innovations suggested by Kaplan, for example, the institution of the comprehensive Jewish communal center. Liebman explains the failure of Reconstructionism to establish itself in the Jewish community as a result of its ideological explicitness. Reconstructionism, Liebman notes, makes a virtue of its ethnic, folk orientation, and "most American Jews are not quite willing to admit to this virtue publicly. The entire basis of Jewish accommodation to America, of the legitimacy of Jewish separateness, has been that Judaism is a religion, like Catholicism and Protestantism, and that Jews are not merely an ethnic group, like the Irish or the Italians" (ibid., p. 96). The article presented above is one of Kaplan's earliest formulations of his philosophy of Reconstructionism.

BERNARD REVEL

31. The American Yeshiva[1]

The Yeshiva ideal of education is based upon the conviction that we serve our country and humanity best by training the growing generation of our youth to live in the ways of Israel's Torah, its moral standards and spiritual ideals.

Not merely does the future of American Jewry depend upon this strengthening in our youth of the bonds of love and understanding of the ideals and eternal truths of Israel, but to a great degree world Jewry is coming to look for its spiritual strength to America. Providence has destined us to play a dominant role in the history of world Jewry and Jewish culture. Many European centers of Jewish learning have suffered greatly from the ravages of the war and the disorganized economic life and spiritual upheaval that have followed it. Russian Jewry, for many centuries the stronghold of Jewish life, learning and idealism, has fallen into temporary confusion and disorganization. The mantle of responsibility is descending upon American Jewry, today the largest single group, as well as the most blessed materially, in the Jewish world. The stream of Jewish learning and idealism from abroad, which has been enriching American Jewish life, is drying up. It is our imperative task to create in this land a Jewish life, inspired and guided by the conceptions and teachings, ideas and ideals, that have ensured the continuity of Israel through all ages and climes, that have been the greatest spiritual force in the history of mankind, and the spirit that guided the minds and inspired the hearts of the Fathers of this Republic. Throughout the ages the historic homes of the Jewish soul, the Yeshivoth, have been the centers of intensive Jewish learning, the reservoirs of intellectual energy and spiritual strength, the conscience of Universal Israel, the instruments for the continued transmission of the divine light of Sinai, to the entire household of Israel. They constitute a glorious chapter in the long history of Israel and, next to the Synagogue, form the most vital institution in the preservation of Judaism. In them the knowledge of and love for the Torah has been cultivated and fostered in the hearts of the Jewish youth. Recognizing that in order to maintain Jewish life and culture in this country as a real and living force, the historic home of the Torah must be transplanted to this land, a small and loyal group of pioneers founded the Yeshiva in America, sanctifying through it the name of the Jewish sage and saint of the last century, Rabbi Isaac Elchanan.

The Yeshiva has sent forth many loyal, spiritually endowed, and mentally equipped rabbis throughout the United States and Canada, who live the life of the Torah, and are constructive forces in their communities for good and for God . . . But the Yeshiva does not exist merely for the training of rabbis and of teachers. Important as this task is, and carefully as the responsibilities it involves are accepted in its Teachers Institute and in its Rabbinical Department, the Yeshiva looks beyond these fields of service to the general development of Jewish life and culture, to the evolving of a system of Jewish education that will bring harmony into the life of the American Jewish youth and will develop not only his usefulness as a member of his community, but his Jewish consciousness and his will to live as a Jew and advance the cause of Jewry and Judaism; an education through

Source: Bernard Revel, "The Yeshiva College" [1926], in Aaron Rothkoff, *Bernard Revel: Builder of American Jewish Orthodoxy* (Philadelphia: The Jewish Publication Society, 1972), pp. 256ff.

which the human conscience and the Jewish conscience develop harmoniously into the synthesis of a complete Jewish personality, that indicates the guiding laws of life in accordance with the immortal truths of Judaism in harmonious blending with the best thought of the age and the great humanitarian ideals upon which our blessed country is founded.

In the fruitful development of the wide field of Jewish learning, which constitutes an integral and vital phase of human knowledge and experience, in the cultivation of the spiritual elements of our faith, harmoniously blended with the general training of high school and college, the Yeshiva and its college will infuse a new note into American education. With the Jewish perspective brought to bear upon the various fields of learning, the Yeshiva will make a lasting contribution to American education, the rich background and point of view that an harmonious Jewish and general training will represent. Thus, in affording the opportunity for this concordant growth, to those American Jewish youth—whatever their future field of activity—who wish to combine the advantages of secondary and higher education with the acquisition of the knowledge of the ideals and truths of historic and living Israel, the Yeshiva at the same time, presents a new force of unique value in American education, the cultural outlook of the educated and Torah-true Jew.

In its high school, the Yeshiva offers an opportunity to those who wish to acquire their general training in a truly Jewish atmosphere while growing in familiarity with the comprehensive sources and the ideals of Judaism. Recognized by the State of New York as of full high school grade, this department of the Yeshiva has established itself prominently among the high schools of New York, being among the first in percentage of State scholarships awarded the graduates, and maintaining an excellent record in the State Regents examinations. During these high school years, while acquiring their general schooling, the students receive, as well, a thorough training in the essentials of Jewish learning, they acquire a living and loving understanding of the tenets and practices of Judaism, and are imbued with love and reverence for knowledge and *idealism* that lead to the formation of character, and are translated into living practice.

In its new home, with adequate facilities and serene academic surroundings, the Yeshiva high school will increase its usefulness, and provide thousands of students with the opportunity of developing their character and preparing themselves in thoroughly Jewish surroundings, for a life of usefulness, bringing them in direct contact with the sources of our faith and culture, deepening their understanding of and loyalty to the Torah and the ideals of Israel—preparing them for their role of true citizens, bringing our children nearer to the faith of our fathers, and helping to insure the continuity of Israel and his incomparable contribution to human progress.

Promising students of the Jewish religious schools throughout this country and Canada come to the Yeshiva to develop under the combined general and spiritual training of the Yeshiva high school, and the Yeshiva proper. By its very existence, then, the Yeshiva helps raise the standard of the work of these schools throughout the land, whose chosen pupils, insofar as present facilities permit, come to continue their study at the Yeshiva. The Yeshiva encourages the establishment of such schools, and of other secondary schools of Jewish learning, and through this development hopes ultimately to systematize and standardize the education of Torah-true American Jewry. At present many tendencies, especially a concentration upon the secular, national and linguistic aspects of Judaism, are shifting the center of gravity of Jewish education, which is essentially spiritual and religious, to the neglect of its high ideals and values. In such an organized system of Jewish education, the Yeshiva College will stand out as the directing and unifying force. Through its requirements for admission and the courses it will offer, the Yeshiva College will help develop a more Jewishly educated and inspired youth.

At present the Jewish perspective in education ceases at the close of the Yeshiva high school work, or severs itself from the general college training. In order to enable young men of Jewish training and love for the Jewish ideals, who wish to dedicate themselves to the service of Judaism, to continue their complete training in one institution, imbued with the spirit and ideals of true Judaism, the Yeshiva College of Liberal Arts and Science is being organized. Its fundamental purpose is to afford this harmonious union of culture and spirituality, and to bring into the field of American education the contribution of the spiritual values of Judaism, of the Jewish ideals of education, of the Jewish perspective upon the learning and knowledge of our age. It is in no sense a duplicate of the general colleges, a refuge for those who, with real or imagined grievances, consider themselves unwelcome in other institutions. It is dedicated to the service of those Jewish young men of ability and high ideals who have already been imbued with the spirit and sanctity of Judaism and its teachings, to whom the message of Judaism is of deep significance and who wish to equip themselves fully, as Torah-true Jews.

The Yeshiva College will extend its usefulness to Jewish youth who consider Jewish learning part of the mental and moral equipment they wish to obtain through a college education, and who are equipped for such a higher education as the Yeshiva College will offer, with the standard college curricula combined with courses in Bible, Hebrew philology, Jewish history and literature, Jewish philosophy and ethics, the Talmud and Rabbinic literature, Jewish archeology, Semitic philology and cognate subjects, offered by eminent scholars of the Yeshiva College Faculty.

In its several departments, the Yeshiva will provide adequate facilities for the education of spiritual leaders, rabbis and teachers who will go forth to continue throughout the Jewish community the work of spreading the spirit and message of Torah, beyond that it will continue the great traditions of scholarship and research that have been a sustaining background to the spiritual and cultural life of Jewry through the ages; and it will bring to ever increasing numbers of American Jewish youth the true perspective of historic Judaism in the complex organization of modern life, combining with the learning of the world today those cultural values and spiritual ideals, the strength of the sustaining faith of our fathers, to the enrichment of the lives of the Jewish community and of America today. The Yeshiva College will in time help span the widening chasm between intellectualism and faith in Jewish life and thought. Throughout the ages the mightiest minds among us have been at the same time our religious guides and our teachers.

It will imbue our Jewish youth with an active and abiding interest in, and a spirit of service to the cause of Israel and help cast the eternal truths of Judaism in the mould of true Americanism upon which our country was founded.

In the pattern and design of American culture, in which are interwoven the finest threads of its varied groups, the Jewish strain of religious and moral fervor and steadfastness shall be firm and distinctive. To perpetuate and advance Israel's spiritual and religious heritage, and the proven idealism of steadfast Israel, that has always valued life *sub specie aeternitatis,* to help make it once more a living force in our daily lives, and to aid in the spiritualization of Jewish life in this land, the Yeshiva and its College are dedicated.

NOTE

1. Bernard Revel (1885–1940), U.S. educator, scholar and leader of modern Orthodoxy in America. Born in Lithuania, where he received a thorough talmudic education, Revel immigrated to

the United States in 1906. In 1915 he was appointed headmaster (*rosh yeshivah*) of the Isaac Elchanan Theological Seminary—a small institution for advanced study of Talmud founded in 1897 in New York City, which included some secular studies in its curriculum, a radical innovation for an Orthodox institution of that period. In 1916 Revel established the first *yeshivah* high school, in which both talmudic and secular studies were taught. Overcoming strong opposition from the Orthodox community, in 1928 he founded Yeshivah College as an extension of the seminary. Yeshivah College represented the first attempt to offer a traditional talmudic education with a modern curriculum of secular studies on a college level. Yeshivah College, which was elevated to university status in 1945, became the center of a distinctive brand of American Orthodox Judaism.

THE ANTI-DEFAMATION LEAGUE
32. A Statement of Policy (1915)[1]

The Anti-Defamation League of America, founded under the auspices of the Independent Order of B'nai B'rith, is the result of a demand by the Jewish people for concerted action against the constant and ever increasing efforts to traduce the good name of the Jew. . . . For the present the League contemplates the following activities:

Educational: 1. Public and university libraries will be furnished with lists of books on Jewish subjects, which, in the opinion of the League tend to show the facts regarding Jewish ethics, customs, history, religion and philosophy.

Where it is found that the endowment of institutions, either private or public, does not permit the procurement of a fairly comprehensive number of books on these subjects, it will be the aim of the League to supply them. Investigations show that a majority of the public libraries of the country do not even possess a Jewish history written by a Jewish historian.

Investigation will be made of the bibliography on Jewish subjects in libraries. Wherever it is found that books which maliciously and scurrilously traduce the character of the Jew are kept for general circulation—especially in public stackrooms—the proper authorities will be urged to withdraw such books from general circulation, or, at least, to place a restriction on their use.

2. The services of prominent lecturers and publicists, regardless of religious affiliation, will be enlisted for the purpose of delivering lectures on Jewish subjects at universities, public schools and at appropriate gatherings.

The League will provide also for the dissemination of literature designed to give the public a true understanding of the Jew and Judaism.

3. The League recognizes the fact that the mind of the growing child must be safeguarded against even a suggestion of prejudice; therefore, where in our educational system, either public or private, text books are used which tend to pervert the mind of the child and create prejudice, a determined campaign will be waged to eliminate all such books from the curriculum.

Vigilance Work: 1. The services of clipping bureaus have been secured to keep the League advised as to matters of interest affecting the Jewish people. Information regarding defamation and discrimination should be promptly sent to the Executive Committee of the League.

2. The League will secure corresponding representatives in every State, who will submit to the central office in Chicago all matters

Source: Report of the Anti-Defamation League, May 1915. Submitted to the Constitution Grand Lodge Convention, Independent Order B'nai B'rith.

pertaining to these subjects which come within the scope of the League.

3. We should find our strongest allies in newspapers, periodicals and magazines, the great mediums for expression and exchange of thought. We therefore heartily endorse and commend the action of certain newspapers in adopting the policy of eliminating mention of the religious denomination of malefactors. We shall bend every energy toward making this policy universal.

4. Where articles appear which present the Jew in a false and unworthy light, we shall endeavor to secure correction either by retraction, or by an answer in the next or early issue of the same publication, thereby reaching the same reading public.

5. The League will attempt to secure the co-operation of the Press in eliminating from foreign and domestic news items, all matters which give an untrue impression of the Jew.

Theaters and Moving Pictures: Investigation will be made of all plays which deal with the Jew. If, after careful study, it is apparent that a play gives an untrue or unfair portrayal of the Jew, the League will endeavor to prevent its production in its offensive form, or if already staged, to secure the elimination of the objectionable matter. Similar measures will be taken in connection with moving picture films.

Legislation: 1. With a view of preventing the presentation, in moving picture theaters, of films which are malicious and scurrilous caricatures, or are objectionable in other respects, the League will endeavor to secure, in the various states of the Union, the enactment of statutes similar to the one recently passed in the State of Ohio, providing for the appointment of a Board of State Censors. Where the passage of such a statute cannot be attained similar relief will be sought from the various municipalities by securing the enactment of appropriate ordinances.

2. The League will endeavor to secure the passage of laws, where the same is practicable, making it unlawful for any hostelry, directly or indirectly, to publish, circulate, issue, display, post or mail any written or printed communication, notice or advertisement, to the effect that any of the accommodations of such places shall be refused, withheld, or denied to any person on account of his creed. . . .

Situation in 1913: When the League was organized in the fall of 1913, an extraordinary situation confronted it. It seemed that whenever film manufacturers desired to depict a hardhearted money-lender, a blackmailer, a fire-bug, a depraved gambler, a swindler, a grafter or a white-slaver, they determined upon a Jewish name for the person in question, and directed the actor to simulate what is popularly regarded as a "Jewish type." There was nothing so unusual in this, as the tendency has been evident since the time of [Christopher] Marlowe's "Barabas." The extraordinary element, however, was that what previously reached the attention of an infinitesimal fraction of the populace, and that fraction a matured and cultured part, was most vividly presented before the eyes of millions of the unmatured, ignorant or the uncultured. A careful survey of the existing situation showed that there were scores of films on the market which were extremely prejudicial to the welfare and happiness of our people. In addition to the criminal characterization, the Jew was often shown in caricature, in a manner similar to that employed on the burlesque and vaudeville stages. These caricaturizations were supposed to be funny, but in many instances the laughter which they stimulated was that which arises from the malicious discomfiture of another. Under the guise of fun, the most sordid, vulgar and unclean characteristics were frequently attributed to Jews in general.

NOTE

1. U.S. organization founded in 1913 by the B'nai B'rith. Its objectives and program are explained in this document.

CONGRESSIONAL COMMITTEE ON IMMIGRATION

33. Temporary Suspension of Immigration (1920)[1]

During the third session of the Sixty-fifth Congress[2] the Committee on Immigration and Naturalization gave thorough consideration to the question of immigration restriction. Several bills were introduced and extended hearings were held. The then chairman of this committee, the late Hon. John L. Burnett, introduced a bill, H.R. 15302, which was reported favorably by the committee January 29, 1919. This bill provided for the prohibition of immigration for a period of four years. The committee was practically unanimously in favor of such a prohibition, and at that time it was thought such a bill could be passed if time for its consideration could be given on the floor of the House. But the House calendars were so congested that the bill did not receive a hearing and therefore failed of enactment. . . .

Since Mr. Burnett's bill . . . was reported, January 29, 1919, almost two years have passed. The flood of immigration which was expected when Mr. Burnett's bill was under consideration did not set in until the summer of 1920. This committee is informed that had steamship accommodations been available, this flood of immigration would have set in more than a year ago. But steamship accommodations were not available, due to the necessities of demobilization of the armies, and it was not until the spring and summer of 1920 that the real effects of unsettled conditions in Europe began to evidence themselves in a stream of emigration from European countries.

It is impossible today to estimate the effect which the Burnett bill would have produced had it become a law during the Sixty-fifth Congress. But of this much we can be certain: That countless numbers of persons now coming to the United States would not have left their homes in Europe during the past year. Half of the four-year suspension period proposed in the Burnett bill has elapsed. The flow of immigration to the United States is now in full flood. The need for restrictive legislation is apparent. The accommodations at Ellis Island are not sufficient for the avalanche of new arrivals; larger cities have not houses for them; work cannot be found for them; and, further, the bulk of the newer arrivals are of the dependent rather than the working class. . . .

Members of the committee found the new immigration at Ellis Island to consist practically of all nationalities except Orientals. It found by far the largest percentage of immigrants to be peoples of Jewish extraction. On the steamship *New Amsterdam*, sailing from Rotterdam, the committee found that 80 per cent of the steerage passengers were from Galicia, practically all of Jewish extraction. On the *New Rochelle*, arriving from Danzig, the committee estimated that more than 90 per cent were of the Semitic race. The committee is confirmed in the belief that the major portions of recent arrivals come without funds. It was apparent to the committee that a large percentage of those arriving were incapable of earning a livelihood. These are temporarily detained, causing great congestion, much delay, and pitiful distress, until relatives or others arrive to give bonds that the newcomers will not become public charges.

. . . The committee has confirmed the published statements of a commissioner of the Hebrew Sheltering and Aid Society of America made after his personal investigation in Poland, to the effect that "If there were

Source: Temporary Suspension of Immigration, Sixty-sixth Congress, Third Session, House of Representatives, Report no. 1109, December 6, 1920.

in existence a ship that could hold 3,000,000 human beings, the 3,000,000 Jews of Poland would board it to escape to America."

In the preparation and presentation of this legislation to the House of Representatives the Committee on Immigration and Naturalization has disregarded the statements of a Polish labor commissioner to the effect that 225,000 Hebrews have been furnished this year with funds for passage to the United States. The committee has disregarded all statements that might give a religious bias of any kind to the matter under consideration. It is fair to state, however, that the largest number of Jews coming to the United States before the war in a single year was 153,748 (1906); while during the one month of October 1920, it is estimated that of the 74,665 immigrants arriving at Ellis Island, more than 75 per cent were of the Semitic race.

Figures available for the fiscal year ending June 30, 1920, show that a very small number of these peoples gave as their reason for coming to the United States the desire to escape religious or political persecution. . . .

Appendix A

Department of State,
Consular Service,
Washington
December 4, 1920.

My Dear Mr. Johnson: In accordance with your request of this morning it gives me great pleasure to send you herewith paraphrases of statements in regard to immigration received from officers of this Government who have visited the countries mentioned. I hope you will find the data of value in connection with the presentation of your bill to Congress.

Very sincerely yours,
Wilbur J. Carr

Hon. Albert Johnson,
Chairman Committee on Immigration,
House of Representatives.

AUSTRIA: *Vienna*—Sixty per cent of the present emigrants are of the Jewish race, 20 per cent are of the German race, and 20 per cent of other races. The favorite occupation of these emigrants is merchant or clerk.

The committee did not investigate charges of extensive funds from America passing through agencies in Warsaw and elsewhere. The committee does believe, however, that these funds, whether large or small, together with generous contributions made both by government and individuals for the relief of distress in central Europe, combined with the reports which have spread everywhere concerning prospects for certain prosperity and immediate wealth in the United States, all combine to play a part in encouraging the downtrodden of all the war-wrecked countries to sell everything and to pay in their depreciated monies $120 to $130 for steerage passage to the United States in addition to $10 for United States consular visa and registration. . . .

GERMANY: *Berlin*—It is estimated that 2,000,000 Germans desire to emigrate to the United States if passport restrictions are removed.

The Germans who proceed to the United States are not of the most desirable class, due to the fact that military service is at present in most cases an absolute bar. Most of those who receive permission to leave for the United States are the aged parents of American citizens or minor children. The wives of declarants who are now permitted to proceed are almost always of the lower classes. The Poles, Austrians, and nationals of the different Russian States who apply for visas are as a rule of the most undesirable type of emigrant. They are usually traders who only increase the number of middlemen or if they work they usually go into sweatshops.

NETHERLANDS: *Rotterdam*—The great mass of aliens passing through Rotterdam at the present time are Russian Poles or Polish Jews of the usual ghetto type. Most of them are more or less directly and frankly getting out of Poland to avoid war conditions. They are filthy, un-American and often dangerous in their habits.

POLAND: *Warsaw*—Concerning the general characteristics of aliens emigrating to the United States from Poland and the occupation or trade followed by them, reports indicate such to be substantially as follows:

1. Physically deficient: (a) Wasted by disease and lack of food supplies. (b) Reduced to an unprecedented state of life during the period of the war, as the result of oppression and want. (c) Present existence in squalor and filth.

2. Mentally deficient: (a) Illy educated, if not illiterate, and too frequently with minds so stultified as to admit of little betterment. (b) Abnormally twisted because of (1) reaction from war strain, (2) shock of revolutionary disorders, (3) the dullness and stultification resulting from past years of oppression and abuse.

3. Economically undesirable: (a) Twenty per cent is given as a round and generous estimate of productive laborers among present applicants for visas. This estimate is meant to include workers or those who may be expected to become workers, from both sexes. The remaining percentage may be expected to be a drain on the resources of America for years. (b) Of the 50 per cent of emigrants from Poland who may be termed efficients, 40 per cent—of the total number of emigrants—will enter a trade as a middleman, not a producer. These will thrive on the efforts of their associates. (c) The productive labor, small percentage as it is, will be found in America, in the sweatshops in the large centers of population. It is decidedly not agricultural, but urban in character. In this report female applicants as housewives, etc., are of course termed as efficients.

4. Socially undesirable: (a) Eighty-five to ninety per cent lack any conception of patriotic or national spirit. And the majority of this percentage is mentally incapable of acquiring it. (b) Seventy-five per cent or upward will congregate in the large urban centers, such as New York or Baltimore, and add to undesirable congestion, already a grave civic problem. (c) Immigrants of similar class are to be found already in the United States who, taken as a class and not individually, have proved unassimilable. (d) All Europe is experiencing in the reaction from the war a corruption of moral standards. This may even be least noticeable in Germany. The introduction of these lowered standards can not fail but have its evil influence in the United States.

NOTES

1. The 1920s saw a rise in anti-Semitism which often expressed itself in a desire to keep Jews from immigrating to the United States. Jews were seen as a detestable, repulsive collection of people who were about to inundate the shores of the United States. Moreover, they were seen as carriers of the Bolshevik revolution, which they intended to use for the purpose of overthrowing Western civilization. It is clear that these views also gained respect in the House of Representatives to whom this report was presented by its Committee on Immigration and Naturalization.

2. From December 1, 1918 to March 4, 1919.

HENRY FORD
34. The International Jew: The World's Problem[1]

The Jew is again being singled out for critical attention throughout the world. His emergence in the financial, political, and social spheres has been so complete and spectac-

Source: Henry Ford, "The International Jew: The World's Problem," *The Dearborn Independent,* May 22, 1920, pp. 1–5.

ular since the war, that his place, power, and purpose in the world are being given a new scrutiny, much of it unfriendly. Persecution is not a new experience to the Jew, but intensive scrutiny of his nature and supernationality is. He has suffered for more than 2,000 years from what may be called the instinctive anti-Semitism of the other races, but this antagonism has never been intelligent nor has it been able to make itself intelligible. Nowadays, however, the Jew is being placed, as it were, under the microscope of economic observation that the reasons for his power, the reasons for his separateness, the reasons for his suffering may be defined and understood.

In Russia he is charged with being the source of Bolshevism, an accusation which is serious or not, according to the circle in which it is made; we in America, hearing the fervid eloquence and perceiving the prophetic ardor of young Jewish apostles of social and industrial reform, can calmly estimate how it may be. In Germany he is charged with being the cause of the Empire's collapse and a very considerable literature has sprung up, bearing with it a mass of circumstantial evidence that gives the thinker pause. In England he is charged with being the real world ruler, who rules as a super-nation over the nations, rules by the power of gold, and who plays nation against nation for his own purposes, remaining himself discreetly in the background. In America it is pointed out to what extent the elder Jews of wealth and the younger Jews of ambition swarmed through the war organizations—principally those departments which dealt with the commercial and industrial business of war, and also the extent to which they have clung to the advantage which their experience as agents of the government gave them.

In simple words, the question of the Jews has come to the fore, but like other questions which lend themselves to prejudice, efforts will be made to hush it up as impolitic for open discussion. If, however, experience has taught us anything it is that questions thus suppressed will sooner or later break out in undesirable and unprofitable forms.

The Jew is the world's enigma. Poor in his masses, he yet controls the world's finances. Scattered abroad without country or government, he yet presents a unity of race continuity which no other people has achieved. Living under legal disabilities in almost every land, he has become the power behind many a throne. There are ancient prophecies to the effect that the Jew will return to his own land and from that center rule the world, though not until he has undergone an assault by the united nations of mankind.

The single description which will include a larger percentage of Jews than members of any other race is this: he is in business. It may be only gathering rags and selling them, but he is in business. From the sale of old clothes to the control of international trade and finance, the Jew is supremely gifted for business. More than any other race he exhibits a decided aversion to industrial employment, which he balances by an equally decided adaptability to trade. The Gentile boy works his way up, taking employment in the productive or technical departments; but the Jewish boy prefers to begin as messenger, salesman or clerk—anything—so long as it is connected with the commercial side of the business.

The question is, If the Jew is in control, how did it happen? This is a free country. The Jew comprises only about three per cent of the population; to every Jew there are 97 Gentiles; to the 3,000,000 Jews in the United States there are 97,000,000 Gentiles. If the Jew is in control, is it because of his superior ability, or is it because of the inferiority and don't-care attitude of the Gentiles?

It would be very simple to answer that the Jews came to America, took their chances like other people, and proved more successful in the competitive struggle. But that would not include all the facts. And before a more adequate answer can be given, two points should be made clear. The first is this: all Jews are not rich controllers of wealth. There are poor Jews aplenty, though most of them even in their poverty are their own masters. While it may be true that the chief financial controllers of the country are Jews, it is not true that every Jew is one of the financial controllers of the country. The classes must be kept distinct for a reason which will appear when the methods of the rich Jews and the methods of the poor Jews to gain power are differentiated. Secondly, the fact of Jewish solidarity renders it difficult to measure Gentile and Jewish achievements by the same standard. When a great block of wealth in America was made possible by the lavish use of another block of wealth from across the seas; that is to say, when certain Jewish immigrants came to the United States with the financial backing of European Jewry behind them, it would be unfair to explain the rise of that class of immigration by the same rules which account for the rise of, say, the Germans or the Poles who came here with no resource but their ambition and strength. To be sure, many individual Jews come in that way, too, with no dependence but themselves, but it would not be true to say that that massive control of affairs which is exercised by Jewish wealth was won by individual initiative....

"To the victor belongs the spoils" is an old saying. And in a sense it is true that if all this power of control has been gained and held by a few men of a long-despised race, then either they are super-men whom it is powerless to resist, or they are ordinary men whom the rest of the world has permitted to obtain an undue and unsafe degree of power. Unless the Jews are super-men, the Gentiles will have themselves to blame for what has transpired, and they can look for rectification in a new scrutiny of the situation and a candid examination of the experiences of other countries.

NOTE

1. Henry Ford (1863–1947), automobile manufacturer and among America's leading businessmen. In 1921 the London *Times* exposed the *Protocols of the Elders of Zion* as a crude forgery. Nevertheless in the United States Boris Brasol, a czarist emigré, persuaded a group of American business leaders, among them Henry Ford, to publicize the *Protocols*. For several years, Ford's private newspaper, *The Dearborn Independent*, quoted literally from the *Protocols* and issued repeated warnings against the "Jewish Menace." The above article was published in his paper. Only in 1927, when a Jewish attorney brought a libel suit against *The Dearborn Independent*, did Ford repudiate his anti-Semitism and issue a public apology.

35. A Protest Against Anti-Semitism (1921)[1]

The undersigned, citizens of Gentile birth and Christian faith, view with profound regret and disapproval the appearance in this country of what is apparently an organized campaign of anti-Semitism; conducted in close conformity to and co-operation with similar campaigns in Europe. We regret exceedingly the publication of a number of books, pamphlets and newspaper articles designed to foster distrust and suspicion of our fellow-citizens of Jewish ancestry and faith—distrust and suspicion of their loyalty and their patriotism.

These publications, to which wide circulation is being given, are thus introducing into our national political life a new and danger-

Source: New York Times, January 16, 1921, pp. 30–31.

ous spirit, one that is wholly at variance with our traditions and ideals and subversive of our system of government. American citizenship and American democracy are thus challenged and menaced. We protest against this organized campaign of prejudice and hatred, not only because of its manifest injustice to those against whom it is directed, but also, and especially, because we are convinced that it is wholly incompatible with loyal and intelligent American citizenship. The logical outcome of the success of such a campaign must necessarily be the division of our citizens along racial and religious lines, and, ultimately, the introduction of religious tests and qualifications to determine citizenship.

The loyalty and patriotism of our fellow citizens of the Jewish faith is equal to that of any part of our people, and requires no defense at our hands. From the foundation of this Republic down to the recent World War, men and women of Jewish ancestry and faith have taken an honorable part in building up this great nation and maintaining its prestige and honor among the nations of the world. There is not the slightest justification, therefore, for a campaign of anti-Semitism in this country.

Anti-Semitism is almost invariably associated with lawlessness and with brutality and injustice. It is also invariably found closely intertwined with other sinister forces, particularly those which are corrupt, reactionary and oppressive.

We believe it should not be left to men and women of Jewish faith to fight this evil, but that it is in a very special sense the duty of citizens who are not Jews by ancestry or faith. We therefore make earnest protest against this vicious propaganda, and call upon our fellow citizens of Gentile birth and Christian faith to unite their efforts to ours, to the end that it may be crushed. In particular, we call upon all those who are molders of public opinion—the clergy and ministers of all Christian churches, publicists, teachers, editors and statesmen—to strike at this un-American and un-Christian agitation.

NOTE

1. The above protest against the burgeoning of anti-Semitic propaganda was signed by President Woodrow Wilson, former President William H. Taft, Cardinal O'Connell of New York City and 116 other prominent men and women of the Christian faith. This protest was initiated by the socialist author, John Spargo, who emphasized that "all the work connected with the protest and all expenses involved represent the contribution of an individual citizen to the defense of American ideals. Neither directly nor indirectly did any person of Jewish ancestry or faith, or any Jewish organization, contribute as much as a postage stamp to the cost of the undertaking" (*New York Times*, January 16, 1921, p. 30).

36. The Columbus Platform (1937)[1]

In view of the changes that have taken place in the modern world and the consequent need of stating anew the teachings of Reform Judaism, the Central Conference of American

Source: W. Gunther Plaut, *The Growth of Reform Judaism: A Sourcebook of Its European Origins* (New York: World Union for Progressive Judaism, 1965), pp. 96–99. Reprinted by permission of the World Union for Progressive Judaism.

Rabbis makes the following declaration of principles. It presents them not as a fixed creed but as a guide for the progressive elements of Jewry.

Judaism and Its Foundations: 1. *Nature of Judaism.* Judaism is the historical religious experience of the Jewish people. Though growing out of Jewish life, its message is universal, aiming at the union and perfection of mankind under the sovereignty of God. Reform Judaism recognizes the principle of progressive development in religion and consciously applies this principle to spiritual as well as to cultural and social life.

Judaism welcomes all truth, whether written in the pages of Scripture or deciphered from the records of nature. The new discoveries of science, while replacing the older scientific views underlying our sacred literature, do not conflict with the essential spirit of religion as manifested in the consecration of man's will, heart and mind to the service of God and humanity. . . .

5. *Israel.* Judaism is the soul of which Israel is the body. Living in all parts of the world, Israel has been held together by the ties of a common history, and above all, by the heritage of faith. Though we recognize in the group loyalty of Jews who have become estranged from our religious tradition, a bond which still unites them with us, we maintain that it is by its religion and for its religion that the Jewish people has lived. The non-Jew who accepts our faith is welcomed as a full member of the Jewish community.

In all lands where our people live, they assume and seek to share loyally the full duties and responsibilities of citizenship and to create seats of Jewish knowledge and religion. In the rehabilitation of Palestine, the land hallowed by memories and hopes, we behold the promise of renewed life for many of our brethren. We affirm the obligation of all Jewry to aid in its upbuilding as a Jewish homeland by endeavoring to make it not only a haven of refuge for the oppressed but also a center of Jewish culture and spiritual life.

Throughout the ages it has been Israel's mission to witness to the Divine in the face of every form of paganism and materialism. We regard it as our historic task to cooperate with all men in the establishment of the kingdom of God, of universal brotherhood, justice, truth and peace on earth. This is our Messianic goal. . . .

9. *The Religious Life.* Jewish life is marked by consecration to these ideals of Judaism. It calls for faithful participation in the life of the Jewish community as it finds expression in home, synagogue and school and in all other agencies that enrich Jewish life and promote its welfare.

The Home has been and must continue to be a stronghold of Jewish life, hallowed by the spirit of love and reverence, by moral discipline and religious observance and worship.

The Synagogue is the oldest and most democratic institution in Jewish life. It is the prime communal agency by which Judaism is fostered and preserved. It links the Jews of each community and unites them with all Israel. . . .

The perpetuation of Judaism as a living force depends upon religious knowledge and upon the Education of each new generation in our rich cultural and spiritual heritage.

Prayer is the voice of religion, the language of faith and aspiration. It directs man's heart and mind Godward, voices the needs and hopes of the community, and reaches out after goals which invest life with supreme value. To deepen the spiritual life of our people, we must cultivate the traditional habit of communion with God through prayer in both home and synagogue.

Judaism as a way of life requires in addition to its moral and spiritual demands, the preservation of the Sabbath, festivals and Holy Days, the retention and development of such customs, symbols and ceremonies as possess inspirational value, the cultivation of distinctive forms of religious art and music and the use of Hebrew, together with the vernacular, in our worship and instruction.

These timeless aims and ideals of our faith we present anew to a confused and troubled world. We call upon our fellow Jews to rededicate themselves to them, and, in harmony with all men, hopefully and courageously to continue Israel's eternal quest after God and His kingdom. . . .

NOTE

1. The Columbus Platform was adopted by the American Reform movement some fifty years after the Pittsburgh meeting of 1885. By 1937, most Reform Jews had moved away from their anti-Zionist position. Although it avoided a clear-cut pro-Zionist position, the Columbus Platform reflected the fact that Jewish peoplehood and Jewish tradition had come to occupy a more significant role within the movement. Rabbi Felix A. Levy presided over the conference, the first avowed Zionist to occupy the chair.

AMERICAN COUNCIL FOR JUDAISM
37. A Statement of Policy (1944)[1]

The American Council for Judaism, Inc., was organized to present the views of Americans of Jewish faith on problems affecting the future of their own lives and the lives of world Jewry in the present hour of world confusion.

The Council reaffirms the historic truth that the Jews of the world share common traditions and ethical concepts, which find their derivation in the same religious source. . . .

As Americans of Jewish faith we believe implicitly in the fundamentals of democracy, rooted, as they are, in moralities that transcend race and state, and endow the individual with rights for which he is answerable only to God. We are thankful to be citizens of a country and to have shared in the building of a nation conceived in a spirit which knows neither special privilege nor inferior status for any man.

For centuries Jews have considered themselves nationals of those countries in which they have lived. Whenever free to do so, they have assumed, and will again assume, full responsibilities of citizenship in accordance with the ancient Jewish command, "The law of the land is the law." Those countries in which Jews have lived have been their homes; those lands their homelands. In those nations where political action was expressed through minority groups, the Jew, following the law of his land, accepted minority status, thereby frequently gaining an improvement over previous conditions of inferior citizenship. Such East European concepts, however, have resulted in a misunderstanding, shared by Jews and non-Jews, a misunderstanding which we seek to dispel. American Jews hope that in the peace for which all of us pray, the old principle of minority rights will be supplanted by the more modern principle of equality and freedom for the individual. The interest of American Jews in the individual Jew in countries where the minority right principle prevailed is not to be confused with acceptance of this East European political principle.

As a result of the bigotry, sadism, and ambitions for world conquest of the Axis powers, millions of our co-religionists who made homes in and were nationals of other lands have been violently deported and made

Source: United States House of Representatives, *Hearings Before the Committee on Foreign Affairs* [February 8–16, 1944] (New York, 1970), pp. 124–26.

victims of indescribable barbarism. No other group has been so brutishly attacked and for one reason only—on the false claims that there are racial barriers or nationalistic impulses that separate Jews from other men.

The plight of those Jews together with millions of oppressed fellow men of all faiths, calls for the profoundest sympathy and the unbounded moral indignation of all freemen. . . .

We believe that wherever possible the forced emigrés should be repatriated in their original homelands under conditions which will enable them to live as free, upstanding individuals.

For our fellow Jews we ask only this: Equality of rights and obligations with their fellow nationals. In our endeavors to bring relief to our stricken fellow Jews, and to help rebuild their lives on a more stable basis, we rely wholly on both democracy and religion, and which have been declared as the principles which shall prevail in the better world for which the United Nations are fighting. . . .

Palestine has contributed in a tangible way to the alleviation of the present catastrophe in Jewish life by providing a refuge for a part of Europe's persecuted Jews. We hope it will continue as one of the places for such resettlement, for it has been clearly demonstrated that practical colonizing can be done, schools and universities built, scientific agriculture extended, commerce intensified, and culture developed. This is the record of achievement of eager, hard-working settlers who have been aided in their endeavors by Jews all over the world, in every walk of life and thought.

We oppose the effort to establish a National Jewish State in Palestine or anywhere else as a philosophy of defeatism, and one which does not offer a practical solution of the Jewish problem. We dissent from all those related doctrines that stress the racialism, the nationalism, and the theoretical homelessness of Jews. We oppose such doctrines as inimical to the welfare of Jews in Palestine, in America, or wherever Jews may dwell. We believe that the intrusion of Jewish national statehood has been a deterrent in Palestine's ability to play an even greater role in offering a haven for the oppressed, and that without the insistence upon such statehood, Palestine would today be harboring more refugees from Nazi terror. The very insistence upon a Jewish Army has led to the raising of barriers against our unfortunate brethren. There never was a need for such an army. There has always been ample opportunity for Jews to fight side by side with those of other faiths in the armies of the United Nations.

Palestine is a part of Israel's religious heritage, as it is a part of the heritage of two other religions of the world. We look forward to the ultimate establishment of a democratic, autonomous government in Palestine, wherein Jews, Moslems and Christians shall be justly represented; every man enjoying equal rights and sharing equal responsibilities; a democratic government in which our fellow Jews shall be free Palestinians whose religion is Judaism, even as we are Americans whose religion is Judaism.

NOTE

1. An anti-Zionist organization founded in 1943, the American Council for Judaism (ACJ) represents the interests of "Americans of Jewish faith." It emphatically maintains that Judaism is a religion of universal values, and not a nationality. Its policy is outlined in this document. The ACJ has remained a small group, with very few synagogues and even fewer Jewish organizations endorsing its program. As the above document illustrates, most American Jews, though they adhere to a firm commitment and allegiance to the United States, also have a special relationship of fraternal affection for the State of Israel.

DAVID BEN GURION AND JACOB BLAUSTEIN

38. An Exchange of Views (1950)[1]

ADDRESS OF PRIME MINISTER DAVID BEN GURION:[2] We are very happy to welcome you here in our midst as a representative of the great Jewry of the United States to whom Israel owes so much. No other community abroad has so great a stake in what has been achieved in this country during the present generation as have the Jews of America. Their material and political support, their warm-hearted and practical idealism, has been one of the principal sources of our strength and our success. In supporting our effort, American Jewry has developed, on a new plane, the noble conception, maintained for more than half a century, of extending its help for the protection of Jewish rights throughout the world and of rendering economic aid wherever it was needed. We are deeply conscious of the help which America has given to us here in our great effort of reconstruction and during our struggle for independence. This great tradition has been continued since the establishment of the State of Israel.

It is our great pride that our newly gained independence has enabled us in this small country to undertake the major share of the great and urgent task of providing permanent homes under conditions of full equality to hundreds of thousands of our brethren who cannot remain where they are and whose heart is set on rebuilding their lives in Israel. In this great task you and we are engaged in a close partnership. Without the readiness for sacrifice of the people of Israel and without the help of America this urgent task can hardly be achieved.

It is most unfortunate that since our State came into being some confusion and misunderstanding should have arisen as regards the relationship between Israel and the Jewish communities abroad, in particular that of the United States. These misunderstandings are likely to alienate sympathies and create disharmony where friendship and close understanding are of vital necessity. To my mind, the position is perfectly clear. The Jews of the United States, as a community and as individuals, have only one political attachment and that is to the United States of America. They owe no political allegiance to Israel. In the first statement which the representative of Israel made before the United Nations after her admission to that international organization, he clearly stated, without any reservation, that the State of Israel represents and speaks only on behalf of its own citizens and in no way presumes to represent or speak in the name of the Jews who are citizens of any other country. We, the people of Israel, have no desire and no intention to interfere in any way with the internal affairs of Jewish communities abroad. The Government and the people of Israel fully respect the right and integrity of the Jewish communities in other countries to develop their own mode of life and their indigenous social, economic and cultural institutions in accordance with their own needs and aspirations. Any weakening of American Jewry, any disruption of its communal life, any lowering of its sense of security, any diminution of its status, is a definite loss to Jews everywhere and to Israel in particular.

We are happy to know of the deep and growing interest which American Jews of all shades and convictions take in what it has fallen to us to achieve in this country. Were we, God forbid, to fail in what we have undertaken on our own behalf and on behalf of our suffering brethren, that failure would cause grievous pain to Jews everywhere and nowhere more than in your community. Our success or failure depends in a large measure on our cooperation with, and on the strength of, the great Jewish community of the United States, and, we, therefore, are anxious that nothing should be said or done which could in the slightest degree undermine the sense of security and stability of American Jewry.

In this connection let me say a word about immigration. We should like to see American Jews come and take part in our effort. We need their technical knowledge, their unrivalled experience, their spirit of enterprise, their bold vision, their "know-how." We need engineers, chemists, builders, work managers and technicians. The tasks which face us in this country are eminently such as would appeal to the American genius for technical development and social progress. But the decision as to whether they wish to come—permanently or temporarily—rests with the free discretion of each American Jew himself. It is entirely a matter of his own volition. We need halutzim,[3] pioneers too. Halutzim have come to us—and we believe more will come, not only from those countries where the Jews are oppressed and in "exile" but also from countries where the Jews live a life of freedom and are equal in status to all other citizens in their country. But the essence of halutziuth is free choice. They will come from among those who believe that their aspirations as human beings and as Jews can best be fulfilled by life and work in Israel.

I believe I know something of the spirit of American Jewry among whom I lived for some years. I am convinced that it will continue to make a major contribution towards our great effort of reconstruction, and I hope that the talks we have had with you during these last few days will make for even closer cooperation between our two communities.

Response of Jacob Blaustein:[4] I am very happy, Mr. Prime Minister, to have come here at your invitation and to have discussed with you and other leaders of Israel the various important problems of mutual interest. . . .

There is no question in my mind that a Jew who wants to remain loyal to the fundamental basis of Judaism and his cultural heritage, will be in the forefront of the struggle for democracy against totalitarianism.

The American Jewish community sees its fortunes tied to the fate of liberal democracy in the United States, sustained by its heritage, as Americans and as Jews. We seek to strengthen both of these vital links to the past and to all humanity by enhancing the American democratic and political system, American cultural diversity and American well-being.

As to Israel, the vast majority of American Jewry recognizes the necessity and desirability of helping to make it a strong, viable, self-supporting state. This, for the sake of Israel itself, and the good of the world.

The American Jewish Committee has been active, as have other Jewish organizations in the United States, in rendering, within the framework of their American citizenship, every possible support to Israel; and I am sure that this support will continue and that we shall do all we can to increase further our share in the great historic task of helping Israel to solve its problems and develop as a free, independent and flourishing democracy.

While Israel has naturally placed some burdens on Jews elsewhere, particularly in America, it has, in turn, meant much to Jews throughout the world. For hundreds of thousands in Europe, Africa and the Middle East it has provided a home in which they can attain their full stature of human dignity for the first time. In all Jews, it has inspired pride and admiration, even though in some instances, it has created passing headaches.

Israel's rebirth and progress, coming after the tragedy of European Jewry in the 1930s and in World War II, has done much to raise Jewish morale. Jews in America and everywhere can be more proud than ever of their Jewishness.

But we must, in a true spirit of friendliness, sound a note of caution to Israel and its leaders. Now that the birth pains are over, and even though Israel is undergoing growing pains, it must recognize that the matter of good-will between its citizens and those of other countries is a two-way street: that Israel also has a responsibility in this situation—a responsibility in terms of not affecting adversely the sensibilities of Jews who are citizens of other states by what it says or does.

In this connection, you are realists and want facts and I wtuld be less than frank if I did not point out to you that American Jews vigorously repudiate any suggestion or implication that they are in exile. American Jews—young and old alike, Zionists and non-Zionists alike—are profoundly attached to America. America welcomed their immigrant parents in their need. Under America's free institutions, they and their children have achieved that freedom and sense of security unknown for long centuries of travail. American Jews have truly become Americans; just as have all other oppressed groups that have ever come to America's shores.

To American Jews, America is home. There, exist their thriving roots; there, is the country which they have helped to build; and there, they share its fruits and its destiny. They believe in the future of a democratic society in the United States under which all citizens, irrespective of creed or race, can live on terms of equality. They further believe that, if democracy should fail in America, there would be no future for democracy anywhere in the world, and that the very existence of an independent State of Israel would be problematic. Further, they feel that a world in which it would be possible for Jews to be driven by persecution from America would not be a world safe for Israel either; indeed it is hard to conceive how it would be a world safe for any human being.

The American Jewish community, as you, Mr. Prime Minister, have so eloquently pointed out, has assumed a major part of the responsibility of securing equality of rights and providing generous material help to Jews in other countries. American Jews feel themselves bound to Jews the world over by ties of religion, common historical traditions and in certain respects, by a sense of common destiny. We fully realize that persecution and discrimination against Jews in any country will sooner or later have its impact on the situation of the Jews in other countries, but these problems must be dealt with by each Jewish community itself in accordance with its own wishes, traditions, needs and aspirations.

Jewish communities, particularly American Jewry in view of its influence and its strength, can offer advice, cooperation and help, but should not attempt to speak in the name of other communities or in any way interfere in their internal affairs.

I am happy to note from your statement, Mr. Prime Minister, that the State of Israel takes a similar position. Any other position on the part of the State of Israel would only weaken the American and other Jewish communities of the free, democratic countries and be contrary to the basic interests of Israel itself. The future development of Israel, spiritual, social as well as economic, will largely depend upon a strong and healthy Jewish community in the United States and other free democracies.

We have been greatly distressed that at the very hour when so much has been achieved, harmful and futile discussions and misunderstandings have arisen as to the relations between the people and the State of Israel and the Jews in other countries, particularly in the United States. Harm has been done to the morale and to some extent to the sense of security of the American Jewish community through unwise and unwarranted statements and appeals which ignore the feelings and aspirations of American Jewry.

Even greater harm has been done to the State of Israel itself by weakening the readiness of American Jews to do their full share in the rebuilding of Israel which faces such enormous political, social and economic problems.

Your statement today, Mr. Prime Minister,

will, I trust, be followed by unmistakable evidence that the responsible leaders of Israel, and the organizations connected with it, fully understand that future relations between the American Jewish community and the State of Israel must be based on mutual respect for one another's feelings and needs, and on the preservation of the integrity of the two communities and their institutions.

I believe that in your statement today, you have taken a fundamental and historic position which will redound to the best interest not only of Israel, but of the Jews of America and of the world. I am confident that this statement and the spirit in which it has been made, by eliminating the misunderstandings and futile discussions between our two communities, will strengthen them both and will lay the foundation for even closer cooperation. . . .

NOTES

1. Even before Israel was established the American Jewish Committee (AJC) received assurances from the Jewish Agency (see document 24, note 1, in chapter 10) that the Jewish State would refrain from interfering in American Jewish internal affairs. Israeli officials continued to assure the AJC on that score after May 1948, when the State was established. However, when in 1949 Ben Gurion called for large-scale immigration to Israel by American Jewish youth, the committee protested vigorously. The AJC sought to work out with the Israeli government a clear and forceful expression of policy on immigration and on the principle of noninterference. The occasion arose in the summer of 1950 when Jacob Blaustein was a guest of the Israeli government. An agreement was sealed in the form of a statement read at a luncheon by Prime Minister Ben Gurion and a response by Jacob Blaustein. Both reaffirmed the agreement in April 1961. (See Naomi Cohen, *Not Free to Desist* [1972], pp. 310ff.)

2. David Ben Gurion (1886–1973), Zionist labor leader, Jewish statesman, architect of the Jewish state and the first prime minister of Israel.

3. Halutz (plural halutzim), a pioneer, especially in agriculture in Israel.

4. Jacob Blaustein (1892–1970), associated with his father, Louis, in the founding of the American Oil Company. Jacob Blaustein was director and member of the board of major companies in the fields of petroleum, insurance and banking; he was reportedly one of the richest individuals in America. Blaustein played an active role in Jewish affairs and had a major commitment to the American Jewish Committee, which he served as president from 1949 to 1954.

X

Zionism

The term *Zionism* was most probably coined by Nathan Birnbaum (1864–1937), a leader of the Hovevei Zion, a loose federation of Jewish groups devoted to the promotion of national resettlement of the Jews in their ancestral homeland. The Hovevei Zion viewed resettlement as the solution to the Jewish question, which they variously defined as the problem of anti-Semitism or the problem of Judaism in a modern, secular world. Significantly, the term *Zionism* reflects both traditional sentiment (the longing for Zion) and a modern political orientation. This fact is clearly reflected in the Bilu Program of 1882 (see document 1).

It is frequently assumed that Zionism is a response to modern anti-Semitism. This is but partially true. As integral to Zionism as its negative reaction to anti-Semitism, is its positive assertion of belief in the messianic prophecy and the historic destiny of the Jewish people. The leading precursors of Zionism, Rabbi Zvi Hirsch Kalischer (1795–1874), Rabbi Judah Solomon Hai Alkalai (1798–1878) and even the socialist Moses Hess (1812–1875), were moved to create a Jewish settlement in Palestine not only by socio-political forces, but also by a deep religious conviction that the time for the ingathering of the exiles had arrived—the prophecy was to be literally acted upon. Theodor Herzl (see document 2), the founder of the World Zionist Organization, was preeminently concerned with the *Judennot*—the distress or problem of the Jews, viz., anti-Semitism. But many of the aforementioned Hovevei Zion groups—which preceded Herzl by almost two decades and which constituted a significant element in the World Zionist Organization—were equally concerned with the *Not des Judentums*, the problem of Judaism. They were thus preeminently devoted to securing the future of Jewish culture both in the Diaspora and in Palestine. To this end they sought to foster the revival of the Hebrew language as the basis of a secular national culture. This position was best articulated by Ahad Ha-Am (see document 5), who did not withhold his criticism of Herzl's *political* Zionism.

In a certain respect, the differences between Herzl and Ahad Ha-Am reflect the differences between West and East European Jewry, stemming from their contrasting political and cultural situations. In Eastern Europe the secularization that affected the Jews was accompanied neither, as it was by and large in the West, by a jettisoning of national culture and identity nor, most importantly, by emancipation. The secularized East European Jew, with rare exceptions, continued to live in a ghetto situation—where opportunities for assimilation were limited—and continued to speak Yiddish, read Hebrew, partake in Jewish folkways and identify ethnically as a Jew. In short, secular Jewish culture was already a reality for many East European Jews. Zionists like Ahad Ha-Am merely sought to give it a specific direction in order to assure its vitality and creativity. Moreover, the multi-ethnic character of some of the states of Eastern Europe theoretically presented the Jews with the possibility of a secular national culture within the context of modern society. However, East European Jewry was forced to face the brutal nature of anti-Semitism in a much more violent fashion than Western Jewry, and because of the exigency of this problem East European Zionists were pressed to develop a program of immediate, practical solutions that involved alternatives that did not require the restoration of Jewish sovereignty in Palestine. This dual emphasis on "interim" solutions and practical action in both Palestine and the Diaspora is exemplified by the policy of *Gegenwartsarbeit* ("work in the present"; see document 13) and by the fact that East European Jewry provided the vast majority of the earlier, i.e. before 1933, waves of immigration (*aliyot*) to Palestine. In contradistinction to East European Zionism, Western Zionism until the rise of Nazism, was largely a philanthropic movement devoted to the welfare of the persecuted Jews of Eastern Europe. The Zionism of Western Jews did not necessarily entail a personal commitment to immigrate to Palestine. It did, however, contribute significantly to the intellectual and ideological fermentation of the Zionist movement of the East and the West.

As can be discerned from the documents, the World Zionist Organization embraced a wide spectrum of ideological positions, from Poalei Zion on the Left to Revisionism on the Right (see documents 12 and 22). What unites these divergent ideological positions is the rejection of Exile (*galut* or *golus* in traditional parlance). "The Zionist attitude begins," as the historian Ben Halpern observes, "with a lively awareness and affirmation of Exile as a condition"; this attitude is inherently problematic for continued Jewish existence. The analysis of this condition varies, of course, according to one's ideological orientation. "The intellectual substance of Zionism," Halpern emphasizes, "is the rejection of Exile: not the denial of Exile, please note, but its rejection. . . . There were two historical attitudes to which Zionism opposed itself, and in opposing, was defined. The first was the acceptance of Exile as a 'commitment'—the attitude, by and large, of Orthodox Jewry at the time [the nineteenth century]. The other was the 'denial' of Exile as a condition—an attitude which arose in Reform Judaism."[1] Thus it is not surprising that within the Jewish community Zionism encountered bitter opposition, from assimilationists, liberals, socialists and traditionalists (see documents 16 and 18).

Zionism acquired a respectability both among Jews and non-Jews with the Balfour Declaration (see documents 19 and 20). This recognition propelled Zionism as a major force not only in Jewish life but also in the international community. Even the gradual erosion of Great Britain's commitment to its Palestine Mandate could not stem the mounting political prestige of the Zionist movement. In the aftermath of the Holocaust this international recognition of Zionism was reinforced by a groundswell of sympathy for the bereaved Jewish people. On November 29, 1947 the United Nations declared the creation of a Jewish state in Palestine. The following year, on May 14, David Ben Gurion on behalf of the Provisional Government formed by the Zionist parties of Palestine officially proclaimed the creation of an independent State of Israel.

1. Ben Halpern, "Exile," *Jewish Frontier* (April 1954), pp. 6–9.

THE BILU
1. Manifesto[1]

To Our Brethren and Sisters in the Exile, Peace be with You!

"If I help not myself, who will help me?" (Hillel.)[2]

Nearly two thousand years have elapsed since, in an evil hour, after an heroic struggle, the glory of our Temple vanished in fire and our Kings and chieftains changed their crowns and diadems for the chains of exile. We lost our country, where dwelt our beloved sires. Into the Exile we took with us, of all our glories only a spark of the fire, by which our Temple, the abode of our Great One, was engirdled, and this little spark kept us alive while the towers of our enemies crumbled to dust, and this spark leapt into celestial flame and shed light upon the faces of the heroes of our race and inspired them to endure the horrors of the Dance of Death and the tortures of the autos-da-fé. And this spark is now again kindling and will shine for us, a true pillar of fire going before us on the road to Zion, while behind us is a pillar of cloud, the pillar of oppression threatening to destroy us. Sleepest thou, O our nation? What hast thou been doing till 1882? Sleeping and dreaming the false dream of Assimilation. Now, thank God, thou art awakened from thy slothful slumber. The pogroms have awakened thee from thy charmed sleep. Thine eyes are open to recognize the cloudy structure of delusive hopes. Canst thou listen silently to the flaunts and the mockery of thine enemies? Wilt thou yield before . . . ? Where is thine ancient pride, thine olden spirit? Remember that thou wast a nation possessing a wise religion, a law, a constitution, a celestial Temple, whose wall[3] is still a silent witness to the glories of the Past, that thy sons dwelt in Palaces and towers, and thy cities flourished in the splendour of civilization, while these enemies of thine dwelt like beasts in the muddy marshes of their dark woods. While thy children were clad in purple and linen, they wore the rough skins of the wolf and the bear. Art thou not ashamed to submit to them?

Hopeless is your state in the West; the star of your future is gleaming in the East. Deeply conscious of all this, and inspired by the true teaching of our great master Hillel: "If I help not myself, who will help me?" we propose to build the following society for national ends: (1) The Society will be named Bilu, according to the motto: "House of Jacob, come, let us go!" It will be divided into local branches according to the number of members. (2) The seat of the Committee shall be Jerusalem. (3) Donations and contributions shall be unfixed and unlimited.

What we want: (1) A Home in our country. It was given to us by the mercy of God, it is ours as registered in the archives of history. (2) To beg it of the Sultan himself, and if it be impossible to obtain this, to beg that at least we may be allowed to possess it as a state within a larger state; the internal administration to be ours, to have our civil and political rights, and to act with the Turkish Empire only in foreign affairs, so as to help our brother Ishmael in his time and need.

We hope that the interests of our glorious nation will rouse the national spirit in rich and powerful men, and that everyone, rich or poor, will give his best labours to the holy cause.

Greeting, dear brethren and sisters.

Hear, O Israel, the Lord our God, the Lord is one, and our Land, Zion, is our one hope.

God be with us!

Source: Nahum Sokolow, *History of Zionism* (London: Longmans, Green & Co., 1919), vol. 2, pp. 332–33.

NOTES

1. The Bilu was a group of young Russian Jews who pioneered the Zionist program of resettlement of the Jewish people in the land of Israel as a solution to the Jewish question. The group derived its name from the Hebrew initials of *Beit Yaakov Lekhu Ve-Nelkha* (Isa. 2:5). A reaction to the 1881 pogroms in southern Russia, the Bilu was founded at the beginning of 1882 with Kharkov as its headquarters; later the headquarters was moved to Odessa. The first Biluim arrived in Palestine in mid-1882. After working in a number of Jewish villages for several years, they founded the settlement of Gederah. The manifesto published here was issued by members of the Bilu in Constantinople in 1882 en route to Palestine.

2. Hillel was a first century B.C.E. rabbinic authority.

3. The Western or Wailing Wall.

THEODOR HERZL
2. A Solution of the Jewish Question[1]

I have been asked to lay my scheme in a few words before the readers of the *Jewish Chronicle*.[2] This I will endeavour to do, although in this brief and rapid account, I run the risk of being misunderstood. My first and incomplete exposition will probably be scoffed at by Jews. The bad and foolish way we ridicule one another is a survival of slavish habits contracted by us during centuries of oppression. A free man sees nothing to laugh at in himself, and allows no one to laugh at him.

I therefore address my first words to those Jews who are strong and free of spirit. They shall form my earliest audience, and they will one day, I hope become my friends. I am introducing no new idea; on the contrary, it is a very old one. It is a universal idea—and therein lies its power—old as the people, which never, even in the time of bitterest calamity, ceased to cherish it. This is the restoration of the Jewish State.

It is remarkable that we Jews should have dreamt this kingly dream all through the long night of our history. Now day is dawning. We need only rub the sleep out of our eyes, stretch our limbs, and convert the dream into a reality. Though neither prophet nor visionary, I confess I cherish the hope and belief that the Jewish people will one day be fired by a splendid enthusiasm. For the present, however, I would appeal in calm words to the common sense of men of practical judgment and of modern culture. A subsequent task will be to seek out the less favoured, to teach and to inspire them. This latter task I cannot undertake alone. I shall take my part in it, in the ranks of those friends and fellow workers whom I am endeavouring to arouse and unite for a common cause. I do not say "my adherents," for that would be making the movement a personal one, and consequently absurd and contemptible from the outset. No, it is a national movement, and it will be a glorious one, if kept unsullied by the taint of personal desires, though these desires took no other form than political ambition. We who are the first to inaugurate this movement, will scarcely live to see its glorious close; but the inauguration of it is enough to bring a noble kind of happiness into our lives. We shall plant for our children in the same way as our fathers preserved the tradition for us. Our lives represent but a moment in the permanent duration of our people. This moment has its duties.

Two phenomena arrest our attention by

Source: *The Jewish Chronicle,* January 17, 1896, pp. 12–13.

reason of the consequences with which they are fraught. One, the high culture, the other, the profound barbarism of our day. I have intentionally put this statement in the form of a paradox. By high culture, I mean the marvellous development of all mechanical contrivances for making the forces of nature serve man's purposes. By profound barbarism, I mean anti-Semitism. . . .

The Jewish Question still exists. It would be foolish to deny it. It exists wherever Jews live in perceptible numbers. Where it does not yet exist, it will be brought by Jews in the course of their migrations. We naturally move to those places where we are not persecuted, and there our presence soon produces persecution. This is true in every country, and will remain true even in those most highly civilised—France itself is no exception—till the Jewish Question finds a solution on a political basis. I believe that I understand anti-Semitism, which is in reality a highly complex movement. I consider it from a Jewish standpoint, yet without fear or hatred. I believe that I can see what elements there are in it of vulgar sport, of common trade, of jealousy, of inherited prejudice, of religious intolerance, and also of legitimate self-defence.

Only an ignorant man would mistake modern anti-Semitism for an exact repetition of the Jew-baiting of the past. The two may have a few points of resemblance, but the main current of the movement has now changed. In the principal countries where anti-Semitism prevails, it does so as a result of the emancipation of the Jews. When civilised nations awoke to the inhumanity of exclusive legislation, and enfranchised us—our enfranchisement came too late. For we had, curiously enough, developed while in the Ghetto into bourgeois people, and we stepped out of it only to enter into fierce competition with the middle classes. Historical circumstances made us take to finance, for which, as every educated man knows, we had, as a nation, no original bent. One of the most important of these circumstances was the relation of the Catholic Church to "anatocism."[3] In the Ghetto we had become somewhat unaccustomed to bodily labour and we produced in the main but a large number of mediocre intellects. Hence, our emancipation set us suddenly within the circle of the middle classes, where we have to sustain a double pressure, from within and from without. The Christian bourgeoisie would not be unwilling to cast us as a sacrifice to Socialism, though that would naturally not improve matters much. But the Jewish Question is no more a social than a religious one, notwithstanding that it sometimes takes on these and other forms. It is a national question which can only be solved by making it a political world-question to be discussed and controlled by the nations of the civilised world in council.

We are one people—One People. We have honestly striven everywhere to merge ourselves in the social life of surrounding communities, and to preserve only the faith of our fathers. It has not been permitted to us. In vain are we loyal patriots, in some places our loyalty running to extremes; in vain do we make the same sacrifices of life and property as our fellow-citizens; in vain do we strive to increase the fame of our native land in science and art, or her wealth by trade and commerce. In countries where we have lived for centuries we are still cried down as strangers; and often by those whose ancestors were not yet domiciled in the land where Jews had already made experience of suffering. Yet, in spite of all, we are loyal subjects, loyal as the Huguenots, who were forced to emigrate. If we could only be left in peace. . . .[4]

We are one people—our enemies have made us one in our despite, as repeatedly happens in history. Distress binds us together, and thus united, we suddenly discover our strength. Yes, we are strong enough to form a state, and a model state. We possess all human and material resources necessary for the purpose. . . . The whole matter is in its essence perfectly simple, as it must necessarily be, if it is to come within the comprehension of all.

Let the sovereignty be granted us over a

portion of the globe large enough to satisfy the requirements of the nation—the rest we shall manage for ourselves. Of course, I fully expect that each word of this sentence, and each letter of each word, will be torn to tatters by scoffers and doubters. I advise them to do the thing cautiously, if they are themselves sensitive to ridicule. The creation of a new state has in it nothing ridiculous or impossible. We have, in our day, witnessed the process in connection with nations which were not in the bulk of the middle class, but poor, less educated, and therefore weaker than ourselves. The governments of all countries, scourged by anti-Semitism, will serve their own interests, in assisting us to obtain the sovereignty we want. These governments will be all the more willing to meet us half-way, seeing that the movement I suggest is not likely to bring about any economic crisis. Such crises, as must follow everywhere as a natural consequence of Jew-baiting, will rather be prevented by the carrying out of my plan. For I propose an inner migration of Christians into the parts slowly and systematically evacuated by Jews. If we are not merely suffered to do what I ask, but are actually helped, we shall be able to effect a transfer of property from Jews to Christians in a manner so peaceable and on so extensive a scale as has never been known in the annals of history.

Everything must be carried out with due consideration for acquired rights and with absolute conformity to law, without compulsion, openly and by light of day, under the supervision of authority and the control of public opinion. . . .

Our clergy, on whom I most especially call, will devote their energies to the service of this idea. They must, however, clearly understand from the outset, that we do not mean to found a theocracy, but a tolerant modern civil state. We shall, however, rebuild the Temple in glorious remembrance of the faith of our fathers. We shall unroll the new banner of Judaism—a banner bearing seven stars on a white field. The white field symbolizes our pure new life, the seven stars, the seven golden hours of a working-day. For we shall march into the Promised Land carrying the badge of labour. . . .

Let all who will join us fall in behind our flag [and] fight for our cause with voice and pen and deed. I count on all our ambitious young men, who are now debarred from making progress elsewhere. . . .

Thus we also need a "gestor" [manager] to direct this Jewish political cause. The Jewish people are as yet prevented by the Diaspora from undertaking the management of their business for themselves. At the same time they are in a condition of more or less severe distress in many parts of the world. They need a "gestor." A first essential will therefore be the creation of such.

This "gestor" cannot, of course, be a single individual, for an individual who would undertake this giant work alone, would probably be either a madman or an impostor. It is therefore indispensable to the integrity of the idea and the vigour of its execution that the work should be impersonal. The "gestor" of the Jews must be a union of several persons for the purpose, a body corporate. This body corporate or corporation, I suggest, shall be formed in the first instance from among those energetic English Jews to whom I imparted my scheme in London. Let that body be called "the Society of Jews," and be entirely distinct from the Jewish Company[5] previously referred to. The Society of Jews is the point of departure for the whole Jewish movement about to begin. It will have work to do in the domains of science and politics, for the founding of the Jewish state, as I conceive it, presupposes the application of scientific methods. We cannot journey out of Mizraim [Egypt] to-day, in the primitive fashion of ancient times. We must previously obtain an accurate account of our number and strength.

My pamphlet [*The Jewish State*] will open a general discussion on the Jewish question. Friends and enemies will take part in it, but it will no longer, I hope, take the form either of violent abuse or of sentimental vindication, but of a debate, practical, large, earnest and political. The Society of Jews will gather all available information from statesmen, parliaments, Jewish communities and societies, from speeches, letters and meetings, from newspapers and books. It will thus find out for the first time whether Jews really wish to go to the Promised Land, and whether they ought to go there. Every Jewish community in the world will send contributions to the Society towards a comprehensive collection of Jewish statistics. Further tasks, such as investigation by experts of the new country and its natural resources, planning of joint migration and settlement, preliminary work for legislation and administration, etc., must be judiciously evolved out of the original scheme. In short, the Society of Jews will be the nucleus of our public organizations. . . .

Shall we choose [the] Argentine [Republic] or Palestine? We will take what is given us and what is selected by Jewish public opinion. Argentina is one of the most fertile countries in the world, extends over a vast area, and has a sparse population. The Argentine Republic would derive considerable profit from the cession of a portion of its territory to us. The present infiltration of Jews has certainly produced some friction, and it would be necessary to enlighten the Republic on the intrinsic difference of our new movement.

Palestine is our ever-memorable historic home. The very name of Palestine would attract our people with a force of extraordinary potency. Supposing His Majesty the Sultan were to give us Palestine, we could in return pledge ourselves to regulate the whole finances of Turkey. There we should also form a portion of the rampart of Europe against Asia, an outpost of civilisation as opposed to barbarism.[6] We should remain a neutral state in intimate connection with the whole of Europe, which would guarantee our continued existence. The sanctuaries of Christendom would be safeguarded by assigning to them an extra-territorial status, such as is well known to the law of nations. We should form a guard of honour about these sanctuaries, answering for the fulfillment of this duty with our existence. This guard of honour would be the great symbol of the solution of the Jewish Question after nearly nineteen centuries of Jewish suffering. . . .

I know full well that in bringing forward a very old idea in a new form, I am laying myself open to derision and to every kind of attack. Gentler spirits will call my idea Utopian. But what is the difference between a Utopian scheme and a possible one? A Utopian scheme may be a piece of cleverly combined mechanism, lacking only the requisite force to set it in motion; a possible scheme on the other hand rests on a known and existent propelling force.

The force we need is created in us by anti-Semitism. Some people will say that what I am doing is to kindle anti-Semitism afresh. This is not true, for anti-Semitism would continue to increase irrespective of my project, so long as the causes of its growth are not removed. Others will tremble for their goods and chattels, and professional business interests. . . .

What form of constitution shall we have? I incline to an aristocratic republic, although I am an ardent monarchist in my own country. Our history has been too long interrupted for us to attempt direct continuity of the ancient constitutional forms without exposing ourselves to the charge of absurdity.

What language shall we speak? Every man can preserve the language in which his thoughts are at home. Switzerland offers us an example of the possibility of a federation of tongues. We shall remain there in the new country what we now are here, and shall never cease to cherish the memory of the native land out of which we have been driven.

People will say that I am furnishing our enemies with weapons. This is also untrue, for my proposal can only be carried out with the free consent of a majority of Jews. Individuals, or even powerful bodies of Jews, might be attacked, but governments will take no action against the collective nation. The equal rights of Jews before the law cannot be withdrawn where they have once been conceded, for their withdrawal would immediately drive all Jews, rich and poor alike, into the ranks of the revolutionary party. Even under present conditions the first official violation of Jewish liberties invariably brings about an economic crisis. The weapons used against us cut the hands that wield them. Meantime, hatred grows apace.

Again, it will be said that our enterprise is hopeless, because, even if we obtain the land with the supremacy over it, the poorest Jews only will go there. But it is precisely the poorest whom we need at first. Only desperados make good conquerors. The rich and well-to-do will follow later, when they will find the new country as pleasant as the old, or even pleasanter. . . .

But we can do nothing without the enthusiasm of our own nation. The idea must make its way into the most distant miserable holes where our people dwell. They will awaken from gloomy brooding, for into their lives will come a new significance. Let each of them but think of himself, and what vast proportions the movement must assume! And what glory awaits those who fight unselfishly for the cause! A wondrous generation of Jews will spring into existence. The Maccabeans will rise again.

And so it will be: It is the poor and the simple who do not know what power man already exercises over the forces of nature, it is just these who will have firmest faith in the new message. For these have never lost the hope of the Promised Land.

This is my message, fellow Jews! Neither fable nor fraud! Every man may test its truth for himself, for every man will carry with him a portion of the Promised Land—one in his head, another in his arms, another in his acquired possessions. We shall live at last, as free men, on our own soil, and die peacefully in our own home.

NOTES

1. Theodor Herzl (1860–1904), father of political Zionism and founder of the World Zionist Organization. While serving as the Paris correspondent for the *Neue Freie Presse* of Vienna, from 1890 to 1895, Herzl—an assimilated Jew of minimal Jewish commitment—was aroused by the growing anti-Semitism in the birthplace of liberalism and Jewish emancipation. The Dreyfus Case—the trial and the public demand of "Death to the Jew"—prompted Herzl to draw the conclusion that the only feasible solution to the Jewish problem was a mass exodus of the Jews from the countries of their torment and a resettlement in a land of their own. He devoted the remainder of his life to the realization of this idea. This article, published in the influential London Jewish weekly, *The Jewish Chronicle*, adumbrates the main points of his *Der Judenstaat: Versuch einer modernen Loesung der juedischen Frage* [The Jewish state: an attempt at a modern solution of the Jewish question] (Vienna: M. Breitenstein, 1896), in which he introduced his plan to the world.

2. Herzl arrived in London on November 21, 1895. Through Max Nordau (see document 7) he met Israel Zangwill (see document 11) who introduced him to some influential people and also obtained for Herzl an invitation to a banquet of the Maccabaeans Club, at which Herzl expounded his ideas and where he established important contacts. Herzl met Asher Myers of *The Jewish Chronicle* at the club. Myers asked Herzl for an article, with the result that *The Jewish Chronicle* preceded *The Jewish State* by four weeks in its publication of Herzl's views.

3. The principle of charging compound interest.

4. This paragraph appears to have been taken verbatim from *The Jewish State.*

5. According to Herzl's plan, the Jewish Company was to be entrusted with the execution of the transfer of the Jews to their own state. The society that Herzl proposed was later to be called the World Zionist Organization.

6. This passage, which also appears in *The Jewish State*, is frequently cited as proof of the colonial, imperialist intentions of Zionism. However, this statement by Herzl must be viewed in light of his vision of the Zionist homeland as an ally of colonized people in their struggle for liberation and restored dignity. See, for example, the passage in his novel *Old-New Land*—Herzl's romantic vision of the New Society of a sovereign Jewry—in which Professor Steineck, head of the Scientific Institute of the New Society, relates to two foreign

visitors, Dr. Loewenberg and Mr. Kingscourt, his hopes for using the institute's knowledge "to open up Africa."

> "Yes, Mr. Kingscourt... I hope to find the cure for malaria. We have overcome it here in Palestine.... But conditions are different in Africa. The same measures cannot be taken there because the prerequisite—mass immigration—is not present. The white colonist goes under in Africa. That country can be opened up to civilization only after malaria has been subdued. Only then will enormous areas become available for the surplus populations of Europe. And only then will the proletarian masses find a healthy outlet. Understand?"
>
> Kingscourt laughed. "You want to cart off the whites to the black continent, you wonder-worker!"
>
> "Not only the whites!" replied Steineck gravely. "The blacks as well. There is still one problem of racial misfortune unsolved. The depths of that problem, in all its horror, only a Jew can fathom. I mean the Negro problem. Don't laugh Mr. Kingscourt. Think of the hair-raising horrors of the slave trade. Human beings because their skins are black, are stolen, carried off, and sold. Their descendants grow up in alien surroundings despised and hated because their skin is differently pigmented. I am not ashamed to say, though I be thought ridiculous, now that I have lived to see the restoration of the Jews, I should like to pave the way for the restoration of the Negroes." (Theodor Herzl, *Old-New Land*, trans. Lotta Levensohn [New York: Bloch Publishing Company and the Herzl Institute, 1960], pp. 169–70.)

PROTESTRABBINER
3. Protest Against Zionism[1]

[A.] We recently received from Vienna the new newspaper of the "Zionists," *Die Welt*.[2] It appeared on the eve of the holiday of the Feast of Weeks, which reminds us more than any other holiday that it was Israel's destiny from the start to be a "Kingdom of Priests." This newspaper contains propaganda for a Congress of Jewish Nationals, called for the twenty-fifth of August of this year [1897] in Munich.

Die Welt is a calamity and must be resisted. As long as the Zionists wrote in Hebrew they were not dangerous, but now that they are writing in German, they must be opposed. It is not a question of refuting their claims. For how can one speak with people who on the one hand are fanatics regarding Jewish nationhood and, on the other hand, complain that the Austrian government required a baptismal certificate from the candidate for the position of secretary of Bukowina. If the Austrian Jews support the efforts of the Zionists, then they should not complain that they are treated by the government like foreigners and are barred from public office.

We, however, can say to our fellow countrymen with complete conviction that we comprise a separate community solely with respect to *religion*. Regarding nationality, we feel totally at one with our fellow Germans and therefore strive towards the realization of the spiritual and moral goals of our dear fatherland with an enthusiasm equalling theirs. Hence, we are permitted to urge the complete implementation of equal rights and to perceive every curtailment of these rights as an injury to our most righteous sensibilities.

What more can one say, if people are so naive as to believe that the West European Jews will hand over their money to purchase Palestine from the Turks and to create a

Source: Allgemeine Zeitung des Judentums, June 11, 1897. Trans. here by M. Gelber. *Berliner Tageblatt* (July 6, 1897), trans. in *The Jewish Chronicle*, July 9, 1897, p. 9.

Jewish organization that will reverse the entire development of the Jewish nation. Eighteen hundred years ago, history made its decision regarding Jewish nationhood through the dissolution of the Jewish State and the destruction of the Temple. Recent Jewish scholarship can count among its highest achievements the fact that this conception has gained the widest circulation among the Jews of all civilized countries.

The Zionists want to provide "an internationally guaranteed place to call home" for those Jews "who cannot or do not want to assimilate in their present places of residence." But where are the Jews who do not want to assimilate? The fact that right now they are still unable to assimilate in many countries makes it precisely our duty to fight in common with the most noble and best men of all confessions for the removal of discriminatory laws. Let us protest in the most decisive manner against such a defamation [implied in the claim that there are Jews who do not wish to assimilate] as well as against the insult that the Zionists level at us in that they speak of a "Jewish distress" which they want to eliminate. In this protest, we shall know ourselves to be in complete agreement with all the Jewish communities of the German fatherland.

We ask the Zionists then, in whose name and by what authority do they speak? Who gave them a mandate to call for a congress in Munich, when it would not even be suitable for Przemysl, Grodno, or Jaffa. We are protesting against the organizers who claim to speak for all of Jewry, but behind whom stands not one single Jewish congregation. We are convinced that no Rabbi or Director of a German congregation will appear at the congress. Thus will be demonstrated to the entire world that *German Jewry* has nothing in common with the intentions of the Zionists.

Dr. S. Maybaum[3], Berlin; Dr. H. Vogelstein,[4] Stettin.

[B.] Owing to the convening of a Zionist Congress and the publication of its Agenda, so many erroneous impressions have gone forth respecting the teachings of Judaism and its efforts, that the undersigned Executive Committee of the Union of Rabbis in Germany deem it their duty to make the following Declaration:

1. The efforts of so-called Zionists to create a Jewish National State in Palestine are antagonistic to the messianic promises of Judaism, as contained in Holy Writ and in later religious sources.

2. Judaism obliges its followers to serve the country to which they belong with the utmost devotion, and to further its interest with their whole heart and all their strength.

3. There is no antagonism, however, between this duty and the noble efforts directed towards the colonisation of Palestine by Jewish agriculturists, as they have no relation whatsoever to the founding of a National State.

Religion and Patriotism alike impose upon us the duty of begging all who have the welfare of Judaism at heart, to hold aloof from the before-mentioned Zionist Movement, and to abstain from attending the Congress, which in spite of all warnings is yet to be held.

The Executive Committee: Dr. Maybaum, Berlin; Dr. Horovitz,[5] Frankfurt; Dr. Guttmann,[6] Breslau; Dr. Auerbach,[7] Halberstadt; Dr. Werner, Munich.

NOTES

1. At the end of May 1897 news reached the German Jewish community that Herzl intended to convene a Zionist congress in Munich on August fifteenth of that year. A united front of German rabbis—both Reform (liberal) and Orthodox—led a vigorous protest against Herzl's planned congress in Munich. We include here two open letters of the *Protestrabbiner* ("protest rabbis"), as Herzl bitterly dubbed them. The second letter, the more formal protest of the two, was written in the name of the German Rabbinical Association (*Rabbinerverband*). Despite its condemnation by a great number of

German Reform and Orthodox rabbis, this letter was endorsed by the general assembly of the Rabbinical Association of Germany convened a year later (July 1-2, 1898), with only one dissenting voice. Due to the storm of protest—not only from the *Protestrabbiner*, but also from the Munich Jewish community, the B'nai B'rith lodge of Munich and others—Herzl decided to transfer the venue of the First Zionist Congress to Basle, Switzerland.

2. *Die Welt* was a Zionist weekly founded by Herzl and published in Vienna from 1897 to 1905, in Cologne from 1906 to 1911 and in Berlin from 1911 to 1914. The first issue of *Die Welt* appeared on June 4, 1897.

3. Sigmund Maybaum (1844-1919), a liberal rabbi in Berlin and lecturer on homiletics at the Hochschule fuer die Wissenschaft des Judentums in that city.

4. Heinemann Vogelstein (1841-1911), rabbi at Pilsen and Stettin, founder and president of the Association of Liberal Rabbis and a vice-president of the Association for Liberal Judaism in Germany.

5. Marcus Horovitz (1844-1910). An Orthodox rabbi at Frankfurt am Main, he was a recognized halakhic scholar and a founder of the Rabbinical Association of Germany.

6. Jacob Guttmann (1845-1919). A respected historian of medieval Jewish philosophy, he served as a Liberal rabbi at Breslau.

7. Avi'ezri Auerbach (1840-1901). A scion of a prestigious German rabbinic family, in 1872 he followed his father as an Orthodox rabbi at Halberstadt.

THE FIRST ZIONIST CONGRESS
4. The Basle Program[1]

The aim of Zionism is to create for the Jewish people a home in Palestine secured by public law.

The Congress contemplates the following means to the attainment of this end:

1. The promotion, on suitable lines, of the colonization of Palestine by Jewish agricultural and industrial workers.
2. The organization and binding together of the whole of Jewry by means of appropriate institutions, local and international, in accordance with the laws of each country.
3. The strengthening and fostering of Jewish national sentiment and consciousness.
4. Preparatory steps towards obtaining government consent, where necessary, to the attainment of the aim of Zionism.

NOTE

1. The historical importance of the First Zionist Congress convened by Herzl in the summer of 1897 was the foundation of the Zionist Organization and the adoption of this official statement of Zionist purpose. While taking into consideration the agricultural achievements of such groups as the Bilu and Hibbat Zion—the movement that constituted the intermediate link between the forerunners of Zionism in the middle of the nineteenth century and the beginnings of political Zionism—the congress endorsed in this statement Herzl's approach, known as political Zionism. According to Herzl, the Jewish problem could only be solved by large-scale migration and settlement of Palestine, which could only be attained through the political assistance and consent of the community of nations. The solution to the Jewish problem would thus be politically and internationally guaranteed by a charter granting the Jewish people (through the World Zionist Organization), the right to reestablish an autonomous homeland in Palestine.

Source: The Jewish Chronicle, September 3, 1897, p. 13.

AHAD HA-AM[1]

5. The First Zionist Congress[2]

"The Congress of the Zionists"—the struggle over which filled the vacuum of our small world during the past months—is now past history.

Approximately two hundred members of the House of Israel from all lands and all countries gathered together in Basle. For three days, from morning to evening, they conducted public proceedings before all the nations concerning the establishment of a secure home for the Jewish people in the land of their fathers.

The *national*[3] response to the Jewish question thus broke the barriers of "modesty" and entered into the public realm. With a loud voice, clear language and proud bearing, a message whose like had not been heard since the time of Israel's exile from its land was proclaimed to all the world.

And that was all. This assembly *could* have done no more and *should* have done no more.

For—why should we delude ourselves?—of all the great aims to which *Hibbat Zion*[4] (or, as they say now, "Zionism") aspires, for the time being it is within our powers to draw near in a truly fitting manner to only one of them, namely the *moral* aim. We must liberate ourselves from the *inner* slavery, from the degradation of the spirit caused by assimilation, and we must strengthen our national unity until we become capable and worthy of a future life of honor and freedom. All other aims, are still part of the world of ideas and fantasies. The opponents of the Jewish state doubt whether it will be possible to obtain the consent of the nations, especially Turkey, to the establishment of this state. It appears to me, however, that there is an even more serious question [that must be asked]. Were this consent to be given would we, in our present moral condition, be capable of seizing the opportunity? Moreover, it is also possible to question the very nature of the proposal for a Jewish state. In light of the prevailing situation of the world in general, would the establishment of the Jewish state in our times, even in the most complete form imaginable, permit us to say that "our question" has been solved in its entirety and that the national ideal has been attained? "According to the suffering—the reward." After thousands of years of unfathomable calamity and misfortune, it would be impossible for the Jewish people to be happy with their lot if in the end they would reach [merely] the level of a small and humble people, whose state is a plaything in the hands of its mighty neighbors and exists only by means of diplomatic machinations and perpetual submission to whomever fate is smiling upon. It would be impossible for an ancient people, one that was a light unto the nations, to be satisfied with such an insignificant recompense for all their hardships. Many other peoples, lacking both name and culture, have been able to attain the same thing within a brief period of time without having had to suffer even the smallest part of what the Jews have suffered. It was not in vain that the prophets rose to the aid of Israel, envisioning the reign of *justice* in the world at the end of days. Their *nationalism*, their love for their people and for their land, led them to this. For even in Biblical times the Jewish state was caught between two lions—Assyria or Babylonia on the one side and Egypt on the other—so that it had no hope to dwell in tranquility and develop in a suitable fashion. Accordingly, "Zionism" developed in the hearts of the prophets, giving rise to the great vision of the end of days when "the wolf shall dwell with the lamb and nation shall not lift

Source: Hashiloah, 2, no. 6 (Elul 5647; August 1897), pp. 568–70. Trans. here by S. Weinstein.

up sword against nation"[5]—and when Israel shall once again safely dwell in its own land. Hence, this *human* ideal was and perforce always will be an integral part of the *national* ideal of the Jewish people. The Jewish state can only find peace when universal justice will ascend to the throne and rule the lives of the peoples and the states.

And so, we did not come to Basle to found the Jewish state today or tomorrow. Rather, we came to issue a great proclamation to all the world: the Jewish people is still alive and full of the will to live. We must repeat this proclamation day and night, not so that the world will hear and give us what we desire, but above all, in order that we ourselves will hear the echo of our voice in the depths of our soul. Perhaps in this way our soul will awaken and cleanse itself of its degradation. . . .

This indeed is what the Basle assembly accomplished at its beginning in a sublime fashion. And for this it would have deserved to have been inscribed in golden letters as a testimony to the generations, were it not for its desire to accomplish even more.

Here, too, rashness—this curse which lies over us and sabotages all our actions—appeared in full force. Had the initiators of the assembly armed themselves with patience and explicitly declared from the beginning that the traces of the Messiah are not yet visible and that for the time being our strength lies only in our mouths and hearts—to revive our national spirit and spread the tidings of this renewal among the public at large—then without doubt the list of delegates would have been much smaller. Instead of three days the assembly could have finished its work in one day, but this day would have been the equivalent of entire generations. Those delegates, the elect of our people—for only the elect would have been attracted to an assembly of this kind—would then return, each to his own country, with hearts full of life, will and new energy, to instil this life and energy into the hearts of all the people.

But now . . .

The initiators of this movement are "Europeans." They are expert in the rules of diplomacy and in the customs of the political sects of our day, and they are bringing these rules and customs with them to the "Jewish state." . . . Emissaries were dispatched prior to the assembly and various "hints" were distributed orally and in writing in order to awaken among the masses an exaggerated hope for imminent salvation. Hearts were inflamed by an idolatrous fire, a febrile passion, which brought to the Basle assembly a motley crowd of youths, immature both in years and in wisdom. This mob robbed the assembly of its splendor and through their great foolishness turned it into a laughing stock.

Large and small committees, endless commissions, a multitude of imaginary "proposals" concerning the "national treasury" and the rest of the "exalted politics" of the Jewish state—these are the "practical" results of the assembly. How could it have been otherwise? The majority of the delegates, the emissaries of the wretched members of our people waiting for redemption, were sent solely for the purpose of bringing redemption with them upon their return. How, then, could they return home without bearing the tidings that the administration of the "state," in all its various branches, had been placed in trustworthy hands, and that all the important questions concerning the "state" had been examined and solved? . . .

The delegates will return [from Basle] with the message that redeemers have arisen in Israel and that all we have to do is to wait for "diplomacy" to finish its task. [But] the eyes of the people will quickly be opened and they will realize that they have been led astray. The sudden fire which ignited the hope in their hearts will once again be extinguished, perhaps even to the final spark. . . .

If only I could enter into a pact with the angel of oblivion I would make him vow to obliterate from the hearts of the delegates all traces of what they saw and heard at Basle, leaving them with only one memory. [I am referring to] the memory of that great and sacred hour when they all stood together as brothers—these forlorn men of Israel who came from all corners of the earth—their hearts full of feelings of holiness and their eyes lovingly and proudly directed to their noble brother standing on the platform preaching wonders to his people, like one of the prophets of days of yore. The memory of this hour, had it not been followed by many other hours which deprived the first impression of its purity, could have turned this assembly into one of the most distinguished events in the history of our people.

The deliverance of Israel will come at the hands of "prophets," not at the hands of "diplomats." . . .

NOTES

1. Ahad Ha-Am, pen name of Asher Hirsch Ginsberg (1856–1927), Russian Jew, Hebrew essayist and leader of Hibbat Zion. He was critical of both political and practical Zionism: of the latter because he felt that the mass resettlement of Jewry in Palestine was unfeasible; the former because he held a profound scepticism regarding the efficacy of its diplomatic program and its neglect of Jewish cultural reconstruction, which he held to be of paramount import. Properly considered, he maintained, Zionism could not solve the "problem of the Jews"—their economic, social and political plight—but it could solve "the problem of Judaism," i.e., assimilation. With the eclipse of religion in the modern period, he observed, Jews are increasingly defecting to non-Jewish secular cultures. Zionist settlement in Palestine should therefore concentrate on fostering a secular Jewish culture based on Jewish national consciousness and the renewal of Hebrew as a means assuring the continuity of Jewish creativity. Palestine Jewry will thereby serve as a "spiritual center" nourishing Jewish life in the Diaspora, where most of the Jewish people will undoubtedly continue to exist.

2. The First Zionist Congress was held in Basle on August 29–31, 1897.

3. All emphases are in the original.

4. Hibbat Zion ("love of Zion"), a movement that came into being in 1882 as a direct reaction to the widespread pogroms in Russia in 1881, for the purpose of encouraging Jewish settlement in Palestine and achieving a Jewish national revival there.

5. Isa. 2:4, 6.

RABBI ZADOK HA-COHEN RABINOWITZ
6. The Zionists Are Not Our Saviors[1]

A voice was heard from on high, a voice of lamentation from the imperial city of Vienna in a matter relating to all of Israel. It concerns the sect which has arisen recently under the name of Zionists. They drag iniquity by cords of vanity and lift up their souls to folly, hoping that in the course of time the sons of Israel will be subdued under their government and subordinated to transgressors. For this my heart grieves exceedingly.

For our many sins, the saying "The face of the generation is as the face of a dog"[2] has been fulfilled among us. We see that their desire to force the whole world to the side of sin, Heaven forbid, is great. Even if in our age the mob will not thank us for uttering words of truth and reproof, I will nevertheless fulfill the commandment "Thou shalt surely reprove"[3] and join in the protest against the Zionists.

Source: Open letter, c.1900, *The Transformation: The Case of the Neturei Karta,* ed. I. Domb (London: Hamadfis, 1958), pp. 192–96. Trans. here by P. Mendes-Flohr and J. Reinharz.

For surely this is not a time to hold one's peace. Heaven forbid that one should show respect for persons in this matter. The danger to the community posed by those who are destructive and who dispute with the *Schechinah* [the Divine Presence] is far too great for that. Concerning them the verse says: "He who observes the wind will not sow and he who beholdeth the clouds will not reap."[4] The Zionists sow wheat and reap thorns and even though the work of Satan should prosper, the end will be, Heaven forbid, what it will be. The House of Israel, the holy and desolate, appears in this hour like a ship sailing without oars in a tempest in the heart of the sea, its helmsmen stricken with blindness.

We surely know that if we were believers and truly trusted in the salvation of the Lord and observers of the commandments of God, we would even today be dwelling in our holy land. For it is known that the land of Israel, by its very nature and the power of its holiness, was created for Israel alone.

It is said in the Midrash that the Holy One, blessed be He, created the land of Israel only for Israel; but it is also known that because of the power of its holiness the land rejects transgressors in the same way that the stomach vomits forth that which is incompatible with its nature. This matter is not subject to dispute. Yet now there have arisen fools and malicious conspirers whose deeds are born of a bitter poison. They proclaim that the life of Israel is in jeopardy and that they, the Zionists, will hasten salvation by founding a state.

They ask why we have been in exile for so long. But this question has already been asked of the sages and the prophets, and has been explained by the Holy One, blessed be He: "Why did the land perish? Because they abandoned My law which I put before them."[5] It has already been made clear that the Zionists reject all the commandments and cleave to every manner of abomination. . . .

Do we not know that the whole purpose of redemption is to improve our ways so that Israel may observe the Torah with all the restrictions that have been placed upon it by our sages who should not, Heaven forbid, be men of power and influence among us. [Moreover] as the prophets foresaw our redemption, we will not require an army and strategies of war. From this we can see that [the aspiration of the Zionists] is opposed to the spirit of Judaism and to the hope of redemption.

I have heard it said in the name of the Zionists that without a state modelled after other states there would be an end to Judaism, Heaven forbid. To them we would reply that the land of Israel and the people of Israel are above the rules of causality and that, thank God, in our day at least the majority of Jews remain steadfast in their faith.

It may be assumed that if the Zionists gain dominion, they will seek to remove from the hearts of Israel belief in God and in the truth of the Torah. [For] the intention of these inciters and seducers is to cast Israel into heresy, that is, to destruction. Moreover, seeing that the Zionists and those among them who at one time had claims to sanctity say that massacres, Heaven forbid, will follow unless their advice is taken, let us emphasize that we have the Divine promise that even though Israel is in exile, nevertheless the memory of Israel will never be erased.

Jerusalem is the height of heights to which the hearts of Israel are directed. Our soul also pants and yearns to breathe her pure and holy air. In Heaven are my witnesses that I would hasten to go there like an arrow from a bow, without fear of the perils of the roads, or of the misery and poverty in the country, but I fear my departure and my ascent to Jerusalem might appear as a gesture of approval of Zionist activity.

With faith in the Lord, my soul trusts in His word that the day of redemption will come. I stand in expectation of the coming of the messiah. [But before his advent] should three hundred scourges of iron afflict me, I will not budge from my place. I will not go up there [to Jerusalem] and join my name to those of the Zionists.

For me the matter is perfectly plain. The

enlightened ones and the reformers who imperil the existence of our people have discovered that through blatant unbelief they will not succeed in driving Israel from its faith and from its religion. Therefore they have thrown off their garment of assimilation and put on a cloak of zeal, so that they appear to be zealous on behalf of Judaism. But they are in fact digging a mine beneath our faith, and seeking to lead Israel from beneath the wings of *Schechinah*.

From all that has been said it emerges that the Zionists and their rabbis are in error when they assert decisively that were it not for the Zionists many of our brethren would have converted. They deceive themselves. The heretics and the transgressors within the camp of Israel do more damage to us than those who have left the community.

Can heretics be regarded as great men? May there not be many like them in Israel! As for us, we need the audacity of holiness and the spirit of self-sacrifice. The counsel to be given to the House of Israel is that they should dissociate from the Zionists and hold themselves apart from this advancing plague. Through the merit of this separation, may we enjoy all the salvations and the comforts and may the Holy One, blessed be He, comfort Zion and build Jerusalem.

NOTES

1. Rabbi Zadok Ha-Cohen Rabinowitz (1823–1900), Hasidic rabbi, known as Zadok Ha-Cohen of Lublin, with a reputation as an outstanding talmudic scholar. Preferring a secluded life of study and devotion, Zadok Ha-Cohen became the spiritual leader of the Hasidim in Lublin after the death of his friend, Rabbi Yehuda Leib Eiger, in 1888. In 1890, following the death of his second wife, Zadok Ha-Cohen sought to immigrate to Palestine, but was discouraged from doing so by his disciples. The letter presented here was written toward the end of his life.

2. Mishnah, tractate *Sotah* 9:15.

3. Lev. 19:17.

4. Eccles. 11:4.

5. Jer. 9:12.

MAX NORDAU[1]
7. Jewry of Muscle

Two years ago, during a committee meeting at the Congress in Basle,[2] I said: "We must think of creating once again a Jewry of muscles."

Once again! For history is our witness that such a Jewry had once existed.

For too long, all too long have we been engaged in the mortification of our own flesh.

Or rather, to put it more precisely—others did the killing of our flesh for us. Their extraordinary success is measured by hundreds of thousands of Jewish corpses in the ghettos, in the churchyards, along the highways of medieval Europe. We ourselves would have gladly done without this "virtue" [i.e., the Christian virtue of corporal mortification]. We would have preferred to develop our bodies rather than to kill them or to have them—figuratively and actually—killed by others. We know how to make rational use of our life and appreciate its value. If, unlike most other peoples, we do not conceive of

Source: "Muskeljudentum," *Juedische Turnzeitung* (June 1903). Republished in Max Nordau, *Zionistische Schriften* (Cologne and Leipzig: Juedischer Verlag, 1909), pp. 379–81. Trans. here by J. Hessing.

[physical] life as our highest possession, it is nevertheless very valuable to us and thus worthy of careful treatment. During long centuries we have not been able to give it such treatment. All the elements of Aristotelian physics—light, air, water and earth—were measured out to us very sparingly. In the narrow Jewish street our poor limbs soon forgot their gay movements; in the dimness of sunless houses our eyes began to blink shyly; the fear of constant persecution turned our powerful voices into frightened whispers, which rose in a crescendo only when our martyrs on the stakes cried out their dying prayers in the face of their executioners. But now, all coercion has become a memory of the past, and at least we are allowed space enough for our bodies to live again. Let us take up our oldest traditions; let us once more become deep-chested, sturdy, sharp-eyed men.

This desire of going back to a glorious past finds a strong expression in the name which the Jewish gymnastic club in Berlin has chosen for itself.[3] "Bar Kochba" was a hero who refused to know defeat.[4] When in the end victory eluded him, he knew how to die. Bar Kochba was the last embodiment in world history of a bellicose, militant Jewry. To evoke the name of Bar Kochba is an unmistakable sign of ambition. But ambition is well suited for gymnasts striving for perfection.

For no other people will gymnastics fulfill a more educational purpose than for us Jews. It shall straighten us in body and in character. It shall give us self-confidence, although our enemies maintain that we already have too much self-confidence as it is. But who knows better than we do that their imputations are wrong. We completely lack a sober confidence in our physical prowess.

Our new muscle-Jews [Muskeljuden] have not yet regained the heroism of our forefathers who in large numbers eagerly entered the sport arenas in order to take part in competition and to pit themselves against the highly trained Hellenistic athletes and the powerful Nordic barbarians. But morally, even now the new muscle-Jews surpass their ancestors, for the ancient Jewish circus fighters were ashamed of their Judaism and tried to conceal the sign of the Covenant by means of a surgical operation,[5] . . . while the members of the "Bar Kochba" club loudly and proudly affirm their national loyalty.

May the Jewish gymnastic club flourish and thrive and become an example to be imitated in all the centers of Jewish life!

NOTES

1. Max Nordau (1849–1923), physician, avant-garde literary critic, novelist. One of the most controversial and influential authors of his day, he was among Herzl's earliest supporters.

2. Congress in Basle, i.e., the Second Zionist Congress, held in Basle, Switzerland during the summer of 1898.

3. At the Second Zionist Congress, Nordau and Max Mandelstamm. (a Russian ophthalmologist and Zionist leader who supported Herzl) proposed a program to promote the physical fitness of Jewish youth. In response, the Bar Kochba gymnastic club was founded in Berlin in 1898. Similar clubs were soon established throughout Europe.

4. Bar Kochba, Simeon (d. 135 C.E.) led the Jewish revolt against Hadrian that broke out in 132 C.E.

5. According to Josephus (a Jewish historian), Hellenized Jews, who in accordance with Greek custom wrestled in the nude, would often undergo surgery in order to disguise their circumcision.

THE MIZRAHI
8. Manifesto[1]

In the lands of the Diaspora the soul of our people—our Holy Torah—can no longer be preserved in its full strength, nor can the commandments, which comprise the entire spiritual life of the people, be kept in their original purity, because the times are besieging us with difficult demands. It is impossible for us to respond to those demands without ignoring the holy treasure entrusted to us at Sinai, without God forbid, turning it into a thing of little value in our eyes, as each of us strays further and further away from the other. Against his will each loses his Jewish self in the [non-Jewish] majority, for only in their midst can he fulfill all those secular requirements which the times demand of him. The people has found one remedy for this affliction—to direct their hearts to that one place which has always been the focus of our prayers, that place wherein the oppressed of our people will find their longed-for respite: Zion and Jerusalem. We have always been united by that ancient hope, by the promise which lies at the very roots of our religion, namely, that only out of Zion will the Lord bring redemption to the people of Israel. The emancipation which our German brethren so desired did much to divide us and keep us scattered in the countries of our dispersion. When the limbs are dispersed, the body disintegrates, and when there is no body, the spirit has no place to dwell in this world.

It has therefore been agreed by all those who love the spirit of their people and are faithful to their God's Torah, that the reawakening of the hope of the return to Zion will provide a solid foundation as well as lend a special quality to ourpeople. It will serve as a focus for the ingathering of our spiritual forces and as a secure fortress for our Torah and its sanctity.

NOTE

1. Mizrahi, religious Zionist movement based on the Basle Program and dedicated to the establishment of the people of Israel in the land of Israel in accordance with the precepts of the Torah. When the Fifth Zionist Congress (Basle, 1901) resolved that the education of the people in the spirit of Jewish nationalism was an important aspect of Zionist activity and an obligation for every Zionist, the religious Zionists felt that there could be no compromise in spiritual matters. They therefore founded in Vilna in 1902 the Mizrahi, an abbreviation of the words *Merkaz Ruhani* ("spiritual center"), adopting the motto: "The land of Israel for the people of Israel according to the Torah of Israel." Mizrahi has remained a faction within the World Zionist Organization. This manifesto was distributed as a leaflet announcing in Hebrew the establishment of Mizrahi.

Source: Kol Koreh (Vilna, 1902). Trans. here by D. Goldman.

SEVENTH ZIONIST CONGRESS

9. Anti-Uganda Resolution[1]

The Seventh Zionist Congress declares:

The Zionist organisation stands firmly by the fundamental principle of the Basle program, namely: "The establishment of a legally-secured, publicly recognised home for the Jewish people in Palestine," and it rejects either as an end or as a means all colonising activity outside Palestine and its adjacent lands.

The Congress resolves to thank the British Government for its offer of a territory in British East Africa, for the purpose of establishing there a Jewish settlement with autonomous rights. A Commission having been sent out to examine the territory, and having reported thereon, the Congress resolves that the Zionist organisation shall not engage further with the proposal. The Congress records with satisfaction the recognition accorded by the British Government to the Zionist organisation in its desire to bring about a solution of the Jewish problem, and expresses the sincere hope that it may be accorded the further good offices of the British Government where available in any matter it may undertake in accordance with the Basle program.

The Seventh Zionist Congress recalls and emphasizes the fact that, according to Article I of the statutes of the Zionist organisation, the Zionist organisation includes those Jews who declare themselves to be in agreement with the Basle program.

NOTE

1. The Seventh Zionist Congress, held in Basle from July 17 to August 2, 1905, was the first congress after Herzl's death in July 1904. The previous congress (August 1903) debated an official offer from the British government, which was willing to allocate a territory for Jewish resettlement in Uganda, East Africa. At that congress, Herzl advanced the Uganda Scheme for serious examination, while simultaneously emphasizing that "our views on the land of Israel cannot and will not be subject to change, Uganda is not Zion and will never be Zion. This proposal is nothing more than a relief measure, a temporary means of allaying distress." By a slim majority, the Sixth Congress voted in favor of the resolution. But those opposed, mostly delegates from Russia, threatened to leave and dissolve the unity of the World Zionist Organization. Only through the personal efforts of Herzl was this prevented. Preserving the fragile unity of the World Zionist Organization was the task of the Seventh Congress. The congress duly re-evaluated the Uganda Scheme, especially after having received from a commission of inquiry a negative report on the conditions in the proposed territory. After acrimonious debate the above resolution was passed on July 30, 1905.

Source: The Jewish Chronicle, August 4, 1905, p. 21.

SEVENTH ZIONIST CONGRESS
10. Resolution on Palestine[1]

The Seventh Zionist Congress resolves that, concurrently with political and diplomatic activity, and with the object of strengthening it, the systematic promotion of the aims of the movement in Palestine shall be accomplished by the following methods: (1) Exploration; (2) Promotion of agriculture, industry, etc., on the most democratic principle possible; (3) Cultural and economic improvement and organisation of Palestine Jews through the acquisition of new intellectual forces; and (4) Acquisition of concessions.

The Seventh Zionist Congress rejects every aimless, unsympathetic and philanthropic colonisation on a small scale which does not conform to the first point in the Basle Program.

NOTE

1. Immediately after the adoption of the anti-Uganda resolution, the Seventh Zionist Congress deliberated upon a statement of policy proposed by Menahem Ussishkin (1863–1941), who was close to the Zionist pioneers (*halutzim*) in Palestine. This proposal reflected the ideas he had developed in a pamphlet, *Our Program* (1905), published on behalf of Russian Zionists opposed to the Uganda Scheme. In this pamphlet he laid the foundation for synthetic Zionism: political action, agricultural settlement, and educational and organizational work among the Jewish people in the Diaspora. The last paragraph of the resolution was an amendment framed by Alexander Marmorek (1865–1923), a French Zionist and close associate of Herzl. He advanced this amendment to prevent the Basle Program, in his words, "from degenerating into a petty Odessa Committee, . . . from drifting back into Hovevei Zionism." The resolution was adopted on July 31, 1905 and represents the policy that thereafter dominated the Zionist movement.

Source: The Jewish Chronicle, August 4, 1905, p. 21.

ISRAEL ZANGWILL
11. A Manifesto[1]

The tragic problem of the Wandering Jew grows daily more insistent. In the language of Dr. [Hermann] Adler, Chief Rabbi of the British Empire, the question of the hour is: *Wohin?* ["Whither?"]

At least a hundred thousand Jews wander forth each year from the lands of poverty and oppression, whether in quest of better life-conditions or actually to escape death by starvation or massacre. The miseries and anxieties of this migration to unknown countries that offer no welcome, the privations and terrors of the journey beset at every turn by harpies and inquisitors, constitute a sum of

Source: The Jewish Chronicle, August 25, 1905, p. 17.

human misery, of which the extinction, or even the alleviation, would be an immense humanitarian achievement.

This emigration comes principally, and, by an automatic law, from the Russian Pale.... The channels sought are principally the United States and England, but Canada, the Argentine, South Africa, etc., etc., all have their streams of Jewish immigration. In all these centres of refuge, the tendency of the immigrants is to remain near their friends and relatives already in the land, and thus to form great ghettos, unhealthily congesting the already-congested towns, and engendering all the spiritual ills which must inevitably accompany the confusion of atmosphere and ideas attendant on a rapid assimilation with its hopeless alienation of parents and children....

But this immigration into particular centres cannot even go long unchecked. Another law of human nature comes into operation to put the brake upon it—a law formulated by the late Dr. Herzl. The stream of emigration, following the line of least resistance, flows into countries with the least anti-Semitism, but by its flowing it increases the local anti-Semitism, till a saturation-point is reached and the immigration is restrained by law.

This point is fast being reached in England, as the Aliens Bill ominously indicates; in America, the just published Report of the Commissioner of the United States Immigration Bureau suggests drastic legislation in the same direction. Is it wise to wait until our hands are forced? Is it wise always to go on hoping that something which we know is bound to occur can be staved off yet a little longer? That is exactly Mr. [Joseph] Chamberlain's[2] definition of absence of statesmanship. Would it not be wiser to face the possibility of all present ports of refuge being closed to Jewish emigration? And would it not be wiser to prevent by anticipatory action a possibility which would cast a stigma upon all Jewry? Should we not hasten, while the gates are still open, to find a land of refuge of our own?

Thus arises the question with which we began: *Wohin?* But it is now combined with the question whether the new refuge, when found, should be merely a temporary convenience like all the others, or whether it should not rather be a permanent Jewish soil? Philanthropy has proved itself unequal to our emigration problem, or, at least, philanthropy split into national sections. The problem cannot be broken into bits, it must be conceived as a whole. It is an international problem, and must be treated internationally. International philanthropy on so big a scale passes insensibly into the sphere of the political, and can only be handled by statesmanship.

And, here, be it remarked that the stream of Jewish emigration, to which so many peoples object on so many grounds, is not a curse but a blessing to the lands over which it flows. It is a stream to fertilise waste places, to turn mill-wheels, and to move machinery. Really feckless and feeble persons have not the energy to tear themselves out of their native environment, and to adventure themselves in another. The Jewish labour-force is, in truth, one of the most potent reservoirs of life and energy in the world. Not its impotency, but its competitive potency, is the true ground of the short-sighted objections to its advent. It is a Nile, which, split into small streams flowing everywhere, loses its force as a Jewish power, though it performs work for other Powers in every quarter. In alliance with Jewish capital it has helped to build up many of the greatest cities and States of the world.

The obvious consideration suggests itself: is it impossible for Jewish labour and capital to create the desired land of refuge? The world still holds—though it will not long hold—vast tracts of comparatively unexploited or neglected territory. British East Africa is only one instance. And the stream of Jewish emigration, though it contains elements that would be useless and even clogging, if turned upon a virgin soil, yet also contains all the elements necessary for pioneer purposes. It includes farmers and artisans, herdsmen and ex-soldiers, miners, and rough labourers, and if these elements were sifted and handled by leaders conversant with Jewish psychology, they could soon prepare the territory for the reception of the general mass of emigrants.

But unless the settlement were made with the full cooperation of the Government of the particular country—and for mutual advantage—the emigration would be attended with great local friction. The territory must be a publicly-recognised, legally-secured home. In this one place of all the world the wanderer must feel himself received not grudgingly, but with the cry of "Peace be to you." Any other form of emigration is, we have seen, inevitably destined to end in local anti-Semitism. And without a certain measure of self-government the better class of patriotic emigrant will not be attracted. Moreover, we have not the right to burden any other nation with the problem of governing our emigrants—a task with which we ourselves are best fitted to grapple. Of course, should the given territory be in a modern constitutional country, local autonomy could be automatically attained by the mere numerical preponderance of our immigrants in the said territory.

It had been imagined that the establishment of such a settlement fell within the scope of the Zionist movement, but the Seventh Congress having declared itself legally incompetent to work except in Palestine and its neighbourhood—districts that at present offer scant prospect of solving our economic problem—it becomes necessary to create a separate organisation *ad hoc*. This organisation, entitled the Jewish Territorial Organisation, takes as a body no position towards Zionism, its members being left free to determine their individual relations in that movement. Naturally, no land whatever is excluded from our operations provided it be reasonably good and obtainable.

1. The object of the Jewish Territorial Organisation is to procure a territory upon an autonomous basis for those Jews who cannot, or will not, remain in the lands in which they at present live.

2. To achieve this end the Organisation proposes: (a) To unite all Jews who are in agreement with this object; (b) to enter into relations with Governments and public and private institutions; (c) to create financial institutions, labour-bureaus and other instruments that may be found necessary.

NOTES

1. Israel Zangwill (1864-1926), Anglo-Jewish novelist (*Children of the Ghetto*, 1892; *King of the Schnorrers*, 1894). Among Herzl's earliest followers, Zangwill was one of the most fervent supporters of the Uganda Scheme. Upon the rejection of this proposal at the Seventh Zionist Congress, he withdrew from the World Zionist Organization, and established the Jewish Territorial Organization (ITO) whose program he delineated in this statement. The ITO endorsed the Basle Program, but held that priority should be given to the most suitable territory—which need not, it was emphasized, be Palestine—for Jewish settlement. The ITO investigated the possibility of settling the Jews in various lands (e.g., British East Africa, Australia, Angola, Cyrenaica, Iraq) but without success. Because of this failure and the lack of the emotional appeal among the Jewish masses that Palestine-centered Zionism possessed, the ITO never commanded the support and credibility enjoyed by the World Zionist Organization. Zangwill was the president of the ITO until its dissolution in 1925.

2. Joseph Chamberlain (1836–1914), secretary of state for the colonies from 1895 to 1902 in the cabinet of Lord Salisbury and from 1902 to 1903 in Arthur James Balfour's cabinet. On April 23, 1903 he suggested to Herzl the establishment of a self-governing Jewish settlement in Uganda. Four weeks later he offered a territory in the East Africa Protectorate.

BER BOROCHOV

12. Program for Proletarian Zionism[1]

The Party's General Program: 1. The primary program of the Party is the proletarianization of the means of production and the transformation of the social structure according to the principles of scientific socialism. The only way of achieving these goals recognised by the Party is through the participation of the Jewish proletariat in the class struggle and in the ranks of the world social-democratic movement.

2. The main item in the Party's secondary program, and that which distinguishes it from other social-democratic parties, is the demand for Jewish territorial autonomy, based on democratic principles, as a necessary condition for the undisturbed development of the forces of production of the Jewish people.

3. Jewish territorial autonomy can be achieved only in the land of Israel, and the Jewish proletariat must contribute to the realization of this aim. . . .

Party Policy in the Diaspora: 1. In the Diaspora the Party aims to achieve maximal democratization of society by means of the class struggle, and thus shares the secondary program of all social-democratic parties.

2. When relating this aim to the national problem, the Party demands national political autonomy, with wide economic, cultural and financial authority in all internal national matters, for those nations whose interests cannot be satisfied in a suitable manner by territorial or regional autonomy.[2] . . .

4. Along with the demand for national political autonomy as the leading formulation of Jewish national rights in the Diaspora, the Party emphasizes, however, that the autonomous political institution described above cannot be considered the sole means of achieving the realization of Zionism, and that until territorial autonomy is acquired, no democratic institutions and no national rights can guarantee a solution to the Jewish problem. Until such a time as those national rights attainable in the Diaspora are in fact realized, the Party proposes the implementation of intermediate reforms: freedom in national education, national cultural autonomy, linguistic equality and proportional representation in legislative, executive and judicial institutions.

Guiding Principles for the Realization of Zionism: 2. . . .Since the bourgeois Zionists often tend to use means and methods which are linked with reactionary and degenerate forms of social organization and which in no way lead to the true realization of Zionism, and since the stages in the realization of Zionism are determined by relations based on Realpolitik and the practical interests to which Zionist polity must continually adapt itself, proletarian Zionism believes that part of its task is to support any policy which rests on real interests and to oppose any policy based on philanthropy, other-worldly idealism, obsequious intercession with authorities, and the like.

3. Proletarian Zionism recognizes that historical necessity leads to the strengthening and expansion of the Jewish positions in the land of Israel and to increasing interests by other nations in a solution to the Jewish question along the following lines: (a) the gradual dissolution of the masses of Jewish petty bourgeoisie (a process involving pogroms and impoverishment, the growth of Jewish revolutionary activity and Jewish emigra-

Source: [Program of the "Poalei Zion—the Jewish Social Democratic Workers' Party in Russia" (1906)], in *Kitvei Borochov*, ed. L. Lavita and D. Ben-Nahum (Tel-Aviv: Hakibbutz Ha-Meuchad—Sifriat Hapoalim, 1955), vol. 1, pp. 383–87. Reprinted by permission of Sifriat Hapoalim. Trans. here by D. Goldman.

tion), has awakened the interest of civilized nations in a territorial solution to the Jewish question; meanwhile the increasing national influence of Diaspora Jewry can enlist this awakening international interest to further the cause of Zionism; (b) the strengthening of the Jewish positions in the land of Israel. . . .

4. Jewish capital and Jewish labor are [dialectically] working in the general directions outlined above: (a) in the Diaspora the struggle between labor and capital draws the Jewish proletariat into the worldwide class struggle and allows him to benefit from the democratization of society, which also entails the strengthening of the national character of society in general and the augmentation of Jewish influence in particular; (b) the struggle between Jewish labor and Jewish capital brought by the immigrants to the land of Israel creates the basis for the progressive democratization of society there.

5. Jewish immigration to the land of Israel is a *stychic*[3] process resulting from the growing difficulties Jews face in acquiring positions on the higher forms of production in those large capitalist countries which formerly absorbed Jewish immigration. At the same time the Jews' need to emigrate, rather than weakening, is becoming even more urgent as their economic position is increasingly undermined by intensive national competition. Today, therefore, Jews are forced to turn more and more to the land of Israel, [an underdeveloped] agrarian country and the only one which is capable of absorbing the immigration of Jewish petty bourgeoisie.

6. Proletarian Zionism, unlike preceding Utopian trends in Zionism, recognizes that Zionism's primary task is not to find a territory, obtain a charter or initiate settlement. Rather, it consists of the programmatic regulation of the *stychic* process of Jewish immigration to the land of Israel and the achievement of political territorial autonomy in the land of Israel itself. . . . The general Zionist institutions can only facilitate, regulate and rationally organize this *stychic* immigration, by relying on the factors mentioned above: international interest, the democratization of society and the augmentation of Jewish national influence.

The Party's Relations with the General Zionist Institutions: 1. Proletarian Zionism recognizes the need to coordinate its activities with those of the bourgeois Zionists in matters relating to the practical work in the land of Israel. This must be done in such a way, however, so that the Party will avoid responsibility for activities opposed to proletarian tactics. . . .

7. Given that the bourgeoisie in general have a role to play in the regulation of those factors which produce the *stychic* historical processes of the capitalist regimes, and given that the role of the proletariat lies in the liberation of the conditions of those processes and the introduction of a revolutionary element into them and that the Jewish bourgeoisie, like all other bourgeois groups, needs the liberating power of the proletariat to carry out its regulating functions in the *stychic* process of the realization of Zionism—the proletarian Zionist party formulated its demands regarding Zionist tactics and policies of the bourgeois Zionist institutions in the conviction that, sooner or later, when reality will have forced bourgeois Zionism to recognize its own interests, our demands will be met.

Practical Work in the Land of Israel: . . . 2. Even before right of free entry for Jews into the land of Israel has been obtained through the class struggle of the Jewish proletariat, even before the foundations have been laid for obtaining other essential legal guarantees by means of the class struggle in the land of Israel, the proletarian Zionist party demands that the World Zionist Organization undertake immediate practical work in the land of Israel. . . .

4. The Party demands the democratization of the internal administration of the Jewish settlements in the land of Israel, based on principles of municipal autonomy and large-scale participation of workers in the self-governing institutions of the settlements. The Party demands that the settlements themselves regulate the relations between

capital and labor within the jurisdiction without the intervention of the Turkish administration. . . .

6. The Party shall organize the Jewish proletariat in the land of Israel and regard the establishment of the World Federation of Jewish Social Democratic Workers, Poalei Zion, as a necessary prerequisite to the undertaking of systematic proletarian work in the land of Israel.

NOTES

1. Ber Borochov (1881–1917), leader and foremost theoretician of the Socialist Zionists. For a generation of Russian Jews drawn to Marxism, Borochov developed a synthesis of the seemingly irreconcilable demands of revolutionary class struggle and the devotion to the national needs of the Jewish people. Based on the precepts of Marxist analysis, Borochov's forceful arguments exercised a commanding influence on the ideology of the emerging Socialist Zionist movement.

Borochov was a delegate of the Poalei Zion ("workers of Zion") to the Seventh Zionist Congress, where he cooperated closely with Menahem Ussishkin (one of the foremost leaders of Russian Zionism) and the struggle against the Uganda Scheme. At the time the Poalei Zion was a loose association of Socialist Zionist groups in Russia. The deliberations of the Seventh Congress exacerbated the ideological dissension between these groups and left the Poalei Zion in disarray. Some groups felt that continued membership in the World Zionist Organization was intolerable, for it entailed cooperation with the Jewish bourgeoisie; others preferred territorialism; still other groups demanded that Zionism should be abandoned altogether, because it was a Utopian ideology that neglected *Gegenwartsarbeit*, i.e., attention to the everyday needs of the Jewish masses in the Diaspora. In early 1906, in the Ukrainian city of Poltava, Poalei Zion groups loyal to the resolutions of the Seventh Zionist Congress founded, under the leadership of Borochov, the Poalei Zion—Jewish Social Democratic Workers' Party in Russia. In the party's program, written largely by Borochov, the ideological challenges presented by the dissident Poalei Zion groups were met, and the participation of Jewish proletariat in the World Zionist Organization justified.

2. The reference is to "extraterritorial" peoples who are not concentrated in a particular region and do not constitute a majority in any single country.

3. A Greek term used by Borochov to designate an "elemental," historically necessary process. The millennial migration of the Jewish people is, according to Borochov, such a process, which will objectively necessitate the territorial concentration of the Jewish masses in Palestine. Zionism appreciates the *stychic* dimension of Jewish history and merely serves it as a "midwife," and it is therefore not a Utopian movement.

HELSINGFORS CONFERENCE
13. *Gegenwartsarbeit*[1]

The third conference of the Zionist Organization in Russia, which took place in Helsingfors, inaugurated a new era in the history of the movement. The conference put an end to the crisis of the last three years.[2] This crisis was not a crisis of objectives, but rather one of tactics. The fundamental goal of Zionism was, and remains, *the political revival of the Jewish people in the land of Israel*. The main error committed by our movement was the blind

Source: [Memorandum of the central committee of the Zionist organization of Russia, December 1906], in I. Maor, *Ha-Tnuah Ha-Zionit be-Russiyah* [The Zionist movement in Russia] (Jerusalem: Hassifriya Haziyonit, The World Zionist Organization, 1973), pp. 318–19. Reprinted by permission. Trans. here by R. Weiss.

faith that our will, and the genius of our leader [i.e., Herzl] were sufficient to obtain almost instantly the land of Israel [for Jewish resettlement]. We expected the Charter[3] to be granted any day, and this expectation caused us to treat with indifference the mundane problems of the present life.

At the time we thought that we must not waste our energies on matters concerning the Jews in the Diaspora [*golah*], but rather concentrate our entire effort toward the realization of our ideal. Our work during that period consisted of soliciting new members, the sale of shares in the Jewish Colonial Trust[4] and the collection of donations to the Jewish National Fund.[5] The optimism which led us to believe that we would imminently get the Charter, prevented us from performing practical work both in the land of Israel and in the Diaspora. But reality destroyed the dream, and we were forced to recognize the evolutionary and developmental nature of Zionism, and accordingly, to change our tactics. To be sure, our goal remains the same, only our tactics have changed. We now understand that only an organized, unified Jewry is capable of mobilizing the vast material and spiritual resources needed to realize our objectives. But the effective organization of Jewry requires two basic elements: an attention to the daily needs of the Jewish masses and the ongoing work, especially that part which can be carried out already in the present, toward the attainment of the ultimate goal of Zionism.

Zionism must address itself to all aspects of Jewish life, and respond to all issues besetting Jewry. [The movement will thereby] tap all the hidden resources of the nation. In consonance with these considerations, it was necessary to prepare an appropriate program. The Conference dealt with this task successfully. . . .

Neither the terrible pogroms [recently perpetrated against our people] nor the shattered hopes that our situation in Russia will change radically in the near future can shake our determination to reach our ultimate goal. On the contrary, both the Jewish bourgeoisie and the Jewish proletariat are convinced, now more than ever, that the basic problems of our nation cannot be solved in Exile [*galut*].

NOTES

1. The Third All-Russian Zionist Conference met from the fourth to the tenth of December 1906 in Helsingfors (Helsinki), Finland. In the wake of recent events—the Revolution of 1905, pogroms, the death of Herzl, the Seventh Zionist Congress, the growing influence of competing ideologies among the Jewish masses—the conference dealt with fundamental issues facing the Zionist movement in general, and Russian Zionism in particular. The program endorsed by the conference constituted a major revision of Zionist policy.

The conference is most famous for its resolution on *Gegenwartsarbeit* ("work in the present"). Prior to the conference the Zionist movement in Russia subscribed to the principle of "the negation of the Diaspora" (*galut*) and correspondingly rejected the possibility of Jewish national existence in Russia. But this position suddenly seemed impolitic, if not sterile. After the Seventh Congress, which betrayed the weakness of diplomatic Zionism, the realization of the Basle Program seemed to lie in the remote future; moreover, the Jewish masses of Russia were being successfully organized by movements such as the Bund, which gave priority to the immediate political and economic needs of the masses. The program of *Gegenwartsarbeit* was formulated as a correlate to the policy of "synthetic Zionism" endorsed by the conference. The latter policy postulated that the attainment of the Basle Program objectives was the ultimate end, but not the precondition of Zionist activity, viz., systematic *aliyah* and settlement in the land of Israel. Similarly, the basic negation of the Jewish future in the Exile (*galut*), does not preclude participation in the struggles of daily life of the Jews in the existing Diaspora (*golah*). Accordingly, the Helsingfors Conference advanced a program to work for the democratization of Russia and the reorganization of Russia as a multinational state that would grant wide, autonomous rights to its non-Russian peoples, including the Jewish nation. Such a policy it was held would transform Zionism into a dynamic movement of the masses. The document presented here is a memorandum sent by the Central Committee of the Russian Zionist Organization to the local branches in Russia explaining the ideological consideration behind the program.

2. I.e., since the Sixth Zionist Congress which first broached the Uganda Scheme and other "temporary solutions."

3. See document 4 in this chapter.

4. Jewish Colonial Trust, bank established in 1899 in accordance with a decision of the First Zionist Congress. The bank assisted in the colonization of Palestine.

5. Called in Hebrew *Keren Kayemet le-Yisrael*, the Jewish National Fund was founded at the Fifth Zionist Congress (1901) to further the acquisition and development of land in Palestine.

HAPOEL HAZAIR
14. Our Goal[1]

Conscious of the fact that our national work is of no value as long as there is no measurably large and measurably strong Hebrew[2] workers' party in the land of Israel, we have set ourselves the goal of creating such a party. How to create it and whether indeed it is possible to create such a party under the present conditions is the central question facing us.

The life of the Hebrew worker in the land of Israel is unlike that of the worker in any other country, as almost everyone who deals with this problem understands. Not everyone understands, however, exactly how the Jewish worker's life here differs from that of the worker in other countries. They do not understand what primary factors force him to follow a unique path in his struggle for survival, what laws he must rely upon as he follows that special path and how he must relate to the world around him; in other words, all the questions concerning how to create in the land of Israel a Jewish workers' party worthy of the name, in terms of both quality and quantity.

Some solve the problem with the facile phrase: "Everything will be created by class struggle." Who are these struggling classes within the Jewish people as a whole and, among the Jews in the land of Israel, in particular? To what extent can this class struggle contribute to the development of an undeveloped land and to the growth of a workers' party in it? Such questions they do not bother to raise.

When we propose, therefore, to publish a newspaper our primary goal is to clarify to ourselves our essential nature as workers, the laws which we must follow in different situations, the extent to which we can utilize means applied in other countries and the point beyond which we must make our own way.

We are not so naive as to believe that we can give a final answer to these questions all at once. A land in the process of development cannot be made to follow predetermined laws; as it develops and is transformed its laws, too, must change. We believe, however, that we can evolve laws suited to the development of the country. If someone comes later and shows us we erred in this or that law, we will not deny it but will readily acknowledge our mistakes. The first part of our newspaper, therefore, will be devoted entirely to the clarification of the questions mentioned above. Study of the conditions of labor and of the life of the worker in the city and village, and careful examination of the development of the country will supply us

Source: "Mataratenu," *Hapoel Hazair* (Iyyar 5667; May 1907). Trans. here by D. Goldman.

with the material we need to formulate our answers.

In addition, we will be on constant guard against the use of false or misleading statements for purposes of propaganda, by various public figures and leaders of Zionist institutions. Our national movement is too genuine to require the use of such impure methods which can only do more harm than good. We shall fight against these methods with all our strength. The second part of our newspaper, therefore, will be devoted to a critique of various Zionist institutions and activities in the land of Israel, to an impartial evaluation of the attitudes of the Zionist leadership on different issues and to a presentation of our views on all these matters.

The newspaper must and can fulfill one other need of ours—the need for information. By maintaining constant contact with our comrades in the cities and villages of the land of Israel, we will always be able to give correct information about working conditions in the country and the demand for workers in specific places. The third part of our newspaper will therefore be devoted to the dissemination of such information. Apart from news items, we will also give our comrades an opportunity to express their opinions on various issues related to life in the land of Israel in general and to their own experiences in particular, in the form of letters to the editor, belletristic essays and popular articles.

At the present time we are unable, both financially and spiritually, to publish a journal that would satisfy all our spiritual requirements. May this modest forum serve our comrades as a central clearing-house for their ideas, and let us hope that it will gradually develop into that larger forum whose lack is so deeply felt here in the land of Israel.

NOTES

1. Hapoel Hazair ("the young worker") was a labor organization active in Palestine from 1905 to 1930 founded by young people who had come to Palestine with the second *aliyah* in protest against the Uganda Scheme and with the determination to demonstrate the possibility of practical work in the country. Unable to identify with any of the existing Hebrew newspapers, the group founded its own organ called *Hapoel Hazair*, which quickly became a leading platform for Socialist Zionist ideas, mainly non-Marxist. Some of the best Hebrew journalists and authors of the period wrote for its pages. The above was the lead article of the first hectographic pamphlet of *Hapoel Hazair*.

2. Indicative of their desire to create a new man, the term *ivri* ("Hebrew") rather than *yehudi* ("Jewish") was employed, as it was—and is—in most Zionist writings.

AGUDAT ISRAEL
15. Founding Program[1]

The purpose of Agudat Israel is the solution of the respective tasks facing the Jewish collectivity, in the spirit of the Torah.

In accordance with this purpose, it sets itself the following goals: (1) the organization, concentration and unification of dis-

Source: "Zum Programm der Agudas Jisroel," in *Agudas Jisroel: Berichte und Materialen*, ed. Provisorischen Comité der Agudas Jisroel zu Frankfurt am Main (Frankfurt am Main: Buero der Agudas Jisroel, 1912), pp. 151–52. Trans. here by J. Hessing.

persed parts of Orthodox Jewry, especially of the Jews in Eastern and Western Europe; (2) the generous promotion of Torah studies, and of Jewish education in general, in countries where this promotion is needed; (3) the improvement of economic conditions of the Jewish masses, not only in Palestine, but wherever they suffer want; (4) the organization and promotion of emergency aid in cases of necessity; (5) the advancement of a press and literature in the [traditional] Jewish spirit; (6) a representative forum of all Jews adhering to the Torah; this forum will parry the attacks directed against the Torah and its adherents.

Against this work of unifying Orthodox Jewry, a stock objection is raised in a part of the national [i.e., Zionist] Jewish press which states that Agudat Israel lacks a clear program. In this respect, Agudat Israel is unfavourably compared with Zionism.

This much is correct: Zionism has not only set up a general program, but is fortunate enough to be able to outline the way in which it hopes to find a definite solution to all Jewish problems. The "national home secured by public law," for which the first battle was fought in Basle, is considered to be the panacea for all national ailments. It is only for this means, transformed into an end, that the Zionists are ready to mobilize and organize their forces.

Agudat Israel, on the other hand—or so they claim—has no program of redemption. And an organization without a program, it is held, is tantamount to an organization without a clear purpose suspended in midair without a foundation and without a supporting pillar.

It can be argued [however] that the general task of Orthodox Jewry has from ancient times been clearly and programmatically defined, and that for its propagation there is no need for any other base than that which has supported and united us through centuries of suffering. New currents and movements must be based on newly created foundations. The work of unification on behalf of Orthodox Jewry does not derive from any new and revolutionary idea. It only wishes to unify, collect and conserve on the basis of our ancient program.

NOTE

1. Agudat Israel ("union of Israel") is a world organization of Orthodox Jewry which had learned from the World Zionist Organization that in order to advance the international and political interests of the Jewish people they must first be organized as a coherent political body. Appreciating the efficacy of politics and mass organization in modern society, Orthodox Jews were alarmed that their secular and assimilated brethren of the World Zionist Organization would assume the mantle of Jewish leadership and the exclusive right to voice the demands and ideals of Jewry before the world. Moreover, modern organizational means have helped the Zionists—and other non-Orthodox and secular trends—to influence Jewish communal and cultural life. The endorsement by the Zionist Congress (1912) of the cultural program of secular Zionism, which was construed by Orthodox Jewry as lending prestige and legitimacy to secular Judaism, was the immediate spur behind the founding of Agudat Israel. The founding convention, initiated by the Neo-Orthodox community of Germany, met at Kattowitz, Upper Silesia, in May 1912. Attended by 227 Orthodox Jewish leaders from Russia, Austria, Hungary, Germany and Palestine, the convention reaffirmed in its program the unimpeachable authority of Torah and Halakha in governing Jewish life and priorities. As a group, Agudat Israel opposed the Zionist program as a profanation of Judaism because it attempted to revive Jewish patrimony in the Holy Land through human agency and because it prompted a secular Jewish society there. On the other hand, Agudat Israel, particularly since the Holocaust, regards the land of Israel as the center—both spiritual and physical—of Torah-true Jewry.

MARTIN BUBER AND HERMANN COHEN

16. A Debate on Zionism and Messianism[1]

BUBER: Herr Professor Cohen, you state that you view nationality only as a "fact of nature." [It is therefore not surprising] that you use the terms "nationality," "stock" [*Stamm*] and "origin" as synonyms. But how could you, from your viewpoint of a strict pristine monotheism, treat the origin [of the Jewish people] as a mere "fact of nature"? The primeval Jewish concept of "seed" appears everywhere that God makes and renews His covenant with Abraham and Abraham's descendents.... And the principle of covenant, you would agree, is not a "fact of nature," but an expression of God's dynamic purpose and presence in history?...

No, nationality cannot be defined through the concept of "fact of nature." Nationality is a historical reality and a moral duty. To be sure, it also has its roots in the natural, but so too does our humanity. Nevertheless, nature cannot contain us within the borders of its [merely empirical] reality. The idea of humanity can only be realized in the spiritual struggle of mankind, in infinite striving. The same is true for love, art and knowledge. They all have their roots in facts of nature. But we cannot become conscious of their meaning until we change "whence" into "whither" and origin into goal, until the understanding of how they became what they are turns into the insight concerning what should become of them, until that which is given us as fact becomes that which is given us as task. It is then that nature becomes spirit....

Zionism never equated religion with nationality, as you claim. But neither will it ever allow nationhood [*Volkstum*] to be relegated to an anthropological means for the propagation of religion. Rather, every Zionist for whom, as for me, religiosity stands at the core of Judaism will, like me, know and acknowledge that Jewish religiosity is a function, the highest function of the dynamic Jewish nationhood.... This Jewish religiosity is a function that is not merely unable to propagate itself without its bearer, as you suppose. No, in such a case it could not continue to exist. Jewish religiosity thrives on the blood of the nation, is nourished by the nation's natural forces and operates through its will. Without the vitality of the nation, without its ardent and long-suffering power, Jewish religiosity would have no place on earth. What is valid for history is also valid for the life of the individual: the idea [of Judaism] cannot be realized if [Jewish] nationhood is not actualized. But what truly matters is the realization. Nationality, as a simple fact of nature, is a fiction, the same way that humanity as a simple fact of nature is a fiction. Only when we first view nationality as a reality of the spirit and ethos can we also turn it into a reality in our own lives....

[You call for a] clarification of concepts—but are concepts the issue here? Can the question of the Jewish people be settled by terminology? Can the naturalness and sincerity of a national feeling be proven by a definition?...

Zionist literature, you write, "indulges in frivolous derision of the most sublime idea of the Jewish religion," namely, messianism. Where and when? I believe I know Zionist

Source: Martin Buber, "Begriffe und Wirklichkeit, Brief an Herrn Geh. Regierungsrat Prof. Dr. Hermann Cohen," *Der Jude*, (July 1916), no. 5, pp. 281ff.; Hermann Cohen, "Antwort auf das Offene Schreiben des Herrn Dr. Martin Buber," *K.-C.-Blaetter*, (July–August 1916), pp. 683ff.; Martin Buber, "Zion, der Staat und die Menschheit," *Der Jude*, no. 7, (September 1916), pp. 425ff. The Buber excerpts are reprinted by permission of Mr. Rafael Buber. Trans. here by M. Gelber and S. Weinstein.

literature well, and I cannot recollect one passage which would substantiate your claim. On the contrary, messianism has been depicted, from Moses Hess[2] up until my own writings (to chose a recent example from the present generation) as the dominant idea of Judaism.

Zionism opposes not the messianic idea, but rather the misrepresentation and distortion of this idea found in a considerable part of Liberal-Jewish, anti-Zionist literature. This misrepresentation and distortion glorifies, in the name of messianism, the dispersion, debasement, and homelessness of the Jewish people as something unconditionally valuable and fortunate, as something that must be preserved because it prepares humanity for the messianic age.

Zionism too sees the goal of Judaism as "the redemption of the human spirit and the salvation of the world."[3] But, we see as the means to the realization of this goal "the liberation of a tormented people and its gathering around God's sanctuary."[4] . . . In the messianic age, let Jewry merge with mankind. But let us make sure that the Jewish people does not disappear *now* so that the messianic age may perhaps come into being *later*. The Jewish people must persevere in the midst of today's human order—not as a fixed, brittle fact of nature appended to an ever more diluted confessional religion, but as a people pursuing its ideal, freely and unhindered, for the sake of this human order. . . . The struggle for a "homeland" is a national struggle. The struggle for Jewish communal existence [*juedische Gemeinwesen*] in Palestine will be a supra-national one. We want Palestine not "for the Jews." We want it for mankind, because we want it for the realization of Judaism.

COHEN: . . . It is characteristic that my opponent irresistably speaks only of people, nation and, if need be, also of religion. He does not mention the state, however, except as it refers to an isolated people. This point of view must be contested. The Jewish question, as it concerns us, deals not with a distinct, cohesive people; but on the contrary, with a people which is dispersed throughout other states and which has to establish and explain its political relationship to each individual state.

I have already referred to the fact that my opposition to Zionism is by no means a matter of apologetics. Rather, I am interested in the general ethical-political problem of preserving nationality. Hence, one may recognize immediately the general reason which led me to attempt to define the difference between nation and nationality. While nationality remains a moral fact of nature, it is only through the state, by virtue of a pure act of political morality, that the nation is constituted. . . .

For us, the state constitutes the hub of all human culture. The "I" of man remains an empirical ambiguity as long as it is not objectified through political self-consciousness. Insofar as I participate in the ideal personality of my state, I may claim a true self-consciousness. Our entire range of feelings is concentrated in our patriotism [*Staatsbewusstsein*]. . . .

The desire of the modern state to be a nation-state presents Judaism and the Jewish people with a dilemma. In that the Jews constitute a distinct ethnic group [*Stamm*], the Jews seem [to non-Jews] to form "a state within a state." In face of this modern dilemma, all Liberal Jews in every state, without prior agreement, exclaim in self-defense: We do not want to form our own state, or, consequently, to be a separate nation. But we are and shall remain a separate religion, we are and shall remain in principle a distinct ethnic group [*Stamm*], a separate nationality.

Can one ethicize nationality—that "fact of nature"—with a more cogent claim than that it is needed for the historical preservation of religion?

Whatever Judaism and its adherents have suffered externally and internally derives from this problem. The states, in their delusion, say: There should be no groups among us that under the guise of some fiction or other lead a separate state-like existence.

And the Jews, oppressed by the ambiguity of modernity as much as by any general distress of our day, who decide to abandon the faith of their forefathers exclaim: There is an irreconcilable conflict between the Jewish religion and the foundations of modern national experience, namely, the nation-state. Our patriotic consciousness of being members of a state [*Staatsbewusstsein*] thus requires renunciation of Judaism.

Modern Judaism counters these two errors with the following thesis: Our religion is the sole and exclusive difference between us and our state, and, accordingly, between us and our nation.

Can the objection dare be advanced now that this thesis is an evasion of the dilemma or even worse, an expression of a cowardly desire to assimilate? Such an objection offends our conviction that we have a moral obligation to the modern state. With such skepticism, one would not desire to take any part at all in the modern state. . . . The Zionist rails pitilessly against us Liberal Jews for imagining that we possess a homeland among the cultures of other countries. This [alleged] delusion is contrasted with the [actual] homelessness of the Jewish people. And, only this homeless Jewish people is considered to comprise the Jewish reality. We "pseudo-Jews," on the other hand, are—rightfully, it is thought—separated from the Jewish people.

In this way Jewish reality is tailored by Zionism to suit its preconceived notion. Further, the implementation of this reality becomes ever more exclusive: Only in Palestine, only in the Jewish state, can the "dilapidated," "fictitious" Judaism be overcome and eliminated. The entire past history of Judaism is misrepresented here as mere ideology. The ghetto mentality is not the ghost, but the true spirit of Judaism and of Jewish reality. The verdict has been reformed regarding all cultural endeavors of Jewish history: these endeavors sow only concepts, but produce nothing real. Furthermore, the modern Liberal movement is considered to be merely the continuation of those earlier, illusory endeavors. These illusions, say the Zionists, must be uprooted altogether. . . .

Does my opponent's statement that there are only two directions for authentic Judaism —that of absolute adherence to Jewish Law and that of Zionism—correspond to the reality of our history? Were all the other directions and turns in our history mere aberrations leading to degeneration? What criterion can there be for deciding the question whether the return to Palestine alone will determine the true nature of the future?

Modern Judaism is historical; through historical development it acquires self-consciousness. And, the guide to our religious development is prophetism, the highpoint of which is messianism.

We interpret our entire history as leading toward this goal of messianism. The downfall of the Jewish state is, in our view, the best example of historical theodicy. The same Micha who coined the phrase "God asks of you: only this, to act justly" (6:8), also coined the providential metaphor: "And the remnant of Jacob shall be in the midst of many peoples, like dew from the Lord" (5:6, 7). It is our proud conviction that we are to continue to live as divine dew in the midst of the peoples and to remain fruitful among them and for them. All of the prophets place us in the midst of the peoples and their common perspective is the world mission of the remnant of Israel.

[Modern, Liberal Judaism acknowledges this messianic mission.] Thus we are free of all discord between our Judaism and our Germanism. Moreover, the Jews of every modern state feel free of any such discrepancies caused by religion. In consequence of its messianic conceptions of God, the Jewish religion is thoroughly a world religion. This messianic faith cannot be impaired by historical reality, by misfortune, or even by the auspicious granting of equal rights. "Happy is he that waiteth" (Dan. 12:12). [Messianic] hope alone confirms our [spiritual and moral] reality. Consequently, hope and trust also shape our fundamental political attitudes.

The practical difference between us and the

Zionists is to be found in what might be called our political religiosity. While the Zionist believes that he can preserve Judaism only through an all-encompassing, unqualified Jewish nationality, we are of the opposite opinion. It is only, we maintain, the universal humanistic Jewish nationality that can preserve the Jewish religion. All the bitterness of the argument becomes understandable and pardonable in light of this difference, which is not merely one of tactics. Both parties fervently desire the continuation of our religion—that I readily acknowledge. To this end I unconditionally favor the preservation of our nationality. But, just as unconditionally, I favor our political integration into the modern nation-state. Political merger conditions and guarantees the perpetuation of our religion. . . .

Palestine is not just the land of our fathers; it is the land of our prophets, who established and perfected the ideal of our religion. Hence, we do indeed regard Palestine as the Holy Land, however only insofar as it is the land from whence came our eternal, sacred heritage. But just as our present religious reality is increasingly and more exclusively directed to the future, likewise, the moral world, as it evolves in history, is our true promised land. . . .

We do not understand the messianic future in terms of the image which suggests that the Lord will appoint a table on Mt. Zion for all peoples. Instead, we refer to the many imageless pronouncements in which the unique God is proclaimed "Lord of the entire earth." We thereby view the entire historical world as the future abode of our religion. And it is only this future that we acknowledge as our true homeland.

BUBER: Hermann Cohen has published an "Answer to the Open Letter of Dr. Martin Buber to Hermann Cohen." In spite of the title, his essay is not an answer but an evasion of the subjects I raised. He speaks not of my words—which he barely tries to refute—but only of what he perceives to be the easily dismissed, fabricated, slogan-laden argumentation of an imaginary "typical" Zionist. . . .

At one point, however, Cohen does not beat around the bush. He recognizes that the core of the argument between us involves the relationship between state and religion. I might also say between state and spirit, or between state and humanity. For me, religion is not, as it is for him, "one of the concentric, special subjects within the unity of moral culture"; nor do I regard the state as "the hub of all human culture." My views are exactly the opposite. Only in religious life is the unity of humanity truly realized.

But, in applying this basic difference between us to the Jewish problem, Cohen goes astray. "Our argument," he supposes, "centers not so much on the Jewish people as it does on the Jewish state. In reality [Cohen continues], my opponent, for his part accepts my definition that the state first defines a people, but he derives from this a particular state for the Jewish people." What a paradox! For me, just as the state in general is not the determining goal of mankind, so the "Jewish state" is not the determining goal for the Jews. And, the "viable ethnic group's need for power," about which Cohen speaks further, is completely foreign to me. I have seen and heard too much of the results of empty needs for power.

Our argument is about something else entirely. It does not concern the Jewish state, that, yes, were it to be founded today would be built upon the same principles as any other modern state. It does not concern the addition of one more trifling power structure. It does, however, concern the [renewed Jewish] settlement in Palestine, which independent of "international politics," can effect the inner consolidation of the energies of the Jewish people and thereby the realization of Judaism.

[Admittedly, in the contemporary Diaspora] there is an awakening of Jews who have been touched by the spirit. Growing from hour to hour, this awakening is animated by the soul's urge to create. . . . But this awakening will subside as all soaring expectations have subsided in the Exile, if the energy of the people is not liberated from the fruitless struggle for bare existence.... This then is what I mean by Palestine—not a state, but only the ancient soil which bears the promised security of ultimate and hallowed permanence. Palestine is the firm sod in which alone the seed of the new unity can sprout, not from a "need for power," but solely from the need for self-realization, which is the need to extend God's power on earth.

"The entire history of Judaism," says Cohen, "teaches, in accordance with the vision of the prophets, that the realization of Judaism is grounded in our dispersion among the peoples of the earth." We have learned the opposite lesson from history, namely, that in a life of dispersion not determined by ourselves, we cannot realize Judaism. We can pray here in the Diaspora, but not act; bear witness to God with patience, but not with creativity; praise the jubilee year, but not usher it in....

This, in brief, is our creed: that Zion restored will become the house of the Lord for all peoples and the center of the new world,... in which "the blood-stained garment of war is burned" and "the swords are turned into plowshares."

The new humanity needs us. However, it needs us not dispersed and working at cross-purposes, but together and united; not befouled by pretences and rumors, but purified and ready; not to acknowledge God with our words while betraying God with our lives, but, to serve God faithfully through the establishment of a human community according to His will. Our contribution to the new humanity consists not in explaining and asserting that there is a God, but in showing how God lives in us—how through a true human life, we realize both ourselves and God within us.

NOTES

1. Martin Buber (1878–1965), since the early 1900s a leading figure in German letters. Buber joined the Zionist movement in 1898 and became one of the opponents to Herzl and political Zionism. He favored a shift of priorities from diplomacy and the drive to obtain a charter to a renewal of Jewish culture, with special attention to youth as the fulcrum of this renewal. Buber's understanding of Jewish culture, however, differed from that other cultural Zionists. For Buber, Jewish culture meant a unique aesthetic and spiritual sensibility, which was ultimately based on what he called Jewish religiosity (to be distinguished from "religion"), that is, a primal awareness of and longing to realize "the Unconditional" in one's actions. Before the development of his philosophy of dialogue in the 1920s, Buber hesitated to identify the Unconditional as the personal God of traditional faith.

Hermann Cohen (1842–1918). One of Germany's most esteemed professors of philosophy, he taught for more than forty years at the University of Marburg; from 1912 until his death he lectured at the Lehranstalt fuer die Wissenschaft des Judentums in Berlin, an institute of advanced Jewish studies associated with Liberal Judaism. His system of philosophical analysis, known as neo-Kantianism, reflects his deep belief in the progress of man as a rational and moral being. He found confirmation for this conviction in the evolution in the modern period of the nation-state, which he viewed as essentially defined by the legal system which aspires to a rational conceptualization of justice and by the tendency of the state to unite within its legal framework and national identity disparate peoples. A world federation of states, Cohen insisted, would be the next and higher stage in the development of man's moral reason; the ultimate goal being an absolute universalism and unity of mankind. Cohen identified this understanding and vision of history with the messianism of the Jewish prophets. He held that the spirit of modern German culture and thought was remarkably consonant with that of prophetic Judaism, and thus as a Jew he felt spiritually at home in German culture. Cohen recognized the Jews as a "nationality" or ethnic group. However, he sharply distinguished nationality from "nation," a designation he reserved for the citizens of a nation-state. Accordingly, since their Exile, the Jews have ceased to be a nation and are simply a nationality. As a nationality Jewry is associated with a particular religion. Indeed, Cohen sought to emphasize the religious vocation of the Jews as opposed to their ethnicity. The Jews' nationality is for Cohen but a "fact of nature," or an anthropological means to support Judaism. The religious vocation of Israel, which required the loss of statehood, is to point to the messianic future of mankind by transcending the concerns of everyday concrete reality and those of one's immediate community. This affirmation of the Diaspora occasioned by Israel's messianic mission placed Cohen ideologically close to the Liberal camp of Judaism.

In June 1916 Cohen wrote in the Jewish journal *K.-C.-Blaetter* a critique of Zionism. Buber published in the July issue of *Der Jude*, a journal that he founded and edited, a response to Cohen, entitled *Begriffe und Wirklichkeit* (Concepts and Reality). The title was an allusion to Cohen's philosophical method which assigned an epistemological role to conceptual constructs. Buber argued in his article that Cohen's understanding of Jewish matters was divorced from reality. Cohen was as deeply hurt by the tenor as by the content of Buber's essay. He responded with a rebuttal in the *K.-C.-Blaetter* issue of July–August 1916. Buber replied to Cohen's rebuttal in an article published in the September 1916 issue of *Der Jude*. Both Buber's and Cohen's arguments were published as separate pamphlets and were widely discussed in Jewish circles throughout Europe; excerpts from their debate are presented above. Although Cohen was not a typical Reform Jew and Buber was hardly a typical Zionist, their debate brought into focus many of the central issues that divided the Liberal Western Jews and the Zionists. These issues were epitomized in their respective understanding of Exile and messianism. Buber advanced the view of Exile as a tragic situation of spiritual and physical homelessness. Cohen denied that the Diaspora was Exile; the Jew was, he affirmed, spiritually, and, since emancipation, politically at home in the Diaspora. By demanding the negation of the Diaspora, Cohen held, the Zionists were negating the messianic vision and task of Israel. Buber countered that Zionism furthers the realization of messianism.

2. Moses Hess (1812–1875), German-Jewish social philosopher, who at one time was close to Marx and Engels. His work *Rome and Jerusalem* (1862) anticipated many of the major tenets of political and Socialist Zionism.

3. Martin Buber, "Renewal of Judaism" [1911], trans. E. Jospe, in Martin Buber, *On Judaism, ed. N. N. Glatzer (New York: Schocken Books, 1967), p. 51.*

4. Ibid, p. 51.

HA-SHOMER HA-ZAIR[1]
17. Our World-View

. . . We believe that the future of the Jewish people is hidden in our youth. We believe that the Jewish people will be revived in the simplest possible way: Youth will renew us.

In bringing out this work-program we are convinced that we can provide a cure for the mortal disease that is consuming our youth. Our meaning is this: We are not complete and healthy men, and we are not complete and healthy Jews; we lack the harmony which should reign between these two fundamental elements of the "I" in us.

Hitherto attention has been paid solely to the lack of Judaism and attempts were made to correct this defect insofar as possible. But no attention whatsoever was paid—or if so then only minimally—to the general human side. For the sake of veracity we must admit that other peoples too, until very recently, worried more about producing good patriotic

Source: Anonymous [The world-view of the Shomer] (Vienna, January 1917), in *Sefer Ha-Shomer Ha-Zair*, eds. Levi Dror and Israel Rosenzweig, 2nd ed. (Merhavia: Sifriat Poalim, 1956), vol. 1, pp. 40–43. Reprinted by permission. Trans. here by L. Sachs.

citizens than about raising whole, healthy men. Only in the last two decades, in fact, has there been a strong movement among the youth—primarily German youth—to break the bonds with which the schools restrained attempts at individual development and to find better forms for the experiences and communality of individuals. But the youth of other peoples have, relatively, a simpler mission to fulfill. For they enjoy a normal national life while we, the children of a people with an abnormal national existence unlike that of any other, have a double task. We wish to save both the man and the Jew together. . . .

Let us look closely at the Jewish youth. Even before he is twenty he is an old man. His soul is shrouded in deep darkness. If he be a superficial man he ultimately becomes an opportunist lacking an independent mind. If he be an intellectual his heart will be eaten by despair and poisoned by pessimism and *Weltschmerz.*

In both cases his soul is bleak and mournful as though in an eternal autumn; he is but a withered flower. Where is the optimism that makes life worth living, that gives strength to bear the sufferings of life and that gives the young man encouragement, joy and vigor? Where is that sincere optimism which imparts a goal and a purpose to life and which every truly young man worthy of the name should profess? Where, we ask, is that fresh and sweet-smelling wind of spring that breathes upon us when we draw close even to a small group of youth?

This and more. In addition to youth, we lack also a pure and true humanity. We stand, therefore, as the miserable inheritors of the faults of our fathers. And these faults are numerous and evil. Truly! Let us not hide within us the words which rise to our lips and demand expression. Our love for our people is strong and loyal. We wish to see our nation great and noble. But precisely for this reason we have a duty to examine our faults and defects. It pains us greatly but we are forced to admit that those traits of character and that nobility of soul which we possess are obscured by the general appearance of the Jewish community today. The average Jew is but a caricature of a man healthy and normal in body and soul. His whole life is but a procession of irregular and unhealthy acts performed to enable him to survive. He is convinced, nevertheless, that he is the most perfect creature under the sun and that his people are a shining example to the family of nations.

Until now it has been thought that a rule requiring the study of Jewish history, or the acquisition of the Hebrew language was sufficient to give us good Jews, even if their value as human beings was small. But the concept of a "human being" is wider and more inclusive than the concept of a "Jew," and it is humanity itself which is the basis of Judaism. It is hard for us to understand how a base human being can be a good Jew.

Until now the individual was not given an opportunity to live a full life in the movement, for the whole system was based on advancing one's studies, on Jewish learning and not on the education of a human being. Therefore, let us establish a new basic element in our program: to give the individual the opportunity to live a full and many-faceted life in our organization. We will do this in the form of small associations of members called "troops." We will endeavor to make our organization a second family, for the youths who join us. In some cases we may be the primary family, for as is well known a blood relationship is not always one of spirit or affinity. But the whole organization can be a "spiritual family" to a young member in the most general and inclusive meaning of the term. Therefore, the form of organization should be a small company of members (a troop) which will constitute a little society unto itself.

And if one of the disciples of extreme individualism should come forward with his theories and claim that, in general, communal life with one's fellowman, even with fellowmen of the same psychological disposition, curbs and restrains the individual, we will reply in brief: Man is a social animal and feels the need to live communally with his fellows—that is, of course, with men who are congenial to him. A man can be compared to a flint which will spray off sparks only when it is struck on another flint. Or in our terms: only through confrontations and communal life can the "I" of a man be molded and forged. For a man yearns for the company of men who will love and understand him and with whom he can share his dreams and ideals, his joys and sorrows.

How can we become young and healthy? It should be pointed out that this problem appeared more than ten years ago in modern Hebrew literature, and many different answers were given. The young and the most extreme coined the phrase: "Let us give up books and grasp the sword!" Only the first part of this slogan is acceptable to us. We agree, in fact we strive, for an end to the idolatrous worship of books which is typical of us. Everything we say or write or think gives off the odor of mold on worn-out pages. Our fathers revered ancient books, and their sons admired modern books also, but the latter brought about no change in the state of affairs. But must the need to abandon books lead inevitably to the second extreme, to the sword? We think that there is yet another way—that is, in becoming close to nature. Undoubtedly, there will be people who will see in this idea a desire, sincere or affected, to return to the bosom of nature or to the natural life in the sense that Ruskin and Rousseau used the terms. This is far from our intention. We mean simply a growing intimacy with nature, and we hope that nature will return to us the freshness, the optimism, the love of beauty characteristic of youth, that it will straighten our crooked back, stretch our muscles and strengthen our resolve. Our young man will cast off the urbanized dress of an old man in the city and put on the many-colored garments of youth! He will bathe in the pure springs of nature and his happiness, his freedom, and his innocence will return to him. . . .

Once we define our belief as a first principle (the belief in optimism and idealism), when we say that the value of life lies not only in what it gives us but also in what we give to it, then we will find it easier to define our duty to the Jewish people. The concept of Judaism has become superficial and its content has been removed. We must rescue the concept of a "true Jew" from the disgrace into which it has fallen. We declare openly and clearly: no one will bear the name of a Jew, or will be numbered in our ranks, who has not absorbed the culture of our people to the depths of his soul. All the arguments about the question of language are ended for us since we proclaim that the Hebrew language is our national language, and that, further, anyone wishing to know our people as it now lives, thinks, and speaks must know the language of the people—Yiddish—and the literature in that tongue. But for us the Bible stands above all; we wish to make it our primer, for it is the never-failing source of idealism, and will forever remain the spring from which the thirsty may drink. We wish to remain young Hebrews, and it will be easier for us to do so if we absorb the spirit of the ancient Hebrews, the spirit of the prophets, the spirit of a moral world-view. . . .

This is how we see our educational tasks. Our ideal is a young Jew of strong body and courageous spirit, whose thoughts are healthy and normal, not hair-splitting and sophistic, who is disciplined and knows how to obey, a Jew to the depth of this heart. His world-view is idealistic; he loves all that is beautiful and noble. We will form a group of such youths—and Zion will be built!

NOTE

1. Ha-Shomer Ha-Zair ("the young guard"), worldwide Zionist youth movement founded in Vienna 1916, merging two groups—Ha-Shomer, a British-styled scouting organization, and Zeirei

Zion, a cultural association—established somewhat earlier in Galicia, then a province of the Austro-Hungarian Empire. Inspired by the revolutionary ferment of the period, but especially by the German youth movement, Ha-Shomer Ha-Zair sought to develop an independent culture and life for Jewish youth. The lifestyle and values of the movement were conceived as an alternative to the life of their parents with its supposed lack of vitality, genuine fellowship, warmth and ideals. Specifically, the movement prepared its members—physically, culturally and morally—for pioneering settlement in Palestine and for the "new" Judaism that would arise there. In the twenties, influenced *inter alios* by Borochov (see document 12 in this chapter), Ha-Shomer Ha-Zair evolved a Marxist-Zionist ideology, which stressed class struggle and pioneering settlement in Palestine, particularly within the framework of communitarian *kibbutzim*. Together with Blau-Weiss, a German Zionist youth movement, Ha-Shomer Ha-Zair was the forerunner of similar youth movements, and was identified with virtually every ideological trend to emerge within Zionism. The youth movements were an important force in Zionist recruitment and in the shaping of the ethos of the Zionist movement.

CONJOINT COMMITTEE OF BRITISH JEWRY
18. An Anti-Zionist Letter to the *Times* (London)[1]

In view of the statement and discussions lately published in the newspapers relative to a projected Jewish resettlement in Palestine on a national basis, the Conjoint Foreign Committee of the Board of Deputies of British Jews[2] and the Anglo-Jewish Association[3] deem it necessary to place on record the views they hold on this important question. . . .

Two points in [the] scheme [recently published by the Zionist leadership] appear to the committee to be open to grave objections on public grounds.

The first is a claim that the Jewish settlements in Palestine shall be recognised as possessing a national character in a political sense. Were this claim of purely local import, it might well be left to settle itself in accordance with the general political exigencies of the reorganisation of the country under a new sovereign power. The Conjoint Committee, indeed, would have no objections to urge against a local Jewish nationality establishing itself under such conditions. But the present claim is not of this limited scope. It is part and parcel of a wider Zionist theory, which regards all the Jewish communities of the world as constituting one homeless nationality, incapable of complete social and political identification, with the nations among whom they dwelt, and it is argued that for this homeless nationality, a political centre and an always available homeland in Palestine are necessary. Against this theory the Conjoint Committee strongly and earnestly protest. Emancipated Jews in this country regard themselves primarily as a religious community, and they have always based their claims to political equality with their fellow-citizens of other creeds on this assumption and on its corollary—that they have no separate national aspirations in a political sense. They hold Judaism to be a religious system, with which their political status has no concern, and they maintain that, as citizens of the countries in which they live, they are fully and sincerely identified with the national spirit and interests of those countries. It fol-

Source: Times (London), May 24, 1917.

lows that the establishment of a Jewish nationality in Palestine, founded on this theory of Jewish homelessness, must have the effect throughout the world of stamping the Jews as strangers in their native lands, and of undermining their hard-won position as citizens and nationals of those lands. Moreover, a Jewish political nationality, carried to its logical conclusion, must, in the present circumstances of the world, be an anachronism. The Jewish religion being the only certain test of a Jew, a Jewish nationality must be founded on, and limited by, the religion. It cannot be supposed for a moment that any section of Jews would aim at a commonwealth governed by religious tests, and limited in the matter of freedom of conscience; but can a religious nationality express itself politically in any other way? The only alternative would be a secular, loose and obscure principle of race and ethnographic peculiarity; but this would not be Jewish in any spiritual sense, and its establishment in Palestine would be a denial of all the ideals and hopes by which the revival of Jewish life in that country commends itself to the Jewish consciousness and Jewish sympathy. On these grounds the Conjoint Committee deprecates most earnestly the national proposals of the Zionists.

The second point in the Zionist programme which has aroused the misgivings of the Conjoint Committee is the proposal to invest the Jewish settlers in Palestine with certain special rights in excess of those enjoyed by the rest of the population, these rights to be embodied in a Charter and administered by a Jewish Chartered Company. Whether it is desirable or not to confide any portion of the administration of Palestine to a Chartered Company need not be discussed, but it is certainly very undesirable that Jews should solicit or accept such a concession, on a basis of political privileges and economic preferences. Any such action would prove a veritable calamity for the whole Jewish people. In all the countries in which they live the principle of equal rights for all religious denominations is vital for them. Were they to set an example to Palestine of disregarding this principle they would convict themselves of having appealed to it for purely selfish motives. In the countries in which they are still struggling for equal rights they would find themselves hopelessly compromised, while in other countries, where those rights have been secured, they would have great difficulty in defending them. The proposal is the more admissible because the Jews are, and will probably long remain, a minority of the population of Palestine, and because it might involve them in the bitterest feuds with their neighbors of other races and religions, which would seriously retard their progress, and would find deplorable echoes throughout the Orient. . . .

NOTES

1. The Balfour Declaration (see the next document) was preceded by protracted negotiations initiated by Chaim Weizmann and Nahum Sokolow on behalf of the World Zionist Organization. There was much discussion on both the formula and timing of the declaration. Despite the support the Zionists enjoyed from such prominent British Jews as Chief Rabbi J. H. Hertz and Herbert Samuel, the presidents of the Board of Deputies of British Jews and the Anglo-Jewish Association issued the above anti-Zionist statement. This statement is said to have induced the British government to adopt a cautious approach and, accordingly, to modify its endorsement of the Zionist aspirations in Palestine.

2. The Board of Deputies of British Jews, founded in 1760, is the representative organization of British Jewry. In 1878, the Board and the Anglo-Jewish Association formed a Conjoint Foreign Committee that operated successfully until 1917 when, discredited by its anti-Zionist line, it disbanded.

3. British organization originally founded, in 1871, for the protection, by diplomatic means, of Jewish rights in backward countries.

19. The Balfour Declaration[1]

Foreign Office
November 2nd, 1917

Dear Lord Rothschild,[2]

I have much pleasure in conveying to you, on behalf of His Majesty's Government, the following declaration of sympathy with Jewish Zionist aspirations which has been submitted to, and approved by, the Cabinet.

His Majesty's Government view with favour the establishment in Palestine of a national home for the Jewish people, and will use their best endeavours to facilitate the achievement of this object, it being clearly understood that nothing shall be done which may prejudice the civil and religious rights of existing non-Jewish communities in Palestine, or the rights and political status enjoyed by Jews in any other country.

I should be grateful if you would bring this declaration to the knowledge of the Zionist Federation.

Yours,
James Balfour

NOTES

1. Chaim Weizmann and Nahum Sokolow, who were instrumental in securing the Balfour Declaration, submitted what they felt to be a moderate formula to the British government to recognize Palestine as "*the* national home of the Jewish people" (emphasis added) and for providing a "Jewish National Colonizing Corporation" for the resettlement and economic development of Palestine. This formula was not accepted. The British government substituted the indefinite article *a* for *the*. The declaration, after having been approved by the British cabinet, was signed by the foreign secretary, Arthur James Balfour, and sent to Lord Rothschild, who was asked to convey it to the World Zionist Organization.

2. Lionel Walter Rothschild, the second Baron Rothschild (1868–1937), honorary president of the Zionist Federation of Great Britain and Ireland at the time of the Balfour Declaration.

Source: "Book of Documents," submitted to the General Assembly of the United Nations by the Jewish Agency for Palestine (New York: The Jewish Agency for Palestine, 1947), p. 1.

WORLD ZIONIST ORGANIZATION—LONDON BUREAU

20. Zionist Manifesto Issued After the Balfour Declaration[1]

To the Jewish People: The second of November, 1917, is an important milestone on the road to our national future; it marks the end of an epoch, and it opens out the beginning of a new era. The Jewish people has but one other such day in its annals: the twenty-eighth of August, 1897, the birthday of the New Zionist Organization at the first Basle Congress. But the analogy is incomplete, because the period which then began

Source: The Jewish Chronicle, December 21, 1917, p. 16.

was Expectation, whereas the period which now begins is Fulfillment.

From then till now, for over twenty years, the Jewish people has been trying to find itself, to achieve a national resurrection. The advance-guard was the organized Zionist party, which in 1897 by its programme demanded a home for the Jewish people in Palestine secured by public law. A great deal was written, spoken, and done to get this demand recognized. The work was carried out by the Zionist Organization on a much greater scale and in a more systematic manner than had been possible for the Hovevei Zion, the first herald of the national ideal, who had tried to give practical shape to the yearning which had burnt like a light in the Jewish spirit during two thousand years of exile and had flamed out at various periods in various forms. The Hovevei Zion had the greatest share in the practical colonization. The Zionist movement wrestled with its opponents and with itself. It collected means outside Palestine, and laboured with all its strength in Palestine. It founded institutions of all kinds for colonization in Palestine. That was a preface, full of hope and faith, full of experiments and illusion, inspired by a sacred and elevating ideal, and productive of many valuable and enduring results.

The time has come to cast the balance of the account. That chapter of propaganda and experiments is complete, and the glory of immortality rests upon it. But we must go further. To look back is the function of the historian; life looks forwards.

The turning point is the Declaration of the British Government that they "view with favour the establishment in Palestine of a National Home for the Jewish people, and will use their best endeavours to facilitate the achievement of this object."

The progress which our idea has made is so colossal and so obvious that it is scarcely necessary to describe it in words. None the less, a few words must be addressed to the Jewish people, not so much by way of explanation, as to demand the new and greater efforts which are imperative.

The outstanding feature of the Declaration is, that what has been a beautiful ideal—and according to our opponents an empty dream—has now been given the possibility of becoming a reality. The aspirations of 1897 now find solid ground in the British Government's official Declaration of the second of November, 1917. That in itself is a gigantic step forward. The world's history, and particularly Jewish history, will not fail to inscribe in golden letters upon its bronze tablets that Great Britain, the shield of civilization, the country which is preeminent in colonization, the school of constitutionalism and freedom, has given us an official promise of support and help in the realization of our ideal of liberty in Palestine. And Great Britain will certainly carry with her the whole political world.

The Declaration of His Majesty's Government coincides with the triumphant march of the British Army in Palestine. The flag of Great Britain waves over Jerusalem and all Judea. It is at such a moment, while the army of Great Britain is taking possession of Palestine, that Mr. Balfour assures us that Great Britain will help us in the establishment of a National Home in Palestine. This is the beginning of the fulfillment.

To appreciate and to understand accurately is the first essential, but it is not all. It is necessary to go further, to determine what is the next step. This must be set forth in plain words.

The Declaration puts in the hands of the Jewish people the key to a new freedom and happiness. All depends on you, the Jewish people, and on you only. The Declaration is the threshold, from which you can place your foot upon holy ground. After eighteen hundred years of suffering your recompense is offered to you. You can come to your haven and your heritage, you can show that the noble blood of your race is still fresh in your veins. But to do that you must begin work anew, with new power and with new means—the ideas and the phrases and the methods of the first period no longer suffice. That would be an anachronism. We need new conceptions, new words, new acts. The methods of the period of realization cannot be the methods of the time of expectation.

In the first place, the whole Jewish people must now unite. Now that fulfillment is displacing expectation, that which was potential in the will of the Jewish people must become actual and reveal itself in strenuous labour. The whole Jewish people must come into the Zionist Organization.

Secondly, a word to our brothers in Palestine. The moment has come to lay the foundations of a national home. You are now under the protection of the British military authorities, who will guard your lives, your property, your freedom. Be worthy of that protection, and begin immediately to build the Jewish National Home upon sound foundations, thoroughly Hebrew, thoroughly national, thoroughly free and democratic. The beginning may decide all that follows.

Thirdly, our loyal acknowledgment of the support of Great Britain must be spontaneous and unmeasured. But it must be the acknowledgment of free men to a country which breeds and loves free men. We must show that what Great Britain has given us through her generosity, is ours by virtue of our intelligence, skill, and courage.

Fourthly, we must have ample means. The means of yesterday are ridiculously small compared with the needs of to-day. Propaganda, the study of practical problems, expeditions, the founding of new offices and commissions, negotiations, preparations for settlement, relief and reconstruction in Palestine—for all these, and other indispensable tasks, colossal material means are necessary, and necessary forthwith. Small and great, poor and rich, must rise to answer the call of this hour with the necessary personal sacrifice.

Fifthly, we need discipline and unity. This is no time for hair-splitting controversy. It is a time for action. We ask for confidence. Be united and tenacious, be quick but not impatient, be free men, but well-disciplined, firm as steel. From now onwards every gathering of Jews must have a practical aim, every speech must deal with a project, every thought must be a brick with which to build the National Home.

These are the directions for your work today.

Worn and weary through your two thousand years of wandering over desert and ocean, driven by every storm and carried on every wave, outcasts and refugees, you may now pass from the misery of exile to a secure home; a home where the Jewish spirit and the old Hebrew genius, which so long have hovered broken-winged over strange nests, can also find healing and be quickened into new life.

N. Sokolow,[2] E. W. Tschlenow,[3] Ch. Weizmann.[4]

NOTES

1. Despite reservations about its ambiguous formulation, the Balfour Declaration—as is reflected in this document—engendered genuine enthusiasm in Zionist circles.

2. Nahum Sokolow (1860–1936). One of the most important figures of post-Herzlian Zionism, he was associated with Chaim Weizmann in the negotiations leading to and following the Balfour Declaration, in connection with which he undertook missions to the French and Italian governments and to the Papal Curia. He was president of the Jewish Agency for Palestine and the World Zionist Organization from 1931 to 1935.

3. Yehiel (Echiel) Tschlenow (1863–1918), a leading figure in Russian and world Zionism.

4. Chaim Weizmann (1874–1952), the most prominent figure in the Zionist movement since the end of World War I. He was president of the World Zionist Organization from 1920 to 1931, and from 1935 to 1946 and the president of the State of Israel from 1949 until his death.

THE COUNCIL OF THE LEAGUE OF NATIONS

21. Mandate for Palestine[1]

Whereas the Principal Allied Powers have agreed, for the purpose of giving effect to the provisions of Article 22 of the Covenant of the League of Nations, to entrust to a Mandatory selected by the said Powers the administration of the territory of Palestine, which formerly belonged to the Turkish Empire, within such boundaries as may be fixed by them; and

Whereas the Principal Allied Powers have also agreed that the Mandatory should be responsible for putting into effect the declaration originally made on November 2, 1917, by the Government of His Britannic Majesty, and adopted by the said Powers, in favour of the establishment in Palestine of a national home for the Jewish people, it being clearly understood that nothing should be done which might prejudice the civil and religious rights of existing non-Jewish communities in Palestine, or the rights and political status enjoyed by Jews in any other country; and

Whereas recognition has thereby been given to the historical connection of the Jewish people with Palestine and to the grounds for reconstituting their national home in that country; and

Whereas the Principal Allied Powers have selected His Britannic Majesty as the Mandatory for Palestine; and

Whereas the mandate in respect of Palestine has been formulated in the following terms and submitted to the Council of the League for approval; and

Whereas by the afore-mentioned Article 22 (paragraph 8) it is provided that the degree of authority, control or administration to be exercised by the Mandatory, not having been previously agreed upon by the Members of the League, shall be explicitly defined by the Council of the League of Nations;

Confirming the said mandate, defines its terms as follows:

Article 1: The Mandatory shall have full powers of legislation and of administration, save as they may be limited by the terms of this mandate.

Article 2: The Mandatory shall be responsible for placing the country under such political, administrative and economic conditions as will secure the establishment of the Jewish national home, as laid down in the preamble, and the development of self-governing institutions, and also for safeguarding the civil and religious rights of all the inhabitants of Palestine, irrespective of race and religion.

Article 3: The Mandatory shall, so far as circumstances permit, encourage local autonomy.

An appropriate Jewish agency[2] shall be recognised as a public body for the purpose of advising and co-operating with the Administration of Palestine in such economic, social and other matters as may affect the establishment of the Jewish national home and the interests of the Jewish population in Palestine, and, subject always to the control of the Administration, to assist and take part in the development of the country.

The Zionist organisation, so long as its organisation and constitution are in the opinion of the Mandatory appropriate, shall be recognised as such agency. It shall take steps in consultation with His Britannic Majesty's Government to secure the co-operation of all Jews who are willing to assist in the establishment of the Jewish national home. . . .

Source: Foreign Office, *The Constitutions of All Countries*, (London: The British Empire, 1938), vol. 1, pp. 539–45.

NOTES

1. The Balfour Declaration was approved by other Allied governments and incorporated in the British Mandate for Palestine on July 24, 1922. The mandate system was created by Article 22 of the government of the League of Nations, which formed part of the Treaty of Versailles of 1919, and then gained the recognition of all states that were members of the League. Article 22 of the Covenant declared that within the ceded territories, inhabited "by people not yet able to stand by themselves under the strenuous condition of the modern world, there should be applied the principle that the well-being and development of such peoples form a sacred trust of civilization," and that the administration of such peoples "should be entrusted to advanced nations" to be exercised by them on behalf of the League. The mandate system applied to the territories ceded after World War I by Germany and Turkey to the principal Allied Powers. The latter appointed mandatories and approved the mandates subject to their confirmation by the League of Nations.

2. Since 1929 the agency established in accordance with this provision was formally known as the Jewish Agency for Palestine.

VLADIMIR JABOTINSKY
22. What the Zionist-Revisionists Want[1]

The first aim of Zionism is the creation of a Jewish majority on both sides of the Jordan River. This is not the ultimate goal of the Zionist movement, which aspires to more far-reaching ideals, such as the solution of the question of Jewish suffering [*Judennotfrage*] throughout the entire world and the creation of a new Jewish culture. The precondition for the attainment of these noble aims, however, is a country in which the Jews constitute a majority. It is only after this majority is attained that Palestine can undergo a normal political development on the basis of democratic, parliamentary principles without thereby endangering the Jewish national character of the country.

"Why proclaim this aim in public?" ask those dreamers who think that Zionism can be turned into a silent conspiracy. They are deceiving themselves. From our standpoint it is first of all useless since all our adversaries not only understand our aims, but also frequently exaggerate them (they say, for instance, that we intend to expel all the non-Jews from Palestine). It is too late to preach a "modified Zionism" [*Kleinzionismus*], for the Arabs have already read Herzl's *The Jewish State* as well as an even more "dangerous" Zionist manifesto—the Bible. Furthermore, the concealment, and particularly the negation of our aims is politically dangerous. It can only lead to the sanction of all preventive measures against Jewish immigration, which, in fact, is what has already happened. [In addition], it provides anti-Zionists with the opportunity to disguise themselves as "cultural Zionists." They argue: "Since the Jews do not wish to form a majority in the country, but rather only intend to create a spiritual center, there is no need to bring tens of thousands of Jews to Palestine annually. For this purpose thousands, and even hundreds, who have been carefully selected and come well-equipped with money, would suffice." . . .

In order to create a solid Jewish majority

Source: Was Wollen die Zionisten-Revisionisten (Paris: Imprimerie Polyglotte, 1926). Trans. here by S. Weinstein.

within twenty-five years in western Palestine we need an average yearly immigration of 40,000 Jews. If we take the area east of the Jordan into consideration, then we will need from 50,000 to 60,000 Jewish immigrants annually.

The immigration of 1924–25 demonstrates that we Jews possess adequate human reserves to support immigration of these dimensions over a long period of time.[2] It must not be forgotten, however, that the economic absorption of such masses in a land the size of ours is a quite complicated task and is nearly unprecedented in the annals of modern colonization. . . .

It follows from this that the creation of a Jewish majority in Palestine requires special measures in order to provide economic opportunities for the new settlers. Our enthusiasm, our national funds, our energy and willingness to sacrifice, as great as they [all] may be, are not sufficient for this. The problem of the orderly absorption of such a large annual influx of people necessitates the direct intervention of governmental authority, that is to say, a whole series of administrative and legislative measures which only a government is in a position to execute.

This is the meaning of the term "political Zionism." No one underestimates the significance of the practical work [being carried out] in Palestine or the importance of our national funds. Zionism is—and must be composed of—90 percent "economics" and only 10 percent "politics." This 10 percent, however, is the precondition, the *conditio sine qua non* of our success. Only a colonization of minor proportions, one which would be capable of creating no more than a minority, that is, a new ghetto, can be realized without the intervention of the state. The formation of a majority and mass immigration are tasks for a state. Their accomplishment demands the active, benevolent and systematic support of the government.

The precise definition of our political demands is thus the first task of political Zionism. It is not enough to speak in general terms of the "fulfillment of [the conditions of] the mandate" or of the "presentation of our political program." Even the friendliest government in the world would only respond to this with the question: "And so, what and which measures are needed?" . . .

The opening up of the area east of the Jordan is the first and most important of the reforms [needed to ensure the absorption of mass Jewish immigration]. To be sure, Trans-Jordan is part of the territory of the mandate, but it was subsequently excluded from the Zionist realm of influence within the mandate.[3] This is a practical and historical injustice. Historically, the area east of the Jordan was always considered to be an integral part of Jewish Palestine. From the practical standpoint of mass immigration Trans-Jordan is perhaps even more important than western Palestine. Its land area is nearly the same, but it has two or three times fewer inhabitants. Also, it possesses more fertile land and more streams. . . . In light of the tremendous Jewish misery in Eastern Europe the exclusion of the best of Palestine from Jewish colonization is also unacceptable from the humanitarian standpoint. . . .

How are these concessions [which we are demanding from the mandatory authority] to be obtained? Suffice it to give a very brief reply to this question: with the same means employed by Herzl, namely, through the instruction, persuasion and organization of public opinion among Jewry, the British and the entire civilized world. This is the sole meaning of the familiar slogan: "political offensive." . . . We have absolute confidence that every just demand, if it is rationally, energetically and boldly defended, will ultimately find a favorable reception among the British people. This is especially true regarding those demands that are in complete harmony with the obligations that England has taken upon herself and whose fulfillment is indispensable for the relief of frightful human suffering. On the basis of this great trust we call upon the Zionist public to renew the Herzlian tradition, [to pursue] the energetic systematic and peaceable political struggle for our demands. . . .

Our attitude toward the Palestinian Arabs is determined by the full recognition of an objective fact: even after the formation of a Jewish majority a considerable Arab population will always remain in Palestine. If things fare badly for this group of inhabitants then things will fare badly for the entire country. The political, economic and cultural welfare of the Arabs will thus always remain one of the main conditions for the well-being of the land of Israel. In the future Jewish state absolute equality will reign between residents of both peoples [*Volksstaemme*], both languages and all religions. All measures must be taken to develop the national autonomy of each of the peoples represented in the country with regard to communal affairs, education, cultural activities and political representation. We believe that in this way the Jewish people in Palestine will in the future be able to convince the Arabs inside and outside the country to reconcile themselves to [a Jewish majority in] the land of Israel.

It is a dangerous falsehood, however, to present such a reconciliation as an already existing fact. Arab public opinion in Palestine is against the creation of a Jewish majority there. The Arabs will continue to fight for a long time—sometimes energetically and sometimes apathetically, sometimes with political means and sometimes with other means—against all that which leads to the creation of this majority until the moment that the overwhelming might of the Jews in the country, i.e., the Jewish majority, becomes a fact. Only then will true reconciliation commence. To close our eyes to this state of affairs is unwise and irresponsible. We Revisionists are keeping our eyes open and want to be prepared for every eventuality. With all the sincere goodwill [we feel] toward the Arab people, we nevertheless firmly believe that the transformation of Palestine into a Jewish state is a postulate of the highest justice and that all opposition to it is unjust. One may neither come to terms with injustice or make any concessions to it. In this case especially, namely, the question of the formation of a majority, there is from our side no possibility to concede anything. One can only struggle against injustice, with peaceful means as long as it is not expressed in acts of violence, and with other means when it assumes the form of violence.

We consider the class struggle within Palestinian Jewry to be an unavoidable and even healthy phenomenon. It is to be noted with satisfaction that the pathos of this struggle in Palestine does not express itself in the struggle over already existing values, as it does elsewhere, but rather in the creation of new values. The working class builds [agricultural] collectives and cooperative workshops while the middle class concentrates [on the development of] private enterprise. Revisionism totally rejects the current fashion of taking a position against one or the other of these methods of construction. . . . The Zionist idea of statehood is obliged to make full use of every form of authentic Jewish energy for the creation of a Jewish majority. The energy of these circles of youths who subscribe to the working-class ideology can be expressed only by the establishment of forms of life in keeping with the spirit of socialism. This is a psychological and organic fact which no argument in the world can alter. To this the Zionist idea of statehood can have only one answer: the workers must establish their own presence in Palestine as they deem fit, and the Zionist movement must support their efforts. It is an equally established fact, however, that the more or less well-to-do Jewish bourgeoisie has completely opposing social tendencies and can establish its own presence in Palestine only on an individualistic basis. To this the Zionist idea of statehood has the same answer: build as you deem fit, I will help. This is the sole correct standpoint for Zionism as a sovereign entity and therefore it is the standpoint of Revisionist ideology. Each form of construction has the right to exist. Each merits assistance and where a conflict between them breaks out the representative of the idea of statehood is to play the role of arbiter. All else is useless polemics. . . .

Zionism appeals to the entire Jewish

people for help in the reconstruction of the land of Israel. We call upon every Jew not only to give but to come and share the responsibility with us. But—and this must remain absolutely clear for all times—*the extent of responsibility depends on what is given*. From the Diaspora Zionism demands not only money, but belief—belief in the Zionist ideal. He who satisfies both these conditions is called a Zionist and is fully entitled to have a voice in decisions concerning budgetary and political problems in Palestine. However, he who offers his money while openly denying that he acknowledges the Zionist ideal is entitled to participate merely in the purely practical questions concerning our enterprise. The political work, the construction of the Jewish state, is the exclusive prerogative of those who profess to be Zionists.

The Jewish Agency—the sole mouthpiece that officially links the Zionist movement to the mandatory power and the League of Nations—must retain this prerogative. Non-Zionists and even assimilationists can be our co-workers, indeed our brothers in the establishment of new settlements. The political struggle for the future, however, can be led only by those who believe in this future—the solution of the Jewish question through the establishment of the Jewish state—and who [wholeheatedly] embrace this belief, which is called Zionism.

NOTES

1. Vladimir Jabotinsky (1880–1940), Russian-born Zionist leader who employed his great oratorical and analytical skill in the advocacy of political Zionism. Like Herzl, he regarded the Jewish problem as preeminently the problem of anti-Semitism and Jewish suffering. Dissatisfied with the acquiesence of the World Zionist Organization to what he believed to be unsatisfactory policies of the Palestine mandatory administration, Jabotinsky resigned from the Zionist Executive in 1923. As an expression of his opposition to official Zionism, he founded in Paris in 1925 the World Union of Zionist Revisionists.

The Balfour Declaration, sanctioned by the League of Nations seemed to fulfill the aspirations laid down in the Basle Program: a home for the Jewish people secured under public law in Palestine. But this formula, like that of the Balfour Declaration, was deliberately vague. To be sure, the Zionists sought territorial sovereignty of the Jewish people in Palestine, but what did this mean concretely. The acquisition of the long sought charter to establish a "home" for the Jewish people in Palestine now obliged the Zionists to determine whether a "home" was communal autonomy or a political sovereign state for the Jews. Ancillary to this question of interpretation of Zionist aspirations were tactical issues that were equally pressing: the implementation of the charter; definition of the territorial boundaries of the mandate; the system and tempo of Jewish settlement; and the determination of Zionist policy for dealing with Arab national claims to Palestine. For a variety of considerations the majority of Zionists initially favored retaining the ambiguous formulation of the Basle Program and followed Weizmann's policy of an "organic" approach for slowly building the Jewish national home. Jabotinsky demanded a radical revision of this policy and called upon the Zionist movement to set as its unequivocal objective the establishment forthwith of a sovereign "Jewish State within its historic boundaries," and to prepare for the evacuation of the Jewish masses to this state. Paradoxically, he made this appeal in the name of Herzl—the author of the Basle Program.

2. In 1924 and 1925 there was a sudden upswing in Jewish immigration to Palestine. In 1924 fourteen thousand Jews entered the country, in 1925 thirty thousand.

MALCOLM MACDONALD

23. White Paper of 1939[1]

In the Statement on Palestine, issued on the ninth of November, 1938, His Majesty's Government announced their intention to invite representatives of the Arabs of Palestine, of certain neighbouring countries and of the Jewish Agency to confer with them in London regarding future policy. It was their sincere hope that, as a result of full, free and frank discussion, some understanding might be reached.... Certain proposals were laid before the Arab and Jewish delegations as the basis of an agreed settlement. Neither the Arab nor the Jewish delegations felt able to accept these proposals, and the conferences therefore did not result in an agreement. Accordingly His Majesty's Government are free to formulate their own policy....

3. The [Peel] Commission and previous Commissions of Enquiry have drawn attention to the ambiguity of certain expressions in the Mandate, such as the expression "a national home for the Jewish people," and they have found in this ambiguity and the resulting uncertainty as to the objectives of policy a fundamental cause of unrest and hostility between Arabs and Jews. His Majesty's Government are convinced that in the interests of the peace and well-being of the whole people of Palestine a clear definition of policy and objectives is essential. The proposal of partition recommended by the Royal Commission would have afforded such clarity, but the establishment of self-supporting independent Arab and Jewish States within Palestine has been found to be impracticable. It has therefore been necessary for His Majesty's Government to devise an alternative policy which will, consistently with their obligations to Arabs and Jews, meet the needs of the situation in Palestine. Their views and proposals are set forth below under the three heads, (I) The Constitution, (II) Immigration, and (III) Land.

I. *The Constitution*

4. It has been urged that the expression "a national home for the Jewish people" offered a prospect that Palestine might in due course become a Jewish State or Commonwealth. His Majesty's Government do not wish to contest the view, which was expressed by the Royal Commission, that the Zionist leaders at the time of the issue of the Balfour Declaration recognised that an ultimate Jewish State was not precluded by the terms of the Declaration. But, with the Royal Commission, His Majesty's Government believe that the framers of the Mandate in which the Balfour Declaration was embodied could not have intended that Palestine should be converted into a Jewish State against the will of the Arab population of the country.

5. The nature of the Jewish National Home in Palestine was further described in the Command Paper of 1922 as follows:

> ... When it is asked what is meant by the development of the Jewish National Home in Palestine, it may be answered that it is not the imposition of a Jewish nationality upon the inhabitants of Palestine as a whole, but the further development of the existing Jewish community, with the assistance of Jews in other parts of the world, in order that it may become a centre in which the Jewish people as a whole may take, on grounds of religion and race, an interest and a pride. But in order that this community should have the best prospect of free development and provide a full opportunity for the Jewish people to display its

Source: British Statement of Policy, May 1939, *CMD*, 6019.

capacities, it is essential that it should know that it is in Palestine as of right and not on sufferance. That is the reason why it is necessary that the existence of a Jewish National Home in Palestine should be internationally guaranteed, and that it should be formally recognised to rest upon an ancient historic connection.

6. His Majesty's Government adhere to this interpretation of the Declaration of 1917 and regard it as an authoritative and comprehensive description of the character of the Jewish National Home in Palestine. It envisaged the further development of the existing Jewish community with the assistance of Jews in other parts of the world. . . .

8. His Majesty's Government are charged as the Mandatory authority "to secure the development of self-governing institutions" in Palestine. Apart from this specific obligation, they would regard it as contrary to the whole spirit of the Mandate system that the population of Palestine should remain forever under Mandatory tutelage. It is proper that the people of the country should as early as possible enjoy the rights of self-government which are exercised by the people of neighbouring countries. His Majesty's Government are unable at present to foresee the exact constitutional forms which the government in Palestine will eventually take, but their objective is self-government, and they desire to see established ultimately an independent Palestine State. It should be a State in which the two peoples in Palestine, Arabs and Jews, share authority in government in such a way that the essential interests of each are secured. . . .

10. In the light of these considerations His Majesty's Government make the following declaration of their intentions regarding the future government of Palestine: (1) The objective of His Majesty's Government is the establishment within ten years of an independent Palestine State in such treaty relations with the United Kingdom as will provide satisfactorily for the commercial and strategic requirements of both countries in the future. This proposal for the establishment of the independent State would involve consultation with the Council of the League of Nations with a view to the termination of the Mandate. (2) The independent State should be one in which Arabs and Jews share in government in such a way as to ensure that the essential interests of each community are safeguarded. . . .

II. [*Immigration*]

12. If immigration has an adverse effect on the economic position in the country, it should clearly be restricted; and equally, if it has a seriously damaging effect on the political position in the country, that is a factor that should not be ignored. Although it is not difficult to contend that the large number of Jewish immigrants who have been admitted so far have been absorbed economically, the fear of the Arabs that this influx will continue indefinitely until the Jewish population is in a position to dominate them has produced consequences which are extremely grave for Jews and Arabs alike and for the peace and prosperity of Palestine. The lamentable disturbances of the past three years are only the latest and most sustained manifestation of this intense Arab apprehension. The methods employed by Arab terrorists against fellow-Arabs and Jews alike must receive unqualified condemnation. But it cannot be denied that fear of indefinite Jewish immigration is widespread amongst the Arab population and that this fear has made possible disturbances which have given a serious setback to economic progress, depleted the Palestine exchequer, rendered life and property insecure, and produced a bitterness between the Arab and Jewish populations which is deplorable between citizens of the same country. If in these circumstances immigration is continued up to the economic absorptive capacity of the country, regardless of all other considerations, a fatal enmity between the two peoples will be perpetuated, and the situation in Palestine may become a permanent source of friction amongst all peoples in the Near and Middle East. His

Majesty's Government cannot take the view that either their obligation under the Mandate, or considerations of common sense and justice, require that they should ignore these circumstances in framing immigration policy.

13. In the view of the Royal Commission, the association of the policy of the Balfour Declaration with the Mandate system implied the belief that Arab hostility to the former would sooner or later be overcome. It has been the hope of British Governments ever since the Balfour Declaration was issued that in time the Arab population, recognizing the advantages to be derived from Jewish settlement and development in Palestine, would become reconciled to the further growth of the Jewish National Home. This hope has not been fulfilled. The alternatives before His Majesty's Government are either (1) to seek to expand the Jewish National Home indefinitely by immigration, against the strongly expressed will of the Arab people of the country; or (2) to permit further expansion of the Jewish National Home by immigration only if the Arabs are prepared to acquiesce in it. . . . His Majesty's Government, after earnest consideration, and taking into account the extent to which the growth of the Jewish National Home has been facilitated over the last twenty years, have decided that the time has come to adopt in principle the second of the alternatives referred to above.

14. It has been urged that all further Jewish immigration into Palestine should be stopped forthwith. His Majesty's Government cannot accept such a proposal. It would damage the whole of the financial and economic system of Palestine and thus affect adversely the interests of Arabs and Jews alike. Moreover, in the view of His Majesty's Government, abruptly to stop further immigration would be unjust to the Jewish National Home. But, above all, His Majesty's Government are conscious of the present unhappy plight of large numbers of Jews who seek a refuge from certain European countries, and they believe that Palestine can and should make a further contribution to the solution of this pressing world problem. In all these circumstances, they believe that they will be acting consistently with their Mandatory obligations to both Arabs and Jews, and in the manner best calculated to serve the interests of the whole people of Palestine, by adopting the following proposals regarding immigration: (1) Jewish immigration during the next five years will be at a rate which, if economic absorptive capacity permits, will bring the Jewish population up to approximately one-third of the total population of the country. Taking into account the expected natural increase of the Arab and Jewish populations, and the number of illegal Jewish immigrants now in the country, this would allow of the admission, as from the beginning of April this year, of some 75,000 immigrants over the next five years. . . .

15. His Majesty's Government are satisfied that, when the immigration over five years which is now contemplated has taken place, they will not be justified in facilitating, nor will they be under any obligation to facilitate, the further development of the Jewish National Home by immigration regardless of the wishes of the Arab population.

III. *Land*

16. . . . The reports of several expert Commissions have indicated that, owing to the natural growth of the Arab population and the steady sale in recent years of Arab land to Jews, there is now in certain areas no room for further transfers of Arab land, whilst in some other areas such transfers of land must be restricted if Arab cultivators are to maintain their existing standard of life and a considerable landless Arab population is not soon to be created. In these circumstances, the High Commissioner will be given general powers to prohibit and regulate transfers of land. These powers will date from the publication of this statement of policy and the High Commissioner will retain them throughout the transitional period. . . .

18. In framing these proposals His Majesty's Government have sincerely endeavoured to act in strict accordance with their obli-

gations under the Mandate to both the Arabs and the Jews. The vagueness of the phrases employed in some instances to describe these obligations has led to controversy and has made the task of interpretation difficult. His Majesty's Government cannot hope to satisfy the partisans of one party or the other.

NOTE

1. As it faced the political exigencies of administering its mandate in Palestine, Great Britain's commitment to the Balfour Declaration underwent continuous re-evaluation. These shifts in policy were largely prompted by the growing Arab opposition to Zionism. In a series of White Papers it was made clear that "a Jewish National Home" did not mean a sovereign Jewish state; moreover, restrictions were imposed on Jewish immigration and areas of settlement. The Arabs, however, were not appeased, and their opposition intensified. From 1936 to 1939 the Arabs of Palestine were in veritable revolt. The Peel Commission's recommendation, published in July 1937, to partition Palestine into separate Jewish and Arab states was reluctantly accepted by the Zionists; the Arab leadership rejected it. In the search for a mutually agreeable solution, further commissions and conferences were held, but to no avail. Exasperated, Colonial Secretary Malcolm MacDonald issued in the name of His Majesty's government the above White Paper. It amounted to a repudiation of the Balfour Declaration, a "death sentence," as Weizmann put it.

THE JEWISH AGENCY FOR PALESTINE[1]
24. Statement on MacDonald White Paper of 1939

1. The effect of the new policy for Palestine laid down by the Mandatory Government in the White Paper of May 17, 1939, is to deny to the Jewish people the right to reconstitute their National Home in their ancestral country. It is a policy which transfers authority over Palestine to the present Arab majority, puts the Jewish population at the mercy of that majority, decrees the stoppage of Jewish immigration as soon as the Jewish inhabitants form one-third of the total [population], and sets up a territorial ghetto for the Jews in their own homeland.

2. The Jewish people regard this breach of faith as a surrender to Arab terrorism. It delivers Great Britain's friends into the hands of those who are fighting her. It must widen the breach between Jews and Arabs, and undermine the hope of peace in Palestine. It is a policy in which the Jewish people will not acquiesce. The new regime announced in the White Paper will be devoid of any moral basis and contrary to international law. Such a regime can only be set up and maintained by force. . . .

5. It is in the darkest hours of Jewish history that the British Government proposes to deprive the Jews of their last hope, and to close the road back to their homeland. It is a cruel blow; doubly cruel because it comes from the Government of a great nation which has extended a helping hand to Jews, and whose position in the world rests upon foundations of moral authority and international good

Source: An Official Communique Issued by the Jewish Agency for Palestine on May 17, 1939, in "Book of Documents," submitted to the General Assembly of the United Nations by the Jewish Agency for Palestine (New York: The Jewish Agency for Palestine, 1947), pp. 137–38.

faith. This blow will not subdue the Jewish people. The historic bond between the people and the land of Israel will not be broken. The Jews will never accept the closing against them of the gates of Palestine, nor let their national home be converted into a ghetto. Jewish pioneers, who in the past three generations have shown their strength in the upbuilding of a derelict country, will from now on display the same strength in defending Jewish immigration, the Jewish home, and Jewish freedom.

NOTE

1. The authority and functions of the Jewish Agency prior to the establishment of the State of Israel were outlined in Article 4 of the British Mandate for Palestine, which provided that "an appropriate Jewish agency shall be recognized as a public body for the purpose of advising and cooperating with the administration of Palestine in such . . . matters as may affect the establishment of the Jewish National Home and the interests of the Jewish population in Palestine," and that "the Zionist Organization . . . shall be recognized as such agency." With the establishment of the State of Israel in May 1948, the Jewish Agency automatically ceased to be the spokesman for the interests of the Jewish population in that country whose internal and external affairs were now conducted solely by its sovereign government, but it continues as an international non-governmental body that functions as the coordinator of all Jewish overseas efforts for Israel.

25. The Biltmore Program[1]

1. American Zionists assembled in this Extraordinary Conference reaffirm their unequivocal devotion to the cause of democratic freedom and international justice to which the people of the United States, allied with the other United Nations, have dedicated themselves, and give expression to their faith in the ultimate victory of humanity and justice over lawlessness and brute force.

2. This Conference offers a message of hope and encouragement to their fellow Jews in the Ghettos and concentration camps of Hitler-dominated Europe and prays that their hour of liberation may not be far distant.

3. The Conference sends its warmest greetings to the Jewish Agency Executive in Jerusalem, to the Va'ad Leumi,[2] and to the whole Yishuv in Palestine, and expresses its profound admiration for their steadfastness and achievements in the face of peril and great difficulties. The Jewish men and women in field and factory, and the thousands of Jewish soldiers of Palestine in the Near East who have acquitted themselves with honor and distinction in Greece, Ethiopia, Syria, Libya and on other battlefields, have shown themselves worthy of their people and ready to assume the rights and responsibilities of nationhood.

4. In our generation, and in particular in the course of the past twenty years, the Jewish people have awakened and transformed their ancient homeland; from 50,000 at the end of the last war, their numbers have increased to more than 500,000. They have made the waste places to bear fruit and the desert to blossom. Their pioneering achievements in agriculture and in industry, embodying new patterns of cooperative endeavor, have written a notable page in the history of colonization.

5. In the new values thus created, their

Source: New Palestine, May 11, 1942, p. 6.

neighbors in Palestine have shared. The Jewish people in its own work of national redemption welcomes the economic, agricultural and national development of the Arab peoples and states. The Conference reaffirms the stand previously adopted at the Congress of the World Zionist Organization, expressing the readiness and the desire of the Jewish people for full cooperation with their Arab neighbors.

6. The Conference calls for the fulfillment of the original purposes of the Balfour Declaration and the Mandate which recognizing *"the historical connection of the Jewish people with Palestine"* was to afford them the opportunity, as stated by President Wilson, to found there a Jewish Commonwealth.

The Conference affirms its unalterable rejection of the White Paper of May 1939 and denies its moral or legal validity. The White Paper seeks to limit, and in fact to nullify Jewish rights to immigration and settlement in Palestine, and, as stated by Mr. Winston Churchill in the House of Commons in May 1939, constitutes "a breach and repudiation of the Balfour Declaration." The policy of the White Paper is cruel and indefensible in its denial of sanctuary to Jews fleeing from Nazi persecution; and at a time when Palestine has become a focal point in the war front of the United Nations, and Palestine Jewry must provide all available manpower for farm and factory and camp, it is in direct conflict with the interests of the allied war effort.

7. In the struggle against the forces of aggression and tyranny, of which Jews were the earliest victims, and which now menace the Jewish National Home, recognition must be given to the right of the Jews of Palestine to play their full part in the war effort and in the defense of their country, through a Jewish military force fighting under its own flag and under the high command of the United Nations.

8. The Conference declares that the new world order that will follow victory cannot be established on foundations of peace, justice and equality, unless the problem of Jewish homelessness is finally solved.

The conference urges that the gates of Palestine be opened; that the Jewish Agency be vested with control of immigration into Palestine and with the necessary authority for upbuilding the country, including the development of its unoccupied and uncultivated lands; and that Palestine be established as a Jewish Commonwealth integrated in the structure of the new democratic world.

Then and only then will the age-old wrong to the Jewish people be righted.

NOTES

1. An extraordinary conference was convened in May 1942, meeting at the Biltmore Hotel, New York City. Since no Zionist congress could be held because of the war, this conference was in effect invested with the authority of a congress. Delegates from every American and Canadian Zionist organization were joined by all European and Palestinian leaders able to attend. Chaim Weizmann, the president of the World Zionist Organization, and David Ben Gurion, the chairman of the Jewish Agency, were in attendance. The conference set a strategy to combat the White Paper of 1939. Ben Gurion, the main force of the conference, explained that Jewry could no longer depend on Great Britain to advance the establishment of a Jewish national home in Palestine, and given the catastrophe currently facing the Jewish people in Europe it was imperative that the mandate be transferred to the Jewish Agency. Some delegates felt that the demand was premature; others urged the adoption of a proposal for a bi-national Jewish Arab state; and some recommended the transference of the mandate to the United Nations. Ben Gurion's position prevailed, and the program was more a symbol than a policy, it was "a slogan, reflecting the radicalization of the Zionist movement as the result of the war and the losses suffered by the Jewish people. It foreshadowed the bitter postwar conflict with the British government" (Walter Laqueur, *A History of Zionism* [New York: Schocken Books, 1976], pp. 548ff.).

2. National Council, executive of the organized Palestinian Jewish community (*Yishuv*). The Va'ad Leumi was recognized by the British mandate as the legal representative of the Yishuv.

HA-SHOMER HA-ZAIR

26. The Case for a Bi-National Palestine[1]

The subject of this memorandum is an attempt to outline a policy for Palestine which, while providing for the ultimate fulfillment of the respective Jewish-Zionist and Arab aspirations is the only one, in our opinion, likely to lead to Jewish-Arab cooperation and to peace and prosperity in this country. . . .

[We hold that] a state is not an end in itself. In its political implications it is only an instrument whereby a people seeks to insure its national welfare and felicity. Assuming that millions of Jews could be saved from their present distress, enabled to build "their own body social in Palestine undisturbed by anyone," yet in no way affect or violate either the Palestine Arabs' "profound attachment to their soil and culture" or their motive of "self-preservation and self-determination"; assuming, furthermore, that adequate safeguards to that effect could be agreed upon and their practicality demonstrated, we fail to see what meaning the controversy of a Jewish *versus* an Arab State would then still possess and why it could not be resolved instead in a form which might be termed a Jewish-Arab State. . . .

We [therefore] suggest that the logical and realistic way out of the situation is an Arab-Jewish State or a Palestinian State which would merit the appellation "Jewish" or "Arab" as little as Belgium deserves to be called Walloon or Flemish, or South Africa—Boer or English. . . . It must be fully grasped and appreciated once and for all that neither in justice nor in practice can either Jews or Arabs maintain exclusive sovereignty over the country. Sovereignty can, however, be exercised *jointly and equally* to the benefit of all concerned. It is this *joint sovereignty* which we have laid down as an essential principal in our efforts to formulate a solution. It is, in fact, the core and substance of bi-nationalism. . . .

Parity in Government has been offered as the practical concept for implementing non-domination in terms of constitution and administration. . . . The essence of parity is in the equality of numerical representation it grants the component units of a state notwithstanding any differences in the numerical voting strength of their electors. It is thus intended as a means of preserving the equality of rights of smaller units against the weight of population enjoyed by the bigger ones. . . . Parity should be regarded as the indispensable constitutional and administrative form of regulating the relations between Jews and Arabs in any system of self-government that may be set up in Palestine. Both peoples are entitled to the maximum amount of safeguards. Any constitution adopted for the country in the future will, in our opinion, have to take special care to provide both communities with adequate means of preventing effectively the enactment of measures designed to encroach upon their vital, legitimate interests. Parity in a legislative body possessing the final vote in passing the important legislation of the country seems to us the most far-reaching of guarantees to either party against eventual domination by the other.

The possibility for constitutionally implementing the principle of joint sovereignty and parity seems to us to lie in a form which we choose to term "Communal Federalism." By this is meant the setting up of a system of government to be constituted as a federation not of territories but of two organized national communities. The territory would re-

Source: Executive Committee of the Ha-Shomer Ha-Zair Workers' Party in Jerusalem, "Memorandum Submitted to the Anglo-American Inquiry Commission" (Jerusalem, 1946), pp. 7, 49, 59ff., 71ff., 126–29, 131, 136.

main undivided and as such would be administered by the Central Government. But this Central Government would, again be set up by two component units jointly administering the country's sovereignty and between them maintaining a state of parity; the demarcation between them, be it noted, would run along national and not along geographical lines.

... The successful operation, however, of any bi-national constitution would require a suitable economic foundation. As long as there continued to exist two distinct national economies within the one country—a Jewish economy and an Arab economy—the functioning of a bi-national state would meet with numerous obstructions. Separate economies tend to become competitive; and economic competition between two races must lead to grave political complications.

Now, the merging of the two existing economies into one broad economic system would depend on an increasing measure of economic cooperation between Jews and Arabs in all walks of life. But this, in turn, would require a greater similarity in their respective living standards as well as in their general social and intellectual levels. Hence, it would be essential to the satisfactory solution of the Palestine problem that the Arab standard of living should be raised as quickly as possible to the present Jewish standard and that simultaneously corresponding changes in the social and educational level should be effected. We have no doubt that it is on the maner in which economic activities in Palestine will affect the Arabs during the next five years that removal of the last vestiges of Arab intransigence depends.

With this in mind, we propose that for the next twenty or twenty-five years Palestine should be placed under the administration of a Special Development Authority the specific objective of which would be:

1. To promote the settlement in Palestine of at least two to three million Jews during the next twenty or twenty-five years by developing the economic possibilities of the country to full capacity.

2. To raise the standard of living and education of the Palestinian Arabs to approximately the present Jewish level during the same period.

3. To promote and actively encourage Jewish-Arab cooperation in every field and by every legitimate means available as well as to encourage the gradual development of self-governing institutions, local and national, on bi-national lines, until the stage of full independence within the framework of a bi-national constitution is reached.

No doubt, it is far from easy to accomplish such a threefold undertaking in a comparatively short time. But, equally we have no doubt that it could be done, given the proper conditions, authority, and leadership....

The other alternative, often spoken of, and advanced with vigour and persuasion by the Royal Commission,[2] is to partition Palestine between the Jews and the Arabs. The Royal Commission started from the assumption that the Jews and the Arabs could not live together. "Half a loaf is better than no bread,"—so let's give each one half the loaf—was the underlying idea behind the Royal Commission's recommendation. It seems simple, it seems easy, it seems plausible. It seems just for an occasion where there is "a conflict of right with right."...

The protagonists of the partition plan cherish the illusion that certain Jewish and Arab circles favour partition as the "lesser evil" so that their support, or at least their acquiescence, might be gained. They overlook the fact that what these Jews and Arabs respectively have in mind is a "good" partition—"good" meaning favourable to their own point of view. But there is no partition that would be "good" for Jews and Arabs at one and the same time. If it were "good" for the Jews, it would rally *all* the Arabs against it, and *vice versa*. Most probably, it would rally both sides against it. The problem would be further complicated by the additional interests bearing on the situation, such as strategic, cultural, commercial, or religious considerations....

[Moreover] these carved out portions of a small country, which would be arbitrarily designated as "states" would be absolutely untenable either economically or politically. Trade and commerce would be strangled. The normal flow of goods and services in a country which naturally presents a single geographic and economic unit would be prevented. It must always be remembered that the reason for any partition would be that "Jews and Arabs will not cooperate." If they could not cooperate in a single Palestine, how would they ever do so across frontiers which each would regard as the burning wounds in their national life? . . . The premise, then, if it is all a true one, that conflict between Jews and Arabs is inevitable, would not be removed by partition. On the contrary, partition would only project it into the future by fixing and amplifying its causes.

By eliminating the unpromising alternatives, once more we reach our original conclusions: that there is no other way out of the deadlock save through a system calculated to bring the Jews and the Arabs together. No matter how much this idea may be criticised as unrealistic by people unable to see beyond a particular, though temporary, situation, we have no doubt that any, or every, other settlement is much more unrealistic. . . .

[A bi-national solution] cannot hope to be carried into effect if Jews, Arabs, and British alike each persist in maintaining that they have always been right while only the others were in the wrong. A thorough heart-searching on the part of all concerned is what is needed. Previous mistakes should be acknowledged. And we hope that the greatness of the cause at stake will not suffer on account of petty considerations. We hope that faith in humanity, in the better qualities of mankind, in progress and the victory of the masses will be the inspiring force in the solution of this grave problem. It is not only Palestine that stands at the cross-roads. The issue affects the entire Middle East. The choice is between friction and harmony, between Balkanisation and cooperation, between fascist reaction and democratic progress. Now is not the time to set the clock back. A wise decision on Palestine will start us off in the right and glorious direction.

NOTES

1. Ha-Shomer Ha-Zair ("the young guard")—a Palestinian political party associated with a Zionist youth movement of the same name (see document 17 in this chapter). In Palestine its members established numerous *kibbutzim*. In 1946 the party received 20 percent of the votes cast in the Histadruth (General Federation of Jewish Labor in Palestine). After the establishment of the State of Israel Ha-Shomer Ha-Zair participated in the formation of Mapam (United Workers' Party).

Since the 1920s various Zionist groups advocated as a solution to the Palestinian conflict the establishment of a bi-national state in which both the Jewish and Arab communities would govern on a parity basis while enjoying communal autonomy. Foremost among the proponents of bi-nationalism was the Brit Shalom, founded in 1926 by Arthur Ruppin; the Ichud, organized in 1942 by *inter alios* J. Magnes and M. Buber; and Ha-Shomer Ha-Zair, which submitted the above proposal to the Anglo-American Inquiry Commission appointed in November 1945 to reconsider the Palestine problem in light of the plight of Jewish survivors of the Holocaust.

2. I.e., the Royal Commission headed by Lord Peel appointed in 1936.

MOSHE SHERTOK[1]

27. Bi-Nationalism Is Unworkable

The [Arab-Jewish conflict in Palestine] can certainly not be met by the adoption of a bi-national solution based on parity. Such a solution, to be operative, presupposes two collective wills acting, by and large, in unison.

It is not a question of individuals combining on some minor matters. Individuals may combine across the barriers of race or community or religion, but on major matters, what one would have to face for a considerable time—heaven knows for how long—would be two national entities, each with a collective will of its own. And to imagine that such a state would be something workable is to presuppose a willingness to walk together on the part of those two national entities.

These prerequisites do not exist, and therefore the issue, I am afraid, is a purely academic one. If, for the sake of argument, I am to assume that it may be practical politics—which I do not—then I would have to say that it would either lead to a state of permanent deadlock on major matters, or that it would lead to the virtual abolition of independence. For in this case again, in order to save the situation from a state of perpetual deadlock, a third party would have to be introduced, either as a result of foresight or as a result of an *esprit d'escalier*.

I do not think I am fully competent to judge the subject from the point of view of comparative constitutional law, but I am not aware of any precedent for such an arrangement. There are bi-national and multinational states in the world, and in all of them, I believe, sovereignty in the ultimate resort is vested in the majority of the population or the majority of some elected assembly. In the last resort the majority prevails, and nowhere do you find two equally balanced communities set against each other. It would have been more logical to expect such an arrangement in those countries than in a country like Palestine, because in those countries there are no such fundamental cleavages and no such diametrical divergencies as we have to face in Palestine. It is not a workable solution.

I must stress again and again that the question is not whether Jews and Arabs can live together within the framework of one state. They can. They do. They will. The question is whether they can operate a state machinery by pulling an equal weight in its councils. They will pull apart. The problem in this country is not how to compose the differences between two static sections of the country's population. If that were the case, it would not be so difficult. The problem is how to reconcile independence with the dynamic development of the Jewish section and of the country as a whole. Perhaps I could formulate it a little differently, and that perhaps would be more correct. The problem is how to make of independence an instrument of development and not a stranglehold on development. But if you assign equality to both statics and dynamics, then the statics will have the advantage. Equality of veto will mean Jewish defeat. What can a Jewish veto do to the Arabs, vitally, crucially? The Arabs are here. Nobody in his senses would try to eradicate them; anyhow you won't do it by a veto. What positive act can doom the hopes of the Arabs to live here, to enjoy prosperity? But an Arab veto could and would prevent Jewish immigration and that is the most fundamental issue for the Jews.

You do not solve the problem by taking

Source: Oral testimony given on July 17, 1947 to the United Nations Special Committee on Palestine, in "The Jewish Plan for Palestine: Memoranda and Statements Presented by the Jewish Agency for Palestine to the United Nations Special Committee on Palestine" (Jerusalem, 1947), pp. 511–13.

immigration out of the context and entrusting it to some ad hoc authority. It cannot be taken out of the context. The problem of immigration is bound up with the whole machinery of Government, with economic policy, with fiscal policy. It is not merely a question of issuing visas and letting people in. It means absorbing those people, providing for them, so shaping the country's economic policy as to enable us to absorb immigrants. If there is harmony between the ad hoc immigration authority and the state machinery, then it is all right. But if there is complete discord, the possibility of it, the certainty of it, then it will not work, and the immigration powers which you might grant to the ad hoc authority would prove a delusion. . . . Again, in a binational state . . . we shall be irresistibly driven to the installation of a third party wielding real power with all the negative results—primarily, no independence.

NOTE

1. Moshe Shertok (1894–1965). From 1933 to 1948 he was the secretary of the Jewish Agency's political department, a position equivalent to the foreign minister of the nascent Jewish National Home. Indeed, with the establishment of the State of Israel in 1948 Shertok (who then Hebraized his name to Sharett) was appointed foreign minister of the Provisional Government.

UNITED NATIONS GENERAL ASSEMBLY
28. Resolution on Palestine[1]

The General Assembly, . . . Considers that the present situation in Palestine is one which is likely to impair the general welfare and friendly relations among nations;

Takes note of the declaration by the mandatory Power that it plans to complete its evacuation of Palestine by August 1, 1948;

Recommends to the United Kingdom, as the mandatory Power for Palestine, and to all other Members of the United Nations the adoption and implementation, with regard to the future government of Palestine, of the Plan of Partition with Economic Union set out below;

Requests that (a) The Security Council take the necessary measures as provided for in the plan for its implementation; . . .

Part I

A. *Termination of Mandate, Partition and Independence*

1. The Mandate for Palestine shall terminate as soon as possible but in any case not later than August 1, 1948.

2. The armed forces of the mandatory Power shall be progressively withdrawn from Palestine, the withdrawal to be completed as soon as possible but in any case not later than August 1, 1948.

The mandatory Power shall advise the Commission, as far in advance as possible, of its intention to terminate the Mandate and to evacuate each area.

The mandatory Power shall use its best endeavours to ensure that an area situated in the territory of the Jewish State, including a seaport and hinterland adequate to provide facilities for a substantial immigration, shall be evacuated at the earliest possible date and in any event not later than February 1, 1948.

3. Independent Arab and Jewish States and the Special International Regime for the City

Source: New York Times, November 30, 1947, p. 1.

of Jerusalem, set forth in part III of this plan, shall come into existence in Palestine two months after the evacuation of the armed forces of the mandatory Power has been completed but in any case not later than October 1, 1948.

D. *Economic Union and Transit*

1. The Provisional Council of Government of each State shall enter into an undertaking with respect to Economic Union and Transit. . . .

Part III—City of Jerusalem

A. *Special Regime*

The City of Jerusalem shall be established as a *corpus separatum* under a special international regime and shall be designated to discharge the responsibilities of the Administering Authority on behalf of the United Nations.

NOTE

1. On February 14, 1947 His Majesty's government announced that given the anarchy reigning in Palestine, the mandate could no longer be properly administered, and that Britain would thus seek to return the mandate to the United Nations (which had replaced the League of Nations). On November 29, 1947 the United Nations General Assembly approved, by a vote of thirty-three to thirteen, of the partition plan for Palestine recommended by the United Nations Special Committee on Palestine. Among the states voting in favor of the plan were the United States and the Soviet Union—Britain abstained. The plan was accepted by the Jews and rejected by the Arabs, who declared that they would do all in their power to prevent its implementation. Britain stated it would do nothing to enforce the plan.

29. Proclamation of the State of Israel[1]

The Land of Israel was the birthplace of the Jewish people. Here their spiritual, religious and national identity was formed. Here they achieved independence and created a culture of national and universal significance. Here they wrote and gave the Bible to the world.

Exiled from Palestine, the Jewish people remained faithful to it in all the countries of their dispersion, never ceasing to pray and hope for their return and the restoration of their national freedom.

Impelled by this historic association, Jews strove throughout the centuries to go back to the land of their fathers and regain their Statehood. In recent decades they returned in their masses. They reclaimed the wilderness, revived their language, built cities and villages, and established a vigorous and evergrowing community, with its own economic and cultural life. They sought peace yet were prepared to defend themselves. They brought the blessings of progress to all inhabitants of the country.

In the year 1897 the First Zionist Congress, inspired by Theodor Herzl's vision of the Jewish State, proclaimed the right of the Jewish people to national revival in their own country.

This right was acknowledged by the Balfour Declaration of November 2, 1917, and reaffirmed by the Mandate of the League of Nations, which gave explicit international

Source: Palestine Post, May 16, 1948, pp. 1–2.

recognition to the historic connection of the Jewish people with Palestine and their right to reconstitute their national home.

The Nazi holocaust, which engulfed millions of Jews in Europe, proved anew the urgency of the reestablishment of the Jewish State, which would solve the problem of Jewish homelessness by opening the gates to all Jews and lifting the Jewish people to equality in the family of nations.

The survivors of the European catastrophe, as well as Jews from other lands, proclaiming their right to a life of dignity, freedom and labor, and undeterred by hazards, hardships and obstacles, have tried unceasingly to enter Palestine.

In the Second World War the Jewish people in Palestine made a full contribution in the struggle of the freedom-loving nations against the Nazi evil. The sacrifices of their soldiers and the efforts of their workers gained them title to rank with the peoples who founded the United Nations.

On November 29, 1947, the General Assembly of the United Nations adopted a Resolution for the establishment of an independent Jewish State in Palestine, and called upon inhabitants of the country to take such steps as may be necessary on their part to put the plan into effect.

This recognition by the United Nations of the right of the Jewish people to establish their independent state may not be revoked. It is, moreover, the self-evident right of the Jewish people to be a nation, like all other nations, in its own sovereign state.

Accordingly, we, the members of the National Council, representing the Jewish people in Palestine and the Zionist movement of the world, met together in solemn assembly today, the day of the termination of the British Mandate for Palestine, and by virtue of the natural and historic right of the Jewish people and of the resolution of the General Assembly of the United Nations, hereby proclaim the establishment of the Jewish State in Palestine, to be called Israel.

We hereby declare that as from the termination of the Mandate at midnight, this night of the fourteenth to the fifteenth of May, 1948, and until the setting up of the duly elected bodies of the State in accordance with a Constitution, to be drawn up by a Constituent Assembly not later than the first day of October 1948, the present National Council shall act as the Provisional State Council, and its executive organ, the National Administration, shall constitute the Provisional Government of the State of Israel.

The State of Israel will be open to the immigration of Jews from all countries of their dispersion, will promote the development of the country for the benefit of all its inhabitants; will be based on the precepts of liberty, justice and peace taught by the Hebrew Prophets; will uphold the full social and political equality of all its citizens, without distinction of race, creed or sex; will guarantee full freedom of conscience, worship, education and culture; will safeguard the sanctity and inviolability of the shrines and Holy Places of all religions; and will dedicate itself to the principles of the Charter of the United Nations.

The State of Israel will be ready to cooperate with the organs and representatives of the United Nations in the implementation of the Resolution of the Assembly of November 29, 1947, and will take steps to bring about the Economic Union over the whole of Palestine.

We appeal to the United Nations to assist the Jewish people in the building of its State and to admit Israel into the family of nations.

In the midst of wanton aggression, we yet call upon the Arab inhabitants of the State of Israel to return to the ways of peace and play their part in the development of the State, with full and equal citizenship and the representation in all its bodies and institutions, provisional or permanent.

We offer peace and amity to all the neighboring states and their peoples, and invite them to cooperate with the independent Jewish nation for the common good of all. The State of Israel is ready to contribute its full share to the peaceful progress and development of the Middle East.

Our call goes out to the Jewish people all

over the world to rally to our side in the task of immigration and development and to stand by us in the great struggle for the fulfillment of the dream of generations—the redemption of Israel.

With trust in the Rock of Israel, we set our hand to this Declaration, at this Session of the Provisional State Council, in the city of Tel Aviv, on this Sabbath eve, the fifth of Iyar, 5708, the fourteenth day of May, 1948.

NOTE

1. At eight o'clock on the morning of May fourteenth, the British lowered the Union Jack in Jerusalem. By mid-afternoon the Arabs' full-scale attack against the Jews was launched. At 4:00 P.M. despite great pressure from the government of the United States and the doubts of many of his colleagues, David Ben Gurion, chairman of the Jewish Agency Executive, read the Declaration of Independence of the State of Israel. The Jewish population of Palestine, except for Jerusalem, which was without electricity, heard the proclamation ceremonies as they were broadcast from the Tel Aviv Museum.

DAVID BEN GURION
30. Address to the Knesset on the Law of Return[1]

. . . The Law of Return and the Law of Citizenship that you have in front of you are connected by a mutual bond and share of common conceptual origin, deriving from the historical uniqueness of the State of Israel, a uniqueness vis-à-vis the past and the future, directed internally and externally. These two laws determine the special character and destiny of the State of Israel as the state bearing the vision of the redemption of Israel.

The State of Israel is a state like all the other states. All the general indications [of statehood] common to the other states are also to be found in the State of Israel. It rests on a specific territory and a population existing within this territory, it possesses sovereignty in internal and external affairs, and its authority does not extend beyond its borders. The State of Israel rules only over its own inhabitants. The Jews in the Diaspora, who are citizens of their countries and who want to remain there, have no legal or civil connection to the State of Israel and the State of Israel does not represent them from any legal standpoint. Nevertheless, the State of Israel differs from the other states both with regard to the factors involved in its establishment and to the aims of its existence. It was established merely two years ago, but its roots are grounded in the far past and it is nourished by ancient springs. Its authority is limited to the area in which its residents dwell, but its gates are open to every Jew wherever he may be. The State of Israel is not a Jewish state merely because the majority of its inhabitants are Jews. It is a state for all the Jews wherever they may be and for every Jew who so desires.

On the fourteenth of May, 1948 a new state was not founded *ex nihilo*. Rather, the crown was restored to its pristine splendor 1,813 years after the independence of Israel was destroyed, during the days of Bar Kochba and Rabbi Akiba. . . .

Source: [Debate on the law of return and law of citizenship, July 3, 1950, Proceedings of the Knesset] 6 (Jerusalem, 1951), pp. 2035-37. Trans. here by S. Weinstein.

The establishment of the Jewish state was not an event limited to the place and time of its emergence. Rather, it is a world event, in the sense of time as well as place, an event summarizing a prolonged historical development. This event has introduced radical reforms and itself serves as a source for alterations and changes exceeding its temporal and spatial framework. . . .

It is not accidental that the Proclamation of Independence began with cogent and succinct passages concerning the perpetual link between the Jewish people and its ancient homeland. Neither is it accidental that as a primary and essential principle governing the direction of the state it was declared before anything else that "the state of Israel shall be open to Jewish immigration and the ingathering of exiles." . . . Just as it was clear that the renewal of the State of Israel is not a beginning, but a continuation from days of yore, so, too was it understood that this renewal is not an end and conclusion but another stage in the long path leading to the full redemption of Israel.

The Diaspora has not ceased with the foundation of the state. In fact, this Diaspora is not a recent phenomenon, having preceded by a long period of time the destruction of our independence. Already in the seventh century B.C.E., simultaneous to the destruction of the First Commonwealth, we find Jews in foreign lands. . . .

In the last meeting of the Zionist Executive in Jerusalem a debate arose concerning the question: ingathering of exiles[2] or ingathering of *all the* exiles? This debate will not be decided by ideology or by political resolutions; only Jewish history can offer a solution. Nevertheless, it is a fact worth noting that foreign volunteers from fifty-five various countries representing all five continents of the world served in the Israel Defence Force [during the War of Independence]. Further, with respect to its scope, dimensions, pace and diversity the return of the exiles taking place in our days has no precedent, even in the annals of the Jewish nation. This is the great, decisive event of our generation that will determine the fate of the State of Israel and fashion the image of the Hebrew nation for many generations; no event in our life from our emergence as a people until the present has been so decisive.

The motives at work in the Jewish immigration [to the land of Israel] in all the generations, including our own, have been many and varied. Longings for redemption, ancient memories, religious feelings, love of homeland and above all, distress—economic, political and spiritual distress. With the foundation of the state a new factor has been added whose strength will continually increase: the power of appeal and attraction [embedded] in the State of Israel. The pace and scope of the return of the exiles will in no small part be dependent upon our capacity to augment this appeal and to turn the State of Israel into the center for the realization of the longings of the nation and for the satisfaction of its material and spiritual needs. In addition, this capacity may very well be the primary factor in attracting immigration from the countries of the new world.

The Law of Return is one of the Basic Laws of the State of Israel. It comprises the central mission of our state, namely, ingathering of exiles. This law determines that it is not the state that grants the Jew from abroad the right to settle in the state. Rather, this right is inherent in him by the very fact that he is a Jew, if only he desires to join in the settlement of the land. In the State of Israel the Jews have no right of priority over the non-Jewish citizens. The State of Israel is grounded on the full equality of rights and obligations for all its citizens. This principle was also laid down in the Proclamation of Independence. . . . The right to return preceded the State of Israel and it is this right that built the state. This right originates in the unbroken historical connection between the people and the homeland, a connection which has also been acknowledged in actual practice by the tribunal of the peoples.

NOTES

1. David Ben Gurion (1886–1973). Chairman of the Zionist Executive and of the Jewish Agency, 1935 to 1948, he also served as the first prime minister of the State of Israel. During the Knesset's deliberations on the Law of Return (see the next document) proposed by the government, Ben Gurion outlined in the above address the rationale of this legislation that would define the infant state as legally committed to the Zionist idea of the repatriation of the "exiled" Jewish people to their ancestral homeland.

2. This ancient expression (in Hebrew, *kibbutz galuyot*), conceptually originating in the Book of Ezekiel, is found in the talmudic literature and in some of the central prayers of the traditional liturgy. The "ingathering of the exiled communities" to the land of Israel was linked with the messianic idea, an association that Ben Gurion acutely appreciated.

31. The Law of Return[1]

1. Every Jew has the right to immigrate to the country.

2. (a) Immigration shall be on the basis of an immigrant's visa. (b) An immigrant's visa shall be granted to every Jew who has expressed his desire to settle in Israel, unless the minister of immigration is convinced that the applicant (1) is acting against the Jewish people, (2) is likely to endanger public health or the security of the state.

3. (a) A Jew who comes to Israel and after his arrival expresses his desire to settle there, is entitled, while he is still in Israel, to obtain an immigrant certificate. (b) The reservations detailed in section 2(b) will also be in force regarding the granting of an immigrant certificate, but a person will not be considered as endangering the public health as a result of an illness he contracted after his arrival in Israel.

4. Every Jew who immigrated to Israel before this law entered into effect, and every Jew born in the country, whether before or after this law entered into effect, shall be considered as having immigrated according to this law.

5. The minister of immigration is responsible for the enforcement of this law, and he is empowered to enact regulations in all matters concerning its implementation as well as the granting of immigrant visas and immigrant papers to minors under the age of eighteen.

NOTE

1. This law was passed unanimously by the Knesset on July 5, 1950.

Source: Reshumot [Official record of the laws of the State of Israel] (Jerusalem, 1951), vol. 51, p. 159. Trans. here by S. Weinstein.

XI

The Holocaust

Holocaust is a term that has come to designate the destruction of European Jewry during the Second World War. The term derives from the Septuagint, the Jewish translation of the Hebrew Scripture into Greek from the third century B.C.E., in which *holokaustos* ("totally burnt") is the Greek rendering of the Hebrew *olah*, the burnt sacrificial offering dedicated *exclusively* to God.[1] Later the term lost its theological nuance and simply denoted sacrifice or vast destruction, especially by fire.

As numbing as it is, the decimation of six million Jews by the Nazis is not an inexplicable, mysterious cataclysm. Although scholars still debate the causes of the Holocaust, all point to a confluence of economic, psychological, political and social factors, among them a history in Germany of political and racial anti-Semitism, a dictatorship, an obedient and disciplined bureaucracy and the technological means for industrial mass murder.

The Nazis initiated their war against the Jews with the rescission of emancipation through a systematic removal of Jewish civic rights and through the legislated de-assimilation of the Jews (see documents 4, 6, 7, 9, 15, 16 and 17). The Jews were forced back into the ghetto—occupational, cultural, social and, in some of the occupied areas, also residential. The ghettoization and induced emigration of the Jews of Europe did not satisfy the demands of the Nazi ideology. By the end of 1941, a policy of extermination of Jewry—the Final Solution—was formulated.

The Final Solution was dutifully and systematically carried out. For the most part it was not executed by rioting mobs and pogroms; rather the Nazis employed the most advanced industrial and organizational means of Western civilization to assure

1. The term *olah qua holokaustos* first appears in the Septuagint, Exod. 18:17. For the meaning of *olah*, see Lev. 1:9.

efficiency and thoroughness (see documents 20 and 25). Puzzling to the student of the Holocaust is the unique morality that guided those responsible for carrying out the Nazi program of genocide (see documents 21, 22 and 26). Also baffling is the apathetic response of the by-standers in the free world. The lack of moral resolve to aid the victims of the Nazi atrocities invites reflection on Goebbel's cynical observation in his diary that the silence of the Churches and the Western democracies indicated implicit approval of Nazi anti-Semitism. In every respect, the Holocaust revealed a profound weakness in the moral conscience of Western man.

ADOLF HITLER

1. A Letter on the Jewish Question[1]

Anti-Semitism as a political movement should not and cannot be determined by emotional factors, but rather by a realization of the facts. And these facts are:

First, Jewry is clearly a racial and not a religious group. . . . All that which is for men a source of higher life—be it religion, socialism or democracy—is for the Jew merely a means to an end, namely, the satisfaction of his lust for power and money.

His actions will result in a racial tuberculosis of peoples [*Rassentuberkulose der Voelker*].

Hence it follows: Anti-Semitism based on purely emotional grounds will find its ultimate expression in the form of pogroms [which are capricious and thus not truly effective]. Rational anti-Semitism, however, must pursue a systematic, *legal* campaign against the Jews, by the revocation of the special privileges they enjoy in contrast to the other foreigners living among us. But the final objective must be the complete removal of the Jews [*die Entfernung der Juden ueberhaupt*].

NOTE

1. Adolf Hitler (1889–1945), Austrian-born leader of the National Socialist German Workers' Party (the Nazi Party) from 1920 and chancellor of the German Reich from 1933 until his suicide on April 30, 1945. Hitler inspired—and was the one ultimately responsible for planning and implementing—the Nazis' "war against the Jews," which culminated in the extermination of European Jewry. He felt himself called upon by Providence to lead the struggle against the Jews. In 1919 he joined a small nationalist, anti-Semitic political circle, the Deutsche Arbeiterpartei (German Workers' Party) and in 1920 he became the Fuehrer of the party which had been renamed the National-Sozialistische Deutsche Arbeiterpartei. Upon the assumption of the leadership of the nascent Nazi Party he declared, "It is our duty to arouse, to whip up, and to incite in our people the instinctive repugnance for the Jews." Hitler's anti-Semitism is an eclectic weave of motifs from Austrian and German political and racial anti-Semitism; his obsession with the world-wide Jewish conspiracy is apparently derived from the *Protocols of the Elders of Zion*, which was translated into German in 1920. (See document 22 in chapter 7.) With the Nazis' accession to power, Hitler's impassioned call for the Aryan peoples to gather together in an apocalyptic effort to check the insidious wiles of Jewry—whom he perceived as the incarnation of absolute evil—gained expression in the policy of "racial purification" and the systematic exclusion of the Jews from German society.

In this letter, which is his earliest extant political statement, Hitler outlined his views on the Jewish question. At the time he was employed as a secret agent of the Press and Propaganda Office of the political department of the Wehrmacht, which was charged with checking the inroads of revolutionary politics within the ranks of the de-mobilizing troops. Adolf Gemlich addressed an inquiry to this office regarding the place of the Jewish question within the Wehrmacht's anti-revolutionary propaganda. Hitler was asked to write the reply to Gemlich, and used the occasion to adumbrate his conception of a rational anti-Semitism (*Antisemitismus der Vernunft*), viz., a two-staged policy of first systematically and legally rescinding the emancipation of the Jews, and then bringing about their total "removal" (*Entfernung*) from German life. (The exact nature of this "final objective" remained for the time being unspecified.) This emphasis on a two-staged solution to the Jewish question continued to characterize Hitler's policy.

Source: Adolf Hitler to Adolf Gemlich, September 16, 1919, Hauptstaatsarchiv Muenchen, in Ernst Deuerlein, "Hitlers Eintritt in die Politik und die Reichswehr," *Vierteljahreshefte fuer Zeitgeschichte*, 7 (1959), pp. 203–5. Trans. here by P. Mendes-Flohr.

ADOLF HITLER
2. Mein Kampf[1]

. . . Today it is difficult, if not impossible, for me to say when the word "Jew" first gave me ground for special thoughts. At home I do not remember having heard the word during my father's lifetime. I believe that the old gentleman would have regarded any special emphasis on this term as cultural backwardness. In the course of his life he had arrived at more or less cosmopolitan views which, despite his pronounced national sentiments, not only remained intact, but also affected me to some extent.

Likewise at school I found no occasion which could have led me to change this inherited picture. . . .

Not until my fourteenth or fifteenth year did I begin to come across the word "Jew," with any frequency, partly in connection with political discussions. This filled me with a mild distaste, and I could not rid myself of an unpleasant feeling that always came over me whenever religious quarrels occurred in my presence.

At that time I did not think anything else of the question.

There were few Jews in Linz. In the course of the centuries their outward appearance had become Europeanized and had taken on a human look; in fact, I even took them for Germans. The absurdity of this idea did not dawn on me because I saw no distinguishing feature but the strange religion. The fact that they had, as I believed, been persecuted on this account sometimes almost turned my distaste at unfavorable remarks about them into horror. . . . Then I came to Vienna. [Gradually], I encountered the Jewish question. . . .

My views with regard to anti-Semitism thus succumbed to the passage of time, and this was my greatest transformation of all.

It cost me the greatest inner soul struggles, and only after months of battle between my reason and my sentiments did my reason begin to emerge victorious. Two years later, my sentiment had followed my reason, and from then on became its most loyal guardian and sentinel.

At the time of this bitter struggle between spiritual education and cold reason, the visual instruction of the Vienna streets had performed invaluable services. There came a time when I no longer, as in the first days, wandered blindly through the mighty city; now with open eyes I saw not only the buildings but also the people.

Once, as I was strolling through the Inner City, I suddenly encountered an apparition in a black caftan and black hair locks. Is this a Jew? was my first thought.

For, to be sure, they had not looked like that in Linz. I observed the man furtively and cautiously, but the longer I stared at this foreign face, scrutinizing feature for feature, the more my first question assumed a new form:

Is this a German?

As always in such cases, I now began to try to relieve my doubts by books. . . .

I could no longer very well doubt that the objects of my study were not Germans of a special religion, but a people in themselves; for since I had begun to concern myself with this question and to take cognizance of the Jews, Vienna appeared to me in a different light than before. Wherever I went, I began to see Jews, and the more I saw, the more

Source: Adolf Hitler, *Mein Kampf*, trans. Ralph Manheim (Boston: Houghton Mifflin Company, 1943), pp. 51-52, 55-62, 64-65.

sharply they became distinguished in my eyes from the rest of humanity. . . .

The cleanliness of this people, moral and otherwise, I must say, is a point in itself. By their very exterior you could tell that these were no lovers of water, and, to your distress, you often knew it with your eyes closed. Later I often grew sick to my stomach from the smell of these caftan-wearers. Added to this, there was their unclean dress and their generally unheroic appearance.

All this could scarcely be called very attractive; but it became positively repulsive when, in addition to their physical uncleanliness, you discovered the moral stains on this "chosen people."

In a short time I was made more thoughtful than ever by my slowly rising insight into the type of activity carried on by the Jews in certain fields.

Was there any form of filth or profligacy, particularly in cultural life, without at least one Jew involved in it?

If you cut even cautiously into such an abscess, you found, like a maggot in a rotting body, often dazzled by the sudden light—a kike!

What had to be reckoned heavily against the Jews in my eyes was when I became acquainted with their activity in the press, art, literature, and the theater. All the unctuous reassurances helped little or nothing. It sufficed to look at a billboard, to study the names of the men behind the horrible trash they advertised, to make you hard for a long time to come. This was pestilence, spiritual pestilence, worse than the Black Death of olden times, and the people was being infected with it! . . .

And I now began to examine my beloved "world press," from this point of view.

And the deeper I probed, the more the object of my former admiration shriveled. The style became more and more unbearable; I could not help rejecting the content as inwardly shallow and banal; the objectivity of exposition now seemed to me more akin to lies than honest truth; and the writers were—Jews.

A thousand things which I had hardly seen before now struck my notice, and others, which had previously given me food for thought, I now learned to grasp and understand.

I now saw the liberal attitude of this press in a different light; the lofty tone in which it answered attacks and its method of killing them with silence now revealed itself to me as a trick as clever as it was treacherous; the transfigured raptures of their theatrical critics were always directed at Jewish writers, and their disapproval never struck anyone but Germans. . . .

The development was accelerated by insights which I gained into a number of other matters. I am referring to the general view of ethics and morals which was quite openly exhibited by a large part of the Jews, and the practical application of which could be seen.

Here again the streets provided an object lesson of a sort which was sometimes positively evil.

The relation of the Jews to prostitution and, even more, to the white-slave traffic, could be studied in Vienna as perhaps in no other city of Western Europe, with the possible exception of the southern French ports. If you walked at night through the streets and alleys of Leopoldstadt, at every step you witnessed proceedings which remained concealed from the majority of the German people until the War gave the soldiers on the eastern front occasion to see similar things, or, better expressed, forced them to see them.

When thus for the first time I recognized the Jew as the cold-hearted, shameless, and calculating director of this revolting vice traffic in the scum of the big city, a cold shudder ran down my back.

But then a flame flared up within me. I no longer avoided discussion of the Jewish question; no, now I sought it. And when I learned to look for the Jew in all branches of cultural and artistic life and its various manifestations, I suddenly encountered him in a place where I would least have expected to find him.

When I recognized the Jew as the leader of the Social Democracy, the scales dropped from my eyes. A long soul struggle had reached its conclusion. . . .

Only now did I become thoroughly acquainted with the seducer of our people.

A single year of my sojourn in Vienna had sufficed to imbue me with the conviction that no worker could be so stubborn that he would not in the end succumb to better knowledge and better explanation. Slowly I had become an expert in their own doctrine and used it as a weapon in the struggle for my own profound conviction.

Success almost always favored my side.

The great masses could be saved, if only with the gravest sacrifice in time and patience.

But a Jew could never be parted from his opinions. . . .

For me this was the time of the greatest spiritual upheaval I have ever had to go through.

I had ceased to be a weak-kneed cosmopolitan and become an anti-Semite.

Just once more—and this was the last time—fearful, oppressive thoughts came to me in profound anguish.

When over long periods of human history I scrutinized the activity of the Jewish people, suddenly there rose up in me the fearful question whether inscrutable Destiny, perhaps for reasons unknown to us poor mortals, did not with eternal and immutable resolve, desire the final victory of this little nation.

Was it possible that the earth had been promised as a reward to this people which lives only for this earth?

Have we an objective right to struggle for our self-preservation, or is this justified only subjectively within ourselves?

As I delved more deeply into the teachings of Marxism and thus in tranquil clarity submitted the deeds of the Jewish people to contemplation, Fate itself gave me its answer.

The Jewish doctrine of Marxism rejects the aristocratic principle of Nature and replaces the eternal privilege of power and strength by the mass of numbers and their dead weight. Thus it denies the value of personality in man, contests the significance of nationality and race, and thereby withdraws from humanity the premise of its existence and its culture. As a foundation of the universe, this doctrine would bring about the end of any order intellectually conceivable to man. And as, in this greatest of all recognizable organisms, the result of an application of such a law could only be chaos, on earth it could only be destruction for the inhabitants of this planet.

If, with the help of his Marxist creed, the Jew is victorious over the other peoples of the world, his crown will be the funeral wreath of humanity and this planet will, as it did thousands of years ago, move through the ether devoid of men.

Eternal Nature inexorably avenges the infringement of her commands.

Hence today I believe that I am acting in accordance with the will of the Almighty Creator: *by defending myself against the Jew, I am fighting for the work of the Lord.*

NOTE

1. In 1923 the National Socialist German Workers' Party attempted a political coup in Munich. Their intention had been to set out from the Bavarian capital to conquer the whole of Germany. The *putsch* ("uprising") failed and Hitler and several of his comrades were brought to trial, a trial which Hitler cleverly used as a forum to publicize the Nazi cause. During the short period he spent in prison, Hitler wrote his autobiography, *Mein Kampf* [My struggle], in which he outlined the program of his movement.

ROBERT WELTSCH

3. Wear the Yellow Badge with Pride[1]

The first of April, 1933, will remain an important date not only in the history of German Jewry, but in that of the entire Jewish people. For the events of the boycott day have not only their political and economic but their moral and spiritual aspects. . . .

It has never been our fashion to lament. To react to happenings of such catastrophic force with sentimental babble we leave to the Jews of that generation which learned nothing and forgot everything. What is needed in the discussion of Jewish affairs is an entirely new tone. We live in a new time. A whole world of ideals and concepts has crashed to ruin. That may give pain to many. But none will be able to sustain himself from now on who shirks realities. We are in the midst of a complete transformation of our intellectual and political, social and economic life. Our gravest concern is this: How does Jewry react?

The first of April, 1933, can be a day of Jewish awakening and Jewish rebirth. If the Jews will it so! If the Jews have the inner maturity and magnanimity. If the Jews are not as their enemies represent them.

Embattled Jewry must affirm itself. . . .

In the midst of all the bitterness that fills us at the reading of the National-Socialist calls to boycott our people and at the false accusations contained therein, for one regulation we are not ungrateful to the boycott committee, which states in paragraph 3: "It goes without saying that we mean business concerns owned by members of the Jewish race. We are not concerned with religion. Jews who have submitted to Catholic or Protestant baptism or have seceded from their religious community remain Jews within the meaning of the order."

That is a sound reminder to all *our* traitors. He who slinks away from his community in order to improve his personal position shall not earn the reward of his treason. In this attitude toward our renegades there may be the faint beginning of a clarification. The Jew who denies his Judaism is no better a citizen than he who affirms it uprightly. To be a renegade is shameful enough. So long as the world seemed to reward this shame, it seemed profitable. The profit is swept away. The Jew is rendered recognizable as such. He wears the yellow badge.

That the boycott committee ordered shields "showing on a black background a yellow spot to be attached to the shops in question," is a terrific symbol. For this shield was supposed to brand us and to render us contemptible in men's eyes. Very well. *We accept the shield and shall make of it a badge of honor.*

Many Jews underwent last Saturday a gruelling experience. Not for an inner conviction, not for loyalty to their people, not for their pride in a magnificent history and in noblest human achievement were they suddenly forced to admit their Jewishness, but by the affixing of a red placard or a yellow badge, sticking their placards to doors and windows and painting the window-panes. For four-and-twenty hours the whole of German Jewry stood, so to speak, in the pillory. In addition to other signs and inscriptions the troopers frequently painted upon windows the *Magen David*. They meant to dishonor us. *Jews, take it upon yourselves, that shield of David, and honor it anew.*

For—at this point begins our duty of self-recollection—if this escutcheon is defiled today, think not that our enemies alone have done it. How many Jews were there among

Source: Robert Weltsch, [Editorial], *Juedische Rundschau*, (April 4, 1933), in Ludwig Lewisohn, *Rebirth* (New York, 1935), pp. 336–41.

us who could not seem to get their fill of undignified self-irony. Judaism was held to be a thing outdated; it was regarded without seriousness; men and women sought to flee from its tragic implications by a grin. But let it not be forgotten that today and for long there has existed a new type, that free and proud Jew, whom the non-Jewish world does not yet know. . . .

Less than thirty years ago it was considered scandalous even to mention the Jewish problem among educated people. The Zionists were regarded as disturbers of the peace haunted by a mania. Today the Jewish problem is such a burning one that every child, every schoolboy, every simple man in the street is ceaselessly preoccupied with it. On April the first every Jew in Germany was stamped as such. According to the latest regulations of the boycott committee it has been determined that, in case of renewal, only two uniform signs are to be employed: "German house" and "Jew." The Jew is known. Evasion or hiding is at an end. The Jewish answer must be clear. It must be that briefest of sentences that Moses spoke to the Egyptians: IVRI ANOCHI, I am a Jew. *We must affirm our Jewishness*. That is the moral meaning of this hour in history. The time is too agitated for argument. . . . But we, the Jewish people, can defend our honor by a moral act. We remember all those who in the course of five thousand years have been called Jews and have been stigmatized as Jews. The world reminds us that we are of them, that we are Jews. And we answer: Yes, it is our pride and glory that we are!

NOTE

1. Born in Prague in 1891, Robert Weltsch served from 1919 to 1938 as the chief editor of the *Juedische Rundschau*, a respected Zionist journal in Berlin. During the Nazi period, the *Juedische Rundschau*, under Weltsch's inspired editorship, sought to instill pride in a humiliated people and to foster Jewish cultural and national consciousness. Since 1940, Weltsch has been a feature writer for the Hebrew daily newspaper *Haaretz* in Tel Aviv, and, since 1956, he has been editor of the *Yearbooks* of the Leo Baeck Institute.

On January 30, 1933, Hitler, as head of the single largest party in the Reichstag, was appointed chancellor of Germany. One of the first acts of the new regime was a program to intimidate its political adversaries, primarily the Socialists and Communists. On March 21, 1933 a concentration camp was established, and within ten days more than 15,000 individuals in Prussia alone were taken into "protective custody." The world-wide protest that ensued was construed by the Nazis as a Jewish plot. This provided them with the pretext to initiate their campaign against the Jews. In retaliation for instigating foreign misunderstanding of their policy to control the intractable opponents of orderly government, the Nazis proclaimed for April 1, 1933 a general boycott of Jewish shops, enterprises and professionals. This boycott was backed by the full weight of the Nazi propaganda machine. On the appointed day, uniformed Nazi pickets appeared in front of Jewish shops, attacked their clients and wrote anti-Jewish slogans on their windows. Students prevented their Jewish classmates and Jewish instructors from entering the universities. Some troops surrounded the courthouses to keep Jewish judges away. The offices of Jewish doctors, lawyers and other professionals were also picketed. In his editorial in the *Juedische Rundschau*, presented here, Robert Weltsch urged the bewildered Jewish community of Germany to respond with inner fortitude and renewed Jewish pride. Weltsch did not, of course, foresee the Final Solution.

4. First Racial Definition (April 11, 1933)[1]

On the basis of paragraph 17 of the Law Regarding the Restoration of Professional Service of April 7, 1933, the following decree is issued:

Addendum paragraph 3. (1) A person is to be regarded as non-Aryan, who is descended from non-Aryan, especially Jewish parents or grandparents. This holds true even if only one parent or grandparent is of non-Aryan descent. This premise especially obtains if one parent or grandparent was of Jewish faith. (2) If a civil servant was not already a civil servant on August 1, 1914, he must prove that he is of Aryan descent, or that he fought at the front, or that he is the son or the father of a man killed during the World War. Proof must be given by submitting documents (birth certificate and marriage certificate of the parents, military papers). (3) If Aryan descent is doubtful, an opinion must be obtained from the expert on racial research commissioned by the Reich Minister of the Interior [*Sachverstaendiger fuer Rasseforschung*].

NOTE

1. Clearly, Nazi policy was to rescind the emancipation of the Jews. The Nazis did not, however, summarily deny the Jews citizenship. They pursued their policy cautiously through the legislature, enacting laws that gradually withdrew Jewish civil rights. The initial legislative stage (from April 1933 to September 1935)—which sought to eliminate the Jews from public office and from economic and cultural life—began immediately after the general boycott of April first. On April 7, 1933 the first anti-Jewish ordinance was passed. The Law for the Restoration of the Professional Civil Service dismissed from the civil service opponents of the regime and non-Aryans. This law included teachers and university lecturers and professors. Similar legislation from the same day prohibited non-Aryans from practicing law. Within the next few months laws were enacted that barred non-Aryans from serving as physicians and dentists in the state social insurance institutions, as patent lawyers, lay assessors, jurors, commercial judges, tax consultants and as editors and publishers. A *numerus clausus* was also introduced in all public educational institutions. The Defense Law of May 21, 1935 excluded non-Aryans from military service. The term *non-Aryan*—used in legal documents until the Nuremberg Laws as a circumlocution for Jews—was defined in the decree reprinted here that was issued on April 11, 1933.

Source: First Decree for the Execution of the Law of Restoration of the Professional Civil Service, in Bernard Dov Weinryb, *Jewish Emancipation Under Attack* (New York: The American Jewish Committee, 1942), pp. 41–42. Reprinted by permission of the American Jewish Committee.

ADOLF HITLER

5. Why the Nuremberg Laws[1]

[With respect to the recent attempts to sabotage German interests in the international arena,] we must point out that we are speaking, almost without exception, of the action of Jewish elements, who stand revealed as factors of incitement and disintegration in the community of peoples [*Traeger dieser Voelkerverhetzung und Voelkerzersetzung*].

Unfortunately it appears that this international ferment in the world has aroused among the Jews of Germany the idea that perhaps the time has come to manifestly oppose the interests of the Jews to the national interests of Germans in the Reich. Bitter complaints have come in from countless places citing the provocative behavior of individual members of this people. On the basis of the striking increase in the number of these occurrences and the similarities among them we may conclude that a certain amount of planning was involved. . . .

Lest these occurrences lead to the outbreak of vigorous defensive actions on the part of the [Aryan] population, we have no choice but to contain the problem through legislative measures. The government of the German Reich is guided in this by the idea that it may nonetheless be possible, through the agency of a definitively secular solution, to create a basis upon which the German people can have a tolerable relation with the Jews. Should this hope not be realized, and Jewish incitement within Germany and outside her borders continue, the situation will be reviewed.

I hereby propose to the Reichstag the adoption of laws which will be read to you by Party Member and Chairman of the Reichstag Goering. . . .

This law is an attempt to find a legislative solution to the Jewish problem; in the event that this attempt fails it will be necessary to transfer the problem, by law, to the National Socialist Party for a final solution [*endgueltige Loesung*]. The National Socialist Party supports all three laws and is in turn supported by the entire German people.

I ask you to adopt these laws.

NOTE

1. In the above speech before the Reichstag, Hitler outlined the ideological objectives of the so-called Nuremberg Laws. For a comprehensive analysis of this speech, see Otto Dov Kulka, "The 'Jewish Question' in the Third Reich" (Ph.D. diss., Hebrew University, 1975), vol. 1, part 1, pp. 200ff.

Source: Adolf Hitler, [Speech before the Reichstag, September 15, 1935], in *Hitler: Reden und Proklamationen, 1932–1945*, ed. Max Domarus (Munich: Sueddeutscher Verlag, 1965), p. 537. Trans. here by L. Sachs and P. Mendes-Flohr.

THE NUREMBERG LAWS (SEPTEMBER 15, 1935)[1]

6. Law for the Protection of German Blood and Honor

Imbued with the conviction that the purity of the German blood is the pre-requisite for the future existence of the German People, and animated with the unbending will to ensure the existence of the German nation for all the future, the Reichstag has unanimously adopted the following law, which is hereby proclaimed.

Paragraph 1. (1) Marriages between Jews and state members [*Staatsangehoerige*] of German or cognate blood are forbidden. Marriages concluded despite this law are invalid, even if they are concluded abroad in order to circumvent this law. (2) Only the State Attorney may initiate the annulment suit.

Paragraph 2. Extra-marital relations between Jews and state members of German or cognate blood are prohibited.

Paragraph 3. Jews must not engage female domestic help in their households among state members of German or cognate blood, who are under forty-five years [of age].

Paragraph 4. (1) The display of the Reich and national flag and the showing of the national colors by Jews is prohibited. (2) However, the display of the Jewish colors is permitted to them. The exercise of this right is placed under the protection of the state.

Paragraph 5. (1) Whosoever acts in violation of the prohibition of Paragraph 1, will be punished with penal servitude. (2) Whosoever acts in violation of Paragraph 2, will be punished with either inprisonment or penal servitude. (3) Whosoever acts in violation of Paragraph 3 or Paragraph 4, will be punished by imprisonment up to one year, with a fine or with either of these penalties. . . .

Paragraph 7. This law goes into effect on the day following promulgation, except for Paragraph 3 which shall go into force on January 1, 1936.

NOTE

1. Despite the discriminatory legislation, all Jews, with the exception of those who were naturalized after September 1918, remained German citizens. Moreover, many Jews were granted extraordinary status, permitting them to practice their professions. By September 1935, however, the Nazi leadership concluded that Germany had reached the political juncture that would allow the full rescission of emancipation. This policy was implemented by the Nuremberg Laws, so-called because they were promulgated at the Nazi Party Congress that met at Nuremberg in September 1935.

Source: Bernard Dov Weinryb, *Jewish Emancipation Under Attack* (New York: The American Jewish Committee, 1942), p. 45. Reprinted by permission of the American Jewish Committee.

THE NUREMBERG LAWS (SEPTEMBER 15, 1935)

7. The Reich Citizenship Law[1]

. . . Paragraph 2. (1) A Reich citizen [*Reichsbuerger*] is only the state member [*Staatsangehoeriger*] who is of German or cognate blood, and who shows through his conduct that he is both desirous and fit to serve in faith the German people and Reich. . . . (3) The Reich citizen is the only holder of full political rights in accordance with the provisions of the laws.

NOTE

1. In effect, the Jews were by virtue of this law and its various amendments deprived of citizenship and all civil and political rights.

Source: Bernard Dov Weinryb, *Jewish Emancipation Under Attack* (New York: The American Jewish Committee, 1942), p. 46. Reprinted by permission of the American Jewish Committee.

A PUBLIC OPINION SURVEY

8. The Response of German Christians to the Nuremberg Laws[1]

KOENIGSBERG: In Allenstein, a town with a predominantly Catholic population, it must be stated that many purchases are still made in Jewish shops. It should also be mentioned that a certain part of the Catholic population displays a friendly attitude toward the Jews and shows little consideration for the race laws. . . . Therefore, no actual success of the anti-Semitic endeavors and no real reduction of the numbers of Jews can be sensed in Allenstein itself. On the other hand, the picture is entirely different in the [predominantly Protestant] cities of the district.

AACHEN: The new laws promulgated in Nuremberg did not meet with unanimous public approval. . . . The church circles do not quite approve of the Jew-legislation, as might have been expected considering the well-known mentality of the local Catholic population. . . . Only the fact that the Jew-legislation would prevent extreme manifestations of anti-Semitic propaganda and riots is received with satisfaction. It would indeed be desirable to stop such anti-Semitic excesses, which are condemned by the greater part of the population.

Source: Report Prepared by the Gestapo and the S.D., September 1935, in Otto Dov Kulka, "The Churches in the Third Reich and the 'Jewish Question' in Light of Secret Nazi Reports on German 'Public Opinion,'" *Proceedings of the Congress of the Commission Internationale d'Histoire Ecclesiastique Comparee (C.I.H.E.C.), Warsaw, July 1978* (forthcoming). We are indebted to Dr. Kulka for bringing our attention to this material.

NOTE

1. Upon their rise to power, the Nazis developed an elaborate system to monitor the public's response to their various deeds and programs. Secret periodical reports—so-called *Lageberichte* or *Stimmungsberichte*—on the mood and attitude of the public were prepared by the security services and various government and party authorities. The picture that these reports reveal, as Dov Kulka observes, "differs from that projected in the daily press and in the official organs and contradicts the image of nation-wide monolithic identification with the regime and its doctrines . . ." (Otto Dov Kulka, "The Churches in the Third Reich and the 'Jewish Question' in Light of Secret Nazi Reports on German 'Public Opinion,'" *Proceedings of the Congress of the Commission Internationale d'Histoire Ecclésiastique Comparée* [*C.I.H.E.C.*], *Warsaw, July 1978* [forthcoming]). We herein present two *Lageberichte* from September 1935, which survey the response of Christian laity to the Nuremberg Laws. The first is from the East German district of Koenigsberg, the second from the district of Aachen in the western part of the country. These similar reports indicate that the response varied, although it had a discernible pattern. "In some areas, we can see that responses denouncing the anti-Jewish policy of the regime came forth from a Catholic minority in a Protestant area or vice versa; in certain sectors, especially in the western part of the Reich, reactions in this spirit were characteristic of the mood of the predominantly Catholic population of these areas" (Kulka, op. cit.). For an extensive study of German public opinion as revealed by the secret *Lageberichte*, see Otto Dov Kulka, " 'Public Opinion' in National Socialist Germany and the 'Jewish Question,'" *Zion: Quarterly for Research in Jewish History*, 40 (Jerusalem, 1975), pp. 186–290.

9. First Decree to the Reich Citizenship Law (November 14, 1935)

. . . Paragraph 4. (1) A Jew cannot be a citizen of the Reich. He cannot exercise the right to vote on political matters, he cannot hold public office. (2) Jewish officials are to be retired on December 31, 1935. In case these officials served either Germany or her allies at the front in the World War, they shall receive as a pension, until they reach their age limit, the full salary last received; they are not, however, to be promoted according to seniority. After they reach the age limit, their pension is to be calculated anew according to the salary last received, on the basis of which their pension was to be computed. (3) Affairs of religious organizations are not affected therewith. (4) The conditions of service of teachers in public Jewish schools remain unchanged until the forthcoming regulation of the Jewish school system.

Paragraph 5. (1) A Jew is anyone who is descended from at least three full Jewish grandparents. (2) A Jewish state member of mixed descent [*Staatsangehoeriger judischer Mischling*] who is descended from two full Jewish grandparents is also considered a Jew, if (a) He belonged to the Jewish religious community at the time this law was issued or [he] joined the community later; (b) He was married to a Jew at the time when the law was issued, or if he married a Jew subsequently; (c) He is the offspring of a marriage with a Jew within the meaning of clause 1, which was contracted after the Law for the Protection of German Blood and Honor of September 15, 1935 went into effect; (d) He is the offspring of extra-marital intercourse with a Jew, within the meaning of clause 1, and will be born out of wedlock after July 31, 1936.

Source: Bernard Dov Weinryb, *Jewish Emancipation Under Attack* (New York: The American Jewish Committee, 1942), p. 46. Reprinted by permission of the American Jewish Committee.

ADOLF HITLER

10. German Economic Goals and the Jewish Question[1]

The Political Situation. Politics are the conduct and the course of the historical struggle for life of the peoples. The aim of these struggles is the assertion of existence. Even the idealistic ideological struggles [*Weltanschauungskaempfe*] have their ultimate cause and are most deeply motivated by nationally [*volklich*] determined purposes and aims of life. Religions and ideologies are, however, always able to impart particular harshness to struggles of this kind, and therefore are also able to give them great historical impressiveness. They leave their imprint on the content of centuries. In such cases it is not possible for peoples and States living within the sphere of such ideological or religious conflicts to dissociate or exclude themselves from these events. . . .

Since the outbreak of the French Revolution, the world has been moving with ever increasing speed towards a new conflict, the most extreme solution of which is called Bolshevism, whose essence and aim, however, is solely the elimination of those strata of mankind which have hitherto provided the leadership and their replacement by worldwide Jewry.

No State will be able to withdraw or even remain at a distance from this historical conflict. *Since Marxism, through its victory in Russia, has established one of the greatest empires in the world as a forward base for its future operations, this question has become a menacing one. . . .*

Germany. Germany will, as always, have to be regarded as the focal point of the Western world in face of the Bolshevist attacks. I do not regard this as an agreeable mission but rather as a handicap and encumbrance upon our national life regrettably resulting from our position in Europe.

We cannot, however, escape this destiny. . . .

It is not the aim of this memorandum to prophesy the time when the untenable situation in Europe will become an open crisis. I only want in these lines, to set down my conviction that this crisis cannot and will not fail to arrive and that it is Germany's duty to secure her own existence by every means in the face of this catastrophe, and to protect herself against it, and that from this compulsion there arises a series of conclusions relating to the most important tasks that our people have ever been set. *For a victory of Bolshevism over Germany would not lead to a Versailles Treaty but the final destruction, indeed to the annihilation of the German people.*

The extent of such a catastrophe cannot be foreseen. How, indeed, would the whole of densely populated Western Europe (including Germany) after a collapse into Bolshevism [*nach einem bolschewistischen Zusammenbruch*] live through probably the most gruesome catastrophe for the peoples which has been visited upon mankind since the downfall of the States of antiquity. *In face of the necessity of defence against this danger, all other considerations must recede into the background as being completely irrelevant. . . .*

I consider it necessary for the Reichstag to pass the following two laws: (1) A law providing the death penalty for economic sabotage, and (2) A law making the whole of Jewry liable for all damage inflicted by individual specimens of this community of criminals upon the German economy, and thus upon the German people. . . .

Source: Unsigned Memorandum on the Four Year Plan, August 1936, *Documents on German Foreign Policy, 1918–1945*, Series C (1933–1937) (Washington, D.C., n.d.), vol. 5, pp. 853–62.

NOTE

1. Anti-Semitism was central to Hitler's political vision and strategy. In this document, an unsigned memorandum on the Four Year Plan of 1936—a plan that was to strengthen the German economy and military preparedness—Hitler presented the ideological rationale of this plan as the "apocalyptic" struggle against Bolshevism and world Jewry. On Hitler's authorship of the memorandum, see *Documents on German Foreign Policy, 1918-1945*, Series C (1933-1937) (Washington, D.C., n.d.), vol. 5, pp. 853ff., n. 1.

R. T. HEYDRICH
11. *Kristallnacht*—A Preliminary Secret Report to H. W. Goering[1]

Re: Action Against the Jews. The reports so far received from the stations of the State Police give the following picture until November 11, 1938:

In numerous cities the plundering of Jewish shops and firms has taken place. In order to prevent further plundering, severe measures were taken everywhere. One hundred seventy-four plunderers were arrested.[2]

The number of pillaged Jewish shops and apartment houses cannot yet be confirmed. The following numbers appearing in the reports—815 destroyed shops, 29 warehouses set on fire or otherwise destroyed, 171 apartment houses set on fire or otherwise destroyed—reflect only part of the actual damage. The urgency with which the reports had to be prepared made it necessary to restrict them to general statements, such as "numerous" or "most shops destroyed." The reported numbers, therefore, will greatly increase.

One hundred ninety-one synagogues were set on fire, another 76 completely demolished. Also, 11 community houses, cemetery chapels and the like were set on fire and another 3 completely destroyed.

About 20,000 Jews were arrested,[3] also 7 Aryans and 3 foreigners. The latter were taken into protective custody.

Thirty-six fatalities were reported, as well as 36 seriously wounded. All fatalities and the seriously wounded are Jews. One Jew is still missing. Among the Jewish fatalities there was one Polish citizen; among the wounded there were 2 Polish citizens.

NOTES

1. Reinhard Tristan Heydrich (1904-1942). In 1931 Heydrich joined the S.S., the private army of the Nazis, as chief of its Intelligence Service. He later became chief of the Gestapo—the German State Secret Police. He was also to play prominent roles in the design and execution of the Final Solution (see document 20 in this chapter).

After the Nuremberg Laws and certain amendments that followed there was a lull in anti-Jewish legislation. After the Anschluss or the occupation

Source: Leon Poliakov and Josef Wulf, eds., *Das Dritte Reich und die Juden: Dokumente und Aufsaetze* (Berlin: Arani-Verlag, GmbH, 1955), pp. 41-42. Trans. here by J. Hessing.

of Austria on March 13, 1938 the pace of legal measures against the Jews suddenly gained momentum. In that year, as a prelude to confiscation, registration of Jewish properties was ordered; the exclusion of Jews from the professions was completed; Jews were issued new passports and identity papers stamped with a red *J* for *Jude*; they were compelled to adopt Jewish names; special taxes were imposed on the Jews; they were required to obtain special permission to open up a new industry or commercial enterprise. Also in that year the Jews of Polish origin who lived in Germany were expelled *en masse*. The Polish government refused to accept the refugees, and they were obliged to live in congested transit camps on the Polish frontier. On November 7, 1938 Herschel Grynszpan, whose family was among the unwanted refugees, assassinated Ernst vom Rath, the third secretary of the German Embassy in Paris. This act provided the Nazis with the pretext to launch the next stage of their Jewish policy: liquidation. Two days later on the night of November ninth a wave of anti-Jewish pogroms swept through Germany and Austria. Although the German government sought to present the *Aktion* against the Jews as a spontaneous protest on the part of the Aryan population, it was clearly orchestrated by the Nazi leadership. Because of the many shop windows broken, the pogroms became known as the *Kristallnacht* or "Night of the Broken Glass." The extent of the pogroms is indicated in this matter of fact "provisional" report made by the head of the Gestapo, Heydrich, to Goering.

Hermann Wilhelm Goering (1893–1946), intimate friend of Hitler from the days of the founding of the Nazi party. With the accession of Hitler to power, he was appointed prime minister of Prussia. In 1936 he was appointed plenipotentiary for the Four Year Plan to prepare the German economy for war. For this purpose he devised a scheme to expropriate Jewish property and wealth.

2. It is hardly to be expected that police intervened in order to protect Jewish property. Goering himself, at a meeting on November 11, 1938, put it very bluntly and cynically: "... Look, gentlemen, I'm quite fed up with the demonstrations. In the end they will not harm the Jews but myself who, in the last resort, is responsible for the economy ..." (cited in Leon Poliakov and Josef Wulf, eds., *Das Dritte Reich und die Juden* [Berlin: Arani-Verlag, GmbH, 1955], p. 41).

3. These Jews were sent to concentration camps at Sachsenhausen, Buchenwald and Dachau. Early in 1939 many were released.

SECURITY SERVICE REPORT ON THE *KRISTALLNACHT*
12. The Operation Against the Jews[1]

The foundations of Jewish life and their internal organization were completely altered as a result of the operation mounted against Jewry in all parts of the Reich in the wake of the murder of the Counsel [of the German Embassy in Paris] Ernst vom Rath by Herschel Grynszpan, a Jew of Polish nationality.

In general the operation took the form of destruction or burning of synagogues, and the destruction of almost all Jewish shops, which were thereby forced to discontinue business. Some Jewish apartments were damaged. Due to lack of attention or ignorance on the part of those involved in the incidents archival materials and valuable art treasures were destroyed.[2] Several Jews were killed or wounded attempting to resist. At the same time, in order to intensify the pressure on emigration, 25,000 Jewish men were brought to concentration camps, in some cases temporarily.

Source: "Die Aktion gegen die Juden am November 9–10, 1938," *Jahreslagebericht des Sicherheitshauptamtes*, vol. 1, pp. 33ff., in Otto Dov Kulka, "'Public Opinion' in National Socialist Germany and the 'Jewish Question,'" *Zion: Quarterly for Research in Jewish History*, 40, nos. 3–4 (Jerusalem, 1975), pp. 283–86. Reprinted by permission of Otto Dov Kulka.

After the conclusion of the operation further steps were taken against the Jews in the form of laws and administrative orders. . . .

Thus the order concerning the arrangement about Jewish property of December 3, 1938 prescribes that the owner of a Jewish business—industrial, agricultural or forestry—can be forced to transfer the business or to close it within a specified period of time. . . . Further decrees were issued forbidding Jews from possessing weapons, and they were decisively excluded from participating in German culture and education.

In addition, a collective fine of one billion marks was imposed upon the Jewish population to compensate for the damages caused by the operation.

Hence, in conclusion it can be stated that Jewry—in so far as German citizens and stateless persons are concerned—has finally been removed from all areas of life of the German people, and Jews, therefore, have only one way to insure their continued existence and that is emigration.

NOTES

1. In its annual report for 1938, the S.D. (the Security Service of the S.S.) provided a lengthy discussion of the *Kristallnacht* and the ensuing legislation against the Jews. In this report the S.D. not only clearly stated the motivations behind the anti-Jewish riots (and later legislation), but also that the S.D. and S.S. had orchestrated the "popular demonstrations against the Jews." This thesis, based on an analysis of previously unpublished materials, is advanced by Otto Dov Kulka ("'Public Opinion' in National Socialist Germany and the 'Jewish Question,'" *Zion: Quarterly for Research in Jewish History*, 40, nos. 3–4 [Jerusalem, 1975], pp. 46–47).

2. The report ascribes this "excess" to the unsupervised actions of forces "who lacked the professional training in dealing with the Jewish Problem." On the night of the riots, Heydrich issued specific orders instructing the S.D. and the Gestapo to protect Jewish archives and art treasures, and generally to observe the "proper" limits of the demonstrations. See Kulka, op. cit., p. 231, n. 114.

H. W. GOERING

13. Decree Regarding Atonement Fine of Jewish State Subjects (November 12, 1938)[1]

The hostile attitude of Jewry toward the German nation and Reich, an attitude which does not even shrink from cowardly murder, demands determined resistance and severe punishment.

On the basis of the Decree of October 18, 1936 for the Execution of the Four Year Plan, I therefore order the following:

Paragraph 1. The payment of an atonement of one billion Reichsmarks to the German Reich is imposed on all Jewish subjects of the State.

Paragraph 2. The Reich Minister of Finance in co-operation with the competent Reich ministers shall issue the regulations for the execution of this decree.

Source: Bernard Dov Weinryb, *Jewish Emancipation Under Attack* (New York: The American Jewish Committee, 1942), p. 53. Reprinted by permission of the American Jewish Committee.

NOTE

1. On the morrow of the *Kristallnacht* Goering convened a conference of Nazi officials to deliberate what punitive action to take against the Jews for the assassination of vom Rath and for thus provoking the "just wrath" of the Aryan masses. The conference decided upon the decree presented here. The same conference also issued a decree compelling Jewish store owners to repair at their own cost the damage incurred to their properties; insurance claims were also nullified. On November 28, 1938 a police order empowered the local authorities to "prevent Jews from entering certain districts or from appearing in public at certain times."

14. Public Response to the *Kristallnacht*

[A] The actions against Jewry in November have been received very badly. . . . The destruction of the synagogues was declared an irresponsible act. . . . It could be observed that the opposition to the anti-Jewish actions was much stronger in the south (with the exception of Ostmark) and in the west of the Reich (with a dense, Catholic and mostly urban population) than in the north (with a Protestant, less dense, and rural population).

[B] Dear Sirs:

The events that occurred amongst our people on and after November ninth of this year [1938] force me to take a clear stand. Far be it from me to disregard the sins that many members of the Jewish people have committed against our Fatherland, especially during the last decades; also, far be it from me to deny the right of orderly and moderate proceedings against the Jewish race. But not only will I by no means justify the numerous excesses against Jewry that took place on and after November ninth of this year (it is unnecessary to go into details), but I reject them, deeply ashamed, as they are a blot on the good name of the Germans.

First of all, I, as a Protestant Christian, have no doubt that the commitment and toleration of such reprisals will evoke the wrath of God against our people and Fatherland, if there is a God in heaven. Just as Israel is cursed and on trial because they were the first who rejected Christ, so surely the same curse will fall upon each and every nation that, by similar deeds, denies Christ in the same way.

I have spoken out of the ardent concern of a Christian who prays to his God everyday for his people and their rulers [*Obrigkeit*]. May God harken to my voice, [I hope] not the only one of this kind. With due respect to the authorities [*Obrigkeit*]. . . .

Source: [A.] Summary statement of a nation-wide *Lagebericht* on the *Kristallnacht* prepared by the S.D., [B.] A Protestant clergyman from Berlin to Hitler, Goering, Goebbles, et al., December 1938. The sender's full name and address were given in the letter. Both *A* and *B* are in Otto Dov Kulka, "The Churches in the Third Reich and the 'Jewish Question' in Light of Secret Nazi Reports on German 'Public Opinion,'" *Proceedings of the Congress of the Commission Internationale d'Histoire Ecclesiastique Comparee (C.I.H.E.C.), Warsaw, July 1978* (forthcoming). We thank Dr. Kulka for bringing these documents to our attention and for granting us permission to cite them.

15. Decree for the Elimination of the Jews from German Economic Life (November 12, 1938)

On the basis of the Decree of October 18, 1936 for the Execution of the Four Year Plan, the following is decreed:

Paragraph 1. (1) From January 1, 1939, Jews are forbidden to own retail stores, mail order houses, or commission houses [*Bestellkontore*] and to engage independently in a trade. (2) They are further forbidden, from that day on, to offer for sale, goods or trade services, to advertise them or to accept orders at markets of all sorts, fairs or exhibitions. (3) Jewish enterprises which violate this decree are to be closed by the police.

Paragraph 2. (1) From January 1, 1939, a Jew can no longer be head of an enterprise within the meaning of the Law of January 20, 1934 for the Regulation of National Work. (2) If a Jew is employed in an enterprise in an executive position, he may be given notice to leave within six weeks. At the expiration of the term of the notice, all claims of the employee, based on the contract, especially such pertaining to maintenance and compensation, expire.

Paragraph 3. (1) A Jew cannot be a member of a cooperative. (2) Jewish membership in cooperatives expires on December 31, 1938. No special notice is necessary.

Source: Bernard Dov Weinryb, *Jewish Emancipation Under Attack* (New York: The American Jewish Committee, 1942), pp. 53–54. Reprinted by permission of the American Jewish Committee.

16. *Numerus Nullus* in Schools (November 16, 1938)

After the ruthless murder of Paris,[1] German teachers no longer can be expected to give instruction to Jewish pupils. It is also self-evident that German students find it unbearable to share classrooms with Jews.

Racial segregation in schools has been carried out in general during the past years, but a small number of Jewish pupils have remained, who can no longer be permitted to attend schools together with German boys and girls. Reserving additional regulations by law, Reich Minister of Education [Bernard] Rust has decreed the following which goes into effect immediately.

1. Jews are forbidden to attend German schools. They are permitted to attend Jewish schools only. Insofar as it has not yet happened all Jewish school boys and girls still attending German schools are to be dismissed immediately.
2. Paragraph 5 of the First Decree to the Reich Citizenship Law of November 14, 1935, specifies who is Jewish.
3. This regulation extends to all schools under the supervision of the Reich Minister of Education, including continuation schools.

Source: Bernard Dov Weinryb, *Jewish Emancipation Under Attack* (New York: The American Jewish Committee, 1942), pp. 54ff. Reprinted by permission of the American Jewish Committee.

NOTE

1. The "murder of Paris" refers to the shooting of Ernst vom Rath, the third secretary of the German Embassy in Paris by Herschel Grynszpan, a Jewish Polish refugee, on November 7, 1938.

17. Ghetto Decreed for Berlin (December 5, 1938)

On the basis of the Police Decree Regarding the Appearance of the Jews in Public of November 28, 1938, the following is decreed for the police district of Berlin.

Paragraph 1. Streets, squares, parks and buildings, from which the Jews are to be banned, are to be closed to Jewish subjects of the State and stateless Jews, both pedestrians and drivers.

Paragraph 2. Jewish subjects of the State and stateless Jews who at the time when this decree goes into effect still live within a district banned to the Jews, must have a local police permit for crossing the banned area.

By July 1, 1939, permits for Jews living within the banned area will no longer be issued.

Paragraph 3. Jewish subjects of the State and stateless Jews who are summoned by an office within the banned area, must obtain a local police permit for twelve hours.

Paragraph 4. The ban on Jews in Berlin comprises the following districts: (1) All theatres, cinemas, cabarets, public concert and lecture halls, museums, amusement places, the halls of the Fair, including the Fair grounds and broadcasting station on the Messedamm, the Deutschlandhalle and the Sport Palace, the Reich Sport Field, all athletic fields including ice skating rinks; (2) All public and private bathing places. . . .

Source: Bernard Dov Weinryb, *Jewish Emancipation Under Attack* (New York: The American Jewish Committee, 1942), p. 56. Reprinted by permission of the American Jewish Committee.

18. The Plight of the Refugees[1]

[A] "German Jews Attempt Suicide After Being Barred in Three Lands" (Cairo, Egypt). After wandering six weeks from port to port in the Mediterranean, eight German Jews attempted suicide by taking poison while their steamer was anchored in Alexandria harbor today. They are six men and two women who left Hamburg by steamer April 22 en route to Alexandria.

They were not allowed to enter Egypt and proceeded with the steamer to Palestine, where their efforts were again unsuccessful. Continuing to Turkey, they were again barred and returned to Alexandria, where

Source: [A] *New York Times*, June 7, 1939, p. 11. [B] "Editorial," *New York Times*, June 8, 1939, p. 24.

their second plea was refused, so no alternative was left but to return to Germany.

When a steward went to their cabins to call them for breakfast he found them writhing in pain, apparently having taken poison. The Alexandria Governor's office was notified, which in turn asked the Ministry of the Interior to be allowed to take them to shore for treatment.

The Ministry ordered a government doctor to examine the victims to determine whether they could be treated aboard ship. The doctor replied that he could not treat them without proper diagnosis, so the refugees were taken to the Jewish Hospital in Alexandria, where they are being cared for.

It is understood the Ministry of Interior has ordered that if they recover they shall again be placed aboard the steamer and deported. How serious their condition is, is still undisclosed.

[B] "The Refugee Ship *St. Louis.*" The saddest ship afloat today, the Hamburg-American liner *St. Louis*, with 900 Jewish refugees aboard, is steaming back towards Germany after a tragic week of frustration at Havana and off the coast of Florida. She is steaming back despite an offer made to Havana yesterday to give a guarantee through the Chase National Bank of $500 apiece for every one of her passengers, men, wome and children, who might land there. President Laredo Bru still has an opportunity to practice those humanitarian sentiments so eloquently expressed in his belated offer of asylum after the refugee ship had been driven from Havana harbor. His cash terms have been met. But the *St. Louis* still keeps her course for Hamburg.

No plague ship ever received a sorrier welcome. Yet those aboard her had sailed with high hopes. About fifty of them, according to our Berlin dispatch, had consular visas. The others all had landing permits for which they had paid; they were unaware that these permits had been declared void in a decree dated May 5. Only a score of the hundreds were admitted. At Havana the *St. Louis*'s decks became a stage for human misery. Relatives and friends clamored to get aboard but were held back. Weeping refugees clamoring to get ashore were halted at guarded gangways. For days the *St. Louis* lingered within the shadow of Morro Castle, but there was no relaxation of the new regulations. Every appeal was rejected. One man reached land. He was pulled from the water with slashed wrists and rushed to a hospital. A second suicide attempt led the captain to warn the authorities that a wave of self-destruction might follow. The forlorn refugees themselves organized a patrol committee. Yet out of Havana the *St. Louis* had to go, trailing pitiful cries of "Auf Wiedersehen." Off our shores she was attended by a helpful Coast Guard vessel alert to pick up any passengers who plunged overboard and thrust them back on the *St. Louis* again. The refugees could even see the shimmering towers of Miami rising from the sea, but for them they were only the battlements of another forbidden city.

It is useless now to discuss what might have been done. The case is disposed of. Germany, with all the hospitality of its concentration camps, will welcome these unfortunates home. Perhaps Cuba, as her spokesmen say, has already taken too many German refugees. Yet all these 900 asked was a temporary haven. Before they sailed virtually all of them had registered under the quota provisions of various nations, including our own. Time would have made them eligible to enter. But there seems to be no help for them now. The *St. Louis* will soon be home with her cargo of despair.

Her next trip is already scheduled. It will be a gay cruise for carefree tourists.

NOTE

1. After the *Kristallnacht* there was absolutely no place for the Jews in the German economic and cultural life; with the banning of the Jewish press and the dissolution of most Jewish cultural and

communal bodies the possibilities of an independent Jewish life also vanished. The pressure on the Jews to emigrate was thus greatly increased. This, of course, was in accordance with Nazi policy. When the Jews still bore German passports emigration was relatively easy. Later, when the deprivation of German citizenship rendered the Jewish emigrants refugees, they increasingly encountered obstacles. For the most part, the existing immigration regulations of such countries as the United States, Britain, Canada and Australia were not eased to accommodate the refugees. Except for Britain in 1938–1939 no entry visas were issued by these countries beyond the scope of the existing emigration quotas. According to estimates of the League of Nations' high commissioner for refugees 329,000 Jews fled Nazi persecution in the years 1933–1939, of whom 315,000 left Germany proper. In June 1933 there were 503,000 Jews by religion in Germany, six years later there were 214,000. The desperate situation of many of these refugees is reflected in these two items from the *New York Times*.

REICHSVEREINIGUNG DER JUDEN IN DEUTSCHLAND
19. A Proposal for Jewish Education in the Face of Catastrophe[1]

[The executive chairman,] Dr. Otto Hirsch[2] . . . stresses the necessity to decide on the principles governing the educational preparations for group and mass settlement [*Gruppen- und Massensiedlung*]. He proposes the following draft for a circular to be addressed mainly to the educators:

The decrease in individual emigration obliged the Reichsvereinigung to prepare group and mass settlement. A reconsideration of the essence of the Jewish community is necessary as a basis for the educational work in the schools, vocational retraining and adult education. This educational work must be guided by the following principles:

1. The Jewish people is the pillar of Jewish communal existence [*Traeger der juedischen Gemeinschaft*]. It is therefore necessary to awaken and strengthen the consciousness of the bonds of nationhood [*volksmaessige Verbundenheit*] in every possible way, especially by stressing the continuity of Jewish history.

2. The Jewish community was endowed with its spirit and character by the Jewish religion. Therefore, access to it must be granted to every individual and every group.

3. Hebrew as the language of the Jewish people and its religion is an essential component of every Jewish education.

4. The demands of mass-settlement call for education towards a social community within the community [*zur sozialen Gemeinschaft in der Gemeinschaft*].

5. The aim of this education is to prepare for life in the Jewish settlement. It is our wish that [this settlement] be realized in the Jewish land of Palestine. However, these principles are valid for educational preparation towards life in any Jewish settlement wherever it may be.

NOTES

1. The National Union of the Jews in Germany, the compulsory organization of all Jews, as defined by the Nuremberg Laws, established on July 4, 1939 by an executive ordinance appended to the Reich's Citizenship Law of 1935. The Reichsvereinigung replaced the previous framework of German Jewry called the Reichsvertretung der Juden in Deutschland (National Representation of the

Source: Otto Dov Kulka, "The '*Reichsvereinigung* of the Jews in Germany' (1938/9–1943)" (Jerusalem: Yad Vashem, forthcoming). We thank Dr. Dov Kulka for bringing this document to our attention.

Jews in Germany). The Reichsvereinigung was supervised by the Ministry of the Interior, i.e., by the security police. Its duties, as specified by law, were to organize Jewish emigration and to administer the Jewish educational and welfare system. The Nazis' interest in the Reichsvereinigung was purely bureaucratic, namely, to facilitate their dealings with the Jews. On June 10, 1943 the Reichsvereinigung was dissolved and its remaining leadership arrested and deported to Theresienstadt. The above document, previously unpublished, is the appendix to the minutes of a session of the executive board of the Reichsvereinigung der Juden in Deutschland, at the end of 1940. Now in the archives of the Reichsvereinigung, this document was recently discovered in the cellar of a destroyed East Berlin synagogue.

In June 1940 the Reichsvereinigung was informed by the security police of "a plan for the comprehensive solution to the Jewish problem in Europe by the deportation of Jews from their countries of residence and their concentration in a reservation [*Reservatgebiet*] in a colonial area." The Nazis had in mind here the island of Madagascar. The Reichsvereinigung was charged with preparing the mechanisms for implementing the plan. The document published here, the only concrete response found in the archives of the Reichsvereinigung, is a proposal for an educational program for the Jewish people in the prospective *Reservatgebiet*. This proposal indicates, according to Dov Kulka, that the Reichsvereinigung was not a helpless body, obsequiously beholden to the Gestapo, as some historians assume. Rather the Reichsvereinigung provided resolute leadership and sought to secure the physical and spiritual existence of the remnant of German Jewry. This document clearly demonstrates that the course adopted to cope with the new situation created in the early 1940s was essentially a continuation of the trends that had forged the character of Jewish education in Germany in the 1930s, when the Jewish community was faced with the rise of the National-Socialist regime. Moreover, although the majority of the members of the executive was not Zionist, we can see the growing influence of the nationalist Jewish concept on its outlook, as expressed by the emphasis placed upon the Hebrew language and historic consciousness. At the same time, the document foresees a central role for Jewish religion, even for those sectors of the public that had become alienated from it, and notes the need to constitute a society based on the principles of social justice in the land to which they would be deported .... On the surface, this document would appear to indicate that the Jewish leadership was oblivious to both the cruel reality of its situation and the gruesome prospect of the "Solution of the Jewish Question" in the near future. But, it also indicates that spiritual and social values still assumed an important role in dictating the direction and priorities of the Reichsvereinigung's practical work. [Otto Dov Kulka, "The '*Reichsvereinigung* of the Jews in Germany' (1938/9–1943)" (Forthcoming).]

2. Otto Hirsch (1885–1941). Before the accession of the Nazis, he was a senior official in the Ministry of the Interior, and active in various Jewish communal organizations. In 1933 he was elected executive chairman of the Reichsvertretung der Juden in Deutschland. Imprisoned several times by the Nazis because of his recalcitrance, he rejected several opportunities to emigrate. Arrested in the spring of 1941, he was murdered at the concentration camp of Mauthausen on June 19, 1941.

20. Protocols of the Wannsee Conference (January 20, 1942)[1]

... Chief of the Security Police Security Service Lieutenant General Heydrich, opened proceedings by addressing the executive charged by the Reich Marshal [Goering] with the preparation of the Final Solution of the European Jewish question, and pointed out that invitations to the conference in progress had been issued to elucidate some questions of principle. The Reich Marshal's wish to obtain an outline of the organizational mate-

Source: Jeno Levai, ed., *Eichmann in Hungary: Documents* (Budapest: Pannonia Press, 1961), pp. 24–28.

rial and financial aspects involved in the Final Solution of the European Jewish question, called for preliminary consultations of all the central authorities directly affected by these problems, in order to develop action on parallel lines.

Concerning elaboration of a final solution to the Jewish question, he stated that regardless of geographical borders, the decision rested centrally with [Himmler], the SS *Reichsfuehrer* and Chief of the German Police.

Then the Chief of the Security Police and Security Service gave a brief survey of the battle waged up to the time of the meeting against the adversary. The essential stages were: (a) removal of Jews from the various walks of life of the German people; (b) removal of Jews from the *Lebensraum* [living space] of the German people.

To accomplish these endeavours, acceleration of the emigration of Jews from Reich territory was to be intensified and supported by planned activity as the only means of solution for the time being. . . .

The work of emigration had become a problem not only to Germany but also to the authorities in the countries of destination, i.e., a problem that had to be dealt with also by the immigration countries. Financial difficulties, increased visa and landing fees exacted by various foreign governments, and lack of shipping space presented growing obstacles, while strict limitation of immigration or complete embargo rendered efforts at emigration extremely difficult. Despite these difficulties, altogether 537,000 Jews had nevertheless been brought to emigrate from the day of the assumption of power until the day of October 31, 1941; of these, 360,000 left the Old Reich after January 30, 1933; 147,000 left Austria after March 15, 1938; 30,000 left the Protectorate of Bohemia and Moravia after March 15, 1939.

Emigration was financed by the Jews and the Jewish political organizations themselves. In order to avoid the stay of indigent Jews, the principle was established and acted on that wealthy Jews had to finance the emigration of the poor ones; a certain amount, commensurate to financial circumstances, was exacted from rich Jews as a contribution to emigration funds employed to cover the emigration costs of needy Jews.

In addition to *Reichsmark* expenses, foreign currency was required for visa and landing fees. In order to spare German foreign-currency holdings, Jewish financial institutions abroad were approached through inland Jewish organizations and requested to provide for adequate amounts of foreign currency. Up to October 30, 1941, the donations of foreign Jewry put at our disposal the sum of exactly 9,500,000 dollars.

In the meantime, with a view to the dangers of wartime emigration and the possibilities offered by the East, emigration of the Jews was prohibited by the SS *Reichsfuehrer* and Chief of the German Police [Himmler].

Instead of emigration, evacuation of the Jews to the East had then been taken into consideration as another possibility of solution, after previous approval by the Fuehrer.

These actions are, however, to be regarded as temporary expedients; practical experiences were nonetheless accumulated here, which are of outstanding importance for the Final Solution of the Jewish question in the future.

This Final Solution of the European Jewish question is estimated to apply to exactly eleven million Jews, distributed over various countries as follows:[2]

Country	*Number*
A. Old Reich	131,800
Ostmark [Austria]	43,700
Eastern Areas	420,000
Generalgouvernement[3]	2,284,000
Bialystok	400,000
Protectorate of Bohemia and Moravia	74,000
Estonia—Free of Jews	
Latvia	3,500
Lithuania	34,000
Belgium	43,000
Denmark	5,600
France, occupied territory	165,000
France, unoccupied territory	700,000
Greece	69,600
Netherlands	160,800
Norway	1,300

	Country	*Number*
B.	Bulgaria	48,000
	England	330,000
	Finland	2,300
	Ireland	4,000
	Italy, including Sardinia	58,000
	Albania	200
	Croatia	40,000
	Portugal	3,000
	Rumania, including Bessarabia	342,000
	Sweden	8,000
	Switzerland	18,000
	Serbia	10,000
	Slovakia	88,000
	Spain	6,000
	Turkey (European part)	55,300
	Hungary	742,000
	USSR	5,000,000
	Ukraine	2,994,685
	White Russia (without Bialystok)	446,484
	Total	over 11,000,000

The figures quoted for various countries refer to Jews of Jewish religion, since the definition of Judaism by racial principles is not yet practised everywhere. . . .

With adequate management the Final Solution is expected to result in Jews being put to appropriate work in the East. In large groups of workers, the sexes separated, able-bodied Jews should be made to build roads in these areas, which would doubtlessly lead to the natural diminution of numbers at a considerable rate.

The final remnant, doubtlessly consisting of the toughest and most resistant individuals, would have to be treated accordingly, since they would have survived by natural development.

When it [comes] to the practical execution of the Final Solution, Europe would have to be combed from west to east; Reich territory, including the Protectorate of Bohemia and Moravia, would have to be exempted, for reasons of housing problems and other socio-political necessities.

The evacuated Jews should be taken in successive trainloads first to so-called transit ghettos, to be transported from there to the East.

An essential precondition, continued SS Lieutenant General Heydrich, for carrying out the evacuation at all, was an accurate basis of criteria concerning the group of persons involved.

It was intended that Jews over 65 years of age should not be evacuated, but transferred to old-age ghettos—presumably Theresienstadt.[4]

In addition to old-age groups—out of the approximately 280,000 Jews living in the Old Reich and Austria, about 30 per cent were over 65 years on October 31, 1941—the old-age ghettos would also take in badly incapacitated Jewish war veterans and Jews holding medals for distinguished military services (Iron Cross First Class). This expedient solution should effectively neutralize the basis for many [foreign] interventions. . . .

Initiation of the several major actions of evacuation would greatly depend on military development. In connection with the handling of the Final Solution in European countries under our occupation of influence, it has been proposed that available experts in this field attached to the Foreign Ministry should discuss matters with the competent executives of the Security Police and the Security Service.

In Slovakia and Croatia the situation had grown less difficult, since the essential and crucial problems have already been solved there in this respect. Also in Rumania, an executive of Jewish affairs has been installed in the meantime. To regulate the question in Hungary it was necessary to force on the Hungarian government a counsellor on Jewish questions without delay.

As concerns the initiation of preparations for settling the problem in Italy, Lieutenant General Heydrich thought it advisable to establish contact with the Chief of Police [Himmler].

In occupied and unoccupied France alike, rounding up Jews for evacuation should in all probability be carried out without any serious difficulties.

Deputy State Secretary Luther [of the Foreign Office] thereupon informed the conference that, upon thorough tackling of the problems, difficulties would arise in several countries, for instance in the northern countries; therefore it appeared desirable to omit these countries for the time being. Owing to the small number of Jews in question, their omission would by no means constitute a noteworthy limitation. On the other hand, the Foreign Ministry did not anticipate too great difficulties in the countries of South-East and South-West Europe. . . .

Efforts to bring about a Final Solution should be based mainly on the Nuremberg Laws, while the solution of mixed marriages and half-blood questions also continued to form a precondition for clearing up the problem completely. . . .[5]

NOTES

1. On September 1, 1939 the armies of Germany invaded Poland. World War II had commenced. By June 1941, the beginning of the campaign against Russia, the Germans had succeeded in conquering most of Europe, inheriting millions of Jews. The Nazis desired an expeditious and radical solution to the Jewish question. But it was soon realized that the policy of forced emigration was no longer a feasible solution. The vast number of Jews in question, the general unwillingness of the prospective countries of refuge to accept these Jews and the fact that most of these countries were now engaged in war against Germany or its allies obliged the Nazis to search for an alternative solution. Sometime in the late spring or early summer of 1941 Hitler issued an oral order for "a Final Solution of the Jewish Question." In Nazi parlance the Final Solution became a euphemism for the physical liquidation of the Jews. In the summer of 1941 construction on the first *Vernichtungslager* ("annihilation camp") was begun. The camp at Chelmno, some twenty-five miles from the Polish city of Lodz, commenced operation on December 8, 1941. The chief of the Gestapo, Reinhard Heydrich, was designated to supervise the overall operational aspects of the Final Solution. On January 20, 1942, he convened a conference of representatives of the various state bureaucracies that would be involved in the Final Solution. The conference, which met at Wannsee, a suburb of Berlin, was of utmost importance, for it set and coordinated the plans for the extermination. The minutes of the conference are presented here.

2. These figures, far from accurate, suggest that Heydrich believed that all of Europe would fall to the Nazis, extending the purview of the Final Solution.

3. The partition and occupation of Poland gave Hitler the opportunity to carry out his racial policies. On October 12, 1939, he issued a decree establishing a civil administration in Poland, called Generalgouvernement, with Hans Frank as governor general.

4. Theresienstadt, near a town in Bohemia of that name, was to become a "model camp," the only one into which the Nazis would permit foreign observers.

5. The conference went on to discuss in detail the status of the *Mischlinge*, i.e., persons of mixed German-Jewish blood. Second degree *Mischlinge*, for instance, being only a quarter Jewish, were in principle to be regarded as Germans. Should these *Mischlinge*, however, have "an exceptionally poor racial appearance" or should "they feel and behave like Jews," they were to be treated as Jews. Regarding the *Mischlinge*, sterilization was proposed by one of the delegates as the most humane alternative to evacuation. This proposal was endorsed by the representative of the Ministry of the Interior, because it would ease the "endless administrative task" of determining the exact status of *Mischlinge*. A representative of the Four Year Plan urged that Jews employed in war industries not be evacuated until replacements were found. The military governor of Poland welcomed the Final Solution, because the Jews constituted "a substantial danger as carriers of epidemics." Moreover, the majority of the Jews in Poland, he held, were useless and not capable of working.

P. JOSEF GOEBBELS

21. The Nazi Response to Resistance[1]

May 27, 1942. . . . An alarming news item has come from Prague. In the suburbs of Prague an attempt has been made to assassinate Heydrich with a bomb. . . . We must be clear about this, such an assassination would become a model for others unless we proceed to take brutal measures. . . .

I shall now likewise complete my war against the Berlin Jews. At the moment I am having a list drawn up of the Jewish hostages to be followed by many arrests. I have no desire to put myself into a position to be shot in the belly by a twenty-two-year-old Jew from the East—such types are to be found among the assassins at the Anti-Soviet Exhibition. Ten Jews in a concentration camp or under the earth are better than one going free. We are engaged today in a fight for life and death and he will win who most energetically defends his political existence. Surely we are the one.

May 29, 1942. [A few days later Goebbels jotted down further details of the new anti-Jewish drive after noticing that Heydrich's condition was very disquieting.[2]] We still don't know the background of the plot. . . . In any case, we are making the Jews pay. I am having my planned arrest of 500 Jews in Berlin carried out, and am informing the leaders of the Jewish community that for every Jewish plot or attempt at revolt 100 or 150 Jews whom we are holding are to be shot. As a consequence of the attempt on Heydrich a whole group of Jews, against whom we have evidence, were shot in Sachsenhausen. The more of this rubbish we get rid of the better for the security of the Reich.

May 30, 1942. The Germans [the Fuehrer recently told me] take part in the subversive movements only when Jews have tricked them into it. For this reason the Jewish danger must be liquidated, cost what it may.

NOTES

1. P. Josef Goebbels (1897–1945), Nazi leader and propaganda minister. He was also *Gauleiter*—the district head—of Berlin. He was among the initiators of the Final Solution.

The Nazi response to armed resistance was swift and brutal. In these entries from his diary, Goebbels refers to two separate incidents of resistance: the first, the assassination on May 27, 1942 of the S.S. leader Reinhard T. Heydrich by the Czechoslovakian underground; the second, a sabotage attempt on an anti-Soviet exhibit in Berlin on May 15, 1942. (Of the twelve saboteurs captured, seven were Jews.) In retaliation the Nazis razed the Czech village of Lidice, executing all of the male inhabitants. At the same time 152 Jews in Berlin were killed in a "special action," and more than 3,000 Jews in the Theresienstadt ghetto were deported to various death camps. The extermination of Polish Jewry was designated by the Nazis *Aktion Reinhard*, in memory of Heydrich.

2. Heydrich died of his wounds on June 4, 1942.

Source: Diary of P. Josef Goebbels', May 27, 29 and 30, 1942, in Ernest K. Bramsted, ed., *Goebbels and National Socialist Propaganda, 1925–1945* (East Lansing: Michigan State University Press, 1965), pp. 396–97. Reprinted by permission of Michigan State University Press.

JUERGEN STROOP

22. The Jewish Residential Area in Warsaw Is No More[1]

The number of Jews taken out of the buildings and arrested was relatively small during the first days [of the operation against the Warsaw Ghetto]. It transpired that the Jews had taken to hiding in the sewers and in specially erected dug-outs. Whereas we had assumed during the first days that there were only scattered dug-outs it transpired in the course of the large-scale action that the whole Ghetto was systematically equipped with cellars, dug-outs and passages. In every case these passages and dug-outs were connected with the sewer system. Thus, the Jews were able to maintain undisturbed subterranean traffic. . . . Through posters, handbills and whisper propaganda, the communistic resistance movement in the former Jewish residential area brought it about that the Jews entered the dug-outs as soon as the large-scale operation started. How providently the Jews had worked can be seen from the fact that the dug-outs had been skilfully installed and equipped with furnishings for entire families, washing and bathing facilities, toilets, arms and munition stores, and large food supplies for several months. There were special dug-outs for rich and for poor Jews. To discover the individual dug-outs was exceedingly difficult for the acting forces, as they had been camouflaged, and in many cases it was possible only through betrayal on the part of the Jews.

Just after the first days it became apparent that the Jews no longer had any intention to resettle voluntarily,[2] but were determined to defend themselves by all means and by using all weapons at their disposal. So-called battle groups had been formed, under Polish and bolshevistic leadership; they were armed and paid any price asked for available arms.

During the large-scale action we succeeded in catching some Jews who had already been evacuated to Lublin or Treblinka, but had broken out from there and returned to the Ghetto, equipped with arms and ammunition. Time and again Polish bandits found refuge in the Ghetto and remained there almost undisturbed, since we disposed of no forces to penetrate into this maze. Whereas it had first been possible to catch considerable numbers of Jews, who are cowards by nature, it became more difficult during the second half of the large scale action to capture the bandits and Jews. Over and over again battle groups, consisting of 20 to 30 or more Jewish fellows, 18 to 25 years of age, accompanied by a corresponding number of women, kindled new resistance. These battle groups were under orders to put up armed resistance to the last and if necessary to escape arrest by committing suicide. One such battle group succeeded in mounting a truck by ascending from a sewer hole in the so-called Prosta, and in escaping with it (about 30 to 35 bandits). One bandit who had arrived with this truck exploded two hand grenades, which was the signal for the bandits waiting in the sewer to climb out of it. The bandits and the Jews—there were over and over again Polish bandits among them armed with carbines, firing hand arms and one light machine gun—mounted the truck and drove away in an unknown direction. . . .

During this armed resistance the women belonging to the battle groups were equipped the same as the men; some were members of the Chaluzim movement.[3] Not infrequently, these women fired pistols with both hands. It happened time and again that they had pistols or hand grenades (Polish "pineapple"

Source: The Report of Juergen Stroop Concerning the Uprising in the Ghetto of Warsaw and the Liquidation of the Jewish Residential Area, ed. B. Mark, trans. B. Dabrowaka (Warsaw: Jewish Historical Institute, 1958), pp. 22–26.

hand grenades) concealed in their bloomers up to the last moment to use them afterwards against the men of the Waffen-SS, Police and Wehrmacht.

The resistance put up by the Jews and bandits could be broken only by energetically and relentlessly using our raiding-parties by day and night. . . . I therefore decided to destroy completely the Jewish residential area by setting every block on fire, including the blocks of residential buildings belonging to the armament works. One factory after the other was systematically evacuated and subsequently destroyed by fire. The Jews then emerged from their hiding places and dugouts in almost every case. Not infrequently, the Jews stayed in the burning buildings until, because of the heat and the fear of being burned to death, they preferred to jump down from the upper stories after having thrown mattresses and other upholstered articles into the street from the burning buildings. With their bones broken, they still tried to crawl across the street into blocks of buildings which had not yet been set on fire or were only partly in flames. Often Jews changed their hiding places during the night, by moving into the ruins of burnt-out buildings, taking refuge there until they were found by our raiding parties. Their stay in the sewers also ceased to be pleasant after the first eight days. Frequently from the street, we could hear loud voices coming through the sewer shafts. Then the men of the Waffen-SS, the Police or the Wehrmacht Engineers courageously climbed down the shafts to bring out the Jews, and not infrequently they then stumbled over Jews already dead, or were shot at. It was always necessary to use smoke candles to drive out the Jews. Thus one day we opened 183 sewer entrance holes and at a fixed time lowered smoke candles into them, with the result that the bandits fled from what they believed to be gas to the center of the former Jewish residential area, where they could then be pulled out of the sewer holes there. A great number of Jews who could not be counted, were finished in the sewers and dug-outs by blowing them up.

The longer the resistance lasted, the tougher the men of Waffen-SS, Police and Wehrmacht became; here, too, they fulfilled their duty indefatigably in faithful comradeship and resisted as models and examples of soldiers. The work often lasted from early morning until late at night. At night, search patrols with rags wound round their feet remained at the heels of the Jews and gave them no respite. Not infrequently they caught and killed Jews who used the night for supplementing their stores from abandoned dug-outs or for contacting neighbouring groups exchanging news with them. . . .

Only through the continuous and untiring work of all forces we succeeded in catching a total of 56,065 Jews whose extermination can be proved. To this figure should be added the number of Jews who lost their lives in explosions, fires and so on, but whose numbers could not be ascertained. . . .

The Polish population for the most part approved the measures taken against the Jews. Shortly before the end of the large-scale operation, the Governor [General of Poland] issued a special proclamation which he submitted to the undersigned for approval before publication, to the Polish population; in it he informed them of the reasons for destroying the former Jewish residential area. . . .

The large-scale action was terminated on May 16, 1943 with the blowing up of the Warsaw synagogue at 20:15 hours.[4]. . .

NOTES

1. Juergen Stroop (1895–1951), S.S. general who was dispatched on April 19, 1943 to Warsaw to crush the ghetto revolt. After the war he was extradited to Poland, where he was sentenced and hanged for his crimes in the Warsaw Ghetto.

German forces entered Warsaw on September

29, 1939. On October 2, 1940 an area of approximately 840 acres was designated as the Jewish ghetto. Within six weeks all Jews residing in Warsaw were to move into the ghetto, while the Aryan inhabitants of the designated area had to leave. Initially some 400,000 Jews lived within the ghetto. With the influx of redugees from the provinces of Poland the ghetto population reached 500,000. Mass deportations to the Treblinka death camp started on July 21, 1942. Between July and September 13, 1942, the ghetto population was reduced to an estimated 60,000 Jews. In the meantime, the Jewish Fighting Organization was established to prepare for armed resistance. On January 18, 1943, the Nazis began a second wave of deportations. They were met with armed resistance, which led to four days of street fighting. The deportations were suspended, but on April 19, 1943, a German force, equipped with tanks and artillery, entered the ghetto in order to resume them. Again, armed resistance thwarted their plan of action. General Stroop took over the command of the German forces and ordered his troops to avoid further street combat with the Jews. Instead, he planned systematically to burn down the ghetto and gas and flood the sewers, which the Jewish fighters used as bunkers. Major resistance continued until May 8, 1943, although sporadic resistance actually lasted until May 16, when Stroop issued the above report to his superiors. The title introducing this document is taken from the subtitle Stroop gave his report.

2. After the suspension of forced deportations in January 1943, the Nazis tried to carry out their objectives through "peaceful" means, namely, by voluntary registration for alleged labor camps in the East.

3. Chaluzim movement, the Zionist movement promoting pioneering settlements in Palestine.

4. As a token of his victory Stroop blew up the Great Synagogue of Warsaw.

23. Bermuda Conference Joint Communique[1]

The United States and United Kingdom delegates examined the refugee problem in all its aspects including the position of those potential refugees who are still in the grip of the Axis powers without any immediate prospect of escape. Nothing was excluded from their analysis and everything that held out any possibility, however remote, of a solution of the problem was carefully investigated and thoroughly discussed. From the outset it was realized that any recommendation that the delegates could make to their governments must pass two tests: Would any recommendation submitted interfere with or delay the war effort of the United Nations and was the recommendation capable of accomplishment under war conditions? The delegates at Bermuda felt bound to reject certain proposals which were not capable of meeting these tests. The delegates were able to agree on a number of concrete recommendations which they are jointly submitting to their governments and which, it is felt, will pass the tests set forth above and will lead to the relief of a substantial number of refugees of all races and nationalities. Since the recommendations necessarily concern governments other than those represented at the Bermuda conference and involve military considerations, they must remain confidential. It may be said, however, that in the course of discussion the refugee problem was broken down into its main elements. Questions of shipping, food, and supply were fully investigated. The delegates also agreed on recommendations regarding the form of intergovernmental organization which was best fitted, in their opinion, to handle the problem in the future. This organization would have to be flexible enough to permit it

Source: Department of State Bulletin (Washington, D.C.), May 1, 1943.

to consider without prejudice any new factors that might come to its attention. In each of these fields the delegates were able to submit agreed proposals for consideration of their respective governments.

NOTE

1. As word of the concentration and extermination camps reached the outside world there was a mounting cry that the Allied governments should work against the diabolical scheme of the Nazis. Under pressure from Jewish organizations, parliaments, churches and humanitarian groups the British Foreign Office, on January 20, 1943, proposed a joint consultation between Britain and the United States to examine the problem and discuss possible solutions. The ensuant Anglo-American Conference on Refugees was held in Bermuda from the nineteenth to the thirtieth of April, 1943. The only positive decision of the conference was to extend the mandate of the Inter-Governmental Committee on Refugees, set up at the Evian Conference of 1938 to organize emigration and settlement of refugees from Nazi persecution. But clearly the problem was no longer one of refugees.

SHMUEL ZYGELBOYM
24. Where Is the World's Conscience?[1]

I take the liberty of addressing to you my last words and through you the Polish government and people of the Allied States and the conscience of the world.

From the latest information received from Poland, it is evident that without doubt the Germans with ruthless cruelty are now murdering the few remaining Jews in Poland. Behind the walls of the ghettos the last act of a tragedy unprecedented in history is being performed.

The responsibility for the crime of murdering all the Jewish population in Poland falls in the first instance on the perpetrators, but indirectly also it weighs on the whole of humanity, the peoples and governments of the Allied States which so far have made no effort toward a concrete action for the purpose of curtailing the crime. By passive observation of this murder of defenseless millions and the maltreatment of children and women, the men of those countries have become accomplices of criminals.

I have also to state that although the Polish goverment [in exile] has in a high degree contributed to stirring the opinion of the world yet it did so insufficiently for it did nothing extraordinary enough to correspond to the magnitude of the drama now being enacted in Poland.

Out of nearly 350,000 Polish Jews and about 700,000 Jews deported to Poland from other countries, there still lived in April of this year, according to the official information of the head of the underground Bund organization sent to the United States through a delegate of the government, about 300,000. And the murders are still going on incessantly.

I cannot be silent and I cannot live while the remnants of the Jewish people of Poland, of whom I am representative, are perishing.

My comrades in the Warsaw Ghetto perished with weapons in their hands in their last heroic impulse.

It was not my destiny to perish as they did

Source: Shmuel Zygelboym to the President and Premier of the Polish Government-in-Exile, *New York Times*, June 4, 1943.

together with them but I belong to them and their mass graves.

By my death, I wish to express my strongest protest against the inactivity with which the world is looking on and permitting the extermination of Jewish people. I know how little human life is worth, especially today. But as I was unable to do anything during my life, perhaps by my death I shall contribute to destroying the indifference of those who are able and should act in order to save now, maybe at the last moment, this handful of Polish Jews who are still alive from certain annihilation.

My life belongs to the Jewish people in Poland and therefore I give it to them. I wish that this handful that remains of the several million Polish Jews could live to see with the Polish masses the day of liberation—that it could breathe in Poland and in a world of freedom and in the justice of socialism in return for all its tortures and inhuman sufferings. And I believe that such a Poland will arise and that such a world will come.

I trust that the President and the Prime Minister will direct my words to all those for whom they are destined and that the Polish government will immediately begin appropriate action in the diplomatic and propaganda fields in order to save from extermination the Polish Jews who are still alive.

I bid farewell to all and everything dear to me and loved by me.

NOTE

1. Shmuel Zygelboym (1895–1943), a leader of the Polish Bund (the General Jewish Workers' Union). When the Germans entered Warsaw and demanded from the mayor twelve hostages, Zygelboym volunteered to be one of these hostages. He was later appointed to represent the Bund on Warsaw's *Judenrat*, the Jewish council established by the Nazis. In January 1940, he managed to escape Poland in order to report to the executive council of the Socialist International in Brussels on the conditions of German-occupied Poland. From there he reached the United States. From the spring of 1942 he resided in London, where he was the Bund's representative at the national council of the Polish government-in-exile. Zygelboym received information about the Nazi program for a Final Solution and implored the Polish, British and other authorities to take retaliatory and rescue action. He was profoundly depressed by the irresoluteness of the Anglo-American Conference on Refugees, held in Bermuda on April 19–30, 1943, and by the brutal suppression of the Warsaw Ghetto revolt. As a protest to the world's indifference to the sufferings of his people, Zygelboym committed suicide on May 12, 1943. The letter he left in explanation is reprinted here.

HEINRICH HIMMLER
25. A Secret Speech on the Jewish Question[1]

. . . May I now, in this most intimate circle, touch upon a question which all of you, members of the Party, have accepted as self-evident, but which for me has become the hardest question of my life: The question of the Jews. You will accept it as self-evident

Source: In Bradley R. Smith and Agnes F. Peterson, eds., *Heinrich Himmler, Geheimreden, 1933 bis 1945 und andere Ansprachen* (Frankfurt am Main, Berlin and Vienna: Propylaen Verlag, 1974), pp. 169–71. Copyright by Verlag Ullstein, GmbH. Reprinted by permission. Trans. here by J. Hessing.

and gratifying that in your districts there are no Jews any more. All German people—a few exceptions notwithstanding—have also understood that we could not have endured the Allied bombardment, nor the hardships of the fourth—and, perhaps, the coming fifth and sixth—war year with this destructive pestilence still in the body of our people. The sentence, "The Jews must be exterminated," is a short one, gentlemen, and is easily said. For the person who has to execute what this sentence implies, however, it is the most difficult and hardest thing in the world. Look, of course they are Jews, it is quite clear, they are only Jews, but consider how many people—members of the Party as well—have sent their famous petitions to me or to the authorities, declaring that all Jews, naturally, were pigs, but that so-and-so was a decent Jew and should not be touched. I dare say that, according to the number of petitions and opinions expressed in private, there were more decent Jews in Germany than the number of Jews that actually were to be found in the entire country. In Germany we have so many millions of people who have their famous decent Jew. . . . I am only saying this because, from your own experience within your districts, you will have learned that respectable and decent National Socialist people all know their decent Jew.

I must ask you only to listen and never to speak about what I am telling you in this intimate circle. We had to answer the question: What about the women and the children? Here, too, I had made up my mind, find a clear-cut solution. I did not feel that I had the right to exterminate the men—that is, to murder them, or have them murdered—and then allow their children to grow into avengers, threatening our sons and grandchildren. A fateful decision had to be made: This people had to vanish from the earth. For the organization in charge of the mission, it was the hardest decision we have had to make so far. It has been executed—as I believe I may say—without damage to the spirit and soul of our men and leaders. This danger was very real. The path between the two existing possibilities, either to become too brutal and to lose all respect for human life, or else to become too soft and dizzy and suffer from nervous breakdowns—the path between this Scylla and Charybdis was frightfully narrow.

All Jewish fortunes that were confiscated —a property of infinite value—were transferred, up to the last penny, to the Treasury of the Reich. I have always insisted on this: if we want to win the war we are obliged to our people and to our race—and obliged to our Fuehrer who is now, once in 2,000 years, given to our people—not to be petty in these matters and to be consistent. From the outset I decided that should a member of the S.S. take only one single Mark, he would be sentenced to death. In recent days I have therefore signed a number of death warrants—I might as well say it, approximately a dozen. Here one has to be relentless, lest the Party and Nation suffer.

I feel most obliged to you—who are the highest commissioners, the highest dignitaries of the Party, of this Political Order, of this political instrument in the hands of our Fuehrer. By the end of this year, the Jewish question in the countries occupied by us will be solved. There will only be remnants of isolated Jews who went into hiding. The question of the Jews married to Gentiles, and the question of half-Jews, will be investigated logically and rationally, decided upon, and solved. . . .

With this I wish to conclude my remarks concerning the Jewish question. Now you know all about it, and you will keep quiet. In the distant future, perhaps, one might consider if the German people should be told anything more about it. I believe it is better that we—all of us—who have taken this upon ourselves for our people and have taken the responsibility (the responsibility for the deed, not merely for the idea), should take our secret to our graves. . . .

NOTE

1. Heinrich Himmler (1900–1945), head of the S.S. A close associate of Hitler from the days of the Munich *putsch* in 1923, Himmler created the S.S., from an elite guard of the party, into a huge "Nordic" army in the service of Nazi ideological goals. Accordingly, Hitler charged Himmler and the S.S. with the implementation of the Final Solution. Following Himmler's arrest by British troops in May 1945, he committed suicide. This speech was given by Himmler at a secret meeting of state and district leaders in Posen on October 8, 1943.

RUDOLF HOESS
26. Commandant of Auschwitz[1]

By the will of the Reichsfuehrer SS [Himmler], Auschwitz became the greatest human extermination centre of all time.

When in the summer of 1941 he himself gave me the order to prepare installations at Auschwitz where mass extermination could take place, and personally to carry out these exterminations, I did not have the slightest idea of their scale or consequences. It was certainly an extraordinary and monstrous order. Nevertheless the reasons behind the extermination program seemed to me right. I did not reflect on it at the time: I had been given an order, and I had to carry it out. Whether this mass extermination of the Jews was necessary or not was something on which I could not allow myself to form an opinion, for I lacked the necessary breadth of view.

If the Fuehrer had himself given the order for the "final solution of the Jewish question," then for a veteran National-Socialist and even more so for an SS officer, there could be no question of considering its merits. "The Fuehrer commands, we follow" was never a mere phrase or slogan. It was meant in bitter earnest....

But outsiders simply cannot understand that there was not a single SS officer who would disobey an order from the Reichsfuehrer SS, far less consider getting rid of him because of the gruesomely hard nature of one such order.

What the Fuehrer, or in our case his second-in-command, the Reichsfuehrer SS, ordered was always right....

Before the mass extermination of the Jews began, the Russian *politruks* and political commissars were liquidated in almost all the concentration camps during 1941 and 1942....

While I was away on duty, my deputy, Fritzsch, the commander of the protective custody camp, first tried gas for these killings. It was a preparation of prussic acid, called Cyclon B, which was used in the camp as an insecticide and of which there was always a stock on hand. On my return Fritzsch reported this to me, and the gas was used again for the next transport.

The gassing was carried out in the detention cells of Block 11. Protected by a gasmask, I watched the killing myself. In the crowded cells death came instantaneously the moment the Cyclon B was thrown in. A short, almost smothered cry, and it was all over. During this first experience of gassing people, I did not fully realise what was hap-

Source: Rudolf Hoess, *Commandant of Auschwitz*, trans. C. FitzGiboon (London: Weidenfeld and Nicolson, 1953), pp. 144–50, 153–55.

pening, perhaps because I was too impressed by the whole procedure. I have a clearer recollection of the gassing of nine hundred Russians which took place shortly afterwards in the old crematorium, since the use of Block 11 for this purpose caused too much trouble. While the transport was detraining, holes were pierced in the earth and in the concrete ceiling of the mortuary. The Russians were ordered to undress in an anteroom; they then quietly entered the mortuary, for they had been told they were to be deloused. The whole transport exactly filled the mortuary to capacity. The doors were then sealed and the gas shaken down through the holes in the roof. I do not know how long this killing took. For a little while a humming sound could be heard. When the powder was thrown in, there were cries of "Gas!," then a great bellowing, and the trapped prisoners hurled themselves against both the doors. But the doors held. They were opened several hours later, so that the place might be aired. It was then that I saw, for the first time, gassed bodies in mass.

It made me feel uncomfortable and I shuddered, although I had imagined that death by gassing would be worse than it was. I had always thought that the victims would experience a terrible choking sensation. But the bodies, without exception, showed no signs of convulsion. The doctors explained to me that the prussic acid had a paralysing effect on the lungs, but its action was so quick and strong that death came before the convulsions could set in, and in this its effects differed from those produced by carbon monoxide or by a general oxygen deficiency.

The killing of these Russian prisoners-of-war did not cause me much concern at the time. The order had been given, and I had to carry it out. I must even admit that this gassing set my mind at rest, for the mass extermination of the Jews was to start soon and at that time neither Eichmann[2] nor I was certain how these mass killings were to be carried out. It would be by gas, but we did not know which gas or how it was to be used. Now we had the gas, and we had established a procedure. I always shuddered at the prospect of carrying out exterminations by shooting, when I thought of the vast numbers concerned, and of the women and children. The shooting of hostages, and the group executions ordered by the Reichsfuehrer SS or by the Reich Security Head Office had been enough for me. I was therefore relieved to think that we were to be spared all these blood-baths, and that the victims too would be spared suffering until their last moment came. It was precisely this which had caused me the greatest concern when I had heard Eichmann's description of Jews being mown down by the Special Squads [*Einsatzkommandos*] armed with machine-guns and machine-pistols. Many gruesome scenes are said to have taken place, people running away after being shot, the finishing off of the wounded and particularly of the women and children. Many members of the *Einsatzkommandos*, unable to endure wading through blood any longer, had committed suicide. Some had even gone mad. Most of the members of these *Kommandos* had to rely on alcohol when carrying out their horrible work. . . .

In the spring of 1942 the first transports of Jews, all earmarked for extermination, arrived from Upper Silesia.

They were taken from the detraining platform to the "Cottage"—to Bunker I—across the meadows where later Building Site II was located. The transport was conducted by Aumeier and Palitzsch and some of the block leaders. They talked with the Jews about general topics, enquiring concerning their qualifications and trades, with a view to misleading them. On arrival at the "Cottage," they were told to undress. At first they went calmly into the rooms where they were supposed to be disinfected. But some of them showed signs of alarm, and spoke of death by suffocation and of annihilation. A sort of panic set in at once. Immediately all the Jews still outside were pushed into the chambers, and the doors were screwed shut. With subsequent transports the difficult individuals were picked out early on and most carefully supervised. At the first signs of unrest, those responsible were unobtrusively led behind the building and killed with a small-calibre gun that was inaudible to the others. The presence and calm behaviour of the Special Detachment[3] served to reassure those who were worried or who suspected what was about to happen. A further calming effect was obtained by members of the Special Detachment accompanying them into the rooms and remaining with them until the end.

It was most important that the whole business of arriving and undressing should take place in an atmosphere of the greatest possible calm. People reluctant to take off their clothes had to be helped by those of their companions who had already undressed, or by men of the Special Detachment.

The refractory ones were calmed down and encouraged to undress. The prisoners of the Special Detachment also saw to it that the process of undressing was carried out quickly, so that the victims would have little time to wonder what was happening.

The eager help given by the Special Detachment in encouraging them to undress and in conducting them into the gas-chambers was most remarkable. I have never known, nor heard, of any of its members giving these people who were about to be gassed the slightest hint of what lay ahead of them. On the contrary, they did everything in their power to deceive them and particularly to pacify the suspicious ones. Though they might refuse to believe the SS men, they had complete faith in these members of their own race, and to reassure them and keep them calm the Special Detachments therefore always consisted of Jews who themselves came from the same districts as did the people on whom a particular action was to be carried out.

They would talk about life in the camp, and most of them asked for news of friends or relations who had arrived in earlier transports. It was interesting to hear the lies that the Special Detachment told them with such conviction, and to see the emphatic gestures with which they underlined them.

Many of the women hid their babies among the piles of clothing. The men of the Special Detachment were particularly on the look-out for this, and would speak words of encouragement to the woman until they had persuaded her to take the child with her. The women believed that the disinfectant might be bad for their smaller children, hence their efforts to conceal them.

The smaller children usually cried because of the strangeness of being undressed in this fashion, but when their mothers or members of the Special Detachment comforted them, they became calm and entered the gas chambers, playing or joking with one another and carrying their toys.

I noticed that women who either guessed or knew what awaited them nevertheless found the courage to joke with the children to encourage them, despite the mortal terror visible in their own eyes.

One woman approached me as she walked past and, pointing to her four children who were manfully helping the smallest ones over the rough ground, whispered:

"How can you bring yourself to kill such beautiful, darling children? Have you no heart at all?"

One old man, as he passed by me, hissed:

"Germany will pay a heavy penance for this mass murder of the Jews."

His eyes glowed with hatred as he said this. Nevertheless he walked calmly into the gas-chamber, without worrying about the others.

I remember, too, a woman who tried to throw her children out of the gas-chamber, just as the door was closing. Weeping she called out:

"At least let my precious children live."

There were many such shattering scenes, which affected all who witnessed them.

During the spring of 1942 hundreds of vigorous men and women walked all unsuspecting to their death in the gas-chambers, under the blossom-laden fruit trees of the "Cottage" orchard. This picture of death in the midst of life remains with me to this day. . . .

This mass extermination, with all its attendant circumstances, did not, as I know, fail to affect those who took a part in it. With very few exceptions, nearly all of those detailed to do this monstrous "work," this "service," and who, like myself, have given sufficient thought to the matter, have been deeply marked by these events.

Many of the men involved approached me as I went my rounds through the extermination buildings, and poured out their anxieties and impressions to me, in the hope that I could allay them.

Again and again during these confidential conversations I was asked: is it necessary that we do all this? Is it necessary that hundreds of thousands of women and children be destroyed? And I, who in my innermost being only fought them off and attempted to console them by repeating that it was done on Hitler's order. I had to tell them that this extermination of Jewry had to be, so that Germany and our posterity might be freed for ever from their relentless adversaries.

There was no doubt in the mind of any of us that Hitler's order had to be obeyed regardless, and that it was the duty of the SS to carry it out. Nevertheless we were all tormented by secret doubts.

I myself dared not admit to such doubts. In order to make my subordinates carry on with their task, it was psychologically essential that I myself appear convinced of the necessity for this gruesomely harsh order.

Everyone watched me. They observed the impression produced upon me by the kind of scenes that I have described above, and my reactions. Every word I said on the subject was discussed. I had to exercise intense self-control in order to prevent my innermost doubts and feelings of oppression from becoming apparent.

I had to appear cold and indifferent to events that must have wrung the heart of anyone possessed of human feelings. I might not even look away when afraid lest my natural emotions get the upper hand. I had to watch coldly, while the mothers with laughing or crying children went into the gas-chambers.

On one occasion two small children were so absorbed in some game that they quite refused to let their mother tear them away from it. Even the Jews of the Special Detachment were reluctant to pick the children up. The imploring look in the eyes of the mother, who certainly knew what was happening, is something I shall never forget. The people were already in the gas-chamber and becoming restive, and I had to act. Everyone was looking at me. I nodded to the junior non-commissioned officer on duty and he picked up the screaming, struggling children in his arms and carried them into the gas-chamber, accompanied by their mother who was weeping in the most heart-rending fashion. My pity was so great that I longed to vanish from the scene: yet I might not show the slightest trace of emotions.

I had to see everything, I had to watch hour after hour, by day and by night, the removal and burning of the bodies, the extraction of the teeth, the cutting of hair, the whole grisly, interminable business. I had to stand for hours on end in the ghastly stench, while the mass graves were being opened and the bodies dragged out and burned.

I had to look through the peep-hole of the gas-chambers and watch the process of death itself, because the doctors wanted me to see it.

I had to do all this because I was the one to whom everyone looked, because I had to show them all that I did not merely issue the orders and make the regulations but was also prepared myself to be present at whatever task I had assigned to my subordinates.

The Reichsfuehrer SS sent various high-ranking Party leaders and SS officers to Auschwitz so that they might see for themselves the process of extermination of the Jews. They were all deeply impressed by what they saw. Some who had previously spoken most loudly about the necessity for this extermination fell silent once they had actually seen the "final solution of the Jewish problem." I was repeatedly asked how I and my men could go on watching these operations, and how we were able to stand it.

My invariable answer was that the iron determination with which we must carry out Hitler's orders could only be obtained by a stifling of all human emotions. Each of these gentlemen declared that he was glad the job had not been given to him.

I had many detailed discussions with Eichmann concerning all matters connected with the "final solution of the Jewish problem," but without ever disclosing my inner anxieties, I tried in every way to discover Eichmann's innermost and real convictions about the "solution."

Yes, every way. Yet even when we were quite alone together and the drink had been flowing freely so that he was in his most expansive mood, he showed that he was completely obsessed with the idea of destroying every single Jew that he could lay his hands on. Without pity and in cold blood we must complete this extermination as rapidly as possible. Any compromise, even the slightest, would have to be paid for bitterly at a later date.

In the face of such grim determination I was forced to bury all my human considerations as deeply as possible.

Indeed, I must freely confess that after these conversations with Eichmann I almost came to regard such emotions as a betrayal of the Fuehrer.

There was no escape for me from this dilemma.

I had to go on with this process of extermination. I had to continue this mass murder and coldly to watch it, without regard for the doubts that were seething deep inside me.

I had to observe every happening with a cold indifference. Even those petty incidents that others might not notice I found hard to forget. In Auschwitz I truly had no reason to complain that I was bored.

NOTES

1. Rudolf Hoess (1900–1947). Member of the S.S., in May 1940 he was appointed first commandant of Auschwitz. At the end of 1941 Himmler ordered him to adapt the camp for the Final Solution. In November 1943 he was transferred to the inspection authority of the concentration camps. In 1944, however, he returned to Auschwitz for a two-month period to supervise the extermination of 400,000 Hungarian Jews. After the war the Polish government tried him, condemning him to death. While in prison Hoess wrote his autobiography, from which this excerpt is taken. He was hanged at Auschwitz in 1947.

Auschwitz, the Nazis' largest concentration and extermination camp, was located near the small Polish town Oswiecim (in German, Auschwitz) in Galicia. Estimates of the victims of Auschwitz's gas chambers vary from 1,000,000 to 2,500,000. In addition to Jews, tens of thousands of gypsies and other prisoners were killed at Auschwitz.

2. Adolf Eichmann (1906–1962), head of the Gestapo Section IV B 4, which dealt with Jewish affairs and the deportation of the Jews to the death camps.

3. These *Sonderkommando*—popularly known as Kapos—were recruited from among the camp inmates.

27. Estimated Number of Jews Killed by the Nazis[1]

	Country[2]	*Jewish population September 1939*	*Number of Jews murdered*[3]	*Percentage of Jews murdered*
1.	Poland	3,300,000	2,800,000	85.0
2.	USSR, occupied territories	2,100,000	1,500,000	71.4
3.	Rumania	850,000	425,000	50.0
4.	Hungary	404,000	200,000	49.5
5.	Czechoslovakia	315,000	260,000	82.5
6.	France[4]	300,000	90,000	30.0
7.	Germany[5]	210,000	170,000	81.0
8.	Lithuania	150,000	135,000	90.0
9.	Holland[4]	150,000	90,000	60.0
10.	Latvia	95,000	85,000	89.5
11.	Belgium[4]	90,000	40,000	44.4
12.	Greece	75,000	60,000	80.0
13.	Yugoslavia	75,000	55,000	73.3
14.	Austria[6]	60,000	40,000	66.6
15.	Italy[4]	57,000	15,000	26.3
16.	Bulgaria	50,000	7,000	14.0
17.	Others[7]	20,000	6,000	30.0
	Total	8,301,000	5,978,000	72.0

NOTES

1. With few exceptions there are no exact statistics of Jews killed. Thus all statistics are estimates.
2. Within its pre-war boundaries.
3. The survivors did not always remain in their countries of origin.
4. The numbers for France, Holland, Belgium and Italy include emigrants from Germany and Austria.
5. N.B., the percentage of victims is for the Jewish population of September 1939. Between 1933 and 1939 an estimated 300,000 German Jews emigrated.
6. Again the percentage of victims is for the population of September 1939. From the *Anschluss* to September 1939 it is estimated that 110,000 Jews left Austria.
7. Danzig, Denmark, Estonia, Luxemburg, Norway.

Source: Leon Poliakov and Josef Wulf, eds., *Das Dritte Reich und die Juden: Dokumente und Aufsaetze* (Berlin: Arani-Verlag, GmbH, 1955), p. 229.

GIDEON HAUSNER

28. Six Million Accusers[1]

When I stand before you here, Judges of Israel, to lead the Prosecution of Adolf Eichmann, I am not standing alone. With me are six million accusers. But they cannot rise to their feet and point an accusing finger towards him who sits in the dock and cry: "I accuse." For their ashes are piled up on the hills of Auschwitz and the fields of Treblinka, and are strewn in the forests of Poland. Their graves are scattered throughout the length and breadth of Europe. Their blood cries out, but their voice is not heard. Therefore I will be their spokesman and in their name I will unfold the awesome indictment.

The history of the Jewish people is steeped in suffering and tears. . . . Yet never, down the entire blood-stained road travelled by this people, never since the first days of its nationhood, has any man arisen who succeeded in dealing it such grievous blows as did Hitler's iniquitous regime, and Adolf Eichmann as its executive arm for the extermination of the Jewish people. In all human history there is no other example of a man against whom it would be possible to draw up such a bill of indictment as has been read here. . . . Murder has been with the human race since the days when Cain killed Abel; it is no novel phenomenon. But we have had to wait till this twentieth century to witness with our own eyes a new kind of murder: not the result of the momentary surge of passion or mental black-out, but of calculated decision and painstaking planning; not through the evil design of an individual, but through a mighty criminal conspiracy involving thousands; not against one victim whom an assassin may have decided to destroy, but against an entire people. . . .

This murderous decision, taken deliberately and in cold blood, to annihilate a nation and blot it out from the face of the earth, is so shocking that one is at a loss for words to describe it. Words exist to express what man's reason can conceive and his heart contain, [but] here we are dealing with actions that transcend our human grasp. Yet this is what did happen: millions were condemned to death, not for any crime, not for anything they had done, but only because they belonged to the Jewish people. The development of technology placed at the disposal of the destroyers efficient equipment for the execution of their appalling designs. This unprecedented crime, carried out by Europeans in the twentieth century, led to the definition of a criminal concept unknown to human annals even during the darkest ages—the crime of Genocide. . . .

Hitler, his regime and crimes, were no accidental or transient phenomenon. He did not come to power as a result merely of a unique combination of circumstances. Historical processes are usually the product of many developments, like many streams flowing each in its own channel until they combine into a mighty river. They will come together only if their flow is in the same general direction.

No doubt various events contributed to the rise of Nazism: the defeat of Germany in World War I; the subsequent economic difficulties; lack of leadership and futile party divisions; fratricidal strife and disunion—all these impelled the German people, disoriented and groping, to turn its eyes towards the false prophet. But Hitler would not have been able to remain in power, and to

Source: Shabatai Rosenne, ed., *Six Million Accusers: Israel's Case Against Eichmann* (Jerusalem: *The Jerusalem Post*, 1961), pp. 29–33, 37–38, 43. Reprinted by permission of the publishers of *The Jerusalem Post.*

consolidate in his support all the strata of the German people, including most of the intellectuals—to win the support of so many university professors and professional men, the civil service and the whole army—if the road to his leadership had not already been paved. Not even the oppressive regime of the concentration camps, and the atmosphere created by the terror so rapidly activated against all opposition by the hooligans of the S.S. and S.A., are adequate alone to explain the enthusiastic and devoted support he received from the majority of the nation, unless it had been preceded by an extensive spiritual preparation. When we read today the declarations of the scientists, authors, and journalists—including many who had not been among his adherents before—who chanted his praises and willingly gave him their support and backing, how they willingly and joyfully accepted his yoke, we must reach the conclusion, however reluctantly, that the people were ready and prepared to crown him as their leader.

Hitler [freed] the hatred of the Jew which was latent in the hearts of large sections of the German people, intensified it and stimulated it into greater activity. The germ of anti-Semitism was already there; he stimulated it and transformed it into the source of an epidemic. For the purposes of Nazi Germany's internal policy, the Jew was a convenient object of hatred; he was weak and defenceless. The world outside remained silent when he was persecuted, and contented itself with verbal reactions that did little harm. The Jew was pilloried as a supporter of Communism—and therefore an enemy of the German people. In the same breath he was accused of being a capitalist—and therefore an enemy of the workers. National-Socialism had found in the Jew an object of hostility appropriate to both halves of its name, and it set him up as a target for both national enmity and class hatred. The Jew was also a ready target through which the attention of the public could be diverted from other problems. This too was an age-old weapon; which had been used by many anti-Semites down the ages. . . .

A confused and blinded world was not alarmed by this campaign of hatred and the denial of human rights. It did not understand that the persecution of the Jews was only the beginning of an onslaught on the entire world. The man whose henchmen howled the infamous words: "When Jewish blood spurts from the knife/Then all goes doubly well!" (*"Wenn Judenblut vom Messer spritzt/Dann geht's nochmal so gut!"*)—the same man would soon, by a natural development and led by the same master-feeling of hate, proclaim that all the cities of England would be subjected to the same fate as bombed Coventry.

In order to complete the picture, we should point out that there were in Germany tens of thousands of scientists and ecclesiastics, statesmen and authors and ordinary people, who dared to help the Jews, to raise their heads in opposition to the iniquitous regime, and even to rebel against it, and among these were men whose names were famous in German science and culture. Thousands of opponents of the bloody regime were imprisoned and were later destined to suffer greatly in concentration camps before the Nazi monster was brought low. Thousands of these died without seeing the day of liberation. Hundreds of ecclesiastics were arrested and imprisoned. There were also examples of personal bravery—like that of a priest who was sent by Eichmann to a concentration camp for intervening openly on behalf of the Jews. There were Germans who hid Jews and shared their rations with them and who at the risk of their lives helped them to hide or to obtain "Aryan" papers, and there were others who maintained an anti-Hitler underground. During the War there were Germans who even protested to Hitler at the disgrace the Gestapo was bringing on the German people by acting like beasts of prey, as they described the extermination of the Jews. There were also soldiers who tried to frustrate the killings by direct intervention.

But after all is said and done, these were a very small minority. The decisive majority of the German people made peace with the new regime, and were phlegmatic witnesses of the most terrible crime ever perpetrated in human history. . . .

There is a Hebrew saying: "The wicked, even at the gate of Hell, do not repent." In April 1945, at the moment of his death agonies, when the Soviet cannons were thundering in the streets of Berlin, when Hitler sat imprisoned in the cellar of the *Reichskanzlei*, his entire world in ruins and his country stricken, over the corpses of six million Jews—at that moment, the Fuehrer wrote his political last will and testament. He bequeathed to his people the injunction of eternal hatred for the Jews, and he concluded:

> Above all, I enjoin the government and the people to uphold the racial laws to the limit and to resist mercilessly the poisoner of all nations, international Jewry.

Even from beyond the grave, Hitler was still trying to sow the seeds of hatred and destruction for the Jewish people.

NOTE

1. Gideon Hausner (b. 1915). The attorney general of Israel from 1960 to 1963, Hausner was the chief prosecutor in the Adolf Eichmann trial. This selection is taken from his speech at the trial, which took place before the Jerusalem District Court and which lasted from April to December 1961. Adolf Eichmann (1906-1962)—who was the Gestapo officer in charge of organizing the deportations of the Jews to the death camps—was charged with "crimes against the Jewish people and humanity." He had been brought to Israel by Israeli security agents who had abducted him from Argentina, where he had been hiding since 1950. The Jerusalem court found Eichmann guilty of the charges against him and condemned him to death. In May 1962 he was hanged in an Israeli prison.

APPENDIX

The Demography of Modern Jewish History

The transformations that characterize the modern period in Jewish history are in part reflected in dramatic demographic changes: a sudden and rapid increase in the population of the Jews, paralleled by major shifts in geographic distribution and by far-reaching changes in social, economic and educational patterns.[1]

Whereas in the classical world the Jewish people was comparatively numerous—at the time of the destruction of the Second Temple in 70 C.E., according to various estimates, there were between four and a half and seven million Jews in the world[2]—the numbers declined drastically during the Middle Ages. The eclipse of commerce and urban life which followed the dismantling of the Roman Empire, together with the restrictions and persecutions which marked the feudal period, led to a sharp reduction in the size of the Jewish population. Thus, by the fifteenth century "on the entire European continent there were probably fewer than 300,000 Jews; in the entire world there were fewer than a million, most of whom were concentrated in the Near East."[3] With the dawn of mercantilism—the revival of commerce and city life and the concomitant relaxation of Jewish disabilities—there was a gradual increase in the population of European Jewry, reaching by the end of the eighteenth century an estimated million and a half, the world Jewish population totaling two and a half million.

Until the beginning of the modern period, the Jews were predominantly a Near Eastern

1. Employing varying criteria and sources, demographers differ, sometimes radically, in their statistical estimates. Our selections in this appendix are based not only on the reliability of a given set of statistics, but also on their value in illuminating what we deem to be salient trends and patterns.

2. Adolf Harnack, *Die Mission und Ausbreitung des Christentums* (Leipzig: J. C. Hinrichs, 1923), vol. 1, pp. 5–19; Arthur Ruppin, *Soziologie der Juden* (Berlin: Juedischer Verlag, 1930), vol. 1, p. 69; Uriah Zevi Engelman, "Sources of Jewish Statistics," in *The Jews: Their History, Culture, and Religion*, ed. L. Finkelstein (Philadelphia: The Jewish Publication Society of America, 1966), vol. 2, p. 1517; *Encyclopaedia Judaica*, s.v. "Population [Jewish]," vol. 13, p. 871. In the Roman Empire the Jews, according to various estimates, were between 8 and 10 percent of the population.

3. Engelman, "Sources of Jewish Statistics," p. 1519.

Table I *Approximate World Jewish Population in 1800*

Place	*Number*	*Percent of World Jewry*
Near East (including Turkey)	1,000,000	40.0
Russian Poland and Western Russia	800,000	32.0
Austria (including Galicia)	300,000	12.0
Bohemia and Moravia	70,000	2.8
Hungary	100,000	4.0
Prussia	100,000	4.0
France (including Alsace)	80,000	3.2
Holland	50,000	2.0
Total	2,500,000	100.0

SOURCES: Compiled on the basis of data presented in Jacob Lestschinsky, "Die Umsiedlung und Umschichtung des juedischen Volkes im Laufe des letzten Jahrhunderts," *Weltwirtschaftliches Archiv,* vol. 30, pt. 2 (Jena, 1929), p. 155; and Arthur Ruppin, *The Jews in the Modern World* (London: Macmillan and Co., 1934), pp. 23–24.

people, but with the numerical ascendancy of European Jewry, they became largely European, as is noted in table 2.

The Jews shared in the general increase of Europe's population which resulted from a marked improvement of economic conditions, sanitation and medical care, extension of life expectancy and a sharp decrease of infant mortality. In the nineteenth century the growth of both the Jewish and non-Jewish populations of Europe was astronomical.

It has been observed that political emancipation was an insignificant factor in the expansion of the Jewish population. For "the major increase . . . occurred in eastern Europe, which remained politically unemancipated." The western countries that granted the Jews civil equality "shared only indirectly in the growth of the Jewish population by accepting the population overflow from eastern Europe."[4] It was this latter area—comprising the Ukraine, White Russia, Lithuania, Poland, Rumania, Galicia and Hungary—which supplied virtually all of the natural increase of the Jewish population in the nineteenth century. In this period, East European Jewry had "a higher rate of natural increase, and a lower standard of living than any of the other Jewish population groups of western and central Europe, or America."[5] Moreover, the increase of East European Jewry exceeded the average growth of the region's non-Jewish population. This rate of growth is not to be explained by a higher Jewish fertility—indeed, the Jews were less fertile[6]—but a higher life-span of the Jews.[7] This fact is generally attributed to Jewish religious and cultural traditions. "There can be no doubt that greater stability of the family, the smaller number of illegitimate children, the infrequency of venereal diseases, the higher status of woman within the family, the care lavished on babies and small children, abstinence from alcohol, the readiness of the individual and the community to undergo considerable economic sacrifice in order to help others and the lengthy tradition of charitable deeds combined, among Jews, to serve as the basis for their demographic development."[8] It may also be noted that East European Jewry lived in far greater proportion than non-Jews in cities where medical care was much more readily available than in rural areas. Moreover, the Jews tended to have a greater trust in medical science, and, accordingly, availed themselves of medical

4. Engelman, "Sources of Jewish Statistics," p. 1521.

5. Engelman, "Sources of Jewish Statistics," p. 1522.

6. See Ruppin, *Soziologie der Juden,* vol. 1, pp. 175–77; Engelman, "Sources of Jewish Statistics," pp. 1524–25.

7. See Ruppin, *Soziologie der Juden,* vol. 1, pp. 237–44.

8. Shmuel Ettinger, "The Modern Period," in *A History of the Jewish People,* ed. H. H. Ben-Sasson (London: Weidenfeld and Nicolson, 1976), pp. 790–91.

Table II *Geographic Distribution of World Jewry*

Place	*Year*	*Number of Jews*	*Percent of World Jewry*	*Year*	*Number of Jews*	*Percent of World Jewry*	*Year*	*Number of Jews*	*Percent of World Jewry*	*Year*	*Number of Jews*	*Percent of World Jewry*
Eastern Europe	1850	3,420,000	72.0	1880	5,812,500	75.0	1939	7,328,000	45.6	1969	4,019,000	29.2
Rest of Europe	1850	688,750	14.5	1880	1,046,250	13.5	1939	1,876,000	11.3	1969		
Americas	1850	71,250	1.5	1880	271,250	3.5	1939	5,556,000	33.4	1969	6,952,000	50.4
Near East	1850	570,000	12.0	1880	620,000	8.0	1939	1,445,000	8.7	1969	2,750,000	19.9
Total		4,750,000	100.0		7,750,000	100.0		16,205,000	99.0		13,721,000	99.5

SOURCES: Compiled on the basis of data presented in Jacob Lestschinsky, "Die Umsiedlung und Umschichtung des juedischen Volkes im Laufe des letzten Jahrhunderts," *Weltwirtschaftliches Archiv*, vol. 30, pt. 2 (Jena, 1929), p. 155; Arthur Ruppin, *The Jews in the Modern World* (London: Macmillan and Co., 1934), pp. 23–25; Arthur Ruppin, "The Jewish Population in the World," in *The Jewish People: Past and Present* (New York: Central Yiddish Culture Organization, 1946), vol. 1, pp. 350–351; and *Encyclopaedia Judaica*, s.v. "History [of the Jews]: Modern Times," vol. 8, p. 730.

Table III *Growth of Europe's Population in the Modern Period*

	1580	*1680*	*1780*	*1880*
England	4,600,000	5,532,000	9,561,000	35,002,000
Prussia	1,000,000	1,400,000	5,460,000	45,260,000
Russia	4,300,000	12,600,000	26,800,000	84,440,000
France	14,300,000	18,800,000	25,100,000	37,400,000

SOURCE: Uriah Zevi Engelman, "Sources of Jewish Statistics," in *The Jews: Their History, Culture, and Religion*, 2nd ed., ed. L. Finkelstein. (Philadelphia: The Jewish Publication Society of America, 1966), vol. 2, p. 1522.

Table IV *Growth of Jewish Population in the Nineteenth Century*

	1825	*1850*	*1880*	*1900*
Western and Central Europe	458,000	693,500	1,044,500	1,328,500
Eastern and Southeastern Europe	2,272,000	3,434,000	5,726,000	7,362,000
Europe (Total)	2,730,000	4,127,500	6,770,500	8,690,500
America	10,000	65,000	250,000	1,175,000
Asia	300,000	320,000	350,000	420,000
Africa	240,000	250,000	280,000	300,000
Australia	1,000	2,000	12,000	17,000

SOURCE: Jacob Lestschinsky, "Di entviklung fun yidishen folk far die letzte 100 yor," in *Yidisher visnshaflekher institut. Ekonomish-statistishe skezie* (Berlin, 1928), vol. 1, p. 6.

care to a much greater degree than the non-Jewish population.[9]

Propelled by acts of discrimination and persecution, the impoverished Jews of Eastern Europe began to emigrate westward to more prosperous and enlightened European countries, and, especially, to the Americas. It is estimated that between 1840 and 1947 there were some four million Jewish immigrants, the vast majority from East Europe.[10]

The United States became the principal focus of Jewish immigration. In the first seven decades of the nineteenth century some 50,000 Jews from Central Europe came to the United States. In the wake of the pogroms of 1881 in Russia, East European Jewry began to emigrate *en masse.* From 1881 to 1900 more than 500,000 Jews emigrated to the United States; smaller numbers went to other countries in the Americas, and others settled in South Africa. But this mass emigration was but a prelude. Between 1900 and 1914 nearly two million Jews left Eastern Europe, 75 percent of whom settled in the United States. It is important to note that this mass emigration of Jews was part of a general wave of emigration from Europe in the period. It is estimated that in the decade prior to the outbreak of the First World War approximately one and a half million Europeans left the continent annually, immigrating chiefly to North America, but also South America, South Africa and Australia. A tenth of these emigrants were East European Jews. See table 6.

As a result of immigration new centers of Jewry emerged, most notably in the Americas. See table 7.

Jewish destiny in the modern period was

9. See Ruppin, *Soziologie der Juden*, vol. 1, pp. 238–41.

10. Jacob Lestschinsky, *Tefuzat Yisrael le-Ahar ha-Milhamah* (Tel Aviv, 1948), p. 31.

Table V *Jewish Migrations, 1881–1930*

To	*From*					
	Russia	*Austria-Hungary (since 1920 from Poland)*	*Roumania*	*Great Britain*	*Other Countries*	*Total*
United States	1,749,000	597,000	161,000	114,000	264,000	2,885,000
Canada	70,000	40,000	5,000	...	10,000	125,000
Argentina	100,000	40,000	20,000	...	20,000	180,000
Brazil	6,000	10,000	4,000	...	10,000	30,000
Other South and Central American Countries	5,000	10,000	5,000	...	10,000	30,000
Total for America	1,930,000	697,000	195,000	114,000	314,000	3,250,000
Great Britain	130,000	40,000	30,000	...	10,000	210,000
Germany	25,000	75,000	...	...	...	100,000
France	40,000	40,000	...	...	20,000	100,000
Belgium	15,000	30,000	...	...	5,000	50,000
Switzerland, Italy, Scandanavian Countries	30,000	...	...	...	...	30,000
Total for Western and Central Europe	240,000	185,000	30,000	...	35,000	490,000
South Africa	45,000	10,000	...	...	5,000	60,000
Egypt	20,000	10,000	...	...	5,000	35,000
Total for Africa	65,000	20,000	...	...	10,000	95,000
Palestine	45,000	40,000	10,000	...	25,000	120,000
Australia and New Zealand	5,000	10,000	...	...	5,000	20,000
Total	2,285,000	952,000	235,000	114,000	389,000	3,975,000

SOURCE: Arthur Ruppin, *Soziologie der Juden* (Berlin: Juedischer Verlag, 1930), vol. 1, p. 157.

to a large measure guided by the emergence of the liberal, democratic institutions, and by the expansion of industry and commerce. Not surprisingly, the Jews were drawn to the focus of these revolutionary economic and political developments—the city. Thus, it may be said that modern Jewish history is associated with the rise of the cities in nineteenth- and twentieth-century Europe and America. It has been calculated that in 1925 45 percent of world Jewry resided in cities with more than 100,000 inhabitants, and that 23 percent lived in cities with more than a million residents. Thus, close to one-fourth of Jewry lived in large cities, nearly one-eighth in New York City alone.[11] In several instances the majority of the Jews of

11. Jacob Lestschinsky, "Die Umsiedlung und Umschichtung des juedischen Volkes im Laufe des letzten Jahrhunderts," *Weltwirtschaftliches Archiv*, vol. 30, pt. 2 (Jena, 1929), p. 147.

Table VI *Jewish and General Immigration into the United States from 1899 to 1914*

Fiscal Years*	*Absolute Numbers*		*Percentage of Jewish Immigrants*	Fiscal Years*	*Absolute Numbers*		*Percentage of Jewish Immigrants*
	Jews	*Total*			*Jews*	*Total*	
1899	37,415	311,715	12.0	1923	49,719	522,919	9.5
1900	60,764	448,572	13.5	1924	49,989	706,896	7.1
1901	58,098	487,918	11.9	1925	10,292	294,314	3.5
1902	57,688	648,743	8.9	1926	10,267	304,488	3.4
1903	76,203	857,046	8.9	1927	11,483	335,175	3.4
1904	106,236	812,870	13.1	1928	11,639	307,255	3.8
1905	129,910	1,026,499	12.7	1929	12,479	279,678	4.5
1906	153,748	1,100,735	14.0	1930	11,526	241,700	4.8
1907	149,182	1,285,349	11.6	1931	5,692	97,139	5.9
1908	103,387	782,870	13.2	1932	2,755	35,576	7.7
1909	57,551	751,786	7.7	1933	2,372	23,068	10.3
1910	84,260	1,041,570	8.1	1934	4,134	29,470	14.0
1911	91,223	878,587	10.4	1935	4,837	34,956	13.8
1912	80,595	838,172	9.6	1936	6,252	36,329	17.2
1913	101,330	1,197,892	8.5	1937	11,352	50,244	22.6
1914	138,051	1,218,480	11.3	1938	19,736	67,895	29.0
1915	26,497	326,700	8.1	1939	43,450	82,998	52.3
1916	15,108	298,826	5.1	1940	36,945	70,756	52.2
1917	17,342	295,403	5.9	1941	23,737	51,776	45.8
1918	3,672	110,618	3.3	1942	10,608	28,781	36.9
1919	3,055	141,132	2.2	1943	4,705	23,725	19.8
1920	14,292	430,001	3.3	1944	. . .	28,551	. . .
1921	119,036	805,228	14.8				
1922	53,524	309,556	17.3	Total	2,082,136	20,059,957	10.4

SOURCE: L. Hirsch, "Jewish Migrations During the Last Hundred Years," *The Jewish People: Past and Present* (New York: Central Yiddish Culture Organization, 1946), vol. 1, p. 409.

*From July first of the preceding year to June thirtieth of the year stated.

a particular country was concentrated in the capital or largest city of that country, as is noted in tables 8 and 9.

As they became urbanized, the Jews also became increasingly middle class, as indicated by their transition from petty trade and handicrafts—typical occupations of the Jews in agrarian and semi-urban societies—to modern urban vocations in commerce and the free professions.[12]

The transformation of the occupational structure of the Jewish community corresponds to its secularization, as is reflected in the remarkable and disproportionate in-

12. "In the countries where there has been no marked development of industry, and where the percentage of Jews has remained comparatively high, say, about 10 percent, their occupational distribution has changed little. Thus in Galicia it is now [1934] practically the same as it was a hundred years ago, while in late Russian Poland, which before the War had become an important industrial area working for export to Russia, many Jews have entered industry.... In Central Europe, where their percentage in the total population was much smaller, there was a marked change: they have entered industry and the professions...." Arthur Ruppin, *The Jews in the Modern World* (London: Macmillan and Co., 1934), pp. 137ff. See tables 10 and 11.

Table VII *The Emergence of non-European Centers of Jewry*

Approximate Number of Jews in the Year	*United States*	*Canada*	*Argentina*	*Palestine*	*South Africa*	*Brazil*	*Uruguay*	*Cuba*	*Mexico*	*Egypt*	*Australia and New Zealand*
1800	2,000	...	...	10,000	...	...	...	...	...	...	...
1850	50,000	500	...	12,000	1,000	...	...	1,000	...	...	...
1880	230,000	2,400	...	25,000	...	...	...	...	...	...	...
1890	500,000	6,400	1,000	35,000	...	...	...	...	...	...	...
1900	1,000,000	16,400	30,000	55,000	30,000	3,000	...	3,000	1,000	27,000	16,000
1910	2,200,000	70,000	90,000	80,000	50,000	5,000	...	...	2,000	40,000	18,000
1920	3,200,000	120,000	130,000	75,000	60,000	7,000	1,000	4,000	...	60,000	24,000
1930	4,400,000	150,000	220,000	170,000	...	40,000	10,000	9,000	12,000	65,000	...
1933	4,500,000	170,000	240,000	220,000	80,000	45,000	12,000	9,000	12,000	70,000	33,000

SOURCE: Arthur Ruppin, *The Jews in the Modern World* (London: Macmillan and Co., 1934), p. 52.

Table VIII *The Urbanization of European Jewry: The Six Most Populous Jewish Cities in Europe*

	*Warsaw**		*Lodz*		*Budapest†*		*Vienna*		*Berlin‡*		*Odessa*	
	Number Jews	*Percent of total pop.*	*Number Jews*	*Percent of total pop.*	*Number Jews*	*Percent of total pop.*	*Number Jews*	*Percent of total pop.*	*Number Jews*	*Percent of total pop.*	*Number Jews*	*Percent of total pop.*
1860	41,000	25.0	3,000	...	...	...	6,217	2.2	18,953	3.5	25,000	...
1870	89,318	32.6	...	...	44,747	16.6	40,227	6.1	36,105	4.4	...	...
1880	127,917	33.4	...	...	70,277	19.7	72,588	10.1	53,916	4.8	...	...
1890	151,076	33.1	...	...	102,377	21.0	118,495	8.6	79,286	5.0	...	...
1900	219,128	34.3	96,671	31.4	166,198	23.6	146,926	8.8	92,206	4.9	138,935	34.4
1910	306,061	39.2	...	...	203,687	23.1	175,318	8.6	144,007	3.9	...	...
1920	310,334	33.1	156,155	34.5	215,512	23.2	200,000	12.8	...	...	...	...
1925	...	...	...	...	207,015	21.5	201,513	10.8	172,672	4.4	153,194	36.4
1929	...	...	195,000	32.7	...	...	201,513	10.8	172,672	4.3	153,194	36.4

SOURCES: Compiled on the basis of data presented in Arthur Ruppin, *Soziologie der Juden* (Berlin: Juedischer Verlag, 1930), vol. 1, pp. 114–15; J. Kreppel, *Juden und Judentum von Heute: Ein Handbuch* (Zurich: Amalthea Verlag, 1925), pp. 301, 323–24, 349; and S. Dubnow, *Die neueste Geschichte des juedischen Volkes* (Berlin: Juedischer Verlag, 1920–23), vol. 2, p. 121.

*In 1813 there were circa 8,000 Jews in Warsaw, constituting 12 percent of the city's total population.

†In 1789 there were only 114 Jews in Budapest, in 1833, 6,730, and in 1849, 19,148 Jews. In the nineteenth century Budapest grew faster than any other European capital. The Jews were demographically so prominent in the Hungarian capital that it was pejoratively called "Judapest."

‡In 1816 there were 3,373 Jews in Berlin, constituting 1.7 percent of the general population. Whereas the total population of Berlin increased twelvefold in the period between 1811 and 1910, the Jewish population of the city increased twenty-sevenfold in the same period.

Table IX *The Jewish Population in the Largest City of Various Countries*

		Number of Jews in country		*Number of Jews in city*	*Percentage of country's Jews in largest city*
1921	Denmark	5,946	Copenhagen	5,482	92.2
1926	France	200,000	Paris	140,000	70.0
1923	Austria	300,000	Vienna	201,513	67.3
1926	England	300,000	London	200,000	66.6
1920	Holland	115,229	Amsterdam	68,758	59.7
1917	Egypt	59,581	Cairo	29,207	49.0
1926	United States	4,000,000	New York	1,800,000	45.0
1921	Hungary	473,310	Budapest	212,736	44.9
1920	Bulgaria	43,232	Sofia	17,038	39.4
1925	Germany	564,379	Berlin	172,672	30.6
1921	Poland	2,829,456	Warsaw	310,334	10.9
1921	Czechoslovakia	354,342	Prague	31,751	9.0

SOURCE: Adapted from Arthur Ruppin, *Soziologie der Juden* (Berlin: Juedischer Verlag, 1930), vol. 1, p. 117.

crease of Jews seeking a secular, general education. See table 12.

The embourgeoisment and secularization of the Jews parallel their unprecedented assimilation in the modern period. In 1904, Arthur Ruppin, a pioneer of Jewish demography and sociology, schematically correlated the adoption of modern education and urban vocations to the degree of assimilation as indicated by four factors: distance from traditional Judaism, decline of birthrate, increase of intermarriage and conversion. Ruppin's scheme, which sought to delineate the prevailing pattern as it emerged in 1900, was, as he admitted, ambitious. Nonetheless, the scheme is illuminating, for as Ruppin explained, "to anyone who has studied the conditions of the Jews in the large European cities [of the nineteenth century], this process [illustrated by the scheme] is as familiar as it is clear."[13] See table 13.

It should be emphasized that this scheme is only a statistical description of certain characteristic phenomena of modern Jewish history; it is not an explanation of these phenomena. In themselves, statistics do not provide an explanation, at the most they alert the scholar to certain correlations and patterns which require independent sociological and historical analysis. What is indeed clear from the statistics is that as the Jews became increasingly middle class and urban, intermarriage and voluntary conversion increased to an unprecedented degree.

The Zionist movement sought to re-direct the course of modern Jewish history. Drawn to the ideals of Zionism, a relatively small but ever increasing number of Jews immigrated to Palestine—the land of Israel—in order to create alternative forms of *modern* Jewish life. Zionist-inspired immigration to the land of Israel was called *aliyah* (plural, *aliyot*), the Hebrew term meaning "ascent" and also traditionally denoting the spiritual elevation associated with permanent settlement in the Holy Land. Initially, Zionist *aliyot* were highly selective groups of pioneers (in Hebrew, *halutzim*) who were pledged to the revival of Hebrew as a spoken language and to the realization of various Zionist social ideals. In the course of time, Jewish refugees joined the *halutzim*. There were seven distinct waves of Zionist-sponsored *aliyot* to the land of Israel.

With the proclamation of the State of Is-

13. Arthur Ruppin, *The Jews of Today*, (New York: H. Holt, 1913), p. 14.

Table X *Occupational Distribution of Jews in Various Countries: Percentage of Gainfully Employed Persons, Excluding Agricultural Labor*

		Industry and Trade		*Commerce and Credit*		*Communications and Transport*		*Public Service and Liberal Professions*		*Domestic and Personal Service*		*Others**	
	Year	*Jews*	*Non-Jews*	*Jews*	*Non-Jews*	*Jews*	*Non-Jews*	*Jews*	*Non-Jews*	*Jews*	*Non-Jews*	*Jews*	*Non-Jews*
Poland	1931	45.4	44.0	38.2	9.3	3.5	7.3	6.1	12.0	3.3	10.9	3.5	11.5
U.S.S.R.	1926	41.5	38.9	23.8	7.9	3.3	10.8	17.5	16.1	...	...	13.9	26.3
Ukraine	1926	43.5	41.7	24.2	5.6	3.5	10.5	14.1	15.2	...	...	14.3	27.0
Central Russia	1926	33.4	38.6	24.4	8.4	2.6	10.8	27.2	16.2	...	...	12.4	26.0
White Russia	1926	49.6	26.1	20.2	4.2	4.0	2.9	11.1	22.6	...	...	15.1	34.2
Germany	1933	18.7	45.6	49.8	15.1	0.3	5.5	9.4	8.3	1.3	5.3	20.5	20.2
Rumania	1930	34.8	47.5	51.5	18.1	2.6	10.1	2.9	13.4	...	...	8.2	10.9
Hungary	1930	32.8	49.5	46.2	10.0	2.0	6.2	8.4	10.4	1.5	11.6	9.1	12.3
Czechoslovakia: Slovakia and Carpatho-Ruthenia	1930	24.8	41.3	46.2	7.4	2.9	8.0	8.3	11.1	2.5	11.1	15.2	21.1
Czechoslovakia: Bohemia, Moravia and Silesia	1930	19.0	53.2	47.1	10.5	1.3	5.8	8.4	6.0	0.9	6.3	23.3	18.2
Canada	1931	33.3	27.1	39.0	12.4	2.9	11.3	5.7	10.4	6.0	13.4	13.1	25.4

SOURCE: Adapted from Jacob Lestschinsky, "The Economic and Social Development of the Jewish People From the Beginning of the Nineteenth Century to the Second World War," in *The Jewish People: Past and Present* (New York: Central Yiddish Culture Organization, 1946), vol. 1, pp. 378–80.

*Includes those living on income not derived from personal labor, such as pensions, welfare, charity, and inherited wealth.

Table XI *The Occupational Distribution of World Jewry: 1929*

Occupation	*Number*	*Percent*
Commerce (including transport, entertainment, trade, and banking)	6,100,000	38.6
Industry (including mining and handicrafts)	5,750,000	36.4
Professions and civil service	1,000,000	6.3
Agriculture	625,000	4.0
Casual laborers and domestic servants	325,000	2.0
Unemployed (living on private means, pensions, charity, welfare)	2,000,000	12.7
Total number of Jews	15,800,000	100.0

SOURCE: Adapted from Jacob Lestschinsky, "A Century's Changes in Jewish Numbers and Occupations," *The Menorah Journal,* 20, no. 6 (1932), p. 177.

rael in May 1948, hundreds of thousands of Jews from the four corners of the earth—among them displaced persons, survivors of the Holocaust, and Jewish communities animated by a messianic enthusiasm—settled in their ancestral homeland.

The establishment of the State of Israel was preceded by the Nazi nightmare in which a third of Jewry was murdered. From close to seventeen million people Jewry was reduced to eleven million (see chapter 11, document 19). In the generation since the Holocaust, Jewry has not grown appreciably. Intermarriage and a low fertility rate have contributed to the virtual demographic stagnation of the Jewish people. According to a recent study completed by O. U. Schmelz of the Hebrew University, the present world Jewish population is considerably lower than it was held to be by previous estimates. Table 18 presents Professor Schmelz's findings.

Table XII *Attendance of Jews at Advanced Academic Institutions and Universities*

Country or City	Types of Schooling	Period	Number of Jewish Students: Absolute No.	Number of Jewish Students: Percent	The Percent of Jewish Students Exceeds Percent of Jews in the Population
Germany*	Universities	Winter Session 1929–1930	2,970	3·4	3·7 times
	Technical Institutes	"	264	1·3	1·4 times
	Art Academies	"	73	1·6	1·8 times
	Together	Winter Session 1929–1930	3,307	2·9	3·2 times
Czechoslovakia	Universities	Winter Session 1927–1928	2,414	14·5	5·6 times
	Technical Institutes	"	1,314	12·2	4·7 times
	Art Academies	"	50	2·2	0·8 times
	Together	Winter Session 1927–1928	3,778	12·8	4·9 times
Vienna	Universities	1928–1929	2,377	21·3	2·0 times
	Technical Institutes	"	328	10·7	1·0 times
	Art Academies	"	239	9·6	0·9 times
	Together	1928–1929	2,944	. . .	. . .
Hungary	All Universities and Advanced Academic Institutions	Winter Session 1930	1,350	10·5	1·8 times
Poland	All Universities and Advanced Academic Institutions	Winter Session 1929–1930	8,711	19·3	1·9 times
Soviet Russia	All Universities and Advanced Academic Institutions	1926–1927	23,699	13·4	5·9 times
Latvia	Universities	1930–1931	744	8·7	1·8 times
Lithuania	Universities	1926	756	31·4	4·1 times
U.S.A.	Universities	1918–1919	14,837	9·7	3·2 times

SOURCE: Adapted from Arthur Ruppin, *The Jews in the Modern World* (London: Macmillan and Co., 1934), p. 313.

*These figures do not include the many East European Jews who attended German universities.

Table XIII *The Four Strata of European Jewry*

Numbers		*Typical Representatives*	*Economic Conditions*	*Religious Outlook*	*Education*	*Birth-rate per 1,000 souls*	*Percentage of Mixed Marriages*	*Conversions Annually per 10,000 souls*
First Stratum	Six million	The great mass of Jews in Russia and Galicia	Workmen, artisans and shopkeepers without means—and of uncertain livelihood	Orthodox	Cheder	30–40	0–2	0–2
Second Stratum	Three million	Settlers in England and America, Rumanian Jews	Artisans and merchants with modest but settled income	Liberal	Jewish elementary schools	25–30	2–10	2–5
Third Stratum	Two million	The mass of German Jews	Well-to-do bourgeoisie	Free-thinking	Christian elementary and secondary schools	20–25	10–30	5–15
Fourth Stratum	One million	Rich Jews and Jews of University Education in all the big towns	Wealthy bourgeoisie	Agnostic	Public School and University	15–20	30–50	15–40

SOURCE: Arthur Ruppin, *The Jews of Today* (New York: H. Holt, 1913), p. 15.

Table XIV *Intermarriage*

	Percent of Jews Marrying Non-Jews			
	Year or Period	*Jewish Males*	*Jewish Females*	*Total*
Germany	1901–1904	8·48	7·41	7·95
	1910–1911	13·49	10·37	11·96
	1928	25·15	16·79	21·19
	1929	27·16	17·82	22·79
	1930	26·60	17·60	22·36
Prussia	1875–1884	4·60	4·98	4·79
	1885–1889	8·29	7·33	7·81
	1905–1908	11·81	10·57	11·19
	1925	23·56	13·97	19·05
	1928	26·06	17·65	22·08
	1929	27·81	18·46	23·47
Berlin	1876–1880	15·69	11·99	13·88
	1901–1904	17·89	12·02	15·06
	1925	30·53	17·90	24·75
	1926	29·19	18·63	24·52
	1929	35·31	21·95	29·21
Hamburg	1886–1890	16·50	9·30	13·10
	1906–1910	26·40	22·20	24·30
	1925	31·82	24·53	28·83
	1928	39·86	26·45	33·83
Bavaria	1876–1880	1·54	2·08	1·82
	1901–1905	4·47	4·04	4·25
	1926–1927	16·90	9·52	13·36
Hungary	1895–1899	2·68	2·73	2·70
	1907–1908	4·12	4·55	4·33
	1925	11·90	10·90	11·40
	1927	11·93	12·06	12·00
	1928	12·50	11·60	12·05
	1929	12·04	11·90	11·97
Budapest	1896–1900	6·71	7·22	6·97
	1925	17·96	15·27	16·64
	1927	16·74	16·18	16·46
	1929	16·61	16·43	16·52
Vienna	1926	12·68	11·71	12·20
	1927	12·16	9·93	11·06
	1928	12·83	10·06	11·47
	1929	13·86	12·02	12·95
Amsterdam	1899–1908	..	..	5·00
	1921–1925	12·66	9·56	11·14
	1926–1927	13·79	12·60	13·20
	1928–1930	17·03	12·49	14·83
Copenhagen	1880–1889	..	..	21·84
	1900–1905	..	..	31·76
Trieste	1887–1890	..	..	14·30
	1900–1903	..	..	17·90
	1927	60·87	50·00	56·10
Galicia	1929	1·02	0·64	0·83
Central Russia	1924–1926	20·68	12·47	16·77
White Russia	1924–1926	1·87	3·73	2·81
Ukraine	1924–1926	4·19	4·90	4·55
Total European Russia	1924–1926	7·41	6·21	6·80

SOURCE: Adapted from Arthur Ruppin, *The Jews in the Modern World* (London: Macmillan and Co., 1934), pp. 318–19.

Table XV *Jewish Conversions to Christianity in the Nineteenth Century*

	Protestant	*Roman Catholic*	*Greek Orthodox*	*Total*
Prussia	13,128		. . .	
Bavaria	330		. . .	
Saxony,	770	5,000	. . .	22,520
Wuerttemberg	115		. . .	
Rest of Germany	3,177		. . .	
Great Britain	28,830	. . .	. . .	28,830
Netherlands	1,800	. . .	. . .	1,800
Sweden and Norway	500	. . .	. . .	500
Denmark	100	. . .	. . .	100
Switzerland	100	. . .	. . .	100
France	600	1,800	. . .	2,400
Austria	6,300	28,200	200	44,756
Hungary	2,056	8,000		
Czarist Russia (including Poland)*	3,136	12,000	69,400	84,536
Italy	. . .	300	. . .	300
Rumania	. . .	. . .	1,500	1,500
Turkey	. . .	. . .	3,300	3,300
Balkan Countries	. . .	. . .	100	100
Asia and Africa	100	500	. . .	600
Australia	200	. . .	. . .	200
North America	11,500	1,500	. . .	13,000
Total	72,742	57,300	74,500	204,542

SOURCE: J. de le Roi, "Judentaufen im XIX. Jahrhundert. Ein statistischer Versuch." *Nathanael: Zeitschrift fuer die Arbeit der Kirche an Israel,* 5, nos. 3–4 (Berlin, 1899), pp. 65–118.

*This figure includes Frankists. The majority of Jewish conversions in Russia were under one form or another of coercion, the most outrageous being the forced baptism of the cantonists. Strictly voluntary conversion in Czarist Russia was relatively rare.

Table XVI *Zionist* Aliyot *to the Land of Israel: 1882–1948*

	Origin	*Motivation*	*Number*
First *aliyah*, 1882–1903	Russia Rumania	Hibbat Zion and Bilu	25,000
Second *aliyah*, 1904–1914	Russia	Labor and Social Zionism	40,000
Third *aliyah*, 1919–1923	Russia, Poland Rumania (Smaller numbers from Germany, Lithuania, United States, and other places)	Hehalutz and Hashomer Hazair	35,000
Fourth *aliyah*, 1924–1932	Poland	Mainly middle-class refugees who left Poland because of anti-Jewish economic measures; four-fifths settled in cities	88,450
Fifth *aliyah*, 1933–1939	Poland, Germany, and Central Europe	Youth *aliyah* Refugees from Nazi persecution	215,222
Sixth *aliyah*, 1939–1945	All of Europe	Refugees from Nazi Europe	62,531
Seventh *aliyah*, 1945–1948	All of Europe	Survivors of the Holocaust, many of whom entered Palestine "illegally"	120,000

SOURCE: Compiled on the basis of data presented in the *Encyclopedia of Zionism and Israel,* s.v. "Immigration to Palestine and Israel." (New York: Herzl Press and McGraw-Hill, 1971), vol. 1, pp. 534–38.

Table XVII *Mass Immigration to the State of Israel: May 1948–December 1951*

All Countries	684,201
Eastern Europe	
Rumania	118,940
Poland	103,732
Bulgaria	37,231
Czechoslovakia	18,217
Hungary	13,631
Yugoslavia	7,595
Soviet Union (incl. Lithuania, Latvia)	4,698
Total	304,044
Western Europe	
Germany	8,856
France	4,008
Austria	2,994
Greece	2,005
Britain	2,143
Italy	1,415
Belgium	1,108
Netherlands	1,102
Spain	412
Sweden	429
Switzerland	386
Other European Countries	147
Total	25,005
Asia	
Iraq	121,512
Turkey	34,213
Iran	24,804
Aden	3,155
Asia (cont.)	
India	2,337
China	2,167
Cyprus	136
Yemen	45,199
Other Countries	3,700
Total	237,223
Africa	
Morocco	30,750
Tunisia	13,139
Algeria	1,523
Libya	30,482
South Africa	584
Ethiopia	83
Egypt	16,508
Other Countries	108
Total	93,177
Western Hemisphere	
United States	1,909
Canada	233
Argentina	1,134
Brazil	442
Other Latin American Countries	870
Total	4,588
Australia	171
Unregistered	19,993

SOURCE: *Encyclopaedia Judaica,* s.v. "State of Israel: Aliyah and Absorption," vol. 9, p. 535. Reprinted by permission of Keter Publishing House.

Table XVIII *World Jewish Population in Thousands: 1975*

Region, Country	*Professor Schmelz's Estimates (rounded)*
Diaspora	
America, Total*	6,417
United States	5,600
Canada	295
Argentina	265
Brazil	110
Other Countries	147
Europe, Total†	1,316
France	535
United Kingdom	400
Other Countries	381
U.S.S.R.‡	1,950
Asia§	88
Africa, Total	177
South Africa, Rhodesia	120
Other Countries	57
Oceania	72
Diaspora, Total	10,020
Israel	2,959
World Total‖	12,979

SOURCE: The table is based on data prepared by Professor Schmelz as part of a comprehensive study on Jewish population trends. We wish to thank Professor Schmelz for his kind permission to use his figures.

*Frequently estimates of the Jewish population include non-Jewish members of Jewish households; Professor Schmelz's figures exclude them.

†Excluding the U.S.S.R., but including the European territories of Turkey.

‡Based on official census results which may actually underrepresent the Jewish population of the U.S.S.R. The estimate given here is based on both the 1959 and 1970 censuses.

§Excluding the U.S.S.R., but including the Asian territories of Turkey.

‖See the *Encyclopaedia Judaica* (vol. 13, pp. 895–96) which estimates the world Jewish population in 1967 to be 13,837,500; and the *American Jewish Year Book* (vol. 75, pp. 562–63) which gives the figure of 14,144,390 for the world Jewish population in 1975.

Index

Entries appearing in footnotes to chapter introductions are designated by page number and *n*; entries appearing in documents and document notes are designated by page number only.